LITERARY BRITAIN

FRANK MORLEY

LITERARY BRITAIN

A Reader's Guide to Writers and Landmarks

HUTCHINSON

London Melbourne Sydney Auckland Johannesburg

To the memory of
Cynthia J. Stevens
of Baltimore, Maryland

Hutchinson & Co. (Publishers) Ltd

An imprint of the Hutchinson Publishing Group

3 Fitzroy Square, London WIP 6JD

Hutchinson Group (Australia) Pty Ltd
30–32 Cremorne Street, Richmond South, Victoria 3121
PO Box 151, Broadway, New South Wales 2007

Hutchinson Group (NZ) Ltd
32–34 View Road, PO Box 40–086, Glenfield, Auckland 10

Hutchinson Group (SA) (Pty) Ltd
PO Box 337, Bergvlei 2012, South Africa

First published 1980
© Frank Morley 1980

Set in Monotype Imprint

Printed in Great Britain by
The Anchor Press Ltd and bound by
Wm Brendon & Son Ltd
both of Tiptree, Essex

British Library Cataloguing in Publication Data

Morley, Frank
  Literary Britain
    1. Literary landmarks – Great Britain
  I. Title
  941   PR109
        ISBN 0 09 139680 8

CONTENTS

ACKNOWLEDGEMENTS

Britain is an island in which a wonderfully active life developed, partly because six arterial roadways to and from London provided for quick circulation of whatever was lively in spirit. The importance of the radial roads in the development of literature is one reason for the arrangement of this book; regional differences appear most naturally with the road-pattern borne in mind.

A gazetteer arrangement, whereby places with literary associations are listed alphabetically, is an alternative adopted by some guides, as notably by *The Oxford Guide to the British Isles*, by Dorothy Eagle and Hilary Carnell (1977). From the Oxford book as from mine, living authors have been excluded (or, in mine, included only very rarely). In the *Oxford Guide* the two compilers pay their respects, as I do also, to the late John Freeman's *Literature and Locality* (1963); in my list of acknowledgements below I record permission for quoting two stories which none could tell so neatly as John Freeman. A work which I found very helpful for checking place-associations in each area has been *A Literary Atlas and Gazetteer of the British Isles* by Michael Hardwick (1973); and for London, on several occasions I have been grateful to consult, and in my text have mentioned, the *Guide to Literary London* by Professor George G. Williams (1973).

Those four are among recent books helpful to explorers in Britain. Since this year is the 75th since I was first taken to see a famous literary site (where two fictional rabbits of childhood, Binny & Bunny, lived near the River Deben) there have been many more friends who have taught me what's in my book, or with whom in a lifetime I have visited the places I mention, or who have helped with the text, than can be individually thanked. Yet I do specially thank my publishers, in both London and New York, for assistances beyond the normal in coping with the maps and indexes which are an integral part of the book. The indexes have been compiled by Sue Major. The sketch-maps are intentionally schematic; motorists always need separate and up-to-the-minute road-maps. Throughout I have tried to avoid giving information of a kind that goes out of date. For 'visiting times' for museums, famous houses or gardens, for instance, since they are subject to alteration, it is wise to check beforehand with a tourist agency or other source for local information.

For special permission to quote from sources in copyright, I greatly thank the following:

Esme Valerie Eliot and Faber and Faber Ltd, *Collected Poems 1909–1962* by T. S. Eliot

Esme Valerie Eliot and Faber and Faber Ltd, Introduction to *A Choice of Kipling's Verse* by T. S. Eliot

Faber and Faber Ltd, *Period Piece* by Gwen Raverat

A. P. Watt Ltd and the National Trust, *Puck of Pook's Hill* by Rudyard Kipling

George G. Harrap and Co. Ltd, *A Shropshire Lad* by A. E. Housman

William Heinemann Ltd, Laurence Pollinger Ltd and the Estate of the late Mrs Frieda Lawrence Ravagli, *Sons and Lovers* by D. H. Lawrence

The Society of Authors as the literary representative of the Estate of John Masefield, 'The Everlasting Mercy' by John Masefield

Martin Secker and Warburg Ltd, *The World of Charles Dickens* by Angus Wilson

The Estate of the late Dr Neil Munro and William Blackwood and Sons Ltd, 'Lament for Macleod of Raasay' by Neil Munro

G. T. Sassoon for the Estate of Siegfried Sassoon, 'At the grave of Henry Vaughan' by Siegfried Sassoon

A. D. Peters and Co. Ltd, Faber and Faber Ltd and the University of California Press, *The Pound Era* by Hugh Kenner

The material from *A Welshman 'Italianate'* by James Morris first appeared in *Horizon*

Chapman and Hall Ltd, *A Short Life of Robert Burns* by Catherine Carswell. The whereabouts of the present copyright holder are not known to me

Lewis Mumford and *The New Yorker*, the quotation from Lewis Mumford

Harcourt Brace Jovanovich Inc., *My Works and Days* by Lewis Mumford

Cassell and Co. Ltd, *Literature and Locality* by John Freeman

The Estate of James Joyce and Faber and Faber Ltd, *Finnegans Wake*

The Estate of W. B. Yeats and Macmillan & Co. Ltd, Yeats' *Collected Poems*

Oxford University Press, *James Joyce* by Richard Ellman

The Estate of Harold Owen and Chatto & Windus Ltd, Wilfred Owen's *Collected Poems*

The Estate of Brendan Behan, *Brendan Behan's Island*

Constable and Co., *The Stricken Deer* by David Cecil

Hutchinson & Co. (Publishers) Ltd, 2nd Revised Edition of *The Concise Encyclopedia of Modern World Literature*, ed. Geoffrey Grigson

Macmillan & Co. Ltd, *W. B. Yeats* by Joseph Hone

Macmillan & Co. Ltd, *A Nest of Tigers* by John Lehmann

Faber and Faber Ltd, *Rupert Brooke: A Biography* by Christopher Hassall

Hutchinson & Co. (Publishers) Ltd, *Byron* by Elizabeth Longford

PREFACE

It may be helpful to explain this book's arrangement.

One advantage of road pattern in an informative book is that regional differences come to notice in a natural neighbourly way, not only large generic distinctions between what has originated in England, Scotland, Wales and Ireland, but vivid differences within each region. After a start in London, my plan is then to make an outward run along each arterial road in turn; on my return from the outward run there is a chance to survey associations in between the road just traversed and the next one. Thus the topography of Britain is covered.

I must make it clear that the six roads of greatest importance, both historically and for present narrative purpose, are the famous old roads each of which has a proper name but which are collectively spoken of as the 'A roads'. The motorways in Britain (marked 'M' on maps) have plentiful uses, but for the users of this book one great virtue of the motorways is that they have relieved congestion of traffic on the 'A' roads and so made travel on the old historic routes all the more enjoyable.

The six main A roads radiating from London and the first to be travelled here, are as follows:

A1 – *The Great North Road*
This link between Northumbria and King Alfred's southland became and remained the premier working road between the capitals, London and Edinburgh. The country in Zone 1 clockwise between roads A1 and A2 includes the North Sea coastal area from the Scottish Border to the Thames estuary; within this area East Anglia claims separate survey.

A2 – *The Dover Road*

From London to Dover is the south-eastern section of the great ancient beltway of Watling Street across the whole island of Britain. In Chaucer's time the Dover Road was the route of pilgrimage to Canterbury and to Rome, and it has remained the traditional most direct surface route to the Continent. Zone 2 between roads A2 and A3 includes Kent, East Sussex, West Sussex and the Isle of Wight.

A3 – *The Portsmouth Road*

This and the Dover Road vie with each other in claiming to be the shortest of the A roads; it passes through country associated with many novelists. Zone 3 between A3 and A4 includes the Anglo-Saxon heartland, Hardy's Wessex, and the heartland of Arthurian legend stretching to Land's End.

A4 – *The Bath Road*

Not only the famous coaching road of Regency times (continuing as such in Pickwick's day) but now the entry to all the coastline of South Wales. Zone 4 between A4 and A5 includes all of Wales south of Snowdonia, together with the valley of the Severn, the Cotswolds, Shakespeare's Avon and the valley of the Thames.

A5 – *The Holyhead Road*

Watling Street, curving westward from St Albans towards Chester, was the rampart supposed to separate the Danelaw of the north-east from the Saxons and Britons of the south and west. The extension of the present A5 throughout North Wales to Holyhead brings us to other and strongly surviving heritages. Zone 5, between A5 and A6, includes the coast of North Wales, also the Lancashire coast, and the many associations of the Lake District.

A6 – *The Manchester Road*

This road branches from St Albans to traverse Sherwood Forest and the Peak Country; from Manchester it leads on through Carlisle to Glasgow. Zone 6, between A6 and A1, includes the region to the Scottish Border, also most of the heartland of the legend of Robin Hood, and the country of the Brontës, of Byron, and of D. H. Lawrence.

It may need to be noted that when my narrative travels outward from London on A1, the countryside to the right of the road (Zone 1) will all be included later in that same chapter; but countryside to the left of A1, having been numbered Zone 6, will be found to be covered in the chapter treating A6. So in general, to read all that may be said about regions on both sides of any main road one has to look at two chapters, both of them relevant. In practice this is less complicated than it sounds in this preamble, for the indispensable indexes are aids for quickly locating what is said about individual persons or places.

The organic road pattern outlined above embraces the whole territory of England and Wales. Separate treatments are accorded to literary associations within Scotland, though in so far as Scottish writers lived and worked in England their stories fittingly enter the English parts of the book. That applies to Irish writers also.

But now, for beginnings, London.

BEGINNINGS

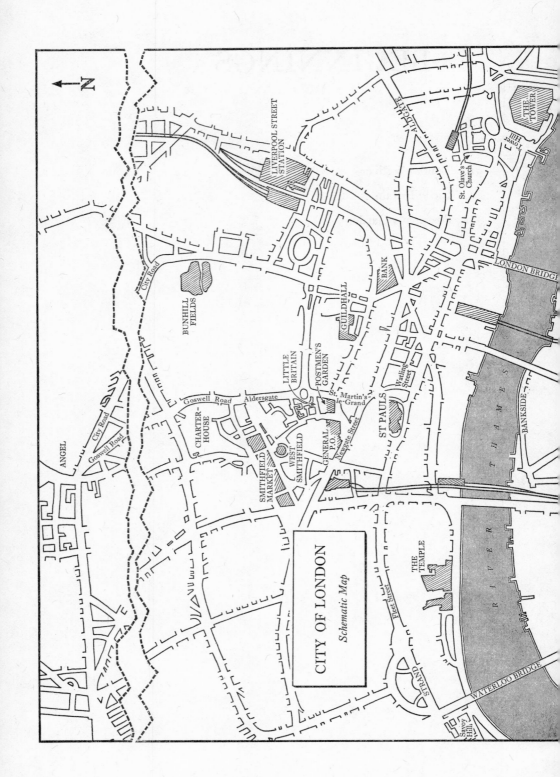

CITY OF LONDON
Schematic Map

1. LONDON'S RIVER

One particular historical episode has often caused me to regard one site in London as the birthplace of English literature. Is that a ridiculous whimsy? I can at least provide some justification.

In present-day London a simple pleasure, known to many, is to step from the Strand on to Waterloo Bridge to look at the reach of London's river as it curves away downstream. Much detail keeps being added to that view from Waterloo Bridge, and it is one of the best views of, for instance, St Paul's – but I don't intend to focus only on the up-to-date visual scene. Here is memory at work; this particular part of the river has been looked at by remembered poets. From the Strand side, from his lookout in the then 'bricky towers' of the Earl of Leicester's riverside house, Spenser caught his catch-line

> Sweet Themmes! runne softly, till I end my song.

A little way downstream and across the river is Bankside; that's where (as Ben Jonson alternately called him) the 'Swan of Avon', 'Star of poets', was producing

> those flights upon the banks of Thames,
> That so did take Eliza and our James.

No scene is closer to the heart of literary tradition than that embraced by Spenser from one side and Shakespeare from the other.

Contemplating this stretch of the River Thames from Lambeth and Westminster to London Bridge and the Tower – the river-mile (or nearer two) which has Waterloo Bridge as the midpoint – it is easy to be persuaded that the roll-call of writers associated with it is unsurpassable. For Elizabethan memories, since I've alluded to Spenser and the literary club (called Areopagus) which Sir Philip Sidney joined at Leicester's house in the 1570s, there is also Raleigh's 'school', possibly alluded to by Shakespeare as a 'school of night', at the neighbouring Durham House. Durham House was another of the 'Stately Structures' along the Strand; its mistress was the 'Stella' of Sidney's *Astrophel and Stella* but, when her father died, that lady (daughter of the then Earl of Essex) was dispossessed by Queen Elizabeth. Then Durham House, which sported a pleasing 'little turret that looked into and over the Thames', was one of the gifts which Elizabeth in 1584 gave to the recently knighted courtier, 'tall, handsome and bold' (but also 'damnable

proud'), named Walter Raleigh. It was presently to Raleigh's 'school' in
the favourite turret, with Raleigh's remarkable mathematical tutor
Thomas Hariot in attendance, that Christopher Marlowe was initiated.
The interchange of verses between Marlowe and Raleigh is thus one of
the mementos of this reach of the Thames.

Not long after the Elizabethans, a boy-apprentice from Cheapside
used the alleyways between great houses of the Strand in order to swim
in this curve of the river. The boy, Robert Herrick, in later country
exile put many 'teares to Thamasis' on paper to recall those 'summer's
sweeter evenings' when he had stripped for his swim along with, he
says, the 'thousand others' of London boys. By Pepys's time and later
one does not hear of bathing from the old strand spoken about with so
much pleasure, but all manner of boating retained its popularity. On the
north bank in the eighteenth century – though there was as yet no such
Embankment as nowadays – there were at least thirty landing-places
between Parliament Stairs and London Bridge where boats waited by the
steps to be hired for passage across or along the river. Westminster's
Horseferry Road is one reminder that there were ferries with platforms
built to carry coach and horses, but until Westminster Bridge was in use
in 1739 the original piers of London Bridge still carried the only actual
roadway over the river.

The earliest street of houses on London's famous bridge was many
times altered and rebuilt and finally the houses were erased to cope with
the increase of traffic, but the wide stone piers in the river, constraining
the stream into twenty narrow arched tunnels under the bridge, had
been so solidly completed in the thirteenth century that they were far
from easy to alter. London Bridge could almost be regarded as a combination of bridge and weir until the ancient piers were finally removed
in 1832. Until that late date it had always been notoriously hazardous
for boats, except at slack tide, to 'shoot the bridge'. An eighteenth-
century saying was that London Bridge was made for wise men to go
over and fools to go under, and Dr Johnson, though he did not invent the
saying, obeyed it. On the fine Saturday morning of 30 July 1763, when
Johnson and Boswell 'took a sculler at the Temple-stairs, and set out for
Greenwich', the boating was done in two bites. Goodhumouredly, when
the boy who rowed them brought them to land just above London
Bridge, they gave him a double fare. Changing then to footwork,
Johnson and Boswell walked to Billingsgate, and there at stairs below
the bridge they again 'took oars and moved smoothly along the silver
Thames' for the day's outing.

Charles Lamb's childhood pleasure in watching river traffic from his
bedroom in the Temple is another of the recollections felt at this reach
of London's river. The whole curving reach between Westminster and

the Tower, for its numerous associations with poets, might well be called the Poets' Curve. In the nineteenth century one thinks immediately of feelings excited in William Blake, George Crabbe and Wordsworth on Westminster Bridge; at London Bridge one thinks of Keats and, in our own time, of T. S. Eliot. But this brief rehearsal of some of the music that has here crept by me on the waters is only preliminary to my point. It may have been agreed that throughout the four centuries between the reigns of Elizabeth I and Elizabeth II, the river has ever been an active partner in whatever process it is that makes poets produce poetry, but that of itself is no proof that this particular river scene can be considered the actual birthplace of literature in English.

Yet boldly to make that claim I have no need to move from Waterloo Bridge. All I need is to view this same curve of London's river as it was two centuries earlier than the 'Sweet Themmes' of Spenser's song.

* * *

From the Strand, the street of entry to Waterloo Bridge is now Lancaster Place. On the Savoy side, just before reaching the bridge, there is a discreet nameplate of the offices of the Duchy of Lancaster. Lancaster, Savoy – those are two strong words that carry us back a full six hundred years. 'Time-honoured Lancaster' (in the opening line of Shakespeare's *King Richard the Second*) was the powerful 'Old John of Gaunt' whose Savoy Palace was in the 1370s much the stateliest of the great houses of the Strand. When John of Gaunt, as England's Regent, was holding court at the Savoy Palace, the 'long age of three hours' between the court's supper and bedtime was occasionally whiled away by recitations or readings by the established court poet, John Gower.

When Edward III died in 1377, his son the Black Prince (popular hero since the winning of the battle of Crécy and even more so after Poitiers) having died the year before, it was the grandson Richard who as a boy at the age of ten inherited the Crown of England. It was not unexpected that John of Gaunt, as Richard's uncle, acquired the power of regent for the boy-king. But the contest then going on between the two tongues in England, English and French, which language was the boy-king going to prefer? (In the teaching of the young in Chaucer's time Latin was a third competitor, and even a century later boys in grammar schools not only stood up in class to translate Latin authors into French or English but out of school hours, G. M. Trevelyan notes, 'no language must be talked except Latin'.) When the boy Richard II came to the throne the Norman imposition of French as the official language in England was, in some areas, becoming relaxed: in 1362 French had been discontinued by statute as the language of England's law courts, and in 1378 the official language of Parliament (as Parliament then was) became English. Nor did John of Gaunt disapprove of Wyclif, who was busy putting the Bible into English for the use of common people. But, for all the inroads that the English tongue was making, it remained *lèse-majesté* within all royal households for upstairs language to be other than French.

Thus poetry readings given by the court-poet John Gower at the Savoy Palace were chosen from his half-hundred French *ballades* or from his first long poem, *Speculum Meditantis*, which though titled in Latin was written in French. John of Gaunt approved for his daughter Philippa such fourteenth-century grammar books as proclaimed (I use a quotation here from J. J. Jusserand) that French was 'the finest and most graceful language, the noblest to speak of in the world after Latin of the schools, and better prized and loved than any other by all men'. There is proof that Philippa of Lancaster wholeheartedly accepted French not only as the normal courtly language of her English home, but also as the tongue that was most 'sweet and lovable' for poetry. Yet the boy-king Richard, eight years younger than Philippa, began to show in adolescence an ability to speak, and even an ill-mannered preference for, the language of England's common people, English.

In the year of Richard's coronation there was an impressive attempt at confrontation between a mob of London citizens and their French-speaking Regent. The noisy mob swelled in the Strand, outside the Savoy Palace, with leaders demanding speech with John of Gaunt in person. Gaunt, who was at dinner, refused to appear. On that occasion the mob was insufficiently prepared to wreak much damage to the Palace; nevertheless Gaunt was accounted lucky to have moved off that evening, by boat and hurriedly, across the river and upstream to Kennington. Far more serious was the countrywide Peasants' Revolt of 1381. This time, when the last straw of a proposed poll tax on every person over fifteen triggered off a general and violent rebellion, the burning of the Savoy Palace was one objective of a determined London mob and much destruction was achieved. John of Gaunt, it seems, was abroad, and the presumption is that as country rebels marched in upon London, Richard II, now a tall slender auburn-haired boy of fourteen, was urged to keep safe within the Tower. With headstrong assurance Richard enforced that he had been anointed to rule, and so it was he, supported by London's Lord Mayor and an array of soldiery, who arrived at West Smithfield to face and parley with the crowd of rebels whose chief spokesman was Wat Tyler.

Which tongue did Richard intend to use in the parley with Wat Tyler?

Froissart, in another connection, tells us that Richard spoke perfect French. It is hardly to be stated for certain in what speech Richard intended to make his temper tell at Smithfield, for the record shows that before Wat Tyler had said more than a few words the Lord Mayor of London, William Walworth, leaped in front of the king and with his dagger stabbed Tyler, swiftly and fatally. This violence interrupted the parley before it had begun. Among the various accounts of what happened after that stabbing (the Lord Mayor's dagger still appears on the shield of the City of London) there is some measure of agreement that the fourteen-year-old king did himself speak up, and with such authority and intelligibility that his promises were trusted by the rebels. One story has it that after Tyler, mortally wounded, had been carried to St Bartholomew's Church, Richard shouted to the people, 'Let me be your leader' and then rode at the head of a following crowd all the way to Clerkenwell Fields. I am no judge of exactly what to believe about that famous Smithfield crisis, yet what comes through is that if there was bandying of words between king and people the language that both used was English.

So now we are ready for the scene on London's river on a summer morning of 1385, four years after the Peasants' Revolt. It is the same scene at which we have been looking from Waterloo Bridge, for the action is below that bridge, on the open river, in full midstream. On the tide flowing up from the then London Bridge I see two boats – one a small rowing boat in which an important-looking gentleman in his fifties is being rowed by a single boatman upstream from Southwark towards Westminster. The other, much more impressive, is the King's Barge, flying the King's Standard, strongly rowed by its many rowers and coming up upon the smaller boat so rapidly that the single boatman is compelled to veer to avoid collision. The king in his barge is Richard II at the age of eighteen. I picture him, with courtier companions, laughing at the discomfiture of the small boat having to get out of the way; and yet, as soon as the king is close enough to recognize the small boat's occupant, it is Richard himself who suddenly tells his men to hold their oars. The gentleman in the small boat is John Gower. The king on the instant has schemed an interview for his own amusement.

The kidnapping of John Gower by Richard on this curve of the Thames is recorded in Gower's own words, though I doubt if Gower saw as much of the all-round comedy as we can. There was humour in the halting of the King's Barge, the surprise of courtiers, the compulsory hoisting of Gower aboard, the resumption of the king's course upstream with the startled passenger, the dropping astern of Gower's disgruntled ferryman who dared express no opinion at the snatching away of his fare. Gower does indicate the banter which it was the king's whim to indulge. The king, said Gower, wished to talk of poetry – and one feels that in such talk the quick intellect of Richard resembled, in wit, Hamlet's, while the part of 'moral Gower' was that of Polonius. During the years from 1382 through 1384 Gower had composed the second of his long major works, his large 'boke' *Vox Clamantis*, reflecting on the recent Peasants' Revolt in Latin elegiac verse of astonishing prolixity. A manuscript had properly been prepared for the king, and by now the king had read as much as he wished of *Vox Clamantis*. Richard's kidnapping of Gower was in order to have a short discussion of the poem as the King's Barge moved upstream.

As regards the Peasants' Revolt, we have seen Richard in the vortex of the actions. None knew more than he of the actualities of the mad moments, the burning of the Savoy Palace, the shouts of fury round the Tower, the shock of the killing of Tyler at Smithfield. If prolix Latin verses interposed a screen upon such actualities, Richard had a right to say so. Whatever Richard in merry mood did say to Gower about *Vox Clamantis* in its Latin we can only guess – all that enters into Gower's own report of the interview is that 'among other things said' by the impetuous young king was that young king's command that Gower should 'boke some newe thing' – in English.

In that episode I see the announcement that English literature was born to full and lusty life. The royal proclamation made on the Thames to Gower, and thereafter publicized by courtiers to others, was that if an Englishman's books were to please both king and people, they had better be put into King's English. The spread of the great assent was from that moment unchecked: obedient Gower promptly began to plan his third long poem, this time in English

> Whiche may be wisdom to the wise,
> And play to hem that list to play.

There was more to Richard's frolic of capturing Gower than the notable conversion of Gower himself into writing in English. The way the story would be repeated meant in effect a simultaneous advancement for the poet Geoffrey Chaucer, whose writings (in English) had been giving pleasure to both Richard and his talented young queen, Anne of Bohemia. Both of them, in the relatively happy early years of Richard's reign, were in their heyday of encouraging artists and poets. Chaucer, when still living in the rooms above the gate at Aldgate, had been able to show, and perhaps to recite, to the king and queen parts of *The Hous of Fame*, *The Parlement of Foules*, and *Troilus and Criseyde*. It may have been due to 'the good queen Anne' that Chaucer in 1385 was allowed to have a deputy to help his work as Comptroller of the Customs; that fits with Chaucer's expression of gratitude to Anne in the Prologue to *The Legend of Good Women*, and fits also with Chaucer's move in 1385 with his wife and son to roomier living quarters, with a garden, at

Greenwich. Although Gower, Chaucer's senior by ten years, held pride of place among elders, there is little doubt that Richard II and his young queen had more affection for Chaucer. In the encouragement of Chaucer lies an acceptable reason for saying that the birthplace of literature in English is that reach of London's river at which we have been looking.

2. LITTLE BRITAIN

The first notable hand-press in England was set up by William Caxton in the 1470s in a house behind Westminster Abbey – the site of that now-vanished house of Caxton's, which housed his apprentices as well as his press, was close to the Abbey's present Chapter House. Five years later Caxton moved from the Abbey precincts into Tothill Street, towards Petty France but still in Westminster. Caxton's name is still recorded on the present Caxton House in Tothill Street.

It was for 'pastime and pleasure', as the schoolmaster Roger Ascham later phrased it, and largely for the pleasure of the nobility and gentry, that Caxton devoted himself to producing his books 'in our English language'. Part of Caxton's problem may be expressed in his own words and his own spelling; in his time 'comyn englysshe that is spoken in one shyre varyeth from another'. Caxton's fame is thus well deserved for his superb example of one printed language that could be common to all shires, common to all who could read, and to the more who could listen. Not till he was fifty-five and had returned to England from a busy life as a textile merchant on the Continent did Caxton set about his book production with missionary zeal. In the fourteen years of life that remained to him he produced nearly a hundred different volumes, many in folio, and he wrote his own translations of as many as twenty of his books. Such industry, it is fair to note, was devoted to putting into print works of an already well established reputation. Caxton was making more widely available books hitherto known through manuscript copies; he could edit if he wished and authors could not interfere, for they were safely dead. An author nearly contemporary with Caxton was Malory, but Malory had been dead for fourteen years before Caxton freely altered and arranged his narratives and so issued the *Morte d'Arthur*. The prevailing Norman tone of the Arthurian legends was advertised by Caxton as 'animated by a high moral and spiritual purpose'. Roger Ascham, the sturdy Yorkshireman who was Queen Elizabeth's tutor, regarded that as false advertisement. The whole pleasure of Caxton's *Morte d'Arthur*, said Ascham, 'standeth in two special points, in open manslaughter and bold bawdry'.

There was a striking contrast between the work done by the hand-presses set up by Caxton beside Petty France in Westminster, and the more numerous hand-presses which came to be set up in Little Britain. Little Britain was the name of the then unsavoury region on the fringe of the ancient city of London – the region tucked in, as the street now bearing the name still is, between West Smithfield and Aldersgate. West Smithfield, at that part where the long façade of St Bartholomew's Hospital leads towards the gatehouse of the church of St Bartholomew the Great, was the scene of the confrontation of Richard II and Wat Tyler; that was the site where Wat Tyler was stabbed to death, and it became the site of the public burnings of martyrs from either side in the bitterness of the religious battles of the fifteenth and sixteenth centuries.

West Smithfield was also an area of smithies and last-minute preparations for taking to the road, for the six great radial roads of England converged then at St Paul's, three roads for the north and west leaving the City at Aldersgate, two for the west and south departing from Newgate, and the Dover Road (continuation of Watling Street to the south-east) leading across London Bridge. For the same reason that there were smithies at Smithfield – adjacency to the road-centre – the hand-presses of Little Britain came into being. The warren of narrow streets of Little Britain was likewise adjacent to the Smithfield burnings; it was where on-the-spot horror accounts of martyrdoms could be put to press hastily, often by stealth, and it was whence news-sheets and pamphlets could be quickly put upon the roads. Little Britain was the suspected source of subversive, Protestant printed matter. By 1524 Cuthbert Tunstall, then Bishop of London, was writing to Erasmus: 'new arms are being added to the great crowd of Wycliffite heretics'. The 'new arms' were the small and fugitive hand-presses of Little Britain.

By the time of the most notorious period of martyrdoms in the short reign of Queen Mary, one of the most daring printers of Little Britain was the hotheaded Protestant, John Day. Day was in custody and waiting his turn to be burned when the death of Mary and the accession in 1558 of her Protestant half-sister Elizabeth gave him reprieve. Freedom then gave Day opportunity to continue stirring 'heat and faction' against Catholics, and the return of the pamphleteer John Foxe from the Continent gave him the chance to print in England the book in Latin which Foxe had issued abroad, and which in its later editions became known as the *Book of Martyrs*. Day brought out the Latin version in 1559, and in 1563 he issued the first enlarged edition of Foxe's book in common English. Day's living quarters were in the gatehouse above Aldersgate; he never tired of speeding copies of the *Book of Martyrs* outward along the great roadway which started below his windows. One of the branches from that road went to Foxe's part of East Anglia – Foxe was a native of Boston in Lincolnshire – and from that region and others the demand for reprints of the *Book of Martyrs* and for further editions was such that publisher Day insisted on author Foxe sharing the Aldersgate household so that they might continuously work together. Four editions of the *Book of Martyrs* were published in Day's lifetime, the last in the year before his death in 1584. Foxe died soon after, but that book from Little Britain continued its career.

By Day's time printings much more elaborate than broadsheets, angry pamphlets and ballads of the kind stocked by Autolycus in *The Winter's Tale*, could be produced in Little Britain. Day himself was the first in England to cast Anglo-Saxon type, and new italic, Roman and Greek types were also introduced by him. During the bitterest period of religious war there was also a surge of competitive writings devoid of propaganda. One of the founder-members of the Stationers' Company in 1557, and influential in the placing of Stationers' Hall between the area of Little Britain and Ludgate Hill, was Richard Tottel. As a publisher mainly of law books Tottel's own headquarters were close beside the Temple, at the sign of the Hand and Star; but now and then Tottel reverted to Caxton's custom of printing literary works of writers no longer living. Thus in 1557 he issued the anthology of *Songes and Sonnets* by Henry Howard (Earl of Surrey), Sir Thomas Wyatt and others, from which is traced an immense effect.

Wyatt had died fifteen years before the printing of 'Tottel's Miscellany', and Howard had also been dead for ten years, but the printed book now brought the sonnet form, and specimens of blank verse, into sudden fashion. With a rapidly widening spread of rival Elizabethan poets, the rage for poetry writing became endemic. Interest in the work of living writers reached to some students in the universities, to some boys at prominent schools (Winchester and Eton), and to some boys at grammar schools – to select one instance, it seems to have reached at least two schoolboys at the free grammar school at Stratford-upon-Avon in Warwickshire. One of these two boys was Richard Field; the other, three years younger, was William Shakespeare. One may make out links between the fathers, though to what extent the boys were friends is pure conjecture. What is known is that the older boy set out from Stratford for London in 1579 apparently with the ambition of becoming a printer and bookseller. What then happened to Richard Field is neatly recorded by Professor Hazelton Spencer: 'having acquired a well-equipped shop by the popular method of marrying his employer's widow', he did well in London. Field was made free of the Stationers' Company in 1587. Shakespeare arrived in London as a man of twenty-two in 1586. I don't know when he first looked up his fellow-townsman, but a firm fact is that when Shakespeare made his bid to promote his own reputation as a poet, Field was the printer and publisher.

The halting of theatre work by the unusually severe outbreak of bubonic plague in the summer of 1592 probably prompted Shakespeare to write *Venus and Adonis*, addressing what he called 'the first heir of my invention' to the twenty-year-old Earl of Southampton, and to take it to Field to be printed. Shakespeare was perhaps repeatedly at Field's house to watch over details of the poem's production, for more special care is evident in the printwork of this, and also of the next poem likewise printed by Field, than Shakespeare gave to any later publications. *Venus and Adonis*, registered by Field at Stationers' Hall in April 1593, sold with gratifying speed. A new printing of *Venus* was prepared for the forthcoming year, and Field registered the next poem, *The Rape of Lucrece*, in May 1594. A new printing of *Venus* appeared in each of four consecutive years and at least ten printings of *Venus* and five of *Lucrece* were printed before 1616, the year of Shakespeare's death.

Within a short step from Little Britain there are reminders of sources of 'copy' which kept various hand-presses busy. Eastward along Cheapside from St Paul's and just before reaching Bow Church is the corner of Bread Street. Milton was born in Bread Street in 1608, and so, a generation earlier, was John Donne (1571–1631). Donne when young attended sessions of the wits at the Mermaid Tavern (on the east side of Bread Street near the junction with Cheapside) in which Marlowe before he was killed (in 1593) had been prominent, and which continued to the pleasure of Beaumont, Fletcher, Chapman, Shakespeare and others. 'What things have we seen, Done at the Mermaid!' Beaumont wrote to Ben Jonson, praising the words exchanged there – words

> So nimble, and so full of subtle flame,
> As if that every one from whence they came,
> Had meant to put his whole wit in a jest,
> And had resolv'd to live a fool, the rest
> Of his dull life.

Keats's exclamation is even more familiar:

> Souls of poets dead and gone,
> What Elysium have ye known,
> Happy field or mossy cavern,
> Choicer than the Mermaid Tavern?

(Keats, by the way, had moved with his brothers into lodgings at No. 76 Cheapside at the end of 1816. He was then still working as a dresser at Guy's Hospital, walking there, and returning, over London Bridge.)

Consider the jobs to be imposed on the hand-presses of Little Britain in the seventeenth century. A brief stroll back from Cheapside to

Aldersgate brings to mind three of them. Gresham Street, parallel to Cheapside, was where the Royal Society held its early meetings, and Edmund Halley, having extracted, piece by piece, the manuscript of the *Principia* from Isaac Newton, carried the text and diagrams along Gresham Street for printers' conferences, to be sure that the complexities of printwork were rightly understood. Halley, who interpreted his function as assistant secretary to the Royal Society as, in part, that of introducing Newton's *Principia* (arranging for the printing of it, correcting all the proofs, and paying all costs of that publication out of his own pocket), deserves the sort of remembrance of which one is aware at the corner where Love Lane enters Aldermanbury.

There the church of St Mary Aldermanbury used to stand. The interior of that church was burnt out by fire-bombs in the Second World War; then after a while the fabric that remained was stone by stone removed, transported, and re-erected at Westminster College, Fulton, Missouri, as a memorial to Winston Churchill and to commemorate the speech made by Churchill at Fulton in 1946. The outer fabric of St Mary Aldermanbury having been whisked away, the small garden through which one used to enter the church is bereft of its former purpose, yet has become more noticeable. Behind the railings in a space barely large enough for a couple of garden benches a statue stands to view – a bust of Shakespeare. Lettering on the plinth explains, however, that the statue is not a memorial solely to Shakespeare: it is dedicated to the two men who collected Shakespeare's plays and published them in the First Folio. The thought that without the efforts of these two theatre comrades, John Heminge and Henry Condell, the world might not have had the book on which all subsequent editions of the plays have depended, led the nineteenth-century Charles Clement Walker of Lilleshall Old Hall in Shropshire to set up this statue to the pair of publishers, both of them men of the parish of St Mary Aldermanbury. The pediment quotes from the Preface to the First Folio: 'We have but collected them, and done an office to the dead . . onely to keepe the memory of so worthy a Friend, & Fellow alive, as was our Shakespeare.'

My few steps from Cheapside back to Aldersgate have already reminded me of other enthusiasts on tour. 'In our little journey up to the Grande Chartreuse', wrote Thomas Gray, 'I do not remember to have gone ten paces without an exclamation, that there was no restraining. Not a precipice, not a torrent, not a cliff, but is pregnant with religion and poetry.' Here in London between the cliffs and precipices of postwar development of the Barbican, discovery of the church of St Giles's, Cripplegate, recalls a creative work that is close indeed to the heart of religion and poetry in England. Lancelot Andrewes (one is glad to see his name on one of the buildings of the Barbican development) was the

incumbent of the living of St Giles's in 1589, and it was while he worked
in this parish that his repute led on to further preferments and to his
becoming a leader in organizing and producing the Authorized Version
of the Bible. St Giles's association with the edition of the Bible which has
been of paramount influence in the English-speaking world is a third
recollection which I take with me across Aldersgate Street and into the
street which now preserves the name of Little Britain. Or perhaps it is
better to find a bench in Postmen's Garden, between Little Britain and
St Paul's, on which to sit and let what I have seen sink in.

3. POSTMEN'S GARDEN

Postmen's Garden, which now contains both open benches and a covered
shelter, is a green space bordering Little Britain, which may be entered
either from Aldersgate or from the side fronting the General Post Office.
It is an acre crowded with memories of how English literature came to
full growth.

When revisiting Postmen's Garden I was thinking, with abiding
wonder, of the small presses of Little Britain managing to cope in the
seventeenth century with the three bundles of book material just mentioned – the Bible (in the version known as 'A.V.') in 1611, the First
Folio of Shakespeare's plays in 1623, and Newton's *Principia* in 1686–7.
Three works, none (in Milton's phrase) 'beneath the reach of any point
the highest that human capacity can soar to', could be not only manufactured, but manufactured worthily. I wondered whether the dissolu-
tion of the monasteries in the previous century had resulted in driving
into London's open market a number of men of letters whose previous
employment had been within the Church; traditions of scholarship and
craftsmanship not necessarily declining when transferred to Grub
Street. The street literally named Grub Street (later called Milton
Street) was across London Wall from St Mary Aldermanbury; Bread
Street with its Mermaid Tavern was another area for the fraternity, both
intellectual and impecunious, that the name Grub Street came to
symbolize. The fraternity of men of letters noticeable round about the
previous old church of St Paul's survived the Civil War, the Fire of
London and the plague years. The closeness of writers and all others
concerned with the book trade toward the end of the seventeenth century
is suggested by a sight familiar in those days, of the tall blind poet John
Milton arm in arm with his bookselling friend Millington as they crossed
Aldersgate Street from Cripplegate into Little Britain. Both of those
men were clearly 'of a quick, ingenious, and piercing spirit', and so

were others then engaged in the corporate activity of book production. It was through able teamwork that the Authorized Version of the Bible, the Shakespeare Folio and Newton's *Principia* could each be parcelled out among several hand-presses and then assembled into completed books.

Among his printer friends in Little Britain blind Milton found concealment in the first months of the Restoration in 1660. Presently he was discovered and apprehended, but after payment of a fine he was released and returned to the composition and dictation of *Paradise Lost*, begun in 1650 yet not completed until 1663. Before *Paradise Lost* was put to press came the interlude when Milton and his three teenage daughters and their stepmother, his third wife, sought refuge from the worst part of London's plague years in the cottage still affectionately preserved at Chalfont St Giles in Buckinghamshire. Milton's return to living quarters close to Aldersgate enabled the printing of *Paradise Lost* to be done in 1667, and from then on Milton had a book of one sort or another on the press each year till his death, at the age of sixty-six, in 1674. Then he was buried beside his father at St Giles's, Cripplegate.

The bustling figure of Samuel Pepys comes into the story of the printing of Newton's *Principia*; his signature, on behalf of the Royal Society, was appended to the *imprimatur* of the first edition. At the other extreme of jobbing printing in Little Britain weekly news-sheets were being produced from early in the seventeenth century, and at the start of the eighteenth century the first daily newspaper in the English-speaking world was produced (in 1702) by Samuel Buckley. Buckley's paper, the *Daily Courant*, was printed in one of the narrow streets just to the north of Postmen's Garden. Seven years later, in April 1709, Richard Steele and Joseph Addison, who had been schoolmates at the Charterhouse off Aldersgate Street nearby, began to have the *Tatler* printed in Little Britain's Cross Key Square. The *Daily Courant*, and Steele's activity in following up the *Tatler* with the *Spectator* and the *Guardian*, soon produced rivals. In 1725, at the age of nineteen, Benjamin Franklin came to Little Britain from Philadelphia to put in his eighteen months' study of London's printing practices and newspaper work. Part of the time Franklin lodged at the inn in Little Britain called the Golden Fan. He was quick to notice that a matter of ever-increasing interest to publishers of periodicals and books was the speed of distribution of their products by road. Mailcoaches ('flying machines' as they were then called) had begun to ply over the main roads after the Restoration, and it was of continuing advantage to have printing works close to the main despatch point at the hub of England's six great radial roads.

The present buildings of London's General Post Office are sited beside St Paul's as if to preserve recognition of this original central despatch point when, from Roman times onward, the main roads all reached outward from here. When Wren's new St Paul's was built after the Great Fire of 1666 the 'riding redoubtable dome of Paul' was as it were the very hubcap at the junction of all main routes. Yet in the eighteenth century, with much increase of traffic and congestion within the City, the starting points for some of the roads tended to move outward, away from St Paul's. The Great North Road, from which the Manchester Road branched off, continued to start from Aldersgate, but presently the London end of the Holyhead Road (resuming its ancient name of Watling Street at St Albans) was regarded as being at Tyburn, and in the nineteenth century the London end of that road was marked by Marble Arch. Similarly, in the heyday of mailcoach days, the Portsmouth Road and the Bath Road were both reckoned to start from Hyde Park Corner, and the Dover Road (south-eastern portion of Watling Street) began at the Southwark end of London Bridge. Furthermore, parliamentary action in the eighteenth century began to cause presswork for newspapers to move away from Little Britain. In 1713 a stamp duty was imposed on newspapers with the object of controlling subversive tendencies, and thereafter – the stamp duty continued until 1855 – newspaper offices tended to move to Fleet Street, for convenience when the stamp office was at Somerset House.

Postmen's Garden in its present quietude did not come into existence until the twentieth century, as the present name of the street at its western end, King Edward Street, indicates. In the eighteenth century Little Britain was still showing more liveliness than appears nowadays. Despite the stamp tax, there were by 1776 fifty-three newspapers being issued in London; most of the printing and posting to all parts of the island was still starting from the traditional hub beside St Paul's; and, as I mused in Postmen's Garden, my thoughts kept dwelling on the ways in which the lust for reading were promoted from this centre. The best description of the eagerness with which many eighteenth-century country-dwellers awaited the arrival of the postman's bag at the village inn is in Cowper's poems.

Hark! 'tis the twanging horn o'er yonder bridge

is the line which opens Book IV of Cowper's *The Task*. The subscriber having obtained his London newspaper, he proceeds to read aloud to his domestic circle all four pages of it:

Now stir the fire, and close the shutters fast,
Let fall the curtains, wheel the sofa round,
And, while the bubbling and loud-hissing urn
Throws up a steamy column, and the cups,
That cheer but not inebriate, wait on each,
So let us welcome peaceful ev'ning in.

The *Tatler*, *Spectator* and the many other periodicals that succeeded them increased the craving for literature. The periodicals from London, so Cowper says, have warmed people to utter

> one gen'ral cry,
> Tickle and entertain us, or we die.

Along with 'the multiplication of accelerated stage-coaches' very noticeable in the 1780s and later, went the spreading appetite for reading; incentives towards reading-matter of one kind or another coursed along main roads and filtered through capillaries to every parish, so it seems, in England. In return for what went out from London, the suction inward of rival talents from the widely differing country provinces was equally increased. The growth and spread of English literature in the eighteenth and nineteenth centuries is clearly linked with the road-building that went on. Two Scottish roadmakers whose works had side-effects on the growth of literature were Thomas Telford (1757–1834) and his almost exact contemporary, John Loudon McAdam, whose name became the synonym for the road surface most suitable for the noble mailcoach and the 'royal magnificence' of its horses.

Postmen's Garden is a portion of significant soil in relation to the development of the English novel – doubly significant, in that in Little Britain the first seedlings were made ready for the market, and from the other side of the garden the Post Office managed the distribution. In Postmen's Garden I never fail to think of Daniel Defoe, the 'link' between the essay-writers of the early eighteenth century and the subsequent great novelists. This very area was Defoe's boyhood playground; his father (whose name was plain Foe) was a butcher in the parish of St Giles's, Cripplegate, but the boy's schooling and aptitudes led him to the journalism of Little Britain. Defoe was sixty when, in 1719, he produced the first volume of *Robinson Crusoe*, which was widely pirated, as was the second volume which he produced in the next year. The *Journal of the Plague Year* and *Moll Flanders* were among other books published for Defoe in 1722, and in Postmen's Garden I don't forget Moll Flanders pictured as passing my bench, carrying her bundle from Little Britain into Newgate Street.

Following *Moll Flanders*, the first part of *Pamela, or Virtue Rewarded* was published for Samuel Richardson in 1740. Richardson, like Defoe before him, knew Little Britain in boyhood; he was a native of Derbyshire, but his schooling was at Charterhouse – Little Britain, between Charterhouse to the north and the Bluecoat School to the south, was presumably out of bounds to both schools, and doubtless more exciting for that reason. Yet in an area where coarseness was common, Richardson moved quietly. As a mouselike boy of seventeen, he was apprenticed to a printer whose daughter he afterwards married; subsequently he set up his own printing works in Salisbury Court, Fleet Street. The success of *Pamela* sparked off Fielding's *The History of Joseph Andrews*; *Tom Jones* appeared in 1749; in the previous year Richardson had published *Clarissa Harlowe* and Smollett had returned to London to enter the lists with *Roderick Random*. The three distinct great names of Richardson, Fielding and Smollett soon attracted lesser rivals, and so began the time that Lady Mary Wortley Montagu could enjoy in Italy, because she could count on receiving boxes full of new novels from her daughter in England. In later developments of the novel – Jane Austen, and Maria Edgeworth setting Walter Scott to dash off the Waverley novels one after another – and even more when the first appearance of novels was in serial form in one or another competing periodical, the correlation between literary creativity and the road network by which it spread ever increases. I have the feeling in Postmen's Garden that I am at the very secret centre whence much has emanated.

I have touched but a moiety of what Postmen's Garden may be a reminder; if one were to bring to it a fully prepared mind, what a comprehensive refresher course of English literature could start from here! The paramount message conveyed by Postmen's Garden is, however, that it is not an acre in which to linger lazily, but from which to start. Sit where you like in the garden, the shadow of the General Post Office Headquarters building will attract your attention, and if you then close your eyes the phantom sound you hear is an echo of what De Quincey heard in the 1820s:

> Every moment you hear the thunder of lids locked down upon the mail-bags. That sound to each individual mail is the signal for drawing off, which process is the finest part of the entire spectacle. Then come the horses into play. Horses! Can these be horses which bound off with the actions and gestures of leopards? What stir! What sea-like ferment! What a thundering of wheels! What a trampling of hoofs! What a sounding of trumpets!

(And what a writer, De Quincey, with his horses like leopards!)

Since I have been convinced of the intimacy in which England's literature and England's roadways grew up together, I have arranged my survey of England's writers in accordance with the road structure. In no literature other than English is 'sense of place' more to be appreciated and enjoyed, and by travelling each traditional road in company with writers that 'sense of place' awakes. Up then, says De Quincey, let us take the road – let us bound away from Postmen's Garden with the actions and gestures of leopards.

*   *   *

But am I to depart from the City of London without further mention of other shrines that London holds for literary pilgrims?

Return a moment to Waterloo Bridge. To make one scene stand out, how many others were obliterated? Suppose a glance upstream had rested on the next bridge, Hungerford Bridge, which carries the railway into Charing Cross station. A straightforward engineering job, confessedly uninteresting, is Hungerford Bridge, not worth the glance – yet stay a second: that bridge carries both railway and footway. It was on that footway of Hungerford Bridge, on the black rain-drenched equinoctial night in September 1887, that Sherlock Holmes allowed the young John Openshaw to be intercepted and lured to death on the Embankment, as five orange pips had fatefully foretold. How could it ever be that on a night when to people indoors 'the wind cried and sobbed like a child in the chimney', Holmes – despite the prescience that had made him twice 'rave in the air' – remained with Watson at the Baker Street fireside, thus sending his client to go it alone to his fate? Well, little doubt the answer is that it made a good story to tickle and entertain readers of the famous *Strand Magazine*.

Hungerford – the sound connects in many ways with writers. 'Until old Hungerford Market was pulled down, until old Hungerford Stairs were destroyed', said Dickens, 'I never had the courage to go back to the place where my servitude began. . . .' Hungerford Stairs was where Dickens as a child was employed (and David Copperfield also) in the servitude of labelling bottles for six or seven shillings a week at the shoe-blacking factory. The emphasis on the first part of the name Hungerford clung to the neighbourhood. Long after the market had been pulled down, 'Harris, the Sausage King' moved into nearby No. 43 Villiers Street, and that meant that a hard-up young writer, Rudyard Kipling, bargained for cheap living quarters there, on the topmost fifth floor. The attraction of those quarters to Kipling was that each morning the Sausage King would allow him enough sausage and mash for tuppence for his daily support. It is not supposed that was good for Kipling's digestion, yet it enabled him to thump out *Barrack-Room Ballads* to the rumble of Charing Cross trains and 'the boom of the Strand' – and thus began Rudyard Kipling's rise to fortune as an author. . . .

My point is that anywhere in central London a glance in any direction leads to some 'literary association', and one identification leads at the instant to another and another and another. Site-seeing in London mostly depends on what's already in the mind, 'who' or 'what' one wishes to look up. London, the Great Wen, the city *a per se*, generally has an answer if one has formed the question. What I have been attempting in a view of London's river, a glimpse of Little Britain and a moment in Postmen's Garden are the large queries, how a literature was bred, how begot and nourished. The interest in who took part depends upon how alive the names become. For instance, I mentioned Samuel Pepys: he comes to mind in Little Britain, as he does so often at many other of London's sites. No man ever comes more fully to life than Pepys does in his *Diary*; of the myriad recollections one may have of Pepys, which scene should be selected?

Pepys came to Little Britain to buy books. Street names in Little Britain have often changed and the street now named as Little Britain was in Pepys's time called Duck Lane and inhabited largely by booksellers. An entry in Pepys's *Diary* in April 1668 (when he was thirty-five) has often caused amusement: Pepys went to Duck Lane 'and there kissed bookseller's wife'. Pepys later revealed the kiss was obtained by taking advantage of her 'in las tenebras' of an alcove; a few days later he walked through Duck Lane 'only to get a sight of the pretty little woman', and again three days after that glimpse he 'did find her sola' in the bookshop, 'but had not la confidence para aller à elle. So lost my pains. But will another time. . . .' But the bookseller's wife showed no wish to be fondled again by Pepys. No less than eight attempts are mentioned, but he 'got no ground', and towards the end dismisses her from the *Diary* as 'not worth seeing' (although, despite that, he tries once more).

The human comedy enacted by both Mr and Mrs Samuel Pepys connects, however, most of all with the other side of London's City – with Tower Hill. Pepys was a man of twenty-two and his wife Elizabeth a girl of fifteen when they were married, and when the *Diary* opens they were barely five years older, living at Axe Yard, Westminster, on a salary of £50 a year. To Axe Yard Pepys might return after an evening of music with like-minded friends to find 'my wife and maid a-washing', and after his writing of an early diary entry the passage ends at past one of the clock when he 'went to bed, and left my wife and the maid a-washing still'. Came then the change of fortune: the monarchy was restored, Pepys's patron was in power, and Pepys was of a sudden jumped up to high position in the Navy Office. The post was completely new to him, and it thrust the young pair suddenly into living at the Navy House on Tower Hill, sandwiched between the two grand admirals, Sir William Penn and Sir William Batten. These were both gentry of the class of £10000 a year. Pepys's basic salary had multiplied to £350. How were the Pepyses to avoid obvious social disparity with such neighbours? Their handling of that question lends delight to a visit to St Olave's, Hart Street, beside Tower Hill.

St Olave's was the parish church attended by officers of the Navy House and their wives, and Pepys's instant ingenuity arranged that a special Navy House gallery was erected within the church wherein the admirals and he, and especially Mrs Pepys and Lady Batten, could be observed to be worshipping side by side. That gallery was a first success – but servants had to be kept out of the gallery, for servants, on the scale natural to admirals, were not within Pepys's means. A next idea about servants induced Pepys to visit his family home at Brampton in Huntingdonshire to lure his younger sister Paulina ('Pall' for short) to enjoy the excitements of London by living and working for him and Elizabeth at the Navy House. Pepys 'told her plainly what my mind was, to have her come not as a sister in any respect, but as a servant, which she promised me that she would, and with many thanks did weep for joy, which did give me and my wife some content and satisfaction'. So with Pall as extra unpaid servant the Pepyses successfully managed their first Navy House dinner in style, and both admirals (and Lady Batten) returned again to supper and to talk till late.

(After six months a sadder entry in the *Diary* is that Pall was becoming 'proud and idle'. It is true that Pall was five years younger than Pepys, but she was two years older than Elizabeth. Pepys at that time made no allowance for Pall, when put upon, to have any 'feelings'. After nine months of being servant at the Navy House 'Pall crying exceedingly' was given twenty shillings by Pepys and sent back by wagon to the parents at Brampton.)

It was nine years after entering the social life of the Navy House on Tower Hill that Elizabeth Pepys contracted one of the fevers which in those days were fatal within a few days. When she died she was only twenty-nine. After the burial at St Olave's Church, Pepys commissioned a marble bust of her which he caused to be placed high on the wall of the church, so that its gaze was directed towards his seat in the Navy House gallery. It was his way of stating that it would help him to go straight if her eye were on him. The Navy House gallery within the church has vanished, and indeed the whole interior of St Olave's, Hart Street, was badly damaged in the Second World War – but by forethought that bust of Mrs Pepys had been removed to safety, and so is now restored to its original place.

Tower Hill is thus the site for a really significant memory of the Pepyses. But if Pepys brings us from Postmen's Garden to look at Tower Hill, there we must either guard against or succumb to other memories. Writers alone range here from Sir Walter Raleigh, prisoned in his apartment in the Bloody Tower and attempting to ease his 'damnable proud' spirit by working on the *History of the World*, to Joseph Conrad who on Tower Hill suddenly understood 'that I had done with the sea, and that henceforth I had to be a writer'.

The visit to St Olave's, Hart Street, was a legitimate digression; yet to guard against too many digressions that Tower Hill might induce, it is better to hasten back to Postmen's Garden and prepare for the first

L.B.—B

of our journeys. If we make six trips, one after another, along England's six major A roads we shall not only survey the whole of England and Wales, but by returning between trips to London shall have the opportunity to pick up many things in several parts of the metropolis. With the wealth of literary gossip of Greater London as a whole, no compiler can cope. Goodness! – even in the little part of Little Britain visible from Postmen's Garden, I have been omitting much. But in our road trips a great sufficiency of Londoners are likely to be met with again, and the road trips are the best way of meeting those writers who began life in the several parts of the country and who were brought to London (permanently or not) by what Geoffrey Grigson has called 'the unpredictable genetics of literature'.

A1

THE GREAT NORTH ROAD

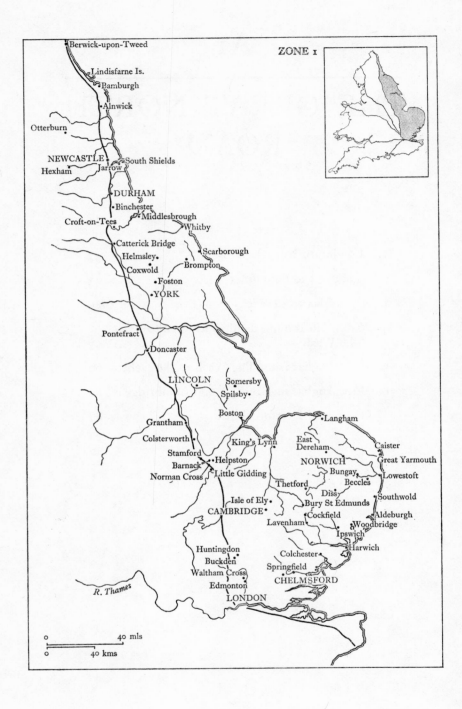

ZONE 1

1 . LONDON TO NORMAN CROSS

The Great North Road whose end in Edinburgh is at the impressive Rock known as Arthur's Seat – that road which from its beginning has partnered the myriad events which crowd its mere four hundred miles – ought, one feels, to give the impression of starting off from London with more of a flourish than it does.

Without fuss A1 takes its departure from Aldersgate. When James Boswell at the age of twenty-two took his departure from Edinburgh, travelling in the opposite direction 'up' to London, he could signal the event by 'bowing thrice to Arthur Seat, that lofty romantic mountain'. For one setting off from London northward a corresponding obeisance might here be made to the dome of St Paul's, but then no further ceremony is encouraged as the remainder of Aldersgate Street bypasses the hidden Smithfield and the hidden Charterhouse to turn itself for half a mile into Goswell Road. In the time of the young Dickens Goswell Road was called Goswell Street, and Dickens had some irreverent fun to make of it. Demonstrably it was Goswell Street that confronted Mr Samuel Pickwick when he burst from his slumbers on a certain May morning of 1827, threw open his chamber window and looked on the world beneath. 'Goswell Street was at his feet, Goswell Street was on his right hand – as far as the eye could reach Goswell Street extended on his left; and the opposite side of Goswell Street was over the way.' The excitement promoted by Goswell Street prompted Mr Pickwick to seek adventure – yet not on the Great North Road, but in the contrary direction.

Goswell Road leads directly to the Angel, Islington, and of the Angel Dickens remarks (in *Oliver Twist*) that for anyone coming into London by the Great North Road it was here, from the crowd of passengers and number of vehicles, that the London of his time began in earnest. Conversely, it was at the Angel that many a traveller northward in the 1820s would join his stagecoach. William Hazlitt, for instance, three years before the start of *Pickwick*, climbed into a northbound coach at the Angel and so met the fellow-passenger, the widowed Mrs Bridge-water, who after that journey together became his second wife. Goswell Street got Mr Pickwick into his breach-of-promise trouble (*Bardell* v. *Pickwick*), and the coach at the Angel was a trap for the widow and Hazlitt. Hazlitt had reason already to consider his temperament un-suited to matrimony, yet that coach journey induced a second try, which presently resulted in a second separation.

We shall meet Hazlitt again, and another whom we shall encounter elsewhere is Edward Lear of the *Nonsense Rhymes*, whose birthplace was close to the coach-road between the Angel and Highgate. The Great North Road was ever a working road, and I had been prepared rather to find individuals of unusual talent using it for travel than to find them born beside it. But Edward Lear is one of the exceptions. Close to the corner where our road crosses Seven Sisters Road was Bowman's Lodge in Bowman's Mews and there, as the second youngest in a family of twenty-one children, Lear was born in May 1812. He was thus an almost exact contemporary of Charles Dickens, who was born in February of the same year, and there were some similarities in the backgrounds of the two boys. Both learned that early Victorian society could be 'a cruel jungle' (in Angus Wilson's phrase) for those whose parents 'clung with difficulty to the ornamental edge of gentility'. Lear's father, with up and down performances at stockbroking, was put into the King's Bench prison in much the same way that Dickens's father was put into the Marshalsea. Mrs Lear (who had originally come from Durham) had an even greater task than Mrs Dickens (or than Mrs Micawber) to keep her troop of children in sustenance. By the time Edward arrived Mrs Lear was no longer much interested; the nurture of the younger children devolved largely on the eldest daughter, and it was to this sister, Ann, that Lear, a weakly child with epileptic seizures and later a somewhat gauche young man, owed a kindly upbringing. It was especially his sister Ann who encouraged the boy's talent for drawing, and when he came of age his expert draughtsmanship of birds brought him to the attention of the Linnaean Society. Edward Smith Stanley, President of that Society, became thirteenth Earl of Derby in 1834; it pleased him to take the young Lear to the noble estate of Knowsley Hall near Liverpool for him to make drawings there of the collection of psittacidae; and presently that was where Lear had the amusement of illustrating his own *Book of Nonsense* for the Earl's grandchildren.

At the present-day Archway Tavern the road north momently divides. The left fork, rising steeply between hospitals, is Highgate Hill. This was to have been Whittington's way out of London; when London's church bells called him back, he turned, as the Whittington Stone has been set by the roadway to testify. Off the High Street at the hilltop, at No. 3 The Grove, Coleridge lived for the last eighteen years of his life. There, a shade of his former self, Coleridge (as Hazlitt said) 'talked on for ever; and you wished him to talk on for ever'. In our time I can remember T. S. Eliot saying (he repeated the remark in print) that he had felt the pale ghost of Coleridge beckoning. There is no knowing whether when Eliot taught in school at Highgate it ever crossed his mind – possibly it did – that Coleridge's remains were then still mouldering below the chapel of Highgate Grammar School. A hundred years after Coleridge's death in 1834 not many people remembered where he had been buried, but in 1961 the remains were disinterred and reburied in St Michael's Church on Highgate Hill.

Before the nineteenth century the way into London from the north had been through Highgate High Street and Highgate Hill. This way Boswell arrived in November 1762. His mode of travel, all the way from Edinburgh, had been by post-chaise. Stagecoaches throughout the eighteenth century had remained slow and heavy vehicles, largely because roads, especially where they crossed heavy clay, remained bad for wheeled traffic. Trevelyan's *English Social History* indicates that it was the efforts of individual turnpike companies, obtaining payment for the maintenance of particular stretches of highway from the actual road-users, which by degrees effected improvement. Yet by the time of Boswell's journey the stagecoaches from Edinburgh 'still had no springs, had heavy wheels like a waggon, carried six inside but had no seats for passengers outside, though the humble were sometimes allowed to cling to the luggage on the roof'. Trevelyan also points out that 'the red-coated guard with his blunderbuss was much in requisition, for the highway-man, still at the height of his glory, could easily ride down any attempt to escape'. Boswell, then, as most other long-distance travellers, preferred to hire a post-chaise. That was expensive, but one could arrange to share the cost with a companion. Post-chaise journeying was rapid, up to a hundred miles a day on thoroughfares where a change of horses at posting inns could be counted on, and, with a chaise, stopping-places could be decided on to allow sufficient time for eating and sleeping. One Monday Boswell was 'bowing thrice to Arthur Seat' and by the succeeding Friday, after four nights on the road, he and his male companion 'came upon Highgate hill and had a view of London'. At that fine sight 'I was all life and joy', exclaims his *Journal*. 'I gave three huzzas, and we went briskly in' – and so, before long, to meet Dr Johnson.

On the road up to London in 1762 Boswell and his travelling companion spent the four nights at Berwick, Durham, Doncaster and Biggleswade. There was nothing unusual in the inconveniences of the journey. Near Berwick 'one of the wheels of our chaise was so much broke that it was of no use'. Between Stamford and Stilton 'there was a young unruly horse in the chaise which run away with the driver, and jumping to one side of the road, we were overturned. We got a pretty severe rap'. Nearing Biggleswade, Boswell confesses that during the last two stages 'which we travelled in the dark, I was a good deal afraid of robbers. A great many horrid ideas filled my mind. . . . However, I affected resolution, and as each of us carried a loaded pistol in his hand, we were pretty secure. We got at night to Biggleswade.' The fears had not been wholly fanciful and the safe arrival at Highgate in 1762 deserved the three huzzas.

Very considerable was the change in conditions of travel by the time of Hazlitt's journey in 1824. After the turn of the century McAdam's ideas for improving the road surface were becoming effective; with the improvement of the road surface there was quick improvement in vehicles, and for the sake of speed sharp bends and hills began to be avoided. Thus Hazlitt's northbound coach would have chosen the right-hand fork where the Archway Tavern is now and by using a milder slope would have bypassed Highgate altogether. Alterations of that kind along the length of the Great North Road caused Walter Scott to say, towards 1830, that the road, though convenient, had become dull. No longer were there so many enlivening accidents and no longer the occasional skirmish with a highwayman.

In Barnet High Street there is a fork in the Great North Road which dictates the method of narration in this book. The left-hand fork in Barnet, the St Albans Road, is the beginning of route A6, the Manchester Road which ultimately, after Carlisle, continues to Glasgow, which I will cover in a later chapter. My present route A1 proceeds through Hatfield, Welwyn, Stevenage, Baldock, Biggleswade, and my first real pause along the Great North Road shall be at Buckden, where a road forks off to Huntingdon.

In *Nicholas Nickleby* Dickens selected the White Hart at Eaton Socon as a stopping-place for Wackford Squeers and his schoolboy victims on their way to Yorkshire. It is for memories of two very different individuals – Oliver Cromwell and Samuel Pepys – that I prefer to halt at Buckden (Laurence Sterne was a curate at Buckden in 1738, but so very temporarily that I leave him out). For the first of these memories, Hinchingbrook House, between here and Huntingdon, belonged to the Cromwell family until 1627. Cromwell, when representing Huntingdon in King Charles's Parliament, rode past the old family house to join the Great North Road at Buckden; but his uncle had been forced to sell Hinchingbrook to the highest bidder, who proved to be one of the Montagu family and who was building a wall round the place. When the big house was sold Cromwell was a man of twenty-eight, married (he was married at St Giles's, Cripplegate) and with a son a year old. Now, passing from the snapshot of Cromwell, unhappy about the state of the nation, riding moodily past Hinchingbrook to London, I skip to the young Edward Montagu, a child of two at the time Hinchingbrook was bought from the Cromwells. At the age of eighteen, he joined the Parliamentary army, proceeded to attract Cromwell's attention by valiant conduct, and went on to hold high office on land and sea during the Commonwealth. This was the same Montagu who after Cromwell's death worked for the restoration of limited monarchy. Charles II at the Restoration created him the first Earl of Sandwich, and so he was in a position to pitchfork his young cousin, Samuel Pepys, into the Navy House on London's Tower Hill. The Montagus did what they could for their poorer relations, the Pepyses; on purchase of Hinchingbrook the Pepys family had been settled into a cottage at Brampton, a dependency of the estate. There Samuel Pepys grew up and was educated at the same school at Huntingdon that Cromwell had attended thirty years before, and after Cambridge was provided by the Restoration with scope for his many abilities.

Buckden reminds me that Pepys's career had awkward moments. The wagon by which his tearful sister Pall was returned to the cottage at Brampton turned off at the road-fork at Buckden. For a long time Pepys's conduct to Pall creates more sympathy with her than with him; it is pleasant to remember that in his will Pepys became kindly to Pall. The scare about invasion by the Dutch in 1667 gave the Pepyses a notable spasm of agitation. Samuel sent off his wife and his father from London for Brampton 'with about £1300 in gold in their night-bag'. A chancy journey on seventeenth-century roads, with that noticeably heavy night-bag; before and after the turn-off at Buckden there may have been anxieties for Elizabeth Pepys and her father-in-law. 'Pray God give them good passage, and good care to hide it when they come home! but my heart is full of fear' is what Pepys said to his diary on 13 June. On the 19th, when Elizabeth had returned to Tower Hill to report, Pepys learned to his horror that when the travellers had safely reached Brampton they had grown careless. The burying of the gold at the cottage had been done on Sunday, 'in open daylight, in the midst of the garden; where, for aught they knew, many eyes might see them'. That put Pepys into such a state that he was 'almost mad' about it.

At Alconbury Hill the Roman Ermine Street comes from Huntingdon to join the Great North Road, and the opening paragraph of Jane Austen's *Mansfield Park* tells how two of the Ward sisters of Huntingdon came journeying this way. 'Miss Maria Ward, of Huntingdon, with only seven thousand pounds, had the good luck to captivate Sir Thomas Bertram, of Mansfield Park, in the county of Northampton, and to be thereby raised to the rank of a baronet's lady, with all the comforts and consequences of a handsome house and large income.' Her elder sister was not regarded as so fortunate; she, half a dozen years after Maria had become Lady Bertram, 'found herself obliged to be attached to the Rev. Mr Norris'. Yet as Sir Thomas was able to provide the clergyman with a living at Mansfield, Mrs Norris – surely one of the most famously diverting of all of Jane Austen's characters – travelled this same road. There is, however, a slight geographical puzzle for the readers of

Mansfield Park. The name Mansfield may have been stored by Jane Austen in her reticule when she was winding up *Pride and Prejudice* and glancing there at the country on the Derbyshire–Nottingham border, yet it is clear that she placed Sir Thomas Bertram's Mansfield Park in the Northampton county adjacent to Huntingdon. Therefore Mrs Norris, on her way to join her sister and thereby precipitate the story, had no very lengthy journey to make on the Great North Road itself. Her chaise had presumably only to cross the road and to make its way beyond Little and Great Gidding.

It was at Little Gidding that Nicholas Ferrar in 1625 founded the small 'Protestant nunnery' which for a generation previous to ours was described in the novel *John Inglesant* by J. H. Shorthouse. In more recent times T. S. Eliot attached a section of his *Four Quartets* to Little Gidding, a place, as he phrased it, 'where prayer has been valid'. Eliot for many years felt an affinity with George Herbert, whose poetry was disseminated through the good offices of Ferrar at Little Gidding. The small partly seventeenth-century church used by the community remains today.

Returning to the Great North Road, a very different literary association is found at Norman Cross. That place-name is a reminder that one of the 'Eleanor crosses' was once by the roadside, but 'Norman Cross' was deemed a more appropriate name when French prisoners were confined in numbers here during the Napoleonic wars. Before the old prison barracks were eliminated, George Borrow came here from Peterborough as a boy of eight with his mother, travelling all of that way by boat. What then happened at the 'strange place it was, this Norman Cross', can be discovered in Chapters IV and V of *Lavengro*, where readers make their first acquaintance with the gipsy Jasper Petulengro.

The sudden reminder that as recently as 1811 journeys perhaps as far as from The Wash to the Great North Road often had to be made by boat, makes us recognize that the initially military road pushed north by the Romans was at this point something like a high-tide mark; the road was borderline to a wide flat treacherously submersible region of fenland. The heritage of the strangeness of the Fenland continued to be felt, being expressed in this century by Dorothy Sayers, who was brought up in her father's rectory at Bluntisham, near the site of Cromwell's one-time grazing-farm at St Ives on the River Ouse. *The Nine Tailors*, in which Dorothy Sayers's feeling for the Fenland is most manifest, was written in the 1930s when she was living at Witham near Chelmsford, but the story was placed at the church of Terrington St Clement, in the wettest part of the Fenland near The Wash and not far from King's Lynn. In the ancient period of four hundred years of Roman rule some efforts were made, yet without much success, to drain the water and reduce flooding of the Fenland. Then the early Church did manage to establish some landmarks, hermitages and even monastic buildings on partially dry islands. The present-day Isle of Ely was a real island when King Canute's barge was rowed across the brackish brown water beside it – as witnessed by the ballad:

> Merrily sang they, the monks at Ely,
> When Canut the King he rowed thereby;
> Row to the shore, men, said the King,
> And let us hear these monks to sing.

When the Normans considered they had conquered most of England, Hereward the Wake was one Fenland hero who, like the Robin Hood of inland country, continued after death to assert through legend the independent spirit of the Danelaw in general, and the spirit of his own Fenland in particular. A characteristic of the Fenland that had emerged in early times was that when floods stood in the land, any eminence was a haven for whatever strange company the emergency might bring together. Where a church was built if only on a slight rise, upon occasion it could be equal sanctuary, for the moment at least, for any refugee, inlaw or outlaw. Church towers came to have a double function as landmarks by day and by night, when so required, as lighthouses. Perhaps the most famous of the 'lantern churches' was Boston Stump; when the floods were out 'And all the world was in the sea', as night fell some who had otherwise lost hope could mark, as in the verse of Jean Ingelow,

> the lofty beacon light
> Stream from the church tower, red and high.

The development of very early hermits' chapels into the later lantern churches, each by both bell and beacon offering a haven, was a theme with which Dorothy Sayers had special sympathy.

2. STAMFORD TO PONTEFRACT

A nineteenth-century writer who spent much of his childhood at the Old Rectory at Barnack, south-east of Stamford, on the fringe of the watery Fenland area surrounding the River Welland, was Charles Kingsley, and one may ponder if childhood familiarity with flooded country had anything to do with the later writing of *The Water Babies* – though the writing of that book was in fact triggered by a later stay of Kingsley at Malham Tarn in Yorkshire. Wholly native to the Welland river area was the ploughman-poet John Clare (1793–1864). I had been thinking (in Postmen's Garden before leaving London) of the way in which lusts for reading spread from main roads into rural parishes, and might instance the delicious passage in *The Winter's Tale* (IV, iv) where Shakespeare has fun with the pedlar Autolycus selling ballads to country folk. That was a picture frequently repeated in the eighteenth century; a case in point was that of John Clare's father, a farm labourer. John Clare recorded the hard conditions of rural life for the labourers in his birthplace, the village of Helpston. John, like his father before him, began his farm-work at the age of seven to add his tiny pittance to the pittance of the family wages. The one escape the father had found, whenever he had a halfpenny to squander, was to acquire a newly printed ballad for his well-worn collection. The boy took to reading even more eagerly, and his heart found its own singing:

> the lark high above charmed me all the day long
> So I sat down and joined in the chorus of song.

Unhappily he suffered in adult life such increase of mental instability that there were many years of total collapse and confinement in the asylum at Northampton. Clare knew long periods of death-in-life, such as were known also to Christopher Smart, Robert Bloomfield and William Cowper. At lucid times memories came back to Clare:

> Summer's pleasures they are gone like to visions every one,
> And the cloudy days of autumn and of winter cometh on.
> I tried to call them back, but unbidden they are gone
> Far away from heart and eye and for ever far away.
> Dear heart, and can it be that such raptures meet decay?
> I thought them all eternal when by Langley Bush I lay,
> I thought them joys eternal when I used to shout and play
> On its bank at 'clink and bandy', 'chock' and 'taw' and 'ducking stone',
> Where silence sitteth now on the wild heath as her own
> Like a ruin of the past all alone.

When Clare was dying it was at his request that a grave was prepared for him where his boyhood had been happy, at Helpston.

Stamford, presumably named for its stone ford over the River Welland, is a pleasing stone-built town where at Ned Drury's shop in the High Street Clare got his books for 'little or nothing'. Drury was a cousin of the publisher John Taylor, and caused Clare's *Poems of Rural Life* to be sent to him. Taylor, publisher likewise of Keats, issued that first book of Clare's in the same year (1820) as Keats's *Lamia, Isabella, The Eve of St Agnes, and other Poems.*

Proceeding over slightly rising country from Stamford towards Grantham, we may recall at Colsterworth that Isaac Newton was born on Christmas Day 1642 at Woolsthorpe Manor, a small compact limestone house nearby. It is fitting to mention Newton again, partly because I spoke of his *Principia* in my preamble and partly to make a point which should be borne in mind when journeys take us on to Cambridge and Oxford. Important as the jostling with others in college life has ever been for the rare individual gifted with genius of the first order, the creative work of such minds has frequently been done not at but away from universities. Especially in realms where apparatus is least essential (as notably in poetry and 'pure' mathematics) the observation may be true. It was certainly true of Newton that when the plague caused him to interrupt his time at Cambridge and return to Woolsthorpe for the years 1665 and 1666, it was in country isolation here that by self-prompting he discovered the binomial theorem, differential and integral calculus, exercises such as the computing of the area of the hyperbola, and implications of the idea of universal gravitation. 'In the two plague years', Newton later reflected, 'I was in the prime of my age for invention, and minded mathematics and philosophy more than at any time since.' Those prime years were, for Newton, the years when he was twenty-one and twenty-two. The writing-out of the *Principia* he achieved when Halley had harried and hounded him to that task. It was in the apple orchard in front of Woolsthorpe Manor that legend asserts the thoughts of universal gravitation were triggered. The Manor and the orchard site are now both cared for by the National Trust, and legitimacy is claimed for at least one descendant of Newton's apple tree.

Because Newton's *Principia* was designed for export beyond the then confines of the English-speaking world, it was written and printed in Latin, and that might seem to remove Newton from my survey. If such objection were pressed I would still bring in Newton for the pleasure of his English prose-writing, notably in his *History of the Jews*. The seventeenth century has often been called a 'century of genius', partly because nobody then writing seemed to fail to write well. Certainly Isaac Newton's English prose, for its lucidity and cadence, is a pleasure to read.

In 1782 the Suffolk poet George Crabbe turned off the Great North Road, perhaps before reaching Newton's village of Colsterworth, to take up his post as domestic chaplain at Belvoir Castle. Crabbe's extraordinary transition from the harsh life at Slaughden Quay beside Aldeburgh to the household at Belvoir Castle was due to Edmund Burke. It may also have been to Burke's secret amusement that the owner of Belvoir Castle – the Duke of Rutland, son of the famous Marquis of Granby who had a record number of inn-signs named in his honour – wished to have the somewhat awkward-mannered poet in residence. There were trials in store for the newly married Crabbe and Mrs Crabbe in their socially uncertain status, a status not regarded amiably by the Servants'

Hall. But the mention of inn-signs calls me back to the road. Dickens had noticed that there were no less than eighteen 'Marquis of Granby' inn-signs in London alone, and many up and down the coaching roads. It was in keeping for him to cause the elder Weller, in *Pickwick*, to be captured in marriage by the hostess of the Marquis of Granby at Dorking. Dickens himself, when considering the inns at Grantham (the town on the road nearest Belvoir) discovered there no Marquis of Granby but settled for the George. At the George Hotel at Grantham Dickens stayed in 1838 on his way to investigate Yorkshire schools, 'Phiz' (Hablot Browne) accompanying him. In a letter to his wife Dickens said the George was 'the very best inn I have ever put up at'. Dickens's high opinion was soon transferred to print – at the end of Chapter 5 of *Nicholas Nickleby* two of the front outside passengers climbed down from the coach and wisely applied for beds at the George as 'one of the best inns in England', while Squeers, Nicholas, the five small pupils and the others wrapped themselves more closely and prepared for the stages to Newark throughout the night of bitter blizzard.

I have said the Great North Road was ever, from the beginning, a working road; always ready to transport men of letters or their works but itself rarely contributing to inspiration. The stretch of road northward from Grantham through Newark-on-Trent and Bawtry to the Yorkshire border at Doncaster is one of those which Walter Scott considered dull. Gonerby Hill (pronounced Gunnerby) just to the north of Grantham had been famous in the Civil War as a site of skirmishing between Royalists and Cromwell's troopers in their new issue of red coats, and Scott used its fame when he gave Jeanie Deans on her walk to London a specially frightening experience in the open ground, intersected with patches of copse and swampy spots, below the north slope of the hill. There (in *The Heart of Midlothian*) footpads stopped Jeanie 'by violence and mastery', and she was compelled to spend the night in the barn in the company of not only the robbers but also Mother Blood and Madge Wildfire. Soon, in the grand high manner of melodrama, that adventure proved to be no isolated episode; through the device of mad Madge taking Jeanie to Willingham Church the plot of Scott's story was sturdily pushed forward. Thus Scott succeeded in livening part of this dull stretch of the Great North Road. Dickens's attempt to do so in *Nicholas Nickleby* was, I feel, much less successful. When Dickens arranged that the coach leaving Grantham on the night of blizzard should be overturned into the snow, he was enabled to work the tales of 'The Five Sisters of York' and 'The Baron of Grogzwig' into his narrative but not even Dickens can make those stories, or the contest between them, thrilling. Apart, then, from the effort made by

Walter Scott, the road offers little of literary interest until one reaches
the traditional gateway into Yorkshire, Doncaster.

Ever since *The Man on a Donkey* by H. F. M. Prescott was published
in 1952, a paramount memory at Doncaster has been of that novel, rightly called by Helen Waddell 'a great and shattering book'. A re-reading
twenty-five years later confirms the reward found in this historical
chronicle in which, as the characters become familiar, their different
stories run together, as Hilda Prescott modestly hoped, 'and are swallowed up in the tragic history of the Pilgrimage of Grace'. What has
to be recalled is that in 1536 there came along the road from London to
this border of Yorkshire the writ from the king, Henry VIII – the
Diktat for the dissolution of abbeys, priories, monasteries, nunneries –
no matter what it meant in the destruction of their hospitals, schools,
libraries and everything they offered in their accustomed ways for welfare of soul and body. This was not reformation, it was peremptory and
universal destruction for great establishments (for instance Fountains or
Rievaulx) and small (for instance the little Marrick Priory in Swaledale).
In 1536 there were many people in Yorkshire as elsewhere who, in Hilda
Prescott's phrase, 'were of the new persuasion, and glad to see the houses
of religion pulled down', but there were also many who rose against this
order of the king. The spontaneous rising in Yorkshire at the start of the
protesting Pilgrimage of Grace brought a rebellious 'army' southward to
Doncaster.

A sixteenth-century picture two-thirds of the way through *The Man
on a Donkey*, when the reader has become engrossed with such men as
Robert Aske and such women as the Prioress of Marrick (and the very
real, if half-crazed, Malle the Servingwoman), is of the confrontation at
Doncaster between the Yorkshire rebels, congregated on the north bank
of the Don, and the king's force, which had hurriedly reached the Town
Moor south of the river. At that moment the host of the commons on the
north bank was fully strong enough to force the town bridge and over-
whelm the vanguard of the king's army and many were eager to do so;
yet the higher purpose of Robert Aske and other leaders of the Pilgrimage of Grace was to present the Articles agreed at Pomfret by the nobles
and commons of the north to the king's Parliament at Westminster.
That was Aske's purpose in the long debate at Doncaster Bridge. The
date was 27 October 1536.

The whole host of the commons lay on the north bank of the Don, the
King's on the other side of the river, and Doncaster between them. Early this
morning thirty of the King's lords and thirty of the commons' leaders had
come together upon the bridge on the north side of the town, the commons to
speak their grievances, the Lords to answer them, that, in the end, some
appointment might be made between them.

It was growing dusk now, and still the conference on the bridge went on. Earlier it had been possible for the commons to see, from where their ranks were drawn up, the crowd on the bridge, thirty lords and gentlemen from their party, and thirty from the King's host. But now, though lights were pricking out in the town beyond, the bridge was drowned from them in the twilight.

For the king, the Duke of Norfolk was able, for that whole day, to stave off the promise that was wanted of him. It was only after the duke had played for time that Aske was able to report at home: 'The Duke read out to us the King's free pardon for us all, and declared His Grace's promise of a free Parliament, and pledged his own word that the Abbeys should stand till that Parliament be met.' Not for the first or last time in history was a promise, so made to quell rebellion, repudiated later; but I know of no other rebellion which has had its chronicle more movingly re-created than this one, in Hilda Prescott's novel. The cruelty of the king's vengeance on Robert Aske, hanged in chains from York keep, is searingly authentic.

When studying *The Man on a Donkey* it seemed to me that strong elements of the spirit of the ancient Danelaw persisted in that chronicle. At this gateway into Yorkshire I become aware of waves of feeling against the 'Norman Yoke', as if tuned in to certain of the feelings likewise in many of the legends of Robin Hood. I have now a twinge of chagrin for calling the stretch of road from Grantham to Doncaster dull; it was I that was dull, for being deaf to signals which might have alerted me to knowing that I was crossing part of what once had been Sherwood Forest. The hints of this were, it is true, concealed, and rapid travel prevents awareness of anything but speed. But on the old road from Doncaster to Pomfret – Pontefract – there was (and I believe it is surviving new roadworks) a piece of evidence. At the side of the road five miles out of Doncaster there is (or was) Robin Hood's Well, and to emphasize that it was Robin Hood's Well Vanbrugh in the eighteenth century designed a square stone cupola to cover it. The part of England we have now reached is really the heartland of the ancient Danelaw, and one of its heritages was Robin Hood. But that thought must now be left, as one leaves a film at the photographer's, for future development. I can as yet say no more than that by pointing to Robin Hood's Well on the way to Pomfret I have made a signal to perceptions that need time to grow. Perceptions, if they continue to grow as I survey Zone 1 and then Zones 5 and 6 of modern England, which go a long way back in tribal memories – connections, it might even be, between Robin Hood, and *cucullati* and woodwoses.

My road has now come to Pontefract, equally called Pomfret, the town that grew up *ad pontem fractam* by the broken bridge which in Roman times had spanned the River Aire. It is not the town but the ruins of the Norman castle – 'Ah, Pomfret, Pomfret, ah, thou bloody prison' – at which one halts in memory of the king whose liveliness in boyhood I was watching at Waterloo Bridge. If the birth of English literature was proclaimed by Richard II, one should surely not desert the plume-pluck'd Richard in the shadow of his sorrow. It was at Pomfret that it came true for Richard to

> sit upon the ground
> And tell sad stories of the death of kings.

Here is where even music maddened the sick king:

> How sour sweet music is
> When time is broke and no proportion kept . . .

until, as Shakespeare tells it, Richard's story was ended by Exton's sword.

3. PONTEFRACT TO BERWICK-UPON-TWEED

There is one large advantage in continuing a swift direct run northward on the Great North Road. No other method of quick survey is likely to bring out a preliminary recognition of the way in which two great groups of legends, the Arthurian legends and those of Robin Hood, emerged from the physical and spiritual conflict of opposing peoples. A later world is apt to disregard the partisan growth of each group of legends, yet I think Britain's North Road, if I attend to it, provides some of the story. The original military importance of the road to the Romans, in subjugating Britain from the south northward, was agreed. The much later Norman conquerors used the same road in the same way, and their buildings followed their conquest. Now I would take a map and place a ruler on it and notice that a straight line of great cathedrals, all representing Norman influence – Peterborough, Lincoln, York, Durham – runs straight as a spear to join the line of the military road at Durham. Look now at each of those cathedrals: I would say each one looks more of a fortress than the one preceding. When you raise your eyes to the great spearhead cathedral, Durham, do you recall anywhere a church that stands more like a fort in hostile country?

My meditation is that by and large this northern part of England was continuing after the Norman Conquest to be as hostile as it could be to the 'Norman Yoke'. A speculation worth pursuing is that one of the instruments for persuading favour for Norman blood was the group of

Arthurian legends: the repetition and identification of special scenes and places with sites in Britain, all accepted by Caxton as of high moral and spiritual purpose, was admirable propaganda. By aiding and evoking local prides the Arthurian legends had been of undoubted use to Norman rule in England's southland and West Country and in Wales. Celtic and Scandinavian imaginations in Scotland seized on French thoughts with kindness when Arthurian heroes were identified with Orkney; there was pride in Edinburgh to speak of Arthur's Seat, and to accept that Arthur and his knights were sleeping beneath the Eildon Hills. It is in keeping, then, to speculate about the Norman scribe who, though the fortress-like Durham Cathedral was the northernmost of its line, aimed a further propaganda spear along that same line – the Norman scribe, whoever he was, who after thought took pen in hand and placed the castle of Sir Launcelot du Lake, the notably French-named castle of Joyeuse Gard, at Alnwick in Northumbria – although some rival copyist soon said it was not Alnwick but Bamburgh.

Such a backward half-look over the shoulder, such a gossamer suggestion that there was a someone who deliberately planted Sir Launcelot's Joyeuse Gard in a hostile part of the Danelaw for propaganda, could hardly expect to be verified. The most one can say is that if there were intentions to appease opinion in the Danelaw by offering hostage, as it were, of one of King Arthur's knights, Launcelot was the one most likely to win favour. The fortress aspect of Durham Cathedral conveys Norman respect for strength of opposition in this northland, and supports the thought that if an Arthurian hero were to be offered as ambassador, it had to be the best. Indeed, so far as I recall from Malory, Launcelot was identified with Northumbria only when he was dying. Joyeuse Gard appears little if at all before that; it was after he sickened and lay mourning on the tomb of King Arthur and Queen Guenever that Launcelot disclosed 'that in Joyous Gard I would be buried'. Then the Bishop and nine knights 'put Sir Launcelot in the same horse bier that Queen Guenever was laid in tofore that she was buried', and all together the Bishop and the nine knights rode with the body of Sir Launcelot along the length of the Great North Road. Within fifteen days the cavalcade with the dead Launcelot ('and ever they had an hundred torches burning about him') reached Joyeuse Gard.

Only at this stretch of road from Doncaster past Pontefract do the trails of Launcelot and Robin Hood coincide. I shall expect to find constant traces of each great legend, separately – the Arthurian traces mainly to the south and west of Watling Street, the traces of Robin Hood mainly on the side of Watling Street where we are now exploring.

*   *   *

A new generation of mapmakers is forced to give up the old division of Yorkshire into 'Ridings'. Having passed through most of the large area administered now as North Yorkshire the road reaches Catterick Bridge, where the River Swale comes down from Swaledale and the high moors of the west, the clear brown river-water having passed beside the Marrick Priory (the scene of much of Hilda Prescott's *The Man on a Donkey*), and under the cliff, as Ruskin says, at Richmond. At Catterick Bridge there came to Ruskin 'one of the great landmarks and pleasures of memory' – recollection of the last, indeed, of those early moments of rapture which acted as impulse throughout the whole of Ruskin's active life. In *Praeterita*, the reflections which Ruskin began to write when in his sixties, he records straightforwardly and simply the rapture, 'a feeling only possible to youth', when his parents' carriage on the journey northward halted for a rest at the old Catterick Bridge over the River Swale:

On the journey of 1837, when I was eighteen, I felt, for the last time, the pure childish love of nature which Wordsworth so idly takes for an intimation of immortality. We went down by the North Road, as usual; and on the fourth day arrived at Catterick Bridge, where there is a clear pebble-bedded stream, and both west and east some rising of hills, foretelling the moorlands and dells of upland Yorkshire; and there the feeling came back to me – as it could never return more.

Repeated efforts that Ruskin made, 'looking back from 1886 to that brook shore of 1837', to identify the passion set up in him by the direct vision of the pebble-bed of the Swale through the clear amber water, are to be found in Ruskin's 'Outlines of Scenes and Thoughts perhaps worthy of Memory in my Past Life' in *Praeterita*.

At Croft-on-Tees are memories of the boyhood of Charles Dodgson ('Lewis Carroll') at the vicarage. Charles had been born in 1832, when the Dodgson family were in Cheshire, but the clergyman-father was presented with the living at Croft in 1843. Charles, as the eldest son and then age eleven, could be sent from Croft to school at Richmond, preparatory to the Rugby and Oxford of his later academic career. It is in the school holidays, in the garden of the vicarage at Croft, that I am inclined to picture the future Lewis Carroll. The vicarage was large, and had need to be, for Dodgson children kept on arriving until there were eleven, seven of them girls, to play, under Charles's instruction, in the garden. What game would the children be playing? One game ranked high at Croft-on-Tees in 1843 and for some years after – the game of trains.

The Tees, from Darlington eastward to Stockton, on its way towards Middlesbrough and the North Sea, is a most remarkably bendy river.

It was because river transport there for heavy goods was infernally awkward that George Stephenson was impelled to extend a colliery rail-way line from Stockton to Darlington, over which colliery trucks might be hauled by a steam locomotive. He further thought to use the same rails for a train for human passengers; and for this designed the specially lively locomotive, Stephenson's *Active*, capable of thirteen miles per hour. The Stockton and Darlington Railway was opened to the public on 27 September 1825, and so began the Railway Age. The experiment was financed largely by Quaker capital, and the wool merchant Edward Pease spoke in good Quaker spirit to a Friend who was doubly shy – shy of the sulphurous smoke of the explosive engine and shy of the danger-ous speed. 'Thou hast the heart of a chicken,' said Pease; 'I am deter-mined to try it.'

By the time the eleven vicarage children were playing in the garden at Croft, it was as natural to play trains as it had been to John Clare to play 'clink and bandy'. The garden was large enough, and the children numerous enough, for a number of stations; for rolling-stock the records mention a wheelbarrow, a garden truck and a barrel; as chief station master, also ticket agent, also writer-out of rules, there was the future Lewis Carroll. Rules, in his handwriting, exist for inspection. Rule 3 is as follows:

> Station master must mind his station and supply refreshments: he can put anyone who behaves badly to prison, while a train goes round the garden: he must ring for the passengers to take their seats, then count 20 slowly, then ring again for the train to start. The L one shall be a surgeon, the wounded must be brought there gratis by the next train going that way and cured gratis. There shall be a place at the L station for lost luggage. If there is anyone to go, a flag is to be hoisted.

The touch about 'the wounded' shows that awareness of risk in early railway travel added drama to the game. The death of the statesman William Huskisson, run over at the opening of the Manchester and Liverpool railway in 1830, was a shock not forgotten. Such accidents were frequently used in fiction; it may be remembered that in *Cranford* (published in 1853) the gallant Captain Brown was run over by a train, having been startled at a moment when he 'was deeply engaged in the perusal of a number of *Pickwick*'. The temporary 'deaths' that might occur to the vicarage children in the garden were all restored at teatime.

A far less happy recollection at Croft-on-Tees is that Byron's three weeks of honeymoon, or, as he later called it with partly self-directed anger, his 'treaclemoon', was spent at Halnaby Hall, two miles from Croft. This followed his wedding in 1815 to Miss Milbanke at Seaham Hall on the Durham coast, the wedding about which he was none the less self-scornful for having himself brought it about. His own mortification at the marriage ceremony, foreknowing by that time that it was a mistake, he was unable to conceal: 'I trembled like a leaf, made the wrong responses, and after the ceremony called her Miss Milbanke.'

Near Croft, though, a more successful marriage may be remembered. Wordsworth's marriage in 1802 came about through the visit that he and his sister Dorothy made, in 1799, to Sockburn Farm, only a few miles east of Halnaby Hall. In 1799 the surgery whereby Annette Vallon and Wordsworth's French daughter were to be wholly cut from Wordsworth's life was an operation not yet completely performed; the visit to the Hutchinson family, a family related to the Wordsworths and living at Sockburn Farm, seemed to make the complete excision of a former part of Wordsworth's life all the more necessary. Wordsworth and Mary Hutchinson were of the same age, both twenty-nine in 1799; the thought of marriage developed happily at Sockburn. Then one reads of the visit that Wordsworth and Dorothy paid to France in 1802, and after that the marriage of Wordsworth and Mary Hutchinson took place in December at Brompton, towards the Yorkshire coast near Scarborough.

Between Darlington and Durham, Binchester (a mile north of Bishop Auckland beside the valley of the River Wear) was the birthplace, in 1811, of Henry George Liddell, who became co-author of the famous Greek–English lexicon known as 'Liddell and Scott'. When Dean of Christ Church at Oxford Liddell very much befriended the young tutor in mathematics, Charles Dodgson, and by taking him into his household as a favourite companion and storyteller for his children, was in effect partner in the creation of *Alice in Wonderland*. I shall be following the emergence of 'Lewis Carroll' out of the young Rev. Mr Dodgson at Oxford and Llandudno, but now continue northward.

Each time I view the Norman 'solidity' of Durham Cathedral (remarked on by Samuel Johnson) I find supported the fortress-like impression which reminded me earlier of the Norman push into this part of England at and after the time of their conquest. The remarkable John Meade Falkner (1858–1932) came to Durham as a young man and was fascinated by the cathedral; whether it was the fortress-feeling that led him into the armaments firm of Armstrong Whitworth I can't say. Falkner's business acumen enabled him to become chairman of that firm, but he kept up his interest in church architecture, heraldry and palaeography, and was thus occasioned to write the novel *The Nebuly Coat*. Falkner's gift for storytelling had been demonstrated previously in *Moonfleet*, a cracking adventure story identified with the Dorset coast, which is where I shall speak of Falkner again – for he was by heritage a man of the south country, whose clergyman-father lived and brought the boy up in Wiltshire, with holidays in Dorset. For what cause Falkner was expelled from Marlborough I don't know, but it did not prevent him from proceeding to Oxford and, as a tutor, to Newcastle, and so to fall in love with Durham.

Before Falkner, Edward Bradley, though a native of Kidderminster, had attended University College, Durham, and under the pen-name 'Cuthbert Bede' wrote his highly successful satire of Oxford's college life called *The Adventures of Mr Verdant Green*. Before 'Cuthbert Bede', another who showed how spirited writings from Durham could be was the sporting novelist Robert Surtees, who produced *Jorrocks's Jaunts and Jollities*. That younger Robert Surtees, not to be confused with the older Robert Surtees, the distinguished antiquary, was, unlike Bradley and Falkner, a native of Durham by birthright. Another birthright native of Durham was the notable travel writer Gertrude Bell (1868–1926).

More complete literary heritages of the country of the Roman Wall, which here stretched across Britain from Newcastle to the Solway Firth, I shall defer until discussion of Zone 6. But after the mention of *Jorrocks* it would be discourteous not to say here that much of the 'Jorrocks country' is to the north of the eastern end of the Wall in Northumbria – a reminder that another famous Master of Foxhounds, John Peel, belongs to the country at the Wall's western end. Hexham, just south of the Wall, where the two branches of the Tyne converge, was the birthplace of Wilfrid Gibson, one of the notable group of poets born in the 1870s (Ralph Hodgson, who was born at Darlington, Walter de la Mare, Edward Thomas and Wilfrid Gibson were all born in that decade, and Robert Frost came from America to join in their company). But London was a magnet drawing together all those named, and others; and Gibson, Thomas, Frost and the slightly younger Lascelles Abercrombie, John Drinkwater and Rupert Brooke joined forces for a time at Dymock in Gloucestershire, not too far from London.

But the Great North Road has now brought us into Northumberland. I spoke perhaps crudely of my impression that the placing of the legendary French-named castle of the Arthurian knight Launcelot in Northumbria was part-inspired by a Norman wish to win sympathy with chivalry. Writers' sympathies likewise affected the writing-out of partisan legends later than their origins. Whether or no partly from wish to please North Countrymen, Malory and Caxton pull out all the stops for the lying-in-state of Sir Launcelot at Alnwick – Malory seems to have favoured Alnwick rather than Bamburgh. I quoted from Malory at Pontefract to give a glimpse of the funeral cortège as he pictured it on the North Road, travelling with its hundred torches ever burning. When Launcelot's corpse was lying in state in the chapel at Joyeuse Gard, Malory then tells how, while men of worship sang and wept, 'there came Sir Ector de Maris, that had seven years sought all England,

Scotland, and Wales, seeking his brother, Sir Launcelot'. Famous indeed is the rhetoric with which Malory gives Ector's lament, when he
had recovered enough from the shock of finding his brother dead to
make his doleful speech beside the bier:

> Ah Launcelot, he said, thou were head of all Christian knights, and now I
> dare say, said Sir Ector, thou Sir Launcelot, there thou liest, that thou were
> never matched of earthly knight's hand. And thou were the courteoust knight
> that ever bare shield. And thou were the truest friend to thy lover that ever
> bestrad horse. And thou were the truest lover of a sinful man that ever loved
> woman. And thou were the kindest man that ever struck with sword. And
> thou were the goodliest person that ever came among press of knights. And
> thou was the meekest man and the gentlest that ever ate in hall among ladies.
> And thou were the sternest knight to thy mortal foe that ever put spear in the
> rest.

'Then', says Malory, 'there was weeping and dolour out of measure.'

That, in the Everyman edition, in spelling only slightly modernized
from the text which Caxton 'chaptered and imprinted', is what seems a
plea for Alnwick to be regarded as a major shrine in Arthurian tradition,
second only to Glastonbury. Yet Alnwick Castle, though dating from
the time of the Norman Conquest and for centuries after the principal
seat of the Percys, has never become a pilgrims' shrine at all approaching Glastonbury, and Bamburgh, the other contender as possible site
of Joyeuse Gard, is more interested in displaying the tomb of Grace
Darling (remembered for her rescue-work by lifeboat) than in memorial-
izing Launcelot. If Malory hoped the Northumbrian people would give
heartfelt welcome to Launcelot that hope was disappointed. Partisan
history was often perpetuated in ballads, and so it is especially appropriate in Northumbria to look at the famous Percy Folio, universally
spoken of as 'the most important single collection of antique ballads
that we have'. If the collection of Percy's *Reliques* were to favour one
group of ballads more than another, it might be expected to give preference to Arthurian heroes. Yet though in the Percy Folio Arthurian
ballads or short romances are well represented, the group of Robin Hood
ballads is more noticeable.

It was natural that Swinburne, in the mid-nineteenth century, should
obtain his passion for the Border ballads in the region where many of
those ballads started. The poet's grandfather, Sir John Swinburne, lived
at Capheaton Hall between Newcastle and Otterburn, and as grandson
Algernon spent many holidays at Capheaton Hall, and was especially
to remember one when he had finally left Oxford at the age of twenty-
two. Swinburne's voracious readings in the Capheaton library, of the
ballads for instance, led to repeated identifications as he rode his pony
to various specific scenes. The 'sense of place' operates in Northumber-

land; Swinburne felt it, as others may, at Otterburn, where the battle
in 1388 between the English under Hotspur and the Scots under Douglas
prompted two ballads, one from each side. In this battle the Douglas
was slain and Hotspur was captured, and the Scottish ballad 'The
Battle of Otterburn' proclaimed victory – 'Harry Hotspur forced to
yield, When the Dead Douglas won the field'. The English ballad, the
famous 'Chevy Chase', probably the earlier in date, was concerned
mainly with compassion for the mutual slaughter:

> And the Lord Maxwell in like case
>   Did with Erle Douglas dye:
> Of twenty hundred Scottish speres,
>   Scarce fifty-five did flye.

> Of fifteen hundred Englishmen,
>   Went home but fifty-three;
> The rest in Chevy-Chace were slaine,
>   Under the greene woode tree.

The sea-coast also held irresistible attraction for Swinburne – I can
believe his pony took him from Capheaton beyond Alnwick to the
hollow ruined tower of Dunstanburgh Castle, spectacular in its now
lonely defence against the sole wild enemies of sea and sea-wind.
Defending the ruined tower of Dunstanburgh are cohorts of seabirds
(kittiwakes, guillemots, fulmars), yet with Swinburne one feels it was
the wind's voice more than the interruptive bird voices to which his
own melody responded. The sea-wind, here as at Dunwich on the
Suffolk sea-coast, always spoke to Swinburne:

> Low and loud and long, a voice forever,
>   Sounds the wind's clear story like a song.

The contribution made by the Holy Isle of Lindisfarne to nineteenth-
century poetry now winds up this part of my survey. One macabre item
can be picked out. Not only the red sandstone ruins of the priory on the
Holy Isle but the report that a skeleton, presumably of an erring nun,
had been found sealed in a wall (the result presumably of being buried
alive), effectively prompted Walter Scott to write *Marmion*. True, Scott
knew of another female skeleton buried alive in a wall elsewhere – it may
be Scott transplanted the story – but the tremendous success of *Marmion*
when published greatly confirmed what he had started with *The Lay of
the Last Minstrel*, which was no less than the creation of a new demand
for poetry. There is much pith in the contention that Saintsbury in his
time put forward, that not only Byron profited because he found 'a
public "ground-baited" to full appetite by Scott', but also Coleridge
and Wordsworth, and Shelley and Keats as well.

4. FROM NORTHUMBERLAND SOUTHWARD TO THE WASH

Ernest Seton Thompson (1860–1946) was born at South Shields, a fact which much surprised me, for my boyhood had been enriched by Thompson's books (notably *Wild Animals I Have Known* and *Two Little Savages*) and from those writings I assumed he had been born and bred in the backwoods of Canada. It is not instantly easy to associate frontier life in Canada with present-day South Shields; nor is it easy to associate the neighbouring industrial Jarrow with the ancient eighth-century monastery once sited there. In that monastery the Venerable Bede wrote his *Historia Ecclesiastica*. Bede was buried at Jarrow, but in the eleventh century his bones were transported so that his tomb might join the tomb of St Cuthbert in Durham Cathedral.

It had been in Cuthbert's time at the Holy Isle of Lindisfarne that Hilda (who like Cuthbert became very worthily 'sainted') founded the monastery at Whitby on the Yorkshire coast and, as Abbess, ruled it with great wisdom. Although I started my whole journey by saying that the birth of English literature was proclaimed (putting the date as late as 1385) in London, the first recorded effort to encourage the writing of 'English' is credited to Hilda, and that is the association which should continue forever to draw literary pilgrims to Whitby. At Whitby, across the harbour from the town centre and high upon the East Cliff, are the conspicuous abbey ruins. These are ruins of the Norman abbey which replaced the original monastery established here for both monks and nuns by Hilda in A.D. 657. Information about Hilda and her monastery comes from Bede at Jarrow, though Hilda died in the year 680 and Bede's life-span is given as 673–735, so, if dates in that period can be relied on, he was a boy of seven when Hilda died.

Bede clearly accepted, and retold as a story to be relished, what Hilda did at her monastery when the odd behaviour of one of the lesser servants was reported to her. The man's name was Caedmon; his function that of a cowman; he was supposed to attend the normal festive meetings at which the harp was handed round and each in turn sang what hymn he could. Complaint about Caedmon had to be made to the Abbess: he made trouble over his singing. It was not that Caedmon refused to sing 'for the love of God' but he would not conform to the purpose of those sessions with the harp, which was for each man to sing 'for the love of God *and of Learning*'. Caedmon wished to sing; he seemed indeed inspired with the wish to sing a sacred poetry of his own – but in his own tongue, not in Latin. It was submitted to the Abbess that Caedmon's preference called for reprimand. Yet her action was twofold. She not only encouraged Caedmon to continue to sing his own hymns in his own 'English', but she also persuaded her scribes to attempt the untried, difficult task of putting that vernacular tongue into communicable writing. Trouble enough Hilda may have had with those scribes, if some of them were such wandering scholars, *vagantes*, as Helen Waddell wrote about, 'yapping Irish hounds, with their sharp filed teeth of grammar'. It was Latin script and Latin grammar with which their teeth were filed; apart from the small sympathy which they might have had with Caedmon, how were those teeth of theirs to grip his most uncouth vernacular?

Hilda forced her scribes to record some of Caedmon's hymns, and Bede in turn came to be impressed with the attempt. It is not recorded that Bede himself mastered the art of writing in 'English', but he lent authority for other scribes to try. The 'English' which had to be transliterated was far from easy to fit into Latin script. Here is a first line of a hymn of Caedmon's, simplified from a manuscript written two or three years after Bede's death:

Nu scylun hergan, hefænricæs uard . . .

That is a beginning of a passage, translated by Dr Dorothy Whitelock into present-day English as:

Now we must praise the guardian of the heavenly kingdom . . .

and the interpretation having been done for us, this particular example is not too difficult to follow. And I derive an impression, not easy to justify perhaps, that the activity of trying to record vernacular speech in writing, started perhaps with great difficulty by Hilda, was becoming, even as early as the eighth century, something of a pleasurable side-activity for clerks, something sometimes of a puzzle or game. It is at least a pleasing fancy to contemplate the strange and scrappy cargo of writings (on whatever scraps could be spared for writing on) carried southward on the road from Hilda's foundation at Whitby and Bede's foundation at Jarrow for the puzzlement, interpretation and, it may be, inspiration, of clerks at London, Canterbury and Winchester. Communication in the vernacular, by writing, between Northumbria and the southland, was being established before the first ferocious attacks of the men in ships with dragon-prows overwhelmed the pious communities at Lindisfarne, Jarrow and Whitby. The 'Danes' (to use the general name for the many raiders and settlers) were arriving in the last quarter of the ninth century, by which time Alfred, fortunately for Britain's southland, had reached manhood. Alfred the Great's first biographer, Asser, mentions that Alfred could not read till he was twelve, but the most significant suggestion is that he learned to read 'English' before he learned to read Latin. Asser may have been emphasizing what Alfred was quick to see, that in the long term, if the Danes could not be beaten off and if they were going to stay and settle in a wide belt across Britain, 'English' would be the means of absorbing them.

My purpose is not to try to follow the story of the English language, but merely to be aware of that story in this neighbourhood, and aware of Northumbria's contribution; from that vast theme, at Whitby, and without losing sight of the abbey ruins on the site of Hilda's even more ancient buildings, I may turn to a smaller item. In 1897, almost exactly a thousand years after the destruction of Hilda's houses by Viking raiders, whom the early Church described as dragons, Abraham Stoker (more widely known as Bram Stoker) reported the entry into England, at the port of Whitby, of another dragon, or at least a dracula. The magical entry of the Count Dracula from his ship into the lower town was achieved in the shape of a black dog; but it is all wrong to speak so coolly of what Bram Stoker reported in *Dracula* with full detail of the appalling menace that was speedily approaching the girl Lucy. The miraculous arrival of the derelict Russian schooner, steered into port by a dead man tied to the wheel with a crucifix and beads, its cargo a number of great wooden boxes filled with mould; the monster dog which leaped ashore and evaded all efforts of capture – but something must have appeared to cause death by fright to the old man on the seat in the churchyard – Lucy's being drawn sleepwalking to that same seat; the moonlight sighting of something long and black and with red, gleaming eyes which bent over the half-reclining helpless girl – result in what thrill of horror! At that nightmare moment, on the East Cliff near the abbey ruins at Whitby, fortune favoured Lucy and the brave Mina. That night the Thing did no more harm to Lucy than to leave two little red points like pinpricks on the skin of her throat; a strange phenomenon, yet causing only one small drop of blood, and easily to be laughed at. But in my edition of *Dracula* that moment at Whitby occurs at page 87 and page 335 must be reached before for the very last time 'the red eyes glared with the horrible vindictive look', and through a final sacrifice 'the curse' of Count Dracula, that 'filthy leech', was ended.

If Whitby is thus to be associated with what Bram Stoker's publishers called 'the most terrifying story ever told', this part of the Yorkshire coast is also the scene of the greater part of what a recent critic termed 'the first, the longest, and the best of modern English detective novels'. The novel thus referred to was *The Moonstone* by Wilkie Collins, and the critic quoted was one not often swayed to speak in superlatives, T. S. Eliot. *The Moonstone* appeared originally part by part in serial publication, and then in book form in 1868; the story was placed twenty years before that, in 'my aunt's house in Yorkshire' in 1848. It is legitimate to ask precisely where upon the coast that house of Lady Verinder's was situated. If the three high-caste Brahmins searching for the diamond were able to locate the house, so should the clever reader be able to find it; Wilkie Collins gives plenty of clues, almost too many. The house was 'high up', 'close by the sea', with 'lonely country' between it and 'the station' (was that the railway station of Frizinghall?). Below the house a path ran down to sandhills and the sea, and there, with the fishing village of Cobb's Hole some way to the side, lay 'the most horrible quicksand on the shores of Yorkshire', the quicksand which plays its sinister part – 'the Shivering Sand'. Several schools of thought exist about the topographical location; adding to the question's importance is that it was here that the great original fictional detective, Sergeant Cuff, made his appearance. Some searchers place the story of *The Moonstone* on the Scarborough side of Whitby and some have explored the coast to the westward – going too far that way has brought some explorers to Middlesbrough, birthplace of E. W. Hornung, who by writing *The Amateur Cracksman* in 1899 introduced the gentleman burglar, Raffles. (As brother-in-law to Conan Doyle, and seven years younger, Hornung was more or less compelled to place his main character, Raffles, on the opposite side of the law to Sherlock Holmes.)

On the Scarborough side of Whitby is Robin Hood's Bay, one more reminder of how dominant is that outlaw's legend in the whole of this zone. Scarborough itself provides a great variety of associations from which to pick and choose. One might look into George Fox's *Journal* to see what he says about being confined in Scarborough's castle in 1665; or Smollett's *Humphry Clinker* or Sheridan's *A Trip to Scarborough* could be consulted for the fashion, beginning to be commended in the eighteenth century, for seabathing. Later on, invalids not strong enough for sea-bathing might yet be brought to Scarborough for the bracing air. It was Scarborough that was recommended for Anne Brontë in the spring of 1849. Emily had died towards the end of the preceding December; the youngest of the three sisters, Anne, 'drooped and sickened more rapidly from that time'. Although her chief support, Charlotte, tried to believe that Anne's illness 'has none of the fearful rapid symptoms which appalled in Emily's case', Anne barely survived that winter at Haworth parsonage and it was not until 24 May that she was strong enough for the two-day journey. Charlotte and Anne broke the journey at York, and arrived at Scarborough, at No. 2 The Cliff (where the Grand Hotel subsequently replaced it), on the 25th. On 26 May Anne enjoyed an hour's drive on the sands in a donkey-cart; on the 27th a seat near the beach was found for her, and later, from her window, she enjoyed the sunset. Then, on 28 May, Anne died, aged twenty-nine. She was buried in the detached part of St Mary's churchyard, east of the church, and Charlotte returned to Haworth parsonage to look after the indestructible widowed father who was fated to survive all his children.

Edith Sitwell was born at Scarborough in 1887, at the family's seaside home, Wood End, by the Crescent – or, as I have also heard tell, at her grandmother's house, Londesborough Lodge. There will be more to record of Edith, Osbert and Sacheverell Sitwell at their main home at Renishaw Hall in Derbyshire, yet John Lehmann in the biographical study *A Nest of Tigers* stresses 'the deep influence of Scarborough' especially on their creativity in childhood. The three Sitwell children spent much of every year first at their grandmother's house, and then from 1902 till 1914 at Wood End, now owned by the Scarborough Corporation as a museum. 'The proof of the deep impression that Scarborough made on the young imaginations of the Sitwells is not only in what they have written, reminiscently, about it', says John Lehmann, 'but in their creative world.'

An American reminiscence might indicate that Scarborough, immediately after the 1914–18 war, failed to exert its full attraction to Lewis Mumford. To those born or brought up in Scarborough, the sands and rockpools, the donkeys and the pierrot troupes on the beach with the castle on the cliff above, possessed an abiding stimulus – not only to the Sitwells, for instance, but to Charles Laughton. Yet postwar Scarborough in 1920 was perhaps not at its most effective. It was in 1920 that Mumford, during a train journey that he was making from London to Scarborough, was faced with a choice. After war service in the American navy he had come to England for a period of study, with particular interest in what was going on in town and country planning. An editorial post in London was tempting him to stay in England instead of returning to his native New York. With him in the train as part of his reading-matter was an issue of the New York *Freeman* and the weekly column in that paper written by Van Wyck Brooks appeared to Mumford at that moment as a clarion call. The emotional effect of the *Freeman* on Mumford was as strong as that of the bells on Dick Whittington; in the train he made his decision to return and join in what that paper was attempting in New York, and his arrival at Scarborough failed to change his mind. Yet if that is the nearest I can get to associating Scarborough with Lewis Mumford, I should add that the American-born T. S. Eliot was to have real and happy associations with Scarborough in his later years.

Inland from Scarborough the Vale of Pickering is entered past Brompton, where in December 1802 Wordsworth was married to Mary

Hutchinson. I propose to return to Pickering for the part it plays in *The Vicar of Wakefield* when there is later opportunity for following that novel of Goldsmith's in a consecutive way. Here, since I have just been mentioning some literary names which were attracting attention in the 1920s and even more in the 1930s, I pass from Pickering towards Helmsley in order to look at Muscoates, the stone farmhouse in which Herbert Read (1895–1968) was born and of which he wrote in *The Innocent Eye*. The stimulus that the coast at Scarborough was to the Sitwells in their childhood – the stimulus that John Lehmann noted as exerting itself continuously throughout all of their creative writings – was paralleled for Read in this inner part of Yorkshire's North Riding. Muscoates is in the vale from which lush narrow dales are like fingers stretching northward into the high hills – the dales which strike 'like green rays into the purple darkness of the Moors' – and the setting in which Read grew up was part and parcel of Read's poems and his imaginative prose writings. In one of the becks which come down from the high moors' purple darkness was a watermill owned by the family and still in operation in Read's boyhood or, when not in operation, providing beside its small millpool a lonely haunt of quiet mystery; that site found transmuted reappearance in Read's romantic prose-work, *The Green Child*. On one of my visits to the Reads at Stonegrave, Read, having first piloted Arthur Wheen and me to pay respects to the Saxon church familiar to him from childhood, asked me to drive my American car (somewhat overlarge for that purpose) as far as a farm track would take us into a far-up vital part of Kirkdale. A permanent reminder of that particular expedition is Read's poem, 'Moon's Farm'. That was after Read's return to live in Yorkshire in 1949. He had written

> God grant I may return to die
> Between the Riccal and the Rye

and when he had purchased Stonegrave House that wish, as near as could be, was granted. Read had nearly twenty years of happy life at Stonegrave (happy except for pressures of overwork) before his death. The stone which marks his grave in the secluded Kirkdale churchyard carries the epitaph that he instructed:

> Herbert Read
> Knight, poet, anarchist.

South-west of Helmsley, in the vale below the southern spur of the Hambleton Hills there is Ampleforth, and west again from Ampleforth is Byland Abbey and Coxwold and Newburgh Priory. Herbert Read firmly supported the legend that Oliver Cromwell's bones were rescued from London and sealed, for their final resting-place, in a wall of

Newburgh Priory. For many visitors, though, the main attraction to Coxwold is the house near the church which Laurence Sterne fitted up when he became perpetual curate at Coxwold in 1760.

We might have had a glimpse of Sterne as a young curate at Buckden near Huntingdon, but that was a temporary post. He had thoughts of a comfortable marriage; there were influences for him at York which would increase his eligibility. The livings of Sutton and Stillington in this part of Yorkshire, coupled with a minor post as prebendary of York, put him in the running for the hand of Elizabeth Lumley who, if not pretty, was of a respected York family and reasonably well-to-do. Sterne married Elizabeth Lumley in York Minster in 1741, when he was twenty-eight. For nearly twenty years after that Sterne was outwardly an easygoing, finicky country clergyman who dabbled at painting, music and writing, and held sound views on local enclosure acts. Among the round of visits at country houses, Sterne, and Mrs Sterne when she was in good health, were often welcomed by Lord Fauconberg of Newburgh Priory, and Lord Fauconberg as patron permitted Sterne to hope that when the perpetual curacy at Coxwold became available, it would be his for the asking. The Sternes had one daughter, Lydia, but after her birth Elizabeth's health was frequently a worry and as Lydia grew up her sympathies tended to be with her often ailing mother rather than with her father. In 1758 acts of unfaithfulness by Sterne, real or fancied, resulted in Elizabeth becoming temporarily 'insane'; after that break-down mother and daughter began to spend more time in travel and less with Sterne at home. Sterne, in 1759, amused himself by starting to put on paper *The Life and Opinions of Tristram Shandy, Gent*. When Elizabeth and Lydia returned from one of their travels, Sterne read aloud to them chapter after chapter of *Tristram Shandy*. He found it unforgivable that they were not much amused.

On New Year's Day 1760 the first volume of *Tristram Shandy* was published in York by the publisher who printed Sterne's sermons, and the copies sent to London caused rapid reprinting there. The calls for the appearance of the hitherto unknown author made Sterne instantly into a literary lion. Sterne rapidly visited London to bask in the applause, which at many routs was all the greater when the book was loudly denounced by Dr Johnson, Richardson, Horace Walpole, Goldsmith and others. At this juncture Sterne had the further gratification of being called back to Yorkshire: the death of the incumbent had made available the perpetual curacy at Coxwold. That appointment, and the house in the village which went with it, pleasingly in the neighbourhood of Newburgh Priory, was his. The house at Coxwold was in no way grandiose; it was no more than a cottage; but he had often eyed it and thought of alterations that could be made, and now he had the opportunity and the means to refit it precisely as he wished. Elizabeth and Lydia were in less of a hurry than he was to inhabit the cottage at Coxwold; and Sterne, when he had it all to his liking, made it perhaps less inviting to them by his new name for it, Shandy Hall.

Despite the pains Sterne had taken to furbish up Shandy Hall, his life there after moving in was only part-time, and Elizabeth and Lydia were even less regular residents. Mother and daughter were away together for long periods, often travelling on the Continent; Sterne, when he was at Shandy Hall, was much of the time preoccupied with the further adventures of Mr and Mrs Shandy, Uncle Toby, Corporal Trim, the Widow Wadman, Dr Slop – characters to whom Sterne gave immortality, and with whom his communions came to be closer than with Elizabeth or Lydia. Between issuing the further parts of *Tristram Shandy* he put together more volumes of sermons and kept up with the correspondence that success had produced. Much of his life he now spent in London and in travelling abroad. From 1762 to 1764 he joined his wife and daughter for many months in France, leaving them behind at Montauban, by their wish, when he returned to London for the publication of Volumes VII and VIII of *Tristram* in 1765. In October 1765 Sterne set out by himself for the seven months' tour of which he was later to make use in *A Sentimental Journey*. The final volume of *Tristram*, with the sentence in it which some have supposed suggested to Burns his lines about the 'guinea stamp', was published in 1767, and in London in that year, at a party given by a distinguished officer of the East India Company, Sterne met a young vivacious married woman of twenty-two, Mrs Eliza Draper. Eliza had been born in India and had married Mr Draper in Bombay, and when her visit to London came to its end she would be compelled, unwillingly it seemed, to return to him. The poignancy of Mrs Draper's marriage to a dull husband led Sterne to confide to her that his case was just the same – if only both Mrs Sterne and Mr Draper were out of the way, how happy Sterne and the young Brahmine (as he began to call her) could be.

Eliza Draper did return to Bombay in the summer of 1767, and as she had predicted, she was discontented at living with Mr Draper, and presently ran away. Sterne meanwhile went back to Shandy Hall and began, simultaneously, to write *A Sentimental Journey* and his *Journal to Eliza*. At that moment Elizabeth arrived at Shandy Hall to see if they might not all live together, past tensions forgotten; but after two months incompatibility had to be agreed; there was nothing for Sterne and the other two except permanent separation. They departed from Shandy Hall, and Sterne reverted to his writing desk for, each morning, the careful work on *A Sentimental Journey* and, each nightfall, his mawkish effusions to Eliza. The way the *Journey* and the *Journal* were kept going side by side 'is curious as few things are in literature' (Saintsbury's phrase), for the brushwork on the *Journey* was careful and scrupulous and much worked over, whereas the kindest way of looking at the effusive *Journal* is to regard it as a safety-valve. Perhaps Sterne did feel at times that other people's faults had caged him as the starling was caged in the *Journey*, but the continuing fantasy that if Elizabeth and Draper were dead the Brahmine would be Shandy Hall's perfect mistress – the stressing of how all the elegant apartments at Shandy Hall, and most of all Sterne himself, were languishing for her – makes the *Journal*, however ordinary to a psychiatrist, a curious device for Sterne to use to cope with his loneliness. The Brahmine, of course, never did see those apartments, which at Coxwold are now maintained for public view. Sterne himself did not live in Shandy Hall much longer, for *A Sentimental Journey* was published in 1768, and he went to his London lodgings in Old Bond Street to enjoy the entertainment that would cause. Unexpectedly, in London he contracted pleurisy and died, at the age of fifty-five. He was buried in St George's cemetery off the Bayswater Road, not far from Marble Arch. Stories grew later that some of the graves in that cemetery had been tampered with; but in 1969 the Laurence Sterne Trust caused Sterne's grave to be opened, and the bones were exhumed and measured. After careful conclusion that the bones so found were Sterne's and none other, they were transferred for reburial outside the church at Coxwold.

*   *   *

York, noble city that it is, and one-time Roman capital of the whole province of Britain, is not especially remarkable for literary associations. In the eighth century there was Alcuin, and gossipers then skip to the eighteenth century and then to Sydney Smith (1771–1845). A clergyman-writer of impeccable social reputation, Sydney Smith was one of the founders of the *Edinburgh Review*; destined eventually to become a canon of St Paul's, he spent an intervening twenty-year period as rector at Foston, north-east of York and not far from Sheriff Hutton. As an essayist and for his letters, Sydney Smith's fame continues, and his writings also intimate that his physical presence, and the spontaneity of his wit in conversation, added much to what's derivable from print. 'Known, liked, and honoured, for his manliness, honesty, and exuberant drollery and wit' was Thomas Seccombe's description of Sydney Smith, and for the period that he was based at Foston (1808–28) he was a very notable figure in the social life of York. In our time W. H. Auden, who was himself born in York (at No. 54 Bootham, in 1907), collected and introduced a volume of Sydney Smith's writings.

L.B.—C

Yet by and large York has achieved many of its literary associations in fiction. Defoe selected the city as the birthplace of Robinson Crusoe – 'born in the year 1632, in the city of York, of a good family, though not of that country' – and Scott gave Isaac of York his dwelling in the Castlegate, where Ivanhoe was nursed by Rebecca. George Eliot brought York into *The Mill on the Floss*, though only for a single night-time. The 'George Eliot country' is specifically the Midlands, yet *The Mill on the Floss* is deliberately placed in eastern England. Perhaps the author wished to avoid Maggie Tulliver's being identified with herself; at any rate her *Journal* for 1859 mentions her 'three days' journey to Lincolnshire and back', and George Lewes accompanying her also recorded the visit, to make sure that her local colour in the story would be accurate. 'Dorlcote Mill' in the novel (though the life in it came from George Eliot's memory of Arbury Mill near her home) was placed at 'St Ogg's', and St Ogg's with its 'aged, fluted red roofs and the broad gables of its wharves', and above all with a river large enough to make credible the flood catastrophe the novel needed, was Lincolnshire's town of Gainsborough. Thus on Maggie Tulliver's madly impulsive northward trip when persuaded to elope with Stephen Guest, she came to be set down from the coach in York, alone and at midnight.

Lincoln, notable like York for much else, is even less prodigal than York with literary associations. There is the little child-martyr, St Hugh, whose shrine is in the cathedral; his story, dating from the thirteenth century, was a frequent theme for early poets – Chaucer refers to it in *The Prioress's Tale* and Marlowe in *The Jew of Malta*. Then there is Tennyson, whom Lincoln has adopted as if he had been a native of the city, with a statue of him beside the cathedral and a Research Centre and a Tennyson Exhibition Room. Clearly Lincoln is the best of centres for Tennyson memorabilia, for Tennyson was a Lincolnshire man, born at Somersby, twenty miles or so due east of Lincoln. Yet Somersby, in the southerly part of the Lincolnshire Wolds, is nearer to the North Sea than to Lincoln City, and Tennyson in boyhood was pulled more towards Willoughby (where Captain John Smith had come from), and Spilsby (birthplace of the explorer Sir John Franklin, to whom Tennyson composed a memorial), and Mablethorpe (where he heard the slap and thunder and hissing of the North Sea on the sands), than to Lincoln. Though Tennyson was often in Lincoln, it is my impression that he was rather a visitor than an inhabitant, and most other literary associations with Lincoln concern visitors. Lincoln's cathedral had specially favoured treatment in Nathaniel Hawthorne's *Our Old Home* (1863). I recall that my writer-brother Christopher, when I had taken him on one of his visits from New York to look at the west façade of Lincoln's cathedral in the slanting rays of a summer's evening, exclaimed that it was 'exactly the colour of treacle tart' – which poetical comparison combined for him the highest of delights.

In the mid-nineteenth century Hawthorne stayed at the Saracen's Head in Lincoln and provided a full description of that famous inn; the Saracen's Head also appears very much in the annals of bomber squadrons of the RAF in the last war. Lincoln's engineering works were the birthplace of tanks in the First World War, and in the Second World War it enters the story of the Dam Busters. This returns us naturally to the Tennyson who 'dipt into the future' and foretold

> a ghastly dew
> From the nations' airy navies grappling in the central blue.

The material gathered and presented by Sir Charles Tennyson and Mrs Hope Dyson in *The Tennysons: Background to Genius* makes it clear that the George Tennyson who was the 'ill, unbalanced, hard-drinking Rector of Somersby', fathered in that country rectory a family of seven boys and four girls who were each to develop some exceeding individual eccentricity. The notable Marx Brothers of later celebrity seem to have had, in combination, a hilarious upbringing on the East Side of New York; but there were only four of them, and on the east side of Lincolnshire at Somersby there were eleven Tennyson children indulging in peculiar antics. Records of their later goings-on make, superficially, hilarious and fascinating reading; beneath the surface the picture of the family at Somersby presents uneasy hints of their future lives. Alfred Tennyson, the fourth son, developed conduct less odd than some of the others of the family, and it seems that after the Somersby days were over, from 1837 (when Alfred at the age of twenty-eight was engaged but not yet married) it was generally thought that on him would fall the chief care of his mother, in her restive years of movings first to Epping Forest, then to Tunbridge Wells, and on to near Maidstone. It was in the years at Maidstone that Tennyson's full future became assured, and there I shall return to him.

A variety of associations cluster in the coastal country between the Humber and The Wash. Just to the north of the Humber estuary Andrew Marvell (1621–78) was born in the rectory at Winestead, attending school at Hull and becoming Member of Parliament for Hull from 1659 until his death. Humberside is thus the region of Marvell's 'green thoughts in a green shade'. In the northern part of Lincolnshire, Robert Burton (1577–1640), the Leicestershire man who had published *The Anatomy of Melancholy* in 1621, became rector of Walesby, just north of Market Rasen, for some years before his eventual return to his final living in Leicestershire.

In the south of the county, near Spilsby, Samuel Johnson stayed at times with Bennet Langton at Langton Hall. Bennet Langton, 'his mind as exalted as his stature', of whom Johnson also said that 'earth does not bear a worthier man', is much remembered as one of Johnson's most valued friends; but a perhaps less generally known uncle, Peregrine Langton, also won Johnson's special affection. Peregrine lived in the village of Partney, an easy walk for Johnson on a summer morning from Langton Hall, and it was the 'piety and œconomy' of his life in that Lincolnshire village which much interested Johnson. Peregrine Langton's income was an annuity of £200; on that income, in the eighteenth century, he and a sister and niece, in a neat house with its two or three small fields, lived as follows:

The servants were two maids, and two men in livery. His common way of living, at his table, was three or four dishes; the appurtenances to his table were neat and handsome; he frequently entertained company at dinner, and then his table was well served with as many dishes as were usual at the tables of the other gentlemen in the neighbourhood. His own appearance, as to clothes, was genteelly neat and plain. He had always a post-chaise, and kept three horses.

Johnson was fascinated with all the details of the 'œconomy' whereby Peregrine's comfortable style of living was managed on £200 a year, and several times himself pondered whether to expend his own pension on a comparably retired country life.

Boston, St Botolph's town at the western corner of The Wash, was the birthplace of John Foxe of the *Book of Martyrs*. John Cotton, vicar of Boston in 1612 and often thereafter accused of Nonconformity, resigned that living in 1633 and sailed with Thomas Hooker and others for New England; from the arrival of this contingent in Massachusetts the name of the township there was changed to Boston. Boston Stump, the famous church tower, stands all the higher in literary annals for its connection with the start of New England's literature. The church itself has a window commemorating Anne Bradstreet, the first of New England's poets, and also Jean Ingelow, who was born in Boston (Lincolnshire), in 1820. 'Play uppe, play uppe, O Boston bells!' is an unforgotten line of Jean Ingelow's ballad, reminder of the part played by the beacon of Boston Stump in flood-time – for all between here and King's Lynn at the south-eastern corner of The Wash is the Fenland which separates East Anglia from England's Midlands.

5. EAST ANGLIA: FROM THE WASH TO THE DEBEN

Literary associations of East Anglia, which in spirit is almost a separate country distinct in itself, are possibly best collected by skirting the coasts of each of the counties of Norfolk, Suffolk and Essex in turn, and in each county glancing at the inland area also before leaving it. Thus having now left Boston and crossed the fen region of Holland (not forgetting Harriet Martineau's story of that area called *The Settlers at Home*) and passed the church of Terrington St Clement (noted earlier as participating in Dorothy Sayers's novel *The Nine Tailors*) I here enter Norfolk at King's Lynn.

Chaucer's friend and rival, the mathematical Nicholas of Lynn, who I think played a part in prompting Chaucer to write his *Treatise on the Astrolabe*, is one of Lynn's early natives of distinction; the remarkable mystic Margery Kempe was another, a few years younger than Nicholas. From Lynn Nicholas sailed on his Arctic voyages, and from Lynn too Margery Kempe took ship for the Holy Land. In the eighteenth century another voyager from Lynn was George Vancouver, who on his long voyage (1792–4) to survey the Pacific coast of North America, upheld the reputation King's Lynn has always had for music by taking with him, aboard ship, his 'music box'. Consider the date: Vancouver's 'music box' was not one of the small tinkling mechanical toys fashionable in the first third of the nineteenth century; it was the eighteenth-century instrument that Goldsmith mentions in *She Stoops to Conquer* (1773), when he speaks of 'Little Aminadab that grinds the music box' – in fact, a barrel organ. As organist at Lynn-Regis (as he preferred to call it), Dr Charles Burney would have encouraged interest not so much in the ordinary street organs (which again were not in use until the nineteenth century), as in the competition engaged in by highly skilled craftsmen to produce instruments of special refinement. An odd future was in store for the barrel organ that Vancouver took to the Pacific. On his way to circumnavigate 'Vancouver Island' he called at the San Carlos Mission on the Californian coast. There the morale of the Mission was temporarily at a low ebb; in distress at the absence of vivacity, Vancouver asked the presiding Father of San Carlos if he might play the music box for them. The instrument afforded such pleasure that Vancouver left it with the Mission as a parting gift.

Dr Burney was a stimulus to literature as well as to music. His daughter Fanny, whose first novel *Evelina* (1778) was a not unworthy forerunner in the realm where Jane Austen would prove supreme, was encouraged to write stories when a child in the house by the river at Lynn; in summertime at the age of ten Fanny Burney was already writing away in a gazebo in the garden. Meanwhile the lively Doctor of Music set forth on a tour of the Continent, gathering notes for his *General History of Music*, and by publishing in 1771 an account of his first jaunt gained such a good reputation for his book that Johnson was prompted to embark on his own Tour to the Hebrides – 'I had that clever dog Burney's Musical Tour in my eye', said Johnson.

Along the coast eastward from King's Lynn another naval man and writer is recalled at Langham, two miles inland from Blakeney; namely Captain Marryat, who was born in the same year that Vancouver was presenting the music box to the Mission on the California coast, and who, after an exceedingly active life, came in his fifties to settle at Langham. Marryat's early novels of sea life, notably *Peter Simple* and *Mr Midshipman Easy*, were based very much on his own adventures. For any occasion of derring-do, afloat or ashore, Marryat had always been, in the phrase of that period, 'true game'; but when he was pensioned off his continuing impulsiveness to have his swing, trying and tasting everything, rendered London too expensive. 'If I were not rather in want of money', he told his mother, 'I certainly would not write any more.' After *Masterman Ready* (1841) he and his favourite daughter Augusta agreed to retire to Langham's Manor Cottage, where there were suitably elegant fittings within doors, and suitably active outdoor sports at hand, ratting, for instance. 'You must know that our Norfolk rats are quite as large as well-grown guinea pigs', he wrote delightedly, and Augusta, when ratting with her father, pleased him by seizing hold of an enormous rat in her bare hands and holding it 'true game'. Within doors, when the captain had arranged the sixteen clocks and chronometers of which he was specially fond, he did his daily stint of writing at the dining-room table, until the final summer of 1848 of which Virginia Woolf wrote in one of her most charming essays, 'The Captain's Death Bed':

The Captain lay dying on a mattress stretched on the floor of the boudoir room; a room whose ceiling had been painted to imitate the sky, and whose walls were painted with trellis work covered with roses upon which birds were perching. Mirrors had been let into the doors, so that the village people called the room the 'Room of a Thousand Pillars' because of its reflections. It was an August morning as he lay dying; his daughter had brought him a bunch of his favourite flowers – clove pinks and moss roses; and he asked her to take down some words at his dictation. . . .

Virginia Woolf continued her essay by giving the words that the captain dictated: his thanks to Augusta for the neatness of the bouquet, just 'three pinks and three roses', his brief counting up of blessings that 'Christianity is true' and that 'God is love', and the two sentences with which he ended – 'It is now half-past nine o'clock. World, adieu.' The oddity on which Virginia Woolf commented lay in the contrast between the rough and often quarrelsome nature of Marryat's life and its quiet ending in the room at Langham with windows open, looking-glasses and painted birds, the many beautifully made chronometers, and the thoughts on God's love and roses. Death did not occur immediately after the two-word sentence 'World, adieu': the captain quietly slipped his cable, none knew quite when, towards dawn of the next morning. After that the bunch of pinks and roses (three of each) were 'found pressed between his body and the mattress'.

Half a century earlier than Marryat, the poet Cowper came to this part of Norfolk for his last years, with Mrs Unwin, the companion of his later life. His cousin John and other friends hoped, when Mrs Unwin's health failed and the two elderly invalids were unable to manage at Olney, that the bracing air of Norfolk might prove better for them. An effort was first made to establish Cowper and Mrs Unwin at Mundesley on the coast; when that failed, they were found lodgings inland at Swaffham; finally in 1796 they were moved to East Dereham, to a house by the market-place (the site now occupied by the Memorial Congregational Chapel). But soon after their arrival at Dereham Mrs Unwin died, and Cowper himself had only three further clouded years of loneliness beside Dereham's 'modest market-place'. Once at least in that last period the power of composition revived in him, when he wrote *The Castaway*. His own life ended in 1800, and his tomb is in Dereham's parish church, with verses on it by the faithful friend Hayley. Cowper's memory was also much respected by Dereham's Nonconformists; it is possible that the Baptist boy Matthew Vassar, coming to Dereham Market from Tuddenham, saw Cowper in the flesh before he himself emigrated to America, eventually at the age of seventy to give his name to Vassar College in New York State.

Following the Norfolk coast from Mundesley past Caister brings us to Great Yarmouth. Caister Castle, built by Sir John Fastolf – Shakespeare's Falstaff – was later the home of the Pastons, and many of the famous fifteenth-century *Paston Letters* were written from the castle. Of the many associations with Yarmouth, where the combined waters of the Yare, the Bure and the Waveney enter the sea, undoubtedly Dickens provides the one which has had most worldwide attention. Yarmouth was for Dickens 'the strangest place in the world', and by placing the Peggotty family (in *David Copperfield*) at home in the ship's hull on the sea front he rendered that site unforgettable. The Peggottys' home must have been not far from the Nelson column; and for an east coast family they were not at all wildly overdrawn by Dickens. The sea-man 'Posh' Fletcher, whom, in his twenties, Edward FitzGerald (three years older than Dickens) took into partnership to operate a herring-lugger, was not only a fairly exact contemporary of Ham Peggotty, but also – six feet tall, blue-eyed, with auburn hair and beard, 'a grand fellow' – pretty much Ham's 'spit and image'. When in the fishery business with Posh, FitzGerald and he often put into Yarmouth, though Lowestoft was really the home port of their lugger, the *Meum & Tuum* (the name chosen by FitzGerald). Of other nineteenth-century associations, Francis Turner Palgrave, who compiled *The Golden Treasury of Songs and Lyrics* in 1861, was a native of Yarmouth; so was Anna Sewell, author of *Black Beauty*, who was born at No. 26 Priory Plain, north of the market-place. South of the market-place, at No. 169 King Street, George Borrow and his wife lodged for long periods in the 1850s, and there he completed the writing of *The Romany Rye*.

Before marriage caused George Borrow to settle at Oulton Broad and Yarmouth, his early upbringing had been largely inland in Norfolk, at Norwich. He was in fact born at Dumpling Green, near East Dereham, in 1803; his journey as a boy along the Great North Road has been mentioned; and when his parents returned from Edinburgh they settled in Willow Lane, Norwich, in what was later named Borrow House. George, while yet at the Norwich Grammar School, spent all the time he could with the gipsies on Mousehold Heath. There he renewed acquaintance with Jasper Petulengro, whom he had met at Norman Cross, and very soon mastered much of the international gipsy lore and gipsy language. At the age of fifteen Borrow was articled to a Norwich solicitor, but at twenty-one was free to stretch his long legs – his height was six foot three – on his preliminary walk, at the steady pace of six miles an hour, to London. There Borrow talked himself into becoming a travelling agent for the British and Foreign Bible Society, and so became intimate with vagrant life and languages in Spain, France, Germany, Russia and the Near East. We shall soon be seeing Borrow again, after his return to England, at Oulton Broad.

A native of Norwich almost exactly contemporary with Borrow and who, like him, achieved her literary reputation by foreign travel, was Harriet Martineau. Borrow had the advantage of a magnificent physique; Harriet Martineau, a sickly child and deaf, was supposedly fated to life-long illness when her father, of Huguenot descent, failed in business and died, leaving her and her brother penniless. (The brother shook loose to become a Unitarian minister in Ireland.) The intense need for eco-nomic reform after the Napoleonic wars made the unknown Harriet, at the age of thirty, produce three short books: *Illustrations of Political Economy, Poor Law and Paupers Illustrated*, and *Illustrations of Taxation*.

With nothing to recommend them beyond their own intrinsic merit these writings reached rapidly from Norwich to London; despite her initial poverty, continuing poor health and deafness she followed her short books to London, was consulted by Cabinet ministers, and promptly entered the swim with other literary celebrities. At that moment there was great interest in the American scene: Mrs Trollope (twenty years older than Miss Martineau) had published her *Domestic Manners of the Americans* in 1832 and Harriet was commissioned to visit the United States and record her own observations. After spending most of three years (1834–6) in America she produced *Society in America* (1837) and *Retrospect of Western Travel* (1838) but these two books are closer to De Tocqueville than to Mrs Trollope. Such was Harriet's repute that she was now persuaded to write a novel, *Deerbrook*, in 1839, and then to have a rest in Venice; but the strain on her health meant collapse for her in Venice. Returned to England, she was firmly ordered to regard herself as a permanent invalid but only a modified version of such orders penetrated Miss Martineau's deafness. For five years she went ahead with many writings (including such delightful adventure stories as *The Settlers at Home* and *Feats on the Fjord*), living quietly until it occurred to her that full activity could be restored by Mesmerism. Sure enough, to the enormous admiration of Wordsworth, Bulwer Lytton and others, Harriet's cure by Mesmerism occurred. Promptly she set off on journeyings in Egypt and Palestine; on her return she built a house near the Wordsworths at Ambleside, and having published *Eastern Life* in 1848 produced her *Complete Guide to the Lakes* in 1855, written in the midst of innumerable articles on every aspect of social reform. Indefatigable to the end, she died in 1876 at the age of seventy-four.

Of the writers not actually native to Norwich but who, as soon as there, tried never to depart, pre-eminent is Sir Thomas Browne. His father, of Cheshire stock, was a London merchant who died when Thomas (born in 1605) was a child. After schooling at Winchester and Oxford the young Browne studied medicine at Leyden, settling in Norwich – after several other trials – in 1636. There he married and remained 'in inoffensive and unmolested prosperity', as Saintsbury put it, for the rest of his life. To my knowledge there is nothing in any of his extensive writings that hints at the tensions and distresses of the Civil War – his *Religio Medici* was singularly detached from current events. He was plain Dr Browne when the *Religio Medici* was published without his sanction in 1642, although he agreed to its reissue in 1643; and that and the later writings suggested the knighthood conferred on him in 1671 when Charles II visited Norwich.

A writer of the twentieth-century war periods who was born in

Norwich and ever returned there as soon as he could was R. H. Mottram, whose best-known work, *The Spanish Farm*, appeared as a trilogy in the 1920s. Mottram became indeed mayor of Norwich, and his successful combination of literary work and banking reminds one of the Gurney family of Norwich's Earlham Hall. Earlham, now encroached on by the expanding city, was charmingly told of in Percy Lubbock's *Earlham*.

Norwich is a great hub from which roads radiate. Due west is 'pretty, quiet Dereham', aforementioned; south-west is Thetford, birthplace of Tom Paine, author of *The Rights of Man* (1791–2), and a statue was set up there by the Thomas Paine Society. Southward from Norwich, after passing Swardeston (birthplace of Edith Cavell), is Diss, where John Skelton was rector before Wolsey, as some suggest, forced him into exile in Yorkshire. The River Waveney, flowing eastward past Diss, becomes the border between Norfolk and Suffolk, and if that river valley is followed to Bungay one comes upon associations with Sir Henry Rider Haggard. Called to the bar in 1884, Haggard preferred writing adventure stories to practising law; *King Solomon's Mines*, published in 1885 while he was living at Hammersmith, proved he made the right decision. His wife inherited Ditchingham House, north of Bungay, and there the Haggards settled in 1889, Rider Haggard continuing, in the midst of other activities, to write his further adventure stories.

The Waveney leads on from Bungay to Beccles, which town received its name, according to the poet George Crabbe, from its fine church – *beata ecclesia*. At Beccles, Crabbe as a young man was nearly drowned in circumstances which he was later able to work into a cautionary tale. While still living twenty-five miles away on the Suffolk coast at Aldeburgh, Crabbe was courting Sarah Elmy of Beccles, and on a summer morning he walked over to join her for a picnic. Sarah had the rowboat ready for the river; her intention was to catch a good supply of the crayfish for which the Waveney at Beccles was particularly noted. Crabbe rowed her to the directed pool, yet feeling himself still overwarm from his walk, proposed to have a dip in the Waveney while Mira, as his verses called her, was still crayfishing. Sea-bathing at Aldeburgh had not taught Crabbe to swim – there from the shingle beach you walked out a few steps until waist-deep, then ducked your head and walked ashore again. But here near Beccles, when Crabbe had stripped and stepped from the river's bank, his feet instantly slipped on the mud – and 'the flood boiled over his head'. Many years later in his *Tales of the Hall* Crabbe reverts to his fright when

> An undefined sensation stopp'd my breath

and despite his frenzied struggles he gave up for lost –

> Hope, youth, life, love, and all they promised, drown'd.

Had Mira not been a prompt life-saver her lover had indeed been lost.

The Waveney, as it approaches and then draws away again inland from Lowestoft, passes Oulton Broad. There Mary Clarke, a widow with one daughter, owned in 1839 a modest estate, a house and summer-house by the side of the lake. Though George Borrow had not yet written *The Bible in Spain*, he was a striking figure; when they happened to meet at Oulton the widow, wrote one biographer, felt 'very kind, very kind' towards him. Borrow had only been passing through Oulton, about to return to his wanderings in Spain, but Mrs Clarke followed right after, and at Gibraltar 'she found him out, having travelled over half Europe in search of him, and took possession of him'. Borrow was not unwilling to be captive at Oulton. There he completed the writings of *The Bible in Spain*, and while engaged on *Lavengro* also 'amused myself by catching huge pike, which lie perdue in certain deep ponds skirted with lofty reeds, upon my land', and at any time was ready to pick up and offer hospitality to vagrants, especially gipsies. This habit proved to be a considerable trial to Mrs Borrow, for Borrow liked to rub it in to respect-able neighbours that, as John Freeman neatly phrased it, 'any except those professing gentility were welcome to call upon him'. *The Romany Rye* was completed during one of the long visits to Yarmouth which gave Mrs Borrow, as her health failed, some escape from the 'affairs of Egypt'. Later Borrow broke away from Oulton for some years, but in 1874 he returned, as he said, to die. The tall mysterious old man with wide black hat and flowing black Spanish cloak was often seen in the Suffolk lanes; 'that King of Gipsies' the children called him as he walked, chanting unintelligible singsong. Increasingly, though, Borrow stayed at home, a sometimes irritable recluse. A good-natured visitor innocently asked how old he was, and Borrow snapped: 'I tell my age to no man!' Then he retired to his summer-house and began an essay with the words: 'Never talk to people about their age.'

Between the coast and Wroxham the Norfolk Broads exerted an appeal to Wilkie Collins in 1864. After the sudden, outstanding, spectacular success of *The Woman in White* Collins fell into eighteen months of 'total literary abstinence', and that, for him, might become a danger: to some extent at least, writing was an antidote to opium-taking. In fact, right after *The Woman in White* a long visit to Aldeburgh had given him local colour for his novel *No Name* (1862); but after that, Collins fell into the lethargy which he shook off in 1864 by visiting the Broads for his project of 'studying localities' and so developed *Armadale*. If I return though to Suffolk's Oulton Broad beside the Waveney, there is a waterway thence to Lowestoft, where again I think of Edward Fitz-Gerald. In the winter before Collins's *The Woman in White* created its sensation, FitzGerald, at the age of fifty, had diffidently offered to the public a poem called the *Rubáiyát of Omar Khayyám*. When the public, as a result of tub-thumping by Tennyson, Carlyle and others, began to pay some attention to the *Rubáiyát*, FitzGerald quietly withdrew from his wife and home near Woodbridge, and instead of continuing the normal life of a modest country gentleman substituted another life of lying under the lee side of fishing boats, beachcombing on the beach at Lowestoft along with the other regular beachcombers. Frank Hussey's recent book on *Old Fitz* adds much amusing detail to the general contrast of FitzGerald, man of letters, and the tall, sea-bronzed waterside character who usually had a bottle of rum in his pocket, and always tobacco, for out-of-work Lowestoft companions.

Blundeston, for the sake of Dickens, was more of a draw to FitzGerald than Oulton for the sake of Borrow. FitzGerald at seventy could burst out: 'I bless and rejoice in Dickens more and more.' Blundeston, between Lowestoft and Yarmouth, was the 'Blunderstone' of *David Copperfield* (to prove which, the round-towered church at Blundeston was restored as a Dickens memorial). Furthermore, Blundeston was associated with the poet Thomas Gray, who used to stay at the rectory. Gray and FitzGerald belong to that group of poets who are chiefly remembered for a single long poem. Gray of the *Elegy* and FitzGerald of the *Rubáiyát* would each have enjoyed the other man's 'melancholy and voluptuous clangour'.

Yet the poet for whom FitzGerald expressed a 'monomania' of admiration was George Crabbe; and for further associations with Crabbe and FitzGerald I move on to Aldeburgh and Woodbridge.

*   *   *

The Suffolk coast offers a wide variety of 'literary items' which could be picked up and examined. Thomas Nash was born at Lowestoft; Teodor Josef Konrad Korzeniowski first landed in England at Lowestoft in 1878, and for some months it became his home port while he served in North Sea coasters. There he improved his English and decided to change his name to Joseph Conrad. At Southwold in the twentieth century Stephen Southwold grew up; he adopted the name of Neil Bell. Eric Blair was also more widely known after he chose as pseudonym the name of George Orwell; he too lived at Southwold (at No. 3 Queen Street) with his parents for several years in the 1930s. Dunwich I have already mentioned for the stimulus the east wind and its own melancholy history had on Swinburne (as on many other visitors). At Theberton Charles Doughty, author of *Travels in Arabia Deserta*, was born, at Theberton Hall, in 1843. That is commemorated in the thatched church; though FitzGerald was more intrigued with that church for its part in contraband – FitzGerald swore that there were (or had been) smuggled 'kegs of Holland under the altar cloth of Theberton Church'.

But these items I must regard as interruptions, and even after reaching Aldeburgh, if I am to recall the 'frowning coast' of the eighteenth century, I must suppress many crowded latter-day memories. Before the throng at Aldeburgh was much increased by the music festivals, at the beginning of this century Edward Clodd was extending the hospitality of his Strafford House to his large circle of notable friends, and Montague James was making other visitors' flesh creep with his Aldeburgh ghost story, *Oh, Whistle, and I'll come to You, My Lad*. Perhaps the way to work back to the earlier, unprosperous, forbidding Aldeburgh of Crabbe's time, may be to quote Wilkie Collins, where he was preparing to use the Aldeburgh setting for a climactic 'sensation-scene' of the novel *No Name*:

It was a dull airless evening. Eastward was the grey majesty of the sea, hushed in breathless calm; the horizon line invisibly melting into the monotonously misty sky; the idle ships shadowy and still on the idle water. Southward, the high ridge of the sea dyke, and the grim massive circle of a martello tower, reared high on its mound of grass, closed the view darkly on all that lay beyond. Westward, a lurid streak of sunset glowed red in the dreary heaven – blackened the fringing trees on the far borders of the great inland marsh – and turned its little gleaming water-pools to pools of blood. Nearer to the eye, the sullen flow of the tidal river Alde, ebbed noiselessly from the muddy banks; and nearer still, lonely and unprosperous by the bleak waterside, lay the lost little port of Slaughden; with its forlorn wharfs and warehouses of decaying wood, and its few scattered coasting vessels deserted on the oozy river-shore. No fall of waves was heard on the beach; no trickling of waters bubbled audibly from the idle stream. Now and then, the cry of a sea-bird rose from the region of the marsh; and at intervals, from farmhouses far in the inland waste, the faint winding of horns to call the cattle home, travelled mournfully through the evening calm.

The description by Wilkie Collins (except for the one detail of the 'martello tower', which came with the Napoleonic wars, later than Crabbe's youth-time) is evocative of Crabbe's surroundings in the poverty-stricken period when he was rolling salt and butter barrels at Slaughden quay. Crabbe, born in 1755 as one of 'the poor laborious natives of the place', was determined to paint Aldeburgh in *The Village* 'as Truth will paint it and as Bards will not':

> Here joyless roam a wild amphibious race,
> With sullen woe display'd in every face;
> Who, far from civil arts and social fly,
> And scowl at strangers with suspicious eye.

The portrait of Aldeburgh was continued in *The Borough*, Crabbe's 'Truth' enforcing fair play between good and bad. His affections enter, and his special feeling for the steep shingle sea-beach of Aldeburgh,

> With all those bright red pebbles, that the sun
> Through the small waves so softly shines upon.

For Crabbe the smiles and scowls of the Suffolk coast both lasted. Once at least in later life, when he was married and settled inland, he rode sixty miles to the east coast in order to dip in the sea 'that washed the beach of Aldeburgh'.

At sixteen Crabbe was apprenticed to an apothecary at Woodbridge, yet in his five years there also diligently practised as a self-taught 'literary Adventurer'. It was Crabbe's meeting with Sarah Elmy of Beccles which stimulated quantities of his early effusions to 'Mira', but it was not until he was twenty-six and in London that Crabbe found his special ability, and by his fortunate appeal to Edmund Burke and Burke's instant recognition and quick friendship, the poet was 'made'. Later 'laborious natives' of the part of Suffolk inland from Aldeburgh have also been recorded. George Ewart Evans has told, in several books, of life for farmworkers round about Tunstall. *Akenfield* by Ronald Blythe might be identified with Charsfield, north of Woodbridge and west of Wickham Market. In Woodbridge the Quaker poet, Bernard Barton (1784–1849) was born. His poems won the friendship of Charles Lamb, and the respect of Southey and others, and caused intimacy with the unusual character whom I have several times mentioned but must now look at a little more closely – Edward FitzGerald.

In the year (1809) that Bernard Barton became a bank clerk (eventually manager) at Alexander's bank in Woodbridge, the boy who was later to be known as Edward FitzGerald was born at Bredfield House, near Boulge (pronounced Bowwidge), two and a half miles north of Woodbridge. He had an older brother, John. What is of relevance is that the family name of the boys' parents was Purcell. The Purcell boys went to the grammar school at Bury St Edmunds, from which John went on, as befitted the Purcell stock, to be a man of business. It was apparently while Edward was still a schoolboy at Bury that he learned that the family name had been changed. His mother was Irish; her maiden name had been FitzGerald; now her father had died, and on condition the name of Purcell was expunged and the name of FitzGerald legally adopted, there was a considerable inheritance. I have been told that Edward's brother John stuck to the name Purcell, but John the father was delighted at the change of fortune. He promptly escaped from rural Boulge, using his new signature of John FitzGerald on the lease of a grander estate on the River Orwell and entered himself as a new member of the Royal Yacht Club as owner of the 50-ton yacht *Ruby*.

Edward also welcomed the name FitzGerald, and proceeding to Trinity College, Cambridge, began a lifelong friendship with another well-to-do undergraduate, Thackeray. His friendship with Tennyson began later – in their college days Tennyson was a hard worker, and FitzGerald showed no ambition for hard work. After Cambridge, at the age of twenty-one, he drifted home to the estate on the Orwell and settled easily into a life of reading, dreaming, smoking, though he also took to sailing with energy and aptitude, and on cruises both long and short proved himself a real and reliable working yachtsman. But after some years the lease of the Orwell estate had to be given up, the yacht *Ruby* was sold, the Royal Yacht Squadron was retired from, and the FitzGeralds are pictured as back in the former Purcell home at Boulge. Edward, now thirty, apparently accepted the change with equanimity; he seems to have given up yachting without repining, and he spent his days at Boulge reading, dreaming, smoking, while routine walks into the market town of Woodbridge formed sufficient activity. Now it was that the banker-poet Bernard Barton warmly promoted the custom whereby the literate, scholarly Edward stopped to have high tea with him and his daughter Lucy at Barton House in the Thorofare at Woodbridge.

Thus passed FitzGerald's life till he was forty; then, in 1849, Bernard Barton, widower, died, but on his deathbed, gossipers asserted, had made FitzGerald promise to take care of Lucy, i.e. to marry her. The only immediate partnership that gossips could observe was that Edward and Lucy prepared an edition of Barton's poems to which Edward contributed, anonymously, a life of the poet. Thereafter he took to visiting London, and in each of three successive years produced books of poetry of his own, a selection from Crabbe's poems, and translations of dramatic poetry from Greek and Spanish. FitzGerald kept returning, however, to Woodbridge, where his bachelor status was protected in 1855 by a visit from Thomas Carlyle. Carlyle and Jane Welsh Carlyle were in a period of domestic discontent; Carlyle arrived in a thundering bad temper – he had made the mistake of journeying from London to Ipswich by railway. The train, he gasped, was 'quite horrible'. For his return he refused utterly to be again suffocated 'like a codfish in a hamper'. FitzGerald therefore drove him to Ipswich and saw him off for London Bridge by steamboat; and Carlyle's further visits were to be made by sea.

It was in 1856 that 'Fitz' revived the excitement of Woodbridge gossips by marrying Lucy Barton, and the pair moved into Farlingay Hall. Three years later his poet-friends succeeded in urging publication of the *Rubáiyát*. As the poem caught on, reprints were called for, and there was eagerness to interview the author. How much of the poem was

Omar, the twelfth-century Persian? How much was FitzGerald? Fitz had no intention of answering questions. Publicity was disgusting: Londoners, on the whole, seemed to him 'a decayed Race'; only on the east coast could he trust in 'the old English Stuff'. As the poem came to be talked about in Woodbridge and Ipswich, Fitz was not pleased with their 'old English Stuff' either. Woodbridge found it humorous to cackle at Fitz for neglecting his wife and fondling Persian fantasies, and as for Ipswich yachtsmen, one recalled the FitzGeralds' former yacht *Ruby*, and the Yacht Club rocked with laughter at his suggestion that book-sellers should be asked for *The Ruby Yacht* by Homer K. Emm. Such level of wit sufficiently explains the outward transformation into 'Old Fitz', the beachcomber at Lowestoft. If FitzGerald's marriage had not been 'ill-fated' before, it was soon after the publication of the *Rubáiyát*. When Fitz returned from Lowestoft to Woodbridge it was to arrange for Lucy to live by herself at Farlingay Hall, while he took up bachelor quarters on Woodbridge's Market Hill. There 'E.F.G.' is recorded by a white stone tablet on the red-brick building, which was his place of residence from 1861 to 1874; after which he moved to the attractive house called Little Grange.

In 1865 FitzGerald had a schooner built at Woodbridge which upon launching he named *Scandal*, because, he said, that was 'the staple product of Woodbridge' – and for emphasis he named her tender *The Whisper*. The *Scandal* was 'not a Racer – but not a Cart Horse – a Sea Boat'; it was 'a splash to Sea' that he liked most. FitzGerald entered her for membership with the Royal Western Yacht Club of Ireland; in June 1866 he announced 'My Ship is afloat with a new Irish Ensign', and it was an ensign that he enjoyed flaunting at Harwich or up the Orwell. (It was when he had taken the *Scandal* to Lowestoft that he embarked on the partnership with Posh Fletcher, equal shares in a herring-lugger.) But by 1873 Fitz had begun, in the seafaring expression, to 'smell the ground'; there was less sailing; he settled into the privacy of Little Grange. Tennyson stayed with him there in 1876, continuing his gentle reproach to his friend for having ceased to publish after the *Rubáiyát*. As Fitz was to enter his seventy-fifth year, Tennyson wrote a graceful birthday greeting:

> Old Fitz, who from your suburb grange,
>   Where once I tarried for a while,
> Glance at the wheeling Orb of Change,
>   And greet it with a kindly smile;
> Whom yet I see as there you sit
>   Beneath your sheltering garden-tree,
> And watch your doves about you flit,
>   And plant on shoulder, hand and knee . . .

The handwriting reached Fitz, although he died before the book which contained the verses (*Tiresias*) was printed.

6. EAST ANGLIA: MID-SUFFOLK AND CAMBRIDGE

Few literary figures come to life so readily as Old Fitz in Woodbridge, where 'with his green Irish cape, flowered satin waistcoat, an old pair of slippers on his feet, and, if the east wind was blowing, a silk hand-kerchief tied over his hat and under his chin', Woodbridgeans today re-main aware of him. Likewise do the pilgrims who come from afar to see if the rose-bushes brought from Omar Khayyám's tomb in Persia and planted over FitzGerald's grave at Boulge – or their descendants or replacements – are properly in bloom. Ipswich, though it grew so much more rapidly in size than Woodbridge, is of lesser importance in literary history. Margaret Catchpole was a spirited nursemaid in service with the Cobbold family in Ipswich, who fell in love with a smuggler and to meet him stole a horse; for that theft she was transported in 1801 to Botany Bay, and in 1845 she was put into a novel by Richard Cobbold. The novel *Margaret Catchpole* survived to be reprinted in 'The World's Classics' in this century for the glimpse it gives of crime and punish-ment at the period described; and it is worth recalling too because Mrs Cobbold, the author's mother and the employer in real life of the energetic nursemaid, was also the lady rudely caricatured by Dickens in *Pickwick* as Mrs Leo Hunter. It has been held that Mrs Cobbold's habit of composing rhymed valentines suggested to Dickens the valen-tine concocted by Sam Weller, addressed 'To Mary, Housemaid, at Mr Nupkins's Mayor's, Ipswich, Suffolk'. Even more remembered is Dickens's use of Ipswich's famous inn, the Great White Horse, for Mr Pickwick's alarming adventure with the middle-aged lady in yellow curlpapers.

Inland from Ipswich is Sudbury, the 'Eatanswill' of the *Pickwick Papers*. To reach Bury from Sudbury, I would make a detour through Lavenham and Cockfield because (apart from Lavenham's church and the colourful streets of 'the most picturesque town in Suffolk') it was at Lavenham, in one of the old houses in Shilling Street, that Ann and Jane Taylor grew up. When they had reached the ages of fourteen and thirteen respectively they were moved away to Colchester, and there at Colchester they presently produced their *Original Poems for Infant Minds* (1804) and also the further nursery rhyme 'Twinkle, twinkle, little star'. Yet I enjoy thinking of Ann and Jane Taylor at Lavenham;

that town still gives the impression in an unspoiled way of having been a happy place for their infant minds to grow in. As for Cockfield, it was at the railway station there that Sidney Colvin, then a young professor of Fine Arts at Cambridge, 'was met on the platform by a stripling in a velvet jacket and a straw hat', who walked with him to Cockfield rectory where both were summer guests. The year was 1873; the stripling was the twenty-three-year-old Robert Louis Stevenson, at a critical moment in his life. He wished to break away from the pattern that was shaping for him in Edinburgh, and live, if he could, by writing. Through the friendships formed at Cockfield rectory with Colvin and the others he was given not merely momentary but continuing encouragement and active help to fulfil this ambition.

Carlyle now waits rhapsodically, at Bury St Edmunds, in *Past and Present*, to grip your arm ('O dilettante friend') to hustle you through the Abbey gate, into the neat and tidy Abbey gardens, and pull and push at you to be sure you look this way and that at the once exceedingly bustling life within 'these old St Edmundsbury walls'. *Past and Present* was published in 1843; academic historians point out that Carlyle's twelfth-century Abbot Samson 'is rather a rhetorical construction than a historical personage'. Never mind, the book was an interpretation of Jocelin de Brakelond's twelfth-century chronicle; and if one wishes to read a slightly later authentic churchman's words about the monastic life here, there is also Richard de Bury's *Philobiblon*.

Mr Pickwick, when he stayed at the Angel, facing the Abbey, had little opportunity to think about Bury's history, for the outwitting of Sam Weller by Job Trotter had a swift and painfully distracting outcome. The girls' school of that adventure was, one imagines, attended a few years later by the remarkable best-selling novelist known as Ouida – the pseudonym of Marie Louise de la Ramée – who was born at Bury in 1839. Moyses Hall, the museum close to Bury's Town Hall, contains mementos of Ouida. Not only are her novels highly rewarding for moments of (sometimes unintended) hilarity, but her escapades in real life were notably high-spirited. I have been told that though Norman Douglas could usually take care of himself, he freely confessed terror of Ouida and her demands when she threatened to visit him in Italy.

Seven miles north-east of Bury are two villages, Honington and Sapiston – not upland villages, but inconspicuous in country that looks past Fakenham and Thetford to the mysterious Breckland and the fens beyond. Robert Bloomfield was born at Honington in the eighteenth century and worked as a farmer's boy at Sapiston. There is nothing apparently magnetic about his life which, after he had been lured to London, continued to be one of unremitting poverty, with less that he liked to look at in London than in the country he remembered, but it was in London in 1800 that he wrote, in *The Farmer's Boy*, his verse description of life in the Sapiston neighbourhood, and there a magnetism does appear. Half a century after publication of the book a copy was part of the stock of a second-hand bookshop in Buenos Aires kept, said W. H. Hudson, 'by a snuffy old German'. Hudson (in *Afoot in England*) describes how, as a ten-year-old American boy, on a trip into the city from the pampas, he browsed in the bookshop, picked up a small volume, and then and later, in a way unanticipated yet irrevocable, was quietly and steadily drawn to come and see for himself the life of the English countryside. Hudson (1841–1922) was middle-aged before he was able to come to settle for the rest of his life in England.

* * *

Cambridge! – how can I deal with its star-cluster of literary associations? A similar problem will have to be faced at Oxford. Let me first consider two general questions which may be asked at both Oxford and Cambridge. Both may be divided into their component parts, city and university, Town and Gown. Then one may ask which notable items of literary interest, in fact or fiction, are going to associate at each place with the town and which with the university. At Cambridge, neither in ancient nor in recent times do outstanding associations with the town, separate from the university, leap to mind. True, in the nineteenth century as soon as Fellows of the monastic colleges were permitted to marry, even before the women's colleges were in full swing, there was an uprush of literary talent among female children of Cambridge men. It was in the 1880s that Rose Macaulay, Gwen Raverat, Frances Cornford were all children growing up in Cambridge, and Virginia Woolf's father, Leslie Stephen, was so much a Cambridge man and so often in Cambridge that she counts as one of that same 'set'. Yet all of these brilliant Cambridge writers, women as much as the men who preceded them or were their contemporaries, were 'university' people. For the literary pilgrim a visit to Cambridge is not complicated by attention demanded by 'Town'; little except 'university' associations cluster there.

Yet from Elizabethan times onward, what a galaxy of poets can the Cambridge colleges present! Marlowe, Spenser, Milton, Wordsworth, Coleridge, Byron, Tennyson – there are seven names to start with. No other university can boast of nursing such a succession of poetical talents of the very first order, and those seven constitute only, so to say, a first team; Cambridge can boast another seven-poet team of almost equal order. I now ask my second general question: to what extent did Cambridge make these poets, or contribute to their development?

Perhaps that is impossible to answer – a parallel question occurred but was unanswered when we looked at the two most transcendent years of Newton's genius. But the question can be rephrased more modestly: to what extent are the years they spent at Cambridge the years of greatest interest to the reader in the lives of the poets mentioned? For Marlowe we are handicapped by lack of knowledge; beyond the details that he entered Corpus Christi about 1580 and received an M.A. degree in 1587 there is not much known about his life at Cambridge. Spenser, a little earlier than Marlowe, had entered Pembroke in the 1560s and at that 'college of poets' was befriended by Gabriel Harvey. In *The Faerie Queene* Spenser spoke with gratitude of 'My Mother, Cambridge' and the 'many a gentle muse and many a learned wit' with which she was adorned. Allowing for the poet's nostalgia, we may nevertheless believe that Cambridge was of positive help to his literary flowering.

One does not doubt that Milton was much 'brought on' by his years (1625–9) at Christ's College. He stayed on in college rooms apparently until taking his M.A. degree in 1632, writing Latin poems on university events, the 'Hymn on the Morning of Christ's Nativity', the sonnet to Shakespeare, and other English poems. It was the death of Milton's fellow-collegian Edward King that later, in 1638, inspired 'Lycidas'. What is traditionally known as Milton's mulberry tree is still in the Fellows' Garden at Christ's College.

It was to St John's that Wordsworth, by what he called

> Migration strange for a stripling of the hills,
> A northern villager,

came for the years 1787 to 1791. He reflects at length, in the third book of *The Prelude*, about the meaning those years at Cambridge had for him. Coleridge's activities at Jesus College – entering in 1791, fleeing 'to debauchery' in London in 1793, impulsively enlisting in the 15th Dragoons under a half-false name (bought out by his brothers), returning in 1794 to find himself in some disgrace confined to college and therefore 'in an inauspicious hour' leaving Cambridge in momentary dudgeon and without a degree – such activities make lively reading, yet indicate that in the Cambridge nursery the 'Archangel' (to use an expression of Charles Lamb's for Coleridge) became a little damaged. Byron's activities when he entered Trinity College in 1805 were also full of vivacity, yet one does not feel that his Cambridge years effected, on Byron, any alteration whatever. Between riding, shooting, boxing and swimming he published two volumes of verse by 1807, which prompted the vigorous controversy with 'Scotch Reviewers'; but Byron and Cambridge got along with singularly little friction.

Tennyson was entered at Trinity in 1827, yet, unable to have his own rooms in college, lodged in Trumpington Street. (FitzGerald, entering Trinity at the same time, also lodged out of college, in King's Parade.) Tennyson's closest friend among the undergraduates at Trinity was Arthur Henry Hallam, who entered from Eton; Tennyson made frequent use of Hallam's rooms in college, and Hallam, one of the earliest members of a select group called the Society of Apostles (which from time to time since has entered into literary annals), brought Tennyson into that Society. With Hallam he travelled in the Pyrenees and on the Rhine in 1832, and it was Hallam's premature death in 1833 that prompted Tennyson to begin expressing his grief in *In Memoriam* and 'The Two Voices'.

In the lives of the seven major poets whom I called, I hope not too flippantly, Cambridge's first team, it would be rash to assume that one could readily tell just how important the Cambridge chapter was in each biography. None of those seven showed signs of being drawn so completely into a collegiate, monastic way of life as were some other poets – Gray, for instance, or A. E. Housman. Yet the college chapter in the life of a man of letters is not to be neglected, and since numbers make it impossible to cope with all chapters in full, my best course is to list some (though not all) of the Cambridge colleges with some (though not all) of the names which provide literary associations:

Christ's: John Milton; Charles Dickens; C. S. Calverley (after his removal from Oxford)

Corpus Christi: Christopher Marlowe

Emmanuel: John Harvard; Hugh Walpole

Gonville and Caius: Jeremy Taylor; J. E. Flecker (after Oxford)

Jesus: T. R. Malthus; Laurence Sterne; S. T. Coleridge; Arthur Quiller-Couch (after Oxford)

King's: Edmund Waller; Robert and Horace Walpole; M. R. James; Lowes Dickinson; Maynard Keynes; E. M. Forster; Rupert Brooke

Magdalene: Samuel Pepys; Charles Kingsley; A. C. Benson (Master)

Pembroke: Edmund Spenser; Gabriel Harvey; Richard Crashaw; Thomas Gray; Christopher Smart

Peterhouse: John Skelton; Richard Crashaw (from Pembroke); Thomas Gray (before Pembroke)

St John's: Thomas Wyatt; Roger Ascham; Robert Greene; Thomas Nash; Robert Herrick; Matthew Prior; Erasmus Darwin; William Wordsworth; Henry Kirke White

Trinity: Francis Bacon; George Herbert; Abraham Cowley; Andrew Marvell; Lord Byron; T. B. Macaulay; Alfred Tennyson; Edward FitzGerald; W. M. Thackeray; Lytton Strachey; Desmond Mac-Carthy; G. M. Trevelyan; A. E. Housman (after Oxford)

Trinity Hall: Robert Herrick (after St John's); Samuel Pepys (before Magdalene); Edward Bulwer-Lytton (after Trinity); Leslie Stephen; Ronald Firbank

To some extent honour is satisfied if the literary pilgrim to Cambridge is aware of such a congregation of shrines that are there for the visiting; though it will be noticed that in the above short list of names there is no pretence of completeness; some men's colleges have been omitted and two famous women's colleges (Girton and Newnham) are not mentioned. All visitors should be aware, for instance, that when Girton moved from Hitchin to Cambridge in 1869–70 some of its pioneers were to go on to have remarkable careers. One of them, Rachel Susan Cook (born at St Andrews), after her Girton years married C. P. Scott of the *Manchester Guardian*; she shared with Scott in the editorial work for the rest of her too short life (she died at fifty-seven) and was one of the writers who lifted that paper to eminence. Eileen Power and Rosamond Lehmann were later notable members of Girton. At Newnham (founded five years after Girton) Katharine Bradley was an early student; and from an invitation to read a paper at Newnham Virginia Woolf's *A Room of One's Own* originated. But in or out of termtime each foundation is busily at its own work, and each porter's lodge is the place inquiry should be made about visiting hours. Because Trinity and King's are prominent as showplaces, other colleges may to some extent be grateful to them for absorbing many of the visitors to Cambridge – the Great Court of Trinity and King's College Chapel are very notable protectors!

The 'south suburbs' of Cambridge, as Grantchester and Trumpington are today, are not to be departed from without recollections of Byron, at the 'Byron's Pool' named after him; of *The Reve's Tale* of Chaucer, placed in the mill which stood over the bridge above the pool; of Tennyson's 'The Miller's Daughter', supposedly suggested by the successor to Chaucer's mill but standing in the same place – all these recollections were alluded to by Rupert Brooke in his poem 'The Old Vicarage, Grantchester':

> Still in the dawnlit waters cool
> His ghostly Lordship swims the pool,
> And tries the strokes, essays the tricks,
> Long learnt on Hellespont, or Styx;
> Dan Chaucer hears his river still
> Chatter beneath a phantom mill;
> Tennyson notes, with studious eye,
> How Cambridge waters hurry by. . . .

The mill that Tennyson had studied was in its place when Brooke wrote in 1912, but it too became a phantom after it was burned down in 1928.

Trumpington holds for me another and different association: it was here that G. A. Henty was born and grew up to write a boys' book, *Out in the Pampas,* in 1868, following that classic with a regular production of boys' books at the rate of three a year (though none to my mind ever came up to *Out in the Pampas*).

7. ESSEX AND HERTFORDSHIRE

It is time, though, to skip without ado from Cambridge back to the east coast and to fulfil my promise of skirting the coast of Essex for its associations. One episode, taking one at once to Colchester and Harwich, must be singled out. Other and very ancient things can be recalled at Colchester: tradition that it was the capital of the British king Cymbeline (or Cunobelin) forges a link for those who wish with Shakespeare's play (though there is not much else in this part of Essex to remind one of Shakespeare, except the 'Manningtree ox' of *Henry IV*, Part One). There are certainly nursery rhyme associations at Colchester with King Cole. Yet the simple little episode which always gives me pleasure to remember is the trip that Johnson and Boswell made here in 1763.

I referred at the beginning to the journey that the young James Boswell, having bowed thrice to Arthur's Seat in farewell to Edinburgh, made along the Great North Road to London. His ambition was to meet the great Dr Johnson, and in May 1763, when Boswell was just reaching the age of twenty-three and Johnson was fifty-four, the meeting took place. The Doctor's abruptness to the young Scottish laird was hardly encouraging, and yet within little more than two months Johnson's pleasure with Boswell was warm and genuine. By the beginning of August the time had come for Boswell, in obedience to his father, to leave London for Utrecht, there to study law. Johnson's horror of loneliness caused him to know, by then, how much he was going to miss the doglike devotion of the younger man. No matter if it was an effort – indeed, partly because it was a considerable physical effort – Johnson insisted on accompanying Boswell all the way to Harwich, as if *in loco parentis* to see a son off. The eighteenth-century coach travel did involve exertion. On 5 August Johnson and Boswell had each managed to get to the point of departure before five in the morning, and the first day by stagecoach got them to Colchester. There, though we are not told at which of the High Street inns they stayed, it was one which provided a supper at which Johnson could talk about good eating 'with uncommon satisfaction'. It was after that, towards bedtime, that Boswell 'teized' the Doctor 'with fanciful apprehensions of unhappiness', until Johnson pointed to a moth which had that moment flown into the candle-flame, with the remark: 'That creature was its own tormentor, and I believe its name was Boswell.'

Next day Johnson and Boswell reached Harwich, for dinner presumably at the Three Cups (which later was Nelson's favoured inn), and after a moment of devotion in the church, it was on the way to the beach that Johnson refuted what Boswell quoted from Bishop Berkeley by stopping at a large stone and 'striking his foot with mighty force' against it. There was then an embrace at Boswell's departure. It could be argued that Boswell exaggerates the 'tenderness' at the parting, but one does not feel so – despite all Boswell's faults, Johnson's love for him is undeniable. They walked down to the water and Boswell was put aboard the packet boat for Helvoetsluys. 'As the vessel put out to sea,' says Boswell, 'I kept my eyes upon him for a considerable time, while he remained rolling his majestic frame in the usual manner; and at last I perceived him walk back into the town, and he disappeared.'

So much for a famous departure from Harwich. An arrival there was once described by G. K. Chesterton. 'Between the silver ribbon of morning and the green glittering ribbon of sea, the boat touched Harwich and let loose a swarm of folk like flies, among whom the man we must follow was by no means conspicuous – nor wished to be.' The man was the detective Valentin, following upon the exceedingly dangerous Flambeau; and it was then in the train from Harwich to Liverpool Street that *The Innocence of Father Brown* materialized into the world of fiction.

*   *   *

The Essex coast from Harwich to Southend is crowded with associations, yet many I fear might be regarded as parochial. On Mersea Island William McFee, then in his heyday as a writer in America of the 1920s yet having a hankering to set up as a publican at Mersea, first introduced me to Margery Allingham. Burnham-on-Crouch was the birthplace of Mrs Gatty; Southend the birthplace of Warwick Deeping. In 1888 Fergus Hume came to settle at Thundersley; that was a year after the publication of his splendid thriller, *The Mystery of a Hansom Cab* – a revival of which has long been overdue. At Hadleigh Castle I am reminded of the novelist Arthur Morrison, and the view towards Canvey Island makes me think specially of some of Austin Freeman's stories. Yet if I look instead into inland Essex I quickly find a site connected with a poem known world-wide – *The Deserted Village* by Oliver Goldsmith. A mile east of Chelmsford, in the valley of the Chelmer, is what in 1770 was the small village of Springfield; it was at Springfield, while staying at a cottage near the church, that Goldsmith continued the composition of the poem, completing much of what had been started earlier.

I am not suggesting that the village of Springfield in Essex is to be regarded as the precise or sole identification of

Sweet Auburn! loveliest village of the plain.

As Edward Dowden put it, one isn't to know 'whether Auburn be an English village or the Irish Lissoy, or both in one. . . . Certainly Auburn is English, but certainly too Paddy Byrne kept school there, and Uncle Contarine or Henry Goldsmith occupied the rectory.' The ten lines of the poem beginning

Dear lovely bowers of innocence and ease,
Seats of my youth, when every sport could please,

were written one morning at Goldsmith's rooms in the Temple, for when a neighbour looked in Goldsmith hailed him and with elation read aloud those ten lines, adding the remark: 'Come, let me tell you this is no bad morning's work – and now, my dear boy, if you are not better engaged, I should be glad to enjoy a Shoemaker's Holiday with you.' Springfield's contribution to *The Deserted Village* is the not negligible one that it provided a habitat congenial to the continuation of the poem, and even perhaps to some of Goldsmith's pictures. A brook tributary to the Chelmer may have been the brook, or a reminder of the brook, from which the 'widowed, solitary thing' was seen to be stripping the watercress.

West of Chelmsford is Waltham Abbey and, over the River Lea, Waltham Cross in Hertfordshire. In 1837–40 Tennyson was living at High Beech in the heart of Epping Forest; family affairs were not very happy; to the bells of Waltham Abbey he addressed the lines 'Ring out the old, ring in the new'. A few years later, from 1859 till 1871, Anthony Trollope lived in much greater contentment at Waltham House at Waltham Cross. The house, unfortunately demolished in 1936, was described by Anne Thackeray as, in winter, 'a sweet old prim chill house wrapped in snow', but in summer, delightfully, parties 'would adjourn after dinner to the lawn, where wines and fruit were laid out under the fine old cedar tree, and good stories were told, while the tobacco smoke went curling up into the twilight'. In health and steadily increasing wealth, with his hunters in the stable, with his family happy and with frequent friendly visitors, Trollope thoroughly enjoyed his dozen years at Waltham House. His regular sessions with Thackeray at the Garrick Club in London led to immense productivity. When Thackeray started the *Cornhill Magazine* in 1860, Trollope was his enthusiastic helper, and the immediate and flattering success of *Framley Parsonage* when it was making its anonymous appearance in the *Cornhill*, was enormously cheering. Among the novels Trollope wrote at Waltham House 'by rising early' was *The Last Chronicle of Barset* (1867). His description of the house as 'a rickety old place' does not disguise his fondness for it.

The crossing of the River Lea has naturally reminded me of another man who found contentment here two centuries before Trollope – this was the Staffordshire man who had become a London ironmonger and wrote a small octavo book, printed in Fleet Street to cost eighteen pence, called *The Compleat Angler*. The year in which *The Compleat Angler* was printed was 1653, the year in which Cromwell overthrew the Long Parliament, the year which saw the beginning of the Protectorate; not a year in which it was easy for a man whose sympathies had been Royalist to be completely happy. But as Izaak Walton's characters in *The Compleat Angler* proceed along the valley of the River Lea, discoursing at a rate of four octavo pages to the mile, it is a restful happiness and peace of mind which the writer clearly seeks. Walton's journey begins at Ponders End; up river past Waltham Cross, the morning draught is taken at the Thatched House in Hoddesdon. The second day begins on Amwell Hill just as the sun is up, and there is a view of the valley where the River Ash comes into the Lea. The boys of Haileybury College were later familiar with that view, and so was Charles Lamb in boyhood. Lamb as a child was taken to Blakesware, three miles or so up the River Ash, where he became acquainted with that 'brawling brook' – and where in adolescence he was in such love with Ann Simmons of neighbouring Widford that he wrote the two sonnets to 'Anna' which Coleridge took charge of and included in his own first published book of poems. Those verses were the first things of Charles Lamb's to be dignified by print. (Lamb never did forget Ann of Widford – she was the 'Alice' of Elia's later essays, 'Blakesmoor in H—' and 'Dream Children'.)

But to return to the view from Amwell Hill as Izaak Walton saw it, it is certainly worth recalling the exact words of *The Compleat Angler*:

Under that broad beech tree [says Walton, with care for its precise location] I sat down when I was last this way a-fishing. And the birds in the adjoining grove seemed to have a friendly contention with an echo, whose dead voice seemed to live in a hollow tree, near to the brow of that primrose hill. There I sat viewing the silver streams glide silently towards their centre, the tempestuous sea; yet sometimes opposed by rugged roots and pebble-stones, which broke their waves and turned them into foam. And sometimes I beguiled time by viewing the harmless lambs; some leaping securely in the shade, whilst others sported themselves in the cheerful sun; and saw others craving comfort from the swollen udders of their bleating dams. As I thus sat, these and other sights had so fully possest my soul with content, that I thought, as the poet hath happily exprest it:

> I was for that time lifted above earth
> And possest joys not promised in my birth.

As I left this place, and entered into the next field, a second pleasure entertained me; 'twas a handsome milkmaid, that had not yet attained so much age and wisdom as to load her mind with any fears of many things that will never be, as too many men too often do; but she cast away all care, and sung like a nightingale. Her voice was good and the ditty fitted it: it was that smooth song which was made by Kit Marlow, now at least fifty years ago; and the milkmaid's mother sung an answer to it, which was made by Sir Walter Raleigh in his younger days.

When Izaak Walton was teased with fanciful apprehensions, this corner of Hertfordshire could enchant them away; it was also, as I was saying, enchanted ground for Charles Lamb; and nearer to our own day there was enchantment here for Beatrix Potter in her childhood. Near Essendon, six miles west of Hoddesdon and near Hatfield, was Camfield Place and there Beatrix Potter used to visit her grandmother. No. 2 Bolton Gardens, Kensington, was where Beatrix Potter was born, and there, somewhat town-prisoned, she lived mostly upstairs with her six years' younger brother; she continued to live in Kensington with her parents until she was nearly fifty. Yet as a child, and even before her brother was born, there were visits to Camfield, the place she wrote of in the memories that she recorded when she was twenty-four as 'the place I love best in the world', and 'where I have been so happy as a child'.

In the new part of Camfield Place, so Beatrix Potter remembered, there were 'two tall mirrors facing one another on the stairs, miles of looking-glasses and little figures in white muslin. I never durst look in them for fear of another head besides my own peeping round the corner'. Most of all she loved 'the old part of the house, the dear realms of *Nanny Nettycoat*, that little old lady with white woollen stockings, black velvet slippers and a mob-cap, who must have been just like my grandmother'. It was when Beatrix Potter was first in touch with her publisher that she rehearsed the childhood memories in which 'all things are a part', in 'this perfect whole', and one clear image quickly revives into another. Several fancies appear to merge into *Nanny Nettycoat* as the memories tell of the little nursery room where there were teas in twilight, and where '*Nanny Nettycoat* presided in the middle of the table, guttering, homely, lop-sided with fascinating snuffers in a tin dish'. The nursery round table 'became sticky when we rested our chins on it. How short we were in those days. The green curtains slid on a long brass pole. I have reason to know it was hollow, for once we took it down to extract a tame fieldmouse.' That tame fieldmouse! – does he not make later re-appearances, possibly one when Beatrix Potter was writing a tale involving 'the days of swords and periwigs'? In 1902 *The Tale of Peter Rabbit* was issued and the regular production of the other tales, for the next eleven years, began. It is right to think of Beatrix Potter at No. 2 The Boltons, as it is right also to think of her as the Mrs Heelis of Sawrey in the Lake District which later she became; yet one should not forget that Camfield Place is what Beatrix Potter called 'my Blakesmoor in Hertfordshire'. (The reference she is there making is to Lamb's essay; and I am very sure that Charles and Mary Lamb would have liked *Nanny Nettycoat*).

That rightly suggests the last stop on this first journey, at the Bell, Edmonton. In Edmonton, Keats Parade at the end of Church Street is a reminder that Keats served his apprenticeship to a surgeon here. The Bell is also the hostelry immortalized by Cowper in the *Diverting History of John Gilpin*. Yet what brings most visitors to Edmonton is Lamb's Cottage, off Church Street, where Charles Lamb brought his sister Mary in May 1833. Eighteen months later he died there; Mary lived on for a further thirteen years, but was then buried beside him in the churchyard. The joint tombstone remains in the churchyard, and in the church are also memorials, side by side, to both Lamb and Cowper.

A2

THE DOVER ROAD

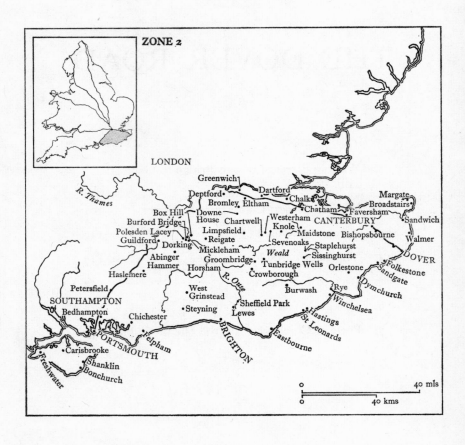

ZONE 2

LONDON

R. Thames

Greenwich
Deptford
Bromley • Eltham   Chalk
Dartford
Margate
Broadstairs
Box Hill   Downe   Westerham   CANTERBURY   Faversham
Burford Bridge   House   Chartwell   Knole   Chatham   Sandwich
Polesden Lacey   Limpsfield   Maidstone   Bishopsbourne   Walmer
Guildford • Dorking   Reigate   Sevenoaks   Staplehurst   DOVER
Abinger   Mickleham   Weald   Sissinghurst   Folkestone
Hammer   Groombridge   Tunbridge Wells   Orlestone   Sandgate
Haslemere   Horsham   Crowborough   Dymchurch
R. Ouse
Petersfield   West   Burwash   Rye   Winchelsea
SOUTHAMPTON   Grinstead   Sheffield Park   Hastings
Bedhampton   Chichester   Steyning   Lewes   St Leonards
Felpham   BRIGHTON   Eastbourne
PORTSMOUTH
Carisbrooke
Freshwater   Shanklin
Bonchurch

0   40 mls
0   40 kms

1. WATLING STREET: LONDON BRIDGE TO GAD'S HILL

In ancient times the sections of highway from Dover to London and from London to Chester were often regarded as one single continuity – one great island-crossing 'Watling Street' with Dover and Chester as terminal points. A bold medieval imagination identified the Milky Way in heaven and this 'Milky Way' of a road across the whole of England; as, for example, that of Chaucer. In *The Hous of Fame* (ii, 431) when Chaucer is lofted by the eagle towards the celestial Milky Way he remarks, as if such wit were natural to Cockneys, that a good many people compliment that prominent sky-path by calling it Watling Street. The earthly Watling Street had been the imagined King's Highway of early British kings: for instance of King Lear. All the heritages attendant on this highway made it all the more important to Chaucer that what was written of it as well as what was spoken on it should be King's English. In the Prologue to *The Canterbury Tales* Chaucer is triumphantly doing for courtiers precisely what he did for 'Litel Lowis my sone' in the opening sentences of *A Treatise on the Astrolabe*. There he excuses Latin folk for writing 'in hir owne tonge, that is to sein, in Latin'. By that same argument the English tongue is for English writers, and if so be, says Chaucer, 'that I shewe thee in my lighte English as trewe conclusiouns touching this matere, and naught only as trewe but as many and as subtil conclusiouns as ben shewed in Latin', then you can 'me the more thank; and preye god save the king, that is lord of this language. . . .'

Whether we speak of the Dover road by the Ministry of Transport's label A2 or by the ancient name of Watling Street, the Borough High Street leads into it from London Bridge by way of the Old Kent Road. Before taking departure, we pay respect in Southwark Cathedral to the tomb of Gower, where the alabaster figure rests its head on the three books, the first two in French and Latin and the third, as Richard II had commanded, in English. At New Cross the Old Kent Road changes its name and presently forks, with a branch to the right through Lewisham and eventually to Folkestone and that part of Kent from which 'moral Gower' came. The Canterbury pilgrims whom Chaucer joined at the Tabard Inn in Borough High Street kept straight on at what we call New Cross to pass between what is now Deptford New Town and Greenwich and thence over Blackheath to Shooters Hill.

In the older part of Deptford near the river, Evelyn Street and Sayes

Court Recreation Ground are present-day reminders that John Evelyn, the seventeenth-century virtuoso and diarist, lived at Sayes Court. Evelyn's property there was wantonly desecrated, he claimed, by the Russian visitors when it was let to Peter the Great in 1698. Of earlier associations with Deptford, the location of the house in which Marlowe was killed is one of the unanswerable questions. One may enjoyably read in Scott's *Kenilworth* of Elizabethan times at Greenwich and of the royal habitations there, and there are spirited scenes in Greenwich Park in the time of James in *The Fortunes of Nigel*. My own recollections of the 1920s remind me that the Ship Inn beside Greenwich Pier was then much favoured by young book publishers for the double function of eating whitebait and promoting attention to forthcoming books. Yet for the greatest of all connections of Greenwich with literature it is hard to point to a visible reminder. Elsewhere in London 'Chaucer' is written up as a street-name, but here, where it belongs, I find no such street-name. I have no particular wish to see a 'Chaucer House' turned into a museum; nevertheless I should like to know where the Chaucers resided, where Chaucer's wife Philippa died, and after that (as he said in berating himself):

> Thou gost hoom to thy hous anoon
> And, also domb as any stoon,
> Thou sittest at another boke
> Til fully daswed is thy loke,
> And livest thus as an hermite . . .

until he roused himself to join the other Canterbury pilgrims.

*   *   *

At the Woolwich side of Eltham is Well Hall Road. Along this, a mile south of the Shooters Hill Road, is Well Hall; the house, apparently in a parlous state when Edith Nesbit purchased it in 1889, was where she lived until 1921. Well Hall was the setting for her novel *The Red House* and for some of the tales of the 'Bastable' family; the house has since been demolished but a Tudor barn was preserved by the council for use as a restaurant and art gallery, and the gardens were opened to the public. Three miles or so south of Eltham and on the far side of Elmstead Woods and the Sundridge Park Golf Course is Bromley, which in 1752 was a town not yet absorbed into the London sprawl; in that year Samuel Johnson, in grief at the death of his wife 'Tetty', agreed that she be buried there. Boswell conjectured that Bromley was chosen, and the arrangements made for Tetty's burial in Bromley Church, by Johnson's friend Hawkesworth, who was a resident of Bromley. More than thirty years later and a few months before his own death, Johnson composed the Latin epitaph to be inscribed on the blue slate slab in the floor at the west end of Bromley Church's central aisle.

Bromley was closer to becoming a part of London in 1866, when H. G. Wells was born there. Wells's father, ex-gardener and professional cricketer, had set up as a general dealer in Bromley High Street, and Wells was born over the shop. His mother wanted the boy to become a draper, and when he was old enough a month's trial with a draper's firm was arranged. Wells himself recorded that after the month the firm rejected him 'as unsuitable for their high trade'. In his thirties Wells lampooned the 'high trade' in *The Wheels of Chance* but in his forties and with deeper humour returned to write of the draper-apprenticeship in *The History of Mr Polly*.

In the story of Mr Polly, in which Wells showed beautifully what V. S. Pritchett called his 'complete power to bounce you off your feet and carry you away with him', there is a list of Mr Polly's books which is reminiscent of Wells's own omnivorous boyhood reading at Bromley. Wells mentions, with an admission of perplexity, that except for the *Pickwick Papers* Mr Polly 'never took at all kindly to Dickens'. This showed disrespect for one who should have been a local hero, for the main road from London onward towards Rochester and Chatham had the closest of associations for Dickens in boyhood and for the whole of his life. In 1816, when Charles was four years old, his father had been appointed to one of the naval dockyards in Chatham, remaining there until Charles was nine. At No. 2 Ordnance Terrace, and for another year at a less genteel address (the move due to the father's financial improvidence), the family's nurse Mary Weller would clear the table for the magic lantern or for Charles's earliest toy theatres; or he would be upstairs in his room reading the books that he mentions in *David Copperfield*. We have Mary Weller's testimony that 'Little Charles was a terrible boy to read'. The passion for reading was encouraged by his mother, and in those happy Chatham years he was his father's companion on long walks. The two of them explored the countryside around Chatham and Rochester; 'it was through Dingley Dell and Muggleton, the very centres of Pickwickian innocence', Angus Wilson points out, that Dickens and his father walked. Charles, the one of the six Dickens children to have most parental attention, enjoyed and remembered those walks. Years later (in 1857) he wrote to a friend that 'Shakespeare's Gads Hill where Falstaff engaged in the robbery' was one of the objectives, and a house there, Gad's Hill Place, was to him at the age of ten 'the most beautiful house ever seen'. In maturity he supposed this was because of its famous old cedar trees. 'And my poor father used to bring me to look at it, and used to say that if ever I

L.B.—D

grew up to be a clever man perhaps I might own that house, or another such. . . .'

Dickens's boyhood at Chatham is pictured as happy; that the family was in for desperately hard times was not foreknown to the children. Up to the age of ten Charles was certainly in danger of becoming 'spoilt'. In 1822 the father's job was transferred to London; Charles had been doing so well at a school started by the son of a Baptist minister at Chatham, and was such a favourite of that young headmaster, that he was left behind as a boarder after the rest of the family had moved to London's Camden Town. (This Chatham school was not among schools satirized by Dickens, and he warmly retained friendship with that head-master, William Giles.) But that protected period soon ended. Around Christmastime 1822 Charles, not yet eleven, was put on the coach from Chatham for London to travel unaccompanied to join his parents.

Through all the years that have since passed, have I ever lost the smell of damp straw in which I was packed – like game – and forwarded, carriage paid, to the Cross Keys, Wood Street, Cheapside, London? There was no other inside passenger, and I consumed my sandwiches in solitude and dreariness, and it rained hard all the way, and I thought life sloppier than I had expected to find it.

That was Dickens's road-journey up to London along this part of Watling Street. Fourteen years later he and his bride were to make an ecstatic journey down this same stretch of road to spend their honeymoon at Chalk – Chalk was in walking distance from Chatham, in the Gravesend direction. It was to country reminiscent to him of his early childhood that Charles at twenty-four brought his bride Catherine, aged twenty. The journey up to London had almost immediately landed the boy in very pitiable tribulations; when the young husband made his triumphant journey down the road, Fortune was being kind – overkind, indeed. Far too much sudden success for any young married pair to contend with accompanied them.

When Dickens had been a young journalist employed by the *Morning Chronicle*, the Fates arranged that George Hogarth, an Edinburgh man, became editor of the newly started subsidiary, the *Evening Chronicle*. Among Hogarth's many friends had been Walter Scott; that had caused Dickens to admire Hogarth. Hogarth in turn was pleased with Dickens and quickly invited the young man to produce pieces for him which he worked into the *Evening Chronicle* as 'Sketches by Boz'. Soon Hogarth was inviting Dickens to visit his home at Fulham, for Dickens 'a meeting place of culture and good breeding'. Of the Hogarth daughters it was to Catherine that Dickens became engaged. One may read pride in social achievement in a letter from Dickens to his uncle announcing his forthcoming union with 'the daughter of a gentleman who . . . was the most intimate friend and companion of Sir Walter Scott, and one of the most eminent among the Literati of Edinburgh'.

With fantastic speed, however, eminence won by virtue of his wedding became 'all very small beer', as Angus Wilson remarks in *The World of Charles Dickens*, 'to the Inimitable Boz, the nationwide notable author of *Pickwick Papers*'. For even before the wedding in April 1836 *Sketches by Boz* in book form was running through its second printing and a rival publisher, Mr Hall, had descended on Dickens in his chambers in Furnival's Inn: *Pickwick Papers* was instantly born. Speed? – Chapman & Hall's offer to publish *Pickwick Papers* was made on 10 February 1836, Dickens 'accepted on 16 February, began writing on 18 February, and the first number was published on 31 March'. The wedding was in April, but the second instalment of *Pickwick* had to be written in time to be illustrated and 'out' by the end of April – and so on, month after month. The honeymoon at Chalk was shortened to cope with the success of *Pickwick Papers*. After a slight initial hesitation the *Papers* 'soared to dizzier sales each month'; further proposals poured in upon young Dickens, and his genius seemed equal to accepting all – in the first year of married life he had a play and operetta put on the stage, he was keeping *Pickwick* going, planning *Oliver Twist*, and by November had agreed with the publisher Bentley to edit a new magazine. In January 1837 he was elected to the Garrick Club; the first issue of *Bentley's Miscellany* under his editorship was 'an instant success', the first number of *Oliver Twist* appeared in the *Miscellany* in February 'with a good deal of acclaim', the monthly *Pickwick* continued to be 'on everyone's lips', and as Angus Wilson indicates by collecting together this much of Dickens's activities, his 'wickedly overworked life' had begun.

While Charles was attracting a rapidly widening number of exciting new friends, Catherine was trying to do her part rightly. Their first child, Charley, was born in January 1837. Catherine, her sister Mary, and the baby, had to fight for home life against the competitive pressures that were piling on, and gaily accepted by, the now famous young Dickens. A gradual success for her husband, no matter how demanding provided it came not all at once, might not have been impossible for Catherine to absorb – that is Angus Wilson's analysis – 'but what came with *Pickwick* was an avalanche that, despite Dickens's real concern for some domestic privacy, took him away from her into more and more work, into ever wider social spheres where she often found it difficult to follow him'. Such, in outline, is the way the stage was setting at the moment the young Mr and Mrs Dickens were visiting the area of his boyhood on their honeymoon. Twenty years later, when it did so happen that the Gad's Hill Place of his childhood memory was available for

Dickens to purchase, to set up house there was a way of fulfilling the father's wish that Charles might grow 'to be a clever man'; yet by that time there was no way for Gad's Hill Place to be a happy family home. Coincidental with the possession of 'the most beautiful house ever seen' was the separation, much publicized, of Dickens and Catherine Dickens.

Gad's Hill Place, halfway between the Chalk of his honeymoon and Rochester, was purchased by Dickens in 1857 and became his more or less permanent address from 1860 until his death in 1870. (At some later date the property was turned into a school. The Swiss chalet, given to Dickens by his protégé Fechter and set up in his garden as a detached writing-room, was preserved by being moved to the grounds of Eastgate House in Rochester – Eastgate House, the Nuns' House of *Edwin Drood*, has been enlarged as a museum.) In Dickens's last decade 'Life at Gad's Hill for visitors', wrote Edmund Yates, a younger journalist, gossip and friend, 'was delightful'. Georgina Hogarth, who had joined the Dickens household in 1843 when a girl of sixteen and who had grown into being the matriarch-housekeeper, had 'early conceived an admiration for her brother-in-law that was absolute'; she remained with Dickens at Gad's Hill, and she and Dickens's daughter Mamie were the indispensable helpmeets for the habitual entertaining.

The differing selves within Dickens became perhaps more noticeably divided in the last decade of his life. At Gad's Hill acting as squire to the locals and as host to the stream of visitors was a source of both amusements and satisfactions, and while Gad's Hill was still a new toy it was pleasant to effect improvements – the tunnel dug under the main road to reach the part of the garden, known as the 'Wilderness', where house-guests (as Yates describes) were wont to smoke morning cigars and loaf, while their host was habitually at work in the Swiss chalet. After Dickens's morning work there were long walks in the afternoons. Yet work, and work that often removed him from Gad's Hill, became for Dickens an increasing obsession. There was work to be done at his magazine office in London; he often had excuse to spend nights in rooms he had furnished over the office. In 1858 Dickens had begun to give public readings; such performances had for him, increasingly, a drug effect; and he managed to fit the consequent movings about in with the secretive life he kept trying to arrange with Ellen Ternan. Despite evidences that health could fail – evidences that Dickens always refused to admit – his energies led him to persist in giving public readings all over England, and this, coupled with his regular and continuing output of writing, seemed to condone short visits to France, mainly Paris, 'each year from 1862 to 1865, and again in 1868'. Many of Dickens's friends endeavoured to dissuade him from over-activity and particularly from the exhausting tours of readings that he made in America in 1867 and

1868. He continued to give public readings after his return from America, but by the summer of 1870, while writing *The Mystery of Edwin Drood* in the chalet at Gad's Hill, overwork struck back; at the age of fifty-eight he collapsed and died.

The great Victorian novelists did not have very long lives: Thackeray died before Dickens, at the age of fifty-two; George Eliot died at sixty-one. None of the three Brontë sisters reached the age of forty. Dickens's friend Wilkie Collins lived to the age of sixty-five, and Thackeray's friend Trollope lived to be sixty-seven. Towards the end of the century novelists tended to live longer. Conrad, it is true, died at sixty-seven, but Henry James lived to be seventy-five, Meredith eighty-one, and Thomas Hardy eighty-eight.

2. WATLING STREET: CANTERBURY TO DOVER

Between London and Rochester, Dickens irresistibly stole the stage. Yet as the road passes Crayford, just to the north, and just before the Thames flows past Erith, are the marshes where Conan Doyle ended the desperate chase after 'the great Agra treasure' in *The Sign of Four*. 'It was a wild and desolate place' where the wooden-legged Jonathan Small ran the launch upon the mudbank and 'the fugitive sprang out, but his stump instantly sank its whole length into the sodden soil', and surely that is a site to be sought by all Sherlock Holmes students. At Crayford, the Manor House just north of the town was the birthplace of Algernon Blackwood (1869–1951), many of whose tales specialized in eeriness. Dartford, a little farther on towards Rochester, was birthplace of the young poet Sidney Keyes, who was killed in the Second World War. Chaucer's pilgrims diverged from our main road to visit Graves-end; I don't think I need to make that sidestep, except to report that W. W. Jacobs, whose short stories delighted in boyhood, lived at Gravesend.

At Rochester and Chatham is the appeal of many associations with Dickens. On the way to Canterbury, Faversham recalls the murder of Thomas Arden in 1550, at his wife's instigation, through the Elizabethan play *Arden of Feversham*. Those who remember M. R. James's *Ghost Stories of an Antiquary* may also recall that the author was born at Goodnestone, near Faversham. At Canterbury, after the murder of Thomas Becket in 1170 and his canonization two years later, the cathedral, as a miracle-working shrine, eclipsed the fame of St Augustine's more ancient abbey and drew, among others, Chaucer's pilgrims. The

supposed demolition of the shrine by Henry VIII in 1538 did not put
an end to pilgrimaging; Christopher Marlowe was born in Canterbury
in 1564, and his father's success in the shoemaking trade may have been
connected with re-shoeing pilgrims. Marlowe's birthplace, No. 57 St
George's Street, was destroyed by bombing in 1942. The birthplace of
a contrasting Canterbury poet, the Rev. R. H. Barham (1788–1845),
author of the *Ingoldsby Legends*, at No. 61 Burgate Street, was also
destroyed. Other associations with poets include the doubtful supposi-
tion that Keats's 'Eve of St Agnes' refers to the cathedral close, and the
certainty that T. S. Eliot's *Murder in the Cathedral* was specially written
for performance in the cathedral precincts.

Even in Canterbury Dickens extends considerable domination. When
Miss Betsy Trotwood sent young Copperfield to school it was the King's
School at Canterbury that was probably the prototype. The King's
School, claiming its foundation as long ago as A.D. 598, may well be the
most ancient school in England. It was ancient when Marlowe studied
there, and of many later students one might pick out Walter Pater, Hugh
Walpole, and Somerset Maugham, who retained bitter memories of
being handicapped, in youth, by a stammer, and satirized Canterbury
(in *Of Human Bondage*) as 'Tercanbury'. Walpole and Maugham both
left bequests to King's School, and forty-six years after the publication
of his satire Maugham revisited the school to open its Maugham Library.
Yet for the majority it remains the schooldays of David Copperfield that
are recalled at Canterbury, and the Sun Inn, near the cathedral, is
believed to be the inn where David, his aunt, Mr Dick and Traddles all
stayed when combining with Mr Micawber in the unmasking of Uriah
Heep. In 1861 Dickens gave a reading from *David Copperfield* in Canterbury, cementing that special connection. Another and curious link
between Dickens and Canterbury is that the issues of the periodical
which opened in 1837 with *Oliver Twist* also contained the first numbers
of the Canterbury-born Barham's *Ingoldsby Legends*.

Richard Harris Barham, a minor canon of St Paul's in London, was
a squat and formidable figure with a crippled arm and a face with
drooping left eyelid and very pale eyelashes, when Dickens first met
him at the Garrick Club in 1837. In that year the young Dickens was
precisely half Barham's age, and there is no evidence that the busy young
man gave much thought to the Rev. Mr Barham. The habitual impression of good humour which Barham both received and returned among
club members covered an inner character in some ways as odd and
melodramatic as any whom Dickens was to imagine in later life (for instance, in *Edwin Drood*). From Barham's birth in Canterbury onwards
circumstances, for him, were as if arranged to be grotesque. Barham's
father was the port-drinking alderman whose house was close to the

precinct gates of the cathedral. Richard Holmes, in an impressive study of Barham in *The Times* (22 December 1973), pointed out that before death the father had become so prodigiously fat (twenty-seven stone) that 'his front door had to be especially widened for the exit of his coffin'. Young Barham was six when he watched the goings-on for the removal of the corpse. His older sister, who chiefly looked after him, was ill at the time of the father's funeral; soon after, she died, and the boy was fostered out 'to maiden aunts'. The alderman's will revealed that neither child was his wife's. In a confusion of claims upon the alderman's estate and throughout subsequent squabbling the illegitimate motherless boy was allowed to infer that some £8000 possibly due to him had been mis-appropriated. Yet when he was sent off to St Paul's school in London it seemed that fate had picked him out for a physical injury that transcen-ded other distresses. On the road the coach crashed. Barham's arm was so damaged that amputation was discussed, though in the event surgeons experimented by rigging up the arm with a contraption of catgut and silver rings.

The prevalence in the *Ingoldsby Legends* of physical dismemberments and an abnormal obsession with 'the dark underside' of morbid themes which Barham in maturity 'systematically *ripped up* for amusement', as one contemporary critic said, is connected by Mr Holmes with actions and happenings that continued throughout Barham's life. Determined to shine at school despite, or because of, the arm, Barham became head boy; then at Oxford, anticipating what money he might inherit, he 'ran somewhat wildly into debt and dissipation'. After his return to Canter-bury he passed through a period of Byronic posing, following this, at the age of twenty-five, by a notably extreme religious conversion. Having taken clerical orders he sought to lose himself in a 'recondite region' (his words) of the Romney Marsh, a region where 'Marsh folk', as Kipling was also later to remind us, were a people unto themselves for knowledge of dark and sordid parts of witchcraft. In his tales of Romney Marsh for children (as in 'Dymchurch Flit') Kipling is not too much concerned with evil intents or practices that might attach to witches' covens, but the diaries kept by Barham in the Kentish marshland reveal obsession to an unusual degree with what he could find of hauntings that were horrible or 'bestial'. In the midst of the Marsh the young Reverend married a 'Marsh girl', bred children, dug a vegetable patch – and kept his diaries. Yet Barham did not lose all connection with Canterbury, and the offer that came to him in his thirty-fourth year of a minor canonry at St Paul's translated him and his family to London. Superficially he resumed friendship with his 'own sort', was a clubbable man with a light and humorous touch in talking of the macabre, and was soon writing up, gaily, some of the horror-themes of the *Ingoldsby Legends*.

The gaiety with which he could 'gambol and slide' in matters essentially of crude horror made the *Ingoldsby Legends* immensely popular in Victorian households, where they could stand on the family shelves with *Pickwick Papers* and Keble's *The Christian Year*. Meanwhile Barham's family of 'Marsh folk' took to London less kindly than he did. One after another Barham watched five of his sons sicken and die. Barham's preoccupation with the macabre did not lessen; he kept in perpetual close touch with Bow Street, where he appeared to revel in the most gruesome cases (such as the Greenacre murder) and in the punishments they earned. Finally in 1844 he himself took sick and he watched his own symptoms to compare them with observations drawn from watching criminals. His lingering throat infection in the spring of 1845 gave him, he wrote, 'the not very pleasant sensation of slowly hanging'. Fifty years after Barham's death a surviving daughter, annotating a later edition of the *Legends*, revealed something of Barham's secret obsessions. The world in general preferred to accept the *Ingoldsby Legends* as good clean fun and not to look for other motives behind the curtain.

Others may have toyed with the thought that this south-east corner of the island of Britain was likely to be singularly prone to sinister superstitions, since in addition to whatever 'voodoo' was native to indigenous Britons this was an area of contagion with perhaps even darker immigrant beliefs and practices. Ever since Romans made landings at Richborough it was obvious that Kent might feel the touch of psychical as well as physical incomers; harmless or not so harmless alien spirits might jostle what Kipling called the local 'Pharisees'. In passing we have already noticed the birth, in this region, of several writers who seemed from childhood singularly interested in the supernatural; to the names of Algernon Blackwood, M. R. James and Richard Barham can be added Walter de la Mare, who smilingly mentioned that because he came from Charlton, beside Barham Downs, south of Canterbury, he might be expected to know about ghosts. However, at Canterbury I must not overplay that thought of extra-sensory distractions. There is no feeling that Richard Lovelace, while he was living here in Stour Street, was ghost-afflicted; nor was Izaak Walton aware of ghosts when he was also living in Stour Street and marrying his first wife in St Mildred's Church.

*   *   *

Margate seems not to share in the dark magic that Barham found at Romney Marsh. It is true that before reaching Margate, one may search for the chalk-pit at Acol (just over a mile south of Birchington, where Dante Gabriel Rossetti died and was buried) which is the scene in the

Ingoldsby Legends of 'The Smuggler's Leap', for which Tenniel provided a suitably horrific illustration. Yet a contemporary critic hostile to the obsessions in the *Ingoldsby Legends* was Richard Hengist Horne (1803–84) who after an adventurous life settled and died at Margate; a no-nonsense 'rational' atmosphere at Margate made it an appropriate birth-place in 1840 for the banker-author Edward Clodd; and, for its health-giving qualities, Margate was the resort recommended to T. S. Eliot in the time of severe strain before he managed to put together *The Waste Land*.

Round the North Foreland from Margate, the watering-place especi-ally fancied by Dickens as 'one of the freest and freshest little places in the world', is Broadstairs. Dickens House at the west end of Victoria Parade is sometimes thought of as the home of Miss Betsy Trotwood, although in *David Copperfield* that home was transposed to Dover. Wilkie Collins shared Dickens's enjoyment of Broadstairs. Towards the end of Collins's life Ramsgate (and an apartment there at No. 14 Nelson Crescent) became for him almost a second home; Broadstairs by then was painfully haunted by the ghosts of Dickens and of Collins's younger brother Charles who had married Dickens's younger daughter Kate, and of others whom Collins had outlived. Broadstairs had also been the place where Wilkie Collins found the title for his book *The Woman in White*. It was Collins's wish to have inscribed on his tomb-stone: 'author of *The Woman in White* and other works of fiction'. At Broadstairs then one may pause to recall how that book came to be written.

It was in London, presumably in 1859, that Caroline came suddenly into Wilkie Collins's life. He and his brother Charles and the painter J. G. Millais were all walking from one of Mrs Collins's parties in Hanover Terrace toward their lodgings in Gower Street. As told by Millais: 'It was a beautiful moonlight night in the summer time and as the three friends walked along chatting gaily together, they were suddenly arrested by a piercing scream coming from the garden of a villa close at hand'. From the iron gate 'came the figure of a young and very beautiful woman dressed in flowing white robes that shone in the moonlight'. She paused for a moment at the sight of the three men but 'moved on and vanished'. ' "I must see who she is, and what is the matter", said Wilkie Collins, as, without a word he dashed after her.' His two companions waited in vain for his return. Next day, Collins wrote: 'She was a young lady of good birth and position, who had accidentally fallen into the hands of a man living in a villa in Regent's Park. There for many months he kept her prisoner under threats and mesmeric influence. . . .' The lady who thus entered the scene was Caroline, who, though they were never married, lived with Wilkie

Collins (and brought her daughter into the household) for the rest of his life. There was one interlude when for a short while Caroline married someone else, but in the 1870s she returned to live with Wilkie Collins, with whom Martha was then living who likewise never married Collins, but who was the mother of his three children. When Caroline and Collins died, both were laid in the same grave in Kensal Green Cemetery; Martha tended it.

Kenneth Robinson observes in his biography of Collins that it was not only that sudden melodramatic appearance of Caroline which started the young writer on his most famous book. When Collins had been in Paris with Dickens in 1856 he had picked up Majan's *Causes Célèbres* in which one case, famous in France in a previous generation, seemed to be almost completely and forcibly reproduced in Caroline's story – in Majan a lady had likewise been abducted for her inheritance, drugged, confined in an asylum, and her identity obliterated – the details, even to the white dress, of the one adventure inextricably blended with those of the other. Instant writing of it all as a serial for Dickens's new magazine *All the Year Round* was simply and intensely forced upon Wilkie Collins. At once he started the writing; the serial was scheduled to start before the end of the year, but autumn arrived before the right title was thought of. Wilkie Collins found that title by going to Broadstairs. It was again on a moonlit night that he strolled along the cliffs towards North Foreland, 'smoking cigar after cigar, racking his brains for the right title'. Then, as Kenneth Robinson describes, 'he threw himself on the grass. Looking across at the white shape of the North Foreland lighthouse, he thought: "You are ugly and stiff and awkward; you know you are as stiff and weird as my white woman . . . White Woman . . . Woman in White . . . the title, by Jove!" ' Dickens immediately liked it: 'I have not the slightest doubt that *The Woman in White* is the name of names and the very title of titles.'

The serial publication duly began before the end of 1859; the book was published in August 1860 and caused such a sensation that (Robinson notes) manufacturers 'were producing *Woman in White* perfume, *Woman in White* cloaks and bonnets, and the music-shops displayed *Woman in White* waltzes and quadrilles. Even Dickens had hardly known such incidental publicity.'

The cliffs at Broadstairs also caused a writer of our time, John Buchan, to think of the title for his bestselling thriller, *The Thirty-nine Steps*. There the plot involved intrigues of German spies in England just before the 1914–18 war. The only clue to the spies' headquarters was in a dead man's notebook: 'Thirty-nine steps – I counted them – high tide, 10.17 p.m.' In due course that led to the hero-narrator being told about 'the Ruff' –

'What's that?' I asked.

'The big chalk headland in Kent, close to Bradgate. It's got a lot of villas on the top, and some of the houses have staircases down to a private beach. It's a very high-toned sort of place, and the residents there like to keep by themselves.'

. . . I closed the book and looked round at the company.

'If one of these staircases has thirty-nine steps we have solved the mystery, gentlemen,' I said.

Buchan had a particular staircase at Broadstairs in mind when writing his book, but all such steps down to the beach along this stretch of coast were demolished in 1940 to hinder possible invaders.

The even more remarkable novel written in 1903 on the theme of an hypothetical German invasion of England – *The Riddle of the Sands* by Erskine Childers – though Chatham is mentioned in it, refers more specifically to that part of the Lincolnshire coast which is locally called 'Holland'. Therefore more than a mere mention of *The Riddle of the Sands* would be out of place here.

*   *   *

It would not be easy to exhaust the numerous associations in the small corner of Kent east of the road from Canterbury to Dover. At Margate I might have brought in Keats, who was there in 1816 and again in the next year. Soon after that Charles and Mary Lamb made their 'first seaside experiment' by visiting Margate in 1821. At Broadstairs George Eliot lived for a while in 1852. The poet Lionel Johnson was born at Broadstairs; the journalist Lord Northcliffe chose the same place for his principal home, and so did Charles Harold St John Hamilton, who, under the pseudonym of Frank Richards, was the creator of 'Billy Bunter'. At Ramsgate I should have paid tribute to F. C. Burnand, of whose books *Happy Thoughts* remains my favourite (it was a favourite of A. P. Herbert's also). Burnand died at Ramsgate in 1917. At Sandwich Tom Paine (of *The Rights of Man*) became discontented with the task of being an Exciseman. Sandwich is supposed to have been the 'Sunwich Port' of some of W. W. Jacobs's stories, and Sandwich Bay is where Ian Fleming made a home, though I am not sure that 'James Bond' originated there. At Deal I recall a terrible predicament into which P. G. Wodehouse's Bertie Wooster was led by that high-spirited girl Roberta Wickham. At Walmer the poet Robert Bridges was born and brought up, and he placed an epitaph in the church of the village of Great Mongeham, a mile inland from Walmer, in memory of his childhood nurse.

Yet at Canterbury is also felt a compulsion to push on straightforwardly to the terminal of the ancient Watling Street. That terminal is Dover.

Therefore, no lingering at Bishopsbourne even though Richard Hooker was rector of the church in the last five years of his life and here completed *The Laws of Ecclesiastical Polity*; and even though in 1920 Joseph Conrad came to live at Bishopsbourne, and lived there until his death in 1924 in the rectory called Oswalds. Alec Waugh, too, lived at Oswalds, in the 1930s.

But then, running on into Dover, which of that town's literary recollections should be selected? In *David Copperfield* there was the battle waged on donkeys by Betsy Trotwood and her maid Janet – though Miss Trotwood's cottage was possibly only transposed to Dover from Broadstairs. (Dickens was staying at Brighton in 1849 when he started the writing of *David Copperfield*. Why he chose Dover as most appropriate 'place' for Betsy Trotwood and Mr Dick is a matter for thought.)

It is as a port from which to leave England that some of Dover's most remembered anecdotes derive. The eighteenth-century poet Churchill was on his way to meet his partner John Wilkes at Boulogne when illness stopped him at Dover. He died in 1764 and was buried at St Mary's in Cannon Street. When Byron, escaping from bailiffs in London in April 1816, drove with Hobhouse and others to Dover, it was Byron's first chance to use the enormous travelling carriage, copied to his order by Baxter the coachmaker from the carriage of Napoleon taken at Genappe – the fittings included 'a *lit de repos* . . . a plate chest, and every apparatus for dining'. The entourage had to wait at an inn for two days until the wind for sailing was favourable. To avoid possible pursuit by bailiffs Byron's Napoleonic carriage was put aboard ship and in the waiting period Byron and Hobhouse spent some time at Churchill's grave. Byron lay down beside it to have his length compared with that of Churchill. After the sailing from Dover and when Byron was in Switzerland he wrote the poem which begins:

> I stood beside the grave of him who blazed
> The comet of a season . . . .

The cliffs of Dover provided Byron with his last sight of England. Dover Town is in a cleft between the East Cliff and the Western Heights, and the steersman of a Roman galley making for this port (which to him was presumably *Dubris*) was aware that the cleft marked the start of his road across Britain. The octagonal *pharos*, standing now within the precincts of Dover Castle at the summit of the East Cliff, marked the landfall for the Romans and, supposedly dating from about A.D. 50, remains today as a relic of the oldest standing building in England, a relic of the original Roman fortress. That physical setting, the cliffs which mark the start of Watling Street, is one of which Shakespeare's audience was aware. Perhaps Shakespeare used that awareness to heighten the feeling in his version of the tragedy of Lear, King of Britain. The 'Shakespeare Cliff' which can be approached direct from the town (bypassing the Western Heights) is commended to visitors for 'association with a famous passage in *King Lear* (IV, 6)' – but I don't feel that a mere pale reference to the association is adequate. Shakespeare in *King Lear* is using Dover and its cliffs as an enhancement for the tragedy because that setting, in his day, could stand up to the requirements not of minor local dignity but of a kingdom's majesty.

Unusual stress is laid upon the very name of Dover at the beginning of the fourth act of *King Lear*. Gloucester, protagonist of the subordinate plot, whom the audience has watched being blinded, has just been uttering, out of pain worse than physical, the lines

> As flies to wanton boys are we to th' gods.
> They kill us for their sport.

Then in that first scene of the act with his mind set on suicide, the blinded Gloucester makes the son whom he cannot see lead him towards the cliff 'whose high and bending head' is the more quickly to be visualized because the Dover setting has been stressed. So in 'the Country near Dover' of Scene 6, though not near the cliff's edge, Edgar may pretend:

> Come on, sir; here's the place: stand still.
> How fearful
> And dizzy 'tis to cast one's eyes so low!
> The crows and choughs that wing the midway air
> Show scarce so gross as beetles; half way down
> Hangs one that gathers samphire, dreadful trade!
> Methinks he seems no bigger than his head.
> The fishermen that walk upon the beach
> Appear like mice, and yon tall anchoring bark
> Diminish'd to her cock, her cock a buoy
> Almost too small for sight. The murmuring surge,
> That on the unnumber'd idle pebbles chafes,
> Cannot be heard so high. I'll look no more,
> Lest my brain turn, and the deficient sight
> Topple down headlong.

What this rhodomontade and grim byplay of the blind Gloucester's thwarted suicide achieve is to heighten the setting for the entry of Lear 'fantastically dressed with flowers' and to the transition to the king's greater tragedy on the highest level. In the last scene of all Lear reappears from the castle with Cordelia dead in his arms; in the cadence of that line

> Never, never, never, never, never!

one is allowed to feel the full tragedy, that Lear dies sane. No analysis reaches the feeling of that ending, yet there is no doubting that the 'never, never, never' repetition is the end of a titanic journey. That the journey ended at Dover was not mere accident. The heath of Shakespeare's time, the storms, the cliffs – especially the symbolism that Dover was the end of a great road – all play their part in *King Lear*.

3. ACROSS THE WEALD OF KENT

A zigzag on the map is the easiest way to arrange for an overall view of the countryside west of the Dover Road.

A first westward course from Canterbury to Guildford starts by following the River Stour from Canterbury upstream. There at a distance of about eight miles is Godmersham Park – an instant reminder of Jane Austen. This part of Kent was of much importance in Jane Austen's short life. The children of the Reverend George Austen all grew up in the rectory at Steventon, in Hampshire – except for one of Jane's older brothers, Edward. A distant connection of the Rector, the wealthy Mr Thomas Knight of Chawton House in Hampshire and Godmersham Park in Kent, was childless; he took a special fancy to Edward and presently adopted him. Thus Edward Knight in due course inherited the Knight properties. Within a less affectionate family this might have created 'differences'. Within the Austen family no chilliness is discernible. Edward, with his rapidly increasing number of children, had just begun to settle in as the new owner of Godmersham Park and into full charge of that considerable estate when the Austen parents and the sisters, Cassandra and Jane, were invited for their first visit. That visit to Godmersham was in 1798 when Jane was twenty-three years old; from that time on she and her sister, sometimes on visits together and sometimes separately, had many occasions to become familiar with the white, wide-stretched, classical building, the impressive central hall paved with marble and the four great side rooms with large windows looking out on different aspects of the beautifully timbered park.

On the first visit to Godmersham, Edward and his wife had only four children; Fanny, the eldest, who was to become Jane's favourite niece, was as yet only five years old. The health and energy of Edward's wife were presently depleted by continuity of child-bearing; in 1808 Fanny at the age of fifteen had ten younger brothers and sisters and she was already taking a share in household arrangements. At that time Fanny made sure that Jane was given the Yellow Room; Jane found her 'almost another sister' and wrote 'I did not think a niece would ever have been so much to me'. By 1813 Edward was a widower; his daughter Fanny was now the young mistress and manager of the household; and from that time she is seen to be providing for her aunt Jane both time and quiet at Godmersham for the writing of *Mansfield Park*. The impression is sometimes given that Jane Austen did all of her novel-writing in the midst of interruptions. At the small cottage at Chawton in Hampshire this was often enough the case; but the opportunities made for her in Kent for undisturbed work should also be remembered. Elizabeth Jenkins points to a letter of Jane Austen's in which, at noon of a November day at Godmersham, she breaks off her work on *Mansfield Park* to say: 'I did not mean to eat, but Mr Johncock has brought in the tray, so I must – I am all alone. Edward has gone into his woods. At the present time, I have five tables, eight and twenty chairs and two fires all to myself.' It was in such circumstances that *Mansfield Park* was completed at Godmersham and *Emma* begun.

The usual way for the Austens to return from Godmersham to Hampshire was to go by chaise up the Dover Road and across London. On the first visit in 1798 Cassandra stayed on at Godmersham Park; Jane and her parents drove off after a heavy shower through 'a very bright *chrystal* afternoon' as far as Dartford, where they arranged to spend the night at the Bull and George. There was a flurry of alarm on arrival, for Jane's writing case and dressing-boxes had been transferred by mistake into a chaise which was just packing up when their chaise arrived at the inn, 'and were driven away towards Gravesend on their road to the West Indies'. Elizabeth Jenkins (from whom I borrow the account) indicates that such alarms were not unusual. A man on horseback was sent off after the missing articles, and 'they were got about two or three miles off'. All was well; as soon as the writing case returned Jane could get on with her letters, while her parents sat by the fire, the Rev. George Austen's book for reading at that moment being, as Jane noted, a supernatural brought from Canterbury, *The Midnight Bell*.

Pursuing a westward course cross-country from Godmersham we pause first at Maidstone. There 'forget not yet' that Sir Thomas Wyatt was born in 1503 at Allington Castle, on the west bank of the Medway, two miles downstream. Wyatt's poem 'Forget not yet' in which his lover beseeched his mistress to bear in mind his 'stedfast faith' and 'tried intent' was first published in *Tottel's Miscellany* in 1557. At Maidstone also William Hazlitt was born in 1778; but Hazlitt himself while still in infancy was taken to Shropshire. The writer most to be thought of at Maidstone is Alfred Tennyson. In 1841, when Tennyson was thirty-two, after several attempts to find a site for living which might suit the health of his widowed mother, he and his mother with his sister Cecilia moved to Boxley near Maidstone (after a year at Tunbridge Wells).

Park House, the home of the Lushington family, was nearby, and the three Lushington brothers were all part of Tennyson's 'set' at Cambridge. Quite soon Tennyson's sister Cecilia was married, at Boxley, to one of the Lushington brothers, Edmund. The epilogue to *In Memoriam*, forming a serene ending to that long poem, recalls the moment of Cecilia's wedding. Tennyson participated in the ceremony by giving away the bride; as one of the wedding party he records, on emerging from the church,

> maidens of the place
> That pelt us in the porch with flowers.

It turned his thoughts to his own prospects. For at least five years there had existed an unconsummated 'understanding' between himself and Emily Sellwood. As if prompted by Cecilia's wedding, their formal engagement was now openly recognized, though Tennyson had no hope of marriage until his financial prospects improved. Yet that is the point about Maidstone, in Tennyson's career: it was at Maidstone that he achieved all-round success.

When Tennyson came to live in the area of Maidstone he had already, for some years, been working on and slowly adding to *In Memoriam*. That long poem had been started in an effort to resolve for himself the feelings caused by the sudden death of his friend Arthur Henry Hallam. This had occurred in 1833; since then the 'more than six score poems' which in the end would make up *In Memoriam* had been accumulating, each individual poem expressed in what at first glance look like similar quatrains of one same and apparently monotonous metre. Saintsbury, writing at the end of the nineteenth century to a captive audience, could point to 'the way in which, side by side with the prevailing undertone of the stanza, the individual pieces vary the music and accompany it, so to speak, in duet with a particular melody'. But in the 1840s how could a little-known poet capture attention for the matter and music so professionally blended?

First, recognition had to be achieved. Tennyson worked for it. Throughout a decade he never deserted poetry 'for lucrative avocations of any kind, even literary'. Then, coinciding with the move to Maidstone, two small volumes were published for him, one a selection of earlier pieces greatly revised and improved, the other of new *English Idylls*. Time would show these two volumes contained many of the now best-known short poems of Tennyson. To a bystander, the reception accorded to these publications of 1842 was hardly overwhelming, and no guarantee that so long a poem as *In Memoriam* would be well received. To Tennyson in his thirties, after years of patient, almost secret, self-improving practice, even the mild applause was exhilarating.

Then Maidstone took its hand in Tennyson's career.

We see Tennyson in 1842, elated, despite his habitual caution, about his work, which even Daddy Wordsworth had condescended to praise. We see him excited by his sister's wedding, excited to the pitch of announcing, at least to intimates, his own engagement. We see him in a burst of sociable party-going – and at that moment Maidstone provided a fête. The fête was organized by Maidstone's Mechanics Institute; the landowner-patron invited Tennyson to join his family in looking on; and the day provided such a lively alternation of visiting

> A Gothic ruin and a Grecian house,
> A talk of college and of ladies' rights,
> A feudal knight in silken masquerade,
> And, yonder, shrieks and strange experiments

that the poet was challenged to transmute the medley into 'A Summer's Tale'. So, in what was for Tennyson a summer of unusual excitement and in a spirit 'part banter, part affection', he at once accepted the challenge and set to work on *The Princess*.

It was five years before Tennyson was sufficiently sure about *The Princess* to release it for publication. Its only possible description was a 'medley'. With awareness in it of 'social wrong' it 'moved as in a strange diagonal' to open a debate about colleges for women and women's rights in general. Half a century after its publication in 1847 so amiable a critic as George Saintsbury could be unsure whether Tennyson was not overstraining himself by attending to anything so 'fantastical in the conception' as equality of education for the sexes. Nevertheless the dream-quality of the central story and the singing-quality of the short lyrics that came into it caused in the 1840s a demand for a second printing; and since it was the lyrics which afforded most general pleasure, for a third printing in 1850 Tennyson 'superadded' six more. By then *The Princess* was felt to be 'a masterpiece', and despite continuing ridicule in some quarters for its attention to women's rights, Saintsbury was forced to sum up the opinion: 'Such lyric as "The Splendour falls" and "Tears, idle tears", with blank verse as that of the closing passage, would raise to the topmost heights of poetry whatever subject it was spent upon.'

All of the lyrics that came to Tennyson at Maidstone while writing *The Princess* linger in memory. 'Ask me no more' provides if you wish a reminiscence of the refrain of the other Maidstone poet, Wyatt. Effortlessly that is followed by the lovely song 'Now sleeps the crimson petal, now the white', containing the metaphor 'Now lies the Earth all Danaë to the stars . . .' For all such moments Maidstone may be thanked for its cooperation. Moreover, the publication of *The Princess* before that of

In Memoriam in 1850 worked out very well for Tennyson. A wide audience was prepared by then to acclaim *In Memoriam*, and the acclamation had for him important results. In 1850 he was appointed Poet Laureate; in his private life his financial position now enabled him to marry Emily Sellwood, an event for which both had long waited. That marriage turned out to be especially happy for Tennyson. Though not devoid of oddnesses, he was devotedly cared for by Emily and spared from the extreme neurotic behaviour exhibited by some of his brothers and sisters.

My route westward very soon presents a choice of three, or indeed four, very famous houses. The largest and grandest of these is Knole, at the Tonbridge end of Sevenoaks, just east of A21. This is the 'grand relation of those small manor houses which hide themselves away so innumerably among the counties'. It is increasingly and intolerably difficult for many of 'those small manor houses' to be kept up, but Knole, exceptional in scale, is one of the most famous of National Trust properties. For ten generations of the Sackville family the house and its beautiful park was their private possession, and her history of *Knole and the Sackvilles* was one of the earlier delightful works of Victoria Sackville-West. Literary associations at Knole are subordinate, although Charles Sackville, sixth Earl of Dorset and Restoration courtier, had there a dining-room known as 'Poets' Parlour' where Wycherley, Prior and Dryden were often guests. Dryden repaid by describing Sackville as 'the best good man, with the worst-natured Muse'; Prior said 'a freedom reigned at his table which made every one of his guests think himself at home' – and all agreed that Charles Sackville was a 'munificent, rakish, witty and florid figure'. (His mind towards the end succumbed prematurely; the Poets' Parlour was therefore closed, and his third wife kept him 'in a sort of captivity in Bath'.)

Victoria Sackville-West and her husband Sir Harold Nicolson lived at Sevenoaks Weald (a mile or so south of Knole Park) until 1930. In more modest circumstances, in 1904, Edward Thomas also brought his wife and young family to Sevenoaks Weald. Thomas rented Else's Farm, opposite the inn; he also rented Stidolph's Cottage in Eggpie Lane as workshop for the often sixteen-hour days of book-reviewing and miscellaneous commissions on which his livelihood depended. At that time Thomas was under incessant pressure, yet was never too hard-up to help others. When the poet W. H. Davies returned from America, penniless and without the leg which had been amputated in his adventures there, it was Thomas who installed that crippled friend in his own writing-quarters at Stidolph's Cottage and provided both the encouragement and the means for writing *The Autobiography of a Super-Tramp*. On occasion there were unusual emergencies: when Davies broke his wooden leg, Thomas got the village carpenter to make another. Davies

was not supposed to reveal that all his support was quietly organized by
Thomas – even 'my rent, coal and light being paid mysteriously by
Thomas and his friends'. The gifts between the two men were not all
one-sided. Davies, the older of the two by seven years, asked the
question:

> What is this life if, full of care,
> We have no time to stand and stare?

Davies was perceptive enough to see that Thomas's own poetic talent
was in danger if he persisted in incessant overwork of a wrong kind, and
Davies's faith in Thomas's poetry was of help to the younger man at a
time when help was needed. Presently Davies was able to be self-supporting and Thomas, in 1906, moved to Hampshire and lived there until
joining up for active service in the 1914–18 war.

Quebec House, at the junction of the Edenbridge and Sevenoaks roads
in Westerham, was the birthplace of General Wolfe and earns a place in
literary pilgrimage from Wolfe's remark to one of his officers before the
battle of Quebec: the writing of Gray's *Elegy* had been a greater
achievement, said Wolfe, than it would be to scale the Heights of
Abraham. Near Westerham on the southern side is Chartwell, the
famous former home of Sir Winston Churchill. In 1954 Chartwell, with
its park, was bought by a group of Churchill's close friends for presentation to the National Trust, though Churchill continued to live there
until October 1964, shortly before his death. Chartwell 'is today the one
property of the National Trust which every Englishman, if he visits no
other, must wish to see'. In the house, the study is kept as it was when
Churchill, at the wide mahogany table, was working at his writings, or
dictations, for *The World Crisis*, *Marlborough*, and *The Second World
War*.

Five miles north of Westerham (as the crow flies) is Downe, or, as it
used to be, Down without the 'e' – another home of great interest. It
was at Down House, now preserved as a museum, that Charles Darwin
wrote the *Origin of Species*. Much could be happily remembered about
the life at Down when the Darwin family lived there. Their occupancy
began in 1842, and attention focuses then on Charles Darwin, in his
early thirties, working with persistent concentration on what became
foundation work 'for the entire structure of modern biology' (the phrase
is Julian Huxley's). But the life at Down was fascinating later than
Darwin's death in 1882, as is most delightfully demonstrated by consult-
ing Gwen Raverat's delicious book, *Period Piece*.

It was after Darwin's five years of voyaging in the *Beagle* that he
interrupted the prodigious labours of classifying the great collection of
specimens he had brought back, by marrying Emma, youngest daughter

of Josiah Wedgwood, and settling after that at Down. Here by 1846 he thought that ten years had completed the description 'of all my *Beagle* materials', but as Alan Moorehead tells there was in fact 'one item left over from the voyage, a tiny cirripede or barnacle, not much bigger than the head of a pin, and the study and classification of this species took up the next eight years of Darwin's life'. Between Charles and Emma Darwin there was lasting sympathy; the fact that his 'observations and experiments' were 'wearisome' to her did not disturb their mutual devotion. Nor did his almost perpetual discomfort and ill-health seem to fret either of them. Alan Moorehead quotes Mrs Huxley's remark about Emma: 'More than any woman I ever knew, she *comforted*.' Darwin's ill-health did not prevent his 'altogether exceptional devotion to his children' – nor the devotion to him of the seven out of ten children who survived childhood. Moorehead cites one of the children at four years old trying to bribe Darwin with sixpence to play with them during his working hours.

I was indicating that a great love for Down House was also felt by the Darwin grandchildren. 'I am afraid it *was* dull for my mother', the granddaughter, Gwen Raverat, confessed in *Period Piece*; but, identifying herself with her father's family:

we Darwins never found it dull there, for we loved every moment of life in the country; and we all, old and young alike, were apt to fly away out of doors and windows, at the first sound of the front-door bell. 'Visitors! Danger!' would be the cry . . . [To] us, everything at Down was perfect. That was an axiom. And by us I mean, not only the children, but all the uncles and aunts who belonged there. Uncle Horace was once heard to say in a surprised voice: 'No, I don't really like salvias very much, *though they did grow at Down*.' The implication, to us, would have been obvious. Of course all the flowers that grew at Down were beautiful; and different from all other flowers. Everything there was different. And better.

Gwen Raverat's grandfather, Charles Darwin, had died three years before she was born, and after his death her grandmother spent the winters in Cambridge and only the summers at Down House. There Gwen, her sister and two brothers 'all went for long walks'. Of the uncles and aunts 'who belonged there', perhaps the most beguiling of all was Aunt Etty. Charles Darwin was sad at losing, in his later years, all the taste for music and poetry that he had when young. His second child, Henrietta (Aunt Etty), married Uncle Richard who before Gwen knew him (he died when she was eight) had done everything that a cultured, enlightened person of his time should do: he 'had adored Ruskin, and worshipped Morris, and had slept for years with a copy of *In Memoriam* under his pillow'; he had read 'all Browning', 'all Wordsworth, and Carlyle, in fact nearly everything'; so it was under Uncle

Richard's influence that 'Aunt Etty had learnt, after her own fashion, to appreciate poetry and music' – and to pass on instruction, after Uncle Richard's death, to her niece.

Unfortunately she had no ear for rhythm, and always applied the full measure of her drastic common sense to all the more imaginative passages of the poets. One would be called upon to read aloud, say, Wordsworth's *Excursion* with her – Wordsworth was her religion – but one was never able to read more than two or three consecutive lines without stopping to discuss *exactly* what the words meant; or, alternatively, for her to give messages to Janet. One of her most engaging habits was to alter a phrase in a poem to suit herself, if she did not happen to approve of the poet's own version; and if she was not satisfied with her alteration, she would apply to Frances, Margaret, or even me, to improve it for her. I remember that Wordsworth's

> The wind comes to me from the fields of sleep

did not please her. What does it mean anyhow? Sleep does not grow in fields. I said, why not try *fields of sheep*. This was not well received . . .

Gwen Raverat went on to mention that Aunt Etty had made a version of Wordsworth's 'Tintern Revisited', entitled 'Tintern Revisited and Improved'. 'The Bard himself was not above amendment, but the alterations have unfortunately been lost.' The lovableness of Aunt Etty is not absent from the niece's account.

4. THE 'SOUTH KINGDOM', SURREY

It is in between the main radial roads out of London that my cross-country route locates writers who were trying to live in a quietly static way in Surrey. Edward and Constance Garnett, for instance, settled at the eastern border of Surrey at Limpsfield Chart, and David Garnett has written of country boyhood there. At Limpsfield Arthur Rackham, widely known for his book illustrations, lived and died. The London–Eastbourne road (A22) is one of the radial roads on either side of which and within twenty miles of London there are patches of real country in which some contest is maintained against the London sprawl. The memory of such a place as Pikes Farm, a house safely hidden, is dear to me because even though I worked in London my young family and I could live there, in country as opposed to suburb. It is a happy memory that T. S. Eliot could find a home with us there in 1933, when and for some time after Pikes Farm provided an 'Uncle Tom's Cabin'. Eliot's creative impulses were at that stage strongly directed to dramatic work. He had been asked to cooperate in a pageant called *The Rock*; Eliot

wrote the choruses for that work at Pikes Farm, and the way was developing for *Murder in the Cathedral*. Of many lively recollections of that
period the scene returns to me now of the planting of forty-five acorns,
all selected from the big oak, to make a circle at the centre of the big
field. The circle of oaks, in commemoration of Eliot's forty-fifth birthday, was intended to grow in due course to a splendid and notable
landmark. We guarded the young oak trees, but during the Second
World War control passed from our hands, and that field and its Eliot
memorial were, for food purposes, ploughed up.

The cross-country route I am following crosses the London–Eastbourne road at Godstone, as indeed in every part of this region, where
there are memories from Cobbett's *Rural Rides*. The next and busiest
of the radials is the London–Brighton road which my route crosses at
Redhill, entering there an area which is nowadays much built-up until
after Reigate. The present-day property development in the Reigate
area is, in a way, a reminder that in the years 1891–3, when Arthur
Conan Doyle was living north of here in London's suburb of South
Norwood (his address there was No. 12 Tennison Road), he could regard Reigate as thoroughly rural. Doyle's friends who visited Norwood
(Greenhough Smith, editor of *The Strand Magazine*, Jerome K. Jerome,
Eden Phillpotts, James Barrie, W. W. Jacobs) could enjoy from his
garden 'an unimpaired view of a broad stretch of fertile open country,
backed by the Surrey hills'. When Hesketh Pearson described those
visits to Tennison Road where Doyle's friends would look up the
athletic doctor (in his 'suit of rough heather mixture' and looking 'like
a Life Guardsman') he may have exaggerated the unimpairedness of the
view southward; yet certainly in 'The Reigate Puzzle', when Watson
diagnosed that Sherlock Holmes would be much the better for 'a week
of springtime in the country', the first thought was a visit to Colonel
Hayter who had a house across those Surrey hills from Norwood in 'the
Reigate depths of country'. Doyle alludes at least four times in that short
story to the thorough countryness of Reigate, and one accepts that before
the motor age that was the case.

Doyle was thoroughly familiar with my route even so far as 'Farnham,
on the borders of Surrey'. In November 1892, having decided that (after
the death of Carlyle) Meredith had become the leading figure in contemporary literature, Doyle lectured on Meredith to the Upper Norwood
Literary and Scientific Society. 'Naturally', Hesketh Pearson wrote, 'he
was invited to see the master at Box Hill'. Meredith was living there at
Flint Cottage, although his second wife had died in 1889, and by the
time Doyle made his visit (driving probably along the road from Reigate
to Dorking) Meredith was beginning to suffer from the paraplegia which
for the remaining nineteen years of his life increasingly disabled him.

It was then still Meredith's custom to struggle up the steep and narrow path to the summerhouse higher up the hill which was his workroom, and (as Doyle recalled in his *Memories and Adventures*) after their lunch Doyle was invited to precede the older man on the climb. In Doyle's words:

The nervous complaint from which he suffered caused him to fall down occasionally. As we walked up the narrow path I heard him fall behind me, but judged from the sound that it was a mere slither and could not have hurt him. Therefore I walked on as if I had heard nothing. He was a fiercely proud old man, and my instincts told me that his humiliation in being helped up would be far greater than any relief I could give him.

Safe in the summerhouse Meredith read aloud to Doyle from his as yet unfinished novel *The Amazing Marriage*, and the visit, despite its awkward moments, ended amicably.

Flint Cottage, where Meredith had lived from 1867 and where he died in 1909, is reached from the lane which turns uphill between the Burford Bridge Hotel and Juniper Hall, or by a track which leads from the grounds of the hotel. Before Meredith's disablement he and Leslie Stephen had been notable members of the 'Informal Order of Sunday Tramps' and in his last years, despite his falls, he was deeply attached to his sloping Box Hill garden – 'the smell of the earth is Elysian', he said. For a year or two before Doyle's visit George Gissing had been living at Dorking and was a frequent visitor to Flint Cottage – Meredith had been one of the earliest appreciators of Gissing's writings. The above-mentioned Burford Bridge Hotel (or a predecessor), beside the River Mole at the foot of Box Hill, was a stopping place much favoured long before Stevenson stayed there for his visits to Meredith. The inn at Burford Bridge provided lodging on occasion for Nelson, and Keats was immensely pleased, towards the end of 1817, to be staying in the room next to the one the hero had occupied. 'I like this place very much', says one of Keats's letters, 'there is hill and dale and a little river – I went up Box Hill this evening after the moon.' 'After the moon' are words with double meaning, for he was then writing *Endymion*. *Endymion* was presently completed at the inn at Burford Bridge. In the 1880s Stevenson stayed four times at that same inn 'with its arbours and green gardens and silent, eddying river'; one result of his visits to Flint Cottage was that Meredith is said to have portrayed him as 'Woodseer' in *The Amazing Marriage*. The track zigzagging up past Flint Cottage leads to the open hilltop, where the springy turf and incomparable views over the Weald are protected by the National Trust but open to all visitors without charge. 'We are going to Box Hill tomorrow: you will join us. It is not Swisserland, but it will be something for a young man so much in want of a change.' Thus, in Jane Austen's *Emma*, her heroine addressed herself to Frank Churchill in the early 1800s, and the expedition to Box Hill is well remembered by all of Jane Austen's readers.

I have never tried to 'place' all the houses and all the episodes in *Emma* precisely, on the map; but it is possible that Emma's drive to Box Hill was up the valley of the Mole from Leatherhead, and it is possible that the site of Donwell Abbey, the seat of Mr Knightley, was in the valley of that charming little winding river. It will be recalled that Jane Austen used Mr Knightley's strawberry party to give a picture of land-scape that was of special loveliness to her for being, she felt, so truly English. With Mr Knightley to show the extent of the grounds, the party began to walk:

It was hot . . . they insensibly followed one another to the delicious shade of a broad, short avenue of limes, which, stretching beyond the garden at an equal distance from the river, seemed the finish of the pleasure grounds. . . . It was a charming walk, and the view which closed it was extremely pretty. The considerable slopes, at nearly the foot of which the Abbey stood, gradu-ally acquired a steeper form beyond its grounds; and at half a mile distant was a bank of considerable abruptness and grandeur, well-clothed with wood; and at the bottom of this bank, favourably placed and sheltered, rose the Abbey Mill Farm, with meadows in front, and the river making a close and hand-some circle around it.

It was a sweet view – sweet to the eye and the mind. English verdure, English culture, English comfort, seen under a sun bright without being oppressive. . . .

At this point of the quotation Elizabeth Jenkins in her delightful book *Jane Austen* breaks off to say that Jane herself seems to have been so penetrated by the loveliness she was describing 'that she made in this passage what is perhaps her one and only mistake on a question of detail, She goes on to describe the surroundings of the farm as "rich pastures, spreading flocks, orchards in blossom and light columns of smoke ascending".' Miss Jenkins then mentions that when Jane's brother, the master of Godmersham, came to this point in reading his sister's work, he said, 'I should like to know, Jane, where you get those apple trees of yours that blossom in July?'

On the uplands west of the valley of the Mole and midway between Dorking and Great Bookham is Polesden Lacey, where the house that was jubilantly bought by the dramatist Sheridan in 1797 was later re-placed by the neo-Grecian mansion which in the twentieth century be-came the home of Mrs Ronald Greville, and which for its very notable collection of works of art and furnishings, and for the garden (which had been started by Sheridan), is one of the National Trust's show-places. But to reach Polesden Lacey from Dorking one passes Camilla

Lacey, and this is a reminder of the romance associated hereabouts with Fanny Burney. Juniper Hall in the valley is nowadays preserved by the National Trust as a field-study centre, but in the French Revolution it was a refuge for some of the most distinguished of the French refugees. Talleyrand and Mme de Staël were among them, and General D'Arblay, who had been adjutant-general to Lafayette. In 1793 Fanny Burney came to visit friends at Norbury Park, across the river from Mickleham; it was natural that the author of *Evelina* and *Cecilia* should meet the French *émigrés* from Juniper Hall, only half a mile distant; less predictably, Fanny Burney (aged forty-one) and General D'Arblay fell so violently in love that nothing – not her own poor health, nor their poverty, nor the initial alarm of Dr Burney, none of these things and no other objections – could prevent their getting married with amazing speed in Mickleham Church in July 1793, the marriage then being repeated with Catholic ceremony in the Sardinian Chapel, Lincoln's Inn Fields. After that they returned to hover at Bookham while Fanny as breadwinner buckled to the writing of her third novel, *Camilla*. This was published in 1796; it was successful enough for them to build their own house, named 'Camilla Cottage', across the river south of Mickleham. There they lived from 1797 until 1802, when the General returned to seek employment in France and she went with him.

On my route from Reigate to Dorking, a quarter of a mile before entering Dorking, was Deepdene, the mansion (later a hotel) where Disraeli wrote most of *Coningsby*. Then at Dorking local rivalries produce three possible sites for the inn which Dickens, in *Pickwick*, refers to as named for 'the Marquis of Granby of glorious memory'. Sam Weller, it will be remembered, made pilgrimage to Dorking expressly to behold his mother-in-law who kept that 'model of a roadside public-house of the better class' and shared his father's displeasure at the habits of the 'deputy shepherd' in dipping his red nose into the often replenished glass of hot pineapple rum and water. In that episode I notice that on the next morning Sam set forward from Dorking 'on his walk to London', as if Dickens's readers would accept that as wholly within normal walking distance. In the very next chapter of *Pickwick* Dickens commends walking twenty-five miles between breakfast and dinner. The amount of footwork in Dickens makes one aware how transport has changed.

Westward from Dorking to Guildford the road passes Westcott and, on the left, the mansion known as The Rookery where Thomas Malthus, author of the *Essay on the Principle of Population*, was born in 1766. Up the long Coast Hill the road passes Wotton Church, where John Evelyn was buried in 1706, and Wotton House, which was the Evelyn family home. Beyond the next side road to the left is Crossways Farm; the name was perpetuated by Meredith in *Diana of the Crossways*. Shortly thereafter is Abinger Hammer, a village well remembered for its remarkable clockhouse. 'Listen to the hammers at Abinger, Abinger Hammer!' is the line repeated by E. M. Forster when recalling the iron furnaces here at the time of the Spanish Armada's threat and of its repulse. Forster reprinted the pageant that he wrote for performance at Abinger, the village he had known all his life, in *Abinger Harvest*; and in that collection he tells how the American royalties for *A Passage to India* enabled him to purchase what he then called 'My Wood' at Abinger Hammer.

The road passes on through Shere, up by Newlands Corner to cross the summit of the chalk ridge and over the Merrow Downs, which bring back the verses of Kipling remembered from childhood. The poem here alluded to was called by Kipling 'Merrow Down', beginning, as usually printed:

> There runs a road by Merrow Down –
> A grassy track to-day it is –
> An hour out of Guildford town,
> Above the river Wey it is. . . .

In the 1920s, when Kipling was among the poets asked to contribute a miniature volume for the library of the Queen's Dolls' House at Windsor, it was one of the ten poems which he copied, by hand, for that purpose. Since is it not particularly short – eleven quatrains, forty-four lines – this is evidence that Kipling was himself fond of it. As he copied he made various small changes, not material corrections but perhaps in the interest of topographical accuracy. The revision of the first line reads 'There runs a road *through* Merrow Down' (my italics) and a little later the statement that the Wey 'Was more than six times bigger than' is altered to 'five times bigger'.

5. BACK TO FOLKESTONE

We have now traversed Zone 2 from Canterbury to its western boundary, the Portsmouth Road, in a line which has taken us through northern Kent and Surrey – and now I should zig-zag first south-east towards Ashford and Folkestone and then turn west again along the seaward side of the South Downs. Having introduced Kipling, it is certainly incumbent to return for traverse of his 'Sussex by the sea'.

South-eastward then from Guildford, two miles before Horsham a left turn at Broadbridge (leading to Warnham) passes within half a mile (on the left) of Field Place. This was where Shelley's parents were living when Percy Bysshe Shelley was born on 4 August 1792. His father could look forward to becoming by inheritance Sir Timothy Shelley, Bart., and the child, as eldest son, could be expected in his turn to be heir to the title and to the Shelley estates. As Leigh Hunt put it, the child who was born at Field Place had only to fulfil easy expectations 'to become a yea and nay man in the House of Commons, to be one of the richest men in Sussex'. The course of schooling chosen for him was not intended to upset such prospects; after some tutoring at Horsham, he was to be a boarder from the age of ten at a school at Brentford, then to proceed to Eton and Oxford, with Field Place to return to for vacations – there he was to learn the real things, how to get on (again to quote Leigh Hunt) with 'fox-hunters and their chaplains'. Of the boarding-school terms at Brentford I know nothing; of Shelley's insubordinations at Eton (which led to his removal before completion of the regular school period) and at Oxford (which led to his expulsion) there are various accounts; but what I wish to know more about, as I pass Field Place, are what refuges the passionate rebel could find there for himself. I am fairly sure it was in a field near Field Place that Shelley heard and saw his first skylark and recognized affinity with that other 'scorner of the ground'. There were not many other affinities to hold him at home.

Shelley was in his nineteenth year when he appeared at the London office where Leigh Hunt was editing the *Examiner*, and Leigh Hunt, eight years the older, though saying little about the manuscript poem that Shelley was offering, was much pleased with the 'youth, not come to his full growth; very gentlemanly, earnestly gazing at every object that interested him, and quoting the Greek dramatists'. That was when Shelley, expelled from Oxford, was trying to live alone in London and was on the point of marriage with the sixteen-year-old Harriet West-brook. This ended with mutual misery, from which her escape was to drown herself in the Serpentine. Then developed the close friendship between Leigh Hunt and Shelley, to which I shall return. Here and independently it was Horsham that brought Leigh Hunt to mind. Two miles from Horsham is the present-day site of Christ's Hospital. The famous Bluecoat School was moved from the Newgate Street site in London in 1902; a poet who attended the school after the move was was Edmund Blunden, but a hundred years before the move Leigh Hunt had also been a Bluecoat boy, following after Coleridge and Charles Lamb.

Other recollections near Horsham provide a rapid alternation between the eighteenth and twentieth centuries. At West Grinstead (south of Horsham) in the Park is 'Pope's Oak' under which Pope is said to have begun the composition of *The Rape of the Lock*, suggested by his friend John Carryll with whom he was staying here in 1712. West of West

Grinstead, two miles up the little River Adur, is Shipley, where Hilaire Belloc lived from 1906 till the end of his life in 1953 in the house (part of it dating from the fourteenth century) called King's Land. Belloc was buried at West Grinstead; Shipley Mill was restored as a memorial to him.

Farther east, Ashdown Forest again suggests associations, one from the eighteenth and the other from the twentieth century. For the second association I would proceed from Fletching around the eastern edge of Ashdown Forest to Crowborough; for here, at the house called Windlesham, Sir Arthur Conan Doyle came to live in 1907, and it remained his home until his death in 1930. For the first, however, I would cross the western edge of Ashdown Forest to pass beside Sheffield Park, and pause there if the date should happen to be one of the Saturdays in early summer and autumn when the gardens are open. The reason for visiting Sheffield Park is, in part, to pay respect to Edward Gibbon (1737–94). The successful completion of *The Decline and Fall of the Roman Empire* owed much to Gibbon's friendship with John Baker Holroyd, who became the first Lord Sheffield; Gibbon's last year from summer till Christmas was spent at Sheffield Place, and he was buried in the church at Fletching.

Most portraits of Gibbon are of his head and shoulders only; the face, despite 'those Brobdignatious cheeks' (as Fanny Burney called them) and double chin, is expressive of dignity, and the eyes show a steady, penetrative gaze. There are some silhouettes of Gibbon in the action of taking snuff which indicate the smallness of his limbs and hands and feet. It is easy to dismiss those silhouettes as caricatures; yet in actuality Gibbon was under five feet in height, and a first impression on meeting him was that his diminutive physique made his behaviour decidedly comical. Thus Fanny Burney recorded of her meeting with Gibbon in 1782:

His neat little feet are of a miniature description and with these as soon as I turned round he hastily described a quaint sort of circle, with small quick steps and a dapper gait, as if to mark the alacrity of his approach, and then, stopping short when full face to me, he made so singularly profound a bow that – though hardly able to keep my gravity – I felt myself blush deeply at its undue but palpably intended obsequiousness.

After this elaborate preparation Gibbon said nothing at all, for her attention was at that moment diverted to her hero Burke, and Gibbon was frequently slow of speech. His dress, even in that colourful period, was noticeably loud. George Colman the younger was a schoolboy of about thirteen when permitted by his father to join the guests at dinner in the Colman house in Soho Square; he recorded that 'On the day I first sat down with Johnson, in his rusty brown, and his black worsteads, Gibbon was placed opposite to me in a suit of flower'd velvet, with a bag and sword'. Colman's own comment, when reflecting later, was that Gibbon's costume was not extraordinary at a time when almost every gentleman came to dinner in full dress, but 'a little overcharged, perhaps, if his *person* be consider'd'.

The satisfaction with his attire, which was part of what Fanny Burney found 'placidly mild, but rather effeminate' in Gibbon, was a not unseemly way of compensating for the unimpressiveness of his physique. Gibbon's 'person' needed some overcharging if he was to hold his own at dinner with Johnson. At the particular dinner mentioned, young Colman attended to the 'measured phraseology' that was used by both Johnson and Gibbon, and later made his famous comparison:

Johnson's style was grand, and Gibbon's elegant; the stateliness of the former was sometimes pedantick, and the polish of the latter was occasionally finical. Johnson march'd to kettle-drums and trumpets; Gibbon moved to flutes and haut-boys; Johnson hew'd passages through the Alps, while Gibbon levell'd walks through parks and gardens.

What won the schoolboy's heart was that Gibbon in the course of the evening talked once or twice especially with him – 'the great historian was light and playful, suiting his matter to the capacity of the boy; – but it was done *more suo*; still he tapp'd his snuff-box, – still he smirk'd, and smiled; and rounded his periods with the same air of good breeding, as if he were conversing with men'. Colman, recollecting that talk more than fifty years later, added a pictorial touch: 'His mouth, mellifluous as Plato's, was a round hole, nearly in the centre of his visage.' Gibbon's use and display of his snuff-box was characteristic. The above-mentioned dinner-party occurred a year before the publication and startling success of *The Decline and Fall*. It was within two months of the appearance of that 'Lo, a Truly Classic Work' that Gibbon had a search made in Paris for a snuff-box sufficiently worthy of him, and from Paris at a cost of £37 5s 6d he obtained the massive gold box embossed on the lid with cupids attending an altar which is now in the British Museum. Display of that box by the small person in 'Burgundy coloured cloth frock with orange shag velvet waistcoat, laced with gold and silver lace' amused and pleased Sir Joshua Reynolds and was well calculated to arouse the bitterest jealous feelings of James Boswell.

The first meeting of Gibbon and Captain Holroyd (later Lord Sheffield) had occurred in 1763 at Lausanne. Peace had been declared and many young Englishmen who could afford it rushed to enjoy a spell of foreign travel. Gibbon at twenty-six had served three years of bloodless campaigning as a captain in the Hampshire Militia; even if the militia had not been the regular army, he never forgot that he had been a soldier. To the same lodgings in Lausanne there arrived in August two English gentlemen, John Holroyd and Edward Manners, each a couple of years older than Gibbon and, so far as army service was concerned, of much more active experience. Both of these visitors were captains of the 21st Light Dragoons, the Royal Foresters, a regiment raised by the Marquis of Granby himself and but lately disbanded. When the two hearty and athletic cavalry officers were smirked at and addressed in rounded periods by a foppish little man announcing himself as captain of Grenadiers in the Hampshire Militia, it was natural for them to laugh at him and for him to react with dudgeon. Yet unexpectedly a friendship of opposites came to pass between Gibbon and Holroyd. The Holroyd who as a young man at Lausanne bathed in the lake every morning, spent the rest of the morning at the riding school and in the afternoon would go shooting, when both had returned to England and especially after the death of Gibbon's father in 1770, became in very many practical ways Gibbon's adviser and increasingly a much-loved kind of guardian. Holroyd had purchased Sheffield Place in 1769; after Gibbon's father's death the Holroyds made both Gibbon and his widowed stepmother very welcome there; it was at Sheffield Place that the Holroyds' small daughter Maria gave him the family nickname 'Gib'. For his part Gibbon was equally imperious that whenever the Holroyds were in town they should make No. 7 Bentinck Street their inn. Having set up his stepmother in Bath, Gibbon and his parrot were looked after in Bentinck Street by Mrs Ford as housekeeper, three men-servants and the 'virgins in the garret'. There he was to write the first half of his History, to enjoy his acceptance as a social figure, and to see the rise and end of his political fortunes, as so pleasingly told of in D. M. Low's biography.

When Gibbon's loss of income in 1782 forced him to return to an inexpensive way of living in Lausanne, it was Holroyd – or Lord Sheffield as he had become – who attended to all the business of selling Gibbon's properties in Buckinghamshire and Hampshire. When Gibbon returned with his completed manuscript of the second part of *Decline and Fall* in August 1787, Sheffield Place was his primary home in England for the nine months of seeing the three volumes through the press. He was troubled with gout, but it was his extreme corpulency that alarmed the Sheffields. Lord Sheffield expressed himself gently in reporting Gibbon's safe arrival:

He amuses himself with the notion that he is not grown fatter, but he appears to me greatly increased in bulk. I was forced to threaten him yesterday that if he would not do as he was bid, we should be obliged to lay him on his back that like the turtle he may not be able to get up. Considering the little exercise he uses, I think he indulges too much with oysters, milk etc. at supper. Two breakfasts are never omitted and at dinner he seems to me to devour much more than he used to do. But he is most provoking on the subject of future residence. He has no view but towards Switzerland.

After the publication of the three volumes which completed *The Decline and Fall of the Roman Empire* and a summer of enjoying his triumph, Gibbon did return to Lausanne for a final five years. In 1793 Lady Sheffield's sudden death, from an infection caught from looking after sick *émigrés* at Guy's Hospital, prompted Gibbon's then wartime journey back to England. The journey aggravated his ailments; after a final summer at Sheffield Place, Sheffield and his daughter Maria doing all that they could for his comfort, he died during medical treatment in London in January 1794. His remains were brought by Lord Sheffield's instruction for burial in the Holroyd family vault in Fletching Church.

*   *   *

The very notable 'country-writer' Richard Jefferies spent a winter at Crowborough, on the eastern heights of Ashdown Forest, towards the end of his short life. At the house called The Downs, on the London Road, he put together his last volume of essays. Of twentieth-century writers who lived and worked and died at Crowborough there was A. S. M. Hutchinson, author of *If Winter Comes*, whose home was New Forest Lodge, Beacon Road, and General Fuller who lived at Forest Gate, as well as Sir Arthur Conan Doyle. It was at the time of his second marriage that Doyle purchased his house here, Windlesham, in 1907. His previous homes had been at South Norwood and, when his first wife's health permitted her to live in England, at the 'considerable mansion' called Undershaw which he built for her at Hindhead. Throughout the Hindhead period (1896–1906) Doyle and the two children of the first family displayed their special feeling for Hampshire. Doyle had met his first wife at Southsea. Minstead plays a particular part in the books especially dear to him, *The White Company* and *Sir Nigel*. From the Sherlock Holmes stories we know that Watson had a yearning 'for the glades of the New Forest or the shingle of Southsea'. S. C. Roberts conjectured that Dr Watson's first honeymoon (for Watson, like Doyle, was twice married) was spent in Hampshire. Yet then the 'Bohemian soul' of Sherlock Holmes tended to drag his creator eastward into Sussex. *Rodney Stone* showed the attraction that Brighton of the Regency period could exert upon Doyle. Sherlock Holmes came to prefer the Sussex Downs and cliffs eastward of Brighton, towards Beachy Head. Holmes and Doyle did not always exhibit the same taste; we know that in 1902 Doyle accepted a knighthood, and that in the same year Holmes refused one. But when Doyle in 1906 was a lonely widower his thoughts, like those of Holmes, turned to Sussex. We see him starting a second home at Crowborough in 1907. In that same year Sherlock Holmes withdrew to his 'villa', 'commanding a great view of the Channel', which I would place as on the coastline of Sussex just about due south of Crowborough (police headquarters for Holmes's neighbourhood were at Lewes).

Doyle was not yet fifty when he regarded Crowborough as home for the rest of his life. He was still to travel widely and to take up many 'causes', some distant, and some local to Sussex, as when he rushed to assist the chambermaids at the Metropole Hotel, Brighton, when the management tried to reduce their salaries. Sherlock Holmes, whom scholars estimate to have been five years older than Conan Doyle, intended to devote his retirement in Sussex to bee-keeping and to the compilation of his *Practical Handbook of Bee Culture, with some Observations upon the Segregation of the Queen*. Holmes's first villa on the coastal side of the Downs was so close to the cliffs that the Channel gales played havoc with his 'little working gangs' of bees, and Henry FitzGerald Heard, in his account of one of Holmes's adventures after retirement (entitled *A Taste for Honey*) told how the bee-keeping fared better after his remove to the village slightly inland, named in Heard's story 'Ashton Clearwater'. Precise identification of the scenes of each Sherlock Holmes adventure is sometimes a quarrelsome matter, but for *The Valley of Fear*, which Doyle issued in 1915, it seems to be accepted that Groombridge Place, a moated house that attracted Doyle's attention on the way from Crowborough to Tunbridge Wells, reappears as Birlstone Manor House.

Groombridge had made an earlier niche in literary annals. Edmund Waller was living there in the 1630s when he was one of the unsuccessful suitors of the attractive eighteen-year-old Lady Dorothy Sidney (grand-niece of Sir Philip Sidney) of Penshurst Place, four miles due north of Groombridge. Penshurst, rich in literary tradition ever since Sir Philip Sidney's day, suggested that Waller should make his courtship known by verses. It was almost compulsory that poets who were guests at Penshurst should commemorate it in rhyme. Ben Jonson paid thanks for being entertained there as a social equal:

> The same beer, and bread, and self-same wine,
> That is his lordship's, shall be mine.

Waller, from his mother's wealth and his own position in Parliament and at court, was likely to feel that he was conferring the favour by paying playful attention to Lady Dorothy. His courtship of 'Sacharissa', the name he gave to Lady Dorothy at eighteen, was publicized for ten

years in many beautifully neat and polished verses until in 1639, the
lady turned away to marry the Earl of Sunderland. The prettiness of
the verses which fluttered from Groombridge to Penshurst had become
famous; for example the lines on Sacharissa's girdle:

> Give me but what this ribband bound,
> Take all the rest the sun goes round

or the song beginning:

> Go, lovely Rose,
> Tell her that wastes her time and me,
> That now she knows
> When I resemble her to thee
> How sweet and fair she seems to be.

The literary courtship was acknowledged at Penshurst Place; one of the
avenues in the park is still called 'Sacharissa's Walk'; but it has often
been questioned whether there was anything more to the affair than a
wish of Waller's to be remembered through Sacharissa as Petrarch
through Laura. In his Life of Waller Johnson mentions that the poet,
after Sacharissa's marriage, promptly found another lady who provided
him with five sons and eight daughters; and when he met Sacharissa in
her old age and she smilingly asked him when he would again write such
verses for her, the wit in his reply is not particularly pleasing. 'When
you are as young, Madam,' said Waller, 'and as handsome, as you were
then.'

Tunbridge Wells was the birthplace of the Fowler brothers, who
produced *The King's English*, *Modern English Usage*, and other notable
concise dictionaries. Charles Doughty (who, though born in Suffolk,
retired to Tunbridge Wells after years of travelling in Arabia) and
Arthur Waley, who was born here, were both poets who preferred to
create some of their own usages of language, rather than always to follow
usages as codified. The mild chalybeate waters of the springs at Tunbridge Wells caused the town to be regarded, from the Restoration onwards, as a leading inland health resort, and if it could not quite rival
Bath, it asserted itself as eminently a watering-place for the serious-
minded. Pages of Macaulay, Thackeray and Meredith, among others,
remind us of the vogue for Tunbridge Wells. The Rev. George Austen,
before the marriage which produced his daughter Jane, had been a master
at Tonbridge School (four miles to the north of Tunbridge Wells), and
when his literary family was growing up in Hampshire and the young
things chatted of Bath, he may have put in a word about the intellectual
advantages of Tunbridge Wells. Thackeray, who was a schoolboy at
Charterhouse in London from 1822-8, spent some of the school

L.B.—E

holidays in Tunbridge Wells at Belleville, a house on the common, and in the summer of 1860 returned to stay in the London Road (now called Thackeray House) and to write and illustrate his essay on 'Tunbridge Toys' in *Roundabout Papers*. Tennyson brought his mother to Tunbridge Wells as a health resort for the year between their stay in Epping Forest and the later and, for them, happier move to Maidstone.

In the ambience of Tunbridge Wells, three miles west of Groombridge, one recalls *The House at Pooh Corner* – for the house at Hartfield, called Gill's Lap, was where Alan Alexander Milne lived and created the characters and verses which (with E. H. Shephard's illustrations) have delighted both children and their parents since the 1920s. Still moving east from Tunbridge Wells, though, one passes Matfield, where Siegfried Sassoon described, in *The Weald of Youth*, what life was like before the 1914–18 war. Sassoon was born at nearby Brenchley. Farther east, after passing through Goudhurst, one notes how literary interests brought about a remarkable renewal of life at Sissinghurst Castle.

Sissinghurst village is in a part of Kent which has attracted various discriminating individuals: Doughty, for instance, moved on from his first retirement and the writing of *Arabia Deserta* at Tunbridge Wells, to spend the rest of his life at Sissinghurst. Doughty died in 1926; at that time Sissinghurst Castle was as forlornly in disrepair as some of the deserted crusaders' castles that Doughty had seen in the East. Sissinghurst Castle may have functioned as a fortress in Norman and medieval times; in the Elizabethan period when building was the way, as Francis Bacon wrote, whereby 'men sought to cure mortality by fame', an ancestor of Victoria Sackville-West purchased the site and he and his sons demolished and rebuilt in lavish fashion. A tall, slender, free-standing tower and a separate Priest's House were features of the Elizabethan establishment; then, in the seventeenth century, the fortunes of that family failed and the house, as Anne Scott-James says in her book *Sissinghurst: The Making of a Garden*, 'met sad vicissitudes'. In the eighteenth century 'it was for a time a disgusting prison for the incarceration of French seamen captured in the Seven Years War' – and Gibbon, as an officer in the militia, was posted for a short time to the keeping guard at Sissinghurst (and hated it). What was left of the buildings and site was on the market as derelict when it came to the attention of Victoria Sackville-West and her husband Harold Nicolson in 1930.

The story now links with Knole, for the daughter of the man who purchased Sissinghurst in Tudor times married the Sir Thomas Sackville to whom Queen Elizabeth, in 1586, presented Knole as a cousinly gift. 'Thus Knole and Sissinghurst had been connected for centuries' – yet though Knole kept and increased its position among the greatest of country houses, Sissinghurst became a wreck. The Nicolsons

in 1930 were themselves in a mood to attempt what Anne Scott-James
calls 'an act of gambler's madness'. Harold Nicolson had by then resigned
from the Foreign Office; life at Sevenoaks Weald for 'Harold and Vita',
as Anne Scott-James calls them, made them feel evicted from Knole
Park and yet rubbed by proximity. The act of madness was to risk whatever they might earn by writings, he as historian, biographer, journalist
and she as poet and novelist, by purchasing Sissinghurst Castle and by
every effort creating there so wonderful a garden as that Sleeping Beauty
of a site deserved. 'Vita's love of Sissinghurst had from the beginning the
intensity of a religion', says Anne Scott-James. As the 'two imaginative
people' climbed the tower at Sissinghurst on their first evening 'the
tower sprang like a bewitched and rosy fountain towards the sky . . .
they climbed the 76 steps of the tower and stood on the leaden flat,
leaning their elbows on the parapet, and looking out in silence over the
fields, the woods, the hop-gardens, and the lake down in the hollow from
which a faint mist was rising'. From then on there was the continuing
satisfaction of re-creating the superb gardens.

Sissinghurst is now cared for by the National Trust. It is pleasant to
remember that Richard Church, whose poems (of which there was a
collected edition in 1948) had won a faithful audience which was much
enlarged by his autobiography *Over the Bridge*, was able to spend his
last years (before his death in 1972) at Sissinghurst. It would be hard to
think of a happier reward for a poet of Church's sensitivity than to live
in the Elizabethan Priest's House (with modernized conveniences) and
with the surrounding gardens.

*   *   *

Eastward from Sissinghurst and south of Ashford there are many
associations with Joseph Conrad, who lived in Orlestone, at Capel House,
from 1910–19. It was fortunate that *Chance*, the novel which brought to
Conrad his first widely popular success, was ready for publication in
1914; his reputation as novelist was securely established before interruptions of wartime. He was first recognized in England some years
earlier when Ford Madox Ford (or Ford Madox Hueffer as his name
was then) serialized *The Nigger of the Narcissus* in the *New Review* in
1897. This encouragement prompted Conrad to leave the sea and live
where Ford lived, at Pent Farm, Aldington, off the main roads between
Ashford and Hythe. There, in the cottage which he rented from Ford
between 1898 and 1909, Conrad worked at *Lord Jim*, *Nostromo*, *The
Mirror of the Sea* and *The Secret Agent*. In this same neighbourhood
and at the same time H. G. Wells was working busily at his own novels.
In 1900 Wells was 'coming on' at a great rate; he built Spade House at

Sandgate, between Hythe and Folkestone, and there, from 1900 until 1911, his work noticeably developed. Inland, at Aldington and Orlestone, Conrad's writings were widening – *The Mirror of the Sea* was the last of his books to be dominated by seafaring. On the coast at Sandgate Wells's scope also widened. He had made his name in the 1890s with the famous scientific romances *The Time Machine* (1895), *The Invisible Man* (1897) and *The War of the Worlds* (1898). This vein was not neglected in the first years at Sandgate, where among other works Wells produced *The First Men in the Moon* (1901) and *The Food of the Gods* (1904), but he displayed (with the 'bounce' that V. S. Pritchett talks of) an enlarged and lively attentiveness to critical moments in human life in England in *Kipps* (1905), *Tono-Bungay* and *Ann Veronica* (both in 1909) and *The History of Mr Polly* (1910).

This part of Kent seemed greatly to stimulate Wells and Conrad, yet I fail to find outstanding literary enterprise associated with Folkestone itself. A well-remembered man of letters of our time, A. E. Coppard (1878–1951), was born here. Several writers came to Folkestone to end their days: C. S. Calverley, the clever parodist known best for his *Verses and Translations*, died here in 1884, and so did George Grossmith in 1912, twenty years after he and his brother had collaborated in writing *The Diary of a Nobody*. Folkestone enters mostly into literary annals as a port for cross-Channel services, especially after the arrival of the Railway Age. Before the Railway Age Dover far outdid Folkestone for departure or arrival of persons of fashion. From Dover Byron's Napoleonic carriage departed; such panache was out of place at Folkestone. When, within a month of Byron's departure, the incomparable 'Beau' Brummell found himself dining alone at Watier's, making a last brief appearance at the opera, and then being driven by night to make his unseen getaway, that departure, though unseen, had to be from Dover. It is noticeable that in the 1830s when Edward Lear was sent off to Rome for his health (he had by then been taken up by his great patron Lord Stanley and was therefore of the household of the Earls of Derby) the Stanley family arranged his trip from Knowsley along the length of Watling Street, to leave from Dover. In the 1840s and '50s, when travelling with Franklin Lushington who was of ambassadorial rank, Lear's port continued to be Dover; but then, when journeying more economically and paying for himself, he began to use the railway line to Folkestone. It was on the Channel steamer from Folkestone that Edward Lear met Thackeray – 'The great man was very amiable and gave me No. 1 of his new magazine, *The Cornhill*'. A year later, after the death of the older sister Ann who had always been more of a mother to Lear than his actual mother, his Diary recorded an episode which is thus picked out in the biography by Vivien Noakes:

The Folkestone train rocked and swayed and jumbled along, and two small children travelling with their nurse were frightened and unhappy. So Lear lifted them onto his knee '& told them my long name & all kinds of nonsense till they forgot the shaking bother. I NEVER saw 2 SWEETER & more intellgent children than those 2: I LONGED to keep them both' wrote the lonely man.

Four years after that, 'the shaking bother' of the Folkestone railway line is recalled by a railway disaster in 1865 at Staplehurst, midway between Ashford and Tonbridge, in which both Dickens and Ellen Ternan were involved, and which cost many lives. Dickens had taken Ellen for a holiday to France; her mother went with them; the trio were accustomed to the intimate private life begun eight years before and kept up steadily, if under cover, ever since. The steadiness of Dickens's love for Ellen Ternan, and his dependence upon her, was concealed from the world in general by elaborate subterfuge, but was not wholly clandestine so far as her mother or his family were concerned. After the separation from Mrs Dickens, gradually, and from the mid-1860s frequently, Ellen, who was of an age with Dickens's daughters, was a house-guest at Gad's Hill. Angus Wilson comments that 'the family sent for her as Dickens lay dying, although she arrived too late to see him conscious', and adds that Dickens's sister-in-law Georgina and his daughter Mamie continued to see Ellen after Dickens's death. Yet however much about the relationship between Dickens and Ellen might be known to a few, it was not to the interest of any of those few to have it a matter of public and probably malicious gossip.

To Dickens and Ellen the train-wreck at Staplehurst dealt a double shock: not only were they trapped among others who were mangled and dying, but anything to do with Dickens was news, and if newsmen pictured Ellen and him together! – the way the lovers coped with that additional alarm shows quick thinking. There were indeed many news reports of Dickens's involvement in the disaster, but they stressed his conspicuous part in giving aid to many of the injured. No one has detected in the news reports any suggestion that the famous man was returning from France with his young actress-friend; the names were not linked; nothing apparently special was noted in the agitation each felt for the other. But the shock and turmoil of Dickens's feelings about the accident had after-effects. Angus Wilson mentions that one of the few letters preserved in which Dickens refers to Ellen was written to his servant, John Thompson, within the days soon after: 'Take Miss Ellen tomorrow morning, a little basket of fresh fruit, a jar of clotted cream from Tucker's, and a chicken, a pair of pigeons, or some nice little bird. Also on Wednesday morning, and on Friday morning, take her some other things of the same sort – making a little variety each day.' The Staplehurst episode gave opportunity for this agreeable cossetting, and it came also to have lasting significance. Travelling and Ellen were more and more to be thought of together – and in these last years Dickens went in for more and more travelling. When planning his American tour in 1867 Dickens hoped to have Ellen's companionship; they might not set sail together, but Dickens arranged a code with his agent to facilitate her arrival in New York. Only after his own arrival in America was he compelled to cancel his plan of her joining him. It wouldn't do. He couldn't lead a natural life with – or without – her, anywhere. The way Dickens was fretted in his last years, without this factor being fully recognized, was noticeable to many, among them George Eliot. Dickens lunched at her house in the spring of 1870. 'I thought him looking dreadfully shattered then', she recalled, and then traced the case back to Staplehurst. 'It is probable that he never recovered from the effect of the terrible railway accident.' Others shared that perception even without knowing anything about Dickens and Ellen Ternan.

6. EAST AND WEST SUSSEX

At Folkestone I turn to follow the coast road through Hythe and westward all the way to Portsmouth and the Isle of Wight. This picks up with a circuit often pursued in the eighteenth century. Thomas Gray, for instance, wrote to a younger Cambridge colleague to say that he had spent part of the summer of 1766 exploring the easternmost ports of Kent, and then westward. He stayed in turn at Margate, Ramsgate, Sandwich, 'and Deal, and Dover, and Folkestone, and Hythe, all along the coast, very delightful'. He reports those travels in a letter which those who are fond of Gray like to quote for the following passage: Gray wrote, he said, 'to inform you that I had discovered a thing very little known, which is, that in one's whole life one never can have any more than a single mother. . . . I never discovered this (with full evidence and conviction, I mean) till it was too late'. Gray looked back with pleasure at having been able to show his mother the *Elegy* in print, three years before she died. Another lonely bachelor, Edward Lear, had little of that closeness to his mother that Gray extolled. Edward, as previously mentioned, was the twentieth of twenty-one children; by his time the mother had small interest in the new arrivals, and his older sister Ann, aged twenty-two, was the one who took charge of the boy. Lear's real mother, when a widow after 1833, went with one surviving daughter to live at Dover, but there is no mention of Edward ever seeing her there. Gray's discovery is more true for one of few children than for a twentieth.

Thomas Gray's circuit of the Kentish coast took in successively three of the original Cinque Ports; he stayed at Sandwich, Dover, Hythe; the remaining two, as originally reconstituted and given peculiar jurisdiction by William the Conqueror, were New Romney and Hastings. The circuit of ports that Gray made by land was frequently made by nineteenth-century men of letters by sea – FitzGerald for instance knew all the Channel ports, and Wilkie Collins, though not so much of a working yachtsman, knew the ports of the Strait of Dover. Yet of writers' voyages round the south coast, the one most worth recalling is that of Leigh Hunt, his ailing wife, their six children and the nanny-goat which had been presented to him by a Hampstead neighbour as a parting present. Leigh Hunt, be it remembered, was the model for Dickens's portrait of Harold Skimpole in *Bleak House*, the innocent prattler, inveterate sponger, who with 'his pretty turn of cynical phrase, never tires of explaining artlessly how he thinks only of himself'. *Bleak House* was being written in 1852–3, by which time Leigh Hunt was approaching seventy, and had published his *Autobiography* and *Table-Talk*. The action of *Bleak House*, however, is set some decades before the middle of the century, and Dickens seems in the caricature to have been imagining Hunt at the period when Charles Lamb (despite his predilection for all Bluecoats) was becoming cool to Hunt, and Keats had become disgusted with him. Dickens's Skimpole squares well enough with the Hunt of 1821 whom Peter Quennell (in *Byron in Italy*) describes as 'the innocent voluptuary' and 'inveterate optimist' who was at that time inviting his friend Shelley (then neighbouring with Byron at Pisa) once again to bail him out of debt. Hunt's sea-voyage round the Kentish coast was a result.

In 1821, when Hunt, as many times before, applied for help, Shelley was himself short of money. Byron's finances had much improved while he was in Italy, and the scheme that Shelley at once put forward was that Byron should advance the cash for Hunt to join them in Italy and they would all combine to continue the production of Hunt's periodical, the *Examiner*, from there. What Hunt delayed revealing was that he had already disposed of the *Examiner*, along with other assets. He was really penniless, and the scheme was that the family should pack up all such belongings as they could ('my books in particular', Leigh Hunt records in his *Autobiography*) and be wafted to the apartment in the Palazzo Lanfranchi which Shelley thought Byron could provide, along with living expenses, indefinitely. The long journey to Italy overland, with the six children and impedimenta, was too formidable for Hunt's wife Marianne (at any sudden exertion she was apt, as Hunt phrased it, to 'expectorate blood'); but Shelley advised that the exodus from London be made by sea. 'Put your music and your books on board a vessel', wrote Shelley, 'and you will have no more trouble.' With roseate hopes that the sea-voyage, even in winter, might benefit Marianne, Hunt embarked the family at the port of London in a small brig, 'a good tight sea-boat, nothing more', on 15 November 1821. The weather was bad with a strong head-wind, and in the river there was a collision, the damage not too serious, yet the fright sufficient to cause Marianne to cough blood. It was on the 19th that 'we passed the Nore, and proceeded the Channel amidst rains and squalls'.

'Rather less apparent', says Peter Quennell, 'now seemed the advantages of a winter sea-voyage.' The cabin, in which Leigh Hunt and Marianne were obliged to sleep upon the floor, while their half-dozen children were packed tight in bunks above, was small and wet as well as atrociously overcrowded. In the Downs the gales were so severe that the brig could make no progress, and by the afternoon of the 21st the captain thought it best to run for Ramsgate harbour; that proved to be lucky, for the rudder was in need of refitting. After three weeks' delay at Ramsgate sail was set at last on 11 December 'in company with nearly a hundred vessels, the white sails of which, as they shifted and presented themselves in different quarters', exhibited 'a kind of noble minuet'.

Yet the fair weather lasted no more than a day, and there then ensued 'such a continuity and vehemence of bad weather as rendered the winter of 1821 memorable in the shipping annals. It strewed the whole of the north-western coast of Europe with wrecks.' For ten successive nights and days the brig laboured heavily onward in the Channel or at times was buffeted back, seas breaking over her, the pump manned constantly. 'The afternoon of the 17th brought us the gale that lasted fifty-six hours', after which the vessel 'looked like a washhouse in a fit'. 'In nothing else that he ever wrote', Quennell exclaims, '(save perhaps in three deservedly famous sonnets) did Hunt's literary virtues find better employment than in his account of their misery. Puking children, danger and cold and dark' – when the family was battened in their coffin-space below deck – 'could not dull his dispassionate appreciation of all that he daily felt and suffered.' Hunt was indeed the only one of his party not prostrate with seasickness; he could clamber from the cabin to the deck, and having noticed that a part of the bulwark had been stove in and that 'we had long ceased to have a duck alive', he saw that 'our poor goat had contrived to find itself a corner in the long-boat, and lay frightened and shivering under a piece of canvas'. The goat, 'a present from a kind friend, anxious that we should breakfast as at home', should at least share whatever cover they had, and he took it down into the cabin, but there, 'not having a berth to give it, it passed a sorry time, tied up and slipping about the floor'. At night the goat was not the easiest of companions for Marianne, attempting to sleep on the same cabin-floor, but by 20 December she appears to have been in a coma, and Hunt in that night-time kept the goat quiet by routing in their food cupboard for all the biscuit he could find, which the animal managed to munch from his hand 'with equal appetite and comfort'.

On 22 December the captain, having failed in several previous efforts to find shelter, managed to put the brig into Dartmouth harbour, and Leigh Hunt, Marianne, children (and, I suppose, nanny-goat) struggled ashore. In six exhausting weeks their first voyage had brought them only as far as Devonshire; there they waited for the further funds from Italy (which in due course were supplied by Shelley from Byron's pocket) for their second voyage, five months later. This voyage in summer was relatively pleasant except for Marianne's continuing ill-health. By the end of June the Hunts were being greeted in Italy first by 'the affable but languid Byron' and then by Shelley, 'shrill, rumpled, enthusiastic, kind as ever'. Shelley saw them installed in the Palazzo and called in a physician to attend to Marianne. The day that Shelley had with the Hunts at Pisa gave them their only sight of him alive, for Shelley returned to Leghorn and there on 8 July the accident occurred in which he and two companions were drowned.

*   *   *

The 'English' Channel, at least ever since the 'Norman Yoke' came into being, has been as much a part of the local background of English literature as any part of England's dry land; I felt no need to apologize for selecting Leigh Hunt's voyage as a token of the many sea adventures to be recalled when looking at the Channel from the white cliffs of Kent. The coastal road westward from Folkestone and Hythe soon leaves the cliffs behind as it passes through Dymchurch and follows the shoreline of St Mary's Bay. All readers of Kipling's *Puck of Pook's Hill* remember Dymchurch for 'The Dymchurch Flit' whereby the Marsh-bred Widow Whitgift with two sons (not wage-earning sons, for the one was born blind and the other had been struck dumb) had enabled the multitude of 'Pharisees' to escape from cruel Old England by giving the sons her 'Leave and Good-will' to ferry them away. When discussing the Rev. Mr Barham I mentioned his obsession with the darker legends of Romney Marsh inland from Dymchurch; the lighter legends that developed there especially pleased Kipling, as also Edith Nesbit, who came here for her last years and was buried in 1924 at the church of St Mary-in-the-Marsh. Farther inland, past the Isle of Oxney and three miles west of Tenterden, is Maytham Hall, which Frances Hodgson Burnett regarded as her English home from 1898 to 1907. Her *Little Lord Fauntleroy* had been a prodigious bestseller for decades after its appearance in 1886; the book which today does more to keep Mrs Hodgson Burnett's name alive is *The Secret Garden*. This later story, begun in

1909 when the author was back in America towards the end of her event-
ful career, and planning the gardens for her new Italianate villa at
Plandome, Long Island, was apparently prompted by the 'regretful
feeling' when she heard, true or not, that new owners were altering her
favourite walled garden at Maytham Hall.

Turning from Maytham towards the coast brings me to Rye, or as
Henry James said, to Rye and Winchelsea, for he was prepared to maintain that the two old towns 'form together a very curious small corner'.
Together in ancient times they had been added with equal privileges to
the Cinque Ports, making the five into seven; though as if in indigna-
tion the sea deliberately then withdrew from the pair of them. Winchelsea
and Rye became 'the two small ghosts of the Cinque Ports family, the
pair of blighted hill-towns that were once sea-towns and that now draw
out their days in the dim after-sense of a mere indulged and encouraged
picturesqueness'. One of the most delightful of Henry James's essays
in his book of *English Hours* is his piece on 'Winchelsea, Rye, and *Denis
Duval*' – *Denis Duval* was the title of the last of Thackeray's novels,
which that practised novelist had planned and of which he had written
as much as two hundred and fifty pages when death stopped him. The
large fragment of *Denis Duval*, studied by Henry James with devotion
and at leisure, fascinates, so far as it goes, with the narrator's 'wondrous
boy-life at Winchelsea and Rye'. The choice of this corner of Sussex
suggested to James that the drama was to have been concerned with the
troubles faced by a French Huguenot family in adjusting to England as
one of the many of the stranger races which struggled to take root in 'the
two small ghosts' of former sea-towns. No overt clue indicates the
development Thackeray had in mind for *Denis Duval* – 'Thackeray
carried the mystery to his grave' – but James goes on to invite his ghost
to come into the garden of his own much-loved Lamb House in West
Street, Rye. There, James knows, 'you may see things'; you may 'keep
remembering and losing there the particular passages of some far-away
foolish fiction'; there

best of all on the open, sunny terrace of a dear little old garden – a garden
brown-walled, red-walled, rose-covered on its other sides, divided by the
width of a quiet street of grass-grown cobbles from the house of its master,
and possessed of a little old glass-fronted, panelled pavilion which I hold to
be the special spot in the world where Thackeray might most fitly have
figured out his story. There is not much room in the pavilion, but there is
room for the hard-pressed table and the tilted chair – there is room for a
novelist and his friends.

At Lamb House, Rye, which James bought in 1899 after leasing it
for two years, *The Awkward Age* was written, and then, among the

successors that he produced with remarkable speed, were *The Wings of the Dove* (1902), *The Ambassadors* (1903) and *The Golden Bowl* (1904). A kindly act of the James family was the presentation, in 1950, of Lamb House to the National Trust. The garden-pavilion (mentioned by Henry James above) was destroyed by an enemy bomb in 1940, but the house, and particularly the rooms in which James worked for the eighteen autumns and winters of his tenure, put the pilgrim in mind not only of the novelist but of the many visitors who there enjoyed his friendliness. Among James's guests at Lamb House as listed by the Trust were Max Beerbohm, Belloc, Chesterton, Conrad, Ford Madox Ford, Gosse, Kipling, H. G. Wells and – last on the list only for alphabetical reason – Edith Wharton, who was a frequent visitor. James's phrase, 'room for a novelist and his friends', was well applied to Lamb House. 'All the good things that I hoped of the place', he wrote, 'have, in fact, properly blossomed and flourished.'

Rye's other literary notabilities – apart from the fictional family of *Denis Duval* about whom Henry James repeats with all emphasis: 'I should, in truth, have liked to lock up Thackeray in our little pavilion of inspiration, the gazebo at Rye, not letting him out till he should quite have satisfied us' – range from John Fletcher the dramatist, 'the Fletcher of Beaumont', to Radclyffe Hall, who wrote *The Well of Loneliness* in 1928. After James's death in 1916 Lamb House itself was for a number of years lived in by E. F. Benson, who made it the setting for his stories of 'Miss Mapp', and his brother, the Cambridge scholar A. C. Benson, also from time to time lived there. A young fellow-American who was making himself noticeable in Rye when Henry James was first living there, and who as a person was not much liked by James, was Stephen Crane, who had written *The Red Badge of Courage* in 1895. I have it only on hearsay that James avoided Stephen Crane; it is certainly more than likely that Crane, well aware that consumption doomed him to an early death, was unable to be other than discordant in the two little Sussex towns which were for James so full of lurking hints and secret memories. Crane had not been at ease in New York where at the age of twenty-two he issued, in 1893, his first novel, *Maggie: A Girl of the Streets*. The objective, reportorial 'realism' of that novel had not been well received. *The Red Badge of Courage*, published two years later, became established as a classic only after Crane's death; during his lifetime the taste for sentimental historical fiction delayed the popularity afterwards given to this novel of the American Civil War. Nor could he count on *The Open Boat and Other Stories*, due to be published in book form in 1898, to provide substantial royalties. In his then state of weak health and weak finances it seems to have been a crazy escape effort, not only to have crossed the Atlantic but in 1899 to have rented the small country mansion of Brede Place in the depths of Sussex countryside, four miles west of Winchelsea.

W. E. Henley, by then nearing the end of his own life, had warmly welcomed young Stephen Crane, and so too had Joseph Conrad. Twenty years later Conrad wrote with friendly memory of the 'young man of medium stature and slender build, with very steady, penetrating blue eyes, the eyes of a being who not only sees visions but can brood over them to some purpose.' Conrad went on to say: 'My wife and I like best to remember him riding to meet us at the gate of the Park at Brede. Born master of his sincere impressions, he was also a born horseman.' The Conrads brought their two-year-old son to visit the American, and Crane gave the boy his first dog. The Conrads' visits were made from Hythe in Kent, but there were not many nearer neighbours who warmed to Crane so readily.

Winchelsea remained cool to his way of attracting attention. A sentence of his from *The Open Boat* reflects his reaction: 'When it occurs to a man that nature does not regard him as important . . . he at first wishes to throw bricks at the temple, and he hates deeply the fact that there are no bricks and no temples.' Crane was ready to try to throw Bohemian bricks 'at the temple', but bricks without straw made little impression. Brede Place was not a large mansion, yet the hours of work he could manage in the small study over the porch could not cover ordinary expenses, let alone 'throwing parties'. His parties gained some local attention, but presently the only way of escape from bankruptcy proceedings was for the sick man to be hurried to the Continent. There the Cranes had reached Heidelberg when Stephen, aged only twenty-eight, could go no farther. He died on 5 June 1900. Some years after, *The Red Badge of Courage* gained the respect given by few in Crane's lifetime but retained since.

Before Henry James chose to settle in Rye, he inspected 'Hastings and St Leonards, with their long warm sea-front and their multitude of small, cheap comforts and conveniences'. He had heard Hastings described as a 'dull Brighton' and this description had 'rather quickened than quenched' his interest. Hastings, he concluded, was an appropriate place for retirement for a quiet old gentleman 'of modest income and nice habits'. Aleister Crowley, although his reputation as practitioner of black magic may have removed him from the pattern of old gentlemen that James had in mind, adopted James's advice, sought seclusion for his last years at Hastings, and died in a boarding-house here in 1947. St Leonards attracted Edward Lear in 1859; he had rooms facing the sea. The novelist Mary Webb died at St Leonards; and here the novelist Sheila Kaye-Smith was born, though much of her life was lived the few miles inland at Brede, and it is with the farming country of the River

Brede valley (and also with Romney Marsh) that one associates the down-to-earth realities of *Joanna Godden* and Sheila Kaye-Smith's other novels. The road inland from St Leonards westward of Brede passes the memorable Battle Hill and Battle, and by turning left at Hurst Green, one reaches Burwash where, at Bateman's (half a mile south of Burwash), Rudyard Kipling lived from 1902 until his death in 1936. The house and gardens of Bateman's are National Trust property; the interior of the house is much as Kipling left it, and his study is a particular focus of interest.

When Kipling and his wife were house-hunting in 1902, the very first sight of Bateman's caused him to exclaim: 'That's her! The Only She!' Inspection of each room then confirmed their satisfaction. One of the abiding pleasures to Kipling of 'The Only She' was that 'the "new" end of her was three hundred years old'. The date on the porch, 1634, was but one of the triggers for Kipling's historical imagination. From the windows of the house a hill was visible; more than just any old hill – demonstrably 'one of my oldest hills in Old England'. Whose was the 'my'? Who 'owned' that hill that the windows of Bateman's looked on? 'Pook's Hill – Puck's Hill – Puck's Hill – Pook's Hill! It's as plain as the nose on my face.' That is how, for Kipling Puck

pointed to the bare, fern-covered slope of Pook's Hill that runs up from the far side of the mill-stream to a dark wood. Beyond that wood the ground rises and rises for five hundred feet, till at last you climb out on the bare top of Beacon Hill, to look over the Pevensey Levels and the Channel and half the naked South Downs.

'By Oak, Ash, and Thorn!' he cried, still laughing. 'If this had happened a few hundred years ago you'd have had all the People of the Hills out like bees in June!'

Certain it is that Kipling 'had a way with him' to bring alive people of all kinds in the episodes of *Puck of Pook's Hill* and *Rewards and Fairies*. When he settled in Sussex, having (as T. S. Eliot said) 'both the humility to subdue himself to his surroundings, and the freshness of the vision of a stranger', Kipling's kind of historical imagination caused him to form into one unit a poem and a story – or a story and two poems – 'combining', Eliot noted, 'to make a form which no-one has used in the same way and in which no-one is ever likely to excel him'. When Tennyson was writing *The Princess* at Maidstone and finding that the lyrics in the early editions gave special pleasure, he skilfully contrived to sprinkle an extra half-dozen lyrics into the third edition; but in *Puck of Pook's Hill* and *Rewards and Fairies* the verses are not an added exhibition of virtuosity – the twins of prose and verse seem to have been there in the same act of creation. This characteristic of Kipling's fascinated Eliot. He saw Kipling as 'completely ambidexterous, that is to say completely able to express himself in verse or prose: but his necessity for often expressing the same thing in a story and in a poem is a much deeper necessity than that merely to exhibit skill. I know of no writer of such great gifts for whom poetry seems to have been more purely an instrument.' Of the verses in these two books I am glad to quote Eliot's appreciation:

There is great variety, and there are some very remarkable innovations indeed, as in *The Way Through The Woods* and in *The Harp Song of the Dane Women* –

> What is a woman that you forsake her,
> And the hearth-fire and the home-acre,
> To go with the old grey Widow-maker?

and in the very fine *Runes on Weland's Sword*.

Sometimes an individual poem has been torn off by readers and separated from the unit within which it was created. Not all who remember Kipling's 'If –' recall its origin in *Rewards and Fairies*.

Five miles west of Burwash one may join the road from Tunbridge Wells which runs due south across the Pevensey Levels that Kipling was fond of mentioning, to reach the coast at Eastbourne. I mentioned Charles Darwin as living in the midst of the North Downs; sheltered under the eastern end of the South Downs, at Eastbourne, Darwin's friend and expositor, Thomas Henry Huxley, lived for his last years. Lewis Carroll in his later years often stayed at No. 7 Lushington Road, Eastbourne. Sherlock Holmes's first experiments with bee-keeping were, I conjectured, on the western side of Beachy Head (perhaps above Birling Gap?); it is to Lewes, whose police had jurisdiction in the Sherlock Holmes story of 'The Lion's Mane', that a literary pilgrim's steps now tend.

The crowd of associations clustering round Lewes has been greatly swollen in recent years by the number of visitors to the Glyndebourne Music Festival; yet apart from mere visitors to the ancient town of Lewes, its inhabitants have included many men of letters from the seventeenth century onwards. Thomas Browne lived here before the move to Norwich and his knighthood there. Southover Grange in Lewes was the boyhood home where John Evelyn lived on and off with his grandparents from 1625 and a dozen years or so after – from the age of five and throughout his schooldays until at seventeen he went on to the Middle Temple, and Oxford, friendship with Charles I and companionship with Edmund Waller. The uninhibited spontaneity of the schoolboy Evelyn, allowed a loose rein by his grandparents, has more appeal for me than his later character. As a schoolboy Evelyn was 'extremely remiss' at his studies, but he had a hand in other activities. Largely at his grandfather's expense, a church (St Michael's) was being built at the adjacent 'suburb' of South Malling; the boy Evelyn took part in the building – 'I laid one of the first stones', was his proprietary feeling. When Evelyn was sixteen in 1636 it was in 'his' church of St Michael's that John Harvard, then a twenty-nine-year-old M.A. of Cambridge, was married to the daughter of a Sussex clergyman. The year after, Harvard and his wife settled in Charlestown, Massachusetts, and the year after that John Harvard died, bequeathing his books and half his estate (a sum of £799 17s 2d) to the college which thereafter bore his name.

In 1772, while stationed as an Exciseman at Lewes and living at Bull House near the West Gate, Tom Paine drew up a statement of the Excisemen's grievances which, as a piece of writing, excited the attention of Benjamin Franklin. When the agitation of the Excisemen failed in 1774 and Paine, parting from his wife, left Lewes for America, his career as sharp provoker of revolutions, first in America and then in France, began on a wider scale. In the twentieth century, it was before the 1914–18 war that E. V. Lucas lived at Kingston Manor, west of the River Ouse; and at Firle, east of the river, Clive Bell attracted Virginia and Leonard Woolf to this part of Sussex. After their marriage and during the 1914–18 war the Woolfs lived near Lewes, and after that war moved into Monks House, Rodmell, for the rest of their lives. During the Second World War, in a recurrence of the mental illness from which she had previously suffered, Virginia Woolf drowned herself in the river at Rodmell. Her ashes are buried in the garden of Monks House.

On the coast south-west of Rodmell is Rottingdean, where the Kiplings lived before the move to Bateman's. It was when living at Rottingdean in North End House (the home of Kipling's uncle, Sir Edward Burne-Jones) that in 1897 Kipling wrote 'Recessional'. Discussion of the South African war was presumably the trigger for the poem, yet as Eliot remarks about 'Recessional', it 'is one of the poems in which something breaks through from a deeper level than that of the mind of the conscious observer of political and social affairs – something which has the true prophetic inspiration. Kipling might have been one of the most notable of hymn writers.' Burne-Jones died in 1898 and the Kiplings lodged awhile at The Elms at Rottingdean, opposite the church. Nearby in The Grange there is a 'Kipling Room', open to visitors. On this Sussex coast within twenty-five miles of each other – here at Rottingdean and twenty-five miles west at Felpham – inspiration prompted two of England's greatest hymns; 'Recessional' is one, and Blake's *Jerusalem* (as the lyric

'And did those feet in ancient time' is often called), written at Felpham,
is the other.

*   *   *

The western part of 'Sussex by the sea' – the actual coastline from
Brighton, Hove, Worthing to Bognor Regis – makes an impression of
one long seaside conurbation. At Felpham, once the village 'In England's
green and pleasant land', it is hard not to feel one is merely in a suburb
of Bognor Regis. Yet inland from the coast there are unspoiled sites
ready to remind the traveller, unexpectedly maybe, of poets. At Steyning,
a little way inland from Hove and Worthing, a plaque on the Chantry
House above the small green records the presence there of William
Butler Yeats. So much of Yeats's life was lived in England – more than
half, if measured by mere count of the calendar – that it is well to think
of Yeats in Sussex (though there were also Hammersmith, Bedford
Park, his years in Bloomsbury and his household at Oxford). It was in
East Sussex, at Coleman's Hatch, that Ezra Pound at several periods
from 1913 to 1916 invited Yeats to spend months at a time at Stone
Cottage. For Yeats, born in 1865, the younger Pound, Wyndham Lewis
and Eliot were '*les jeunes*'; he did not wholly catch on to what they were
trying to do, but Pound he liked as 'a learned companion and a pleasant
one'. In a preceding winter in Bloomsbury Ezra had spent countless
evenings reading aloud to Yeats when the older man's eyes were bad and
digestive disorders meant his living on a milk diet, and when Dorothy
Shakespear married Ezra she greatly helped to make Yeats's visits to
Stone Cottage recuperative. Though, after 1915, '*les jeunes*' became a
little tired of Yeats living 'as if nothing had occurred but Irish troubles',
the 'breathing' of the Irish poet, as he paced the downstairs room at
Stone Cottage, intoning, was hearkened to by Ezra. Often, later, Pound
quoted Yeats as saying of a poem 'I made it out of a mouthful of air'.
Visits to the Pounds in Sussex proved important also to Yeats in that
they kept him in touch with Dorothy Pound's 'cousin by marriage' who
in 1917 was to become Mrs Yeats. Ezra attended the pair to the Register
Office as witness. Twenty years after East Sussex contributed his happy
marriage, Yeats, on a visit from Ireland, was brought by Edmund Dulac
to West Sussex to see Edith Shackleton Heald and her sister at their
home, Chantry House at Steyning. Yeats was charmed with the Misses
Heald and they with him and thereafter, in the 1930s, when visiting
England Yeats stayed at Steyning with those friends working on his last
play and some of his last poems in what came to be called 'his room'
at Chantry House, with its window looking on the village street.

The direct road from London to Brighton divides West Sussex from

East Sussex psychologically, and that road is an instant reminder of all that is to be associated with the goings-on of England's Regency period. That period, dated formally from 1811 to 1820, in effect began when the Royal Pavilion at Brighton was built to the command of the then Prince of Wales in 1784. Before the days of the Royal Pavilion the efforts of the south-coast fishing port to become a health resort that might rival Bath are illustrated by Mrs Thrale's decision to take a house in Brighton's West Street for Mr Thrale's convalescence when his health was breaking up. Samuel Johnson was at that time one of the Thrale household, and the social life of Brighton was enlivened for him by the presence there of Fanny Burney; yet Thrale had lost heart after the untimely death of his son, and both before and after Thrale's own death the Brighton sojourns were never such as to put Johnson in much good humour.

When the Prince of Wales took residence in the Pavilion, however, Brighton suddenly threatened to outclass Bath in the world of fashion. By the time of the specific Regency period, when the Prince Regent's coach was in frequent rapid transit between London's Carlton House and the Pavilion, Brighton had really earned its sobriquet of 'London by the Sea'. 'Beau' Nash, described in the eighteenth century by Oliver Goldsmith as 'King of Bath', had caused more attention to be paid in Bath to fashionable dress and manners; but though Goldsmith, Gibbon and Sterne might wish to dress as Bath approved, a greater influence on writers was exerted in the Regency period, directly and indirectly, by the *arbiter elegantiarum* for the Prince of Wales, 'Beau' Brummell.

Brummell's influence on English literature is worth a moment's attention. Virginia Woolf dwelt on the Beau's direct influence on Byron; she pointed out that Byron, ten years younger than Brummell, 'always pronounced the name of Brummell with a mingled emotion of respect and jealousy', a respect whose echoes can be heard in parts of Byron's *Don Juan*. The 'certain exquisite propriety' which Byron remarked in Brummell's dress 'stamped his whole being, and made him appear cool, refined, and debonair among the gentlemen who talked only of sport, which Brummell detested, and smelt of the stable, which Brummell never visited'. In his immaculate toughness Brummell exhibited, and Byron and others popularized, a kind of hero who has often reappeared in various guises, in fiction. P. G. Wodehouse's creations of Bertie Wooster and Jeeves are perhaps descendants of the Prince Regent and Brummell. Indirectly, 'Beau' Brummell influenced literature through his superiority in the art of tying neckcloths to perfection and the Prince's reaction to this: with the Prince of Wales sitting by and watching, while he demonstrated that art, the 'Beau' exhibited something 'which it were too heavy handed to call a philosophy of life, but served the purpose'. The Prince's own attempts at rivalry in dress, and the admission that in such deportment he was outranked, is held to have reinforced his competitiveness in other appetites and interests where his own appreciations were superior. Whatever his faults, his meanest detractors admit that in all arts he had an eye for style, and in the realm of reading-matter his perceptions transcended those of his favourite Brummell. The outstanding and mature example is the famous way in which he fell upon each of Jane Austen's books as they appeared: when he was Regent he not only read each of her novels, but returned to read and re-read them, and his ever-deepening pleasure in them dictated that whenever he travelled all of Jane Austen's books should be at hand in any house where he had to stay.

A Regent who had such affection for Jane Austen cannot have been all bad, yet from the moment the Prince was made Regent in 1811 young left-wing poets vied with each other in total condemnation. Winthrop Mackworth Praed was scarcely out of school before he produced a pretended epitaph for the Prince Regent:

> A noble nasty course he ran!
> Superbly filthy and fastidious.
> He was the world's first gentleman
> And made the appellation hideous.

Shelley, in his first period of living on his own in London, studied a newspaper account of the exceedingly ostentatious banquet at Carlton House to celebrate initiation of the Regency, dashed off a doggerel address, had it printed as a broadsheet, and for a day or two attempted to thrust copies of it into the hands of those whose carriages approached the terrace of 'Nero's Hotel'. The 'shrill, rumpled' Shelley was pushed away but not imprisoned for this action; it was two years later that Leigh Hunt was gaoled for continuing to lampoon the Regent in the *Examiner*. Hunt's sentence immediately brought sympathetic visits to the gaol by diverse literary figures – Moore, Bentham, Lamb, and, notably, Byron. Hunt was not very ill-treated; he was able to have quarters in which his wife and children joined him; he was not stopped from continuing to edit the *Examiner*, and at least one of his ardent readers was headmaster of a school at Enfield who sent his son on weekly visits to the prison in Horsemonger Lane with baskets of vegetables and eggs for Hunt and his family. That son was Cowden Clarke, tutor to his slightly younger companion John Keats. Clarke's admiration for Leigh Hunt continued after Hunt's release and so did his companionship with Keats throughout the period when Keats was dressing the part of a poet with collar turned down and 'neck nearly bare à la Byron'. Naturally Clarke introduced the young poet to Hunt, and Hunt introduced him to Shelley, and Shelley then, although advising Keats that book publication might as yet be premature, appears to have introduced Keats's first collection of poems to his own publishers – and so *Poems* (1817) by John Keats was launched. The collection included the famous sonnet on Chapman's Homer which Swinburne was much later to call, in its context, a singular 'example of a stork among the cranes'.

After the Regency period Brighton proved convenient to Dickens as a work place. The writing of *Dombey and Son*, with its many echoes from his own childhood in the first part of Paul Dombey's story, was completed at Brighton in March 1848. A year later, in February 1849 and also at Brighton, Dickens began *David Copperfield*, written with what he described as 'a very complicated interweaving of truth and fiction'. Brighton turned Dickens's thoughts not only to his own upbringing but, in *Dombey and Son*, to an attack on wider aspects of life that had been seen in Brighton. Angus Wilson, in *The World of Charles Dickens*, very pertinently observes that 'in Mrs Skewton and Major Bagstock, Dickens produced the funniest, the most violent and the most frightening attack upon worldly values embodied in Regency manners, in the whole of his work' and analyses the contribution that Mr Toots and Cousin Feenix make to the novel. Thackeray's Brighton scenes in *The Newcomes* are less intense. Gradually in English fiction Brighton becomes a convenient setting in which (as in *The Moonstone*) the pace of a story may momentarily slow down; and then in some recent storytelling it becomes (as in Graham Greene's *Brighton Rock*, or Dick Francis's *Dead Cert*) a locale for crime.

7. POETS AT CHICHESTER AND THE ISLE OF WIGHT

Keats, in his explorations of the south coast, did not (so far as I know) visit Brighton. Like Henry James, he appears to have preferred Hastings; but his associations are more with Chichester and the Isle of Wight. Moving in that direction, Lancing claims it was by living there that Anna Sewell gained the love of horses which led her to write *Black Beauty*. Broadwater cemetery, now within the built-up area of Worthing, contains the graves of two great lovers of the English countryside: Richard Jefferies and W. H. Hudson. Jefferies had been born to English farmland; Hudson came to it after a life in South America, but took to England's country things so naturally that Conrad exclaimed to Ford: 'He [Hudson] writes as the grass grows. The Good God makes it be there . . .' Inland from Worthing is Storrington, where the monks at Storrington Priory did what they could for Francis Thompson who,

like Keats, was condemned to die of pulmonary tuberculosis, then and
later called 'consumption'. At Storrington Thompson wrote *The Hound
of Heaven*. Still farther inland is Petworth, where the paintings proved
to be an immense stimulus to (among many others) the young Edward
Lear when as a boy that 'lovable oddity' was put to stay with his cousins
at Lyminster, between Arundel and the coast.

From Arundel or Lyminster one quickly reaches Chichester. The
earliest of the eighteenth-century poets to emerge from Chichester was
the sweet-natured though unhappy William Collins – 'with whom I
once delighted to converse, and whom I yet remember with tenderness',
said Dr Johnson. Those who recall Collins's 'Ode to Evening':

> Now air is hushed, save where the weak-eyed bat
> With short, shrill shriek, flits by on leathern wing;
>   Or where the beetle winds
> His small but sullen horn . . .

will not quarrel with the epithet 'sweet-natured'. He was unhappy in
that the brain-disease which overtook him resulted in 'that depression
of mind', as Johnson put it, 'which enchains the faculties without des-
troying them'. Another poet born at Chichester, a boy of fourteen when
Collins died there, was William Hayley. If Collins suffered 'a deficiency
rather of vital than of intellectual powers', Hayley has ever been recorded
as the opposite. He was the inveterate, energetic, extreme type of romantic 'Man of Feeling', who, fairly well set up at Eartham House (about
five miles north-east of Chichester and four miles east of Goodwood)
called himself 'Hermit of Eartham', and did actually make Eartham
'a minor centre of the world of art and letters', as Lord David Cecil
describes in *The Stricken Deer*. Into Hayley's library at Eartham, under
a large picture of 'Sensibility watering the sensitive plant' by Romney,
the Hermit's hero-worship managed from time to time to gather, separately or together, Gibbon, Howard, Romney, Flaxman and many lesser
men and artists. Hayley's wife, 'brilliant and elegant, but too exquisitely
sensitive to stand the rough friction of common life', had retired from
the attempt to live with him – but no matter how 'trying' there was
something in Hayley's irrepressible goodwill which retained most of the
friendships that he went out of his way to seek.

To scrape acquaintance with Cowper, Hayley journeyed from
Chichester to Buckinghamshire; that friendship quickly burgeoned, and
when Mrs Unwin suffered a sudden recurrence of her illness Hayley
promptly prescribed a visit to Eartham as the best of cures. In August
1792 a phenomenal event therefore occurred: Cowper, the partially
paralysed Mary Unwin, their faithful cousin Johnson and three servants
uprooted themselves from the Midlands and made the journey of three

days and nights by coach to Eartham. Cowper's own stability, in his sixty-second year, was very insecure. The travellers crossed the Surrey hills at night; to his uneasy mind they were 'as tremendous as the Himalayas', and in the baleful moonlight 'a thrill of elemental terror ran through him'. At Eartham Hayley had restrained himself to a modest welcoming party, and laid himself out to cosset his invalid guests. Sadly, though, Mrs Unwin's health did not improve. After six weeks 'Johnny' conducted the return journey, and then made all his further efforts to find lodgings for the invalids in Norfolk.

Hayley's own private campaign to obtain a government pension for Cowper started early in 1792. With Hayley, says Lord David Cecil, 'to think was to act':

At first it seemed likely that his attempt would share the fate of most of his other schemes. For, as usual, the almost supernatural indefatigability with which he pursued his end was only equalled by the eccentricity of the means by which he sought to achieve it. At a critical period of English history he thrust himself upon eminent statesmen whom he hardly knew, harangued them for hours in a high-flown style, and when he could not see them bombarded them with letters both in prose and verse.

Thurlow, Pitt, Lord Spencer of the Admiralty (who presently singled out Nelson and sent him to win the battle of the Nile) – Hayley bombarded them all with bursts of lyrics and sonnets of increasing earnestness and (no matter how horrified Cowper would have been had he known of Hayley's methods) in the end, after two years of persistence, the pension was awarded. Hayley was himself in want of money and moved from Eartham House in 1800, after Cowper's death, to the smaller Turret House at Felpham. There he set to work on his *Life of Cowper*, and likewise continued his edition and commentary of Milton; it was to help with this that he invited Blake to come to Felpham and live in the cottage (which has survived) next to Turret House.

On arrival at the country cottage Blake exclaimed at the contrast from Lambeth; at Felpham 'the sweet air and the voices of winds, trees and birds, and the odours of the happy ground, make it a dwelling for immortals'. Blake then had his own visions to contend with; talk of Milton set him off on his own prophetic poem in which 'And did those feet in ancient time' appeared in the preface. Before long he found it troublesome to be 'pestered with Hayley's genteel ignorance and polite disapprobation', and in 1803 was about to return to London when there occurred the episode of the drunken soldier, who entered his cottage garden, was roughly turned out by Blake, and retaliated with a charge of seditious assault against Blake. The quarrel required Blake to stand trial at Chichester in January 1804. He was acquitted, but the delay prevented his return to London until that year.

Exactly fifteen years later, in January 1819, Keats was staying in Chichester. A plaque at No. 11 Eastgate Square (which was the home of the parents of Keats's friend Dilke) commemorates that Keats worked there on 'The Eve of St Agnes'. At the Mill House in Bedhampton (thirteen miles west of Chichester and part now of the Portsmouth–Havant conurbation) another plaque was set up in 1964 bearing the words: 'In this house in 1819 John Keats finished his poem "The Eve of St Agnes" and here in 1820 he spent his last night in England'. Dilke's sister lived in the Bedhampton house, and after four or five days at the Dilke house in Chichester Keats had walked to Bedhampton to stay with her. The story behind both plaques is that at Christmas-time 1818 Keats, in overwhelming preoccupation with Fanny Brawne at Hampstead, had totally neglected two other Christmas engagements. His friends the Dilkes, and Brown, had expected him in Hampshire over Christmas and on the January visit Keats was trying to make amends. One hears as yet of no open confession of the distracting love for Fanny Brawne, but if Dilke's sister (herself a married woman) was given 'The Eve of St Agnes' to read she may perhaps have pierced Keats's secret.

Keats's last night in England was spent at Bedhampton, at the end of September 1820, because the brig in which he and Severn were voyaging to Italy unexpectedly put in to the Solent and was detained there by contrary wind. Keats was not yet given to discussing with Severn the particular agony of leaving Fanny Brawne forever, and seized the opportunity of a last night ashore with the friendly family at Bedhampton's Mill House; whether or no Fanny Brawne was spoken of out loud, there was a special sympathy there on which Keats could draw before what he believed to be final departure. It was the next day, still held up by weather off Yarmouth, Isle of Wight, that Keats wrote to his closest male friend, Brown, 'my last letter', asking Brown to be 'a friend to Miss Brawne when I am dead'.

*   *   *

Portsmouth, chief port for reaching the Isle of Wight, belongs in my next chapter. Topographically, I should defer associations with the Isle of Wight till then. At Portsmouth, though, novelists come first to mind but since the poet Keats brought my thoughts here to the Isle of Wight, his and other poets' connections shall here be my concern.

The first of two considerable visits of Keats to the Isle of Wight occurred in April 1817, when, at Hampstead, he had been growing away from Leigh Hunt's obsessive companionship and in a mood of emancipation thought of escaping somewhere on his own. The younger brother

Tom, for the good of his weak health, had been packed off to Margate; Keats felt the Isle of Wight to be of the right size for his own exploration and some solitary thinking. Carisbrooke was his choice as a centre from which to explore on foot, and at first his April expeditions were reward- ing – the Isle of Wight ought, he wrote, 'to be called Primrose Island; that is, if the nation of cowslips agree thereto'. But a week by himself on the Isle of Wight was at that time more than enough for Keats. In the absence of communication of his feelings to brothers and friends he felt 'narvus'. He found himself 'obliged to be in a continual burning of thought', inescapably questioning without relief 'why I should be a Poet more than other Men, – seeing how great a thing it is . . .' It was probably by bargaining with the skipper of a coasting vessel that Keats, in his 'some sort of sailor costume', was taken aboard and in due course landed at Margate, there to join with young Tom. Tom, who worshipped John, was of immediate encouragement for Keats at Margate to be 'gathering Samphire' – 'the Cliff of Poesy Towers above me'.

Tom died from consumption in December 1818; it was after that, and after he had spent that Christmas Day with Fanny Brawne, and visited Chichester and Bedhampton to apologize, that the second of his visits to the Isle of Wight took place, in the summer of 1819. Throughout the early months of 1819 many of Keats's finest poems had poured out: in January 'The Eve of St Agnes', in February the fragment of 'The Eve of St Mark', in April 'La Belle Dame sans Merci', the 'Ode to Psyche' and the 'Ode on a Grecian Urn', in May the 'Ode to a Nightin- gale'. Such things brought in no ready money, and Keats by the summer was hard up for cash. The expedient his medical training offered was to spend the summer at a cottage at Shanklin on the Isle of Wight looking after his friend Rice, who had been ill. Throughout July Rice remained depressed and Keats, with recurrence of sore throat and the perpetual fight against a conviction that his end was as inescapable as his brother Tom's, could not avoid morbid feelings in the 'little coffin' of a bedroom at Eglantine Cottage. At the end of July, however, Rice was moving away; Brown came to Shanklin, and Brown and Keats planned regular work together on the drama *Otho the Great*, which was to make their fortune. Brown had brought with him the latest news of Fanny Brawne, and Keats at once wrote to her the letter confessing that he would be looking at her star that night from his bedroom window:

I will imagine you Venus to-night and pray, pray to your star like a Heathen.
Yours ever, fair star.

It is supposed that the sonnet 'Bright Star, would I were stedfast as thou art' was composed by Keats at that time, at Shanklin. That sonnet was copied by Fanny Brawne into the copy of Cary's *Dante* that Keats had given her, as companion to the 'Dream' sonnet that Keats had himself written in that volume. When the brig was finally bearing them away from the Isle of Wight to Italy in 1820 Keats is said to have repeated the 'Bright Star' sonnet aloud to Severn, and Severn at once begged for a copy. Certain it is that Keats did write the sonnet out for Severn on a blank page in an edition of Shakespeare's poems – the page opposite one that was headed 'A Lover's Complaint'.

Those were Keats's associations with the Isle of Wight. Longfellow also stayed at Shanklin as a visitor in 1868 – he wrote some verses for the drinking-fountain near the Crab Inn. By that time Tennyson had been a resident on the island for nearly twenty years. After his marriage to Emily Sellwood the Tennysons settled at Farringford House, west of Freshwater, near the western tip of the island. Edward Lear stayed with them there in 1859, and Vivien Noakes pictures Lear 'striding over the downs beside Alfred', who with 'tousled black beard and flowing cloak' was 'booming out his new "idylls of the King" in a deep measured voice'. On that visit Lear, when not playing with the two boys who were now seven and five and 'very darling chaps indeed', was keeping a most sympathetic eye on Emily Tennyson. She looked to him 'tired and ill, and he thought Alfred should have realized that she was wearing herself out working for him'. Lear at that time wrote: 'I should think computing moderately that 15 angels, several hundreds of ordinary women, many philosophers, a heap of truly wise and kind mothers, 3 or 4 minor prophets, and a lot of doctors and school-mistresses, might all be boiled down, and yet their combined essence fall short of what Emily Tennyson really is.'

Back in Rome in 1860 Lear entered in his diary: 'O dear Emily T! & various people! How I live a living death here!' As time went on, he found Tennyson increasingly egocentric, but remained particularly faithful to Emily Tennyson as a friend to whom he thought he could always talk. The house he built for himself at San Remo he called Villa Emily. He pretended to questioners that it was named for his niece in New Zealand; but when he left England forever in 1880 and built the second house in San Remo in which to live till he died, he named that permanent home Villa Tennyson, and gave up pretending there was anyone he could be really fonder of than 'Emily T'.

At the time the Tennysons were settling into Farringford House, a house called East Dene at Bonchurch, nestling below the Downs at the south-east of the island, was often a boyhood home for Algernon Charles Swinburne. Swinburne was twelve years old when Dickens brought his own family to Bonchurch in 1849, and his son Charley played with the 'golden-haired lad' of the same age whom Dickens was later to congratulate for *Atalanta in Calydon*. The Swinburne family were not so much pestered by admirers as the Tennysons. In 1869, to obtain some privacy, Tennyson built the house at Aldworth on the Sussex slope of Blackdown, and for many years used both homes; it was on one of his annual crossings of the Solent that he is credited with composing 'Crossing the Bar'. He died in Sussex, although on the island there are appropriate reminders of his years of residence. Of the poets mentioned here, Swinburne is the only one whose body was brought to the island after death. He was buried in 1909 in the churchyard above the village of Bonchurch.

A3

THE PORTSMOUTH ROAD
AND
SOUTH-WEST ENGLAND

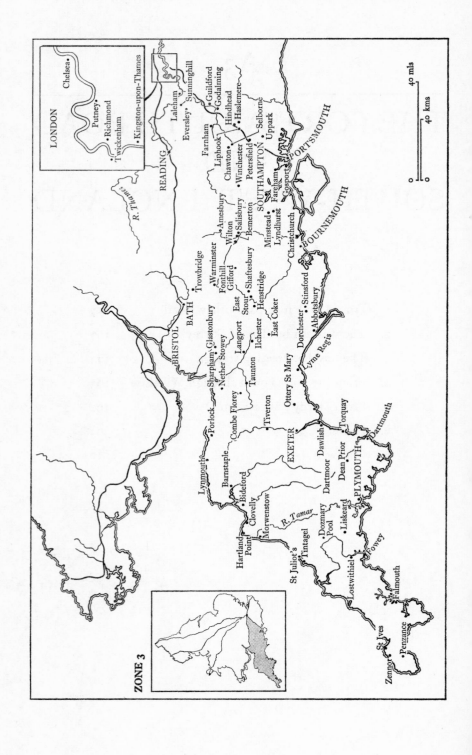

ZONE 3

LONDON
Chelsea
Putney
Richmond
Twickenham
Kingston-upon-Thames

R. Thames

READING

Laleham
Eversley
Sunninghill
Farnham
Guildford
Godalming
Liphook
Hindhead
Haslemere
Chawton
Selborne
Winchester
Petersfield
Uppark
SOUTHAMPTON
Fareham
Gosport
PORTSMOUTH

Amesbury
Wilton
Salisbury
Bemerton
Minstead
Lyndhurst
Christchurch
BOURNEMOUTH

Trowbridge
Warminster
Fonthill
Gifford
Shaftesbury
Henstridge
East
Stour
Ilchester
East Coker
Dorchester
Stinsford
Abbotsbury
Lyme Regis

BATH

BRISTOL

Sharpham
Glastonbury
Nether Stowey
Langport
Combe Florey
Taunton
Porlock
Ottery St Mary
Tiverton

Lynmouth
Barnstaple
Bideford
Clovelly
Morwenstow
Hartland
Point
St Juliot's
Tintagel

EXETER
Dawlish
Dartmoor
Dean Prior
Torquay
Dartmouth

PLYMOUTH

R. Tamar
Dozmary
Pool
Liskeard
Lostwithiel
Fowey
Falmouth
St Ives
Penzance
Zennor

40 mls
40 kms

1. FROM LONDON ACROSS PUTNEY HEATH

The two main roads from London so far discussed were both regarded as starting from the City. London's West End developed so rapidly throughout the eighteenth and nineteenth centuries that it became customary to consider the start of the next two great roads, the Portsmouth Road (A3) and the Bath Road (A4), as Hyde Park Corner. In the days of post-chaises and stagecoaches Hyde Park Corner was the point from which mileages along these roads were usually measured. The Portsmouth Road, which I here take as introducing the wealth of literary associations of south-west England, is most directly to be reached from Hyde Park Corner by forking from Knightsbridge into the Brompton Road, and forking again into the Fulham Road so as to cross the Thames by Putney Bridge.

A turning off the south side of the Brompton Road is Beauchamp Place, and there, at a pub called the Grove, there were regular Thursday lunchtime gatherings in the 1920s for a few men who made a habit of keeping in touch with friends in various posts in the South Kensington museums. The special bond of interest which brought this group together was the quarterly periodical which T. S. Eliot had started in 1922, *The Criterion*; in 1925, when Eliot was no longer obliged to keep office hours at Lloyds Bank in the City, he was able to join the lunches, and Herbert Read (then at his post in the Victoria and Albert) found that the Grove in Beauchamp Place could offer a room (downstairs in a cellar) for the sessions. With Eliot and Read as regular attenders, the cellar table was customarily filled once a week, until Eliot went as Visiting Professor to Harvard in 1932. The lunches were a useful way of keeping up with what was going on abroad, on the Continent and in America. Various Americans were naturally visitors to the Grove. It was Eliot, I think, who brought along Robert Frost one Thursday; in 1929 I took Allen Tate, already known to Eliot and Read by correspondence, to Beauchamp Place to meet those men in person. There were many luncheon-groups in London of the 1920s. The Grove stands out in my memory.

Any residential area of London contains a highly heterogeneous sprinkling of literary associations. Along the Brompton Road, the next turning after Beauchamp Place is Ovington Gardens, leading into Ovington Square where, at No. 1, Oscar Wilde's mother was living in the early 1880s. In 1884, at the age of thirty, Wilde had settled into the house in Tite Street, Chelsea, where he lived until the time of his imprisonment in Reading Gaol (1896–8). In 1886 his mother, Lady Jane Wilde, known as 'Speranza' – Irish patriot, poet in her own right, pamphleteer, and conductor of a salon which attracted Robert Browning, Edmund Gosse, Ouida, and, on occasion, Oliver Wendell Holmes – moved to Oakley Street, a little nearer to her son. The year that Oscar Wilde went to prison was also the year of Lady Jane Wilde's death.

In Pelham Street near 'South Ken' station lived Olive Schreiner at the time that her most important novel, *The Story of an African Farm* (1883), gained its rightful attention. In nearby Pelham Crescent lived (intermittently) until his death in 1881 the adventurous Edward Trelawney. As an impetuous 'younger son', he had been in company with Shelley and Byron in Italy, and was the leader in arranging the funeral pyre for Shelley's body on the shore where it was washed up after the drowning. No less remarkable as an adventurous transgressor of our day, and more accurate as an autobiographical writer, was Negley Farson, who in the 1920s and 1930s was living hereabouts, some years in Walton Street, some in Pelham Street and Pelham Crescent. Eve Farson's uncle, Bram Stoker (author of *Dracula*), had preferred living in Chelsea.

Shortly after Pelham Crescent a turning to the left off Fulham Road is Sydney Street, which leads to St Luke's Church, where Dickens and Catherine Hogarth were married in 1836. Elm Park Gardens is farther along Fulham Road towards Beaufort Street: Sinclair Lewis and his first wife moved from a hotel in Sloane Street for a longer stay in a hotel in Elm Park Gardens (No. 58) in their first years in London, 1922–4. Drayton Gardens, a turning off the north side of Fulham Road (a continuation of Beaufort Street), leads on in Old Brompton to Bina Gardens, where in the 1930s John Hayward, confined for life to his wheeled chair, could be regarded as a highly intelligent spider at the centre of a widespread web, so sentient was he to all that went on in the literary scene.

Gilston Road, next turning north from Fulham Road, leads to The Boltons; here W. S. Gilbert, when the operas he and Sullivan wrote were in the full burst of creation, lived and worked on *The Pirates of Penzance, Patience* and *Iolanthe*. After four years at The Boltons Gilbert moved for his longer stay at No. 39 Harrington Gardens, near Bina Gardens. Beatrix Potter was a child of ten at No. 2 The Boltons when Gilbert moved into No. 24, but I know of no indication that either paid attention to the other. It was when returning to the upper floor of No. 2 The Boltons from her grandmother's country place at Camfield in Hertfordshire that Beatrix is credited with bringing with her the fieldmouse which had been accustomed to explore the hollow brass curtain rod of the Camfield nursery.

So the catalogue of who, in this part of London, resided where, and when, seems quite various. Redcliffe Road, next turning to the north off Fulham Road, brings in memories of Middleton Murry, Katherine Mansfield and Wyndham Lewis before the 1920s; across Fulham Road on the south is St Stephen's Hospital where in the 1940s Dylan Thomas was renovated from at least one bout of alcoholic gastritis. Next to St Stephen's Hospital is Netherton Grove where, at No. 6, Arnold Bennett lodged after he came to London from Burslem – later, in the 1920s, Bennett was proud of the way he had risen to his much more prosperous home in Cadogan Square, where the surprisingly large number of mirrors startled H. G. Wells. Bennett was twenty-two in 1891 when he first arrived in London; G. B. Shaw was twenty when he joined his mother in lodgings in Netherton Grove in 1876. By the time Bennett arrived, Shaw had moved on to progressively better bachelor quarters in Fitzroy Street and Fitzroy Square until his marriage in 1898, when he and his wife settled into her rented quarters at No. 10 Adelphi Terrace.

The list of such items could be endless: at least since the eighteenth century, there were many men of letters (though it was not of men of letters that W. S. Gilbert was thinking) who pranced 'from their abode in Fulham Road through Brompton to the City'. Animals in fiction, as well as writers, also enter the catalogue. Let it not be forgotten that the Hound of the Baskervilles was 'bought in London from Ross and Mangles, the dealers in Fulham Road'. ('It was the strongest and most savage in their possession.') But a reason for harking back to the eighteenth century is that all who read modern novels ought to find pleasure in recalling the short plump nervous man, 'the first great English novelist', Samuel Richardson (1689–1761). After his printing prospered, Richardson, at whom we glanced in Little Britain, was able to set up a correctly managed 'country box' in this neighbourhood. The 'box', which if it did not claim to be 'situated in a spacious park' was nevertheless a neat, plain villa 'built in the rustic taste', was first at North End, off the Fulham Road towards what is now West Kensington. He later built a second, even neater villa, at Parson's Green off the south side of the Fulham Road and on the way to Putney Bridge, and there he lived till his death. His body was then taken for burial to St Bride's Church, near his Fleet Street printing works.

Chelsea's King's Road and Cheyne Walk are apt to loom more important in guidebooks than the route by the Fulham Road to Putney Bridge, but the area assumed such airs only relatively recently. It is true that about the same time that Richardson was provoking Henry Fielding and Tobias Smollett to create novels an alternative amusement was being promoted at Ranelagh Gardens, at the Westminster side of the Chelsea

Royal Hospital. There the great Rotunda was erected in 1742, and the promenaders circling round it, criticized by those who sat and took refreshments in the Rotunda's tier of boxes, made Dr Johnson admit that Ranelagh was, in some ways, the finest thing he had seen. 'Every night constantly I go to Ranelagh', wrote Horace Walpole, and added, 'My Lord Chesterfield is so fond of it that he says he has ordered all his letters to be directed thither.' Yet few of the 'literary' sites in Chelsea relate to people who lived here earlier than the nineteenth century. Wellington Square is where Thomas Wolfe stayed in 1926 while working on *Look Homeward, Angel*. Smith Street contains Durham Place where Bram Stoker lived till 1912 at No. 4. Off Smith Street just before Durham Place is Tedworth Square; a tablet on No. 23 reminds us of Mark Twain's stay there in 1896–7. Tite Street leads thence to the Chelsea Embankment; the vogue which took Whistler and Sargent, as well as Oscar Wilde and Laurence Binyon, to live in Tite Street is a reminder that at the end of the last century Chelsea attracted painters as well as men of letters. The Embankment, towards the Albert Bridge, leads into Cheyne Walk; at No. 4 George Eliot died in 1880, less than three weeks after moving in. The painter-poet Dante Gabriel Rossetti was then living at No. 16 – the 'conjectural and mysterious' Rossetti, as Max Beerbohm called him. Rossetti's house was filled with curios and the garden with a strange collection of animals. There is 'a somewhat indistinct story' (John Freeman's words) that Meredith was invited to live with Rossetti but after trial could not stand the Bohemian ménage. Swinburne, however, stayed with Rossetti on and off after that for two years. Rossetti continued to keep open house for friends whom some neighbours thought odd, until his final illness caused his removal to Birchington in Kent in 1882.

Cheyne Walk proceeds across Oakley Street (Oakley Gardens is where George Gissing managed to live for a time) and the entrance to Cheyne Row is indicated by a statue to Thomas Carlyle, reminding visitors that No. 24 Cheyne Row is the house where Carlyle and Jane Welsh Carlyle lived from 1834 – she for the thirty-two years until her death in 1866, and he for the fifteen years more before his own death in 1881. The house is kept as a museum and Professor George G. Williams in his *Guide to Literary London* advises that it 'should be visited', though E. V. Lucas in his day found some of the relics off-putting, despite thoughts of Tennyson and Edward FitzGerald going there to smoke a pipe with Carlyle. 'If there is any man's wash-handstand and bath, any woman's bed and chair, that I feel there is no need for me or the public generally to see', said Lucas, 'they are Mr and Mrs Carlyle's.'

I confess I have never been inside the Carlyle house, but I have frequently entered what Professor Williams calls the 'large and rather pretentious apartment complex called "Carlyle Mansions" ' at the corner of the next street (Lawrence Street) and Cheyne Walk when, after the last war, T. S. Eliot and John Hayward shared a flat there. During the 1914–18 war, until his death there in February 1916, Henry James used a flat in Carlyle Mansions when he was in London. James has a commemorative tablet in Chelsea's Old Church nearby, and another commemoration is provided by Hugh Kenner in *The Pound Era*. The scene is in one of the last evenings 'of a gone world, the light of its last summer' (i.e. 1914) finding and suffusing 'the red waistcoat of Henry James, lord of decorum, *en promenade*, exposing his Boston niece [Margaret] to the tone of things'. On the stately promenade in Cheyne Walk there came along to present themselves for James's inspection young Ezra Pound and his newly married wife Dorothy (née Shakespear). Ezra had at that time a greater devotional respect for Henry James than perhaps for any other man alive. After the introductions, as James permitted Dorothy Pound and his niece Peg to walk ahead, 'Dorothy heard from behind her, addressed to her husband of two months, in the slow implacable voice the great expatriate's overwhelming question, as who should ask, animal, vegetable, or mineral: "And is she a com-pât-riot?": the syllables spaced, the accented vowel short'. The anecdote is memorable for James's 'fierce need to "place" and categorize'.

I don't think the great painter, Turner, dressed as carefully as James when he emerged from his house (No. 119) at the westernmost end of Cheyne Walk. That was the house to which Turner (about the time that Henry James was in petticoats) retreated to live alone, away from friends, and unknown to neighbours in Chelsea except as a pretence character, 'Admiral Booth'. Left to himself, Turner in his seventies was not too infirm to maintain his habit of climbing to the roof of No. 119 in his dressing-gown at daybreak, to watch the sun rise. When Whistler first made his home in London, he lived at this western end of Cheyne Walk (No. 101), and from this point of view preferred the wonderful night-time vision of old Battersea Bridge, the river scene that Whistler 'was born to do above all other men'. Earlier, this western part of Cheyne Walk attracted a Mr and Mrs Stevenson, and Elizabeth Cleghorn Stevenson was born at No. 93 in 1810. Soon after, the death of both parents caused the child to be brought up by an aunt in Knutsford, Cheshire, and there she grew to become the writer Mrs Gaskell.

If from Cheyne Walk one steps up Oakley Street and then to the left into the King's Road to turn up Manresa Road one can reach a flat where Dylan and Caitlin Thomas lived for about three years. My little tour, however, hastens westward into the New King's Road in order to return to where, boxed between it and the Fulham Road, lies the little triangle of Parson's Green. There I can again pay tribute to the strange little figure of Samuel Richardson, born nearly three centuries ago, who then at the age of fifty accidentally but effectively set about establishing the novel as a means of watching and appreciating and communicating the workings of the human heart.

The wonderful contribution to the modern novel made by the man who looked 'like a plump white mouse in a wig, at once vivacious and timid' is simple to state: he started it. A theatrical decline in the mid-eighteenth century in London prepared one kind of audience for the novelists, and Leslie Stephen discussed another effective coefficient in the need for novels up and down the country – 'winter evenings were long in the country and the back parlours of tradesmen's shops'. Delivery of periodicals by mailcoach and post-boy had greatly spread the reading habit. Letter-writing was more and more widespread and not for the next hundred and fifty years did such a substitute as the telephone interfere. It was the growth of letter-writing that by happy accident suggested to publisher friends of Richardson that he be asked to compose for them, in 1739, a volume of *Familiar Letters* – a handbook for beginners. The friends knew that as a boy in Derbyshire Richardson had displayed such skill in letter-writing that girls of the neighbourhood employed him to concoct their love-letters. Increasing subjection to attacks by sudden tremors and dizziness on his way to his printing works made Richardson, by the age of fifty, no longer happy about riding from his 'country box' to Fleet Street. In the privacy of his house he kept a 'chamber-horse', a wooden animal on which he sometimes exercised, but to have an excuse for not riding to his office suited Richardson nobly. He devised *Pamela* as a cautionary theme for young serving-women who were exposed to temptation, and, becoming totally absorbed in Pamela's character and in the conditions for women in eighteenth-century life, he gave up 'wine and flesh and fish' and completed two volumes of his heroine's story, told in letters, within three months. It was not the handbook that had been asked for. It was something better. Richardson had transformed the assignment into a first modern novel, and a novel to arouse social conscience.

Pamela was published in 1740 and the current greed for reading-matter gave a warm (though varied) welcome to the two volumes. Henry Fielding promptly regarded Pamela's 'strange conjunction of purity and precaution' as a challenge to a man who considered he knew more about life than Richardson. Thus Fielding, hitherto not greatly successful as a playwright, at the age of thirty-three set out to write an outright burlesque of *Pamela*. The hero of *The History of Joseph Andrews* is an imagined brother of Richardson's Pamela, and for five short chapters the satire on Richardson seemed Fielding's only object; but then the characters (and especially Parson Adams) take on a life and spontaneous activity entirely of their own. Fielding's novel was published in 1742, and the bitter resentment of Richardson and his admirers (female and male) may have added to the circulation of both experimental novels. Richardson and Fielding were each conscious that their first efforts could be improved upon, and after a period of gestation, and with Smollett as a third rival, a series of what remain as masterpieces were produced in quick succession – *Clarissa*, *Roderick Random*, *Tom Jones*, *Peregrine Pickle*, and *Sir Charles Grandison*. A few years more, and with other writers now in competition, there was another burst of shooting stars for admiration – *Tristram Shandy*, *Rasselas*, *The Castle of Otranto*, and *The Vicar of Wakefield*.

Brilliantly as some of this last-named group still shine, one agrees with Gosse that they are 'satellites in attendance on the three great lights of eighteenth-century fiction, on Richardson, Fielding, and Smollett, and when the third of these departed, the art of novel-writing ceased to progress, in any large sense, until it was taken up forty years afterwards by Jane Austen and Sir Walter Scott'. The earlier Defoe had been a precursor, but not only did Richardson start off the novel-writing of the mid-eighteenth century, but the touches by which he brought his characters 'into a stereoscopic distinctness' also played much part, as Elizabeth Jenkins notes, in encouraging Jane Austen's revival of the art. The hold that *Sir Charles Grandison* took on Jane Austen's imagination, Miss Jenkins points out, 'was extraordinary':

Henry Austen said that she remembered and would speak of any date throughout the year on which any episode of the book was said to have taken place; on one occasion she was to wear a cap of white satin and lace, 'with a little white flower perking out of the left ear, like Harriet Byron's feather', because Harriet's costume for the fatal masquerade included 'a white, Paris sort of cap, glittering with spangles and encircled by a chaplet of artificial flowers, with a little white feather perking from the left ear'.

Passing Parson's Green, one may pause to recall Richardson's 'country box'. The parlour of that neat villa in the 1750s had stiff old-fashioned furniture and a window offering a glimpse of garden. In that parlour one can see a circle of ladies sitting for the daily reading: Richardson's chair is so placed that he uses the light from the window to read aloud from the work in progress. Leslie Stephen refers to that picture, Richardson sitting in his usual morning dress, 'a kind of brown dressing-gown with a skull cap on his head, filling the chair with his plump little body, and raising one foot . . . to point his moral with an emphatic stamp'.

To later historians of literature, however, Leslie Stephen was wide of the mark in harping on the personal shyness and foibles of the 'plump white mouse in a wig' without recognizing at all the powerful effect that

Richardson's novels would have in initiating and supporting the fight for women's rights. Christopher Hill, writing half a century later than Stephen, is better able to show the general fight that was being made in England against the 'Norman Yoke', and Richardson's effective contribution to a part of that fight which specially concerned women. In *Puritanism and Revolution* Christopher Hill points out that the social background 'of which Richardson was part and parcel, and which was the main novel-reading public', was the then 'developing bourgeois society'. 'The aristocracy owed its continuing predominance in part to its concentration of family property by entail and marriages for money. Political compromise between aristocracy and bourgeoisie had been arrived at in the seventeenth century; but compromise in the realm of ideas was still being worked out.' Pertinently, in *Clarissa* Richardson was seriously examining 'the effect on men and women of property marriage and all that goes with it'. Other critics nowadays tend to be in full agreement that with *Clarissa* Richardson 'stumbled on a situation fully tragic'; whatever its weaknesses, the enormous advance in *Clarissa* 'beyond the conventional "marriage-covers-all" morality' of *Pamela* makes Christopher Hill begin a chapter in his above-mentioned book with the forthright statement that *Clarissa* seems to him 'one of the greatest of the unread novels'. That is to say, *Clarissa* is comparatively unread today because as a tract its purpose has long been achieved; but it was certainly read with effect by eighteenth-century Dissenters such as Mary Wollstonecraft and William Godwin. (It interests me to observe that names of those who prepared women to become aware of 'the necessity of their emancipation' tend to come from a line of country on the Danelaw side of Watling Street – Godwin from Cambridgeshire and Richardson from Derbyshire, while Wollstonecraft is said to be a Lancashire and Cheshire name.)

Putney Bridge recalls Mary Wollstonecraft's second attempt at suicide, by throwing herself from the old toll-bridge into the river on a cold, dark evening of rain in October 1795, half a century after the time that Richardson was offering his ladies cups of chocolate along with the readings. But contemporary with Richardson's readings, across the river in a large house (later known as Lime Grove) at the foot of Putney Hill, the little boy Edward Gibbon was growing up. He was the eldest child, and the only one who survived infancy, of a mother who in the first ten years of marriage had given birth to seven babies and who then died in a final child-bearing. A chief abiding memory that Edward Gibbon had of his mother was connected with a certain spot on Putney Common where, when driving him as a boy of eight to his first school, she impressed upon him that he was to think and act for himself. When Edward was ten and his mother had died, his impulsive father promptly got rid of Lime Grove, gave up his London life and drove down the Portsmouth Road to live at Buriton, south of Petersfield. For the next four years young Gibbon was planted as a boarder with his aunt Catherine Porten, who kept house for a number of boys attending school at Westminster. This aunt became, to Gibbon, 'Dear Kitty', and such was his affection for her that he propounded, as a schoolboy, a theological conundrum: ought he to kill her? She was so good, the schoolboy argued, that she was bound to go to heaven; while if she went on living, she might become wicked.

It was only for the first ten years of his life that Gibbon lived in the big house at Putney; later on and by contrast, Swinburne spent the last thirty years of his life living modestly with Theodore Watts-Dunton at The Pines (now No. 11 Putney Hill). Swinburne's retired life from 1879 until his death in 1909 was described in a famous essay by Max Beerbohm ('No. 2, The Pines') and there is a sketch by Arnold Bennett in *Books and Persons* which conveys his impression of the sight of Swinburne out for his regular walk on Putney Heath. Beerbohm also stressed those walks – Swinburne's slight, almost childish figure carried 'with his long neck strained so tightly back that he all receded from the waist upwards', and with tiny hands fluttering 'helplessly, touchingly, unceasingly'. On the Heath 'the eyes of a god, and the smile of an elf' lit up and his step was singularly quick and springy at any instant magnetism of a nursemaid with perambulator. 'Well do I remember', wrote Beerbohm, 'his ecstasy of emphasis and immensity of pause when he described how he had seen in a perambulator on the Heath to-day "the most BEAUT–iful babbie ever beheld by mortal eyes".' Nursemaids were not relieved from Swinburne's idolatry for 'babbies' until his own eyes were closed, and his coffin made its journey for burial in the Isle of Wight.

To the west of the Portsmouth Road is Richmond Hill, and Richmond Hill on one side of the River Thames and Twickenham on the other are a simultaneous reminder of the two eighteenth-century poets, Alexander Pope and James Thomson. The fact that they settled on opposite banks of the river emphasizes that their poetry was of different schools, and it is, I think, a mark of generosity in Pope (the elder of the two by twelve years) that at a time when by immense and disciplined hard work he had become England's foremost poet, he gave unstinted praise to an opposite kind of writing by the relatively unsophisticated young Scot who had come to London from the northern slopes of the Cheviots, near the Border. Profits from his translation of Homer enabled Pope to dress his five acres of Twickenham to advantage and to entertain such intimates as Gay, Swift, Arbuthnot and Lord Bolingbroke; the apparently artless Thomson sought to gain the attention of the *cognoscenti* with a poem entitled *Winter*, which he managed to get published in 1726, with hopes of later completing *The Seasons*. *Winter* was not in the least influenced by metropolitan wit but was written in blank verse with rhythm of its own, not imitative, and presented country pictures enjoyable by everybody – as of the robin, who when the snow bears hard on all wild life, pays annual visit to the farmstead and to the house itself:

> Half-afraid, he first
> Against the window beats; then, brisk, alights
> On the warm hearth; then, hopping o'er the floor,
> Eyes all the smiling family askance,
> And pecks, and starts, and wonders where he is –
> Till, more familiar grown, the table-crumbs
> Attract his slender feet.

It contradicts the assertion that Pope's temper was usually fretful and waspish to find him praising *Winter* on its first publication, and for reasons which Johnson later put: 'The reader of the *Seasons* wonders that he never saw before what Thomson shews him, and that he never yet has felt what Thomson impresses.' Thomson completed his four *Seasons* with no loss of his gift for attracting readers to 'country' poetry. *The Seasons* retained its widespread popularity throughout the eighteenth century and later. Coleridge's pleasurable excitement at finding a dog-eared copy on an inn windowsill is one instance of the continuance of Thomson's influence on readers and on poets. 'The honor, yea, the redeemer of Scotland' is a phrase that Coleridge once applied to Thomson. And if W. H. Hudson's fascination with the English countryside began by his finding Bloomfield's poems in a bookshop in Buenos Aires, that fascination was promptly increased by his purchasing, in that same bookshop, Thomson's *Seasons*.

Of Thomson's ventures in poetic drama, one song is generally remembered. On 1 August 1740 a masque entitled *Alfred*, written by Thomson and Mallet, was performed at Cliveden on the Thames before the then Prince of Wales. The music was provided by the thirty-year-old composer Thomas Arne, and a song written by Thomson for the second act and set 'to still-living strains' by Arne was 'Rule?, Britannia!'. On the Portsmouth Road, famed as the route of so many famous naval men setting forth to rule the waves, it has not been inappropriate to mention Thomson.

2. THE WESTERN BORDERS OF SURREY

The narrow slice of Surrey and Hampshire bounded by the Portsmouth Road and the almost parallel radial road from London to Southampton contains a wealth of associations which especially tie into the history of the English novel. Had I kept on the northern side of the Thames I should have found, at the Holly Road in Twickenham where the river bends around Eel Pie Island, the Fielding Cottages marking the site where Henry Fielding in 1749 was writing *Tom Jones*. Two of the great early novelists, therefore, were doing their writing within the sliver of territory bounded between the first furlongs of the roads mentioned. Now I ask: where did those next great originators – Jane Austen and Sir Walter Scott – find their respective triggers, in what surroundings, to set them off? Where did the name Waverley first so excite Scott as to become the label for the Waverley novels? Where was the cottage with the creaking door which gave Jane Austen protection and encouragement to write? The answer is that the stimulus for both occurred in this countryside that on the map is a thin slice between the Portsmouth and Southampton roads. Richardson and Fielding, Jane Austen and Walter Scott – that's a notable quartet of novelists. When you go on to find various formative associations that this slice of England also had for three great Victorians, Dickens, Thackeray, George Eliot, you begin to wonder what radioactivity worked in this strip.

Yet the roads that mark each side of this radioactive sliver of land have rarely, as roadways, aroused much special adoration. Walter Scott's remark about the Great North Road, that it was 'a dull road, but convenient', has been also remarked by others of the roads from London to Portsmouth and Southampton. In April 1817 the twenty-two-year-old Keats, setting out for his first visit to the Isle of Wight, might have been expected to find excitement in his overnight journey by coach along the road to Southampton. His picture of the journey, as written to his brothers, however, is not much romanticized. The coach left London about four in the afternoon:

I did not know the Names of any of the Towns I passed through all I can tell you is that sometimes I saw dusty Hedges sometimes Ponds – then nothing – then a little Wood with trees look you like Launce's Sister 'as white as a Lilly and as small as a Wand' – then came houses which died away into a few straggling Barns then came hedge trees aforesaid again. As the Lamp light crept along the following things were discovered: 'long heath brown furze' – Hurdles here and there half a Mile – Park palings when the Windows of a House were always discovered by reflection – One Nymph of Fountain *N.B.Stone* – lopped Trees – Cow ruminating – ditto Donkey – Man and Woman going gingerly along – William seeing his Sisters over the Heath – John waiting with a Lanthen for his Mistress – Barbers Pole – Doctor's Shop – However after having had my fill of these I popped my Head out just as it began to Dawn – *N.B. this tuesday Morn saw the Sun rise* – of which I shall say nothing at present . . . from dawn to half past six I went through a most delightful Country – some open Down but for the most part thickly wooded. What surprised me most was an immense quantity of blooming Furze on each side of the road cutting a most rural dash. . . .

Nicholas Nickleby and Smike travelled the Portsmouth Road by foot. Theirs also was a springtime journey, but there was nothing to be seen on the first day that called for comment. (What I notice about that age of walking is that to reach Godalming, only 'some thirty and odd miles from London', could be regarded as an easy first day's step.)

The westward arm of the crossroad at Cobham leads to Laleham, the birthplace of Matthew Arnold. In Ashford Road, Laleham, there is (or used to be) a cedar tree which by local repute stood formerly within the grounds of the now vanished house in which, on Christmas Eve 1822, Arnold was born. In that house his father's profession was the teaching of private pupils; six years later Thomas Arnold was appointed head-master of Rugby School, and when the family moved Matthew and his younger brother perforce left Laleham, although between the ages of eight and fourteen young Matthew went back from Rugby to live at Laleham with his maternal uncle. The place continued to draw him: after Winchester and Oxford, despite the physical moves of his life, three of his children, when they successively died young, were buried in Laleham churchyard. For the final fifteen years of his own life Matthew Arnold lived at Pain's Hill Cottage, Cobham, and that was as if returning to home ground. When he died in 1888 he too was buried in Laleham churchyard.

On the Portsmouth Road at Guildford I halt for the associations there with Charles Dodgson (Lewis Carroll). It was in his later life that Mr Dodgson (to his sisters he remained 'Charles' rather than 'Lewis') used to stay in his sister's house, named The Chestnuts, on Castle Hill. He was there for his last Christmastime; taken ill, he died at The Chestnuts on 14 January 1898. He was buried in the Mount cemetery at Guildford. From fiction I remember Nicholas Nickleby, and how he first met the notable actor-manager Mr Vincent Crummles on the Portsmouth Road, just after the said Mr Crummles and two boys had been 'fulfilling an engagement at Guildford with the greatest applause'. Dickens is soon providing a very fair prognostication of the real-life

Portsmouth actor-parents Ben and Sarah Terry and their girls Kate and Ellen – Kate, the older sister, in the beginning outstarring Ellen as an Infant Phenomenon.

Ben Terry and his wife Sarah were with a company of strolling players on a 'wandering speculation' (to borrow the phrase from *Nicholas Nickleby*), when Ellen was born at Coventry in 1847. Thereafter Ben Terry had two girls to train to act. For serious work the girls and Ben became part of the Keans' troupe at London's Princess Theatre, but for at least one summer (1857) there was an all-Terry season of farcical entertainments at a pavilion rigged up by Ben as a playhouse at Ryde on the Isle of Wight. There Ben, Kate and the ten-year-old Ellen cavorted to make fun for summer visitors. Ellen Terry had made her London début the year before, in a performance of *The Winter's Tale*. That performance had been attended by Queen Victoria herself and, it so happened, by young Charles Dodgson, who had just begun his workaday occupation during termtime at Oxford as tutor in mathematics.

The eye of the future Lewis Carroll was at once attracted to Ellen; in his description of the players in his diary he wrote that he 'especially admired the acting of little Mamillius, Ellen Terry, a beautiful little creature who played with remarkable ease and spirit'. Much later, George Bernard Shaw was to testify that 'every famous man of the nineteenth century', provided he were a playgoer, had been in love with Ellen Terry. Charles Dodgson was one of the first of all those worshippers. Those who adored her were indeed a varied company – of a vintage earlier than Shaw and H. G. Wells, they included Tennyson, Matthew Arnold, Oscar Wilde, Sargent, Burne-Jones, Oliver Wendell Holmes and, in a more restrained way, Henry James (who sent Ellen one of his plays in hopes that she would act in it – hopes that were unfulfilled).

Ellen Terry herself came to evaluate Dodgson's affection. 'He was as fond of me', she wrote, 'as he could be of anyone over the age of ten.' Dodgson was twenty-four when he wrote in his diary about the 'beautiful little creature'. He was thirty-two and a zealous amateur of portrait photography when he sought for an introduction to the Terry family and first met Ellen face to face. Many might think Dodgson's intrusion upon the Terrys was a crude display of a photographer's self-interest. Ellen, at the age of seventeen, was topic of incessant gossip. Offstage she had already been the model of the painter George Frederick Watts, and then, in a wedding much laughed at, his wife; now the gossip was that she, still seventeen, was leaving Watts and, in the dubious social status of ex-wife, returning to live with her parents. With gossip at its height, the young Rev. Mr Dodgson hired a cab to transport his camera tripod and equipment to the home of the Terrys, to take away pictures of all and especially of Ellen. It was cunning of Dodgson first to find three younger children in the Terry family whose ages were on the right side of ten; with them the photographer made friends. That gave excuse for further visits by the Oxford don, until – a day to be specially marked in Dodgson's diary – Ellen appeared and took his presence and the photography as a matter of course. On one July day that Dodgson had engaged to spend with the Terry family, his diary shows he was delayed by a stop at the office of the Macmillans, his publishers, to autograph twenty copies of *Alice in Wonderland*, then fresh from the press. Of the day's two engagements, Dodgson records the photography at the Terrys' as of higher importance than the sight of a first consignment of *Alice*.

In the following six years when Ellen was living with Edward Godwin near Wheathampstead in Hertfordshire, producing two children without benefit of marriage rites, she was regarded by most of society as an outcast. It was unlikely that close friendship with the Oxford don would burgeon in such circumstances, and it does not appear that Dodgson attempted to make it burgeon. When Ellen's older and closer friend Charles Reade did persuade her back to the stage by making her leading lady in his play *The Wandering Heir*, Dodgson went to see the play but did not make his presence there known to Ellen. It was still another six years to the time when Ellen married (in order to make school life less awkward for her children), and it was then that Dodgson wrote to suggest resumption of the friendship. They did meet, and Dodgson tried to interest Ellen's son Teddy in a puzzle about getting five sheep across a river in a boat. Teddy was bored, and friendship with Ellen never really revived. Yet I think that when Dodgson at Guildford was reviewing his memories, he would not have forgotten Ellen Terry.

'Farnham, on the borders of Surrey' was described by Sherlock Holmes as being in 'a beautiful neighbourhood, and full of the most interesting associations.' A side-trip from Guildford along the Hog's Back finds one such association in the ruins of Waverley Abbey in the lovely valley of the Wey, two miles south-east of Farnham. A loyal Scottish writer (Dawn Macleod) has been known to say that when young and travelling the east coast route to Scotland 'those old steam trains seemed always to beat out the refrain of *Sir Walter Scott, Waverley, Waverley, Waverley*, as we approached the Border'. Edinburgh's Waverley Station – the name is absolutely Scottish. Yet was Waverley a Scottish name before Scott made it so?

Warm friendship with an older Englishman, George Ellis, is held to have encouraged Scott in the period before he was certain of his own powers. On his visit to London in 1801 Scott met Ellis who, with Canning, had started the *Anti-Jacobin*, to which Scott eagerly contributed; but in addition to political agreement the friendship was also immediate and intimate in every other way. Ellis, senior by eighteen years, promptly invited Scott to stay at his house at Sunninghill, near Ascot, and for fourteen years thereafter, until Ellis's death, that was where Scott on his visits to London was accustomed often to stay. Scott praised his host also as a 'converser'; much later, in 1826, he recorded: 'Mr Ellis was the first converser I ever knew.' The interpretation is that on these visits Ellis took pleasure in showing Scott the countryside, talking about the points of interest, and stimulating the comparison of scenes, traditions, and social conditions in the two countries.

The stimulus to begin the novel *Waverley* is thus held to have been prompted during Scott's visits to Sunninghill. Part of the first two cantos of *Marmion* were written at Sunninghill, and the introduction of the Fifth Canto is addressed to 'Dear Ellis', named there 'My guide, my pattern, and my friend!' It was while *Marmion* was being composed that Scott was, he says, 'induced to think' of a portrayal in prose of Scottish traditions of the mid-eighteenth century, such as would be exhibited with appropriate liveliness by imagining a young Englishman of good family introduced and by degrees entwined with Scottish families of equal rank. In 1829 Scott reminisced that 'it was with some idea of this kind, that, about the year 1805, I threw together about one-third part of the first volume of *Waverley*'. It is assumed that the name of Scott's English hero was prompted by a visit made with Ellis from Ascot to Waverley Abbey; that a 'Waverley of Highley Park, com. Hants.', if adopted into the succession of the hereditary estate of Waverley-Honour, would be just right as a visitor 'To Cosmo Comyne Bradwardine, Esq. of Bradwardine, at his principal mansion of Tully-Veolan, in Perthshire, North Britain'. As a 'character' Waverley was not meant to be the centre of interest; it was the Scottish scenery and manners to which the hero (and the reader) were to be introduced that would be the main focus of the novel.

The first six chapters of *Waverley* were then thrown together about the year 1805, while the contrast of country roundabout Waverley Abbey and Scottish glens was fresh in mind. Yet those six chapters, when shown 'to a critical friend' of Scott's Edinburgh circle were not approved, and, unwilling to risk the loss of the 'poetical reputation' that his name had achieved, he at once laid the prose work aside. Ballantyne had advertised the book for publication 'under the name of *Waverley, or 'Tis Fifty Years Since*', but that was allowed to be forgotten. One of the circumstances which some years later revived Scott's memory of his prose manuscript – he could not locate the papers, for in the move to Abbotsford they were mislaid – was the great success accorded to Maria Edgeworth, 'whose Irish characters have gone so far to make the English familiar with the character of their gay and kind-hearted neighbours of

Ireland, that she may be truly said to have done more towards completing the Union, than perhaps all the legislative enactments by which it has been followed up'. This was in keeping with the conversations with George Ellis; Scott had never failed to wish to introduce Scottish characters, both of 'the elder, as well as more modern race' in 'a more favourable light than they had been placed hitherto, and tend to procure sympathy for their virtues and indulgence for their foibles'. The mislaid chapters of *Waverley* fortunately did turn up; he determined to complete them. The subtitle was altered to *'Tis Sixty Years Since*, Waverley and the Highland cateran Bean Lean were set off on their adventures, and the book, although the name of the author was cautiously withheld, was published in 1814. The secret of the authorship and the subsequent publication of other highly successful novels 'by the author of *Waverley*' came to make 'Waverley' almost a Scottish name.

* * *

The literary associations of Waverley Abbey are not confined to Sir Walter Scott. Near the entrance-lodge is 'Stella's Cottage', and it was at neighbouring Moor Park that Swift, then secretary to Sir William Temple, first met Stella (Esther Johnson) in 1697. He was thirty, and she sixteen. Swift had been ordained in Ireland, but his satirical tongue seemed to be delaying preferment in the Church; while waiting for an appropriate 'living', among other writings at Moor Park he composed the powerful attack on theological shams and pedantry called *The Tale of a Tub* – whose irony went very much wider and deeper than the ostensible satire on religious conflicts. Temple died in 1699, leaving Swift his literary executorship and a small legacy. Swift then returned to Ireland, although (especially in the next decade) he made visits to London and to friends throughout England. *The Tale of a Tub* was published, together with *The Battle of the Books*, in an anonymous volume in 1704. The story has often been repeated of how Swift, in later days, happened to pick up and re-read a copy of the *Tale* and exclaimed 'What a genius I had when I wrote that book!' Queen Anne, reading it, was struck by pious horror at Swift's pessimism; her opinion, it is said, prevented him from obtaining a Church position higher than the Deanery of Dublin. But one of the most interesting influences of *The Tale of a Tub* was on William Cobbett (1763–1835).

Cobbett was born at Farnham, reputedly in the house which is now the inn called the Jolly Farmer by the bridge over the River Wey, only two miles from Moor Park. Cobbett had no schooling to speak of. His prospects were those of a farm labourer; but when at the age of eleven he was working on the flowerbeds at Farnham Castle the head gardener told him about Kew Gardens, and the next morning the boy set out to walk to Kew to find employment there. Having reached Richmond, so he tells, he saw in a shop window a copy of Swift's *The Tale of a Tub*. He was tired and hungry and yet the sight of the small book aroused curiosity; he had the necessary threepence and, although that was all the money he had, he bought the *Tale*, found a haystack beside which to sit and read it, and read on till darkness came. Many years later he described that experience as the 'birth of intellect'. The *Rural Rides* of Cobbett's maturity show that intellect, when grown, darting about like a dragonfly, his style always direct, vivid and beautiful ('vernacular made literary', it has been called) as stimulated in the boy by Swift.

The borders of Surrey and Hampshire were always a favourite scene for Cobbett's *Rural Rides*. He died near Guildford; the burial was in the churchyard of the parish church at Farnham, and on the south wall of the church is a tablet and commemorative bust. The writer of the hymn 'Rock of Ages' (Augustus M. Toplady) is also commemorated in Farnham Church. Farnham Castle, which rises above the town, was at one time a residence of the bishops of Winchester; the castle owes its present form mainly to the seventeenth-century Bishop Morley, Izaak Walton's friend when Walton was spending the latter part of his life at Winchester. Along the river-banks of Hampshire Walton is claimed, almost everywhere, to have fished; sometimes at least, he preferred periods of rest at Farnham Castle.

3. THE NOVELIST-CREATING TRIANGLE

Attending earlier to the fancy of this radioactive triangle, I mentioned George Eliot. What do I see as its effect on her? Under her real name, Mary Ann Evans, she was born in 1819 at Arbury in Warwickshire; the 'George Eliot country' is firmly identified with the Midlands. That is not disputed. She lived till the age of thirty in or near Arbury – but was not as yet writing, or at least not publishing, anything. Her religious views having altered, at the age of thirty she was translating freethinking works. She visited Geneva, and returning to London obtained rooms in the Strand in the house of the editor of the *Westminster Review*. For that periodical she worked industriously for years and might have continued at such office work indefinitely had she not met George Henry Lewes, and gone to live with him, first at Richmond and then at Shepperton. So, towards the end of the 1850s, at the age of thirty-eight, she turned into a novelist, with *Scenes of Clerical Life* in 1857 and *Adam Bede* in

1858. There had been no premonition that Mary Ann Evans had such a gift; whether living with Lewes acted as catalyst or whether it was by moving to the magic territory that the transformation occurred – for which reason or for both or neither – I don't pretend to say. The life George Eliot wrote about was life in the Midlands, but the trigger which caused the writing was released in the slice of land traversed by the Portsmouth Road. Once she had begun to be a professional novelist she went on to write wherever she happened to be; though I noticed that for the writing of *Middlemarch* she chose to work at Haslemere.

Another novelist to be much associated with the Portsmouth Road is George Meredith. He was nine years younger than George Eliot. Petersfield claims he was born there; after boyhood in Portsmouth he moved up the road to London. Meredith's first wife was a daughter of Thomas Love Peacock, who lived at Lower Halliford; for the decade of that marriage the Merediths lived nearby at Shepperton; in the same vicinity in which George Eliot produced her first novel, Meredith, two years later, produced *The Ordeal of Richard Feverel*. After the break-up of his marriage Meredith settled near Esher. Long walks in Surrey were his favourite recreation; exploring the valley of the Mole led him to notice Flint Cottage, at Box Hill, and in 1867 he bought that house as permanent home for the rest of his long life.

I have to admit that Box Hill is off to one side of my triangle, and farther south beside the Portsmouth Road (though not far away from the triangle) is South Harting in West Sussex where Anthony Trollope came to live in 1880 for the last two years of his life. It was also in 1880 that H. G. Wells's mother became housekeeper to the family at Uppark, near South Harting. From the age of fourteen Wells was thus familiar with Uppark, which appears as 'Bladesover' in *Tono-Bungay* (though the housekeeper in the novel is not to be identified with his mother). It was an enormous stimulus to Wells as a boy to have the run of the library at Uppark, and adventures in that part of the country entered later into fiction – the apprenticeship as pharmacist in Midhurst appears in *Tono-Bungay*, and the experience as a draper's assistant in King's Road, Southsea (Wells worked there for two years, mainly to please his mother) is very much a feature of *Mr Polly*.

At Godalming Aldous Huxley was born in 1894, but associations with earlier novelists are my present concern. Charterhouse School, which was moved from London to its present site at Godalming, in 1872, brought with it an archway from its former site, carved with names of former Carthusians. Thackeray was one such who will soon come in for mention; here at Godalming the manuscript of *The Newcomes* is one of the treasures of the Charterhouse School Library. The old Portsmouth Road (rejoined by the Guildford bypass at Milford) rises through heathy country to Hindhead. Here for ten years before the death of his first wife in 1906 Conan Doyle lived in the house he had built and named Undershaw – the site had been chosen for Mrs Doyle's health, for Grant Allen had told Doyle that the soil and air of Hindhead were a cure for consumption. Doyle himself was often away as man of action in various causes, including the services during the Boer War which brought him his knighthood in 1902. With their mother an invalid, the two children of that marriage had much freedom, as boy and girl, to roam the countryside, and their summer holidays at Seaview, near Ryde, were enjoyed without much supervision from their seemingly slightly frightening father.

The occasion in Conan Doyle's own childhood when Thackeray momently appeared, as if one of the family, in the Doyles' home in Edinburgh, will be mentioned when I journey in Scotland. Doyle's childhood background there made it natural for him to take to writing; while a medical student he tried his hand at stories; then in his first years as a doctor in Southsea it was imperative to have additional earnings, and a first notable success was a story accepted by the *Cornhill*. To the young doctor (aged then twenty-four) the payment of twenty-nine guineas was wonderful; but the greater elation was that his own writing appeared in the magazine founded and edited in the beginning by Thackeray. Throughout Conan Doyle's life one of his deepest wishes was that his historical novels might put him into the company of the author of *Henry Esmond*.

Where the old Portsmouth Road skirted the Devil's Punch Bowl at Hindhead, Dickens stopped to look at the memorial stone which attested to the murder there of a sailor and to the fate of the assassins – for Dickens describes Smike listening to that inscription 'with greedy interest' when Nicholas Nickleby read it out to him. From the crossroads at Hindhead a short run south reaches Haslemere, where George Eliot wrote most of *Middlemarch*, while living at Shottermill for several months in 1871. Another writer associated with Haslemere is George Macdonald, whose *At the Back of the North Wind* was written in the same year as *Middlemarch*. Then leaving Haslemere by Tennyson's Lane one reaches Blackdown, with Tennyson's view of the Sussex Weald – 'Green Sussex fading into blue, with one gray glimpse of sea'. Tennyson built his house Aldworth, where he died in 1892, on the eastern slope of Blackdown.

At Liphook, the Portsmouth Road has entered Hampshire. Here Sidney and Beatrice Webb, the prominent Fabians, lived and worked; Sidney Webb, who became Lord Passfield, died here at Passfield Corner in 1947. And now we swing away westward, to pass through Selborne and to reach, towards Alton, the village of Chawton. At Chawton, the very centre of my novelist-creating triangle, the irresistible impulse of the area seems quite independently to have stimulated Jane Austen. Jane's brother Edward organized the move to Chawton in 1809 for the widowed Mrs Austen, the friend Martha Lloyd, and Cassandra and Jane, the two unattached daughters of the Austen family, who had continued to lodge at Bath after the death of the Rev. George Austen in 1805. They had then moved to Southampton, but needed a permanent home and Edward, the older brother who had been adopted by the childless and wealthy Thomas Knight and who had now inherited the beautiful landed properties of Godmersham in Kent and Chawton in Hampshire, offered his mother a choice of two convenient houses. One of these was near the grounds of Godmersham and the other stood in the village street of Chawton, opposite the Great House. The ladies happily accepted Chawton. Time and road-making have altered the village: in their day the house, near the crossroads leading respectively to Gosport and Winchester, fronted on the street and was alive to what Mrs Austen is said to have enjoyed, the 'stimulating noise of wheels and hoofs'. (The old lady's granddaughter Caroline, when staying there as a child, maintained it was greatly comforting 'to have the awful stillness of night frequently broken by the sound of passing carriages'.) Edward had the big window to the left of the front door bricked up and that room was allowed to look out upon the garden. However, the window of the right-hand room remained peno to the street, and after the four ladies were installed a gentleman who was travelling by their door in a post-chaise reported that they were 'looking very comfortable at breakfast'.

From the time of arrival at Chawton Mrs Austen gave over the affairs of the household entirely to Cassandra and Jane, while she supervised the garden and its produce, on occasion putting on 'a round green smock like a labourer's' and digging the potatoes. Within doors the energetic elderly mother (she was to survive Jane by ten years) worked on a splendid patchwork quilt, and also took to knitting gloves. Jane's special charge was seeing that breakfast was prepared every day at nine and she also looked after the store cupboard. To replenish supplies of tea, sugar and wine, and for other shoppings, Jane enjoyed driving herself by donkey-cart into the nearby town of Alton. All other housekeeping duties seem to have been assumed by Cassandra, apparently as pleased as was Jane that the Chawton household should be arranged to allow Jane to return to the writings which had been interrupted by her father's death and the temporary stay at Southampton. The left-hand parlour at Chawton was the larger of the two, and there was Jane's piano. She could have that room to herself before breakfast, and customarily played to herself every morning – the piano was solely for Jane's own pleasure, her nieces thought, for the others did not much care for music and she was never known to play in company. The room to the right of the front door was in general the common sitting room, and contained Jane's mahogany writing desk. There, overlooking (and sometimes looked into from) the street, Jane did find opportunity to revise *Sense and Sensibility* and wholly re-create *Pride and Prejudice* for publication, and in subsequent years to work on *Mansfield Park*, *Emma* and *Persuasion*. All biographers have commented on her ability to concentrate despite interruptions of callers or children (nephews and nieces from Steventon) walking in. 'Her sole protections against the world were a door which creaked, whose hinges she asked might remain unattended to because they gave her warning that somebody was coming, and the blotting paper under which she slipped her small sheets of exquisitely written manuscript when a visitor was shown in.'

Much has been made of that 'creaking door that shielded a novelist from the world', yet the writings Jane achieved in the eight years of her life at Chawton suggest that her devoted elder sister Cassandra was responsible for a great deal of protection for her work. It was not so much visitations that bothered Jane as the full drag of daily housekeeping at such times as Cassandra (who was in much demand from her brothers when their wives were childbearing) was taken away. Then, in Cassandra's absence, Jane really could complain: 'I find composition impossible with my head full of joints of mutton and doses of rhubarb.' When Jane herself was away from Chawton, as in the months spent at Godmersham in Kent, her niece Fanny (as mentioned earlier) was able to give an almost embarrassing amount of luxurious quiet to the author-aunt. Yet Jane did not like Kent or Canterbury so much as Hampshire; she called herself one of 'the Hampshire-born Austens', and throughout the eight years that the pleasure was granted she is imagined as returning very happily to Chawton and the house with the creaking door.

By 1815, though, Jane's health was a matter of secret concern, and by the next year the whole family was beset with troubles. A lawsuit had developed over Chawton Manor; Edward was in danger of having to hand over the Chawton property. Simultaneously the brother Henry, by then a banker in London, who regarded himself as the closest of Jane's literary advisers and who from the beginning had been her agent in publishing matters, was causing acute anxiety. In 1815 Henry had been much involved in the transfer of Jane's publishing rights to the celebrated Mr Murray; Henry had also indirectly been the cause of the Prince Regent's invitation to Miss Austen to be shown the library at Carlton House, where the suggestion was made (or so she *thought*) that the Prince Regent would take it kindly if her next novel were dedicated to him. But in that autumn, while Jane was with him in London, Henry had suddenly been so alarmingly ill with an inflammatory fever that

Jane hurriedly sent for Edward, James and Cassandra. For a week the whole family thought Henry to be dying. After that Jane stayed in London to nurse him. Presently the mercurial Henry bounced back into activity, but only to find himself in sudden and acute financial disaster. The bank at Alton, of which he was a backer, had failed; he was involved to such an extent that in March 1816 he was declared bankrupt.

Henry Austen's happy disposition was such that on being declared bankrupt, with cheerfulness and conviction he rapidly brushed up his knowledge of the Greek Testament and applied for ordination in the Church. The lawsuit had cost Edward much worry and money – and Henry's failure had also involved him in considerable loss – but he managed to retain Chawton, and so the ladies there were not evicted. But for Jane the strain of nursing Henry and of the other family worries was more dangerous than even she recognized. She did become aware, in her forty-first year, that she could not count on health for much longer. Work at the writing desk seems to have taken on all the more importance. In 1816 she finished *Persuasion*, a very short novel yet the favourite of many; it was in one sense finished in July 1816, but there is some evidence to indicate that in March 1817 she was still keeping the manuscript by her for possible revisions. Meanwhile she was thinking about, and in January 1817 began to write, the unfinished novel to which her family attached the name *Sanditon*. Henry Austen also arrived at Chawton to place on her writing desk the manuscript of *Northanger Abbey*, which for thirteen years had been lying unused in the office of a Messrs Crosby in London. That manuscript was the early novel which Henry on Jane's behalf had sold to Crosby in 1803 for a sum of ten pounds; everybody then appeared gradually to forget about it. Yet 'before the transformation of Henry' (as Elizabeth Jenkins puts it) from London banker into country clergyman, his memory, as if prompted by bankruptcy, recalled the neglected asset; he visited the Crosby office, repaid the ten pounds, and bore away the old manuscript to return it to Jane. In the January of 1817 Jane had no energy to spare for anything but *Sanditon*; she did nothing about *Northanger Abbey* except to add a prefatory note and to put it 'upon the shelf for the present'.

By the middle of March 1817 Jane Austen's condition was too poorly for her to continue with *Sanditon*. She wished to get out of doors and breathe fresh air but walking exhausted her. Edward and Cassandra rigged up a saddle for her to ride on one of the donkeys, and with him on one side and Cassandra on the other they had at least one short triumphant outdoor round, which Jane wrote to her niece Fanny that she had liked very much. 'Aunt Cass is such an excellent nurse,' her letter said, 'so assiduous and unwearied! But you know that already.' At the beginning of April her spirits were suddenly dashed by the failure to materialize of an expected bequest to Mrs Austen. This bequest, from Mrs Austen's well-to-do and only brother, the ladies at Chawton had come to count on for their future security. The news that there was no such bequest was a general shock, and to Jane, in her physical weakness, the shock caused an alarming relapse. Within weeks further and severe symptoms caused Mr Lyford, a highly skilled apothecary of Winchester, to be sent for; he did what he could, but the patient grew weaker. Towards the end of May Cassandra drove with Jane in Winchester, where a pleasant lodging had been found, close to the school, overlooking the headmaster's garden on the opposite side of the lane. There Mr Lyford could be in regular attendance, and there June passed into July. Jane's brothers visited; she read and re-read letters from friends and family and nieces in particular – Fanny's letters gave perhaps the most pleasure of all – and Cassandra was steadily and always there for talk and comfort. But her illness (probably Addison's Disease) was incurable. At half-past four on the morning of 18 July 1817 Jane died in the arms of Cassandra.

Her contemporary Walter Scott often communed with himself about novel writing. On 14 March 1826 his diary records this:

Read again for the third time at least, Miss Austen's finely written novel of *Pride and Prejudice*. That young lady had a talent for describing the involvements and feelings and characters of ordinary life which is to me the most wonderful I ever met with. The big Bow-Wow strain I can do myself like any now going; but the exquisite touch which renders ordinary commonplace things and characters interesting from the truth of the description and the sentiment, is denied to me. What a pity such a gifted creature died so early!

The house at Chawton has now been restored as nearly as possible to the state in which Jane Austen knew it, and it is preserved as her museum.

*   *   *

When I skipped away from the Portsmouth Road at Liphook to swing west through Selborne for Chawton, I was too concerned with Jane Austen to stop at Selborne to look into the home of Gilbert White (1720–93), the naturalist. The many who come here for memory of his *Natural History and Antiquities of Selborne* and for his famous *Letters* – the many who, to quote W. H. Hudson, 'love the memory of Gilbert White, and regard the spot where he was born, to which he was so deeply attached, where his ashes lie, as almost a sacred place' – find that his house, since 1955, has been opened as a museum and library. From Hudson's own books I judge he would have had mixed feelings about making Gilbert White's home into a showplace. Hudson's own first visit to Selborne is recorded in the last chapter of his book *Birds and Man*, and many of his further rambles in this countryside, with his own naturalist's eye on everything from the grasshoppers to the yew trees, and on human species also, are in his *Hampshire Days*. Hudson was living at Bournemouth when he wrote several of his most delightful books about the English countryside.

Another 'countryside' writer, the poet Edward Thomas (1878–1917), is particularly associated with the hamlet at Steep, near Petersfield. In the sixty years since Thomas's death interest and pleasure in his poems have steadily increased. Although he was killed in battle, at Arras in 1917, Thomas's permanent fame is not as a war poet but as an observant lover of the country, and friend especially of the corner of Hampshire around Petersfield. Two lancet windows have been designed by Laurence Whistler to be placed in the parish church of Steep to commemorate the centenary of Edward Thomas's birth.

Yet having returned at Petersfield to the Portsmouth Road, it is to Portsmouth and Fareham that I hurry on to continue the associations with novelists. For after Austen and Scott there was another waiting period, though only a short one, before further novelists of an indisputably top class arrived at the base of my triangle – Dickens at Portsmouth, Thackeray at Fareham.

The house in Portsmouth that Dickens was born in, No. 1 Mile End Terrace, Landport, was at some time renamed as No. 393 Commercial Road, and was opened to the public as a Dickens museum. In that house John Dickens, a clerk in the Navy Pay Office, proposed to support the eighteen-year-old Elizabeth Barrow when they were married in 1809. It had been impressed on John Dickens that he had to live in a style suitable to the bride's father, who was no less than Charles Barrow, Chief Conductor of Moneys in the Navy Pay Office. I notice that in his study of Dickens Angus Wilson attends to the 'social tight-rope acrobatics' whereby John Dickens kept up with the Barrows. The Barrow daughter Elizabeth, aged eighteen, had chosen to fling herself away on the histrionic young clerk whose parents – this was the blot on the Dickens scutcheon – had been domestic servants. That had to be concealed; yet a year after the marriage a much bigger skeleton (as Angus Wilson expresses it) suddenly appeared in the cupboard of the Barrow family. Charles Barrow, the genteel honoured Chief Conductor of naval moneys, was found to have been for years embezzling them. When this was discovered, he fled abroad, later settling in the Isle of Man, safe at that time from English legal jurisdiction. The young Dickenses, both strongly given to self-dramatization, found an element of enjoyment mixed with the excitement; though the rest of the Barrow family were horrified at the scandal the Dickenses seem to have taken it relatively lightheartedly. They already had one daughter, Fanny, but promptly named their firstborn son Charles after the defaulting grandfather.

The young Dickenses carried on in Portsmouth in what was to become the Micawber tradition, cheerfully overspending at No. 1 Mile End Terrace. When the baby Charles was seven months old, debts forced them to move to cheaper quarters at No. 16 Hawke Street (now vanished). In later life Dickens claimed to have some memories from the Portsmouth life which he left before he was three. It is more than likely that throughout the ups and downs of family life the often-rehearsed stories of events and people of the Portsmouth period contributed, for one example, to the creation in *Nicholas Nickleby* of the Crummles family – and privately I have sometimes thought of Mrs Nickleby (brought up, it is indicated, near Dawlish in Devon) as not unrelated to the Barrows. It was Elizabeth, his grandmother, that Dickens spoke of as wishing, in her old age, to be got up in sables 'like a female Hamlet'. Portsmouth was then, for Dickens, much more than merely a birthplace from which he was taken away. *Nicholas Nickleby* indubitably shows his imagination playing with the Portsmouth background.

The importance of Fareham in Thackeray's life he himself recognized in his later years. After his mother's death in India, Thackeray was 'sent home' to England at the age of six and deposited with relatives, the Bechers, at Fareham. He was to be a boarder at a school in Southampton, where the contrast from a protected life in the prosperous household in Calcutta was sharp; when not at school he was with the Bechers, who noticed his instinct to secrete himself in the garden behind the house on the High Street to lose himself in a book. In that garden at Fareham Thackeray read his first novel, which he records as having been *The Scottish Chiefs*.

It was clear to the Bechers that the child was unhappy at school, so in 1818 (when Thackeray was seven) he was transferred to what they hoped was a better school up the length of the Portsmouth Road at Chiswick. At that school he was a boarder for the four years until he entered Charterhouse. Thackeray's description of Henry Esmond's lonely boyhood is thought to reflect some of his own feelings at the school in Chiswick and of the time out of school at Fareham. A happier period in his 'education of a gentleman' began when he entered Charterhouse in 1822, lasting through the further eight years of Charterhouse and Cambridge. The generally enjoyable period of inheriting and rapidly spending his fortune was followed by the hard period of unlucky marriage to the wife who became insane after the birth of their third child. Throughout this time before and after he separated from his wife Thackeray struggled for support from journalism. 'Success', such as had come swiftly to Dickens, was achieved only slowly. But by 1848 the *Book of Snobs* and *Vanity Fair* had established his reputation, and for the next fifteen years that part of the public who did not feel that pre-eminence belonged to Dickens, regarded Thackeray as the greatest living novelist. Life for Thackeray ended, though, at the age of fifty-two. He was found dead in his bed at his house in Kensington on Christmas Eve 1863.

In Thackeray's last years his thoughts reverted to Fareham. A sketch drafted by him has an account of life in 'the little old town of Fareport in Hampshire'. In what he named 'Fareport society' he recalled 'scarcely any men' but many widows and daughters, relics of deceased commodores and captains, of families much connected with Portsmouth. Fareham people kept up appearances by various contrivances – it was hard to tell how many families would manage to club together to take in the Portsmouth paper. Life there was in his later recollection so 'like a novel by Jane Austen' that he could wonder: 'Was she born and bred there?' The boyhood vacations at Fareham perhaps influenced him in two ways; he had there begun to be observant of 'life' going on around him, and there he cultivated a fascination with novels in the garden where first of all he had read *The Scottish Chiefs*. I notice now that Thackeray has another connection with my novelist-creating triangle, for it was to Kensington that he was drawn for the years of his own novel-writing: 'his' Kensington from 1847 to 1863 was still the 'old court suburb' where sheep might graze in Kensington Gore and leafy lanes wound on to Fulham. It is natural for Thackeray that the school from which Becky Sharp was to emerge in *Vanity Fair* should be placed at Chiswick. From base to tip my obsessive triangle associates itself with Thackeray.

Just outside my novelists' triangle, between Aldershot and Reading, is Eversley. There, at the rectory, in the midst of many activities from 1842 to 1859, Charles Kingsley wrote busily. His *Westward Ho!* (1854) belongs to that period; *The Water Babies* (1863) was prompted by re-visiting Yorkshire, but there is a claim that most of the actual writing was done at Itchen Abbas, north of Winchester.

Across the mouth of Portsmouth Harbour, at one southern corner of the novelist-producing territory, is Gosport. In our own century unusual talents have continued to outcrop hereabouts, as Arthur Upfield proves. It was in Australia that marks of genius in a number of detective novels concerning a half-aborigine Inspector Napoleon Bonaparte, were first noticed and then widely recognized. Something of a flurry occurred to find out where such genius originated. The answer was – Arthur Upfield was born in Gosport.

4. FROM THE NEW FOREST THROUGH WILTSHIRE

Southampton, at the south-western corner of the triangle that I am now leaving, was the birthplace of George Saintsbury, but Saintsbury, when compiling the histories of English literature from which I have frequently quoted, displayed no favouritism towards fellow-townsmen. Southampton is, for example, the 'Bevishampton' of Meredith's *Beauchamp's Career*. In the eighteenth century the town had a period of great fashion as a spa; among visitors drawn there were Pope, Swift, Voltaire, Gray and Horace Walpole. Southampton also had its own home-talents: for instance, Isaac Watts (1674–1748). Watts, son of a Nonconformist schoolmaster, began to be known for his hymns when he was about twenty; he was encouraged to write out copies by hand to be sung in the Above Bar Chapel. That chapel has vanished, but one at least of Watts's hymns is not forgotten: 'O God, our help in ages past'. When, as here, something breaks through from a deep level, the fact of its being a hymn need not prevent literary appreciation. I thus add Watts to Kipling and Blake as south-coast hymn-writers; but Saintsbury mentions not Watts. I am also distressed that when discussing Captain Marryat, Saintsbury does not refer to Marryat's *The Children of the New Forest*, nor has he any reference to R. L. Stevenson's *The Wrong Box*, for both of those romances are to be remembered pleasurably in the 'forest' country between Southampton Water and the Hampshire Avon.

My excuse for including the Isle of Wight in my previous chapter was that the pursuit of poets led me peremptorily across to the island. Here I keep to the mainland. Traversing the New Forest straightaway from Southampton to Bournemouth, there is suddenly, near Christchurch, a reminder of Walter Scott. Memorials of Shelley are more to be expected: in the churchyard of St Peter's at Bournemouth both Mary Wollstonecraft and Mary Shelley are buried, and it is reputed that Shelley's heart, taken by Trelawny from the body before the burning on the beach near Spezia, was buried there also. In the priory church at Christchurch is a monument to Shelley with Mary, placed here when it had been rejected for Westminster Abbey. The connection with Walter Scott is at Mudeford, east of Christchurch at the entrance to Christchurch Harbour. Here William Rose, to whom Ellis had introduced Scott four years earlier, invited Scott for a visit in the spring of 1807. With Rose, Scott had 'various long rides in the New Forest, a day in the dock-yard of Portsmouth, and two or three more in the Isle of Wight'. Some of the proof-sheets of *Marmion* were corrected and sent off to Edinburgh during this stay in Hampshire, and it is possible that Scott talked with Rose of his design of *Waverley*. (It is an odd though not very important coincidence that the lady whom Waverley was to bring to Hampshire from Scotland was given the christened name, by Scott, of Rose.)

At Bournemouth Stevenson lived for three years (1884–7), and in the house called Skerryvore in Alum Chine Road (destroyed in an air raid in 1940) completed *Kidnapped* and *Dr Jekyll and Mr Hyde*. It was after leaving Britain in search for bodily health and in temporary quarters at Saranac in the Adirondacks that his thoughts, and the independent promptings of the young Lloyd Osbourne, made them combine to produce *The Wrong Box*, the story whose crucial episode is placed in the New Forest. The actual writing at Saranac proceeded with 'such high spirits and hilarity' and the copy was made ready for the press with such 'ease and facility' that *The Wrong Box* played a signal part in the affairs of the Stevensons, making possible the chartering of the yacht *Casco* and the eventual haven-finding in Samoa.

Locating precisely the part of the New Forest that Stevenson had in mind for the train-wreck which was to cause the essential mix-up in *The Wrong Box* is an amusement which requires a close look at a map. Since it was on the railway line of the London and South-Western Railway that the victims encountered 'the apocalyptic whistle and the thundering onslaught of the down express', the scene is not especially close to either Lyndhurst or Minstead – place-names to which quite different literary memories attach. Stevenson's train from Bournemouth with the two old gentlemen in the attire prescribed by the medical baronet Sir Faraday Bond, had passed Christchurch, Herne and Ringwood before it turned eastward to reach the station that Stevenson named Browndean. Some students have identified Browndean as Brockenhurst; but I am of the school which prefers Holmsley. That would place the cottage used by the Finsbury brothers as in the region of the Wilverley Inclosure. The public house which supplied whisky which was 'the worst in Hampshire' (an expression used by Stevenson as a superlative of considerable force) is not to be identified. Each lover of *The Wrong Box* may place the scenes as he pleases.

The other and different memory at Lyndhurst is the grave of Mrs Reginald Hargreaves. Her maiden name was Alice Liddell, and in childhood at Oxford she was the original of Alice in Wonderland; her married life was mostly at Lyndhurst and she was buried here. The other allusion, to Minstead (north of Lyndhurst), will be recognized by readers of Conan Doyle. Minstead's part as the home of Sir Nigel, in *The White Company* and *Sir Nigel*, comes readily to mind, and Conan Doyle's own affectionate pride in those books and his affection for what

Minstead had meant to him were such that they received posthumous recognition. He died at Crowborough in 1930, but after the Second World War his remains were transferred from Crowborough for burial in the churchyard at Minstead.

*   *   *

Revisiting Winchester can lead on to the remaining half of Hampshire and to south Wiltshire. Methodical stock-taking of place-names to be noted in south-west England calls then for survey in turn of Dorset and Somerset, and continuance through Devon and Cornwall. As mileages increase, sites of significance are (perhaps fortunately) less thick on the ground: where separate individual memorials become less crowded, all the more awareness is possible of larger tribal memories, of identifications that are general, regional, and not narrowly confined. Entering south-west England I am aware of entering, in succession, different heartlands. Farther to the west of the Portsmouth Road is the heartland of certain very ancient and perennial 'once and future' impulses, in the land of the Arthurian legends. But first at Winchester I approach one of the other large memories which attach to another whole national background – the background of the Free Anglo-Saxon. At Winchester there is pause in special tribute to Alfred the Great.

Many lesser literary tributes can also be paid there. On the way to Winchester from the south one passes Twyford; at Twyford House in 1771, while in England as agent for the commonwealth of Pennsylvania, Benjamin Franklin put on paper part of his autobiography. Before and after that fairly recent period the list of writers associated with Winchester is formidable. Izaak Walton at the age of eighty-five settled for his last five years with his son-in-law, a canon, at No. 7 The Close; Walton's tomb is in the cathedral. Writers who attended William of Wykeham's famous Winchester College form a notable compilation, from Sir Thomas Browne to Matthew Arnold and later names. Lionel Johnson's poem 'Winchester' rehearses the record of former 'high companions' there. Yet among men of letters at Winchester the name of Alfred is highest of all, for at least one paramount reason. Alfred was the greatest early promoter of the existence of a written English language.

Alfred is credited with picking up every suggestion made by Hilda of Whitby and others of Northumbria before the Danes invaded Britain, to create writings in Anglo-Saxon that might communicate as universally as possible throughout the island. He is also believed to have sponsored the concept of a united English nation with one language nationwide. He himself wrote in 'English', and bore down upon churchmen for their neglect of learning if they were versed only in Latin and not devoted to the new tongue. It has been argued that Alfred's insistence upon his language was in the end the means of amalgamating the Danish invaders. There was no way of preventing Danes from consolidating their monstrous area of the Danelaw, or of preventing immigrants from continuing to seep into it; yet if the Danelaw could be contained by Watling Street as a boundary, and if Danes of their own volition were to feel as much right to snatch the Anglo-Saxon's language as to snatch his lands, there could be an ultimate absorption. That settlers in the Danelaw did in time adopt 'English', did add their own flavours to it, and presently did defend the tongue against Norman-French with as much spirit as if it had been altogether of their own invention, has always seemed of prime importance in the history of the island; and in so far as Alfred foresaw that his 'English' might have power over Danes (and others) his memory may be esteemed for that, more than even for his actions as a warrior with sword or with his long ships. Though many battle-sites recall Alfred, the most significant of sites for those who make use of written words is Winchester. Here was Alfred's best-known workshop, where Asser of South Wales and John the Saxon were brought to manage and assist in the practical work of making the vernacular literary. The greatness of Alfred is not to be pinned for any single reason to any single spot: he is remembered too at Wantage, in the Vale of the White Horse, where, more than eleven hundred years ago, he was born. But after his death the King's body is said to have found its final resting-place at Winchester (the precise location seems now to be unknown) and I venerate Winchester as much for Alfred's language-workshop as for his other achievements.

*   *   *

The road from Winchester westward through Stockbridge passes, soon after entering Wiltshire and six miles before reaching Salisbury, the Pheasant Inn, two miles north of the village of Winterslow. *Winterslow: essays and characters written there* is the title of a volume by William Hazlitt, published posthumously, by which the name of the village became known to distant readers. When at the age of thirty Hazlitt married Sarah Stoddart in 1808, they came to live in one of the cottages she owned here. Charles and Mary Lamb paid them a visit in the following summer, taking what were for the Lambs very long walks to Salisbury, Wilton, and northward to Stonehenge. The visit was memorable, and Charles and Mary repeated it in the following year, but by 1812 the Hazlitts had been forced to move to London for the sake of more income, and in London Hazlitt was one of the early visitors to Leigh Hunt in prison. (The Lambs – both Charles and Mary – Leigh Hunt recorded

also as coming to comfort him 'in all weathers, hail or sunshine, in daylight and in darkness, even in the dreadful frost and snow of the beginning of 1814'.) Hazlitt was one of the few from whom Leigh Hunt would
take 'advice or remonstrance with perfect comfort', for 'notwithstanding
his caprices of temper' Hazlitt was capable of giving genuine disinterested
counsel. ('Lamb could have done it, too; but for interference of any sort
he had an abhorrence.') By 1822, Hazlitt's 'caprices' led to divorce from
Sarah; the absurdities of his *Liber Amoris* in 1823 flaunted his amour
with Miss Walker; his friends supposed that publication was made 'to
burn her out of his thoughts'. Then his sudden marriage to Mrs Bridge-
water, whom he met on the coach journey on the Great North Road
startled Hazlitt's young son, who disliked that widow; but she was 'worth
£300 a year' – and after that marriage Hazlitt, son, and stepmother all
set off on long Continental tours at Hazlitt's wish. On the second tour
'Ill-conduct of the boy' caused the second Mrs Hazlitt to remain in
France and let the two return without her. On these adventures Lamb
looked with concern, though without interference. Curiously, throughout aberrations Hazlitt remained faithful to Winterslow, after his fashion.
Troubles, always accompanied by stomach troubles, had not prevented
his returning to the Pheasant Inn, called affectionately Winterslow Hut;
and he retained the habit.

Much earlier, in June 1668, Pepys and his wife, making a summer
jaunt in considerable style (Pepys having with him his chief clerk, W.
Hewer, and Elizabeth having with her the two maids, Deb and Betty),
came in his own coach to Salisbury from Hungerford, passing 'all over
the Plain by the sight of the steeple' and arriving after dark at the George
Inn, which is still there. That night the maids did not have to sleep in a
truckle-bed beneath Pepys and Elizabeth; the Pepyses had 'a silk bed'
to lie in 'and very good diet'. Next morning Pepys, as others since, found
Salisbury 'a very brave place'. The river, to his delight, went 'through
every street'; the market-place was capacious and 'the Minster most
admirable'. To do everything properly, though saddle-horses would be
very dear, Pepys sent a boy (another 6*d*) for saddle-horses for the party
for the visit to Stonehenge, known to Pepys as 'Stonage'. There were
three other men in the party, so the three women could ride pillion
behind them. Pepys reserved the right to ride single. And so 'to Stonage,
over the Plain and some great hills, even to fright us. Come thither, and
find them as prodigious as any tales I ever heard of them, and worth
going this journey to see. God knows what their use was! they are hard
to tell, but yet may be told.' Pepys's report upon Stonehenge is as good
as that of most people.

If the party had returned to Salisbury along the valley of the Avon
they would have joined that river-road two miles below the rectory at

Milston, where in 1672 Joseph Addison was born; the road from Stonehenge would have brought them to the Avon at Amesbury, where in
Amesbury Abbey, then the seat of the Duke of Queensberry (but destroyed by rebuilding in 1840), it has been said that 'John Gay wrote
The Beggar's Opera in a stone room rather like a cave, known as the
Diamond, on a bank overlooking the River Avon'. Thackeray disputed,
however, that Gay was ever so austere as to use that stone room for
writing. The Duchess's hospitality and his own taste were such that
Gay's life at Amesbury 'was lapped in cotton'. In his last years with the
Queensberrys at the Abbey Gay, in Thackeray's description, 'had his
plate of chicken and saucer of cream, and frisked, and barked, and
wheezed, and grew fat, and died'.

The Beggar's Opera was first produced in 1728, and, much as Pepys
would have enjoyed it, the advent of John Gay, like the advent of
Addison, was for him in the unrevealed future. It was Wilton House,
the great mansion of the Earls of Pembroke, that Pepys had a mind to
see, on his way back from Stonehenge; but when the party had ridden
round that way the moment of arrival at Wilton was inconvenient; they
were not permitted to enter the house and so, in Pepys's diary (in a
mood of sour grapes) he decided it would not have been worth seeing.
Pepys's mood towards the end of that day in Salisbury was less cheerful
than at the beginning. When they were all back at the George Inn, and
had dined, and Pepys had to pay the reckoning, it was 'so exorbitant'
that he 'was mad'. Off he set in his own coach along the road to Warminster, but having been late in starting, by ten at night they could not
get to a town and had to turn into 'a little inn, where we were fain to go
into a room where a pedlar was in bed, and made him rise; and there
wife and I lay, and in a truckle-bed Betty Turner and [Deb] Willett'.
On that next morning, when they got up, they agreed their beds had
been 'good, but lousy; which made us merry' – on Pepys's part to
some extent because the reckoning there was not going to be exorbitant.

In the wide cathedral close at Salisbury, which Pepys admired,
Fielding used to stay as a boy with his maternal grandmother at No. 14.
The first-floor library of Archdeacon Fisher's house in the close, where
John Constable stayed for three extended visits, looked southward over
the water-meadows to Harnham. The depressed remark of an earlier
bishop, that 'Salisbury is the sink of Wiltshire plain, the close is the
sink of Salisbury, and the bishop's palace the sink of the close', indicates
what was the greatest attraction, to Constable, of the cathedral. Turner
made wonderful architectural watercolours at Salisbury, but in almost
all Constable's views of the cathedral, whether pencil, oil or watercolour,
he chooses to have water in the foreground. Water seemed almost as
requisite to Constable as his 'chief organ of sentiment', his skies – that

is to say, as requisite to Constable as a painter – for Salisbury as a place, painting apart, he had no special affection: he called it 'muggy'.

Another visitor to Salisbury who was delighted, like Pepys, to find the river flowing under the streets and 'the Minster most admirable', was Anthony Trollope, who after ten years of working for the Post Office in Ireland had been moved, in 1851, to work which covered Gloucestershire and Somerset. Not confined to those counties, he records in the *Autobiography*: 'Wandering one mid-summer evening round the purlieus of Salisbury Cathedral I conceived the story of *The Warden*, from whence came the series of novels of which Barchester, with its bishops, deans and archdeacons was the central site. . . .' He makes a point in the *Autobiography* of recalling 'the little bridge in Salisbury' where he had stood for an hour planning the spot on which Hiram's Hospital should stand. Rather more than twenty years before him Constable had lingered beside that same Harnham Bridge (over which goes St Nicholas Road, which passes St Nicholas's Hospital) – as is proved by a pencil sketch in the British Museum and by his oil painting in the Wernher Collection. It is pleasant today to pause on that Harnham Bridge; but Michael Sadleir's study of Trollope makes it clear that 'Barchester' derives as much or more from Winchester as from Salisbury; and the county of 'Barset', which Trollope says in the *Last Chronicle of Barset* 'to me has been a real county', is probably largely Somerset, yet with admixture of Dorset, Gloucestershire and Wiltshire, 'over nearly every acre of which he is known to have travelled'. Trollope wrote 'from experience selected and carefully mixed', said Sadleir, and in his book reproduces Trollope's own sketch-map of 'Barsetshire', and two other maps worked up from details (often contradictory) given in the various novels, by two devoted Trollopians to whom Sadleir gives full credit, 'Mr Spencer van Botekelen Nichols in America and Father Ronald Knox in England'.

Three miles west of Salisbury is the carpet-making town of Wilton; the great Wilton House, south of the town, was the seat of successive Earls of Pembroke (of the Herbert family) from the fifteenth century onwards. Many of the family were buried in Salisbury Cathedral: one diamond-shaped stone near the altar is inscribed to 'Sidney's sister, Pembroke's mother'. Sir Philip Sidney began and wrote much of *Arcadia* when staying with his sister either at Wilton House or (according to John Aubrey) at Ivy Church nearby. Tradition says that in the great hall at Wilton House Shakespeare acted in a performance of *As You Like It* given there in the presence of King James I.

The names of Spenser, Ben Jonson, Massinger, and later Izaak Walton and Aubrey, can also be associated with Wilton. I select, though, the seventeenth-century poet George Herbert. Induced to adopt religious life by Nicholas Ferrar and ordained as priest, Herbert was appointed to the benefice, in 1630, of Bemerton, halfway between Wilton and Salisbury, a low-lying parish sometimes flooded by the River Nadder. Herbert was thirty-seven when he became incumbent of what Izaak Walton called the 'more pleasant than healthful parsonage'; he had barely three full years there in which to perform his duties and also write the poems which from his deathbed he sent to Ferrar at Little Gidding, before in March 1633 he died of consumption. Ferrar saw to the publication of the poems, *The Temple*, within the same year. Nearly forty years later Walton wrote the short *Life of Herbert* (1670) which, taken together with *The Temple*, gave to the Church of England what Helen Gardner calls 'a legend and an ideal'.

There is pleasure in going to Walton's pages for his account of 'Herbert's aristocracy of temper, his exquisite courtesy, and power to win hearts'. On one of his twice-a-week walks to Salisbury for his 'Music-meetings', Walton says:

he saw a poor man with a poorer horse, that was fallen under his load: they were both in distress, and needed present help; which Mr Herbert perceiving, put off his canonical coat, and helped the poor man to unload, and after to load his horse. The poor man blessed him for it, and he blessed the poor man; and was so like the Good Samaritan, that he gave him money to refresh both himself and his horse; and told him, 'That if he loved himself he should be merciful to his beast'. Thus he left the poor man: and at his coming to his musical friends at Salisbury, they began to wonder that Mr George Herbert, which used to be so trim and clean, came into that company so soiled and discomposed: but he told them the occasion. And when one of the company told him 'He had disparaged himself by so dirty an employment', his answer was, 'That the thought of what he had done would prove music to him at midnight; and that the omission of it would have upbraided and made discord in his conscience, whensoever he should pass by that place: for if I be bound to pray for all that be in distress, I am sure that I am bound, so far as it is in my power, to practise what I pray for. And though I do not wish for the like occasion every day, yet let me tell you, I would not willingly pass one day of my life without comforting a sad soul, or shewing mercy; and I praise God for this occasion. And now let's tune our instruments'.

Perhaps the oddest of writing-characters in the whole of this part of Wiltshire (if not John Aubrey, who lived for periods at Broad Chalke) is the William Beckford (1759–1844) who wrote *Vathek*. His father, also named William Beckford, had been the Lord Mayor of London who in 1770 laid the first stone of Newgate Prison, and in that same year he died, leaving to the eleven-year-old son at the family mansion at Fonthill Giffard (twelve miles west of Wilton) a million pounds and the not inconsiderable income of £100,000 a year. The boy was soon on tour abroad with a private tutor; he wrote *Vathek* in French, in his early twenties; on return to England he gradually retired into an almost complete seclusion at Fonthill Giffard. He rebuilt his father's house, and then demolished it. He commissioned Wyatt, the architect who was reviving interest in the Gothic style, to build for him a 'convent partly in ruins and partly perfect'. The 'Fonthill Abbey' so constructed was then fantastically decorated and supplied with a wide collection of works of art and curios. Hazlitt inspected it, reporting that it was 'a glittering waste of laborious idleness, a cathedral turned into a toyshop'. By 1822 Beckford's extravagance recoiled upon him; he was compelled to dispose of Fonthill, retiring into even more seclusion; all that now remains of his Abbey is one of the smaller towers.

At Trowbridge in 1814 George Crabbe, whose early years we saw in Suffolk, became, as a widower at the age of sixty, resident rector for the remaining eighteen years of his life. The East Anglian Crabbe, with his genetic links to the ancient Danelaw, was not readily accepted by everybody in this Wiltshire region, whose racial tradition was that of King Alfred's Wessex. The pious William Lisle Bowles (whose poems galvanized young Coleridge) observed with alarm some of the sparks when East Anglian flint struck West Country granite. For a parliamentary election shortly after his installation as rector Crabbe spoke in favour of the candidate 'to whom the manufacturing interest, the prevalent one in his parish, was extremely hostile'. In the account by Bowles: 'A riotous, tumultuous, and most appalling mob, at the time of election, besieged his house, when a chaise was at the door, to prevent his going to the poll.' Crabbe came out, spoke to 'the furious assemblage', told them 'they might kill him if they chose', but short of that nothing should prevent his voting according to his promise. There must have been something in his presence to calm the mob, for Crabbe drove to the poll unhurt.

Other conflicts in Crabbe's first years at Trowbridge eased, and as he aged his social behaviour, especially to ladies, softened to what Saintsbury called 'an easy *bonhomie*, which sometimes approached the childish'. Thomas Moore's friendship with Crabbe increased after he likewise settled in Wiltshire (Moore lived at Chittoe till 1852 and was buried at Bromham, north of Devizes); he remarked that in the older man's manner to women there was 'a sweetness bordering rather too much upon what the French call *doucereux*', and he quoted one lady as saying, in allusion to this excessive courtesy, 'the cake is no doubt very good, but there is too much sugar to cut through in getting at it'. Crabbe's conversation contrasted with the poems which, after a lapse of twenty years in middle life, he resumed producing in his fifties. In public conversation his absence of sporting talk with men and his archness of manner with women might be noticed, but in the poems there continued to be the same sure, original, astringent touch in accurately painting 'as Truth will paint it, and as Bards will not' that in his younger days had much pleased Burke and Johnson. Thus *The Borough* (1810) gave solid satisfaction to Jane Austen; of such poems none could say that there was too much sugar to cut through before getting to the cake. The earning-power of Crabbe's later poems was surprising. Mr Murray the publisher paid £3000 outright for *Tales of the Hall* in 1819, and as the elderly poet pocketed bankbills for that sum he had innocent pride in reflecting that it was a thousand times his once total monetary capital, which had been £3 when as a young man he had worked his sea-passage from Aldeburgh to London.

5. FROM HARDY'S WESSEX TO DEVON

Dorset is the heart of Thomas Hardy's Wessex. The map of Wessex in his novels, thoughtfully placed by Messrs Macmillan in their editions of the books, shows where each of his episodes are located, and pilgrimage to almost every scene that Hardy writes about has thereby been made easy. The total area over which readers of Hardy claim jurisdiction is wide – not quite so wide as the land to which King Alfred had prior claim, yet wide enough – from Hardy's 'Solentsea' of the Portsmouth area to the north coasts of Devon and Cornwall, and from Oxford ('Christminster') to the Isle of Portland (the 'Isle of Slingers'). The central area about which Hardy's readers may feel most possessive is the area in which he was born and, for the most part, lived: that part of Dorset which surrounds Dorchester (which in the novels is 'Casterbridge').

The small thatched cottage where Hardy was born in 1840 had been built by his great-grandfather in the hamlet of Higher Bockhampton, three miles north-east of Dorchester, off the road towards Puddletown and Tolpuddle. The cottage –

> It faces west, and round the back and sides
> High beeches, bending, hand a veil of boughs,
> And sweep against the **roof**

– is now a National Trust property. Care had been taken to preserve the room in which, at a table by the window, and after his return from his five years in the architect's office in London, Hardy worked at *Under the Greenwood Tree*, the first really successful effort to prove that he might turn from the profession of architect to that of novelist. In that book he wrote with the affection derived from childhood of 'the Mellstock Quire', 'Mellstock' being Stinsford, a mile nearer Dorchester, where it had been traditional for the Hardys to take part in instrumental music at Stinsford parish church. Then his mood was good, but more than forty years later he less happily brooded on his other self revisiting the cottage, yet too uneasy to linger:

> And I make again for Mellstock to return here never,
> And rejoin the roomy silence, and the mute and manifold
> > Souls of old.

After his long life ended in 1928 Hardy did 'make again for Mellstock': although his ashes went to Westminster Abbey, it was thought right for his heart to be buried in Stinsford churchyard. In that same churchyard is the later grave, within a few feet of Hardy's, of the poet Cecil Day Lewis (1904–72).

When *Under the Greenwood Tree* was published in 1872, Leslie Stephen was so much impressed by it that he invited Hardy to write a serial for the *Cornhill*. The result was *Far from the Madding Crowd*, completed at the table by the window of the Bockhampton cottage, and published in 1874. But before Hardy gave up architectural work he visited St Juliot's, on the Cornish coast near Tintagel, to restore the church; there he met and quickly fell in love with Emma Lavinia Gifford, who in 1874 became his first wife. The couple then for some years lived in various places. In 1885 Hardy built a house of his own design just outside Dorchester, on the Wareham Road. (The Dorset poet, William Barnes (1801–86), who lived in South Street, Dorchester, was regarded as the town's chief literary figure until Hardy was awarded that position.) At this house, Max Gate, Hardy lived for the rest of his life, and the bulk of his writings was done here; the study at Max Gate has been reconstructed at the Dorset County Museum in Dorchester, and the manuscript of *The Mayor of Casterbridge* is one of the relics preserved there.

During the 1920s the number of notable people who sought to visit Hardy at Max Gate was very large; among the many was the consciously eccentric T. E. Lawrence, whose fame as 'Lawrence of Arabia' was not dimmed by his entering the RAF in 1922 as an aircraftman under the name Ross, or by the later alteration of his name by deed poll to T. E. Shaw. When serving temporarily as 'Private Shaw' in the Tank Corps with duty at Bovington Camp, Lawrence rented a derelict cottage at Clouds Hill, nine miles east of Dorchester. In 1935, when discharged from the Services, Lawrence returned to live at Clouds Hill; but within a short time there was the fatal crash on his fast-ridden motorcycle. The cottage at Clouds Hill, which contained Lawrence's gramophone, books, furniture and other relics, was taken over and is preserved by the National Trust. Lawrence's literary fame was achieved mainly by his large work *Seven Pillars of Wisdom*, of which an abridgement, *Revolt in the Desert*, had previously won spectacular success in 1927. A century before the First World War Lady Hester Stanhope had shown that an intrepid English eccentric could establish fervent devotion among Arab revolutionaries; the 1914–18 war enabled Lawrence to step into that tradition and, as a guerilla leader of genius, to improve upon it. Yet, after the war, in the occasional meetings and correspondences which he initiated, one felt at once both power and emptiness; I recall a secretary exclaiming that he was 'a terrifying little man'. The sitting-room at Clouds Hill, left I suppose as Lawrence left it, gives to me a painful impression of unhappiness.

A happy memory of the Dorset coast hereabouts is provided by J. Meade Falkner's *Moonfleet*. The publication of Stevenson's *Treasure Island* in 1883 had whetted a demand for rival adventure stories: Rider Haggard consciously competed with Stevenson when he produced *King Solomon's Mines* (1885) but the African setting avoided invidious comparisons with *Treasure Island*. *Moonfleet* (1898), in so far as the boy-hero is involved with smugglers and a sea-adventure, is more nearly in the *Treasure Island* pattern, and in my view has several points of superiority. Falkner's firm writing achieves effect without the taint of over-writing; and a singular pleasure of *Moonfleet* is the abiding feeling it conveys for the Dorset coast from Portland Bill to St Albans Head, and the tunnels and caves within Purbeck itself. Meade Falkner was born in 1858 at Manningford Bruce in Wiltshire, the son of a poor clergyman. As a boy he knew intimately the Dorset quarry coast, and the feeling for it stayed with him throughout his unusual career. We have already mentioned that he became chairman of the armaments firm of Armstrong Whitworth, and combined the life of a businessman of great ability with the function of Reader in Palaeography at Durham University. He died at Durham in 1932 and was buried at Burford, in Oxfordshire.

South-west of Dorchester, after passing Maiden Castle and over Black Down, is Abbotsbury, and on the coast beyond Abbotsbury – beside the western end of the Chesil Bank – was a pair of former coastguard cottages, which I remember inhabited during summers, in the late 1920s, on one side by Middleton Murry and on the other by H. M. Tomlinson. I have a personal fondness for one of Tomlinson's books, *A Mingled Yarn*, in that some of the essays there collected have reminders of many talks at Tulk's Hill beside the Chesil Bank. I was not at Tulk's Hill, though, when Thomas Hardy visited Tommy there, as recorded in the essay 'A Brown Owl'. The owl, Joey, had joined the Tomlinson family, and if they were to be visited by Mr Hardy, so was he:

I believe that great man had a special regard for owls; the author of *The Dynasts*, we may fairly suppose, would know why the owl is Athene's familiar. In any case, the venerable poet and Joey unexpectedly confronted each other. It was a strange experience for the rest of us, who stood and watched them. They did not speak; they regarded each other intently, but I do not know what passed between them. Presently the poet turned sadly away; and the owl directed his gaze elsewhere as though entirely satisfied.

* * *

Lyme Regis takes one swiftly back to Jane Austen's *Persuasion*. The stone pier, called the Cobb, was pointed out to Tennyson as the place where the Duke of Monmouth landed to raise the rebellion against James II which was crushed at Sedgemoor. 'Don't talk to me of the Duke of Monmouth,' said Tennyson. 'Show me the exact spot where Louisa Musgrove fell "and was taken up lifeless".'

Inland from Lyme, and about halfway between Lyme and Crewkerne, is Racedown Farm, below Pilsdon Pen, the highest hill in Dorset. Wordsworth and his sister Dorothy were allowed to live at Racedown rent-free for the two years 1795–7. There Wordsworth wrote *The Borderers*; the perceptive Swinburne remarked on the strange tensions that tragedy displayed, and wondered what was on Wordsworth's mind when writing it. One unrevealed strain was the poet's concealment of his love affair in the first years of the French Revolution with Marie-Anne Vallon, and the consciousness of responsibility for some of the care, to which he was unable to contribute, of his illegitimate French daughter. No one in England except Wordsworth's sister Dorothy as yet knew Wordsworth's secret. Coleridge came to visit the Wordsworths at Racedown, and Wordsworth and Dorothy repaid by visiting Coleridge in Somerset. Thoughts of issuing the *Lyrical Ballads* were on the way. In the summer of 1797 the Wordsworths moved into Somerset in order to be nearer Coleridge, who with his young wife Sarah, of whom he had not yet tired, was living, in dynamic spirits, at Nether Stowey.

The outline of Dorset on the map is the shape of a left fist punching northward; at the second knuckle of the pugnacious fist is Shaftesbury. The description of the old town, dramatically situated on its cliff, is vivid in *Jude the Obscure* (where Hardy calls it 'Shaston'). It was to a manor house at East Stour, four miles west of Shaftesbury, that Fielding's parents moved when Henry Fielding was three, and where the boy was presently tutored by the parson not very kindly depicted as Parson

Trulliber in *Joseph Andrews*. Fielding was then schooled at Eton, where he was contemporary with Pitt and Fox, and returning to Dorset fell somewhat tempestuously in love with a young heiress of Lyme Regis. An attempted elopement was thwarted by an angry guardian; the violence that Fielding and his manservant were alleged to have threatened was unsuccessful; the lady, torn away from Fielding, was married to another. Fielding was packed off by his father to study law at Leyden. When he returned, the lady whom he did marry in 1734 – his first wife – was affectionately portrayed as 'Sophia' in *Tom Jones*, when Fielding was writing that novel after her death. For a short time after their marriage Henry and his 'Sophia' lived in the now vanished manor house at East Stour, before the pull of London took them back to Town.

On the way from East Stour to Sherborne, at the crossroads at Henstridge, is the inn where the maid (whose name I have failed to find) doused Sir Walter Raleigh with the contents of a tankard as he sat in the sunshine on the bench outside. The action as I conceive it was done from within the open window, and it was an action eminently reasonable and quick-witted, for smoke was rising around the gentleman's head and flames might blaze at any minute. This happy episode, deserving much reflection, occurred in the early 1590s, when Raleigh held a long lease of Sherborne Castle, and was there (rebuilding the central portion of it in 1594) because Elizabeth considered that his conduct had disgraced her court (according to Aubrey's account, it had).

The road that I have been following from Shaftesbury through Sherborne proceeds into Somerset just before Yeovil. A few miles south of Yeovil is East Coker, where T. S. Eliot's Somerset forebears lived. Eliot visited East Coker with thoughts of the house, in the double sense of that word, started by his ancestor, the Sir Thomas Elyot who was born (some editors estimate) exactly four hundred years before the Thomas Eliot whose birth had come about in 1888 in St Louis. After 'our' Eliot the male line of that house – of his particular branch – was to become extinct. I know our Eliot had feelings that the former Elyot was the beginning of an era of which he was the ending. As for the lines which conclude the first stanza of 'East Coker' –

> Houses live and die: there is a time for building
> And a time for living and for generation
> And a time for the wind to break the loosened pane
> And to shake the wainscot where the field-mouse trots
> And to shake the tattered arras woven with a silent motto

– I can supply a comment. The spelling of the word *arras* in the last line above is as Geoffrey Faber insisted that it should appear in the printed *Four Quartets*. In the typescript which Eliot mailed to me for the

American printing, the above last line had been restored by him to the way he had written it:

> And to shake the tattered arasse woven with a silent motto.

The reason for spelling *arasse*? It is the way Sir Thomas Elyot had spelled it in *The Governour* four centuries before. 'With riche arasse or tapestrye' is what is found in the earlier Elyot with whom the later Eliot was expressing identity: they were beginning and end of the same house – the house whose motto of reticence, *tacet et fecit*, is one to which Eliot often referred. Faber as publisher felt the antique spelling would confuse most readers. Faber had his way, but the modern print rankled with Eliot.

> The village of East Coker is approached by the deep lane
> Shuttered with branches, dark in the afternoon,
> Where you lean against a bank while a van passes,
> And the deep lane insists on the direction
> Into the village, in the electric heat
> Hypnotised . . .

St Michael's Church, on the hillside above the village, contains the oval memorial plaque, set into the wall above Eliot's ashes, with quotations from the first and last lines of 'East Coker': 'In my beginning is my end' and 'In my end is my beginning'.

To the west of Yeovil, in the thirteenth century, this countryside produced Roger Bacon. That is to say, tradition holds that Bacon's birthplace was Ilchester, yet experts refuse to be too certain about the place, or date, or as to which of several families he may have belonged. The historian Lynn Thorndike pictures Bacon as being at Oxford sometime about 1230 writing textbooks for students, and there he 'worked so hard that men wondered that he still lived'. Some time later he joined the Franciscans, and said that after becoming a friar he was able to study as much, yet in conditions that were easier. From about 1266 Bacon was putting on parchment his *Opus Maius*, a compendium of all branches of knowledge. Thorndike's opinion is that 'there is no other book quite like the *Opus Maius* in the Middle Ages, nor has there been one like it since; yet it is true to its age and is still readable to-day. It will always remain one of the most remarkable books of the remarkable thirteenth century.'

It was convenient to have had a gentle nudge backward to the thirteenth century, for in the fenland and sedgy moors to which we are introduced at Ilchester imagination has swiftly to range even farther back in time. This wide green plain of central Somerset, flat as a seabed, you have to think of as the legend tells, when the waters were upon it, and here and there the hills that now rise up were islands. These hills were the Isles of Avalon, King Arthur's country. A little to the east of Ilchester is what we now call Cadbury Castle; a little to the north is Glastonbury Tor.

There are firm present-day arguments for Arthur of Britain as a genuine historical figure. I turn to Alcock's *Arthur's Britain* for a vision of his Arthur, whose major victory, the siege of Mount Badon, was fought against the 'ancestral English' about 490, perhaps on a hill near Bath. Alcock uses the term 'ancestral English' to embrace the incoming Germanic peoples, and visualizes Arthur's fight or fights against these pagan intruders at Badon (for there is mention of two battles of Badon) as checking the further penetration of the settlers who had already reached the upper Thames valley. The interpretation is that the decades after Badon saw the consolidation of English settlements from the Channel to the Tees, rather than their expansion. Yet presently there were more Anglo-Saxon beach-heads on the south coast; there was the 'ancestral English' capture of the Isle of Wight, and further push inland; and the 'strife of Camlann', the internecine battle between Britons in which Arthur and Modred perished, must have facilitated the English advance. Alcock refers to one British counter-attack on the grand scale, in which Cadwallon overthrew Edwin at Hatfield and proceeded to ravage Northumbria; yet that resulted in the end in defeat of Cadwallon. So, among the British, legends grew round Arthur as 'once and future king'; legends all the more to be cherished as a relief from lamentations by a people not so much defeated as hemmed in.

Such, in summary, is Leslie Alcock's survey of the 'Arthur of history': a sturdy Briton, winning fame as soldier, fighting battles in various parts of Britain in the late fifth and early sixth centuries. The Roman legions having been withdrawn, the island was open to invasion by Picts and Scots as raiders and Anglo-Saxons or 'ancestral English' as settlers. The year A.D. 367 is regarded as marking the first major barbarian attack on Britain, and A.D. 634 as marking the failure of the last great British counter-attack. Arthur appears at the midpoint of those events. Yet the subsequent exaltation of Arthur into the legendary 'once and future king', with his Knights of the Round Table and the quest of the Holy Grail, was far from a parochial promotion or creation, as it were, solely for British self-encouragement.

This same Somerset fenland with the hills that were once islands was peopled with local British memories, but who – was it William of Malmesbury? – brought hither Joseph of Arimathea? Teachers tell that William recorded what tradition may have told him, that Joseph of Arimathea had been given an isle in Avalon on which to build his church. Doubts there might have been as to which isle; one contender may have been

Cadbury Castle; but Glastonbury Tor stood out with greater certainty as the island which received St Joseph and his eleven companions. There, where St Joseph placed his staff, sprang up the Glastonbury Thorn which was to blossom every Christmas-tide; and there those faithful carriers of the sacred chalice built the *Vetusta Ecclesia*, the primitive church of wood and wattlework which was the earliest Christian foundation in England, a foundation which survived Saxon, Danish and Norman conquests and was not extinguished until the Reformation.

The welding of legends enlarged the 'Arthur of history', and made him meaningful to other peoples, and yet the tales of each generation tell us more about the story-tellers in their changing generations (from Malory who died in 1471 to T. H. White who died as recently as 1964) than about the enigmatic king. To the historian the final battle in which Arthur and Modred perished may have been at the Irthing valley towards the western end of Hadrian's Wall – Alcock favours, I think, that site. Tennyson places the final hours of the wounded king in fabled Lyonnesse, on a dark strait of barren land:

> On one side lay the Ocean, and on one
> Lay a great water, and the moon was full.

It was into the mere that the king told Sir Bedivere, the last of all his knights, to fling his sword Excalibur far into the water, and when at the third time of trying Bedivere finally brought himself to do it, then he beheld the arm 'clothed in white samite, mystic, wonderful' that caught the great sword by the hilt, and brandished it three times, and drew it under in the mere. When the dusky barge appeared at Lyonnesse ('dark as a funeral scarf from stem to stern') that must have been (I felt, as a boy) on the Ocean side of the barren land, for the barge was to convey the stricken king somehow oversea to Glastonbury Tor. But like Bedivere I was desolated that the whole Round Table was dissolved, and not wholly comforted by Arthur's final message:

> The old order changeth, yielding place to new,
> And God fulfils Himself in many ways,
> Lest one good custom should corrupt the world . . .

*   *   *

At Sharpham, two miles south-west of Glastonbury, in a manor house which before the Dissolution had belonged to the Abbey, the Fieldings lived before their move to East Stour, and it was here that Henry Fielding was born. (*Tom Jones*, it is to be recalled, begins and ends in Somerset.) At Langport, farther to the south-west from Glastonbury, Walter Bagehot was born, and here returned to die (in 1877) and to be buried, after his life as banker, editor of *The Economist* and literary critic. He was one of the great 'all-rounders' of the nineteenth century, his genius being 'regulated' rather than 'irregular' (his terms); he was himself an example of 'the exact combination of powers suited to graceful and easy success in an exercise of mind great enough to task the whole intellectual nature'. To the south-east from Glastonbury and close to Castle Cary is Ansford, where Parson Woodforde followed his father in the eighteenth-century parsonage; his *Diary of a Country Parson*, published during the 1920s, pleases us with the daily doings and communings of the diarist with himself.

I turn here from central Somerset to Taunton, the county town, notable as such, and notable also because at Wilton House, at the top of High Street, there was born the author A. W. Kinglake, who wrote the travel book *Eothen* (1844). I must now connect Kinglake, and this part of Somerset, with Lady Hester Stanhope, whom I mentioned as one of the precursors of Lawrence of Arabia. The richness of associations hereabouts is indicated by various memorial pillars. One is on the road from Glastonbury to Taunton, which crosses the now drained marshes to the Isle of Athelney, where King Alfred gathered his forces for the critical struggle with the Danes in 878. There the memorial pillar is also a reminder that this is the scene of Alfred and the burned cakes. But a much taller pillar is the Parkfield Monument, on the southern side of the sedge moor, erected by the first Earl of Chatham (the elder William Pitt) to the gentleman who had bequeathed to him the neighbouring mansion of Burton Pynsent. That gives the connection with Lady Hester Stanhope. Her mother was sister of the second William Pitt, and Lady Hester Stanhope herself, as a girl, sided strongly with her uncle when he and her father (Earl Stanhope) severed relations because of violently opposite attitudes to the French Revolution. The daughter elected to grow up in Lady Chatham's household at Burton Pynsent.

At Burton Pynsent the stables, to the young Lady Hester, were the greatest attraction; and among the young ladies of Taunton – Alexander Kinglake's mother had been one – the aristocratic girl established a clientele as riding-master and horse-trainer. It was 'during that inglorious period of the heroine's life' that the future Mrs Kinglake and Lady Hester Stanhope became friends. Pitt, however, presently persuaded his niece to London, where she was his housekeeper and trusted confidante from 1803–6, until his death. Lady Hester's feelings after Pitt's death, the death of a favourite brother, and finally the death of Sir John Moore at Coruña, drove her abroad; and so, after pilgrimage to Jerusalem, she adopted Eastern habits, journeyed with Bedouins, and settled at Mount Lebanon, building there a walled group of houses, as

ruler and champion of the rebel Druses. A quotation from *Eothen* shows
the effect on Kinglake's childhood:

You may suppose how deeply the quiet women in Somersetshire must have
been interested, when they slowly learned, by vague and uncertain tidings,
that the intrepid girl who had been used to break their vicious horses for them
was reigning in sovereignty over the wandering tribes of western Asia. I know
that her name was made almost as familiar to me in my childhood as the name
of Robinson Crusoe; both were associated with the spirit of adventure: but
whilst the imagined life of the castaway mariner never failed to seem glaringly
real, the true story of the Englishwoman ruling over Arabs always sounded to
me like a fable. I never had heard, nor indeed, I believe, had the rest of the
world ever heard anything like a certain account of the heroine's adventures:
all I knew was, that in one of the drawers, the delight of my childhood, along
with the attar of roses, and frequent wonders from Hindostan, there were
letters carefully treasured, and trifling presents which I was taught to think
valuable because they had come from the Queen of the Desert – a Queen who
dwelt in tents, and reigned over wandering Arabs.

When Kinglake at the age of twenty-six made his own Eastern tour
described in *Eothen*, he found at 'Beyrout' that the standing topic of
interest in all society continued to be Lady Hester Stanhope, whose
repute among the people of the mountains had enlarged into a claim
that she was superhuman. It was understood that she refused to be
visited by Europeans, but Kinglake petitioned, and Lady Hester Stanhope, remembering his mother as 'a sweet, lovely girl', allowed him to
make the day's journey to her mountain fortress. The interviews which
ensued form a long and interesting chapter of *Eothen*. Kinglake later
followed the English expeditionary force to the Crimea, and was notable
for his skilled and careful history of the Crimean War in eight volumes;
his place here is due to his visit to the 'Queen of the Desert', once his
mother's riding-mistress at Burton Pynsent.

Another writer of soldier-stories remembered by a window in the
parish church at Trull, two miles south of Taunton, is Juliana Horatia
Ewing, *née* Gatty. Six miles north-west of Taunton is Combe Florey
where another church window commemorates Sydney Smith. The last
sixteen years of his long career as clergyman, man of letters and wit,
were spent as rector of Combe Florey, until his death in 1845. From
1956 to 1966 the manor house at Combe Florey was the home of Evelyn
Waugh; and he wrote here the last volume of his war trilogy, *Uncondi-
tional Surrender*. Farther in the same direction and halfway towards
Minehead is Stogumber, a name which recalls to me one of H. C. Bailey's
detective stories (*The Wrong Man*).

It is, however, on the opposite eastern side of the Quantocks, and
reached most readily from Bridgwater, that there happens to be the

place-name which in literary interest dominates all others in this district – Nether Stowey. A tablet in the church and a pleasing description of his hospitality in De Quincey's *Reminiscences of the English Lake Poets* commemorate Thomas Poole of Nether Stowey, who at the end of 1796 provided Coleridge and his wife and baby (Hartley) with the cottage 'at the foot of Quantock' which is now maintained by the National Trust as 'Coleridge Cottage'. In the nineteenth century the cottage was somewhat altered from what it was in its Coleridge period, when it was a low, thatched dwelling with a clear brook running before the door, and the garden as described in 'This Lime-Tree Bower my Prison'. The extraordinary and amazing stimulus that Coleridge exerted in the first two years of living at Nether Stowey is perhaps best evidenced by Hazlitt's tribute (in 'My First Acquaintance with Poets'). Hazlitt shows the impact Coleridge made not only on himself but on his father, even adding the touch that Coleridge's presence in his father's house made the food taste better – 'I remember the leg of Welsh mutton and the turnips on the table that day had the finest flavour imaginable' – a tribute which is meaningful from a man who all his life had stomach trouble. Another example of Coleridge's power was the rapidity with which Wordsworth and Dorothy rented for themselves the manor house at Alfoxden, near the village of Holford, to be near him. What Stephen Potter calls the 'two great years' of Coleridge's life, 1797 to 1798, 'when he came near to being really happy, when his health was still good, his domestic life fairly calm, and when he was on terms of perfect understanding with his best friends, Poole and the Wordsworths', must have been something of a strain at times to 'my pensive Sara', who had little Hartley to look after, while catering, without resources, for guests whom Coleridge, without prior consultation, was ever ready to invite.

'The Rime of the Ancient Mariner' and the first part of *Christabel* were both produced at Stowey. The occasion for Coleridge's writing 'This Lime-Tree Bower my Prison' was the visit to the cottage of Charles Lamb (and Mary?) in June 1797. Lamb, one feels sure, was little trouble as a house-guest, but there were others in that party, and other visitors at other times who were less accommodating to Sara than Lamb. De Quincey, whose personal acquaintanceship did not begin until ten years later, and whose petty gossip becomes the more suspect the more its writing became his means of income, dwells at length and possibly with exaggeration on the 'bitter trial' and mortification daily renewed to Sara by having Dorothy Wordsworth arrive with her brother to carry off her husband on the walks and picnics which the three of them enjoyed the more if Sara stayed home. De Quincey alleges that Dorothy 'had no personal charms' but 'intellectually she was very much superior to Mrs Coleridge', and that throughout the years 1797 and 1798 intellectual sympathies welded the three (Coleridge and the two Wordsworths) into a triad of mutual admiration which excluded Sara.

In those two years at Stowey, Coleridge was often away on other activities, often on the preaching engagements such as described by Hazlitt – and once at least by himself on the trip which led to writing 'Kubla Khan'. That was later in the summer of Lamb's visit; Coleridge said that 'in ill health' he took himself off 'to a lonely farm-house between Porlock and Linton, on the Exmoor confines of Somerset and Dorsetshire'. At the farmhouse, supposedly above Ashley Combe just to the west of Porlock, in the Culbone Hills (not quite so far west as the Doone Valley), the famous episode took place of Coleridge waking from his daydream, instantly and eagerly writing down all that is preserved of 'Kubla Khan', until interrupted by the 'person on business from Porlock'. The fragment, and the as yet incomplete part of *Christabel*, were not included in *Lyrical Ballads*, which Wordsworth made ready for publication in 1798. Coleridge then decided to use the unexpected annuity from the Wedgwoods to go travelling with the Wordsworths in Germany. This, if De Quincey is right about Sara Coleridge's feelings, was unlikely to cheer her. Coleridge probably put off going until after the birth of his second child, who, however, sickened and died while Coleridge was in Germany. In May 1799 Coleridge was writing to Poole that there were moments when he laid 'the blame of my child's death to my absence'. That made him think of his first-born son, Hartley: 'I hope he won't be dead before I get home.' In 1799 Coleridge returned, but Nether Stowey was not then to be 'home'. First he followed the Wordsworths for a tour of the Lake District, and then, in 1800, decided to live there. Sara and Hartley followed. The Coleridges had two more children, but the rift between him and Sara widened, and there was little further family happiness.

6. DEVON

Mention of the Doone Valley in Exmoor has carried me from Somerset into north Devon – or since Badgeworthy Water, which runs through the valley, marks the county line, the 'Doone country' can be equally claimed by both counties. R. D. Blackmore, whose novel *Lorna Doone* initiated what has become a steadily increasing attraction to the Doone Valley, was not himself a West Countryman by birth. He was born at the vicarage of Longworth in Berkshire, but his father transferred to Ashford near Barnstaple and then to Culmstock east of Tiverton, and in boyhood Blackmore achieved enough intimacy with Exmoor to feed his imagination when, as a middle-aged schoolmaster in Teddington, he set himself to the writing of *Lorna Doone* (published 1869). Gomer House, Teddington, is where Blackmore wrote this, the best-known of his fifteen novels. His writing was done in between schoolmastering and tending his vegetables and orchard, and he may be forgiven if his description of the faraway Doone country and its characters is considerably heightened. Blackmore ascribed the epileptic attacks which afflicted him in middle life to the rough treatment that he had in boyhood at Blundell's School, Tiverton, yet he chose that school for his hero, John Ridd, giving him heroic spirit, as, presently, heroic physique, to see him through all his troubles. The natural defences of the valley of the Doones and the physical effort John Ridd had to make to meet Lorna are a credit to Blackmore's power of enhancing his story; to a less romantic writer the terrain might not suggest so much. The little church at Oare on the Somerset side of the county line is where Blackmore placed the marriage of Lorna Doone to John Ridd, and where the (almost) fatal shot from Carver Doone's carbine rang out. Never in boyhood reading was there a greater thrill than when John Ridd as avenger caught up with the bearded Carver, and 'grasped his arm, and tore the muscle out of it (as the string comes out of an orange)'. I could never quite believe in that muscle-tearing, despite the suggested comparison; but the thrill was undeniable, and was and is shared by natives of the Doone country, as witnessed by the medallion portrait of Blackmore in Oare Church.

Along the north coasts of Devon and Cornwall are fewer literary memories than cluster along the south. Southey, and Shelley too, had normally happy relaxed periods at Lynmouth. To Southey Lynmouth was 'the finest spot, except Cintra and the Arrabida' that he ever saw. At the age of twenty, Shelley, in the summer of 1812, brought Harriet Westbrook, in the first and still happy year of their marriage, to the 'myrtle-twined' cottage in Lynmouth, where he proselytized for vegetarianism and political freedom until the natives were roused to active protest and the Shelleys departed. Barnstaple claims interest as birthplace of John Gay. He was of an old Devonshire family and had his schooling at the grammar school at Barnstaple; yet I obtained a clearer snapshot of the mature Gay when he was living with the Queensberrys in Wiltshire. A traveller who came to rest near Barnstaple was Negley Farson (1890–1960), who wrote *The Way of a Transgressor*. Farson, when he knew his wanderings were over, settled for his journey's end at the Grey House, Braunton, to be beside what he called 'one of the most noble stretches of sea and sand anywhere in the world'.

Literary recollections in north Devon would be grossly incomplete, though, without mention of Bideford, where the room in which Charles

Kingsley worked on *Westward Ho!* is shown at the Royal Hotel. Kingsley was born at the vicarage of Holne, on Dartmoor; his father moved to the rectory at Clovelly, and the boy grew up in that most picturesque of fishing villages, described by Dickens in 'A Message from the Sea' (one of Dickens's Christmas stories in *All the Year Round*). When Kingsley's novel had been published in 1855 its popularity became such that a residential development on the coast west of Bideford was named Westward Ho! Kingsley himself was embarrassed by that naming, yet the place-name continued, and Westward Ho! became the site for the United Services College. Rudyard Kipling was put to school there from 1878 to 1882; it later prompted the writing of *Stalky & Co.* Hartland Point (pointing out to Lundy Island) marks the westward end of Barnstaple or Bideford Bay; at Hartland's church (whose tower is high as a mark for seamen) there is the grave of John Lane (1854–1925), 'a devoted son of Devon' who made his name as a London publisher, and also a memorial tablet to Sir Allen Lane (1902–70), even better known for his chief contribution to readers – Penguin Books. The coastline south of Hartland Point very soon belongs to Cornwall, but I will not yet enter that land of King Arthur and attendant legends. One odd item before leaving the neighbourhood of Bideford is that this is where Mrs Pepys came from. Her French father and her mother tried to settle near Bideford, while the daughter grew up; but how Elizabeth St Michel came to meet Samuel Pepys and to be married to him at the age of fifteen, is, as far as I know, unrecorded.

*   *   *

I return to south Devon. Ottery St Mary is still aware of 'the pale ghost of Coleridge', the thirteenth and last child of the rector of Ottery St Mary; after his parents' death friends secured entry for the boy into Christ's Hospital in London which school became in effect his mother and father. I don't think Coleridge often returned in maturity to the

Dear native Brook! wild Streamlet of the West!

of which he wrote in his sonnet to the River Otter of childhood memory. The Coleridges' rectory has disappeared. There is another connection of Ottery St Mary with the City of London's literary schoolboys. When young William Makepeace Thackeray left Charterhouse, conscious at that time of being very well-to-do, before entering Trinity College, Cambridge, he spent the interval at what he lightheartedly in lordly manner spoke of as 'my country seat'. That was Larkbeare House, a mile and a half north of Ottery St Mary – close enough for Ottery to become 'Clavering St Mary' in Thackeray's *Pendennis*.

To the north-west of Ottery St Mary is Tiverton. The River Exe flows south from there to Exeter and Exmouth. The smaller River Otter calls to mind not only Coleridge but Sir Walter Raleigh, born at Hayes Barton where the Otter flows to the sea past East Budleigh. The scene of Millais' famous painting of 'The Boyhood of Raleigh' is legitimately taken to be the beach of Ladram Bay. Strangely, the Exe and Exeter fail to bring such vivid associations. A literary thought is that the words of 'Onward, Christian Soldiers' were written by Sabine Baring-Gould, who was born at Exeter. The sixteenth-century Richard Hooker was also born here (or rather at Heavitree, the eastern suburb), as is recorded by the statue beside the cathedral. Yet though in the map of Hardy's Wessex Exeter is 'Exonbury' his use of the city does not leap to attention, and though George Gissing is reputed to have lived here for a time, I cannot feel for certain that the setting of *Private Papers of Henry Ryecroft* was the countryside round Exeter. Is the best item connecting Exeter and literature an alleged mention of Exeter in *Pickwick Papers*?

I don't recall much of Exeter in *Pickwick*, but more exciting is the thought that Dickens in 1839 was making efforts to settle his parents into Exeter's southern suburb of Alphington, at Mile End Cottage. He was at that same time juggling things together for *Nicholas Nickleby*; and the superb comic creation of Mrs Nickleby relates in some part to Dickens's affectionate struggles with his mother's flow of genteel memories of her West Country upbringing. Mrs Nickleby and the Crummles episodes are the transcendent creations of this novel, and whereabouts does Dickens let Mrs Nickleby originate, at the moment he is settling his own mother into Alphington? He places her when young, both before and after her marriage, as having been brought up near Dawlish, on the Devon coast due south of Alphington. Thereupon one gains from her, with spontaneous increase, the fascination of the departed glories of the Dawlish neighbourhood. It was probably at Mrs Nickleby's papa's household that there was the footboy whose nose had not only a wart but a wen also, 'and a very large wen too, and he demanded to have his wages raised in consequence'. That may have been before Mr Nickleby won her away from a dozen suitors, not counting the young gentleman who used to go to the same dancing school, 'and who *would* send gold watches and bracelets to our house in gilt-edged paper (which were always returned)' or that other young gentleman 'who sat next to us at church, who used, almost every Sunday, to cut my name in large letters in the front of his pew while the sermon was going on'. (By the by, what was Mrs Nickleby's full maiden name?) It was after marriage to Mr Nickleby that the pair of them, being a great deal sought after, used, in the Dawlish neighbourhood, 'to keep such hours! Twelve, one, two, three o'clock was nothing to us. Balls, dinners, card-

parties! Never were such rakes as the people about where we used to
live' – including, we learn, the Dibabses with their earwigs (and frogs
behaving like Christians) and also 'those Peltiroguses', who were visited
by turning sharp off to the left by the turnpike where the Plymouth
mail ran over the donkey. The full and glorious social life of Dawlish,
revealed by Mrs Nickleby, hilariously makes up for any inadequacy of
material at Exeter.

Associations with Torquay must be bravely presented if they are to
compete with Mrs Nickleby. Elizabeth Barrett Browning was sent there
at the time that her father was treating her as a confirmed invalid. She
lived at Bath House, which subsequently became the Regina Hotel; but
there was tragedy for her when her brother was drowned in Babbacombe
Bay. Bulwer-Lytton died at Torquay in 1873. Kipling was at nearby
Maidencombe in 1896–7. We remember rather, however, the writers
Eden Phillpotts, who lived in Torquay before settling for his last years
at Broad Clyst, north-east of Exeter – and Agatha Christie, who was
born at Torquay and was encouraged to write by Eden Phillpotts. Two
very different writers whose circle of readers was never so large as that
of Phillpotts and 'the Queen of detective fiction' were Sean O'Casey,
who after living at Totnes when he left Ireland came to live at Torquay
from 1955 until his death in 1964, and Neil Bell, who in his last years –
he also died in 1964 – was living across Tor Bay at Brixham. To complete my list of hymn-writers along England's south coast, I should
notice that Henry Lyte was vicar at Brixham for twenty-five years, and
wrote 'Abide With Me' at Berry Head, at the south of Tor Bay. Was it
one of Lyte's parishioners who wrote 'The Wives of Brixham'?

Ten miles inland from Tor Bay and on the southern edge of Dartmoor
is the village of Dean Prior, where for two long portions of his life
Robert Herrick resided as vicar; he came here from London in 1629
when he was thirty-eight, and because he was a Royalist he was ejected
from that living at the age of fifty-six by the Parliamentarians; at the
Restoration Herrick was reinstated at Dean Prior – he was then seventy-
one and continued to live at the old vicarage until his death at the age
of eighty-three. A modern tablet and window commemorate him in the
church. In Rose Macaulay's novel *They Were Defeated* there is a brilliant
and thoroughly sympathetic picturing of Herrick's life in Devonshire.
When the lonely man relived 'the *Lyrick* Feasts' with Ben Jonson and
the 'clusters' round him at 'the *Sun*, the *Dog*, the triple *Tunne*', certainly
the comparative dullness of middle-aged routine beside 'Dean-bourn,
a rude River in Devon' seemed to excuse self-pity, and to invite comparison with Ovid

. . . by hard fate sent
Into a long and irksome banishment.

It does not stand out that Herrick felt much concern for, or even interest in, his Devonshire parishioners,

> A people currish; churlish as the seas;
> And rude (almost) as rudest Salvages.

Yet within his 'Grange', looked after by his maid ('my *Prew* by good luck sent'), he was clearly and frequently granted the supreme pleasure of knowing that in his 'numbers' he had found perfection of expression. Within his circle in Devon he must have had some friends, such as the lady to whom he sent a 'pipkin of Jellie' and who enjoyed the perfect touch with which his numbers were played; but the impression is that he played as well or better if playing solely for himself. 'No one has ever been quite certain', Saintsbury said long ago, 'what the word "Protestant" means in the celebrated verse beginning, "Bid me to live and I will live, Thy *Protestant* to be" ', yet 'Protestant' could not be changed for any other word without loss. 'Prewdence' Baldwin – she who kept house for him – is transmitted to us as an actual person, and in a sense she lives, in the short epitaph Herrick wrote for her. To what degree Anthea, Julia and the other mistresses are actual or imaginary is guesswork. When Herrick was evicted from Dean Prior in 1647 he took with him to London all the scraps and pieces that he had written in Devon, both *Noble Numbers* and *Hesperides*; there the two collections of verses, produced in banishment, were published together, and in those disturbed years very few readers paid any attention. It was not till the end of the eighteenth century that Herrick was 'discovered'.

To the north and west of Dean Prior is the wide tract of Dartmoor. Dartmoor is featured in Blackmore's romance *Christowell*; in more recent times it has been the setting of many notable novels of Eden Phillpotts; but probably the story set in the wildest part of Dartmoor which has had widest circulation is *The Hound of the Baskervilles*. In the maps that have been made of Sherlock Holmes's adventures, Dartmoor ever holds its honoured place, and not only for the Baskervilles. Did ever a volume open better than:

> 'I am afraid, Watson, that I shall have to go,' said Holmes as we sat down together to our breakfast one morning.
> 'Go! Where to?'
> 'To Dartmoor; to King's Pyland.'

That, of course, is the conversation which introduces 'Silver Blaze', the first story of the *Memoirs*. The mapmaker is going to be in for a slight confusion, for the training stable at King's Pyland is to begin with placed in the north of Dartmoor, but on the next page is within two miles or so of Tavistock, which is at the western edge of the area, not north. No matter: 'Silver Blaze' is one of the most immortal of the immortal stories, and are not some of the tales loved all the more for what, if you did not love them, would be peccadilloes?

Mapmaking for *The Hound of the Baskervilles* is bound to lead to argument. The prose narrative at emotional moments has the cadency of verse, and might be printed as such:

> The driver pointed with his whip.
> 'Baskerville Hall,' said he.

Precisely where should the map pinpoint the cup-like depression in the moor where the Hall's two high, narrow towers rose over the trees? The parishes of Grimpen, Thorsley and High Barrow for which the Dr Mortimer who introduced the mystery was medical officer are all perhaps in the southern half of Dartmoor; one remembers that Stapleton brought the hound from Ross and Mangles in London's Fulham Road to Dartmoor by the North Devon line and walked it 'a great distance over the moor so as to get it home without exciting any remarks'. To mention *The Hound of the Baskervilles* right after mentioning Herrick has made me aware of a coincidence. The portrait of the Cavalier which fascinated Holmes when he was supping at the Hall – the wicked Hugo Baskerville 'who started the Hound of the Baskervilles' – had a date on the back of the canvas. That date, possibly marking the year that the hell-hound caught up with the wicked Royalist Hugo, was 1647, the same year that the harmless gentle Royalist Herrick was evicted from the neighbouring parish of Dean Prior.

Many writers and journalists of recent times were born at Plymouth, among them Desmond MacCarthy, Derek McCulloch, John Squire and L. A. G. Strong. Of earlier vintage, Plymouth produced Henry Austin Dobson (1840–1921); his *Eighteenth-Century-Vignettes* exhibit his charm as essayist in the climate of the 1890s, and in that period of rondeaus and triolets, his were of the neatest:

> I intended an Ode,
>   And it turn'd to a Sonnet
> It began *à la mode*,
> I intended an Ode;
> But Rose cross'd the road
>   In her latest new bonnet;
> I intended an Ode;
>   And it turn'd to a Sonnet.

A generation before Dobson, Stephen Hawker (1803–75) was born at Stoke Damerel, now in the western part of Plymouth and though rector of Morwenstow in North Cornwall for forty years, he was buried in Plymouth in Ford Park Cemetery.

7. CORNWALL

For most of the whole coast of Cornwall, from Rame Head at the entrance to Plymouth Sound westward to Land's End, and then along the north coast from Land's End to the Devon border, quietly intrepid walkers may find rights of way for distances totalling over three hundred miles of paths along the famed sea-cliffs. Something over a quarter of this coastline now belongs to the National Trust. Footwork is occasionally needed, and especially if searchings are dominated by such great tribal memories as those of Arthur, and of King Mark, and Tristan and Iseult. Some inland haunts of the old legends are reached almost before expected, from the road from Plymouth through Liskeard. Liskeard is a 'Stannary' town, and it once returned Edward Gibbon to Parliament, but that need not prevent me aiming north-west, where, before reaching St Neot's Church on the southern edge of Bodmin Moor, there is a road north past Brown Gelly to the very centre of this wild moorland – and there is Dozmary Pool.

Here and unequivocally anything that I said earlier in Somerset about King Arthur's command to Sir Bedivere to fling the sword Excalibur into the mere must be emended. True, when I am at Land's End and facing toward the Scilly Isles, I know those islands to be the only visible relic of the Lyonnesse where Arthur fought the final battle – that land of legend which now lies forty fathoms deep, between the Scilly Isles and Cornwall – and it is farther than a narrow space from there to Dozmary Pool. Yet nothing else that's said before or after alters the equal truth that on Bodmin Moor it is certain that it was into the waters of Dozmary Pool that Bedivere cast the great sword. Here, then, is one reality where the arm of the Lady of the Lake, clothed in white samite, reached up to catch and brandish Excalibur. On that dark day the arm in gleaming white showed well against the darkness of the mere, and the remembrance stayed with Sir Bedivere as he lived out the rest of his life in prayers and fastings, and great abstinence, in the hermitage beside Glastonbury.

A left-hand fork of the road after Liskeard leads away from Bodmin Moor to Lostwithiel, and if Liskeard boasted Edward Gibbon as Member of Parliament, Lostwithiel once had Joseph Addison as representative. Restormel Castle north of Lostwithiel is a reminder of the much more ancient and more legendary sites near Fowey, where Castle

Dore, now a gorse-clad mound, was once the palace of King Mark, and where Golant was one of the scenes of the romance of Tristan and Iseult. Twentieth-century associations with Fowey include pre-eminently Sir Arthur Quiller-Couch. He was born at Bodmin but came to live here, at The Haven; 'Q' made Fowey famous as 'Troy Town' in several novels. At Fowey I break my rule of not mentioning living authors to say that Dame Daphne du Maurier lives at nearby Par. Kenneth Grahame was married at Fowey, with Anthony Hope Hawkins as best man. Clearly that enhanced his pleasure in describing, in *The Wind in the Willows*, 'the little grey sea town I know so well, that clings along one steep side of the harbour'.

Modern associations with Truro connect mainly with Hugh Walpole, who lived here in childhood at the time the cathedral was being completed, for the reconstituted see of Cornwall. Truro is the 'Polchester' of Walpole's novels; and his place-names are hardly disguised – the Lemon Street of Georgian architecture is named by Walpole 'Orange Street'. At Falmouth the White Cottage came to be the home of Howard Spring, who used Falmouth and its neighbourhood as settings in several novels. Helston, famous for the 'Furry Dance' each May, is famous also for the nearby Looe Pool between the town and the coast – this pool vigorously contests with Dozmary the possession of King Arthur's sword Excalibur. Mount's Bay, where St Michael's Mount preserves romantic relations with Mont St Michel in Normandy, claims to be the landing-place for Sir Walter Raleigh and Edmund Spenser when Raleigh, in 1589, had looked up Spenser in Ireland. In Ireland, at Kilcolman, it had not taken long for Raleigh to persuade Spenser to put the first instalment of *The Faerie Queene* in his portmanteau so that the two of them might make as speedy a presentation of it as possible to Elizabeth,

> Whose grace was great, and bounty most rewardfull.

Promptly they set sail, as Spenser rehearses in *Colin Clouts Come Home Againe*, daring the 'stinking Seales and Porcpisces together', and passed Lundy, and as some read into the poem, rounded Land's End and made port, close to St Michael's 'loftie mount', at Penzance. Raleigh's rapid return to London's court, and Spenser's, was in that year most graciously received; Elizabeth was pleased to accept the dedication of *The Faerie Queene*, the first instalment was soon published, and the 'newe poete' entertained for eighteen months or so vain hopes of exorbitant reward. Spenser did in fact receive a life-pension, and though Burghley saw to it that the sum was not large, Spenser presently came to agree that for him a life in Ireland, with visits to England from time to time, was far more serene than hanging around the Elizabethan court. Spenser was relatively fortunate. At Penzance a more recent poet, John Davidson, reduced to despair by ill-health and poverty, drowned himself in 1909.

Rounding Land's End in the direction opposite to that taken by Raleigh and Spenser in 1589, one reaches St Ives; the distance inland across the peninsula from Penzance to St Ives is naturally much shorter, but the coastal road enables one on the way to pass, downhill and up, through Zennor. At Zennor D. H. Lawrence lived in 1916 and 1917, while writing *Women in Love*, and Katherine Mansfield and John Middleton Murry stayed there with Lawrence. In the 1880s and throughout Virginia Woolf's childhood, her father Leslie Stephen ('L.S., the most lovable of men', said Lowell) rented Talland House, St Ives, each summer. His mountaineering feats were by then over, but as his daughter described, he could still spend all day striding across the moors of Penwith, alone or with one companion, and no doubt studying the various sites along the sea-cliffs which have now been selected as rock climbing centres. Virginia Woolf returned to St Ives in 1926 – at least, friends have reported that she wrote *To the Lighthouse* at St Ives, and that the lighthouse to which 'they should have gone already – they had to catch the tide or something', is the lighthouse on Godrevy Island at the far side of St Ives Bay. Edith Mary Lees, a native of Cornwall and herself a novelist, was born at St Ives; she married Havelock Ellis and they lived at Carbis Bay, where Ellis turned from general medical practice to the profession of writer.

It is a good many miles along the cliffs and beaches of the holiday coast of north Cornwall, from Godrevy Point past Newquay, Padstow and Port Isaac, before the strength of the Arthurian legend, as popularized in Victorian times by Tennyson, is fully felt at Tintagel. The 'wild Tintagel by the Cornish seas' was one of the earliest sites to receive some protection from the National Trust; fortunately so, for the King Arthur Castle Hotel, placed above Barras Nose by the Great Western Railway, was only the most prominent of many efforts which might have degraded the ruins. The legend that Tennyson followed for the coming of Arthur recalls that in King Uther's time that king so lusted for the wife of the prince and warrior who held Tintagel that he fought and killed the husband, captured the castle, 'and with a shameful swiftness' wedded the widow.

> . . . afterward,
> Not many moons, King Uther died himself,
> Moaning and wailing for an heir to rule
> After him, lest the realm should go to wrack.
> And that same night, the night of the new year,
> By reason of the bitterness and grief

That vext his mother, all before his time
Was Arthur born, and all as soon as born
Deliver'd at a secret postern-gate
To Merlin, to be holden far apart
Until his hour should come . . .

The ruins of the castle are there, and the visitor may judge for himself the location of the secret postern-gate where Merlin spirited away the child.

Tintagel Castle has been identified as the burial place of Tristan and Iseult, a vine and a rosebush over their graves having at times intertwined to symbolize the eventual union of the lovers. I am, though, less concerned with specific linking of this coast with the European myth of Tristan, widespread as that is throughout history, than I am with recalling that Boscastle, on the coast just north of Tintagel, is the 'Castle Boterel' of Hardy's novel *A Pair of Blue Eyes*. Two miles up the River Valency from Boscastle is St Juliot's, which in the novel is 'Endelstow', and where at the vicarage (perhaps very much as in the novel) Hardy portrays his first meeting with Emma, his first wife. The half-dozen *Satires of Circumstance*, poems in which Hardy in the spring of 1913 seems to be deliberately rehearsing memories of the spring of 1870, justify accepting portions of *A Pair of Blue Eyes* as autobiographical. In that 1870 spring Hardy, as young architect, went to Cornwall to restore the church of St Juliot's, and whether the real Emma Gifford was the daughter, sister, or sister-in-law of the rector (as she is variously described) hardly matters; we accept that Emma Gifford was the young woman at the vicarage to whom Hardy became engaged and whom in 1874, when he could afford marriage, he married; all near enough to the novel to suggest some mixture of fact with fiction. Yet the fiction is highly melodramatized. The 'enormous sea-bord cliff' which figures in an episode which gave Hardy some lasting pleasure (for he refers to it in a preface written in 1895) is almost certainly High Cliff, the highest in Cornwall, which rises 731 feet above the fearsome wicked beach named the Strangles.

The whole of the north Cornish coast and the cliffs onward to Hartland Point in Devon have always earned the seafarer's warning:

From Padstow Bar to Lundy Light
Is a sailor's grave, by day or night.

At Morwenstow sixty acres of cliff-top between the church and the sea are a National Trust memorial to the Rev. Stephen Hawker (1803–75), the Plymouth-born parson-poet who placed over his Cornish vicarage door the inscription in Old English lettering:

A House, A Glebe, a Pound a Day,
A Pleasant Place to Watch and Pray;
Be true to Church, Be Kind to Poor,
O Minister! for evermore.

The vicarage, with chimneys designed by Hawker after the towers of neighbouring churches, nestled in the valley. The approach to the cliff is past the Norman church, which is surrounded by the graves of drowned sailors. On the very edge of the 450-foot Vicarage Cliff Hawker built his 'Hut'; it is said to have been constructed of driftwood dragged up from the rocks below. As a young man Hawker had been at Pembroke College, Oxford, where he was a Newdigate prizeman for poetry; he was thirty when he settled as vicar at Morwenstow. His reputation for eccentricity was partly caused by his refusal to wear black – in church he wore at first a brown cassock, later a long blue coat over a fisherman's blue jersey. When off duty he spent much time in the rough hut on the lip of the cliff working, in the fisherman's jersey that he favoured, on his long ambitious poem, *The Quest of the Sangreal*.

Hawker did not publish this major effort until 1864, but his researches into Arthurian legends were spoken of, and Tennyson, making his tour of the West Country in 1848, set out to call at Morwenstow. The story (as told by John Freeman) goes that Tennyson, when asking the way to the remote vicarage, happened to speak to Hawker's brother-in-law, who directed him to the hut; and there, though not disclosing his name, Tennyson ventured to intrude. 'King Arthur' was the password; the two men were soon talking. Presently Tennyson questioned Hawker's apparent isolation; Hawker in response quoted from *Locksley Hall*. 'That man appears to be your favourite poet,' said Tennyson. 'Not mine only, but all England's,' replied Hawker, and at that Tennyson disclosed himself. Hawker was generous to his younger rival, supplied such help for *Idylls of the King* as Tennyson desired, and if Tennyson stayed for dinner I feel sure that Hawker dressed for it in the claret-coloured coat with long tails which has been often mentioned as another peculiarity of 'Passon' Hawker's.

The parish of Kilkhampton, south-east of Morwenstow, belonged to the Grenvilles of Stowe. Stowe House, which is described in Charles Kingsley's *Westward Ho!*, was the home from which Sir Richard Grenville departed for his last sea-fight, his 'little *Revenge*' in single battle against the Spanish fleet. Tennyson put the story into words that generations of boys and girls later learned by heart:

At Flores in the Azores Sir Richard Grenville lay,
And a pinnace, like a flutter'd bird, came flying from far away:
'Spanish ships of war at sea! we have sighted fifty-three!'

Hawker was good at ballads, but the touch for that one lay with the younger poet. Remembrance of Tennyson and Hawker on the sea-cliffs by Morwenstow, discussing Grenville, discussing Sangreal, is a chord on which to end these associations found in south-west England.

A4

THE BATH ROAD AND INTO WALES

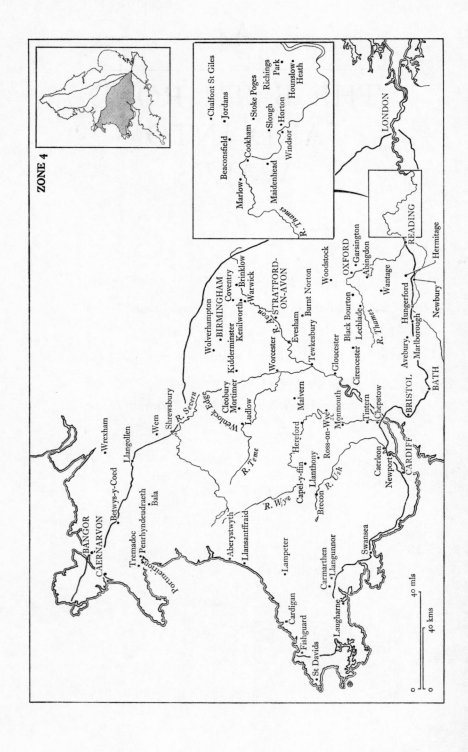

ZONE 4

Chalfont St Giles
Jordans
Stoke Poges
Richings Park
Beaconsfield
Cookham
Slough
Horton
Hounslow Heath
Marlow
Maidenhead
Windsor

LONDON

R. Thames

READING
Hermitage
Newbury

Wrexham
Langollen
Wem
Shrewsbury
R. Severn
Wenlock Edge
Cleobury Mortimer
Ludlow
R. Teme
Wolverhampton
BIRMINGHAM
Coventry
Brinklow
Warwick
Kidderminster
Kenilworth
STRATFORD-ON-AVON
R. Avon
Worcester
Evesham
Tewkesbury
Burnt Norton
Woodstock
OXFORD
Garsington
Abingdon
Wantage
Gloucester
Black Bourton
Lechlade
Cirencester
R. Thames
Avebury
Hungerford
Marlborough
BRISTOL
BATH

Hereford
Malvern
Monmouth
Ross-on-Wye
Capel-y-ffin
Llanthony
Breon
R. Wye
R. Usk
Caerleon
Newport
CARDIFF
Tintern
Chepstow

BANGOR
CAERNARVON
Betwys-y-Coed
Tremadoc
Penrhyndeudraeth
Bala
Portmeirion
Aberystwyth
Llansantffraid
Lampeter
Cardigan
Fishguard
St Davids
Carmarthen
Llangunnor
Laugharne
Swansea

40 mls
40 kms
0
0

1. LONDON TO READING

The era of stagecoaches began three hundred years ago, coincidental with the Restoration of England's more limited monarchy. *Coaching Days and Coaching Ways* by W. Outram Tristram mentions the following advertisement as posted up in London in the 1660s:

FLYING MACHINE

All those desirous to pass from London to Bath, or any other Place on their Road, let them repair to the Bell Savage on Ludgate Hill in London and the White Lion at Bath, at both which places they may be received in a Stage Coach every Monday, Wednesday, and Friday, which performs the whole journey in Three Days (if God permit), and sets forth at five in the Morning

The first stage for the early 'flying machines' going westward ended at what is now, appropriately enough, Heathrow Airport. As the coaching era developed, at this point of Hounslow Heath there came to be kept a total of 2500 horses for the demands of posting and coaching. That number gives an idea of the amount of roadwork by the time of Pickwick, when passengers leaving the White Horse Cellar in Piccadilly at 7 a.m. could count on being deposited by 7 p.m. of the same day at the White Hart, opposite the Pump Room at Bath. In the beginning the relative lack of organization and the state of the roadways were not the only reasons for the caution that in the 1660s a passenger might get to Bath 'in Three Days (if God permit)'. The roadway itself was bad, frequently waterlogged, with eight inches of slippery sludge in wet weather leading to dangerous ruts and trenches when dry. In the 1660s the 'flying machine' could not be other than a slow coach – and therefore an easy mark for highwaymen.

One of the first, and certainly one of the most notorious, of the gentry that passengers feared to meet on Hounslow Heath was Claude Duval, a Frenchman. It was in 1670 that Duval was hanged. He was captured when drunk, thrust into Newgate, arraigned, convicted, condemned and, though not before flamboyant 'Dying Confessions' could be released for sale, hanged before a large crowd at Tyburn. His career ended in the twenty-seventh year of his age; he was reputed to have been as notable for gallantry as for his robberies, and efforts were made to use his name to set a pattern. His body, when cut down from the gibbet, was given leave to lie in state in the Tangiers Tavern, St Giles, in a room draped with black and with eight wax candles burning beside the coffin. It was then reported (and no later denials gained credence) that Duval had been buried in the middle aisle of Covent Garden Church under a wide white marble stone with 'Du Vall arms' and an inscription, because he had been born in Normandy, to 'The second Conqu'ror of the Norman Race'. The broadsheets made out that the eight-line epitaph in the church ended with proper tribute to

> Old Tyburn's glory, England's illustrious Thief,
> Du Vall the ladies' joy: Du Vall the Ladies' Grief.

The pattern of gallant-highwayman lasted, in some imaginations, for fifty years or so. In the provinces the pattern lasted longer, and in fiction the romantic gay cavalier-desperado is one of the hardiest perennials. There is substantial evidence that Epping Forest went on sheltering the low-grade Dick Turpin until the 1730s, yet before then interference by highwaymen on Hounslow Heath, such as started by Duval, seems to have fallen off. The network for crime organized in London by Jonathan Wild, and useful to the higher grades of highwaymen, failed to hold together after Wild was hanged at Tyburn in 1725. By 1728 Gay was able to be sportive with the theme of highwaymen in *The Beggar's Opera*. Hounslow Heath may have been in Gay's mind when he named his hero Macheath; and I am taking the instant popularity of *The Beggar's Opera* as an indication that the once notoriously dangerous route could by 1728 also be regarded with lightheartedness. Further evidence of the reasonable safety of this part of the Heath is that Richings Park, just to the north of Colnbrook, was, in the first third of the eighteenth century, the seat of the Lord Bathurst who much enjoyed dining and wining many of London's literary wits. Matthew Prior is spoken of as a visitor to Richings before his death in 1721, and Congreve and Swift, Addison, Steele, Pope and many of their friends are said to have driven out from Town to dine with Lord Bathurst. It was reputed that a bench in the grounds of Richings had initials or autographs of these and other names scratched, carved or in some other way perpetuated on it. Without stressing the story of the bench, Lord Bathurst's entertaining does suggest a fair amount of easy-going carriage traffic using that route without much fear.

It was in the rougher times of the seventeenth century that Milton's father, in 1632, had retired to the village of Horton – Colnbrook is mid-point between Richings to the north and Horton to the south – and it was at Horton that Milton lived, studied and practised poetry for the five years after leaving Cambridge. In this low-lying part of the Colne valley Milton wrote the companion pieces 'L'Allegro' and 'Il Penseroso' in 1632; the landscape in those poems derives perhaps more from his inward eye than from actual surroundings. Although apparently isolated at Horton and away from main roads, Milton managed to keep in touch with active friends – for instance, with Henry Lawes the musician, who was then in the household of the Earl of Bridgewater at Harefield, ten miles up the valley of the Colne, past Uxbridge. When Milton wrote the two masques *Arcades* in 1633 and *Comus* in 1634, Lawes contributed the music; the performance of *Comus* in the West Country at Ludlow brought wider attention to both of its creators. Another friend of Milton's, from Cambridge days, was Edward King, whose death by shipwreck on the way to Ireland in 1637 caused the writing of 'Lycidas'. In that same year Milton's mother died. She was buried in Horton churchyard; then John Milton the elder returned to live his last years in London, and John the younger set out on his European travels, chiefly in Italy, in 1637-9.

*   *   *

Dickens in 1867 rented Elizabeth Cottage in the High Street of Slough probably because it was as safe a place as possible wherein to be anonymous. His hope was there to have the occasional comfort of companionship with Ellen Ternan. I referred earlier to Dickens's besetting need for Ellen in the late 1860s, and the strains that the relationship imposed on both of them. Almost as soon as Dickens and Ellen were together in Slough, he was off again to America on the exhausting tour on which he had tried (but found it impossible) to have her company and when he returned, Slough proved less convenient for them than Dickens had hoped. Elizabeth Cottage was presently rented to other tenants; it was later destroyed by fire, and I am not sure that its site in Slough's High Street is positively known.

Thomas Gray (1716–71), when not living in college at Cambridge, remained with his mother at Stoke Poges. His deceased father, a London 'citizen and money-scrivener' (which was, I suppose, an early phrase for 'stockbroker'), was called by one biographer 'a selfish, extravagant, and violent man'; he died in 1741, when Gray had been to Eton, to Cambridge, had travelled for two years on the Continent and reached the age of twenty-five. Mrs Gray was described by her son Thomas as the 'careful tender mother of many children'; he was the only child who survived her. She settled at Stoke as a widow and Gray, dividing his time between fellow-collegians and his mother, was quietly pleased when his poetry gave pleasure to both. He was in no hurry to print for a wider public. The 'Ode on the Prospect of Eton', for instance, was probably written at Stoke, perhaps in 1742; it pleased Gray's mother, and it seems partly for her further pleasure that five years later Gray had it printed. It was his first publication, and 'little notice', Warton said, 'was taken of it'. Presently the *Elegy written in a Country Church-yard*, and written likewise partly for his mother, was put into print in 1750. The printer, Dodsley, told Gray that he had instantly achieved a 'reputation'; but Gray himself was unchanged by that. The moment the poem was famous, suggestions were made that it was to be identified with churchyards other than Stoke Poges; the theme is agreed to be general, yet there is no need to deny its link with the particular church to which Gray and his mother were both devoted. When she died in 1753 Gray arranged for her burial in a vault outside the east end of the church, and when he died at Cambridge in 1771, it was in the same vault at Stoke Poges that in accordance with his wishes he was buried.

After some years the old Manor House in Stoke Park, written of by Gray in 'A Long Story', came to be rebuilt by a John Penn who was a grandson of the great William Penn who founded Pennsylvania. Two of William's grandsons were named John; the one referred to was the miscellaneous writer who had gone to Pennsylvania at the winding-up of family affairs in that territory, and with his share of reward, returned to England, settled in this part of Buckinghamshire, and went on producing poems, plays, pamphlets, and putting up memorials. With praiseworthy concern to honour Gray's memory, and with fortune well able to do so, John Penn commissioned the imposing monument, a stone sarcophagus on a tall square plinth in best classical style, which stands today in a field next the churchyard. This 'Gray's Field' and the monument now belong to the National Trust.

This part of Buckinghamshire is 'the Penn country'. The Friends' Meeting-house at Jordans, beside which William Penn's remains are buried, is, as the crow flies, five miles due north of Stoke Poges; thereabouts, within short compass, are Chalfont St Peter, Chalfont St Giles and Amersham, all of which were made important in the life of William Penn, and Chalfont St Giles in the life of John Milton also, by the energy of one of the most active young Quakers of that time, the admirable Thomas Ellwood. Ellwood, five years older than William Penn, had been accepted as a student by Milton in his hard times of blindness and poverty after the Restoration; and Milton's manner of teaching Ellwood the proper foreign mode of pronouncing Latin made them firm friends. Both men were under threats of persecution; Ellwood, for conscientious objection to swearing the oath of allegiance, was thrown into Newgate in 1662 and from time to time was in other prisons. He was in danger of prison sentence when Milton asked for help in getting out of London – the story is best told in Ellwood's own words:

Some little time before I went to *Aylesbury* Prison, I was desired by my *quondam* Master *Milton*, to take an House for him in the Neighbourhood where I dwelt, that he might go out of the City, for the Safety of himself and his Family, the Pestilence then growing hot in *London*. I took a pretty Box for him in Giles-Chalfont, a Mile from me, of which I gave him Notice, and intended to have waited on him, and seen him well settled in it, but was prevented by that Imprisonment.

The 'pretty Box' in the main street of Chalfont St Giles (Deanway) was purchased by subscription in the last century and has become a well-kept museum. (On the opposite side of the Deanway and somewhat above Milton's Cottage, is a curious phenomenon – a dwelling-house with a front entrance through the pillars of, formerly, a fourposter bed. There is a story behind that: the once highly popular author of boys' books Captain Mayne Reid built a large and elaborately furnished house, The Rancho, at Gerrards Cross, but after only a few months of occupancy was forced to sell everything. It was the whim of a Chalfont builder to convert Mayne Reid's fourposter into a porch. Thus in the nineteenth century Chalfont St Giles came to have two showpieces: Milton's Cottage and Captain Mayne Reid's Bed.) Returning from that parenthesis to the dignity of seventeenth-century puritans, one of Ellwood's charms was that he could be gay without being flippant. As soon as he was released from gaol in Aylesbury he visited Milton to make sure his blind friend was well settled. Presently Milton called, presumably to one of his daughters, for a manuscript of his, which he handed to Ellwood with instruction that it should be taken home, read at leisure, and then returned with the young man's 'Judgment thereupon'. As regards this considerable assignment, I refer again to Ellwood's words:

When I came home, and had set myself to read it, I found it was that excellent Poem which he entituled PARADISE LOST. After I had, with the best Attention, read it through, I made him another Visit, and returned him his Book, with due Acknowledgement of the Favour he had done me in communicating it to me. He asked me, *How I liked it, and what I thought of it?* which I modestly but freely told him; and after some further Discourse about it, I pleasantly said to him, Thou hast said much here about *Paradise lost*; but what hast thou to say of *Paradise found?* He made me no Answer, but sate some Time in a Muse; then brake off that Discourse, and fell upon another Subject.

After the Sickness was over, and the City well cleansed and become safely habitable again, he returned thither. And when afterwards I went to wait on him there (which I seldom failed to do) he showed me his second Poem, called PARADISE REGAINED; and in a pleasant Tone said to me, *This is owing to you; for you put it into my Head by the Question you put to me at* Chalfont *; which before I had not thought of.*

In those years 'friends Meeting' was forced to be kept in secret, the Quakers being in perpetual danger from informers. One place that was favoured for meeting was Jordans Farm, where the road from Chalfont St Giles, turning into Jordans Lane, meets Welders Lane. Here, at Old Jordans Farmhouse (converted by the Society of Friends in 1911 into Old Jordans Hostel), after one raid Thomas Ellwood was able to secure the conviction and punishment of some informers for perjury. That provided a measure of protection, and a small piece of land below the farmhouse was made into the little Quaker graveyard – it began to be used as such when the farmhouse was still the meeting place. The present Meeting-house, sited just below the older burial-ground, was built as soon as the Acts of Toleration made open worship possible for congregations not within the Church of England. After the death of Charles II in 1685 (an apoplectic stroke was fatal even though the king's head was 'plied with frying pans'), Penn, who had returned from his first visit to Pennsylvania, was one of the chief contributors to the fund for building the Jordans Meeting-house; and it was his long-standing personal friendship with James II (which horrified some Quakers, for James was openly a Roman Catholic) that enabled him to work for inclusion of all Nonconformists in the then current moves for toleration. It was in large part through Penn's influence that the building of Jordans Meeting-house could begin in James's reign; the Meeting-house was completed and in use before the 'bloodless revolution' enthroned the Protestant William of Orange.

Old Jordans Hostel and Jordans Village (organized by some leading Quaker families after the 1914–18 war, and pleasingly sited on the crest of rising ground above the Meeting-house) have been hospitable or neighbourly to various modern writings; it was for instance in Jordans that *All Quiet on the Western Front* was translated by A. W. Wheen in 1928, and in the house that Herbert Read built in the valley below Jordans he wrote, in the 1930s, *The Innocent Eye* and *The Green Child*. The many other writings which grew in this area (for instance George Orwell's *Animal Farm* at nearby Gerrards Cross) indicate that this part of the country retained the stimulus it had variously exercised on Penn and Burke (I am thinking of their writings), Milton, Waller, Gray, Shelley – and Mary Shelley. Beaconsfield illustrates the possible medley of recollections: it has been of significance to writers who range from Waller, Burke and Crabbe to G. K. Chesterton and Robert Frost.

Remembrance of Edmund Waller's poetry is often confined to the verses addressed to Sacharissa; I referred to those when mentioning Waller at Groombridge in Kent and his courtship of Lady Dorothy Sidney ('Sacharissa') at Penshurst. The Wallers had been a well-known family in and around Beaconsfield since the fourteenth century. The poet was born at Coleshill; his father died and the mother pushed her son into becoming Member of Parliament for Amersham when he was barely sixteen; the large property of Hall Barn at Beaconsfield was bought for him when he was eighteen; and his marriage with a very wealthy London heiress when he was twenty-five was also attributed to the mother's management. Waller's mother, as a Royalist, was accustomed to hector Cromwell at the time the Civil War was brewing (although Cromwell called Mrs Waller 'aunt' and her son 'cousin' there was no actual relationship). When the Civil War became inevitable and Cromwell found that 'she was more in earnest than he in jest' and was working for the Royalists, 'he put her under the custody of her daughter'.

Edmund Waller's wife died after three years of marriage. Waller then used his position in Parliament to act as leader in a plot ('Waller's Plot') to seize London for Charles I, in May 1643; a further treachery attributed to him was that he informed against his fellow-plotters to save his own life. He was expelled from the House of Commons, imprisoned, fined and after a while banished. This enabled him to marry again and withdraw to Paris, where he printed his poems and proceeded to raise a second family, while his mother continued to be in charge of children and estates at Beaconsfield.

Perhaps it was partly Cromwell's liking for that old forthright enemy of his, the 'aunt', that persuaded him in 1651 to secure pardon for his 'cousin' Waller. This caused publication of Waller's laudatory verses on Cromwell and, as soon as they were appropriate, his contrary poems of rejoicing at Cromwell's death and of welcome to Charles II at the Restoration. By then Waller was planning to settle again in Buckinghamshire. He died at Hall Barn, Beaconsfield, at the age of eighty-one. Near the churchyard wall at the centre of the old town of Beaconsfield is a conspicuous monument to Waller, with elaborate and laudatory Latin inscriptions; yet visitors to the church tend to show less attention to that ornate memorial than to the simple brass and tablet within the church, recording the burial-place of Edmund Burke.

As early as 1704 a wealthy London family called Gregory built a house called Gregories; which, with surrounding lands, has now been completely overbuilt by the new town which grew around Beaconsfield's railway station. Possession of Gregories reverted for a while to a branch of the Waller family until in 1768 Edmund Burke bought the house, enlarged it, and changed its name to Butler's Court. From Ralph Robinson's *The Penn Country and the Chilterns* I borrow comments on the improvidence of Burke's purchase:

Burke had to borrow nearly all the money, and his hospitality to visitors and generosity to neighbours kept him constantly in debt. When Mrs Burke sold the property in 1812, the original mortgage of £14000 was still upon it; the house was burned down in the following year and never rebuilt. But Edmund

Burke loved it and found it convenient: it was but twenty-four miles from London and within an easy ride of his constituency at Wendover. Of his life at Butler's Court much has been written; how he kept open house, with creditors at his door, befriended the despairing poet Crabbe, or fed the poor with flour ground from his own corn in his own mill. . . .

Burke farmed 160 acres of grass and 160 of arable, and Arthur Young, the writer on agriculture, noted that Burke had his own idea of ploughing twice as deep as the normal practice of his neighbours. This meant extra hard work for his oxen and ploughman, but he himself would take a hand with the ploughing – a custom which at least once was of double advantage. On that occasion a solicitor's clerk who had been sent to serve a writ on Burke, asked of a man ploughing in a field near the house if Mr Burke was at home. 'Mr Burke is out,' said the ploughman (Burke himself) and the writ for that instant was unserved.

Burke was perpetually pressed for money, which may make less surprising his sympathetic response to a long letter which came out of the blue in 1781 from 'the despairing poet Crabbe'. Nothing would have been easier for Burke than to excuse himself at that time from reading an appeal from a long-winded indigent poet who begged for an interview next day. The whole quality of Burke's attentiveness to Crabbe's letter and the orderly sequence of further diagnoses and actions betokened Burke's genius. There was nothing flash-in-the-pan about the help that he gave Crabbe, who was taken into the household at Butler's Court, where Burke, after studying all the poet's manuscripts, judged rightly which to take to the office of the same Mr Dodsley who (or whose father) had published Gray's *Elegy* thirty years before. Burke himself carried the manuscript poem to Dodsley, read parts aloud to that bookseller with comments, and was in general so effective a literary agent that Dodsley agreed not only to print the poem as a pamphlet, but to pay all costs and turn over to the author every bit of profit that might in usual way accrue to him as publisher and vendor. Burke then sailed on to introduce Crabbe and his works to Reynolds, Johnson and others of his wide circle. Crabbe's own merits resulted in his being, from the hour that he met Burke, 'a made man'.

G. K. Chesterton was fond of repeating that when Burke in the 1790s was contemplating retirement, it was proposed to make him a peer under the title of Lord Beaconsfield; but Burke, saddened by the death of his son Richard, had for that reason refused such an hereditary honour. To Chesterton, Burke's refusal emphasized Disraeli's impudence in selecting the title 'Earl of Beaconsfield' when he had no connection with the place. Chesterton and his wife moved from Battersea to Beaconsfield in 1909; he tells in his *Autobiography* how as a young married couple on exploration by foot they had come to 'a sort of village', had bed and

breakfast 'at an inn called The White Hart', learned that a local pronun-
ciation of the place-name was 'Beconsfield', and then and there decided
it was where 'some day we will make our home'. After waiting for seven
years they were able to purchase their first house in Beaconsfield,
Overroads. Here Chesterton was between 'Old Town' and 'New Town'
and for a time went in turn to a barber shop in each, until the bold
project was conceived of having the barber attend to him at Overroads
– for he never managed comfortably to shave himself. Among the stream
of visitors to the 'little triangular house' was Father O'Connor who
generally carried a large umbrella and many brown paper parcels and
was admittedly the prototype of Father Brown of Chesterton's detective
stories. Those stories were written at Overroads, and it was a sketch of
Father O'Connor which appeared on the wrapper of the first edition of
The Innocence of Father Brown.

In 1922 the Chestertons moved into their second house in Beaconsfield, called Top Meadow. It grew from a huge room or studio built in
the field opposite Overroads, and here they lived for the rest of their
lives. When Eric Gill moved to Speen in the Chilterns, he was a fairly
frequent visitor, and after Chesterton's death in 1936 Gill designed the
memorial monument in the churchyard of Beaconsfield's Catholic church.

I mentioned the name of the American poet Robert Frost in association with Beaconsfield. The link may have been Ezra Pound. Pound,
angry at what he felt to be the stagnation of poetry in America in 1909,
had arrived in London at the age of twenty-four. He paid unusually
careful attention to who was who among London publishers, not only
with regard to the then fashionable publishers for poetry (such as Elkin
Mathews and John Lane) but also to the less famous (such as David
Nutt), keeping an eye on any who might be useful to himself or other
American poets. When Robert Frost's early poems had been, in Pound's
phrase, 'long scorned by the "great American Editors" ', it occurred to
Frost to try his hand in England. I don't know who suggested his lodging in Beaconsfield, but that was his 'home from home' for periods between 1912 and 1914. I have no hard evidence to prove that it was Pound
who introduced Frost to David Nutt; I only say it would have been
typical of Pound; and it is true that even before David Nutt 'at his own
expense' published Robert Frost's first book, *A Boy's Will*, Pound had
prepared a review to salute its appearance. That was in 1913. The
London publication was not much noticed in America. When David
Nutt continued with Frost's *North of Boston* in 1914, Pound wrote about
it for *Poetry* (Chicago): 'It is a sinister thing that so American, I might
almost say so parochial, a talent as that of Robert Frost should have to
be exported before it can find due encouragement and recognition'.

*   *   *

I am not here going afield to Hughenden Manor, where Disraeli became a landed proprietor and where he wrote his later novels; nor even to Marlow, with the recollections there of Thomas Love Peacock and Shelley and their wandering little walking tours together while Mary Shelley, more closely tied to Marlow by her pregnancy, stayed within Albion House to write *Frankenstein*. To Eton and Windsor such a complex of memories attach that I select only one reference which combines both. In the Preface to Roger Ascham's Elizabethan treatise on practical education, *The Schoolmaster*, it is told that when the great plague was at London in the year 1563, the Queen's Majesty, Queen Elizabeth, lay at her castle of Windsor; and Ascham, as her private tutor, was dining there. As 'so many wise and good men together, as hardly then could have been picked out again, out of all England beside', began their dinner, their host prompted discussion of 'strange news' that had been brought to him that morning. The news was 'that divers scholars of Eton be run away from the school, for fear of beating'. What discipline, and of what sort, did each of these 'wise and good men' think was best suited to instil learning? Roger Ascham had his say along with most of the others, and then left the table to go upstairs for his customary period of reading with the Queen.

'We then read together in the Greek tongue', said Ascham, 'that noble Oration of Demosthenes against Aeschines, for his false dealing in his ambassage to King Philip of Macedonia.' Sir Richard Sackville, who like Ascham had permission to enter her Majesty's privy chamber, entered quietly without interruption of the tutorial. Presently the Queen was occupied by herself in performing some task set by the tutor, and Sackville took Ascham by the hand and led him to a window-embrasure for private talk. With reference both to the discussion at dinner and the Queen's evident proficiency in learning, Sackville earnestly and quietly beseeched the tutor to put into a treatise his own experience of learning and teaching, and how he 'did teach the Queen'. Their side-talk was interrupted by Elizabeth's suddenly calling for Ascham's attention, yet that evening prompted Ascham's famous book. *The Schoolmaster* remained unfinished – perhaps it is in the nature of the best treatises on practical education to remain unfinished.

At Maidenhead, where the Bath Road crosses the Thames, there are two associations I have been waiting for. One is the recollection of Hugh Lofting, who was born here. The many delightful stories of *Dr Doolittle* grew from letters he wrote home to his children from the Western Front in the 1914–18 war.

The other association is that in the years before that war, when for many who lived beside the banks of the Thames above Maidenhead there might be *nothing* – if I may quote –

'nothing – absolutely nothing – half so much worth doing as simply messing about in boats. Simply messing', he went on dreamily: 'messing – about – in – boats; messing – '

'Look ahead, Rat!' cried the Mole suddenly.

It was too late . . .

There might seem nothing, I was about to say, to interrupt happy total immersion in *The Wind in the Willows* by Kenneth Grahame. From many little clues not too difficult to put together it was easy to locate the homes of Mole and Water Rat and of Mr Toad of Toad Hall in or on the river banks where the Thames flows by Cookham. Kenneth Grahame lived at Cookham as a child in the 1860s, and was living here again when, primarily for the pleasure of his own son, he wrote *The Wind in the Willows* in 1908. (For topographical identification of 'The Wild Wood' one may remember that what was large for animals was small for humans. Some vast distances, though, are in the book: the Berkshire Downs, and faraway Fowey in Cornwall.)

Kenneth Grahame later moved up the Thames past Reading to Pangbourne, where, at Church Cottage, he died in 1932. I suppose Oscar Wilde's imprisonment in Reading Gaol (1895–7) is still the most notorious literary reminiscence at Reading. Wilde wrote *De Profundis*, as if a long letter to Lord Alfred Douglas, while in the gaol at Reading, but *The Ballad of Reading Gaol* was written and published in 1898, after his release.

With a shockingly abrupt change of reminiscence, one finds, near the gaol in Reading, the Old Abbey Gateway – the gatehouse once occupied by the girls' school which was attended for a short time by Jane Austen and a decade later also by Mary Russell Mitford (1787–1855). Very much earlier in time the canon 'Sumer is icumen in', the earliest known piece of music for several voices, was composed by one of the monks of the Abbey and was sung here from about 1240, as a tablet within the ruins commemorates. There is a tablet also on the house in the London Road to which Mary Russell Mitford was brought as a girl of ten; the story of all that was beautifully told by Anne Thackeray Ritchie:

Dr Mitford, having spent all his wife's fortune, and having brought his family from a comfortable home, with flowers and a Turkey carpet, to a small lodging near Blackfriars Bridge, determined to present his daughter with an expensive lottery ticket on the occasion of her tenth birthday. She had a fancy for No. 2224, of which the added numbers came to 10. This number actually came out the first prize of £20,000, which money started the family once more in comparative affluence. Dr Mitford immediately built a new square house, which he calls Bertram House, on the site of a pretty old farmhouse which he causes to be pulled down. He also orders a dessert-service painted with the Mitford arms; Mrs Mitford is supplied with a carriage, and she subscribes to a circulating library. . . . The next two or three years were brilliant enough; for the family must have lived at the rate of three or four thousand a year. Their hospitality was profuse, they had servants, carriages, they bought pictures and furniture, they entertained. . . . The Doctor naturally enough invested in a good many more lottery tickets, but without any further return. . . .

Of Dr Mitford a friend remarked that his 'manners were easy, natural, cordial, and apparently extremely frank', but he 'was prepared to allow himself any insincerity which seemed expedient. He was not only reck-lessly extravagant, but addicted to high play'. He had apparently run through £50000 of his wife's as rapidly as he proceeded to run through the £20000 of the daughter's, but 'his wife and daughter were never heard to complain of his conduct, nor appeared to admire him less'. Presently, when Miss Mitford was in her twenties, even more when she was in her thirties, the three of them (infirm mother, feckless father and herself) were dependent on what her pen could earn; she had been known to say she had rather be a washerwoman than a literary lady, but it was the earning-power of the pen that forced her into the company of Mesdames Bailey, Edgeworth, Opie, Trollope – and the many other women-writers of that period who had to be family breadwinners. After the lush years at Bertram House the Mitford family had moved five miles from Reading to a labourer's cottage at Three Mile Cross; 'there I had toiled and striven', Miss Mitford remarked in a letter late in life when she was leaving the poor cottage, 'and tasted as bitterly of bitter anxiety, of fear and hope, as often falls to the lot of women'. That particular letter described her move from Three Mile Cross, in 1851, to Swallow-field, where the cottage in which she lived for her last four years is still to be seen 'where three roads meet'.

A little earlier, though, in 1844, there is a picture of Miss Mitford that is nice to remember. Her father had died after a long and trying illness in 1842; the £1000 of debts that he left had been paid off – friends helped in that, as friends had also seen that she had a Civil List pension. In 1844 Miss Mitford had enough 'ease' to organize a school-feast for 'our village', with buns and flags for the children who rode in waggons decked with laurel, Miss Mitford leading the way, and eight or ten neighbouring carriages following – 'the whole party waiting in Swallow-field Lane to see the Queen and Prince Albert returning from their visit to the Duke of Wellington'. In reporting the outing, 'Our Duke went to no great expense', said Miss Mitford. This she examines in detail. 'One strip of carpet the Duke did buy, the rest of the furniture he hired in Reading for the week. The ringers, after being hard at work for four hours, sent a can to the house to ask for some beer, and the can was sent back empty.' The Doctor, her father, had been dead for two years. Her incorrigible love for him, despite – perhaps because of – his irresponsible extravagances, shines through each of these comments on the Duke. How much better the royal visit would have been treated by her father!

2. THE BERKSHIRE DOWNS, BATH AND BRISTOL

The part of Berkshire between Newbury and Oxford holds many memories of writers of the 1914–18 war period and the decades that followed. Before the war Robert Bridges had built Chilswell House at Boar's Hill, and from there had produced his anthology *Spirit of Man* in 1916 and in 1918 the complete edition of the poems of Gerard Manley Hopkins, which had much influence on later twentieth-century poetry. Dr Bridges produced his own *Testament of Beauty* in 1929; when he died in 1930 he was buried at Yattendon, on the southern side of the Berkshire Downs, near Newbury. Two miles from Yattendon and closer to Newbury is Hermitage, where D. H. Lawrence rented a cottage in the winter of 1917–18 and again in 1919. Richard Aldington also settled into a cottage near Hermitage after his demobilization, and he used to speak of visits paid to him there by Harold Monro and T. S. Eliot. Aldington, even more than Lytton Strachey, suffered from unusual jealousies, his occasional way of easing (so it seemed) some internal hidden mortification; I would not advise believing what Aldington's ill moods made him say about such one-time close friends of his as D. H. Lawrence, Monro, Pound and Eliot.

It was before the war and higher on the Downs at East Ilsley that Lytton Strachey had to a considerable extent overcome the jealousies which were the reverse side of his unhappiness; having grown his psychological beard, he decided there to use 'Lytton Strachey' as his pen-name ('rather theatrical, I think') and began to think about applying a carefully measured injection of malice to various of the eminent Victorians. Strachey's life during the period of writing *Eminent Victorians* alternated between Berkshire and London; for a time he was at Pangbourne; but some time after the publication of the book in 1918, and when it was being hailed as 'the first book of the Twenties' – Strachey revelling in that success – he settled into Ham Spray House, near the Downs between Newbury and Hungerford, as home for the rest of his life. It was at Ham Spray House that Strachey died in 1932.

Immediately to the south of Newbury is the country of *Watership Down*, the story by Richard Adams of the small band of rabbits who, when their territory was about to be developed by hostile Newbury builders, were forced to set out from their warren on a long and dangerous journey. All the places where the rabbits' adventures occur are, as the author promises, real places and the map reproduced in the book must have tempted many ardent readers, both children and adults, to search out scenes that are described. Often Mr Adams's text assists his map, as when, at the start of a new journey, Hazel (leader of 'our' rabbits) is guided to a patch of thorn from which he and a companion looked out across the open ground ahead.

Two or three hundred yards away and directly across their line, a belt of trees ran straight across the down, stretching in each direction as far as they could see. They had come to the line of the Portway – only intermittently a road – which runs from north of Andover, through St Mary Bourne with its bells and streams and watercress beds, through Bradley Wood, on across the downs and so to Tadley and at last to Silchester – the Romans' Calleva Atrebatum. Where it crosses the downs, the line is marked by Caesar's Belt, a strip of woodland as straight as the road, narrow indeed but more than three miles long. In this hot noon-day the trees of the Belt were looped and netted with darkest shadow. The sun lay outside, the shadows inside the trees. All was still, save for the grasshoppers and the falling finch-song of the yellow-hammer on the thorn. Hazel looked steadily for a long time, listening with raised ears and wrinkling his nose in the unmoving air.
'I can't see anything wrong with it,' he said at last.

After that aside the adventures continue.
Across the Berkshire Downs from east to west the Icknield Way or Ridgeway led very anciently to Avebury, and beyond the Ridgeway at the northern escarpment of the Downs lies Wantage, in the Vale of White Horse. Wantage, traditional birthplace of King Alfred the Great, and the Vale of White Horse, setting for one of the legendary combats of St George and the Dragon, were at the very central heartland of Saxon England. Respectful tribute of one kind to the Vale of White Horse is shown in the opening chapters of *Tom Brown's School Days*. Deeper tribute was shown by the late J. R. R. Tolkien, Professor of Anglo-Saxon at Oxford, whose feeling for the Anglo-Saxon shires, as felt for instance here and in the Vale of Evesham, created *The Hobbit* (1937). Here, adapted for juveniles, the Hobbits themselves embodied what Tolkien loved best in the Saxon-English character. It is likely that the Hobbits may contribute more lasting resistance to the destructions caused by witless bureaucrats and industrial developments than can be communicated in stories of humanized animals. Tolkien felt his measure-

less deep reservoir of latent courage in England's Midland shires and I shall return at Evesham to his feeling for 'the Shire'.

It was not unnatural that in Sir Walter Scott's *Kenilworth*, when Tressilian (Chapter 9) had set out by night from Cumnor for Devonshire, the morning should have found him 'only in the vale of Whitehorse, memorable for the defeat of the Danes in former days, with his horse deprived of a forefoot shoe, an accident which threatened to put a stop to his journey'. The region in which Tressilian found himself in that plight was immediately beneath White Horse Hill, where the figure of the horse cut in the turf was in Scott's time frequently associated with Alfred's victory over the Danes at Ashdown. Here the traveller was surrounded by sites to which legends were attached; within short compass is the Blowing Stone, and the detached knoll called Dragon's Hill, where at the end of one of his many combats with St George the dragon breathed one of his lasts. Then from the oval earthwork called Uffington Castle on the top of White Horse Hill the Ridgeway leads on to the dolmen known as Wayland Smith's Cave. It was the legend attaching to this last-named site which Scott adapted to his own purpose in *Kenilworth*; and if the horse had to be led quite a way uphill to be shod, the adventure with the impersonator of Wayland Smith, as Scott tells it, was worth the telling.

Hungerford did not enter very much into literature until Hazlitt wrote his essay about the fight (on the gentle eminence 'a mile to the left of Hungerford') between the Gas-man and Bill Neate. Scott took his travellers in *Kenilworth* farther westward from Wayland Smith's Cave over the Marlborough Downs to Marlborough, though the inn at which they alighted was not the famous Castle Inn of the heyday of the coaching era. Stanley Weyman's romance *The Castle Inn* reported the early history of the fine house in Marlborough which (a century later than the period of *Kenilworth*) was built as a mansion for the Royalist Lord Seymour. At Christmas-time in 1648 a number of Royalist gentlemen were collected there, ostensibly for a day of sport with the hounds and a good hunting dinner, among them John Aubrey, then aged twenty-two. The Meet was at the Greywethers; in Aubrey's words:

'Twas here that our game began and the chase led us (at length) through the village of Aubury, into the closes there: where I was wonderfully surprised at the sight of those vast stones, of which I had never heard before, as also the mighty bank and graffe [ditch] about it. I observed in the enclosure some segments of rude circles made with these stones, whence I concluded they had been in the old time complete. I left my Company a while, entertaining myself with a more delightful indagation: and then (steered by the cry of the Hounds) I overtook the company and went with them. . . .

The place-name Avebury has had many spellings. Some villagers who left England for Pennsylvania shortly after John Aubrey's time named their new estate in Philadelphia with the old place-name, although spelled Awbury. Yet, disregarding spelling, what Anthony Powell rightly points out in *John Aubrey and His Friends* is that the above sentences, 'even if he had taken no further interest in such matters, would alone have given Aubrey a place in the annals of English archaeology'. Bearing in mind the years of neglect of the extraordinary archaeological interest of this prehistoric centre, before, and indeed after, John Aubrey, it is fitting to speak of him as the discoverer of Avebury.

While thinking of John Aubrey and his further 'indagations' in archaeology, I remember also that Lord Seymour's house in Marlborough was in the eighteenth century a home of Frances, Countess of Hertford, well-known in her time for insistence on sham ruins in her gardens, artificial cascades and grottoes intended to outdo Pope's grotto at Twickenham. She was a generous patron to 'grotto poets', and won more respect than that phrase might suggest: it was the worthy Mrs Rowe who addressed the Countess in verse as 'Cleora', and to the exceedingly worthy Isaac Watts she was 'Eusebia'. I suspect that these names flew round at poetry readings at Richings (near Heathrow) after that house had passed in 1739 from Lord Bathurst to the Earl of Hertford. It was supposedly some years earlier and when James Thomson was a guest at Marlborough that he offered to the Countess the dedication of his poem *Spring*, the third part of his *Seasons* to be composed. The Countess had proposed an evening of reading her own poems, but Thomson and his host spoiled her evening by lingering unforgivably over their wine. Thomson's effort to appease the lady –

> Hertford, fitted or to shine in courts
> With unaffected grace, or walk the plain
> With Innocence and Meditation joined
> In soft assemblage –

was unavailing. His visit to that family seat of the Seymours was summarily cut short; nor was he again received by the Countess. When the Hertford household removed from Marlborough, the house was turned into the Castle Inn, for more than a century the 'best' in England, and clearly the most fashionable for, as Mr Tristram says in his *Coaching Days and Coaching Ways*, 'it had the advertisement of all the nobility, wealth, fashion of a century that thronged as all history in those days thronged, to that centre of the valetudinarian and the voluptuary, Bath'. The fortune of the house altered once more in 1843, when it became the first of the buildings in which Marlborough College was housed.

On the Marlborough Downs north of Marlborough is the prehistoric camp called Barbary Castle, one of the favourite haunts of Richard

Jefferies; it is described, as is much else of this part of Wiltshire, in his *Wild Life in a Southern County*. Jefferies was born in 1848 at Coate Farm close to Swindon; the farmhouse, which is near the entrance to Coate Reservoir from the Marlborough Road, continues to house many relics of Jefferies, whose childhood and youth here gave rise to *Bevis* and *The Story of My Heart*.

I now return to the Bath Road by way of the Avebury which John Aubrey's further studies convinced him surpassed Stonehenge as much 'as a cathedral doth a parish chuch'. Even to those who bypass Avebury, Silbury Hill, rising beside the main road and showing itself as the largest artificial mound in Europe, may cause astonishment – that singularly massive monument remaining from we don't know when to signify we don't know what. Passing Beckhampton and Calne (where Coleridge lived for two unhappy years and possibly put together the end-part of the *Biographia Literaria*) the main road goes through Chippenham and we recall that Aubrey was born at Easton Piercy to the north, and two hundred years later the also voluble Thomas Moore settled at Bromham to the south. Then the coaching road takes us downhill through Box (and past a road-sign 'Pickwick') over the Avon into Bath.

*   *   *

Bath has been important in social and hence in literary history since the reign of Queen Anne and as a result of two men, Ralph Allen (1694–1764) and 'Beau' Nash (1674–1762). Throughout the turmoil of the seventeenth century the reputation of the baths had been such as to attract visits from, for instance, both Evelyn and Pepys. Pepys, his wife and the whole of his coachload whom we saw at Salisbury, were carried 'one after one another' into the temperate Cross Bath, where there was 'much company' and 'very fine ladies; and the manner pretty enough, only methinks it cannot be clean to go so many bodies together in the same water'. Yet by the time of Pepys's visit people of fashion, according to Oliver Goldsmith, were already also making Bath a summer retreat where 'they might have each other's company, and win each other's money, as they had done during the winter in town'. Social amusements were beginning to be organized under the direction of a Master of Ceremonies; balls were soon to be held in the town hall; but in Goldsmith's account the gaming-table was chiefly 'the salutary font to which such numbers flocked'. Goldsmith goes on to say that until the eighteenth century the amusements of Bath were neither elegant nor conducted with delicacy. 'Smoking in the rooms was permitted', people were disrespectful as regards dress and in their manners. 'The lodgings for visitants were paltry, though expensive; the dining-rooms and other chambers were floored with boards, coloured brown with soot and small beer, to hide the dirt. . . . The city was in itself mean and contemptible.' It was about the year 1703 that Queen Anne came to Bath for her health, and after that in both manners and architecture the city really took itself in hand. The two John Woods, father and son, found their design of a new city immensely supported by the wealthy Ralph Allen, who built the magnificent Prior Park, where Pope and other writers made lengthy visits. Fielding has a particular connection in that not only were parts of *Tom Jones* written there, but Allen was recognizably the original of 'Squire Allworthy'.

It was the appointment in 1704 of 'Beau' Nash as Bath's Master of Ceremonies that 'introduced order and method into the gaieties and social life of the place', says Muirhead's *England*, and that excellent guidebook refers to the pictures of that life drawn 'by innumerable authors – Smollett, Sheridan, Fanny Burney, Jane Austen, Thackeray, and (as regards a later period) Dickens'. The influential Richard Nash was by origin the son of an obscure Welsh gentleman of Swansea; he had a modicum of wit but such maximum of assurance as on a ball-night at the Assembly Rooms to strip even the Duchess of Q— of the white apron in which she had appeared. The 'King of Bath', with his aversion to white aprons, was determined to allow no deviations from the rules which he placarded in the Pump Room. Nash himself, Goldsmith says, was not cut out by nature to be a Beau. 'His person was clumsy, too large and awkward, and his features harsh, strong, and peculiarly irregular', yet 'he had assiduity, flattery, fine clothes, and as much wit as the ladies he addressed'. He had less trouble in persuading the ladies to conform to his rules than to make men give up wearing swords or forbid country squires from dancing in riding-dress and boots. In time, however, Nash managed to enforce the codes of conduct proper for the assemblies, public places and gaming-tables of Bath. When Bath had been merely a place for taking the waters, music, as Pepys had found ('musick extraordinary good as ever I heard at London almost, or any-where'), was an attraction; the first care of the 'King of Bath' had been to promote a more general music subscription, and the theatre, built in 1705, was prompt also in the 'rotation of diversions'. Every amusement so much improved under the management of Richard Nash that 'we see a kingdom beginning with him, and sending off Tunbridge as one of its colonies'.

Remarkable as were Nash's achievements, not even Goldsmith could make him out to be a very interesting person. But almost everything that happened to Goldsmith himself has charm, and one example is found in an episode more amusing than anything 'Beau' Nash offers. It occurred in the period between the writing of *The Deserted Village* and *She Stoops to Conquer* when Goldsmith was staying in Bath with his friend and patron Lord Clare at No. 11 North Parade – formerly a residence of Edmund Burke – and the story is neatly retold by John Freeman:

> One morning when Goldsmith was returning from a walk he went absent-mindedly into the neighbouring house, which happened to be that of the Duke of Northumberland. The duke and duchess talked amiably to him, Goldsmith supposing them to be guests of Lord Clare's, but when asked to breakfast he realized his error. The duke and duchess said that it was a most fortunate error for them, and made him promise to come to dinner.

Such unpremeditated and comical little adventures were part of the spice of life among well-mannered first-class passengers in Bath. What sort of lively marriage market it might be for the young at the very end of the eighteenth and beginning of the nineteenth century is the delicious subject of the story Jane Austen began to write after her own visits from the parsonage at Steventon to her aunt, her mother's sister-in-law Mrs Leigh Perrot. Mrs Austen's brother, Mr Leigh Perrot, is described by Elizabeth Jenkins as a man known to be of considerable wealth, by nature stiff, reserved, 'fastidious almost to a fault'; he and his wife were childless and lived in 'a somber and sunless dwelling', No. 1 Paragon near the upper end of the town. Visits to the uncle and aunt in Bath were not 'the unmixed delight' to the nieces Cassandra and Jane Austen, for though the aunt meant to be kind her own manner 'was not prepossessing, and her temper was rather gloomy and uncertain'. Nevertheless the nieces did make repeated visits to No. 1 Paragon, and to Jane those visits prompted her story of a heroine who also 'having been brought up in a remote country parsonage, was taken for a season to Bath'. Miss Jenkins's fitting comment continues:

> Jane chose a heroine for this novel with a healthy love of pleasure, an enthusiasm for dancing and novels and dearest friends and the society of young men, and with just that degree of *naïveté* that enhance the bustle and elegance of Bath into something absolutely glamorous. The exquisite naturalness of this story of a girl's holiday owes some of its convincingness at least to the manner in which, by touches so small and yet so sure, Jane Austen calls up around her walks and streets and buildings in so solid a form that when one visits those parts of Bath mentioned in *Northanger Abbey* after one has read the book, the experience strikes one as a confirmation.

I mentioned the Leigh Perrots partly to bring in an adventure that befell them that was very far from comical. In 1799, on an early afternoon in August, Mrs Leigh Perrot stepped into a milliner's shop in the centre of Bath to buy some black lace. A little later she repassed the shop with her husband, the parcel still under her arm, when one of the shop assistants 'ran out and charged her with having a card of stolen lace in the parcel as well as what she had paid for'. The parcel was there and then undone 'and sure enough disclosed a second card of lace'. The street-scene that followed, with the shopman and assistant loudly charging Mrs Leigh Perrot with theft and Mr Leigh Perrot taking his wife away with hot denials, was such as one might have expected to find in *Moll Flanders* (who in her time did have adventures in Bath) rather than in connection with members of the Austen family. Mr Leigh Perrot was not a man to compromise; he utterly denied the charge. Two days later the shopman lodged a formal accusation with the magistrates who had no option except to hold Mrs Leigh Perrot for trial at the next Assizes. These would be held at Taunton in March, eight months away; and in the meantime the law committed her to Ilchester gaol.

In telling about this Miss Jenkins assures us that none of Mrs Leigh Perrot's friends remotely supposed her to be guilty, but nobody could be unaware of the gravity of the punishment if the trial went against her. Since the value of the alleged theft was above five shillings, the legal penalty could be hanging. Reprieve from that extreme was probable, but the all too likely alternative was transportation to Botany Bay for fourteen years. Mr Leigh Perrot faced up to this possibility; he made tentative plans to sell his property so that if his wife were transported he could go with her. In the meantime, for the eight months until the Assizes, he shared her imprisonment – his money procuring such advantage as was possible – which was for both to share the squalid living-quarters of the prison-keeper and his family. There was talk of Cassandra and Jane Austen going to stay at Ilchester, either in the same prison-quarters or nearby, to be of help to their aunt and uncle throughout their extreme discomfort, and it was also suggested that they might sit by their aunt at the trial. But Mrs Leigh Perrot was firm in her refusal to allow her nieces to come to such a scene as she was undergoing, and the impulse was allowed to pass. At the end of March 1800 the case was tried and the jury took less than fifteen minutes to return a verdict of not guilty. Mr and Mrs Leigh Perrot returned to Bath poorer in health, and poorer in pocket by about £2000 from the unpleasant experience. So far as concerns Jane Austen the episode contradicts any impression that life in her family was uneventful.

The first writers in Bath I think of are novelists. I recall Defoe only as passing through Bath on the way to interview Robinson Crusoe – or rather Alexander Selkirk, the original of Robinson Crusoe – at Bristol; and similarly Swift placed Gulliver's story as starting from Bristol and was not specially concerned with Bath. Yet Smollett, if it was as a surgeon that he first went to Bath, returned because of its stimulus to him as novelist. It is probable that Smollett began the writing of *Humphry Clinker* (part of which is laid in Bath) when staying in Gay Street, and some have traced the influence on that novel of Christopher Anstey's amusing satire *The New Bath Guide* (1766). Sterne, having left his wife and daughter in France as a prelude to permanent separation, came to Bath in 1765, visited Ralph Allen at Prior Park, had his portrait painted by Gainsborough at a single sitting, and set off on the seven months' tour which was the basis for *A Sentimental Journey*.

Towards the end of the eighteenth century, if Bath was not for all novelists a place in which to write, it was the best place to come to hear people talk about what you had written. Fanny Burney was brought here in 1780 by the Thrales, to hear *Evelina* being discussed on all sides; and Horace Walpole in 1766 visited Bath to revel in hearing that grown-up people were positively frightened by *The Castle of Otranto*, which had appeared anonymously in the previous year. *The Castle of Otranto* soon stimulated imitations and though 'tales of terror' as produced by Mrs Radcliffe (her *Mysteries of Udolpho* appeared in 1795) were mildly ridiculed by Jane Austen in *Northanger Abbey*, remarks there indicate how compulsive the fashion was both to read novels and to chat about them.

Walter Scott mentions that it was in Bath that he learned his letters when as a child he was taken by his aunt to spend a year here for the cure, if possible, of his paralysed leg. Scott says he 'went through all the usual discipline of the pump-room and baths, but I believe without the least advantage to my lameness'. Yet what Scott remembered about Bath throughout life was that there he had learned to read and there he had his first visit to the theatre – the play was *As You Like It*, and he never forgot 'the witchery of the whole scene'.

I have sometimes wondered if it was from Dickens's first visit to Bath that the name of Pickwick stuck in his mind. As I've said, in recent times there has been a road-sign 'Pickwick', and both Upper and Lower Pickwick, though not conspicuous on most maps, are not far east of Bath. But were there road-signs to little villages off the Bath Road in Dickens's day? Or was it, as Chapter 35 of *Pickwick* may suggest, that before ever going to Bath Dickens's quick eye had noticed what Sam Weller speaks of in the text, that the name of the proprietor of at least one Bath coach 'was the magic name of Pickwick!' By 1840 Dickens, Forster and Maclise were very well pleased to spend time with Walter Savage Landor in the city that Landor called 'the Florence of England', but Mr Pickwick's earlier visit, although he was to spend two months in Royal Crescent, is really somewhat sketchy. It is the side-journey onward to Bristol and to Clifton which advances the plot and the central theme of *Pickwick*, which has now become 'Pickwick and principle!' and the developing relationship of Mr Pickwick and Sam.

*   *   *

Johnson and Boswell had made a side-trip from Bath to Bristol in 1776, so that Johnson might on the spot test the claims made for the antique 'Rowley's poetry' which had been produced by Thomas Chatterton. The suicide of Bristol's 'marvellous boy' was still widely lamented. Johnson's opinion, later proved correct, was that 'Rowley' was an invention of Chatterton's, yet he felt that the lament for the adolescent Chatterton was justified. 'This is the most extraordinary young man that has encountered my knowledge', said Johnson. 'It is wonderful how the whelp has written such things.' Presently Southey (who was born in Bristol, at No. 9 Wine Street, two years before the visit of Johnson and Boswell) championed Chatterton's poems and prompted their republication.

If in Bath one thought primarily of novelists, it is poets one thinks of in Bristol; and partly because at Bristol's Cross (the junction of the four streets, High Street, Wine Street, Broad Street and Corn Street, where the High Cross once stood) there was the bookshop of Joseph Cottle. Cottle's immortality was earned by publishing Coleridge's *Poems* in 1796 and Southey's *Joan of Arc* in the same year – Cottle advanced them money, thirty guineas to Coleridge, fifty guineas to Southey – and further, and certainly with scant expectation of profit, brought out *Lyrical Ballads* by Coleridge and Wordsworth in 1798.

On the Clifton side of Bristol (Sam Weller found that it's 'all uphill' at Clifton) Thomas Lovell Beddoes was born in 1803. He was the son of a famous physician who died when the child was six; his mother was a sister of Maria Edgeworth. His gifts showed early and his first work *The Bride's Tragedy*, written when he was sixteen, achieved some notice when it was published three years later. He published another volume and started on a wild Elizabethan play called *Death's Jest-Book*, never wholly completed, which he kept with him during his years as medical student and then as medical practitioner in Germany and Switzerland. Beddoes was apparently much involved in liberal politics on the Continent, and the circumstances of his illness at Basle in 1848 and his death in January 1849 remain a mystery. If Beddoes's death was suicide, as it was alleged to be, the cause was probably not disappointment about the reception of his poetry. Of his poems he spoke sardonically as being 'entertaining, very unamiable, and utterly unpopular'; there is no intimation that he had any special hankering for momentary popularity. After his death the impact of his writings grew and some of his lyrics clearly influenced various twentieth-century poets – Walter de la Mare and Ralph Hodgson come to mind, as you read Beddoes's invocation to *Dream-Pedlary*:

> If there were dreams to sell,
>   What would you buy?
> Some cost a passing bell;
>   Some a light sigh,
> That shakes from Life's fresh crown
> Only a rose-leaf down.
> If there were dreams to sell,
> Merry and sad to tell,
> And the crier rung the bell,
>   What would you buy?

Shortly after the founding of Clifton College, one of the masters there was T. E. Brown. He was a native of the Isle of Man and made his reputation at first for narrative verses in the Manx dialect, but was prolific also in the English of the mainland. Later generations have not been wholly respectful to his lyric with the first line:

> A garden is a lovesome thing, God wot!

Yet Brown was an inspiring teacher, and he and John Addington Symonds (who like Beddoes was the son of a Bristol medical man) made Clifton, in the late 1860s, a stimulating place for literary-minded school-boys. (William J. Locke was also a master there, before he became a highly popular novelist.) T. E. Brown's best-known pupil, though, had been at the Crypt School, Gloucester, before Brown's appointment to Clifton – that pupil was W. E. Henley. As a boy of twelve Henley was discovered to have a tubercular disease which after some years caused the amputation of one foot and which before he was twenty was threaten-ing the other leg. It was Brown that Henley always credited with his start, despite physical handicaps, on his much-valued literary career. In Henley's early twenties he was sent to Edinburgh to become a patient of Sir Joseph Lister, who placed him in Edinburgh Infirmary, and for two years that hospital, 'cold, naked, clean, half-workhouse and half-jail', was his university. From the 'transformed back-kitchen where he lay' while Lister struggled with his condition he sent his *Hospital Verses* to the *Cornhill Magazine*. Those verses caused the editor, Leslie Stephen, to visit him and to introduce him to Robert Louis Stevenson. The friendships matured; when Henley was twenty-eight he was well enough, though crippled, to attempt a 'Grub Street' life in London, and so spotted Conrad, and published *The Nigger of the Narcissus* in his own *New Review*. Collaborations with Stevenson produced four plays, among them *Deacon Brodie*; in Stevenson's essay 'Talk and Talkers'

Henley is portrayed as 'Burly', yet the more widely seen portrayal by Stevenson of Henley (with some of his qualities suppressed) is the one-legged John Silver of *Treasure Island*.

Henley drew me away from Bristol, where there are many other names for mention. Hartley Coleridge, who classed himself among 'the small poets', was the first-born son of 'S.T.C.', born at Bristol, though brought up in the Lake District. At Clevedon, on the coast west of Bristol, Tennyson's friend Hallam, commemorated in *In Memoriam*, was buried. Thackeray was a frequent visitor to Clevedon Court, and part of *Henry Esmond* was written there; Thackeray was also attentive to Bristol's early trade with the Americas in *The Virginians*. More recently, the novelist Mary Webb lived for some years a little farther along the coast, at Weston-super-Mare. On Bristol's northern side, at Stapleton, Hannah More was born (1745), and at Stapleton too Frances Milton, who became Mrs Trollope and Anthony's mother, was born and brought up.

To the list of poets who have been born in Bristol there may be added the name of Isaac Rosenberg (1890–1918). Most of Rosenberg's upbringing was in the East End of London; his genius had few of what are sometimes called 'advantages' to help (or hinder) its growth, and towards the end of the 1914–18 war he was killed on active service in France; yet more than half a century after Rosenberg's death the stature of his poems is noted more widely than it was in his lifetime, and Bristol can claim the pride of having been his birthplace.

3. THROUGH SOUTH WALES TO ST DAVID'S

Instead of taking the M4 motorway over the Severn Estuary and so into Wales, I prefer to go northward as far as Gloucester before crossing the Severn. From Bath to Gloucester I like the road along the Cotswold Edge through Stroud, partly because Catherine Morland started off that way in General Tilney's fashionable chaise-and-four from Bath for Northanger Abbey, in the earliest of Jane Austen's novels; and after leaving Bath I like to pause at Petty France for no better reason than that there Catherine Morland 'baited' and had the happiness of changing from the grander carriage into the curricle driven by Henry. Jane Austen's characters forked to the right on the way to her Abbey, but I go on through Nailsworth (where W. H. Davies spent his last years; he died at Nailsworth in 1940) and Stroud and Gloucester (Henley's birthplace there was No. 2 Eastgate Street) in order to cross the river and pass through the Forest of Dean to Ross-on-Wye. (It was to Ross-on-

Wye that Captain Mayne Reid, after the loss of his home in Buckingham-shire, eventually retired.) From Ross-on-Wye, by going down the Wye Valley to Monmouth, I would then achieve a respectfully gradual transi-tion from Saxon into Celtic country. In Monmouthshire (I am as yet hardly accustomed to the new county-name of Gwent), I am well aware that my ambition has to be much more limited than that, for instance, of George Borrow, when he began his book *Wild Wales*. Borrow, in his intention of regarding no place as obscure 'which has produced a poet', had this advantage – he could speak and read the Welsh language. My inventory is restricted to writers in Wales, whether natives or visitors, who used English.

From Monmouth, a side-trip north from Abergavenny into the Black Mountains would provoke memory of Walter Savage Landor at Llanthony and of Eric Gill, David Jones and others at the monastery at Capel-y-ffin. Llanthony Priory in the Vale of Ewyas originated in the twelfth century; the ruins adjacent to the present Abbey Hotel are a memento of many troubles. The revolt in 1399 of Owain Glyndwr – no less than twenty-one times does Shakespeare spell the name of that irregular and wild hero in the way with which I am more familiar, but Owain Glyndwr is the spelling commanded now – the revolt of Glyndwr so weakened the Priory that there was little to be dissolved at the dissolu-tion of 1538. In 1807 what remained of the Priory building and the estate were bought impulsively by Landor. Landor's plans for Llanthony in-cluded planting thousands of cedars of Lebanon and importing merino sheep from Spain; the chief handicap on such schemes' success was Landor's exceeding propensity for quarrels and litigation. After six stormy years of ownership Landor left Llanthony forever in 1813 and went successively to Jersey, France and Italy. There he had moments of recollecting Llanthony Priory –

> Llanthony! an ungenial clime,
> And the broad wing of restless Time,
> Have rudely swept thy mossy walls
> And rockt thy abbots in their palls.
> I loved thee by thy streams of yore,
> By distant streams I love thee more;
> For never is the heart so true
> As bidding what we love adieu.

It was twenty-five years later that Landor returned from Italy for his lengthy stay in Bath, and thereafter set forth again as an old man for his final years in Florence.

Llanthony Priory is about ten miles north of Abergavenny, and four miles farther up the mountain pass is the Llanthony Monastery at

Capel-y-ffin. This monastery was partially built in the 1860s by the Anglican preacher who became known and greatly admired as Father Ignatius. Circumstances brought Eric Gill and Donald Attwater (whose 'trade was in letters') here from 1924 to 1928, and then from time to time David Jones and others 'formed an extended family of like-minded craft and literary workers, during four years of intensive activity'. Much of Gill's own *Autobiography* (one of the permanent books of our time) was written when revisiting Capel-y-ffin in the last year of his life, and in it he looked back with his customary humour to the move from Sussex for the first 'assault on Capel-y-ffin'.

Three families left Ditchling – three fathers, three mothers, seven children (of whom the eldest was nineteen and the youngest five years old) one pony, chickens, cats, dogs, goats, ducks and geese, two magpies and the luggage. We hired a lorry at Pandy, twelve miles away (the nearest station at which the pony could be detrained) and arrived at Capel about tea time in a typical steady Welsh downpour. . . .

It was probably after that period that *In Parenthesis* by David Jones began to be written. His painting skill may have contributed even before his writing skill to the communal needs; but what's to be observed is that the good life of the small community was bursting into creativity of many kinds. The creativity displayed at Capel-y-ffin was not something separated from work on the upkeep of the remote and dilapidated monastery ('without any of the things they call modern conveniences – except water, and of that there was plenitude') but was part of, and grew out of, the spiritual decency in which the small group lived. An instance that I find charming arose out of the way those living in the monastery were troubled by visitors. In his *Autobiography* Eric Gill burst out: 'You can't imagine, unless you're one yourself, their impudence. They would walk in without asking and you would find them wandering in and out of your bedrooms. And when you asked them what . . . they were doing, they would say: Can we see a monk?' So Gill painted 'a lot of notice boards', and for that purpose devised 'a sort of free sans-serif lettering'; and presently 'Douglas Cleverdon, a forward-minded book- seller of Bristol' made Stanley Morison aware of that lettering. Morison asked Gill 'to draw an alphabet of sans-serif letters for the Monotype Corporation' – and so began the 'lots of other typographical and type- designing' for which, among many works, Gill is remembered.

'All enlightenments', Gill says somewhere, 'are the same enlighten- ment. Different things are illuminated, but it is the same light.' The statement, exemplified at the monastery at Capel-y-ffin, provides a right mood for returning to the main road through the mountains from Abergavenny to Brecon and for pausing in the valley of the Usk at the place where Henry Vaughan (1622–952) was born, where he lived for most of his life, and where his grave remains. When writing of his birth-place Vaughan rarely used the Welsh name Trenewydd but usually the English form, Newton or Newton-by-Usk. The Newton estate, accord-ing to an inventory made in the year of Vaughan's father's death, would make out the Vaughans as then being among the poorest of Welsh gentry; yet at the date of that inventory (1658) the purging of defeated Royalists by victorious Parliamentarians was a very real threat, and any listing of possessions which might risk exactions from those whom Royalist gentry regarded as 'Devills and destroyers' (a phrase used by Henry Vaughan for the Puritan 'propagators') was likely to be minimal. The country house at Newton-by-Usk where the twin brothers Henry and Thomas Vaughan grew up was at any rate sufficiently well found for both boys to be sent to Oxford, and Henry thence to an Inn of Chancery in London for the general knowledge of law which every country gentleman required.

It seems that Henry Vaughan saw some military service in the first part of the Civil War. He probably fought for King Charles at the battle of Rowton Heath near Chester in September 1645, the battle which the king is supposed to have watched from the Phoenix Tower on Chester's city wall, and which began well for the Royalists but ended disastrously. Vaughan was then among those who found temporary refuge at Beeston Castle, nine miles south-east of Chester, a Royalist stronghold which held out for a further two months. Part of the evidence of Vaughan's active service is the humorous poem which, on discharge into civil life, he sent to the friend who had lent him a voluminous armoured cloak, also returned. In what Vaughan describes as this *'Compendious hutt'* of a garment he must have found it hard to be a swordsman; it had 'stiffe, hollow pletes' and wire supports; having one night to lie out naked ex-cept for the cloak, its 'villanous, biting, *Wire-embraces*' had by morning marked his body with *'Characters* and *Hierogliphicks'*. Vaughan wore the cloak 'on the stormy winter's day', as Dr Hutchinson narrates in his *Life* of Henry Vaughan, 'when the garrison of Beeston Castle surrendered after two months' siege, and were allowed to march out with drums beating and to cross the Dee on their way to Denbigh'. On returning the cloak to his friend the verses say:

> Hadst thou been with me on that day, when wee
> Left craggie *Biston*, and the fatall *Dee* . . .
> I know thou wouldst in spite of that day's fate
> Let loose thy mirth at my new shape and state.

The uplift presently and suddenly to enter majestically into Vaughan's poems:

> I saw Eternity the other night
> Like a great *Ring* of pure and endless light,
>   All calm, as it was bright . . .

came after his return to Newton-by-Usk. The worldly fortunes of the
Vaughans and their defeated Royalist friends were being steadily ground
down. Henry Vaughan's twin brother Thomas had become rector of
their parish, Llansantffraed, but in 1650 was evicted from his benefice
by the Parliamentarians, and after returning to Oxford he went on to
find sufficient patronage for his chemical researches to take him to
London. Thomas Vaughan thus drifted away from Llansantffraed, but
to Henry in his new-found intensity of feeling for and sympathy with
the poetry of George Herbert, the church of Llansantffraed, almost especially if desecrated, took on more meaning. In the 1650s many of
Vaughan's friends and relations came to accept office under the Commonwealth, and he did not dissuade them, yet for himself he was un-
compromising. He would not 'collaborate' –

> I'le not stuff my story
> With your Commonwealth and glory.

So (as one of his most devoted admirers, the American poet Louise
Imogen Guiney, pointed out) Vaughan's 'sole asylum, since he was thus
cut off from the reconstructing Commonwealth which he abhorred, was
in the interior life'.

The opening poem of *Olor Iscanus* (the 'Swan of Usk'), by *Hen:
Vaughan Silurist*, had expressed the relatively light and literary conceit
of the way his feelings were attached to the clear running river beside
which he had grown up:

> *Poets* (like *Angels*) where they once appear
> *Hallow* the *place*, and each succeeding year
> Adds *rev'rence* to't, such as at length doth give
> This aged faith, *That there their Genii live.*

But after Vaughan's conversion and in the turning to the interior life,
he viewed his childhood beside the Usk with renewed directness:

> Happy those early dayes! when I
> Shin'd in my Angell-infancy.
> Before I understood this place
> Appointed for my second race,
> Or taught my soul to fancy ought
> But a white, Celestiall thought,
> When yet I had not walkt above
> A mile, or two, from my first love . . .

The sweetness of the singing that continued to come to Vaughan

from time to time indicates the solace he had found against an increasingly troublesome exterior life. In the 1650s there was ill-health (he was then
at times prepared 'for a *message* of *death*'). Vaughan's first wife, who had
borne four children who survived, died toward the middle of that
decade; Vaughan rather swiftly (about 1655) married his deceased wife's
younger sister who likewise proceeded to bear him four children. None
of the children were as yet 'disobedient and rebellious', though in the
next decade family dissensions and lawsuits would flare up, but in the
1650s there was still Henry's 'very decrepit' father to be looked after,
and the increase of mouths to feed, and the steady erosion of resources
during the Puritan regime. All these things interfered with a wished-for
life of quiet and reflective study.

Hutchinson expresses wonder how in the remote Welsh village
Vaughan managed to obtain the very remarkable range of books of some
rarity which his writings prove that he was reading between 1648 and
1655; he was still able to spend money and time on 'works of piety,
primitive, medieval, and of his own day'. With the end of the Puritan
regime Vaughan hoped for better times, yet the Restoration did not ease
money matters at Newton-by-Usk. So in the 1660s, because his talents
extended to 'physic' and because it brought reward, we hear increasingly
of Vaughan's medical practice. That practice became 'great & steady'
and by the 1670s he was in professional demand over a wide area of
Breconshire and possibly even into what was then Glamorgan. In later
life, indeed after 1655, he is seen less as writer than as an active, busy
doctor in physic, described by Miss Guiney: 'One can picture him on
his hardy Welsh pony, drenched in the mountain mists, close-hatted,
big-cloaked, riding alone, and looking abroad with those mild eyes
which were a naturalist's for earth and sky, and a mystic's for the
spiritual world.'

Vaughan died at Newton on 23 April 1695, and he was buried within
sight of the Brecon Beacons and the river which made him call himself,
when young, the Swan of Usk. The grave is in the churchyard of
Llansantffraed, which is the native name of the place of St Freda, Bride,
or Bridget; Vaughan used to write of himself as of 'the parish of S.
Brigets'. The description 'Silurist' (which he used of himself because
Silures was the name used by Tacitus for the British tribe inhabiting
this part of Wales, who offered strenuous resistance to the Romans) is
repeated on the tombstone. Siegfried Sassoon, in *The Heart's Journey*,
paid tribute in a sonnet 'At the Grave of Henry Vaughan' to the feeling
that

> . . . this lowly grave tells Heaven's tranquillity
> And here stand I, a suppliant at the door.

*   *   *

I thought it right to plunge at once into the region where Vaughan the Silurist spent almost his entire life because to many readers he remains, as Dr Hutchinson expressed it, 'the most Welsh of all who have written English poetry'. Vaughan ever acknowledged the depth of his debt to George Herbert, the 'dear friend' whose 'holy, ever-living lines' encouraged the expression of his own 'bright *shootes* of everlastingnesse'. The 'bright *shootes*' are in English words, yet with cadence and arrangement that are felt to be Welsh. His contemporary and 'Honoured Cousin' John Aubrey spoke of Vaughan's Silurist nature as 'ingeniose but prowd and humorous', but that was chiefly because of Vaughan's delays in answering Aubrey's chatterbox letters, and was not intended as literary criticism. Yet for an orderly invasion of Wales I ought now to retreat from Brecon to follow the beautiful valley of the Wye from Monmouth to Chepstow, momently pausing as Wordsworth and his sister Dorothy did at Tintern Parva. It was in 1798 when the Wordsworths were temporarily away from Coleridge that they paid the visit which Wordsworth made memorable first to Dorothy and then to others by his 'Lines, composed a few miles above Tintern Abbey'. A different association hereabouts is that in 1872 at Trelleck, within a few miles of Tintern, there was born Bertrand Arthur William Russell. Downriver from Tintern, 'the beautiful Wye joins the noble Severn', at what the British called Aber Wye, but the Saxons termed Chepstow, as the site of a notable 'cheap' or market.

Cognoscenti will note that I have already begun to quote from George Borrow's book, *Wild Wales*. Chepstow was the end-point of the journey Borrow had made by foot in 1854. He had entered North Wales from Chester; no longer in youth's first flush (he was fifty-one) he was nevertheless able to walk for as long as he wished, in top hat and with umbrella, satchel on his shoulder, at his old normal rate of six miles an hour. It was in November, after four months of exploration, that Borrow ended that journey. His recollection that Chepstow had been made illustrious by Scott's ballad 'The Norman Horseshoe' contributed to his finale:

I went to the principal inn, where I engaged a private room and ordered the best dinner which the people could provide. Then leaving my satchel behind me I went to the castle, amongst the ruins of which I groped and wandered for nearly an hour, occasionally repeating verses of the Norman Horseshoe. I then went to the Wye and drank of the waters at its mouth, even as some time before I had drunk of the waters at its source. Then returning to my inn I got my dinner, after which I called for a bottle of port, and placing my feet against the sides of the grate I passed my time drinking wine and singing Welsh songs till ten o'clock at night, when I paid my reckoning, amounting to something considerable. Then shouldering my satchel I proceeded to the railroad station, where I purchased a first-class ticket, and ensconcing myself in a comfortable carriage, was soon on the way to London, where I arrived at about four o'clock in the morning.

Entering South Wales where Borrow was leaving it, I bid him farewell for the moment. Before moving along the coastline from Newport to St David's, even at the risk of seeming fanciful I must confess that what stirs me in these parts is not contemporary scenes and recent associations half so much as the whiff here and there of an ancient Arthurian magic. Was not Carmarthen, farther along this coast, named for Arthur's chief magician, Merlin? Merlin or Merlinus is but the Latinized form of the name, popularized by Geoffrey of Monmouth in his *Historia Britonum*. Latin in the twelfth century 'was not foreign in any country, just as it was mother tongue in none', and Merlin was the way in which the Welsh-spoken Merddin or Myrddin was circulated; although to us the Latin form obscures that the name Carmarthen means 'Merlin's camp' or 'fortress'. At Carmarthen itself there are still the remains of a Merlin's Oak, bolstered to avert the prophecy:

> When Merlin's Tree shall tumble down,
> Then shall fall Carmarthen Town.

Yet it is not so much the other heritages along the coast of South Wales that will keep pulling me up with reminders of Arthurian legends as what appears as an ordinary topographical feature, the shoreline of sands. On the Welsh side of the Severn Estuary, towards Cardiff, the sands are much to be mentioned, as farther west, the sands of Swansea, and all the remarkable stretches of sand around Carmarthen Bay. Here, then, we enter on romance that is not to be escaped – romance spelled in the very first sentence of Book VII of *Le Morte d'Arthur*, which starts 'at a site and a castle upon the sands that marched nigh Wales'.

I am aware that those particular 'sands that marched nigh Wales', as spoken of by that Warwickshire-Welsh writer Thomas Malory, are not to be too categorically identified. The castle to which Malory refers at the beginning of Book VII, where at the feast of Pentecost the king would not go to meat until he had heard or seen of a great marvel, was in those days called 'Kynke Kenadonne'. As for the spelling of the castle's name, that depends on who is editing Malory; as for the castle's site, Cornishmen have argued for Cornwall. Yet what is peculiar about this tale of Sir Gareth of Orkney that wedded Dame Lyonnesse of the Castle Perilous (and also 'Sir Gaheris that wedded her sister, Dame Linet, that was called the damosel Savage') is that it seems to be the single one of Malory's stories for which there is no acknowledged prior source. The special interest for us here in this unique and well-told invention of Malory is that wherever one places the preamble, the action of the story is promptly in South Wales. After the twelvemonth that the hero spent in the kitchen of King Arthur's court, the feast of the next Whitsuntide was placed at Carlyon – indubitably today's Caerleon, on the River Usk above Newport. Thence began Gareth's journey to relieve the Lady Lyonnesse, leading to the happy ending of the pair being duly wedded at Michaelmas at 'Kynke Kenadonne by the sands', the ceremony being performed by the Bishop of Canterbury.

To Caerleon came Tennyson to study the terrain for *Idylls of the King*, and he used Caerleon especially in his 'Geraint and Enid'. Entering this region, then, we may often expect coastal sands and rivers and the Welsh hills (especially Snowdonia) to offer memories of *Le Morte d'Arthur*. The power of Malory remains such that even recent memories are over-shadowed. Arthur Machen (1863–1947) was born at Caerleon, and W. H. Davies (1871–1940) at nearby Newport; Davies in particular made efforts to escape, emigrating to the United States and living as described in his *Autobiography of a Super-Tramp*. Cardiff, noble city in many ways, retains few literary associations; of recent natives of literary talent, Howard Spring and Ivor Novello went elsewhere. Was it in part the old Arthurian enchantments of the valley of the Usk that Eliot was expressing in his poem, 'Usk'?

> Do not suddenly break the branch, or
> Hope to find
> The white hart behind the white well.
> Glance aside, not for lance, do not spell
> Old enchantments. Let them sleep.

Why have I been stating that the Warwickshire Sir Thomas Malory was a Welshman? Ernest Rhys, himself a Welshman, quoted the old identification of Malory as *Britannus natione*, that is to say, Welsh, and within Wales I would not think of disagreeing.

*   *   *

Dylan Thomas (1914–53) was born and started life at No. 5 Cwmdonkin Drive, Swansea. His early *Eighteen Poems* were published in 1934, and it was two years later that Edith Sitwell wrote in the *London Mercury*: 'I know of no young poet of our time whose poetic gifts are on such great lines.' Thomas was twenty-two at that time and Edith Sitwell wrote directly to him about his poem 'A Grief Ago': 'I know now, without any possibility of doubting it, that in you we have a poet from whom real greatness may be expected.' Thomas's second book, *Twenty-five Poems*, was published that year; Miss Sitwell reviewed it with unlimited praise in the *Sunday Times*. She sought their meeting, 'was immensely struck by his look of "archangelic power"' (as is told by their friend John Lehmann), and at once set out to make the young man into a national celebrity. Thomas, in John Lehmann's observation, was 'always a little shy of her *milieu*' yet naturally welcomed the generous friendship of Miss Sitwell and the promotion which by the end of the 1930s had made him a well-known poet.

Dylan Thomas's 'Swansea period' ended when he moved to London in 1936. In 1938 he began to make summer visits, repeated in the next two years, to Laugharne, where the Rivers Towy and Taf enter (between the sands) Carmarthen Bay. Laugharne was (I believe) initially suggested to the Thomases by Richard Hughes, author of *A High Wind in Jamaica*, *In Hazard*, and other writings of lasting distinction, whose own love of sailing had caused him to settle in the uplands above. Thomas was to comment of Laugharne that: 'Its literary values are firmly established: Richard Hughes lives in a castle at the top of the hill; I live in a shed at the bottom.' The valleys of the Taf and Towy had attracted writers in earlier centuries. Grongar Hill in the Vale of Towy 'invites my song', wrote the eighteenth-century poet John Dyer; and he continued:

> Grongar, in whose mossy cells
> Sweetly-musing Quiet dwells;
> Grongar, in whose silent shade,
> For the modest Muses made,
> So oft I have, the evening still,
> At the fountain of a rill,
> Sate upon a flow'ry bed,
> With my hand beneath my head;
> While stray'd my eyes o'er Towy's flood,
> Over mead, and over wood,
> From house to house, from hill to hill,
> 'Till Contemplation had her fill.

Dyer was born at Llanfynydd, a few miles north of Grongar Hill. On the south bank of the Towy at Llangunnor, a mile east of Carmarthen, Sir Richard Steele sought retirement in a modest farmhouse called Ty-Gwyn, within distant sight of his friend Dyer's Grongar Hill. It was not a wholly happy retirement for Steele, for even at Ty-Gwyn he was pursued by London creditors. Though also paralytic in his final years, Steele's kindly cheerfulness was much loved in Llangunnor. There is a memorial to him in Llangunnor's church, and another memorial in St Peter's Church in Carmarthen – for medical treatment Steele had been moved into the house in Carmarthen which is now the Ivy Bush Hotel, where in 1729 he died.

Laugharne itself had been visited by poets long before Richard Hughes suggested Thomas's visits; Coleridge, for instance, had described epitaphs and graves in the Laugharne churchyard. Thomas was mostly in London during the war period, where in the winters his short, stubby, pear-shaped appearance in a too-big overcoat and green pork-pie hat was a familiar sight in Chelsea.

Between the end of the war and the return of Thomas and his wife Caitlin to Laugharne, Edith Sitwell was convinced that Thomas's '*great* genius' would benefit by a complete change of scene. A fund was available, and Miss Sitwell was determined that an award should enable Thomas and his family to spend a year abroad. The award was designed for 1947, but when communicated to Thomas, Miss Sitwell was shocked by his instant intention of using the money to visit America. In haste she wrote to John Lehmann:

America. I was aghast when I heard he was going there. I've tried *everything* – imploring, owl-like prognostications of disaster – saying that Caitlin will have a rotten time because she isn't rich. *Nothing* sways him. And his hostess at Oxford . . . says it is like measles – you have to have it and get over it – I mean this mania to go to America.

Edith Sitwell was not in a strong position to disinfect Thomas's mania, for she and her brother Osbert were themselves busily planning their own visit to America for which they set sail in October 1948. Yet Thomas's ambition was at that time appeased; he was persuaded into going, with his family, to Italy, and those who sponsored that stay abroad may have hoped that Thomas would then return to continue writing poetry within Britain, even in Britain's austerity period. It was then, in May 1949, that the Thomas family turned for a permanent home to Laugharne and took occupancy of The Boathouse below the cliff, where there was a wooden outhouse suitable for a study and workroom. Whether Richard Hughes, who in later years lived near Harlech, was wholly pleased to have Thomas permanently at his doorstep I can't tell. Thomas had moods in which he could speak with hostility towards 'gentry' who lived in uplands above Laugharne, and he could be prickly also with some of the natives of the estuary town with its history of cockle-fishing – 'where they quarrel with boathooks', so he said, and 'All the women there's got web feet. Mind out for the evil eye! Never go there at the full moon!' Stephen Dixon in the *Guardian* (29 July 1975) reported how men of Laugharne tended to regard all strangers 'with cool and good-humoured insolence', and according to one of his Laugharne informants, Thomas seemed to the native-born 'shy, reserved, nervous, tense . . . always conscious of his lack of height . . . a genius, I think, but he was a user, a cadger, and when he had money he used it to buy friends. He was a lonely, cut-off kind of man.' At The Boathouse Thomas completed his most widely known work, the radio play *Under Milk Wood*. Locally there was not going to be universal approval in Laugharne for the 'borrowing our pub gossip and spinning it into a classic translated into 26 languages'. But before it appeared in book form Thomas was dead. His 'mania to go to America' had been ineffectively repressed; he had already succumbed to the temptation of crossing the Western Ocean to make lecture tours and 'readings'. Some money might be pocketed if his physique could stand the strain. But the combined impact of American hard liquor and anti-booze tablets proved fatal for him in 1953. He had set out from The Boathouse on 9 October that year, and on 9 November died in New York.

Dylan Thomas's body was brought back for burial in the churchyard at Laugharne. There are plans now for yearly summer festivals in his memory. In July 1975 Stephen Dixon described the opening festival in the *Guardian*:

Laugharne has been celebrating its first Dylan Thomas Festival, and the tiny estuary town is lively with bright nylon and Crimplene as the students and the journalists and the trippers move in, past Milk Wood, down the tortuous main street, past the pubs where the loud and lonely poet so eagerly squandered his money and played double or quits with his fragile constitution. The Boathouse, where he lived for years and where he created the enchanted (and, in Laugharne, resented) village of Llaregyb, is open to the public. There's a Milk Wood Restaurant and trips around the bay in the Polly Garter. In St Martin's churchyard the white wooden cross (mark IV; its predecessors purloined by Thomas groupies), with its jam jar of dying wild flowers, seems ostentatiously modest set against the ornate marble and angel carvings of the other graves.

*   *   *

Few are the further associations, within South Wales, with Welsh-born writers who chose to write in English. No dearth, I hasten to add, of Welsh writers: witness the annual Eisteddfod. Yet writings in Welsh are to me a sealed book, and possibly even monastic Latin loses less than Welsh may lose in translation. I have been able to look into the twelfth-century *Giraldus Cambrensis* (Gerald the Welshman) with happy pleasure, but then his *Itinerarium Cambriae* has been kindly Englished. Gerald, churchman of the royal blood, was born into a very stormy life at Manorbier Castle on the west side of Carmarthen Bay. After travels, outlawry, imprisonment and release he died at St David's, and his grave is there. One might indeed trace innumerable visits of other writers to Pembrokeshire (now blanketed with Cardiganshire under the revived ancient name of Dyfed). Close to the site of Manorbier Castle, I remember visiting Walter de la Mare in 1923, when the de la Mares were having a family holiday at Skrinkle. The only special link with the Pembroke-shire site (it was before the county name was changed) that I recall was that someone raised the idle question: how many times was Milford Haven mentioned by Shakespeare? The question and the answer (is the number of mentions as large as fourteen?) are perhaps as idle to remember as that the Thomas Bowdler who expurgated Shakespeare died near Swansea and was buried near Mumbles Head.

4. NORTH TO THE MENAI STRAIT

As I go north through Dyfed I note that the novelist Caradoc Evans was born at Llandyssul in 1878; the valley of the River Teifi provided the setting and incentive for most of his work – West Wales was 'his' part, and he returned to die at Aberystwyth in 1945. It is also to be remembered that another (and less deeply angry) novelist of that genera-tion, Oliver Onions (1873–1961), lived a little farther up the coast of Cardigan Bay at Aberdovey. Inland from Aberystwyth and up the Rheidol valley, one passes the birthplace of Dafydd Ap Gwylym, and in the chapters of *Wild Wales* in which Borrow treats of his stay at the inn now named for him at Ponterwyd, and of his visits to the Devil's Bridge, is his spirited tribute to the fourteenth-century Ap Gwylym, 'the greatest of his country's songsters'. Borrow asserts that 'the genius of this won-derful man' was first recognized when the young Ap Gwylym was taunted about the circumstances of his birth, and 'retorted in an ode so venomously bitter that his adversary, after hearing it, fell down and expired'. Yet with fitting mixture of light humour and seriousness Borrow does convey that his own appreciation of Ap Gwylym is almost equal to the encomium of Iolo Goch, the bard of Owain Glyndwr. Iolo Goch 'went so far as to insinuate that after Ap Gwylym it would be of little avail for anyone to make verses', according to the interpretation of the bard's verse which Borrow translated:

> To Heaven's high peace let him depart,
> And with him go the minstrel art.

Continuing to follow *Wild Wales* in the reverse direction from south to north – turning the reel so that Borrow travels backward – I see him at Machynlleth, inspecting Owain Glyndwr's parliament house and introducing again Welsh poets of the fifteenth century, not only Iolo Goch but Lawdden. At Machynlleth I cross the Dovey Valley into the large county now named Gwynedd. To pursue Borrow I would pres-ently turn eastward towards Bala, but other excitements take me due north, either by the inland road or by the coast road from Barmouth through Harlech, to sites which have attracted worldwide notice, Penrhyndeudraeth and Portmeirion.

James Morris has written of the approach to this coastline from the sea:

Through binoculars the shoreline of Tremadoc Bay, where the mountains of North Wales meet the Irish Sea, looks majestically austere; moorland and mountain above, long lines of empty sand, a huddle of grey where the little slate port of Portmadoc stands beside its harbour.

Harlech Castle juts pugnaciously from a ridge; all is fierce, misty, Byronic – 'There is no corner of Europe that I know', wrote Hilaire Belloc, 'which so moves me with the awe and majesty of great things as does this mass of the northern Welsh mountains seen from this corner of their silent sea.'

But as the stranger sweeps his glass around this tremendous panorama, something bright, small and incongruous strikes his eye; and incredulously focusing his lens upon it, he finds it to be a sort of Faerie settlement, half hidden by woods at the water's edge. A golden ball flashes on a tower. What looks like a campanile protrudes above the trees. Bright Italianate pavilions cluster beside the sea. It seems to be a cross between Portofino and one of Canaletto's architectural caprices; in fact it is the sprightliest of modern English follies, Portmeirion.

Morris calls the spirit of Portmeirion 'English', for though 'it stands in one of the Welshest corners of Wales', and though 'Portmeirion is the creation of a Welsh patrician', one may feel that the creator, Clough Williams-Ellis, has brought into being, with superb panache and supreme architectural skill, the sort of 'folly' mostly hitherto associated with eighteenth-century England. Yet the sparkle and grace of Portmeirion is likewise practical and self-supporting:

to finance the thing [Morris goes on to observe] Williams-Ellis built his folly as a hotel. The original mansion is the core of the complex, with a restaurant, bars, and sumptuous public rooms. Scattered through the village are cottages and apartments which the visitor may rent, discreetly tucked away in unsuspected privacy.

When Lewis Mumford described his visit in the *New Yorker* he reminded himself that he was in the country of Thomas Love Peacock:

. . . perhaps the way to describe Portmeirion is to say that it is Peacock's Crotchet Castle come to life, with its contending dinner-table opinions taking concrete architectural form in an amusing array of politely incompatible, argumentative, but elegantly phrased buildings.

Williams-Ellis's 'spirit of nimble improvisation' shown in Portmeirion's terraced gardens, cobbled square, slim Italianate bell tower and in 'its constant effort to give human emphasis, by leaping walls and pinnacles, to the natural rhythm of the landscape' was not the only pleasure Mumford commented on; he likewise records the use made of the magnificent beauty contributed by the trees and banks of flowers:

Portmeirion, an artful and playful little modern village, designed as a whole and all of a piece, on a sea-girt peninsula, and the rhododendrons alone justify a pilgrimage to it, though there is more to be seen in this lively landscape than their great bushes and trees, and the equally lush camellias, azaleas, and hydrangeas.

But what I notice at Portmeirion is the way this piece of Welsh peninsula under the Snowdonian mountains evokes something much wider and larger in spirit than Morris and Mumford suggest. Bear in mind 'this mass of the northern Welsh mountains seen from this corner of their silent sea'. Bear in mind George Borrow: 'Oh, the wild hills of Wales, the land of old renown and of wonder, the land of Arthur and Merlin!' Bear in mind not Peacock's Crotchet Castle, but Malory. Think first of Snowdon. Borrow rehearses some of the events that took place in the wilds of Snowdon: Vortigern calling here on the counsels of Merlin ('said to be begotten on a hag by an incubus, but who was in reality the son of a Roman consul by a British woman'); and Merlin advising him, in a wind-beaten valley of Snowdon, near the sea, to build his castle, whence in the end his dead body decked in green armour was carried to where the mound of earth and stones was raised over it. Nearby 'the brave but unfortunate Llywelin ap Griffith' made his last stand for Cambrian independence. It was to Snowdon also that Owain Glyndwr sometimes retired and then emerged at will to chase away the numerous armies of Harry the Fourth.

Above all other history, it is Arthur and his knights who people Snowdon. Not only Welsh and Breton minstrels tell you that, but Scotsmen also:

> . . . Stirling's Tower
> Of yore the name of Snowdoun claims.

Where have you been all these years if you don't know Scott's *Lady of the Lake* by heart, or remember that the ring in the Castle park at Stirling, within which jousts were practised, was often called the Round Table? Even more to the point here, recall that the official title of one of the Scottish heralds – I quote on the authority of Scott – was 'Snawdoun'. This Welsh Snowdonia is then the great progenitor of other of Arthur's seats elsewhere; all are akin; and everything that Malory tells of is akin to the hills, woods, shores of this Snowdonia. Read once again that wonderful seventh book of Malory, where he is most himself, and where the braw lad from Orkney (momently called Sir Beaumains) ambles along, suffering patiently great rebukes from the damosel yet scuppering as they go false knights of any colour, and – here is my point – in such travel and with the precision of magic there spring up to greet them gay pavilions, castles, unexpected arches, alcoves, emblazoned coats of arms, stone walls and balustrades, pinnacles everywhere, flights of stone steps up and down. It is in the heritage of all that, from Malory, that Williams-Ellis managed to contrive Portmeirion.

* * *

To reach Portmeirion from the south by road the River Dwyryd, which flows from the Vale of Ffestiniog, is crossed at the small town of Penrhyndeudraeth; here, at Plas Penrhyn, Bertrand Russell settled at the age of eighty-two for the remaining sixteen years of his very long life. Across the flat expanse of Traeth Mawr from Penrhyndeudraeth and under the cliffs where the foothills rise dramatically towards the range of Snowdon was the estate of Tan-yr-allt, where early in the nineteenth century the philanthropist W. A. Madocks reclaimed a large acreage of Traeth Mawr by building an embankment to reduce the estuary. Madocks founded the town of Tremadoc, and Shelley, enthusiastic over Madocks's schemes, spent six months at Tan-yr-allt in 1812–13. Here occurred the strange adventure, or hallucination, which Shelley believed to be an attempted assassination.

Towards the end of the century the younger son of an Anglo-Irish family who started life as Thomas Robert Chapman but altered his last name to Lawrence, settled at Tremadoc, and T. E. Lawrence ('Lawrence of Arabia') was born there, second in a family of five sons. Lawrence reputedly learnt his letters from hearing his elder brother being taught. Precocity was natural with him; he was reading newspapers and books at four, beginning Latin at six, and entering Oxford High School at eight. It was helpful to the family that from the age of twelve Lawrence could earn all of his tuition expenses by scholarships at school and a Welsh exhibition at Jesus College, Oxford. His interests at Oxford led to his joining the British Museum expedition which was excavating, from 1911 to 1914, the Hittite city of Carchemish, and that again led to his becoming, in the 1914–18 war, 'Lawrence of Arabia'.

Caernarvon, with its very famous castle, is now barely twenty miles ahead – and there, perhaps repeating the walk which Borrow took to the top of Snowdon, the itinerary of this section of literary pilgrimage reaches its northernmost point. I do not here traverse the Menai Strait from Caernarvon to Bangor, for Bangor is on the great arc of road, the dividing line of great significance, that runs from Holyhead across the whole of the island to Dover.

L.B.—I

5. FROM CAERNARVON TO BIRMINGHAM

I have already adumbrated the historical significance when this cross-island Watling Street (as singular on earth, said Chaucer, as the Milky Way in heaven) was thought of by Englishmen as the dividing line between Saxon land and Danelaw. One way of expressing the importance of Watling Street to men of Saxon heritage was to think of it as the line along which St George fought the Dragon. Another way is to recall that to the north-east of that line the Robin Hood legend originated; south and west of it is the heartland of Arthur. Such antique distinctions have become so blurred as to seem, it may be, now meaningless; and yet strong trace-elements of ancient differences remain. Within Wales itself, however, the border that counts between Britons and Saxons is the anciently defined north–south line of Offa's Dyke – though none can now say for certain whether Arthur's Ninth Battle (as numbered in *Historia Britonum*) was fought at Caerleon-on-Usk or at Chester-upon-Dee.

Yet, topographically, the Holyhead Road from Anglesey to Llangollen and Shrewsbury is a convenient boundary and to the next chapter, then, I relinquish Anglesey, Bangor, the north coast of Wales and Chester. Consider, though, the wealth I have yet to explore if I turn at Caernarvon and head again for London, not as yet crossing the singular rampart of Watling Street. South of the Holyhead Road I might explore the Lleyn Peninsula which juts out below Caernarvon Bay because the sprightly, diminutive Mrs Thrale who played much part in Dr Johnson's life was born at Bodvel Hall, inland from Pwllheli, in 1741. On a tour of North Wales with the Thrales in the summer of 1774, Johnson and the others fell in with Mrs Thrale's wish to visit Bodvel. I do not, though, propose to follow them, for she and the others found the visit to scenes of her early childhood – I borrow the word that Johnson used – 'melancholy'. So at Pwllheli they 'bought something to remember the place', and departed. They went back along the coast of North Wales to what had also been Mrs Thrale's father's property of Bach-y-graig in the Vale of Clwyd. It was in that neighbourhood that most of Johnson's visit to Wales was spent, a visit which is commemorated by the monument set up to him at Gwaenynog, near Denbigh.

Yet I have here forsworn the north coast of Wales, and have turned south and eastward, and my departure from the principality must be quicker than De Quincey's. De Quincey was a boy of seventeen, wandering on foot through Wales in 1802, stopping with anyone with whom he might hold lengthy conversation, when the narrative in his *Confessions* then makes him skip to Oswestry and Shrewsbury, where he whirls away in the Holyhead Mail for London. Skipping ground like De Quincey, I keep to the south of him, crossing the Severn (which here flows north) at Welshpool and paying farewell to Wales for the moment at Montgomery Castle, where George Herbert was born in 1593. Thence I cross the line of Offa's Dyke to reach, south of Shrewsbury, Wenlock Edge.

Westward from Wenlock Edge one sees Housman's 'quietest places':

> Clunton and Clunbury,
> Clungunford and Clun
> Are the quietest places
> Under the sun.

A. E. Housman (1859–1936) was not a native of Shropshire (renamed now with the old name Salop). He was born at Valley House, now called Housmans, at Fockbury, a few miles south of Birmingham. Housman's brother Laurence was born six years later at Bromsgrove, and both went to Bromsgrove School. Laurence Housman's writings (novels, e.g. *An Englishwoman's Love Letters*, and plays, e.g. *Victoria Regina*) have not lasted so powerfully as have the poems of the more reticent older brother. Shropshire, and specifically Wenlock Edge, were evocative to A. E. Housman; he wrote most of the poems of *A Shropshire Lad* (1896) during the ten years that he was working as a clerk in HM Patents Office; then, after becoming Professor of Latin in London and, after 1911, holding a similar high academic chair at Cambridge, he issued, in 1922 and 1936, two further companion collections of short poems. *A Shropshire Lad* played a part, I think, in stimulating Hardy's publications of Wessex poems; the contrast in the reflective use Hardy makes of Wessex heights and the use Housman makes of Wenlock Edge is as noticeable as the similarities.

Housman is not always looking from his Edge westerly towards Clun Forest. Sometimes he looks north, over Much Wenlock, towards the Wrekin:

> On Wenlock Edge the wood's in trouble;
> His forest fleece the Wrekin heaves;
> The gale, it plies the saplings double,
> And thick on Severn snow the leaves.

In winter or summer the Wrekin, which some geologists think the core of an extinct volcano, is a central feature of Shropshire. It was impudent of Arnold Bennett to speak of it as nothing but 'a swollen bump'; it is more fitting to recall the famous Shropshire toast 'All friends round the Wrekin'. As Housman's verse reminds one, it is the Wrekin which has caused the River Severn, after making its wide arc from Wales to Shrewsbury, here to turn southward past Much Wenlock to Worcester; and this mention of the Severn makes one wonder exactly where P. G. Wodehouse placed Blandings Castle, the famous country seat of Lord Emsworth, where there happened many matters of much importance. The likely original of Wodehouse's Market Blandings has been identified by Colonel Michael Croft as the village of Buildwas, three miles from Much Wenlock. Other experts may add further evidences for the exact position of Blandings Castle; I rely on this description (by Wodehouse) of the scene that spread itself beneath Lord Emsworth's window:

> The scene . . . was a singularly beautiful one, for the castle, which is one of the oldest inhabited houses in England, stands upon a knoll of rising ground at the southern end of the celebrated Vale of Blandings in the county of Shropshire. Away in the blue distance wooded hills ran down to where the Severn gleamed like an unsheathed sword; while up from the river rolling park-land, mounting and dipping, surged in a green wave almost to the castle walls, breaking on the terraces in a many-coloured flurry of flowers as it reached the spot where the province of Angus McAllister, his lordship's head gardener, began.

While looking for Buildwas on my map, I note that Stella Benson was born at Much Wenlock and that Mary Webb, author of *Precious Bane*, was born at Leighton, a little closer to the Wrekin. The 'Sarn Mere' of *Precious Bane* is easily to be identified with Bomere Pool, two or three miles south of Shrewsbury. I move on farther south, past Wenlock Edge, to Ludlow, where A. E. Housman was buried in the churchyard of St Lawrence.

Milton's masque of *Comus*, prepared in Middlesex with music fitted by his friend Henry Lawes, was first performed in the Great Hall of Ludlow Castle. The imposing ruins of the castle and of the hall (though now roofless) render it possible to visualize the occasion for *Comus* when the Earl of Bridgewater, on taking up his appointment as Lord Lieutenant of Wales in 1634, brought with him to Ludlow his household from Harefield, including his musician Lawes. There is apparently no record whether Milton was or was not included in the party at Ludlow for the first performance.

A very different literary figure of the seventeenth century, the Samuel Butler who wrote *Hudibras*, took up residence at Ludlow Castle in 1660. Son of a Worcestershire farmer, Butler throughout the Parliamentary regime had been clerk to various puritan Justices of the Peace, but at the Restoration he was appointed secretary to the Lord President of Wales.

This meant that he was steward of Ludlow Castle; he occupied the rooms over the gateway by which the Castle Green is still entered; and here, it is supposed, *Hudibras* began to be written. This long, satirical and often extremely caustic poem was taken by many to make great sport for the 'winning side', but an initial popularity for the first part began to fade after parts two and three. Such 'scorn made metrical' as brilliantly applied to those who

> Compound for sins they are inclined to
> By damning those they have no mind to

was not restricted by Butler merely to the Presbyterians who occasioned that remark. When there was seen to be something deeper and more general to Butler's scornfulness than partisan malice, Royalist partisans were 'disobliged', and, as Aubrey pointed out, Butler then had enemies all round. There are many and totally contradictory stories of what happened to the witty, disobliging Butler after he left (or was dismissed from) Ludlow and went to London. The third part of *Hudibras* was published there in 1678, and two years later Butler died – all the differing stories agree he died in poverty.

Ten miles east of Ludlow is Cleobury Mortimer, where the church has a *Piers Plowman* window commemorating that William Langland, famous contemporary of Chaucer and Gower, was born there. This claim is contested by Ledbury, and also by faraway Wychwood in Oxfordshire. Whichever may have been Langland's birthplace, the prologue of *Piers Plowman* associates the beginning of the poem with the Malvern Hills west of the Severn Valley, below Worcester. Before joining Langland beside one of the Malvern springs I ought not to leave the road from Ludlow to Hereford without recalling that in the church of All Saints in Hereford's High Street is registered the birth of David Garrick. Among the other individuals of genius who were born at Hereford was Thomas Traherne (*c.* 1637–74), who became vicar of Teddington. His manuscript poems and *Centuries of Meditations* remained unpublished for more than two centuries after his death; then the rediscovered beauty of his spirit placed him, for readers, in the loved company of George Herbert and Henry Vaughan. Hereford should very specially honour the man who spoke of childhood there as Traherne did in the section (III, 3) which begins: 'The corn was orient and immortal. . . .' Traherne's clerical gentleness, and advice that 'to think well is to serve God in the interior court', contrasts with the fourteenth-century Langland's active revivalist energy. I know no portrait of Traherne but would imagine from the report of the exceedingly neat and beautiful and exceptionally small characters of his handwriting, that his physique was likewise neat and not overlarge; Langland's admission that his nickname

was Long Will and characteristics revealed in *Piers Plowman* have provided the also contrasting physical picture that Langland was tall, gaunt,
and of sometimes forbidding demeanour.

There are other literary associations with Ledbury. Early years of
Elizabeth Barrett Browning were spent nearby, and John Masefield was
born and brought up here, as allusions in his early poems indicate. Yet
it is Langland who continues to capture attention here; wherever he was
born, all traditions suggest he was educated at Malvern Priory, at the
eastern side of the short but remarkable range of Malvern Hills. The
remains of British forts on the hills indicate battles there from earliest
times: this setting stimulated Elgar to compose his oratorio *Caractacus*,
in tribute to the British chieftain's choice of headquarters here. The
much later Normans used the Hereford Beacon as a fort against the
Welsh, and a vigorous attempt to retake it was made by Owain Glyndwr
in 1405. It was in about 1362, a relatively peaceful period for Malvern,
half a century before the battle made by Glyndwr, that Langland began
at the age of about thirty to write the long poem which, in its three
versions, was going to occupy him during a great part of his later life.
The beginning is precisely pictured: 'on a May morning on Malvern
hills' (in modernized wording) it was natural for the poet to fall asleep
beside one of the springs for which the Malvern Hills are still famous.
But as he slept there befell to him a marvel, the vision of a tower, high
in the rising sun, and in the shadows beneath a deep and dreadful
dungeon, and in between the 'fair field full of folk' of every kind – that
is, as visions succeed and replace each other, into the poet's field of view
come the many forms of English life and fourteenth-century institutions
with Heaven and Hell alongside. In the first draft of the poem worldly
scenes appear and are criticized with 'homely earnestness' and 'hearty
hatred of untruth in every form', and a homily is added 'with the title of
Do-well, Do-bet [i.e. Do-better], and Do-best'. The loose structure of
The Vision of Piers the Plowman reminded Professor Skeat (from whom
I have been quoting) in this one respect of *Hudibras*, in that in each case
the structure permits the author to say many things 'by the way'.

Generally speaking, the first draft of *Piers Plowman* is the vision (or
kaleidoscope of visions) as seen by the Malvern countryman. It seems
that subsequent to the first draft Langland was resident in London,
housed on Cornhill, and Skeat encourages us to visualize the tall, severe
'Long Will' of Malvern striding towards his clerical occupation at
Westminster Hall 'saluting no man . . . loath to reverence lords or ladies,
or persons dressed in fur and wearing silver ornaments, and not deigning
to say "God save you" to the serjeants whom he met'. The second and
third versions of the poem, each completely reworked about the years 1377
and 1393 respectively, are each longer than the first; reform of the world,

as viewed from London, was less susceptible to simple homily. Langland's strong faith in the Christ who descended into Hell and rose again
found renewal of expression, though, in his third version. I quote from
Canto 21 as Skeat modernized it 'because the language is a little difficult'.
In the night-time, in the house on Cornhill, Langland was dreaming of
the Resurrection until at dawn the church-bells rang to greet Easter:

> · and with that I awaked,
> And called Kitte my wife · and Calote my daughter,
> 'Arise! and go reverence · God's resurrection,
> And creep on knees to the Cross · and kiss it for a jewel,
> And rightfullest relic · none richer on earth!
> For God's blessed body · it bare, for our boot,
> And it a-feareth the Fiend · for such is the might,
> May no grisly ghost · glide where it shadoweth.'

That the word *boot* signifies 'redemption' is a needed explanation;
otherwise, how clearly Langland calls across the centuries – and how
the call to wife Kitte and daughter Calote (Colette? Nicolette?) brings
the whole picture alive!

*   *   *

It is scarcely more than five miles from Great Malvern to the outskirts
of Worcester, and here I have to make a choice of direction. There is
much to be associated with Worcester, yet of its literary connections all
that comes to me is that Mrs Henry Wood, daughter of a Worcester
glove manufacturer, married and lived here – but when widowed went
to London and achieved the fame of writing *East Lynne*. The poet Lord
Alfred Douglas who became associated with Oscar Wilde (a friendship
which ultimately resulted in Wilde's imprisonment) was born at Ham
Hill nearby. Otherwise at Worcester I might record that the County
Cricket Ground, in a bend of the River Severn, overlooked by the
cathedral from the other bank, is one of the pleasantest in all England.
The choice here is to go south or north. Seagoing vessels ascend the
Severn as far as Worcester Bridge; I might follow them downstream, to
pause at Tewkesbury where, past the Abbey and the Mill, Shakespeare's
Avon comes to join the Severn. Shakespeare mentions 'Tewkesbury
mustard', but it is not mentioned that Pickwick, dining at the Hop Pole
with Bob Sawyer and Ben Allen, partook of it. For a lengthier appearance
in literature, Tewkesbury acts as 'Nortonbury' in Mrs Dinah Craik's
John Halifax, Gentleman. The Abbey Mill and the Bell (the house of
Abel Fletcher in that book) are among the attractions of Tewkesbury.
It was before her marriage, though, and under her maiden name of
Miss Mulock, that *John Halifax, Gentleman* was published in 1857.

Dinah Mulock was not a native of Tewkesbury; she had been born at
Stoke-on-Trent, went to London at the age of twenty, and made a name
as a writer of children's books. Seven years after the great success of
John Halifax, Gentleman she married George Lillie Craik, then a partner
in Macmillans, the publishers, and she turned from writing fiction to
writing didactic essays. On the way from Worcester to Tewkesbury it
could also be recalled that Samuel Butler was born at Strensham in the
seventeenth century, and Bredon Hill is there nearby, the setting of
Housman's poem 'In Summertime on Bredon' in *A Shropshire Lad*.

Yet I am inclined to return to the Vale of Evesham through which the
Avon (Shakespeare's Avon) flows to Tewkesbury, after I have first
taken a northward course from Worcester to Birmingham. This course
takes in Kidderminster, birthplace of Edward Bradley, who under the
pseudonym of Cuthbert Bede wrote the lighthearted *Adventures of
Mr Verdant Green, an Oxford Freshman* in the mid-nineteenth century.
(This reminds me that 'the prince of parodists', C. S. Calverley, who
went to Oxford as well as Cambridge to enjoy the mid-nineteenth-
century fun of both places, was likewise a Worcestershire man, born at
Martley, west of Worcester.) From Kidderminster, Birmingham is entered by way of Halesowen, where Francis Brett Young (1884–1954)
was born. Birmingham, with the country to the west, comes into many
of Brett Young's novels. Paramount, though, to me over all other of
Birmingham's associations with literature is that here Samuel Johnson
first had effective help in coping with the 'dejection, gloom, and despair'
which, combined with physical disorders, did really threaten to unhinge
him in his early twenties.

Forty and more years later in Johnson's life, when he gossiped as much
as he chose with Boswell and Hester Thrale, he was reticent about his
early manhood. He revealed to Boswell that it was in his twentieth year,
while at home in Lichfield during the Oxford vacation of 1729, that there
was violent onset of the 'morbid melancholy' from which he was to suffer
periodically throughout life. 'I did not then know how to manage it' was
the gist of Johnson's comment. He had applied to his godfather, the
Lichfield physician, but there was no mutual understanding, and no useful advice for the overgrown gawky young man. He was frightened with
fear of insanity; the hint he obtained was to beat the 'horrible hypo-
chondria' out of his system by violent physical exercise; excessive
exertions in fact made him so languid and inefficient that he could not
distinguish the hour on the town clock – the large clock referred to
stuck out from the church tower in Lichfield, across the street from the
Johnson house, and was in prominent view from the windows. Yet
though in that summer Johnson was seriously unwell, the worry dissolved,
and he was able to return to Oxford.

At Oxford he was well aware that there was laughter at his oversized awkwardness and mannerisms that were often made more noticeable through his own slow bodily reflexes, poor eyesight and seeming deafness. Undeniably he was a great ugly duckling. His face bore traces of both scrofula and smallpox; when talking with others or when walking by himself he was given to making unexplainable involuntary gestures and motions; when alone he frequently talked to himself, and sometimes loudly. The Master of Pembroke College was not above listening to and repeating to others a soliloquy that he heard coming from Johnson's college room. Yet though at Oxford Johnson was often ill at ease, and always (and bitterly) made aware of his poverty, his self-esteem was strong enough to rouse his fighting power – he tried, as he expressed it, 'to fight my way by my literature and my wit'. His wit gathered cronies, and as for his 'literature', it prospered: his capacity for putting his mind to whatever he read increased; he read voraciously, and what he read, he remembered. All in all, the return to Oxford fortified the cure from the temporary despondency of his twentieth summer. Presently, though, the small legacy which had enabled him to go to Oxford was all spent. There was no more money in the Johnson family wherewith to pay the college bills for Samuel, and it was a real blow when lack of money forced him to leave Oxford without the chance of taking a degree. Boswell says that Johnson had college residence for three years, but others have found that his Oxford period lasted no more than fourteen months. It was on Samuel's return to Lichfield as a failure that there began his really prolonged attack of 'dejection, gloom, and despair'.

The next period (1730–3) was one which in later life he did not talk about. Those years were to be recalled only 'with the strongest aversion, and even a degree of horror'. Johnson erased those years so far as possible and Boswell shortened them. Samuel's younger brother Nathaniel was of some help to the ailing father in bookselling; of such help Samuel was incapable. More and more his own consciousness of failure was rubbed in. There were friends at Lichfield; yet he could feel his abilities and powers to be at Lichfield almost totally unwanted; scholarly capacities about which he had felt cocksure seemed wholly wasted. At the end of 1731 his father died. In the replanning, Mrs Johnson and Nathaniel were to carry on with the Lichfield house and bookshop; there was hardly any money, and it was imperative for Samuel to become self-supporting. After some unsuccessful efforts, a school at Market Bosworth, about twenty miles east of Lichfield, did accept Johnson's application to become an 'usher'. Thither the uncouth new employee trudged on foot in mid-July 1732 and at the instant of presenting his rawboned, untidy appearance to the patron of the school, a coarse country baronet, was regarded by that patron with contempt. The undisguised hostility and 'intolerable harshness' with which the patron treated the large clumsy usher gave both staff and schoolboys every scope to make Johnson's life miserable. 'A few months', says Boswell, was all that Johnson could stand of the humiliations at that school before trudging, or stumbling, the twenty miles back again to Lichfield. The period that then ensued at Lichfield, when everything rubbed into him his total incapacity to cope, threatened a lasting melancholia far more violent than before. That can justifiably be called Johnson's worst climacteric.

The medical man who made that diagnosis was Johnson's friend and former schoolmate Edmund Hector, who had the wisdom to see that the cure for Johnson was Birmingham. Hector was then setting up in Birmingham as a physician and lodging in the house of Mr Warren, a leading Birmingham bookseller. What he prescribed for Johnson (and what's more, persuaded him to accept) was to transfer from Lichfield to the larger city, and share Hector's lodgings and board as Hector's guest for an indefinite duration. The skill of Hector's treatment was superb. When Johnson complained of suffering from 'constitutional indolence' and refused to get out of bed, Hector connived with the bookseller to provide chores for which being in bed was no preventative.

In talk about books he had read at Oxford, Johnson happened to mention the experiences of a seventeenth-century Jesuit, Father Lobo, in Abyssinia. The book had been written in Portuguese, and a French version in the Pembroke College library had caught Johnson's attention. Hector and the bookseller-landlord were on to this at once; Hector procured the college copy of the French version of Lobo from Oxford, and Johnson was coerced into translating the book into English for publication by Mr Warren. Thus Johnson was made to exert (in Boswell's words) 'the powers of his mind, though his body was relaxed. He lay in bed with the book . . . and dictated while Hector wrote.' The book was completed ('the first prose work of Johnson', Boswell calls it) and published by Warren in Birmingham (although with a faked London imprint) in 1735. Boswell, fifty years later, comments that Warren paid Johnson 'only the sum of five guineas'. That was one of Boswell's jealous pinpricks. Gratitude is due to the physician and bookseller that after six months of their free care and intelligent treatment Johnson felt strong enough to hire modest lodgings on his own and, with the continuing assistance of connections suggested by Hector and Warren, to attempt to make a go of things, if only as a literary hack, for a time, in Birmingham.

Among friends whom Johnson now made at Birmingham were Mr and Mrs Porter. Mrs Porter was twenty years older than Johnson, and her grown-up children failed to see what she could find attractive in the conversation of the poorly dressed man of twenty-six who to them looked like a scarecrow. Mrs Porter's daughter told Boswell that Johnson

was then lean and lank, so that his immense structure of bones was hideously striking to the eye, and the scars of the scrofula were deeply visible. He also wore his hair, which was straight and stiff, and separated behind; and he often had seemingly convulsive starts and odd gesticulations, which tended to excite at once surprise and ridicule.

The daughter expressed her disapproval to her mother. The mother answered shortly: 'This is the most sensible man that I ever saw in my life.' It happened that Mr Porter's death afforded Johnson opportunity both to console and presently to propose marriage to Mrs Porter. In July 1735 she married him.

On a wintry day many years later Boswell found Johnson sitting alone in his London room, roasting apples at his fireplace and reading a history of Birmingham. Few friends who first came to know Johnson in the later life knew, to the full, what Birmingham had done for the great Doctor. The cure that his friend Hector started was completed by Johnson's wife, who throughout her far from easy life and after her death remained to Johnson 'dear Tetty'. There were plenty of hard knocks and prolonged distresses to come to Johnson and to her after he and Tetty had left Birmingham, but it was there that he had been restored to fight. It was in Birmingham that he found his trustiest helpers when help was most needed. Well might he solace a lonely hour in later life by roasting apples and reading about Birmingham.

6. SHAKESPEARE'S AVON AND RIVER THAMES

Birmingham, Coventry, Rugby are all just within the south side of the large curve of Watling Street, and again I recall that this ancient road marked, a thousand years ago, a recognized border between Saxon England and the Danelaw. The first two hundred years or so of active conflict of all kinds between Saxons and Danes along and across this borderline were interrupted and in a large way overlaid by the Norman Conquest, but the Saxon–Dane rivalry, of which trace-elements remain, was an occasionally active ingredient in ordinary life of the English Midlands, at least into Elizabethan times. Here I select only one suggestive example: if you look into 'Hock-tide' customs you find that, along the Saxon side of Watling Street, into the traditional celebration, on the second Monday and Tuesday after Easter Sunday, were woven many strands. Tied in with Hock-day dividing the rural year (Hock-day and Michaelmas being days for paying rents), the two-day festival which heralded summer included the seizing and binding, by women on Monday and by men on Tuesday, of persons of the opposite sex, who released themselves by paying a forfeit. This cheerful fun was condoned by the Saxon Church: some forfeits might be paid in cash, and if so the cash went into parish funds. Into this custom, which could in part be taken as a parody of the once ferocious levying by Danes of Danegelt, there were woven various forms of exhibiting, in Saxon parishes, a 'scorning and contempt' for Danes. Sometimes the date would coincide with the celebration of St George's Day (23 April), and as Easter-tide had been identified ever since the time of the Venerable Bede with raids of the dragon-prowed Viking ships, the Church gave approval to interpreting St George v. Dragon as Saxon v. Dane. Weaving in also to the medieval patterns for Hock-tide, at least at this part of the Watling Street borderland, were play-performances by strolling players. As record that this was a Hock-tide custom lasting into the Elizabethan reign, let one quotation from Dugdale's *Warwickshire* (1575) suffice: 'Hither came the Coventre men, and acted the ancient Play, long since used in that City, called Hocks tuesday, setting forth the destruction of the Danes in King Ethelred's time.'

Dugdale's 'hither' perhaps refers to Warwick, ten miles south of Coventry. After the Coventry men had played their play at Warwick, did they stroll on the further eight miles to Stratford-on-Avon? Or did an eleven-year-old Stratford schoolboy run with others to Warwick to take advantage of the Hock-day holiday by watching the play about Danes? Answers are not within the realm of proof; all one can say is that in that year or other years the young Will Shakespeare may have watched the Coventry players, may even have talked with them, and it is as easy and natural in this Warwickshire setting to picture a boy in conversation with a strolling play-actor as it was for Millais to picture the boy Raleigh conversing with a seaman beside the Devon sea.

One of the happinesses in re-reading Shakespeare, or re-viewing

> Those flights upon the banks of Thames
> That did so take Eliza and our James

is the noticing of touches that perhaps derive directly from the countryside that he grew up in. I have sometimes even felt traces of Warwickshire Hock-tide in Shakespeare's own play about Danes; yet as example of sudden recognition of where a fancy was bred, I would here turn to something that was taught me by Hugh Kenner. Mr Kenner asked in *The Pound Era*: 'How do words found in 1611 stir us now?'; and quoted:

> Fear no more the heat o' the sun
>   Nor the furious winter's rages;
> Thou thy worldly task hast done,
>   Home art gone, and ta'en thy wages;
> Golden lads and girls all must
>   As chimney-sweepers, come to dust.

I have an idea that Mr Kenner was a boy in Canada when he first read that stanza of Shakespeare's song. As a mature teacher in American universities he went on pondering the phrase 'Golden lads' as fine words for caressing our sensibilities. I quote:

English lads, perhaps, with yellow hair; 'golden', because once precious when they lived; 'golden', touched with the nobility and permanence of gold (that royal metal, colored like a cold sun, in which wages are paid), as now, gone home, they receive the wages of immortality; 'golden', in contrast to 'dust': a contrast of color, a contrast of substantiality, a contrast of two immemorial symbols, at once Christian and pagan: the dust to which all sons of Adam return, the gold by which human vitality braves time; dust, moreover, the environment of chimney-sweepers, against whose lot is set the promise of shining youth, *la jeunesse dorée*, who may expect to make more of life than a chimney-sweeper does, but whom death at last claims equally. 'Golden', magical word, irradiates the stanza so that we barely think to ask how Shakespeare may have found it.

Yet a good guess at how he found it is feasible, for in the mid-20th century a visitor to Shakespeare's Warwickshire met a countryman blowing the grey head off a dandelion: 'We call these golden boys chimney-sweepers when they go to seed.'

'And all is clear?' continues Mr Kenner, having sprung his pleasing surprise, how much the local country voice and idiom has added to what else there is in Shakespeare's lines.

Having now in my journey circled into 'Shakespeare's country', the Stratford where he grew up and to which he chose to retire when he had ta'en enough wages from London, what I may gain from the actuality of being here is the occasional consciousness of seeing what he saw, and sometimes of noticing (as with the dandelion) what use he made of something that you see he had his eye on. It is probable that the nine lines of 'Hark, hark! the lark' and the first stanza of 'Fear no more the heat o' the sun' are about all that many people remember of the play of *Cymbeline*. Not everybody has relished *Cymbeline* – you will recall Samuel Johnson's dismissal of the play as a whole: 'To remark the folly of the fiction, the absurdity of the conduct, the confusion of the names and manners of different times, and the impossibility of the events in any system of life, were to waste criticism upon unresisting imbecility....' Nevertheless I don't see why I should stubbornly resist the more than occasional invitations to true enjoyments freely offered by this imperfect play, this so-called 'imbecility', *Cymbeline*.

It isn't likely that it occurred to Johnson, predominantly attracted as he was to city streets, that at the back of Shakespeare's mind when writing *Cymbeline* there might have been personal thoughts about retiring to the country. Here's guesswork with a vengeance! I have dipped into other urbanized critics since Johnson; many of them intimate that Shakespeare, when writing *Cymbeline*, was slipping; and perhaps that is what I am fancying, that some of his thoughts, behind the scenes, were slipping away to this particular countryside. Evidence for the fancy is that the scenery of *Cymbeline* is spread out before you as a map of Britain at its widest, from Cymbeline's court at Colchester to the far west of Milford Haven, as if a man reflecting about retirement were spreading a map to see where – and plumping for what was familiar in childhood. The work itself, the play to be put on the boards, seems momently, now and then, of less actuality than some of the intruding thoughts, pictures conjured of field and country. An invitation in the first act of *Cymbeline* is to notice that the 'violets, cowslips, and the primroses' as mentioned are not artificial flowers; they are not stage-flowers, nor gardeners' or florists' flowers; they are field-flowers, and, as they ought to be, field-flowers growing in Warwickshire fields. Presently one of the 'retirement to Warwickshire' thoughts at the back of the author's mind is going to introduce the dandelion, which as Hugh Kenner says, will establish Fidele's death in *Cymbeline* (or any death, even Shakespeare's?) as an assimilable instance of nature's custom.

But return a moment to another of the field-flowers that is here in Shakespeare's eye: the cowslip. Supposing you have really looked at an English cowslip, then from your own observation you know that deep within the inside of each small pale yellow cup there is the signature of a tiny tattoo-mark, five extremely slight and soft red accents, the merest touches of a fine-pointed brush. I doubt if Samuel Johnson ever saw the delicate red five-point within the cowslip's cup, for it needs better eyes than, more was the pity, he had been given. But you who have seen the cowslip's birthmark may know for certain Shakespeare saw it – for that's the mark he makes you see on Imogen:

> On her left breast
> A mole cinque-spotted, like the crimson drops
> I' the bottom of a cowslip.

So far as the plot of the play goes, Imogen's birthmark is a supposedly secret voucher on which some of 'the folly of the fiction' will depend. It is strange that in *Cymbeline* the flowers of the field do make their presence felt so instantly, vividly, lastingly, and almost independently of their stage use. The dandelion remains more distinct to me than the character of Fidele; the cowslip is more real to some than Imogen.

A pleasure of visiting the town of Stratford resides in dutifully sharing the homage to Shakespeare that (it can't be denied) is a 'must'. Yet after I've shared as much as I may of Stratford, I remember how much of 'Shakespeare's country' is rural, and not a matter of showplaces. Or rather, with that Saxon gift of gab of his he is ready to show, if you are ready to see. He shows you Warwickshire's golden lads and chimney-sweepers, which are not hard to find. It is rarer now than in Shakespeare's day to find the cowslip growing wild, but when you do (mid-April to mid-May) don't pick but go on your knees to confirm the good eyesight that made appropriate use of the birthmark in the tiny but up-standing cowslip's pale cup.

*   *   *

I have not forgotten that Malory (no matter if Welshmen claim him) was a Warwickshire man. Brinklow, between Coventry and Rugby, is a site where he is supposed to have worked on the immortal legend, before his own violent misconducts meant continuance and completion of the work in gaol. Perhaps I derive my impression from a sentence from Dugdale's *Warwickshire* that Brinklow beside Coventry may have been one of the outposts from which, on the southern side of the no-man's-land of Watling Street, there was anciently, in Saxon–Dane hostility, the tradition of hurling 'scorning and contempt' at the Danelaw. In the atmosphere of Midland shires there is some suggestion that the Arthurian legend, in its centuries of retellings, came to be played up differently from the 'Celtic twilight' of Cornwall and Wales. A. L. Rowse has emphasized: 'It was the hero of the losing side, King Arthur, who imposed himself on the imagination, the chief and lasting contribution of the Celts to the mind and literature of Europe.' Very true, and when Norman rule came to the island one feels the effective appeasement to 'British' feelings in the promotion of the tremendously great legend of 'the once and future king'. The impression that lurks with me, however, is that as the legend of Arthur and his knights came to be presented to the 'English', parts that took the Saxon fancy and were emphasized by Saxons had less to do with lamentation than with the heartiness, whether right or wrong, of the adventures.

The downgrading of women under the guise of chivalry seems to have been included in the specifically French contributions to the retellings of the epic as it returned from French courts to English. T. H. White, in his immensely entertaining modern retelling in four parts under the collective title of *The Once and Future King* (1958), indicates that it was appropriate that a Warwickshire knight, Malory, should be the man to restate (as if spokesman for England's heartland) the ideals of Arthur and his knights. Yet men and women of the different Danelaw heritage, before and after Malory's time, were not subscribing without resistance to a life patterned on the Arthurian legend. Especially they were not subscribing to a pattern flung at them highhandedly over the border of Watling Street. In proper Danelaw tradition the Yorkshire schoolmaster Ascham was ready to hurl back the *Morte d'Arthur*:

> The whole pleasure of this book standeth in two speciall poyntes, in open manslaughter and bold bawdrye; in this booke may be counted the noblest, knightes that do kill most men without any quarrell and commit fowlest adoulteries by subtlest shiftes; as Sir Launcelote, with the wife of king Arthure his master; Sir Tristram, with the wife of king Marke his uncle; Sir Lamerocke, with the wife of king Lote, that was his own aunte. . . .

According to Danelaw feelings, how right it was for Ascham (himself an expert archer) to prefer the Robin Hood legend.

On the northern side of Watling Street it may again be felt how the Robin Hood legend grew in the Danelaw, promoted perhaps in conscious opposition by dissenters against an élite. From the conflict represented in the two great legends, of Arthur and Robin Hood, many smaller conflicts peel off. (George Eliot, born right on the line of Watling Street and closer than other novelists to the 'matter of Dissent' in Victorian times, presents one of those conflicts.) Here my present wish is to return from Watling Street through Shakespeare's country along the course of the River Avon, which will also return me to the Vale of Evesham. North of Warwick the stripling Avon, which at one time carried Wyclif's ashes from Lutterworth to the Severn and the sea, avoids both Coventry and Kenilworth. The Earl of Leicester's specially lavish entertainment of Queen Elizabeth in 1575 at Kenilworth Castle (chosen by Walter Scott to mark the climax of his novel) was what Ascham, when tutor to the young Queen, had advised her to beware of as a trap. Ascham had been dead for seven years in 1575, and his had not been the only voice that taught the Queen to look about her. Today in the castle ruins at Kenilworth the site of the Pleasance and the Swan Tower, near which Scott's *Kenilworth* makes Amy Robsart be discovered by Elizabeth and a plot suspected, is more or less identifiable. (How much appreciation for Scott's novels increases, when, in maturity, they are re-read!) Yet, as I was saying, the course of the Avon bypasses Kenilworth and brings me, before entering Stratford, to Charlcote Park.

In 1583 Shakespeare, so the story goes, was arraigned in the great hall of the 'goodly dwelling and rich' of Charlcote Park and duly fined for poaching deer. Charlcote Park is now a property of the National Trust and a 'Shakespeare herd' of deer in the park recalls the story. After Shakespeare's day successive owners altered much of the buildings; that part that remains as he saw it is the pink brick gatehouse. The Avon as it flows on to Stratford, under the bridge and below the Memorial Theatre, is now a good-sized river, and swans in midstream are well contrived to call attention to the 'Swan of Avon' and to the proper business of the visitor, looking at what is signposted to be seen, and looking for what's also useful, the place to eat. Here, though, I am following the road out of Stratford which keeps beside the right bank of the Avon for the dozen miles to Evesham. Halfway to Evesham this road passes close to the village of Broom with its inn and goes through Bidford where there was the inn called in Shakespeare's time the Falcon.

Beggarly Broom and Drunken Bidford

is the last line of a quatrain enumerating the 'Eight Shakespearian Villages' (each rewarded with its epithet), supposedly composed by young Shakespeare at the Falcon at the end of a twenty-mile pub-crawl. In the effort of returning to Stratford from this carouse Shakespeare is said to have struggled so far as a crab-apple tree a mile east of Bidford, and there to have lain down to sleep. The crabtree (or a successor) is sometimes pointed out.

At Evesham, the River Avon heads north to curve through Pershore. The one-legged Jonathan Small, a character of boyhood importance in Conan Doyle's *The Sign of Four*, was a native of Pershore; but now at Evesham I wish to study the view south-east across the fruit-growing Vale of Evesham to the high edge of the Cotswolds. Out of this part of the Shire country there developed the great fantasy of Middle-Earth which J. R. R. Tolkien (1892–1973) wrote of in his three-volume epic, *The Lord of the Rings*.

That Tolkien's epic (not to be thought of as allegory but as imagined history of Middle-Earth in its Great Year) is to be especially associated with the Vale of Evesham is evidenced by the fact that his mother's family, the Suffields, were originally of Evesham. John Tolkien was the elder of two sons born to the Tolkiens in Bloemfontein, South Africa, but the father died when John was four years old and the mother returned with the children to live in Worcestershire. It was from his mother that Tolkien felt he had derived an 'almost idolatrous' love of the trees and flowers of the Worcestershire countryside; in letters likewise she was his first teacher, and along with introducing him to classical mythology, Arthurian romance and the stories of the more nearly contemporary George Macdonald, she aroused his early interest in linguistics. At the age of eleven the future professor gained a scholarship to King Edward's School, Birmingham, and his form-master, noticing the boy's gifts, lent him an Anglo-Saxon grammar. Tolkien's mother died when he was twelve, yet something that had been of mutual fascination continued, a hearkening for 'the horns of Elfland' blowing in a country which was at once both imaginary and very closely attached to the Midland shires of Old England. Elfland and Vale of Evesham could on occasion fuse completely as a portion of real Middle-Earth, of which some of the inhabitants, Hobbits for instance, might show in their blood something that was Evesham-earthy-human, something Elvish, and a dash of something that may have come from George Macdonald's Goblins.

The Vale of Evesham seems thus to have been, for Tolkien, an early area of tangency between the worlds of England and of Middle-Earth. First acquaintances in Middle-Earth were the go-between Hobbits, and in their shire were other peoples not altogether strange – elves, dwarfs, trolls. The imaginative boy was impelled to attend to languages from, as it were, the inside: how should he go about putting together a real 'Elvish tongue'? – not a mere gabble, but a language with 'consistent roots, sound laws, inflexions, even poetry, of its own. Tolkien's private linguistic searchings in Mercian, Gothic, Anglo-Saxon, Welsh continued throughout his undergraduate period at Oxford before the 1914–18 war, and after the interruption of army service the invention of 'Elvish' was resumed; yet having come to the conclusion that every language presupposes a mythology, Tolkien's private occupation came to be (as the obituary notice in *The Times* expressed it) 'to fill in the mythology presupposed by Elvish'. Renewed 'in-dwellings' within the Middle-Earth showed that the shire area which with its little peoples had been the otherworld of Tolkien's childhood, was surrounded by other territories inhabited by other creatures – many of Tolkien's creations (revealed to him as it were by his philology) display an individual and vivid vitality. Grigson's *Encyclopedia of Modern World Literature* rightly picked out, for instance, the delightfulness of 'the Ents', the tree-shepherds, of Middle-Earth, 'like nothing anyone has imagined before': 'As tall as trolls they were, twelve feet or more in height; their strong bodies, stout as young trees, seemed to be clad with raiment or with hide of close-fitting grey and brown. Their limbs were long, and their hands had many fingers; their hair was stiff, and their beards grey-green as moss. They gazed out with solemn eyes.'

To Tolkien in his maturity there came from contemplation of the Vale of Evesham something that broke through from a deeper level than that of the mind of the conscious observer; what broke through was a spectacle of warfare which his prose had an unusual power to depict, and when it was fitting for verse to be called on in the epic, Tolkien's skill with verse-rhythms was reminiscent of Kipling's. The war in the Great

Year in the history of Middle-Earth was a contest, at times fearful in intensity, of good and evil. The 'responsibility of saving the sum of things' eventually fell upon two reluctant heroes out of that special tribe of small beings who had been Tolkien's known familiar friends ever since he and his mother first saw them in the Vale.

*   *   *

Henry James, in his book *English Hours*, returned from Stratford to Oxford and London by way of Compton Wynyates, which gave him opportunity to mention how Walter Scott had his eye on that 'seat of enchantment', transferring as much as he could to the description of the dwelling of the old Royalist knight in *Woodstock*. Thoughts evoked by *The Lord of the Rings* and the Vale of Evesham lead me to follow a route to Oxford in a circuit through Cheltenham to Cirencester and thence along the valley of the stripling Thames. The straight route from Evesham might have been across the Vale to Broadway, up Broadway Hill and over the Cotswolds; or a detour northwards along the Edge of the Cotswolds from Broadway would have put me in the neighbourhood of Eliot's *Burnt Norton*. Yet Tolkien's sturdy Little People in the Vale of Evesham have brought to mind three of their fellows I once saw in a Romano-British sculptor's bas-relief in the Cirencester Museum. That sculpture showed three small creatures of a tribe not wholly unrelated to Hobbits; but these little tribesmen, when seen by Romans, were always wearing hoods which hid their faces, so that the Romans called them *cucullati*, and never did see what they had under their cloaks; they were far too shy, and ran very fast. 'Not far from Cirencester' and close no doubt to one of those many Roman roads that meet here, the three *cucullati* of the museum had been seen long enough to be recorded.

'Not far from Cirencester' is a magic phrase; you will find it effectively used in John Aubrey's *Miscellanies*: '*Anno* 1670, not far from Cirencester, was an apparition: being demanded, whether a good spirit, or a bad? returned no answer, but disappeared with a curious perfume and most melodious twang. Mr W. Lilly believes it was a fairy.' Aubrey in 1670 was considerably involved in astrological inquiries, and it was natural that he consulted his leading astrologer-acquaintance William Lilly. It was the 'curious perfume' that was significant to Lilly and Aubrey, Aubrey quoting a parallel adventure from Propertius, in which he translated the line of Latin as 'the remaining scent a goddess did declare'. Byron used the phrase 'melodious twang' as a quotation in his *Vision of Judgment*. Scott also quoted Aubrey's anecdote in *The Antiquary*, where Oldbuck, the antiquary, comments on 'the concise style of Old Aubrey' in the making of the report. One notes that though 'Old Aubrey' uses the magic phrase 'not far from Cirencester' to place the event, his style is too concise to allow the day or night to be dated. Was it on a Midsummer Night that this fairy appeared? – in search, most likely, for the companions that Shakespeare had been watching some few years before and not far from what he called (albeit in another connection) 'our town of Cicester in Gloucestershire'.

Many would agree that this area between the Fosse Way and the Roman road from 'Cicester' to Cricklade, was part of Shakespeare's fairyland. It is a region of the shire in which there are the sources of the River Thames, and that is important, for what makes the character of the lower river far from ordinary are the legends and pre-legends of the shire where it is born. Appropriate happenings are the moonlight goings-on of *A Midsummer Night's Dream*. Nobody is taken in by the pretence that the scene of that play is 'Athens, and a wood near it'. The impression for the London Thames-side playgoer is that for his entertainment an essential part of England's country has floated itself downstream. I feel that if Shakespeare's Avon had directed its course towards Elizabeth's courts and London's theatres, the *Dream* might have come from near the source of Avon, instead of from a source of Thames; but that's no matter, Shakespeare is as much at home with one wood and meadow and its denizens as with the other. (His favourite cowslips come into the *Dream* as Titania's pensioners, and the same delicate birthmark in the cowslip's cup is mentioned as in *Cymbeline*.) If there is a little fun made of rural theatricals, it is not unfriendly mockery; though if the dramatist was turning Shire memories of his own into 'a musical' for the abridgement of a patron's evening, it might have been wise to identify the locality as, if not near Athens, rather 'not far from Cirencester' than anywhere close to Stratford.

I spoke of 'sources' of the Thames, for there are various opinions and something depends upon the climate. A source asserted with assurance by the British Tourist Authority is in a glade called Trewsbury Mead, where at times there is sufficiency of shallow water to be pointed to as proof. A site was here pinpointed in 1938 (pleasingly, close to such a 'duke's oak' as Quince appointed for the rehearsal in *A Midsummer Night's Dream*) where the Conservators of the Thames placed a reclining stone statue within supposedly protective iron railings 'to mark the source of the river'. The statue was of a venerable partly clad athlete somewhat twice as large as life, with long-flowing hair and beard, in recumbent position, staring as he rested at something that he seemed about to dig, for his right hand clasped the handle of a shovel, the blade of which was at the moment on his bare shoulder. There was an oddity about this recumbent leg-draped statue of a man with his shovel, and an oddity also about its history. Within living memory it had been one of the assortment of statuary placed in the grounds of the Crystal Palace in South London. After the burning of the Crystal Palace in 1936, in the remodelling of the Palace's grounds the statue was one of those regarded as redundant. Viewers throughout the years had speculated at the profession symbolized by the recumbent man with the shovel; after the fire the suggestion that it betokened Father Thames led to its being placed at Trewsbury Mead. There for half a lifetime the statue remained in its enclosure, gazing past its neighbouring oak tree at the Trewsbury glade. Sometimes the scene at which the statue looked was muddy, sometimes there was enough shimmer of water to carry even a light portable boat. Many visitors took pleasure from the sight of the statue at that site; some commented on the facial expression – there was indeed a sort of puzzlement reminiscent of Demetrius (*A Midsummer Night's Dream*, III, 2) waking to his new scene and observing: 'Crystal is muddy.' But in the spring of 1974 vandals conceived the thought of smashing up the statue; to some extent damage was achieved; the battered statue was then taken away by the Conservators, restored, and placed at a new and it may be hoped safer riverside home at St John's Lock, near Lechlade.

Several companions assure me it has been no mistake to mention in the same breath Shakespeare's *Dream* and the birth-region of the River Thames. One such companion is Thomas Love Peacock's character, the Rev. Dr Opimiam who (in *Gryll Grange*) expresses approval of connecting 'the immaterial world with the material world, as far as you can'. Peacock and Shelley, on their walking trip in search of the headwaters of the Thames, presently absorbed the dream quality of the region and forgot any other duties in the enjoyment of making paper boats to sail along the little creek from Cricklade to the navigable stream at Lechlade, the 'little paper argosies which trembled down the Isis'. Downstream from Lechlade, Kelmscott Manor preserves within its high wall the dream quality which, when he first saw the house in 1871, caused William Morris to exclaim 'a Heaven on earth'. After Morris had made Kelmscott his home for twenty years he there wrote the book which he called *News from Nowhere or An Epoch of Rest*, and after his death at Hammersmith in 1896 his coffin was brought to Kelmscott for burial, in the grave which later was shared by his wife Janey. All along the quietly flowing river past Bablockhythe to Oxford, the suggestion as each bend of Thames draws on to the 'city of dreaming spires' is of one summer's daydream after another; the gentle green hillsides sloping to the stream bring memories of Arnold's 'The Scholar-Gipsy':

> O born in days when wits were fresh and clear
> And life ran gaily as the sparkling Thames,
> Before this strange disease of modern life.

It was in a riverside meadow at Godstow, just above Oxford, that on 4 July 1862, one special dream occurred. Oxford that Friday afternoon felt sultry, but the three young daughters of the Dean of Christ Church had been invited to go on the river. Lorina Liddell, the eldest, was only thirteen, Alice was ten, and Edith was eight; all were rather special friends of Charles Lutwidge Dodgson, tutor in mathematics at Christ Church, and as soon as they had collected him from his rooms in college, all set off, as often before, to their light rowing boat at Folly Bridge. Alice Liddell later supplied visual details:

Mr Dodgson always wore black clergyman's clothes in Oxford, but when he took us out on the river, he used to wear white flannel trousers. He also replaced his black top-hat by a hard white straw hat – but of course he retained his black boots, because in those days white tennis shoes had never been heard of. He always carried himself upright, almost more than upright, as if he had swallowed a poker.

As Alice reported, a river-party usually consisted of five – 'one of Mr Dodgson's men friends as well as himself and us three. Our most usual fifth was Mr Duckworth, who sang well.' On this particular Friday it was the Rev. Robinson Duckworth who, also in white flannels, had the rowing gig ready at Folly Bridge. The gear was stowed: 'When we went on the river for the afternoon with Mr Dodgson, he always brought with him a large basket full of cakes, and a kettle, which we used to boil under a haycock, if we could find one.' It was the custom for Duckworth to row stroke and for Dodgson to row bow, and as they went up the river towards Godstow, Dodgson began to tell them all a story. In Duckworth's account, 'The story was actually composed and spoken over my shoulder for the benefit of Alice Liddell, who was acting as "cox" of our gig. I remember turning round and saying, "Dodgson, is this an extempore romance of yours?" And he replied: "Yes, I'm inventing as we go along." ' At Godstow, when a hayrick had been found, the tale of *Alice's Adventures Underground* – as *Alice in Wonderland* was initially thought of – was continued.

Miss Joanna Richardson began a very delightful article in *History Today* by putting together those quotations, which make it possible to visualize in precise detail the Thames-side picnic of that particular Friday. All readers recall that early in the adventures, when Alice and the animals were beside the pool of tears, among the creatures were a Duck and a Dodo, a Lory and an Eaglet; what is to be added from visualizing the picnic, is: 'The Lory, of course, was Lorina Liddell, Alice's elder sister, and the Eaglet was her younger sister, Edith. The Duck was Robinson Duckworth.' As for the Dodo, Miss Richardson suggests that Dodgson was thinking of the dodo which visitors could see at the University Museum; it is also possible that if Duck stood for Duckworth, Dodo might partially suggest Dodgson, which fits with the presentation of the prizes, after the caucus race, by the Dodo. Yet the identification to which Miss Richardson introduces me, and which supports my feeling that nowhere along the river is it forgotten that its flow begins in the country of Shakespeare's *Dream*, is that Dodgson had noted in his diary, a few years earlier than the picnic at Godstow, that among the 'wonderful points' in Landseer's painting called 'Titania' were 'the ass's head and the white rabbit especially'. It is the 'White Rabbit with pink eyes', coming from Shakespeare's *Dream* by way of Landseer, that Dodgson says 'sent my heroine straight down a rabbit-hole, without the least idea what was to happen afterwards'.

* * *

Before and after the riverside picnics of the Lory, Alice, and Eaglet, squired by two Fellows of Oxford colleges (Duck and perhaps Dodo), plentiful are anecdotes that could be recalled on the terrace of the Trout Inn at Godstow; and if there are fairly recent recollections there of Aldous Huxley and A. P. Herbert, stories of Godstow go back at least to Fair Rosamund of song and legend. Yet if I pause for more than a moment on the river above Folly Bridge, to give equal treatment to the rest of Oxford's river, and to Oxford itself (both Town and Gown), would prove impossible. At Folly Bridge one may meditate upon the older narrow stone span which carried the three-storeyed stone tower with Friar Bacon's study at the top. The noisiness of bargemen attempting to navigate under the awkward bridge was less perhaps in Bacon's thirteenth century than at the start of the seventeenth, when Robert Burton used to find relief from the *Anatomy of Melancholy* by strolling from Christ Church down to Folly Bridge.

I have heard [said Bishop Kennet] that nothing at last could make him laugh, but going down to the Bridge-Foot in Oxford and hearing the Barge-men scold and storm and swear at one another, at which he would set his Hands to his Sides and laugh most profusely: Yet in his College and Chamber so mute and mopish that he was suspected to be Felo-de-se.

On his summer outing of 1668 Pepys stayed long enough in the butteries and cellar of Brasenose College (Burton's other college) to warrant a tip of two shillings to the 'Butler'; as climax of Pepys's entertainment he too strolled down to Folly Bridge and climbed into the tower to see Friar Bacon's study. 'I up and saw it', said Pepys, 'and give the man 1s.' By the end of the eighteenth century the three-storey tower on the bridge was deemed to be unsafe, and it was demolished. From the present Folly Bridge one looks downstream on the river of Oxford's boating men and the towpath recalled, for instance, in Max Beerbohm's *Zuleika Dobson*.

As at Cambridge, the sheer number of writers who spent their prentice years (and sometimes their maturities) within university circles forces me to present a mere and incomplete catalogue of some of the colleges and some of the names associated with them.

Balliol: Robert Southey; A. H. Clough; C. S. Calverley (sent down); Matthew Arnold; Andrew Lang; Benjamin Jowett (Master); Algernon Swinburne; Gerard Manley Hopkins; Anthony Hope Hawkins; Hilaire Belloc; Aldous Huxley; Ronald Knox

Brasenose: Robert Burton; Walter Pater (as Fellow); R. H. Barham; John Buchan; Charles Morgan

Christ Church: Thomas More; Philip Sidney; Richard Hakluyt; R. Burton (from Brasenose); William Penn; John Wesley; John Ruskin; Charles Dodgson (Lewis Carroll); W. H. Auden

Corpus Christi: Richard Hooker; Robert Bridges; Henry Newbolt

Exeter: J. A. Froude; R. D. Blackmore; William Morris; E. Burne-Jones; Alfred Noyes

Hertford: John Donne; J. M. Falkner; Evelyn Waugh

Jesus: Lancelot Andrewes; Henry Vaughan; 'Beau' Nash; T. E. Lawrence

Lady Margaret Hall: H. M. F. Prescott; Helen Waddell; C. V. Wedgwood

Magdalen: John Foxe; Joseph Addison; Edward Gibbon; Charles Reade; Oscar Wilde

Merton: Richard Steele; George Saintsbury; Max Beerbohm; T. S. Eliot; J. R. R. Tolkien; Louis MacNeice; Stephen Spender

New College: Sydney Smith; Lionel Johnson; John Galsworthy; A. P. Herbert; R. C. Sherriff

Oriel: Gilbert White; J. H. Newman (as Fellow); A. H. Clough (as Fellow); Thomas Hughes

Pembroke: Samuel Johnson; T. L. Beddoes

Queens: Walter Pater

Somerville: Rose Macaulay; Dorothy L. Sayers; Vera Brittain; Winifred Holtby; Margaret Kennedy

Trinity: W. S. Landor (sent down); J. H. Newman; A. Quiller-Couch; J. E. Flecker; Ronald Knox (as Fellow)

University: P. B. Shelley (sent down)

Wadham: C. Day Lewis

Worcester: Richard Lovelace; Thomas De Quincey

At Cambridge I mentioned a galaxy of seven great poets, from Marlowe to Tennyson, who had all been members of Cambridge colleges, and Cambridge men used to claim that for poets Oxford was outranked. Oxford men used to promote, as best they could, Sidney, Raleigh, Donne, Shelley, Landor, Matthew Arnold, Clough, Swinburne. After 1914 Oxford put forward Eliot, Auden, Spender and in the postwar period it was Cambridge's turn to be relatively modest. Yet that is comparing the two universities. If Town associations are added to those of Gown, consider the additions to be made at Oxford. River and road brought outside poets to Oxford. River, for instance, brought Keats, who on his visit in 1817 'had regularly a boat on the Isis, and explored all the streams about, which are more in number than your eyelashes. We sometimes skim into a bed of rushes and there become naturalized river-folks – there is one particularly nice nest, which we have christened "Reynold's Cove", in which we have read Wordsworth, and talked as may be.' And who else should have been brought by road to Oxford – who but Shakespeare?

Aubrey tells that Shakespeare 'was wont to goe to his native Country once a yeare', and elsewhere adds that he commonly stopped in Oxford at the Crown, in Cornmarket Street, 'where he was exceedingly res-pected'. It has, though, been pointed out that the establishment referred to was a tavern, not an inn. The tavern, kept in Shakespeare's time by John Davenant, was next door to the inn then called the Cross (now, it is assumed, the Golden Cross), and that is the inn regarded as Shakes-peare's sleeping-place. The tavern's attraction was said by Aubrey to be Mrs Davenant; Aubrey followed persistent traditional gossip that Mrs Davenant's son William (later to become Poet Laureate) was not only Shakespeare's godson, but also (as stated bluntly, a century later, by the Oxford antiquarian Thomas Hearne) 'in all probability he got him'. It is an unverified story of a type not difficult to invent. Deliberately fictional tales of Oxford life in later centuries range from those of Thomas Hughes and Cuthbert Bede to Thomas Hardy and many more recent. Hughes's *Tom Brown's School Days* led naturally to *Tom Brown at Oxford*. Cuthbert Bede's *Mr Verdant Green* was assumed to be a farcical narrative by an Oxford man of Oxford in the 1850s 'to the life'. The writer in fact was Edward Bradley, born in Kidderminster, whose under-graduate experience and BA degree were derived from University College, Durham (the pseudonym, Cuthbert Bede, intentionally sugges-ted Durham). 'Bede' made Verdant Green start his Oxford life at the Mitre, in the High Street, which was to Nathaniel Hawthorne 'the noblest old street in England'. Thomas Hardy was concerned rather with opposing Town to Gown, and it was the bar of Shakespeare's inn, the Golden Cross, which he prefers, and to which he allows Jude entry, in *Jude the Obscure*.

In 1892 Hardy visited Oxford to confirm details for scenes in *Jude the Obscure*; the publication of that novel in 1895 aroused such confused and bitter controversy that Hardy thereafter abandoned fiction and returned to his first love, poetry. He later recorded what his feelings had been at the height of the *Jude* controversy:

Poetry: perhaps I can express more fully in verse ideas and emotions which run counter to the inert crystallised opinion – hard as a rock – which the vast body of men have vested interests in supporting. To cry out in a passionate poem that (for instance) the Supreme Mover or Movers, the Prime Force or Forces, must be either limited in power, unknowing or cruel – which is obvious enough, and has been for centuries – will cause them merely a shake of the head; but to put it in argumentative prose will make them sneer, or foam, and set all the literary contortionists jumping on me. . . . If Galileo had said in verse that the world moved, the Inquisition might have let him alone.

Nowadays opinions on *Jude the Obscure* seem to be less affected than Hardy makes out by Hardy's personal sombre pessimism.

Thoughts of novelists remind me that in following the course of the Thames towards Oxford, I neglected to mention that Black Bourton (north of the river, between Kelmscott and Witney) was birthplace of Maria Edgeworth; interest in her novels, and in the way she stimulated both Scott and Jane Austen, has much increased in the 1970s. Early in the eighteenth century Black Bourton was an estate 'of eight hundred pounds a year, highly improvable, well wooded and within a ring fence', belonging to the Hungerford family (which had given its name to Hungerford Market at Charing Cross in London – and preserved it in London's Hungerford Bridge). The Hungerford heiress who inherited Black Bourton was apparently not a good manager, nor was her indolent husband; they had several pretty daughters of marriageable age, but the estate was disintegrating when it happened that the seventeen-year-old Richard Lovell Edgeworth, of an Anglo-Irish family, was placed at Black Bourton as a home from home while entered at Corpus Christi College, Oxford. This Richard Edgeworth will be referred to later as a man of exceptional vitality and abilities; here the point is that before his three years at Oxford were completed he was married to the eldest daughter at Black Bourton, Anna Maria, and was father of his first son. The young couple presently moved to a rented house in Hare Hatch, a Berkshire village between Reading and Maidenhead. Anna Maria's intellectual limitations and Edgeworth's incessant energies (mental, physical and social) made them ill-matched. Edgeworth spent most of his time in London. Anna Maria returned to Black Bourton for the birth of her second child; it was a second son, dying within a month of birth in 1766. The following year she was pregnant again, and again went to

Black Bourton; this time it was Maria Edgeworth who there came into the world on 1 January 1768.

While still in country west and north of Oxford, I should mention Charlbury as the home, towards the end of her life, of Hilda Prescott – her greatest book, *The Man on a Donkey*, was quoted earlier. At Woodstock there was born, and at Bladon was buried, Winston Churchill, whose claim as a novelist is that he published *Savrola* in 1900. To the north-east of Oxford is Elsfield, where John Buchan lived at the manor and where he is buried in the churchyard. At equal distance to the south-west of Oxford is Boar's Hill, where among the many to be remembered lived Gilbert Murray and the twentieth-century Walter Raleigh, and where Robert Bridges lived and composed his *Testament of Beauty* (1929).

Six miles or so south-east of Oxford is Garsington. In 1915 Bertrand Russell introduced the newly married T. S. Eliot and his wife to Lady Ottoline Morrell and (as T. S. Matthews has expressed it) to 'all the Comus crew that battened on her at Garsington Manor for well-fed weekends – Leonard and Virginia Woolf, Katherine Mansfield, Middleton Murry, Aldous and Maria Huxley, Vanessa and Clive Bell, Duncan Grant, Lytton Strachey, and lesser lights'. At that time of his visits to Garsington Eliot was 'a virtually anonymous foreigner', though it is now in recollection of him that many visitors think of Garsington 'with the flower of Bloomsbury strewn amid the trees'. Garsington Manor plays a large part in biographies of Bertrand Russell and Lytton Strachey; yet here I prefer to point from Oxford south to Abingdon. Abingdon itself has much to please and many associations (not least, that John Ruskin chose to live at the Crown and Thistle Inn while first Slade Professor of Art at Oxford in 1871), but I prefer to pause a further mile or two in the neighbouring Sutton Courtenay on a backwater of the Thames. At the church in Sutton Courtenay there was buried in 1928 the Earl of Oxford and Asquith; in 1950 – this is why I stay – Eric Blair, whose pen-name was George Orwell, was buried here.

Should Orwell's *Animal Farm* require introduction, I might quote from Geoffrey Grigson's *Concise Encyclopedia of Modern World Literature* (1972):

Animal Farm (1945) is Orwell's only real achievement as an artist. Here his deliberately colourless style was given a melancholy elegance by the fact that this account of a revolution betrayed was devised as a fairy tale. The recollection of childhood always meant a great deal to Orwell, and the fate of Boxer, the carthorse of the revolution, whose remedy for every setback is to work a little harder, is tenderly but unsentimentally rendered. Certain phrases in the book have passed into current use – 'All animals are equal, but some are more equal than others' – and these, too, generally derived from childhood sayings. The whole story is written with a delicacy and sensibility shown nowhere else in his work.

It was not easy for Orwell and his literary agent to find a publisher for this work which Grigson, some decades later, picked out as Orwell's 'only real achievement as an artist'. Whatever the permanent beauty of the fairy tale, in 1945 a number of publishers found reasons to avoid printing it before Frederick Warburg rose to the occasion and issued the little book in London; except for paper shortage, copies of *Animal Farm* would have multiplied in Britain much faster than they did. The New York publisher who then purchased the American publication rights was under no such handicap, and the timing of publication there ensured for Orwell's fable a circulation immensely beyond his expectation. In March 1946 Winston Churchill delivered his 'Iron Curtain' speech at Fulton; the period of 'the Cold War' was on its way; *Animal Farm* when published in late summer clicked with the mood in America, and sales there ran rapidly towards and past two million. Few people in England then recognized the immense impact of *Animal Farm* across the Atlantic.

It is with respect for George Orwell that I pause at All Saints Church, Sutton Courtenay. As I now return Londonwards past Wallingford, I note other respects to be paid: about three miles north-east of Wallingford is Ewelme, notable for its beautiful almshouses, and remembered also because Jerome Klapka Jerome was buried here in 1927 – interest has revived in recent years in his *Three Men in a Boat*. At an equal distance south-west of Wallingford is Cholsey, where after her magnificent long lifetime as Queen of mystery story writers, Agatha Christie was buried in 1976. Towards London then I could find Ipsden beneath the north edge of the Chilterns and it is here that Charles Reade was born, his wonderful energy now perhaps chiefly remembered for *The Cloister and the Hearth*. Then in the Chiltern Hills on the way to Henley is Nettlebed, where Peter Fleming lived at Merrimoles House, and died there in 1971. Before the last war I remember that Patrick Hamilton (whose best-remembered play was *Rope*) was living for some years in Hart Street, Henley. Eastward from Henley I am quickly back to the scene whence this particular expedition started.

A5

THE HOLYHEAD ROAD AND NORTH TO SOLWAY FIRTH

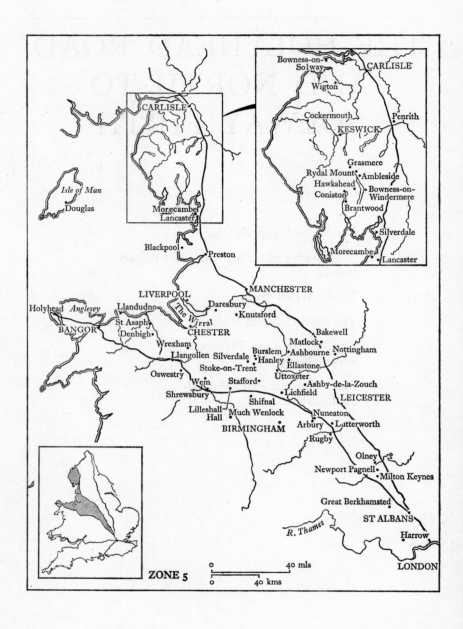

Isle of Man
Douglas

CARLISLE

Bowness-on-Solway
Wigton
Cockermouth
KESWICK
Penrith
Grasmere
Rydal Mount
Ambleside
Hawkshead
Coniston
Bowness-on-Windermere
Brantwood
Silverdale
Morecambe
Lancaster

Morecambe
Lancaster

Blackpool
Preston

MANCHESTER

LIVERPOOL
Daresbury
Knutsford

Holyhead Anglesey
Llandudno
The Wirral
Bakewell
St Asaph
BANGOR
Denbigh
CHESTER
Matlock
Ashbourne
Nottingham
Wrexham
Burslem
Llangollen Silverdale
Hanley
Ellastone
Stoke-on-Trent
Uttoxeter
Oswestry
Ashby-de-la-Zouch
Wem
Stafford
Lichfield
LEICESTER
Shrewsbury
Shifnal
Lilleshall
Hall
Much Wenlock
Nuneaton
BIRMINGHAM
Arbury
Lutterworth
Rugby

Olney
Newport Pagnell
Milton Keynes

Great Berkhamsted
ST ALBANS
R. Thames
Harrow
LONDON

ZONE 5

40 mls
40 kms

1. LONDON TO COWPER'S OLNEY

I now propose to venture forth on Watling Street and to visit regions to the north of that rampart. But when setting out from London what nowadays do we regard as the starting-point for Watling Street – or that long part of it which runs north-west from London? The answer to that preliminary problem is that the Edgware Road from Marble Arch is the start now of the A5. It promptly crosses Blomfield Road and changes its name to Maida Vale; yet the glimpse of canal should be a reminder of what sites, at starting, are passed on the left. Blomfield Road is here the north bank of the Regent's Canal; a short way along Blomfield Road and one is looking over the water at the site of No. 30 Maida Avenue, where John Masefield (1878–1967) was living at the time he wrote 'The Everlasting Mercy'. That was the poem which brought him much attention and which then, in English verse, seemed revolutionary:

> 'You closhy put.'
> > 'You bloody liar.'
> 'This is my field.'
> > 'This is my wire.'
> 'I'm ruler here.'
> > 'You ain't.'
> > > 'I am.'
> 'I'll fight you for it.'
> > 'Right, by damn.'

A mile to the west of Maida Avenue Ford Madox Ford (or Hueffer, as his last name was until 1919) was at that time living at No. 84 Holland Park Avenue (near Holland Park Station) and editing, at that address, the *English Review*. His contributors included Hardy and Conrad; of younger writers he was not afraid to publish Wyndham Lewis, and in the same year (1911) in which he was introducing D. H. Lawrence to the public, Hueffer (or Ford) accepted 'The Everlasting Mercy'. Christopher Morley, a Rhodes Scholar at Oxford in 1911, never forgot the way in which 'Masefield burst upon us. Almost overnight every one was reading "The Everlasting Mercy". Does a thrill like that come to every undergraduate generation? Somehow I doubt it.' It was 'The Everlasting Mercy' which to that undergraduate (who himself later masqueraded under the name John Mistletoe) 'suddenly spoke as poetry should'.

Blomfield Road, after its short stretch of looking across the canal at what used to be Maida Avenue, continued then to look across a wider triangular lake of water, on the far side of which was Warwick Crescent, and of No. 19 of that crescent, facing the water, Robert Browning was householder. He returned to live there for sixteen years after the death of his wife in Italy in 1861, and had spent some years there when Edmund Gosse settled in to No. 29 Delamere Terrace, the westward continuation of Warwick Crescent. Edward FitzGerald (who had lodged for a short time on the other side of Maida Vale, in St John's Wood) was no admirer of Mrs Browning's poetry, but 'Fitz' was in no proximity to the widower; it was Gosse, when living close to Browning and wishing to court the older man, who was cautious in expressing what he and up-coming critics of the 'delicate ear' school objected to in the 'vulgar' rhymes which they felt to be 'a most terrible drawback' occasionally in Browning's verse, and habitually in the poems of Mrs Browning. Saintsbury, of the then younger school, was most outspoken about the pain that Mrs Browning caused him. 'The positive anguish which such hideous false notes as these must cause to anyone with a delicate ear, the maddening interruption to the delight of these really beautiful pieces of poetry, cannot be over-estimated.' (The examples which had maddened Saintsbury were that Mrs Browning, despite her Greek, had rhymed *idyll* to *middle* and *pyramidal* to *idle*.) Browning's father and sister shared No. 19 Warwick Crescent with the widower, as well as his son; all were capable of defending Mrs Browning's foibles, and in that neighbourhood Gosse kept guard on his tongue. I am not sure if the Browning rowboat was still being kept in front of No. 19 when Gosse became a neighbour; if so, he probably on occasion joined with the younger Browning in rowing the writer of 'Rabbi ben Ezra' along the not yet fully built-up canal as far as Kensal Green. But by 1887 Browning (then aged seventy-five) was hankering for the other canals of Venice, where in 1889 he died, the last volume of his poems, *Asolando*, appearing in England on the day of his death.

The Edgware Road, after the segment of it named Maida Vale, in its straight course onward through Kilburn bears the name Kilburn High Road and then, straight again through Cricklewood, is there called the Broadway. It is to the east of the Edgware Road's straightforwardness that the Finchley Road makes its curving way from the north into London – it was on that highway, which could eventually link Wilkie Collins's characters with Cumberland, that in the hour past midnight at the end of a mid-nineteenth-century July there was the initial and mysterious appearance of 'The Woman in White'. Collins in the text is precise about the scene. The narrator (Walter Hartright), walking from Hampstead in the moonlit night, had just turned left at Swiss Cottage:

. . . when, in one moment, every drop of blood in my body was brought to a stop by the touch of a hand laid lightly and suddenly on my shoulder from behind me.

I turned on the instant, with my fingers tightening round the handle of my stick.

There, in the middle of the broad, bright high-road – there, as if it had that moment sprung out of the earth or dropped from the heaven – stood the figure of a solitary Woman, dressed from head to foot in white garments, her face bent in grave inquiry on mine, her hand pointing to the dark cloud over London, as I faced her . . .

The strange woman spoke first.

'Is that the road to London?'

The Warwick Crescent to which Browning came (in the same year that *The Woman in White* was published) is in the neighbourhood of what Blake called 'mournful, ever-weeping Paddington'. The region through which the Edgware Road leads is what Blake saw as part of his Jerusalem:

> Pancras and Kentish-town repose
> Among her golden pillars high,
> Among her golden arches which
> Shine upon the starry sky.
>
> The Jew's-harp-house and the Green Man,
> The ponds where Boys to bathe delight,
> The fields of Cows by Willan's farm,
> Shine in Jerusalem's pleasant sight.

'What melodies, I wonder,' asked Ivor Brown, when commenting on these lines, 'came out of the Jew's-harp-house and where did Willan farm? Was it in Willesden?' Blake (as Browning also) was a Londoner born and bred; his Delectable Mountains were not identified with any personal nostalgia for country boyhood. But the road leading out of London towards Shropshire – this Edgware Road – reminds one how the direct influence of Blake's music, coupled with nostalgic feelings from boyhood in the country, shared in producing A. E. Housman's *A Shropshire Lad*.

'*A Shropshire Lad* was written at Byron Cottage, 17 North Road, Highgate, where I lived from 1886 to 1905', wrote Alfred Housman in a brief autobiographical note for his brother Laurence. It was a taciturn and sour young man who took the bachelor lodgings at Byron Cottage; his moodiness had to an extent caused, and was certainly exacerbated by, his disastrous career at Oxford. There Housman had taken a First in 'Mods' but was ploughed altogether in 'Greats', after which catastrophic failure he could obtain no better job than a minor post in HM

L.B.—K

Patent Office. That made him take the Highgate lodgings, to which he rarely returned till night, for 'while I was at the Patent Office I read a great deal of Greek and Latin at the British Museum of an evening'. His long hours of disciplined self-training led then to his teaching post in Classics at University College, London. While teaching, Housman continued to remain living alone in the Highgate lodgings. In 1895 three-fourths of the poems in *A Shropshire Lad* were written, feelings of adolescent boyhood seemingly returning with a rush, though the expression was carefully and expertly modulated by the mature scholar of thirty-six. The woe as at the age of seventeen about

> graves of lovers
> That hanged themselves for love

and a welter of thoughts of death and love, and (as has been said) 'preferably of both together', were set to verbal music by the man who loved and studied Blake as poet not much less than he loved and studied the diction of *The Greek Anthology*. There may be speculation how it was that the Worcestershire-bred man chose to place the local habitation for his feelings in an adjacent county. Sometimes in later life Housman disclaimed any special affinity with Shropshire. 'Very little in the book', he said of *A Shropshire Lad*, 'is autobiographical.' Now that I am away from Shropshire, I may quote Housman's disclaimer. 'I had', he said, 'a sentimental feeling for Shropshire because its hills were our western horizon. I know Ludlow and Wenlock, but my topographical details – Hughley, Abdon-under-Clee – are sometimes quite wrong.' When Housman first put the collection of poems together for offering to Macmillans the title he provided was '*Poems* by Terence Hearsay'; it is not surprising that the offering so entitled was declined. It was Housman's friend Alfred Pollard who suggested that *A Shropshire Lad* would be an appealing title. Possibly Pollard divined that the associations with Shropshire were more real than Housman had wished openly to admit.

Having taken departure along Maida Vale (Browning to the left, and Lord's Cricket Ground and the Hospital of St John and St Elizabeth to the right – where Francis Thompson died in 1907) I find few pauses to make until past the Welsh Harp (my guess is that was the most populous of Blake's 'ponds where Boys to bathe delight') and indeed past Edgware – except at Harrow on the Hill. Among Harrow schoolboys who turned to literature in the eighteenth century was Richard Brinsley Sheridan, who, after leaving school, returned to live in The Grove, on the north side of the church. While living at The Grove Sheridan won success as a playwright; his early comedy, *The Rivals*, was when first produced a failure, but the man who had fought two duels to win his wife did not lack either courage or wit to try the stage again. *The School for Scandal* was among the productions for which Sheridan became rapidly famous. When he had ceased to live at The Grove it presently became a school boarding-house. In a subsequent generation Byron was at Harrow from 1801 to 1805; there he proved to be an indifferent scholar, a considerable reader, and a good boxer and batsman, despite his lameness. The church at Harrow, with its slender tall white spire making, on the hilltop, so notable a landmark that the Prince Regent considered it to epitomize 'the Church Visible', returned to Byron's memory in 1822 in a way that provoked by intention or not, parochial embarrassment.

That story recalls the short life of Byron's daughter, the child born into such unhappy circumstances as made her seem to have been misnamed Allegra. When Byron had escaped from Dover to the Continent in 1816, he was met in that summer at Sécheron by Shelley, who was accompanied by Mary Godwin and Mary's stepsister, Clara Mary Jane Clairmont, who called herself 'Claire'. Thereafter Claire, pregnant by Byron, returned to England with the Shelleys in August and Allegra was born at Bath in January 1817. Byron evaded all Claire's efforts to rejoin him, yet in 1818 he acquiesced in the despatch of the baby to Venice, for him to accept and bring up. The wife of the British Consul in Venice then came to Allegra's rescue; yet as Byron kept moving, on Allegra's fifth birthday he placed her in a convent near Ravenna. Three months after that, in 1822, the child died. It may be that Byron thought again of his own 'Lines Written Beneath an Elm in the Churchyard of Harrow', in which, when he was eighteen, he had expressed the wish that 'here my heart might lie'. At any rate it is reported that he was determined that Allegra's body should be transported to Harrow and buried in Harrow's church. Thus came the problem for Harrow; was one who had disowned allegiance to the Church to claim church burial as of right for his illegitimate child? The conclusion (I am told) was that the body of the ill-starred Allegra was accepted for interment within the porch.

Anthony Trollope was not in happy circumstances when he was a boy at Harrow. In his childhood the family had been comfortable in a fine house called Julians on the south side of Harrow Hill, and then were in a nearby smaller farmhouse, Julians Hill – which later reappears in Trollope's *Orley Farm*. Trollope himself, in 1827 at the age of twelve, was entered at Harrow School as a town-boy. The disadvantage to him of this status might not have caused unhappiness if the family home had been stable; but the half-baked father was setting off on the wild American adventure which resulted in the building of Trollope's Bazaar in Cincinnati. That building, locally spoken of as 'Trollope's Folly', remained in Cincinnati long after the total failure of the adventure – Harriet Martineau mentioned the Trollope building in 1838 as 'the great deformity of the city'. For Anthony the American adventure meant that his father, his elder brother and his mother – described as 'a vulgar, brisk and good-natured kind of well-bred hen-wife, fond of a joke and not troubled with squeamishness' – were all far away while he was an awkward penniless teenager being kicked around at school. With her immense energy, on her return the mother (Frances Trollope) set to work at writing her *Domestic Manners of the Americans* which, when published in 1832, caused a furore and put her in the way of repairing, by incessant further writings, the finances so totally dissipated by her husband. He rewarded himself by complete immersion, till death stopped him, in his unfinished ecclesiastical encyclopedia. Home life for Anthony's later years as day-boy at Harrow was spent at the 'wretched tumbledown farmhouse' at Harrow Weald, three miles away, to which Mrs Trollope had been forced to move her husband. Anthony walked the three miles of dirty lanes twice a day to the school which he hated, to return to a home where both parents were far too preoccupied to show any interest in him. Release from both school and home came when he was nineteen. Then, in 1834, Trollope escaped from Harrow to become a junior clerk at £90 a year, in the London General Post Office at St Martin's-le-Grand.

Most famous of all recent Harrovians is undoubtedly Winston Churchill, who wrote of his schooldays in *My Early Life*. Of those who have lived at Harrow without special connection with the school, I think in the nineteenth century of Matthew Arnold, and in our time of the painter-writer David Jones. On returning to the Edgware Road by way of Harrow Weald, there is recollection of W. S. Gilbert at the edge of Harrow Weald Common. In 1890 Gilbert gave up the town house in Harrington Gardens which he had designed in his peculiar combination of medieval Dutch and Victorian English styles, and bought a house and estate at Harrow Weald, partly for the pleasure of the small lake within the grounds. But in the very warm summer of 1911, when one of his guests, a young lady, got into difficulties while swimming, Gilbert suffered a heart attack in the sudden exertion of the rescue, and died at the age of seventy-five. After cremation his ashes were buried in Great Stanmore churchyard.

* * *

The Edgware Road, continuing past Edgware, though steadily bearing the label A5, is locally defined as Elstree Road until at the crossroads after Elstree Hill that part of Elstree Road turns sharp left, taking its name with it. The straight road ahead at the crossroads is hereabouts taken to be the true beginning of Watling Street. A pub, a school building and churches (both Established and Nonconformist) and what was anciently a blacksmith's forge, and remains a 'Blacksmith Fabricator', support the view. The road now is Watling Street, past Aldenham Park and Kendal Wood, and straight through Radlett and Watford North. Momently the street is forced off course by modern St Albans, but the ancient line of it is soon resumed, and Watling Street, having at times divided the island of Britain as a tide-rip marks division in the sea, proceeds in its great curve across the Midlands – on the map the eye makes short steps on to Dunstable and Stony Stratford, then longer strides past Rugby to Tamworth and Shrewsbury, and may choose then to fork either to Holyhead or to Chester and Liverpool.

The solidity of the Roman remains at St Albans induces anyone to believe that the great link-road across the land to Chester was intended to last. A double purpose as rampart and as military road makes itself felt. As road, one feels it ever ready for heavy duty. The 'street' was not engineered to be scenic or pretty, nor was it prettiness that counted when it was fought over by Saxons and Danes. Its practical utility for any kind of rough and ready use – and devil take the hindmost – is dominant in the character of Watling Street. Indeed, that most sovereign action of all – outrunning the devil – was Wyclif's reason for valuing the street, and for setting up his Bible factory at Lutterworth. Rough and ready was the conduct Watling Street continued to call for; even if a preacher preached complete non-violence he might have to speak with vehemence, as indeed George Fox (born beside this road at Fenny Drayton) spoke to those who drew swords at him. A road in every way accoutred to heavy duty, but not a road on which to carry, without most cautious packaging, a precision instrument of unusually delicate balance. Perhaps this should have warned of what was to happen in 1737 when William Cowper, after the death of his mother, was sent at the age of six to the boarding-school at Markyate Street, a little market town a few miles north of St Albans on Watling Street.

The first six years in the life of the small human atomy called William Cowper were spent in his father's comfortable rectory of Great Berkhamsted; the child had the patronym of his prosperous Anglican parent, who had an amiable reputation as composer and singer of ballads. As for the child's nature, it may be that a chief share came from his mother, whose family were the Donnes who had generated the great seventeenth-century 'metaphysical' poet and Dean of St Paul's, John Donne. Yet when Cowper's mother died, his father, with no doubt best intentions of toughening the previously 'mother's boy', sent the innocent to board in the bullying exercise-ground of Watling Street. The result of the Markyate Street school, for a six-year-old child devoid of aggressiveness, was to turn him (as Lord David Cecil expresses it in his biography of Cowper, *The Stricken Deer*) into a 'quivering jelly of fear'. How long

that period of total torment lasted is not precisely measurable, and at
one of his most homesick moments a vivid vision did come to him of his
mother reading to him and a fragment of the words from her Bible: 'I
fear nothing that man can do unto me.' The strength of a spiritual
exaltation did, for its moment, flicker intensely. That moment vanished.
'But that moment', says Lord David Cecil, 'had made as deep an impression on him as the sufferings that preceded it. He never forgot what
he had felt. In the brief prologue of his first school-time, the two
protagonists of his mental tragedy, the demon of his despair and the
angel of his consolation, had both made their appearance on the stage.'

After the nearly fatal experiment of Markyate Street, the remainder
of Cowper's school-years at Westminster went on with no apparent
breakdowns. At Westminster he boarded, made good friends, did well in
scholarship and at cricket, and on 'leave-out' days went with other boys
on usual excursions. Schoolboy outings included a visit to stare at the
lunatics at Bedlam, and he recorded that along with his companions 'it
was impossible not to be entertained' at the conduct of the poor cap-
tives, 'at the same time that I was angry with myself for being so'. His
own highly strung spiritual and mental nature showed as yet no overt
signs of derangement; between the ages of twelve and twenty the
periods of overconscientious depressions and insecurities seemed little
more than normal nervous sicknesses. It was in the next decade, when
he had spent years in desultory preparation for the law, and was a
young barrister with rooms in the Temple, that 'the demon of his
despair' really and fearfully got at Cowper. Unnecessary here to attempt
to trace the increasing torments Cowper suffered before his first and
apparently total collapse; suffice it to say that in 1761 his brother John,
now a don at Cambridge, arrived at the Temple to find the nervous,
scholarly barrister in the agony of repeated efforts at suicide. Cowper's
hallucinations had actually increased his torment; even self-destruction
failed. John Cowper had no alternative but to conduct his insane
brother to Dr Cotton's Home for Madmen at St Albans, where at first
he had to be tied to his bed for fear he should succeed in killing himself.

The fact that John Cowper was able to place William with Dr Cotton
and avoid the horrors of Bedlam was a wonderful mercy, for not only
was Cotton a wise, experienced physician but in religion he was a
moderate Evangelical, and able presently to talk with Cowper in the
same language. For when after months of nursing Cowper's physical
and mental health was better, there was a day when he felt God's grace
had come upon him, and his conversion to the faith of the Evangelicals
was ecstatic. In his first euphoria, 'Lyrically, incoherently, garrulously,
he proclaimed and re-proclaimed the glory of his redemption. The
quiet Hertfordshire garden used to ring with his rhapsodies. . . . Poor

Dr Cotton! He sometimes wondered if Cowper saved was much saner than Cowper damned.'

After more than a year, in May 1765, when Cowper was thirty-four, Lord David Cecil describes him as safe to leave St Albans. 'But where was he to go?' That was when, and with John Cowper's help, the good angel stepped in; for brother John found lodgings for Cowper at Huntingdon, and the good angel arranged that there he should presently join the household of the pious Unwin family, and begin to learn the pleasures of gardening. When the elderly Mr Unwin died after a bad fall from his horse and the Huntingdon home perforce broke up, the natural arrangement was for Cowper and Mrs Unwin to set up house together. Then the dynamic Evangelical clergyman John Newton (author of the hymn 'Amazing Grace') decided that the pair should settle as close as might be to his pulpit, which meant that Cowper would be living at Olney, a little to the north of Watling Street, just north of the modern town of Milton Keynes. There Cowper was to remain for the period which was most creative for his poetry, from 1773 to 1786.

Bletchley and Milton Keynes, prominent on most maps nowadays, were scarcely noticeable in Cowper's eighteenth century. Newport Pagnell, in the preceding century, was well established: Gayhurst, the estate where Sir Kenelm Digby was born and which he inherited, was close and at Newport Pagnell in the first phase of the Civil War there was maintained a Parliamentary garrison, in which it is supposed John Bunyan served from his sixteenth till his eighteenth year. Bunyan's characters Greatheart, Valiant-for-Truth, and Saddai's captains in *The Holy War* are taken as evidence of his service with fighting-men who, in Cromwell's phrase, knew what they fought for and loved what they knew. In Cowper's time, life was outwardly composed in this northern corner of Buckinghamshire. Many of the fields were brilliantly yellow with the mustard for which Newport was famous. The life of the country-side, hard as it was for the farm labourer, was even for him and his family not wholly devoid of humour. At Stony Stratford, which is in the Newport 'Hundred', the Bull and the Cock had been rival inns from ancient times; they are side by side and their rivalry in producing tall tales is said to have given rise to the phrase 'a cock and bull story'. The fine steeple of Hanslope Church, nearer to Olney, led to the twisting of one tall story into a Buckinghamshire riddle: 'If Hanslope Spire was ten times higher, I could still take off my shoe and hop over it.' An old inhabitant, who had been a child in Newport Hundred, said he found this very confusing until it was spelled out.

To this 'tame and trivial' area, as it might seem then, came Cowper and Mrs Unwin, though not long after arrival at Olney, partly as a result of his brother John's unexpected death, he suffered a recurrence of despairs and a breakdown even worse than that of ten years earlier. This time, what saved him was a two-year period of day and night attendance by the devoted Mrs Unwin. After this second recovery he did not become euphoric yet achieved a measure of happiness from the garden, the neighbouring countryside, and the three hares which kindly neighbours had presented as pets. These hares ('Bess, Puss and Tiny') became for a long time a dominating interest in his life. But the appalling strain of coping with that two years' illness of Cowper's impaired Mrs Unwin's own health for ever.

As Cowper's health returned their life together paced forward slowly, gently, within its small circumference. I take it that with Mary Unwin guarding their joint income there was enough for modest upkeep, even for Cowper to display in dress what Lord David Cecil calls 'a sober foppishness': when clad for the afternoon in blue coat and green satin waistcoat, he himself said that he looked, as he approached the age of fifty, 'a very smart youth for his years'. His days in summer were often spent in the garden, where presently he had a tiny greenhouse, in which he could grow rarities, even a New Zealand flower only recently brought back by Captain Cook, called the Browallia – when he called to Mary to come and see the blossom they agreed it was 'the most elegant flower they had ever seen'. In winter Cowper's days were mostly confined to the little wainscoted parlour of Orchard Side where, and especially of an evening, Mary and he would sit together and he would read aloud to her and they would talk or relapse into a placid silence. Sometimes when the none-too-steady card table on which they had had tea had been cleared and candles lit, Cowper would pass the time penning a letter of what Lamb called his 'divine chit-chat', such as this to Mary Unwin's son William in 1778:

We are indebted to you for your political intelligence, but have it not in our power to pay you in kind. Proceed, however, to give us such information as cannot be learned from the newspaper; and when anything arises at Olney, that is not in the threadbare style of daily occurrences, you shall hear of it in return. Nothing of this sort has happened lately, except that a lion was imported here at the fair, seventy years of age, and was as tame as a goose. Your mother and I saw him embrace his keeper with his paws, and lick his face. Others saw him receive his head in his mouth, and restore it to him again unhurt – a sight we chose not to be favoured with, but rather advised the honest man to discontinue the practice – a practice hardly reconcilable to prudence, unless he had a head to spare.

As the correspondence continues, Cowper is presently enclosing verses that he has written:

I shall charge you a half penny apiece for every copy I send you, the short as well as the long. This is a sort of afterclap you little expected, but I cannot possibly afford them at a cheaper rate . . .

The ease and fun of Cowper's chitchat in the letters and verses in the first years at Olney suggest that he was eager for some excitement to be added to the Olney routine. Wherefore on an afternoon in July 1781 Cowper's good angel arranged that into sight from his parlour window there appeared two ladies, one known to him ('wife of the clergyman of the neighbouring village of Clifton') but the other an unknown and instantly attractive visitor. Impulsively Cowper at once besought Mrs Unwin to ask the ladies in to tea; they accepted; the visiting widow, Lady Austen, was as instantly charmed by Cowper as he was by her – and for the next three years she, Cowper and Mary Unwin were close companions. I say the good angel had a hand in this for the companionship was now perfect to awake Cowper's talents to the full.

In 1782 Lady Austen rented the neighbouring house with garden which adjoined Cowper's Orchard Side; a door was cut in the garden wall; and for hardly a moment were the three separated. Cowper preened himself on their different modes of pleasing him. 'One of the ladies', he wrote, 'has been playing on the harpsichord, while I, with the other, have been playing at battledore and shuttlecock.' Of an evening all three sat together, and when Cowper's malady threatened to return – each approaching winter brought its threat – it was Anna with her vivacity who had new means of diverting the sudden fits of gloom with which insanity began. Lord David Cecil provides the marvellous account of how Anna with Mary abetting staved off one acute threat by forcing Cowper's attention to her high-hearted story about John Gilpin. Her well-told story, once she had made it captivate him, roused him from dejection and led him to lie awake that night putting it into verse. When he wrote and recited it to them Anna and Mary both were so delighted, and Cowper also, that arranging for publication of *John Gilpin*, and then the comic poem's success in London, saw him through that winter, safe from madness. More than that, Anna's faith in his powers gave him faith also to produce more than comic poems. She had both faith and wit to start him off. Let me quote Lord David Cecil about Lady Austen urging Cowper to write a meditative poem in blank verse.

'I have no subject,' he said.
'Write about anything,' she returned impetuously. 'Write about the sofa.'
He took her at her word. And a few days later, began a poem which started, as required, about the sofa, but gradually blossomed into something bigger; in fact, into the biggest work he ever wrote: 'The Task.'

The six books of *The Task*, with their many lasting pleasures for readers of maturity and leisure, were also a health-giving activity to Cowper; he was now well started into the creative period which out-lasted the triangular ménage at Olney. The good angel who had brought Anna Austen into Cowper's life in 1781 removed her from it in the summer of 1784. 'No man in the world', says Lord David Cecil, 'can live permanently in the same house with two strong-willed women, both violently in love with him.' Anna was the one to go, and the good angel so arranged it that after a while she found a French husband and was whirled away to live in France. She had been a livening and wonderful companion for the short term, but had the rivalries had much further time to develop, some fuses somewhere would have blown. Anna's de-parture did not remove the stimulus that she had given Cowper; he was more of a fine fellow for having both attracted that entrancer and put her away. With renewed contentment Cowper resumed growing his cucumbers on their stercoraceous heap, and arm in arm with Mary Unwin – so long as her health lasted – strolled, with an eye that was ever attentive to the slightest of nature's changes, toward Weston Under-wood. There, less than two miles from Olney (in the direction of the Hanslope spire which reminded you to take off your shoe and hop over it) Cowper and Mary found new congenial friends with whom to taste 'the cups that cheer but not inebriate' (a phrase which, by the way, he borrowed from Berkeley's *Siris*). Elsewhere in this book, at Chichester and in Norfolk, I have followed Cowper and Mary as, for so long as they could, they supported each other after the long period, with mo-ments good to remember, at Olney and Weston Underwood.

2. THE COUNTRY OF GEORGE ELIOT AND RUPERT BROOKE

Something to read was an increasing necessity through the eighteenth century. 'Tickle and entertain us, or we die', said Cowper, commenting in part on the spate of 'sensation-novels' that were becoming available. New ground for romantic fiction had been, as Bonamy Dobrée has said, 'volcanically broken' by the appearance of Horace Walpole's *The Castle of Otranto* in 1764. In that year Ann Ward, later Mrs Radcliffe, was born. Ann Radcliffe is to be associated with my present journey partly because when she died in 1832 she was buried in St John's churchyard just north of Hyde Park near the beginning of the Edgware Road, but more particularly because most of her travels were on, or bounded by, Watling Street. She was a Londoner by birth and upbringing; a sufferer all her life from asthma. After her marriage at the age of twenty-three to an Oxford graduate who was studying for the law, both she and her husband lived quietly in the neighbourhood of Gray's Inn, a chief excitement being holiday jaunts by carriage to St Albans, or more adventurously but still within the bounds of Watling Street, into Warwickshire. Her fancied travels were not so bounded. Confined by her health much of the time to her London fireside and less from any particular wish to enter literary life than for self-entertainment, she began writing the novels of which the most famous was the four-volume *The Mysteries of Udolpho*. That work, immediately after its publication in 1794, became and for at least fifty years remained, again to quote Professor Dobrée, a 'must' for all readers of fiction. Not only did Jane Austen assume that readers would automatically pick up allusions to characters and episodes in *The Mysteries of Udolpho*, but Thackeray, writing in 1840, could make the same assumption.

It was to the characters in Ann Radcliffe's novels that Thackeray chiefly referred; Jane Austen pokes fun at the romanticized scenery and settings which attracted Ann Radcliffe's readers and made her, as De Quincey said, 'the great enchantress of that generation'. Her glamorous descriptions of the scenery in southern France and 'Swizzerland' and Italy were wholly derived from pictures and prints. She and her husband managed one trip abroad, to Holland and the borders of Germany; but the settings of *Udolpho* were entirely from 'Phantasie'. The Radcliffe influence was so strong a help in bringing about a type of make-believe to which other writers could appeal, that Scott entitled her 'the first poetic novelist' in English literature. As for poets, Dobrée quotes the amusing statement that 'Byron modelled his scowl on that of Schedoni' (one of Ann Radcliffe's characters) and indicates how Keats took full advantage of romantic traditions formed by *Udolpho*. In private letters Keats made fun of the way in which the often housebound Ann Radcliffe heightened her imagined scenic settings. In a letter to Reynolds in 1818 Keats proposed 'to tip you a Damosel Radcliffe – I'll cavern you, and grotto you, and waterfall you, and wood you, and immense-rock you, and tremendous sound you, and solitude you' – yet at the same time he was choosing what he calls 'fine Mother Radcliffe names' for his poems. Although privately apologizing 'it is not my fault – I do not search for them', Keats specifies 'the Pot of Basil, St Agnes Eve and the Eve of St Mark' as 'Radcliffe' titles that lay to his hand. Likewise, conventional trappings of Gothic romance were so much accepted and expected that Keats without question adopted them. Martha Hale Shackford observed that common to both *Udolpho* and Keats's 'The Eve of St Agnes' are not only 'the solid grandeur of the ancient Gothic castle, with shadowy galleries, moonlit casements, and gorgeous apartments hung with arras glowing with medieval pageantry', with old retainers serving an arrogant master and his carousing friends – and the lonely maiden – but also 'even the lute left conveniently lying about to assuage the heroine's melancholy moments'.

When Ann Radcliffe and her husband drove out from London and along Watling Street and (as she recorded) into Warwickshire, it was a holiday from writing thrillers. In the same part of Warwickshire at which the Radcliffes looked as summer visitors from London, there grew up as native to it the girl who later chose the pen-name 'George Eliot'. It is interesting that as the world revolves towards the end of the twentieth century, George Eliot's stature as novelist is far from diminishing. In an issue of *The New Yorker* in 1976 I notice the instruction that *Middlemarch* remains 'the most adult, comprehensive fiction in English literature'. The country girl whose writings were to cause such admiration far away in space and time was born on the estate of Arbury, near Nuneaton, in 1819; her name was Mary Ann Evans, her father was land steward to the estate, and when as a child she drove with him among the Warwickshire farms not only were her own eyes observant but she also learned much from her father's comments. The drives with her father were recalled in a passage in *Middlemarch*, as she remembered how they lay through

. . . a pretty bit of midland landscape, almost all meadows and pastures, with hedgerows still allowed to grow in bushy beauty and to spread out coral fruit for the birds. Little details gave each field a particular physiognomy, dear to the eyes that have looked on them from childhood: the pool in the corner where the grasses were dank and trees leaned whisperingly; the great oak shadowing a bare place in mid-pasture; the high bank where the ash-trees grew; the sudden slope of the old marl-pit making a red background for the burdock; the huddled roofs and ricks of the homestead without a traceable way of approach; the grey gate and fences against the depths of the bordering wood; and the stray hovel, its old, old thatch full of mossy hills and valleys with wondrous modulations of light and shadow such as we travel far to see in later life, and see larger, but not more beautiful. These are the things that make the gamut of joy in landscape to midland-bred souls – the things they toddled among, or perhaps learned by heart standing between their father's knees while he drove leisurely.

Henry James in his *English Hours* saw this part of Warwickshire, not then endangered by the outspreading growth of Coventry, as sturdily and centrally 'George Eliot's country'. To his American audience James reported:

It was in one of the old nestling farmhouses, beyond a hundred hedgerows, that Hetty Sorrel smiled into her milk-pans as if she were looking for a reflection of her pretty face; it was at the end of one of the leafy-pillared avenues that poor Mrs Casaubon paced up and down with her many questions. The country suggests in especial both the social and the natural scenery of *Middlemarch*.

Yet it is of singular interest to watch the battle Mary Ann Evans had to grow into her full human development in the 'social scenery' of her native countryside. A firm Evangelical in girlhood, she became as firm a freethinker in her twenties, when living with her father in Coventry to which he had by then moved. The 'movement and mixture' of the old provincial society described in *Middlemarch* did not supply, or at least in Coventry she did not find, the full nourishment she craved: Virginia Woolf wrote with understandable sympathy of Mary Ann Evans in youth as in maturity 'reaching out with "a fastidious yet hungry ambition" for all that life could offer the free and inquiring mind and confronting her feminine aspirations with the real world of men'. When she was thirty her father died and presently she lit out for a year of study at Geneva. There she worked hard and on return to England, with the intention of writing for the *Westminster Review*, sought successfully to live as paying guest in the house of the editor, at No. 142 Strand, London. Before long she was the indispensable assistant editor of the review, and her life might have continued as that of a subordinate editor, essayist and translator if the editor and Herbert Spencer had not introduced her to the clever George Henry Lewes, 'a sort of miniature Mirabeau in appearance', and just the man, as it proved, to perceive and nurse the genius latent in Mary Ann Evans.

Lewes was separated from his wife but her existence and that of Lewes's school-age sons were impediments to the completely shared life together without which Lewes could hardly have provided for her genius the catalytic agency for which that 'miniature Mirabeau' is now chiefly remembered. In 1854, however, the permanent union with Lewes began, and under his masterly prompting in her late thirties her gift for fiction came into its flowering. Lewes acted initially as salesman for her *Scenes of Clerical Life*, and the pen-name of George Eliot was a joint composition – she chose 'George' because it was Lewes's name, and 'Eliot' they both felt to be 'a good mouth-filling easily-pronounced word'. The publication of *Scenes of Clerical Life* and subsequently of *Adam Bede* with their distinct vein of thought and feeling caused much speculation about the identity of George Eliot. Dickens thought he recognized a 'woman's hand', while Thackeray was sure they were 'not written by a woman'. One characteristic of George Eliot was a much closer understanding of the spirit in the Midlands of Nonconformity, and of the heritage of Dissent along the tide-rip of Watling Street, than had been exhibited by other novelists; another characteristic was the vein of humour which gave to Leslie Stephen such intense delight in *Silas Marner*:

It might throw some light upon George Eliot's peculiar power if we could fairly analyse the charm of that little masterpiece. . . . Why are we charmed [in the party in the 'Rainbow' parlour] by Ben Winthorp's retort to the parish clerk: 'It's your inside as isn't right made for music; it's no better nor a hollow stalk;' and the statement that this 'unflinching frankness was regarded by the company as the most piquant form of joke;' or by the landlord's ingenious remarks upon the analogy between a power of smelling cheeses and perceiving the supernatural; or by that quaint stumble into something surprising to the speaker himself by its apparent resemblance to witty repartee, when the same person says to the farrier: 'You're a doctor, I reckon, though you're only a cow-doctor; for a fly's a fly, though it may be a horsefly'?

Leslie Stephen enjoyed the great spirit of sympathy with which George Eliot gathered into a large grasp a great bunch of the main elements of human nature in the English Midlands; for that he compared her with Scott, Fielding and Thackeray for what they had done, each in another special sphere. Leslie Stephen's daughter, who became Virginia Woolf, yielded to nobody in admiration for 'the mature *Middlemarch*, the magnificent book which with all its imperfections is one of the few English novels written for grown-up people'. (Re-reading *Middlemarch*, how up-to-date more than a century afterwards is her incidental use of such a phrase as 'bloody-mindedness'.) Detached amusement was part of the pleasure with which Leslie Stephen read George Eliot, but his daughter Virginia Woolf read with much more passionate identification with the woman within, the 'troubled spirit, that exacting and questioning and baffled presence who was George Eliot herself'. Leaving aside others of George Eliot's characters in which the novelist 'shows herself', there is poignancy in Virginia Woolf's special and intimate attention to *Middlemarch* 'and Dorothea seeking wisdom and finding one scarcely knows what in marriage with Ladislaw'.

*　　*　　*

Without moving off the modern roadway one can watch for an inconspicuous low brick parapet signifying a small stream beneath. Underneath the red-brick parapet there is indeed one of the channels, not wide, which is carrying through the water-meadows swift-moving waters of the little River Swift, the stream which having just passed Lutterworth to the north is on its way to join the Avon. Why pause for the River Swift, which is easy to cross without noticing? Remember John Wyclif and his achievement.

John Wyclif, spoken of in older centuries as 'the morning star of the Reformation', was of Yorkshire stock – his family took its name from Wycliffe-on-Tees in the heart of the Danelaw – but it was as rector of Lutterworth, resident in that parish until his death in 1384, that he raised his very lasting stir against the then overlords of the Church in England. The firmness of his stand that the Bible was man's true source of knowledge of God's will, coupled with determination to make the full text of the Scriptures available to all Englishmen in English, set him not only to organizing translation work at Lutterworth but also to send forth his band of Poor Preachers. At first, in 1377, Wyclif's Poor Preachers were priests in close agreement with him, living under a rule of poverty and footing up and down the length of Watling Street preaching and teaching Bible Christianity. Presently other laymen and 'Lollards' who preached differing and violent remedies for social discontent were by many confusingly identified with the Poor Preachers, and after the general alarm and cross-currents of fury of the Peasants' Revolt of 1381, a feeling grew that Wyclif had been, by his dissent from orthodoxy, a dangerous instigator.

Personal violence to Wyclif as a Dissenter was not strenuously offered in the short years of his life after the Peasants' Revolt was suppressed. For those two years he lived and went on preaching, writing and translating at Lutterworth until, at about the age of sixty-five, a stroke resulted in paralysis and death. But in 1428, forty-four years after Wyclif's burial at Lutterworth, indignity was done to his coffin. Rivals of Richard Fleming, Bishop of Lincoln, dragged up the scandal that, when younger, Fleming had been a Wycliffite. The Bishop himself was condemned to prove his later orthodoxy by having Wyclif's remains exhumed, removed from Lutterworth churchyard and flung into the River Swift, which joins the headwaters of the Avon at Rugby. The memory of what had been done to Wyclif's body in 1428 was preserved from generation to generation of Dissenters by the rhyme which reads (in modern spelling):

> The Avon to the Severn runs,
>   The Severn to the sea;
> And Wyclif's dust shall spread abroad
>   Wide as the waters be.

Literary associations immediately remembered at Rugby relate less to the joining of the little rivers, Swift with Avon, than to the school which came to great fame in the nineteenth century not alone for 'Rugby football' but for its influence on such men when young as Walter Savage Landor, Matthew Arnold, Arthur Hugh Clough and 'Lewis Carroll'. In the twentieth century I think of Rugby School especially in connection with two distinctively different schoolboys, Wyndham Lewis and Rupert Brooke. Lewis (1884–1957), born off the coast of Maine in his father's yacht, was placed by his mother, when she came to England, at school at Rugby. I think that Lewis, even as a schoolboy, must have been inordinately suspicious of other people, and to other schoolboys at Rugby he very likely seemed an unattractive oddity. Brooke (1887–1915), though three years younger than Lewis, was son of a house-master, and even before his own schooling was very much an alert and active part of the whole establishment. As a boy Brooke was probably wholly unaware of such a restive ugly duckling as I imagine Lewis to have been before he was at length removed to practise painting at the Slade School of Fine Art.

Looking backward it is easy to conclude that the Lewis who was something of a dropout at Rugby was actually at heart a good deal more sure of himself than the Brooke to whom at school admiration was attached with an extraordinary readiness, both by his elders and by companions of his own age. As a boy he was obvious for his intelligence, good looks, and unusual capacity to charm. Still a schoolboy, he was scrutinized by Lytton Strachey as a likely candidate, if he should be going to Cambridge, for election to the Society of Apostles – that selective Cambridge fraternity admitted a few undergraduates into close companionship, in termtime and in vacations, with elders such as Bertrand Russell and G. E. Moore, E. M. Forster and Lowes Dickinson, Maynard Keynes and Lytton Strachey himself. Rupert Brooke, aware that he was being discussed for this secret society under a code-term 'Sarawak' (because of a fancied connection with the Brookes who were Rajahs of Sarawak), was nicknaming his mother 'the Ranee' even before he was at Cambridge. There he was then subjected to the powerful flattery of quick acceptance by the Apostles – 'it is terrible to move in the best society' was his mock-humble report about that, to 'the Ranee'. Presently his natural ability as an actor, his good looks, and his graceful gifts for 'serious light verse' all contributed to his being likened to 'young Apollo'. That phrase was first applied to Brooke by Frances Cornford, and later was by her much regretted, for the amount of adulation heaped upon Brooke in his Cambridge career made it extra difficult for him to learn to know himself and come to terms with his real condition of inward insecurity.

Looking at the years in England immediately before 1914, one has to remember that many of the then young poets who later moved in contrary directions were not as yet hostile to one another. For example, in October 1912 Ezra Pound (two of whose poems had been chosen by Quiller-Couch for inclusion in *The Oxford Book of Victorian Verse*) was commended by Brooke to Edward Marsh and was invited, with T. E.

Hulme, Wilfred Gibson and all of Marsh's other choices, to contribute to the first 'Georgian' anthology to be published by Harold Monro at the Poetry Bookshop. Seeking out and meeting other poets was a main and energetic occupation of Brooke's in 1912, an activity conducted in parallel with working for the Fellowship at King's College which he was awarded in March 1913. I find no mention of any attempt by Brooke to look up his fellow-Rugbeian Wyndham Lewis, but the tally of the poets with whom he tried to establish personal friendship was large. Writing to Mrs Cornford about the 'lot of poets' he had been meeting, Brooke expressed the feeling 'they *were* so nice: very simple, and very good-hearted. I felt I'd like, almost, to live with them always (and protect them).' Edward Marsh was doing much to establish Brooke in a position above the ordinary: the dinner party he arranged at his rooms in Gray's Inn to celebrate Brooke's Fellowship was made up of Yeats, Brooke and their host as the three men, and Miss Violet Asquith (the Prime Minister's daughter), Lady Cynthia Asquith, and Mrs Winston Churchill as the three ladies. All the ladies were much pleased with Brooke. Yet the social whirl among top people and the success as poet (even the wish to be patron to other poets) did not conceal that Brooke was inwardly distressingly insecure. His love affairs, in particular the intense emotional relations with Ka Cox, had gone most disturbingly wrong. Brooke's understanding and trusted adviser, Frances Cornford, was urging him, he said, 'to go to America or somewhere for a year for Ka's sake, for mine, and for everybody's'. Lowes Dickinson offered to help him with the expenses.

Brooke's year of absence from England (May 1913 to June 1914) is recorded in Christopher Hassall's biography under the chapter title 'A Deep Sleep'. It seems as if only part of himself is in leisurely motion across North America and after that in the islands of the South Seas. On return to England he took the train to Rugby, and the greeting of 'the Ranee' at their home in Bilton Road was 'as if he had only been away for a long week-end'. He then rushed to London for a party to be arranged by Marsh, and he and Marsh became instantly busy planning a second volume of *Georgian Poetry*. After a renewal of superficial activity in various directions he was back at Rugby with his mother and younger brother for his twenty-seventh birthday on 3 August. On the 2nd, the last Sunday of the old world at peace, the brothers borrowed 'the Ranee's' car for a drive in Warwickshire. In a letter written that evening Brooke described the outing:

It's the sort of country I adore. I'm a Warwickshire man. Don't talk to me of Dartmoor or Snowdon or the Thames or the lakes. I know the *heart* of England. It has a hedgy, warm bountiful dimpled air. Baby fields run up and down the little hills, and all the roads wriggle with pleasure. There's a spirit of rare homeliness about the houses and the countryside, earthy, uneccentric yet elusive, fresh, meadowy, gaily gentle. It is perpetually June in Warwickshire, and always six o'clock of a warm afternoon. Of California the other States in America have this proverb: 'Flowers without scent, birds without song, men without honour, and women without virtue' – and at least three of the four sections of this proverb I know very well to be true. But Warwickshire is the exact opposite of that. Here the flowers smell of heaven; there are no such larks as ours, and no such nightingales; the men pay more than they owe; and the women have very great and wonderful virtue, and that, mind you, by no means through the mere absence of trial. In Warwickshire there are butterflies all the year round and a full moon every night. . . . Shakespeare and I are Warwickshire yokels. What a county!

'This', Brooke has the grace to add, 'is nonsense' – for Hampden-in-Arden, which the brothers had set out to visit, 'was just too full of the plutocracy of Birmingham, short, crafty, proudly vulgar men, for all the world like heroes of Arnold Bennett's novels'. Arden – a name to dream about: 'Perhaps one shouldn't have *gone* there', said Brooke. 'But it *is* lovely.'

In Brooke's 'first deep estrangement from one he loved' he had felt himself split into two halves, the upper part dashing aimlessly to and fro from one half-relevant thought to another, 'the lower, unconscious half labouring with some profound and unknowable change'. In his year of travel the feeling of duality went with him; travel had not shaken him together, nor did his return to England of itself heal the inward rift – part of its pain was that he would feel guilty if the wound were healable. Immediately after Brooke's birthday at Rugby, he set forth to join his closest of friends, the Cornfords, on the Norfolk coast. He arrived with an armful of newspapers with word of the ultimatum to Germany, and on the next morning he and the Cornfords woke to learn that England was at war. They uttered no words about that all day, but at evening, Rupert, alone with Frances, started talking of Ka. 'The best possible thing that could happen for her', he said, 'is that I should be blown to bits by a shell. Then she would marry someone else and be happy.' In the next months, into his complex of feelings about the war entered the sudden happiness of having the deep private turmoil of his own wholly resolved, his pain healed not by any action of his own, but by the overwhelming counter-effect of general disaster. In his biography Christopher Hassall points out this element of private happiness in Brooke's enlistment. 'If there was no other way out of the "muddle", as he called it, here was the chance not only of going blameless but with honour.' The war, then, effected Brooke's re-integration, and the happiness of being at one with himself, and more himself as one of a number with others, added much to the power of his '1914' series of poems.

Brooke had already drifted apart from some of the Apostles and from the Bloomsbury set in London – 'In fact Bloomsbury was against him and he against them', wrote Virginia Woolf – but though she thought him 'the ablest' of young men 'because he had such a gift with people' she did not think much of his poetry. Virginia Woolf stood up for Brooke when the others in Bloomsbury 'all cried him down'; yet it was the man, not the poet, that she admired; Brooke's war poems seemed to her mere 'barrel-organ music'. When in 1915 Brooke died in the hospital ship in the Aegean and was buried on Skyros before his companions reached Gallipoli, it was largely his own sonnet about 'some corner of a foreign field That is for ever England' but also in part the quick opportunism of Winston Churchill that made Rupert Brooke into a legend: he became 'the youth of our race in symbol'. The circulation of his poems posthumously increased throughout the war and throughout the postwar decade. On shipboard on the way to Gallipoli he had written to his mother that all monies that might have come to him after his debts were paid, including any royalties from his poems, were to go to three poets whom he named as his heirs: Wilfred Gibson, Lascelles Abercrombie, and Walter de la Mare. Hassall's biography records that the three heirs became materially blessed beyond their benefactor's dreams. The London publisher added up the sale of his main editions of Brooke's poems to the end of 1926 as amounting by then to 291,998 copies; a paper-bound edition and all of the sales in the USA and elsewhere were not included in that figure.

3. TO THE WELSH BORDER

Watling Street pursues its westward course, passing between Birmingham and Lichfield. Thirty years after Samuel Johnson and David Garrick left Lichfield by road from the Midlands to London, the Lunar Society of Birmingham was formed. This group grew to as many as fourteen ingenious, energetic individuals (including from the beginning Dr Erasmus Darwin of Lichfield, Josiah Wedgwood of Etruria, Matthew Boulton and, when they had arrived from Scotland, James Keir the chemist and James Watt the engineer) who from 1765 onwards met at Boulton's house near Birmingham on Mondays nearest to the full moon – moonlight made the journey easier for those who came from a distance. Ideas emergent from the Lunar Society were communicated to correspondents in Glasgow and Edinburgh; there were close ties with London and with experimental work on the Continent; letters passed to and fro between them and Benjamin Franklin in Philadelphia.

The home of the Franklin family, from which Benjamin's father had emigrated to New England, was some forty miles eastward (at Ecton, near Northampton); had father Franklin stayed at home, the forty miles of the Watling Street journey would hardly have prevented Ben from meeting with the Lunar Society – it was an active-minded club that would have suited him. It was likewise perfectly suited to Richard Lovell Edgeworth, the lively, inventive young Irishman who had called upon Dr Darwin at Lichfield in the summer of 1766, and whom Darwin promptly sponsored in Lichfield's social circle and as a member of the Lunar Society. Both introductions play a part in the story of Edgeworth's daughter, the novelist Maria Edgeworth. The Lichfield intellectuals offered to Edgeworth more excitement than he could find in the company of his first wife; when she died in 1773 at the age of thirty (having provided Edgeworth with five children in the nine years of marriage) he promptly, within four months of being a widower, married Honora Sneyd of Lichfield, 'a woman that equalled the picture of perfection'. Maria, who was five years old when her mother died, remembered little of her in later life except 'she did recollect that she was always crying'. Maria remembered her first stepmother Honora – she was to have two more stepmothers, for Edgeworth married four times – chiefly for the repressiveness of the new dispensation. It bore especially hard on the older Edgeworth children that Honora and Edgeworth were experimenting for his book on *Practical Education*. The story as it later reached Coleridge from the Wedgwoods was that 'the Edgeworths were most miserable when children; and yet the father in his book is ever vapourizing about their happiness'.

Yet Maria early and late did revere and love her father, and Mrs Marilyn Butler, in her recent book *Maria Edgeworth*, very effectively proves how her devotion to Edgeworth affected her own career and influence. Mrs Butler sees the importance of Erasmus Darwin, and Lichfield and the Lunar Society, in stimulating ideas which came to govern her own work. 'Through her devotion to Edgeworth, and despite herself, Maria brought Lunar practicality and the Lunar social ethos into the novel, and in doing so helped to set it on a course which it held for over half a century.'

The 'Lunar practicality' of the West Midlands, if brought into the novel by Maria Edgeworth, was strongly reinfused into fiction by George Eliot; in moving westward along my route I do not forget the memorial garden to George Eliot that is still to be found at Nuneaton. Yet the road leading me on between Lichfield and the northern outskirts of Birmingham has also and suddenly reminded me of something now vanished yet very much a feature of Midlands life until eliminated by 'the Lunar social ethos': I mean the road, in bypassing present-day

Walsall and Wolverhampton, has reminded me of Mumpers' Dingle.

At the end of *Lavengro* and at the beginning of *The Romany Rye* George Borrow is reasonably precise in his location of Mumpers' Dingle; it was near to Willenhall, where the gipsies took Borrow with them to church. Mr and Mrs Petulengro, and the gigantic Tawno Chikno also, all dressed partly in Romany fashion, by that action brought Borrow back to the custom of church-going, which for him had been for years interrupted. Willenhall is halfway between Walsall and Wolverhampton, but Mumpers' Dingle, where Borrow set up his forge, and which was a hollow where anyone was free to settle as he or she chose (there is a splendid engraving of it at page 444 of my edition of *Lavengro*) seems to have been exterminated. But in this neighbourhood in 1825 Mumpers' Dingle still existed. It was there that there was the visit of the Flaming Tinman, and the battle in which Borrow eventually felled the Tinman with the right-handed blow which caused the famous exclamation from Isopel Berners: 'Hurrah for Long Melford! There is nothing like Long Melford for shortness all the world over.' Since Borrow's success in this contest resulted in the instant transfer of Isopel's allegiance to him and since his life with that proud girl in the dingle continued for the last sixteen chapters of *Lavengro* and the first sixteen chapters of *The Romany Rye*, there ought at least to be a memorial garden to record the dingle's existence. However, by the mid-nineteenth century the lane leading to Mumpers' Dingle was being called Momber or Monmer Lane, and Borrow's peripatetic smithy was replaced by the Monmer Lane Ironworks, and gipsy occupancy, as Jasper Petulengro foretold, was eliminated.

Escaping from the environs of Birmingham, the ancient route of Watling Street proceeds through Wellington to Shrewsbury. Before Wellington, a mile or two south of the road is Shifnal, which Dickens described in *The Old Curiosity Shop* and which claims attention also as the birthplace of the Thomas Brown who wrote 'I do not love thee, Dr Fell'. Inquisitive about the origin of so forceful a statement, I re-learned what was familiar to an older generation, that the Dr Fell was the famous seventeenth-century Dean of Christ Church College at Oxford who gave each member of his college each year a copy of some classical author. Such generous action failed to win the heart of the Salopian Tom Brown who had entered Christ Church in 1678, and, when he had struggled as far as the thirty-second epigram in the first book of Martial ('Non amo te, Sabidi, nec possum dicere quare'), turned it into the remembered lines:

> I do not love thee, Dr Fell.
> The reason why I cannot tell;
> But this I know, I know full well,
> I do not love thee, Dr Fell.

Shrewsbury, county town of Shropshire (now re-named with the old name Salop), where the town centre is on a rising peninsula almost wholly encircled by the Severn, is often recalled by Falstaff's claim to have slain Hotspur there after the single combat lasting 'a long hour by Shrewsbury clock'; or also by the famous school attended in their different centuries by Sir Philip Sidney, Fulke Greville, Judge Jeffreys, Charles Darwin and the Samuel Butler who wrote *Erewhon*. A statue of Darwin seated in bronze is in front of the Museum and Free Library; he was born in Shrewsbury, as also were Charles Burney, the musician, and John Reynolds, Keats's friend. Yet of the many memories which could be investigated, Hazlitt records a notable one. In the year 1798 Coleridge came to Shrewsbury by coach from Somerset, leaving Nether Stowey for a trial period as a Dissenting minister in spiritual charge of Shrewsbury's Unitarian congregation. He held the good town, so Hazlitt wrote twenty-five years later, 'in delightful suspense for three weeks that he remained there, "fluttering the *proud Salopians*, like an eagle in a dove-cote"'.

Ten years before, the Hazlitt family had returned from New England, where Hazlitt's father, himself a Dissenting minister, had founded the first Unitarian Church at Boston. The Hazlitts on return settled at Wem, ten miles north of Shrewsbury, and young William (at the age of twenty) lived with his parents, reading voraciously but very uncertain as to his own vocation. The father's wish that William Hazlitt might become a minister had been abandoned, yet the talk at Wem about Coleridge coming on trial to Shrewsbury incited young William to hear his first Shrewsbury sermon. 'A poet and a philosopher getting up into a Unitarian pulpit to preach the gospel, was a romance in these degenerate days, a sort of revival of the primitive spirit of Christianity, which was not to be resisted.' So, rising on a January morning before daylight, Hazlitt walked ten miles in the mud from Wem to Shrewsbury, to hear Coleridge preach. 'Never, the longest day I have to live,' he said later, 'shall I have such another walk as this cold, raw, comfortless one, in the winter of the year 1798.' Nevertheless the sermon was rewarding 'even beyond my hopes', and two days later, when Coleridge had already agreed to visit Wem to see the senior Mr Hazlitt 'according to the courtesy of the country', young William's 'rather resentful attitude towards the world' was for the moment very much changed.

Years after, in one of his own lectures, the glow with which Hazlitt spoke revealed the power that Coleridge had in the early days exerted on him, a power also exerted on such different characters as Charles Lamb, Southey, and Dorothy and William Wordsworth.

I may say of him here [Hazlitt said of Coleridge in that latter-day lecture] that he is the only person I ever knew who answered to the idea of a man of genius. He is the only person from whom I ever learnt anything. . . . His genius at that time had angelic wings, and fed on manna. He talked on for ever; and you wished him to talk on for ever. His thoughts did not seem to come with labour and effort; but as if borne on the gusts of genius, and as if the wings of his imagination lifted him from off his feet. His voice rolled on the ear like the pealing organ, and its sound alone was the music of thought. His mind was clothed with wings; and raised on them, he lifted philosophy to heaven.

Coleridge, 'the only person from whom I ever learnt anything', activated the young Hazlitt. On his visit to Wem he stayed overnight with the Hazlitts, and on the following morning the twenty-year-old William walked back toward Shrewsbury with him as far as the six-mile stone. Coleridge did the talking:

As we passed along between Wem and Shrewsbury, and I eyed their blue tops [the Welsh mountains] seen through the wintry branches, or the red rustling leaves of the sturdy oak-trees by the road-side, a sound was in my ears as of a Siren's song; I was stunned, startled with it, as from deep sleep; but I had no notion then that I should ever be able to express my admiration to others in motley imagery or quaint allusion, till the light of his genius shone into my soul, like the sun's rays glittering in the puddles of the road. I was at that time dumb, inarticulate, helpless, like a worm by the way-side, crushed, bleeding, lifeless; but now, bursting from the deadly bands that 'bound them,

'With Styx nine times round them',

my ideas float on winged words, and as they expand their plumes, catch the golden light of other years. My soul has indeed remained in its original bondage, dark, obscure, with longings infinite and unsatisfied; my heart, shut up in the prison-house of this rude clay, has never found, nor will it ever find, a heart to speak to; but that my understanding also did not remain dumb and brutish, or at length found a language to express itself, I owe to Coleridge.

Hazlitt's report of Coleridge's talk as they went along suggests that views that Coleridge had planned to express in two further sermons at Shrewsbury would have disqualified him from becoming the pastor of the congregation; but in fact such trial was evaded, for a letter just received from his friend Thomas Wedgwood offered him £150 a year, should he choose to waive the ministry and devote himself entirely to poetry and philosophy. Coleridge's undisguised pleasure at accepting the annuity and at thoughts of studying, perhaps abroad, did not prevent him noticing the woebegone expression of the awkward, tongue-tied Hazlitt. At the instant the young man was smitten with hero-worship, the hero was talking of departure! With ready affection Coleridge repeated his warm invitation, that Hazlitt should visit him at Nether Stowey. Sara's hospitality was taken for granted, and thus was Hazlitt winkled away from life with his parents at Wem and introduced into the active company of Coleridge's friends, and to the start of his own career.

* * *

Watling Street, which I have now followed far enough west to call the Holyhead Road, crosses the Welsh Border (the ancient north–south line of Offa's Dyke) beyond Oswestry; but one does not pass by Owestry without memory of the poet Wilfred Owen (1893–1918), who was born there. In this Welsh Border country, which had given birth to George Herbert, Henry Vaughan, Thomas Traherne, the arrival of another poet with some spiritual affinities to them is not unnatural. Vaughan and Traherne lived through actualities of war, yet the poetry for which they are remembered was mostly composed when actual combat was over. We don't know how Owen's poetry would have later developed, for after serving as infantry soldier in France throughout the trench warfare of the Great War, he was killed in November 1918, a week before the Armistice.

Owen himself mentions his awareness of 'poethood' as a child. He noted that his own 'poethood was born' during a happy visit to Broxton in Cheshire in the summer of 1903. After his schooldays, perhaps partly to please his mother, he became a lay assistant to the vicar of Dunsden. His religion deepened as he matured, but the narrowness of interpretations thrust at him by sectarianism led him to escape from Dunsden. Before 1914 he was supporting himself by schoolteaching and tutoring in France. Came then the war and his enlistment in the British army. Like Brooke and others, Owen felt the initial and normal elation at being recruited for expeditionary action: 'There is a fine heroic feeling about being in France', he wrote in 1915. But as trench war went on front-line troops in France stopped writing that way. Owen was with the Manchester Regiment on the Somme. Then on 16 January 1917 he wrote to his mother: 'I can see no excuse for deceiving you about these last 4 days. I have suffered seventh hell.' In the summer of 1917 Owen was in hospital at Craiglockhart near Edinburgh; there he was presently joined by a fellow infantry officer, Siegfried Sassoon, Owen's elder by seven years. Both were poets who felt the need to write effectively of the real and hideous experience of modern war. Sassoon's anger lashed out the more directly at anyone who condoned the horrors or who offered a gloss of any kind of pious justification. Owen's reaction was seemingly slower, yet sixty years afterwards it is his voice which of those two is the stronger.

In the preface to his war poems Owen wrote of his intention: 'Above all, I am not concerned with Poetry. My subject is War, and the pity of

War. The poetry is in the pity.' He said further: 'All a poet can do today is warn. That is why true poets must be truthful.' In the 1970s Richard Harries included Wilfred Owen in his studies of literature and religion, and points out that the word *warn*, as used by Owen, bears an unusual amount of weight. Steeped as Owen was in the language of the Author-ized Version of the Bible he evoked Ezekiel's passionate statement of the watchman's duty to warn. As for the originality of the verse in which Owen's messages come through, the perceptive contributor to Geoffrey Grigson's *Modern World Literature* speaks especially about the poem 'Exposure'. 'Here the imaginativeness of Owen's mind unites with his technical inventiveness in a splendid combination of sharp images and ominous, uneasy rhythms; and this is perhaps more memor-able than any simple outcry against the facts of war could have been . . .' 'Exposure' is the poem which begins:

> Our brains ache, in the merciless iced east winds that
>   knive us . . .
> Wearied we keep awake because the night is silent . . .
> Low, drooping flares confuse our memory of the
>   salient . . .
> Worried by silence, sentries whisper, curious,
>   nervous,
>   But nothing happens.
>
> Watching, we hear the mad gusts tugging on the wire,
> Like twitching agonies of men among its brambles.
> Northward, incessantly, the flickering gunnery
>   rumbles,
> Far off, like a dull rumour of some other war.
>   What are we doing here?

Mr Harries does not fail to say that when Owen got out of hospital he rejoined his men in the front line. It was not Owen's way 'only to utter moral truths'; it was also 'to stand beside those on whose behalf he was pleading'. In 1918 he was back again with his company. 'My senses are charred', he said of himself in that last year. Charred or frozen – the words are almost interchangeable – it was frequently of the lack of any warmth in a soldier's dying of which he wrote, as in the last verse of 'Exposure':

> To-night, His frost will fasten on this mud and us,
> Shrivelling many hands, puckering foreheads crisp.
> The burying-party, picks and shovels in their shaking
>   grasp,
> Pause over half-known faces. All their eyes are ice,
>   But nothing happens.

4. THE COAST OF NORTH WALES

When my road has entered Wales, just beyond Oswestry, the right-hand fork leads north past Wrexham to Chester; the Holyhead Road continues westward through the Vale of Llangollen. It was possibly where the road crosses the Morlas Brook, before the bridge crossing the larger River Ceiriog, that George Borrow halted in the year 1825 and refused the cordial invitation of Peter and his wife to enter, with them, into Wales. It is well to pinpoint the scene if we can, for in *Lavengro* Borrow has a good account of the reception he would expect from Welshmen. Here is the text, from *Lavengro*:

We proceeded till we had nearly reached the brook. 'Well', said Peter, 'will you go into Wales?'
'What should I do in Wales?' I demanded.
'Do!' said Peter, smiling, 'learn Welsh.'
I stopped my little pony. 'Then I need not go into Wales; I already know Welsh.'
'Know Welsh!' said Peter, staring at me.
'Know Welsh!' said Winifred, stopping her cart.
'How and when did you learn it?' said Peter.
'From books, in my boyhood.'
'Read Welsh!' said Peter, 'is it possible?'
'Read Welsh!' said Winifred, 'is it possible?'
'Well, I hope you will come with us,' said Peter.
'Come with us, young man,' said Winifred; 'let me, on the other side of the brook, welcome you into Wales.'
'Thank you both,' said I, 'but I will not come.'
'Wherefore?' exclaimed both simultaneously.
'Because it is neither fit nor proper that I cross into Wales at this time, and in this manner. When I go into Wales, I should wish to go in a new suit of superfine black, with hat and beaver, mounted on a powerful steed, black and glossy, like that which bore Greduv to the fight of Catraeth . . .'

Borrow, who at the age of twenty-two had translated the works of the great Ap Gwylym, with notes critical, historical and explanatory, might very properly demand a grand reception, and it is sad that in 1825 he felt himself unproperly dressed and his pony unworthy. It was in fact twenty-nine years later, in the summer of 1854, that Borrow did actually cross the Border for the extended journey which he recounts in *Wild Wales*. On that trip he was accompanied, at the start, by his wife Mary and his stepdaughter Henrietta. The ladies went on ahead by train from Chester to Llangollen; Borrow preferred to walk the twenty miles with tall hat and umbrella and a satchel slung from his shoulder. He breakfasted at Wrexham and inspected the church. Elihu Yale was buried there in 1721, and in recognition of his gift to the college at New Haven, Connecticut, which grew in due course to Yale University, a replica of Wrexham church tower is one of that university's buildings – rendering the original tower at Wrexham a sight very familiar to all Yale men. Yet it was tombs of poets that fascinated Borrow. 'Can that be an obscure place which has produced a poet?' was the question governing his Welsh journey. He made no mention of Elihu Yale. The truth is that at Wrexham Borrow did not yet feel that he was actually within Wales. It was when he reached Llangollen that he felt sure of being in the land of the Celt rather than of the Saxon.

At Llangollen almost the first item in Borrow's account is that the church contains the tomb of the bard Gryffydd Hiraethog, and the first exciting expedition that he offers is the search in the Ceiriog valley to find the birthplace of Huw Morus or Morris and the stone chair in the wilderness above the gorge – whose back showed three carved letters 'H.M.B.', signifying Huw Morus Bard, in memory of the seventeenth-century 'Nightingale of Ceiriog' whose songs continued to make Borrow's 'eyes overflow with tears of rapture'. Borrow pictures his search and its happy conclusion:

I then sat down in the chair, and commenced repeating verses of Huw Morris. All which I did in the presence of the stout old lady, the short, buxom and bare-armed damsel, and of John Jones the Calvinistic weaver of Llangollen, all of whom listened patiently and approvingly, though the rain was pouring down upon them, and the branches of the trees and the tops of the tall nettles, agitated by the gusts from the mountain hollows, were beating in their faces, for enthusiasm is never scoffed at by the noble simple-minded, genuine Welsh, whatever treatment it may receive from the coarse-hearted, sensual, selfish Saxon.

After that the Holyhead Road drew Borrow onward at his usual fast walking pace through Corwen and past Betws-y-coed and Capel Curig in Snowdonia and so at length to the town of Bangor. The poets Borrow wished to celebrate there were the fifth-century Taliesin and the sixteenth-century Edmund Price. Over the Menai Bridge in Anglesey lay even richer ground for Borrow, for there a side-skip from the main road to the north coast, through Pentraeth to Llanfair beyond the Red Wharf Bay, brought him to the birthplace of the great Gronwy Owen (1723–69). If Borrow was not absolutely certain that he had located the house in which Anglesey's finest poet was born, at least he obtained the autograph of a little stubby girl of about eight, with a broad flat red face and grey eyes, dressed in a chintz gown, with a little bonnet on her head. This courteous small creature, 'looking the image of notableness', consented to inscribe her name in Borrow's pocket-book, as 'Ellen Jones yn perthyn o bell i gronow owen', which is to say, 'Ellen Jones belonging from afar to Gronwy Owen'. When Borrow saw the name of Ellen he had no doubt of the authentic relationship – one of Gronwy's best-known poems was addressed to the memory of his daughter Ellen.

After George Borrow in 1854 had paid such fitting and proper respect to the north coast of Anglesey, he marched at his six miles per hour pace onward to Holyhead Island. In the town of Holyhead he recalled the immortality of Lewis Morris, who had rescued Gronwy Owen and sent him to America to become master of William and Mary College, Williamsburg, Virginia.

Borrow parleyed with the gang of Irish workmen waiting at Holyhead's quay for the ferry to Ireland – the quay is much the same nowadays, but the present-day ferry to Dun Loaghaire is British Rail's sturdy car ferry. Then Borrow set his long legs to climbing Holyhead Mountain and felt 'all the intensely Welsh thoughts which crowded into my head as I stood on the Cairn of the Grey Giant'. He cooled off by drinking his fill of the Fairies' Well and contentedly returned to Bangor by rail.

On the quay beside Holyhead's harbour, this end of the road between Holyhead and London is formally marked by an impressive stone arch, as the London end of A5 is marked by Marble Arch. The Holyhead Road deserves, I think, a special salute for having been so favoured with a notable arch at either end.

*   *   *

Turning back from Anglesey, it is an easier and safer drive now on the coast road from Bangor than it was for the four-horse coach belonging to Mr Thrale, when the Thrales, accompanied by the bulky Samuel Johnson, were returning this way to St Asaph in August 1774. Miss Margaret Lane has recently related that in the last ten years of Johnson's life he was almost more often on the road than at home. Not so much from Boswell as from other sources one learns how, in Johnson's sixties, sometimes most acute and painful fears of madness occasionally recurred to torment him. There were times when London city dwelling was violently intolerable. 'Insane thoughts of handcuffs and fetters' which hitherto had been confided, in Latin, to his private diary were, by 1773, sometimes transmuted into the morbid practice of persuading Mrs

Thrale to be his gaoler, keeping him as a captive penitent padlocked into his 'own room' at Streatham in what Miss Lane speaks of as a 'weird make-believe' of absolution. The death of her mother in June of that year had left Mrs Thrale emotionally prostrated, and she urged Johnson to go away; it was altogether better for Johnson to seek 'dissipation' far away from London. She encouraged his trip to the Hebrides. 'Dissipation is to you a glorious medicine', wrote Mrs Thrale, commending at that time Boswell as Johnson's best physician. 'Farewell', she wrote, 'and be good; and do not quarrel with your governess for not using the rod enough.'

By the next summer of 1774 Johnson, at the age of sixty-five, put the first sheets of his *Journey to the Hebrides* to the press and was ready for another three months of rambling, this time with the Thrales into Mrs Thrale's homeland of North Wales. On the death of her uncle Mrs Thrale had inherited an estate of Bach-y-Graig in the Vale of Clwyd, midway between St Asaph and Denbigh. One purpose of the journey was to inspect the estate, and Mr and Mrs Thrale and their daughter Queeney made room for Johnson to accompany them in Thrale's own comfortable four-horse coach. Queeney, eldest of the Thrale children, was then ten years old, and a favourite of Johnson's.

To journey leisurely from London to Bach-y-Graig, taking three weeks on the way, suited Johnson very well. Lodgings obtained were good or bad, according to luck, yet in the area of Lichfield Johnson could take charge of arrangements, and he made sure that district should be toured in style. In Lichfield itself the party stayed at the Swan and the Thrales were introduced to the variety of Johnson's friends; the coach and party then moved on for the handsome entertainments provided by Johnson's old host Dr Taylor at Ashbourne. There, on the southern verge of the Derbyshire Peak District, Johnson was forcible in praise of the scenery. They visited Dovedale, which in Johnson's writings suggested the 'Happy Valley' of *Rasselas* (Dovedale also appears as the 'Eagle Dale' of George Eliot's *Adam Bede*). 'He that has seen Dovedale has no need to visit the Highlands' was Johnson's remark both made aloud to the Thrales and jotted into his diary. Yet though for Johnson the travel provided effective remedy for the 'vacuity of life', it was not all pleasure for the others. Queeney caught cold and coughed incessantly, and Margaret Lane points out Mrs Thrale's secret tribulation – bouts of sickness on the journey told her that she was again pregnant.

Childbearing was by then no novelty to Hester Thrale; it was an inescapable routine. In sixteen years of marriage to Thrale (until his health collapsed) she gave birth to twelve children, of whom only four survived. 'Almost every winter,' says Margaret Lane, 'she found herself contending with the fatigues and discomforts of pregnancy, almost every spring she gave birth to a child more likely to die than to survive.' She herself, Miss Lane observes, 'was a born survivor', but that does not mean that she welcomed finding herself pregnant on this summer trip. She had moments of tiredness and flashes of irritability; she startled Johnson by wholly losing her temper when he had been walking with Queeney on the walls of Chester beyond the child's hour of going to bed. When they had gone on from Chester into Wales and had passed from Mold to Lleweney Hall, where Mrs Thrale's cousin was to put them all up for three weeks while they examined the estate of Bach-y-Graig, disappointment awaited them, especially Mrs Thrale. Bach-y-Graig, instead of being an estate worth 'at least, five hundred a year', was found to be impoverished and the mansion thoroughly dilapidated. Johnson's diary indicates that Mrs Thrale, having entered the house, was so disgusted as to refuse to look at it room by room. Johnson dismissed her 'chatter' about the inspection being 'tiring' and forced her 'to go to the top', making her observe that everything from the upstairs floors had been stolen and the windows stopped.

The journey of the Thrales and Johnson into North Wales can hardly be presented as a success. In memory of Johnson's visit a monument was later to be set up in a field at Gwaenyog, a mile or so west of Denbigh, but at the time Mrs Thrale was ready enough to return after, as she privately put it, 'three months from home among dunces of all ranks and sorts'. Tiresomely from her point of view the return was not to Streatham but to the gloomy house at the brewery in London's Bankside; for Parliament had been dissolved, and Thrale and Johnson also would be in a bustle of canvassing for Thrale to retain his seat for Southwark. However, Mrs Thrale loyally and vigorously supported the electioneering. Thrale was returned to Parliament, the tedious winter days were ticked off by Mrs Thrale and in April her expected child was born. The baby was a girl and died before the summer. In July the younger of the Thrales' two sons also died, apparently of meningitis. Even bearing in mind the eighteenth-century death rate, they were having bad luck. Yet soon after that Johnson, eager for a ramble, and Mrs Thrale, 'born survivor' and 'for once not pregnant', were badgering Thrale to treat them to another journey. Thrale was persuaded, and in September 1775 he paid the bills for the party as before, including this time Johnson's old friend Joseph Baretti as tutor for Queeney and courier and interpreter for all, for a lively and expensive month in Paris. An even more ambitious tour of Italy in 1776, talked of and greatly looked forward to by Johnson, never took place: the sudden death of young Harry Thrale, Thrale's only surviving son and heir, destroyed that felicity. Young Harry's death (third death in the Thrale family within a twelvemonth) was a cause contributing to a quite rapid decay of relationships between the Thrales, and in their relationships with Johnson.

*   *   *

The coast road that Johnson and the Thrales had followed on their return from Bangor towards St Asaph bypassed the peninsula where the port of Llandudno, small in their time, was in the nineteenth century to grow with speedily increasing popularity into a seaside holiday place. A statue of Lewis Carroll put up to overlook the Model Yacht Pond at Llandudno commemorated much more than the mere fact that in both of his costumes (whether dressed as Lewis Carroll or as the Rev. Mr Dodgson) he had been a visitor: it was to draw attention to the participation of this part of the Welsh coast in some of the best-remembered moments of *Alice in Wonderland.*

I could spoil the case to be made by overstating it. A cardinal fact to remember, when pointing out the Welshness of *Alice,* is the complexity of the Welsh connections of Dr Liddell, the Dean of Christ Church, who regarded the young college tutor (Dodgson) as one of his family. When Dr Liddell's duties at Oxford did not require his entire household to be there, it was to Llandudno that the household repaired. Earlier in this book I referred to the scenery, the banks of the Thames near Oxford, where the storytelling of *Alice in Wonderland* started, for the benefit of the three Liddell daughters (Lorina, Edith and especially Alice), who no doubt offered interjections as the tale went on. I noted that 4 July 1862 was the date on which the story started; very soon after, the Liddells' house at Llandudno was opened for their summer holidays, and Lewis Carroll, if he had not journeyed with them, was quickly sent for. The Liddells' house was not at all one of the long line of boarding-houses which, with the many hotels, now form Llandudno's long, curving and, viewed as a whole, very pleasing esplanade; it was on the westward side of the spectacular high peninsula called Great Ormes Head, on the site now occupied by the Gogarth Abbey Hotel.

It was while Lewis Carroll was staying with the Liddells and being driven in the dog-cart to see the local sights that I visualize him using features of local scenery in his continuation of the *Alice* story; part of the deliciously teasing quality of *Alice* for the Liddell children was the storyteller's twist of lending unexpected happenings to familiar scenes. To a man who played with words and names as Lewis Carroll did, the coast of North Wales must have given delightful opportunities, and the sights which he and the children visited creatively cooperated. The bay with its sands which is known now as Colwyn Bay was in 1862 called, by those who drove to Rhos-on-Sea for picnics, Rhos Bay. Assonance hints that these sands were habitat for the Walrus. I would not press too hard the association of those two immortal beachcombers, the Walrus and the Carpenter; conceivably the amount of building going on at Llandudno had something to do with the Carpenter. Yet not to be heavy-handed as to the light quick way that Carroll's wit worked, and not to impose hidden meanings, there is one swift observation at Llandudno sufficiently convincing for my present purpose. If from the front of the Gogarth Abbey Hotel, site of the Liddells' house, you look out at low tide over the area of Conwy Sands, will you not agree those were the very same grey sands to give seven maids with seven mops plenty of work for half a year?

I could go on brooding about Welsh elements in *Alice*. (How natural it was that the most perfect illustrator for Alice and her adventures should be the artist whose name retained the proud Welsh spelling, Tenniel.) Yet I must move with speed now for St Asaph, in the region whose poverty depressed Johnson and the Thrales. Poverty, in and around St Asaph, remained an acute problem in the nineteenth century; it is the famous workhouse to the south of the town which I select as the feature which, indirectly, kept St Asaph in literary annals. The earlier of two names to be mentioned is that of a vivacious and courageous lady, Felicia Hemans. In the south aisle of St Asaph Cathedral (of which Johnson had remarked that though not large it 'has something of dignity and grandeur') a tablet records that for most of the time between 1809 and 1827 St Asaph was Mrs Hemans' home. Felicia Browne, as her name had been, was born at Liverpool in 1793; she moved to St Asaph as a girl and was only eighteen when impulsively swept into marriage by the military Captain Hemans. Six years later, after Captain Hemans' debts had exhausted her resources and the pair had separated, leaving her to look after the children, she had no course except to return to St Asaph and wonder however to manage to keep those children out of the threatening workhouse. To what was she to turn for bread-winning? Verse-making? Was there any chance of making a livelihood that way? It is true that in the 1820s a young lady in London whose signature was 'L.E.L.' was making more than pin-money from her verses in London newspapers, literary albums and *Souvenirs*. But 'L.E.L.'s' full name was Letitia Elizabeth Landon; she was of a well-to-do family which was automatically close enough to the professional swim for her contributions not only to be placed but paid for. I cannot believe it was readily predictable that a twenty-five-year-old mother, tied to a house with the unknown address of Bronwylfa, St Asaph, was going to achieve by verse-writing the money that she needed. Yet there was St Asaph's workhouse on the same side of the town as Bronwylfa, and to keep her boys out of that workhouse was an impulse that lent crispness to the rhythm of

> The boy stood on the burning deck,
> Whence all but he had fled.

What Felicia Hemans' surcharge of feelings managed to put into some of her lines was 'unforgettability'. Her verses came to the attention of Sir Walter Scott (it is probable that she sent them to him) and he noted her tendency to 'over-do', to be 'somewhat too poetical for my taste'; yet he noted also the gift she had for openings that caught attention and were rememberable:

> The stately homes of England!

or, in 'The Landing of the Pilgrim Fathers',

> The breaking waves dashed high
> On a stern and rock-bound coast . . .

Scott took the trouble to aid Felicia Hemans in the production of a play, and he was notably among those who helped her towards professional success.

So through her own ardency and work, and with good luck, the unpredictable was achieved: Mrs Hemans became the person whose portrait may be looked at in the National Portrait Gallery – there is at least an outward picture there of an engaging face with bright eyes and good complexion surrounded by dark glossy curls. In June 1830 there came to her the accolade of an invitation to stay with the Wordsworths at Rydal Mount, in the Lakes, as a house-guest. She took with her as a present for Wordsworth's daughter Dora, on whom at Rydal Mount the management of housekeeping was largely falling, a little prettily bound album for visitors to write impromptu verses in. It was a gift which Dora was to make use of and to value all her life. Dora was touched by Mrs Hemans' special thought for her, though Wordsworth ('benignant-looking old man,' said Mrs Hemans – Wordsworth was then sixty – in a letter reporting her visit) considered that total attentiveness to his own brand of wisdom was incumbent on all visitors.

One of the most wonderful comments ever made to Wordsworth was made by Mrs Hemans early in that visit to Rydal Mount. It is recorded in Mrs Hemans' above-mentioned letter. 'I laughed', she says, 'to find myself saying on the occasion of some little domestic occurrence, "Mr Wordsworth, how *could* you be so giddy?"' *Giddy!* There is perhaps no guessing what the domestic occurrence was, but no one had ever before, in his dignity at Rydal Mount, called Wordsworth to his face 'giddy'. That barb went beneath the skin. Next morning Wordsworth took Mrs

Hemans aside in his 'richly shaded grounds' and told her that poets he admired were such as Spenser, notable for 'earnestness and devotedness'. He intimated solemnly that she was too flippant to be a poet, and that anyway a woman's proper work was housekeeping. This, to her who had achieved in practical self-support far more than Wordsworth ever had to think of, might be thought gorgeous impertinence on his part. Yet Wordsworth even more comically returned to telling of his duty to improve Mrs Hemans. Many years later he dictated this note about her:

Her education had been most unfortunate. She was totally ignorant of housewifery, and could as easily have managed the spear of Minerva as her needle. It was from observing those deficiencies, that, one day while she was under my roof, I *purposely* directed her attention to household economy, and told her I had purchased *Scales* which I intended to present to a young lady as a wedding present; pointed out their utility (for her especial benefit) and said that no ménage ought to be without them. Mrs Hemans, not in the least suspecting my drift, reported this saying, in a letter to a friend at the time, as a proof of my simplicity.

I take back what I said about not being able to identify the moment when Felicia Hemans told William Wordsworth not to be so giddy. It was the moment of his talk about the kitchen '*Scales*'. All in all I regard Mrs Hemans as having had the better of the exchange. Apparently the quick encounter with her wit went on rankling, now and then, for Wordsworth's remaining twenty years. Physical death came to Mrs Hemans more quickly. She died five years after this little episode, at the age of forty-two. By odd coincidence Wordsworth's daughter Dora, instinctively Felicia's friend, was to die at just about the same too early age.

For others besides Mrs Hemans St Asaph's workhouse was a warning of what might await fatherless children. One such child of six, by name John Rowlands, born at Denbigh in 1841 to a mother unable to support him, was planted there and remained in what Alan Moorehead calls an 'awful Dickensian childhood' till the age of fifteen. At that age the boy emerged from the workhouse to fend for himself. His mother would have nothing to do with him and after three years of drifting in and out of casual work he shipped as cabin-boy on an American packet for New Orleans in 1859. There the young Welshman jumped ship and having obtained work from a cotton-broker named Henry Stanley, he so much pleased his employer that the older man adopted him as son. The boy assumed the name of Henry M. Stanley, became a naturalized American, and embarked on his extraordinary career. He was in both armies in the Civil War, first fighting for the South and then, when captured, fighting for the North; when invalided from the army he joined the US Navy;

and when the Civil War was over began as a journalist. Under James Gordon Bennett of the *New York Herald* he became what Alan Moorehead (in his book *The White Nile*) calls 'the most assiduous foreign correspondent who ever lived'. Moorehead retells the famous journey Stanley made for his paper to obtain kudos by finding Livingstone when that great missionary seemed to have disappeared in darkest Africa.

Three months of companionship with Livingstone in Africa had more effect on Stanley's character and on his subsequent career than he had expected. Then Livingstone, on a final journey with none but native friends, died in central Africa in 1873. His remains, embalmed and carried to the African coast by two companions, Susi and Chuma, were transported for burial in Westminster Abbey on a day of national mourning. Stanley was one of the pallbearers at the Abbey. Presently he embarked on his own explorations in Africa, and we now see how immensely consequential they proved to be. It was Stanley's traverse of equatorial Africa from the Indian Ocean to the Atlantic which for the first time opened up the heart of the continent to foreigners. The 'waif from Wales' now, both for his adventurings and for the immense appeal of his books, had won for himself, as Moorehead comments, 'kudos galore'. Stanley's marriage to Miss Dorothy Tennant in Westminster Abbey was a famous occasion; he was re-naturalized as a British subject, was elected a Member of Parliament and awarded a KCB. Yet in his house at Furze Hill, near Pirbright, though willing enough towards the end of his life to point out features in his garden which had been named after notable discoveries of his in Africa, he apparently never forgot the hardness of his start in life at Denbigh and St Asaph. Professor Coupland's summing up of Stanley's nature is: 'No other famous man of his time got so high from a start so low. No one who can understand him forgets that. He never forgot it himself.' The St Asaph workhouse has turned now into a very good-looking hospital. If Stanley never forgot it, it has not forgotten him – the signboard is proud in its proclamation: YSBYTY H. M. STANLEY.

5. THROUGH THE LAKE DISTRICT TO THE SOLWAY FIRTH

Liverpool, to which Mrs Hemans moved for the last eight years of her life, and where she lived at High Street, Wavertree, was acquiring many literary associations in the nineteenth century. Augustine Birrell, long-lived man of letters, was born in 1850 at Wavertree. The poets Arthur Hugh Clough and Richard Le Gallienne were both born at Liverpool;

Matthew Arnold collapsed and died at Dingle, and Sir William Watson was buried at Childwall. Walter Crane was born in Liverpool in 1845, the time at which Edward Lear was becoming one of the household at the Earl of Derby's seat, Knowsley Hall – it was in 1846 that Lear's *Book of Nonsense*, compiled for the children at Knowsley, was published. Among American writers, Washington Irving owed the start of his successful career to Liverpool, although the debt was indirect: it was Irving's lack of success in business as merchant in Liverpool that turned him to writing *The Sketch-Book*, an immediate and notable bestseller in America when published in 1819. Nathaniel Hawthorne's period as US Consul at Liverpool was later (1853–7); the travel sketches of England which he published in book-form as *Our Old Home* in 1863, retain their charm today. It is not forgotten in Liverpool that the great Gladstone, who could be classed as a man of letters as well as Liberal Prime Minister, was a native of the city, born at No. 62 Rodney Street.

Yet the moment one mentions Chester, the nineteenth-century associations of Liverpool seem relatively parvenu. I don't propose to refer to Roman times, when Chester was named *Castra Devana*, the 'camp on the Dee', the Dee then being far more important than the Mersey. (In song, Merseyside began to gain a reputation with sea-shanties, and football-singing and disco-pop; a contrasting older vintage of Deeside is of Mary calling the cattle home, and the self-sufficient Miller of the Dee.) Miracle Plays were performed at Chester in medieval times, and Chester's neighbourhood (the Wirral), was the setting for the ancient poem *Sir Gawaine and the Green Knight*. This curious work has been transmitted to us in, I suppose, pretty much the form in which it was recited about the year 1400, the time of the great exploits of Owain Glyndwr. The boundary marked most of the way from the Severn estuary to Chester by Offa's Dyke – the boundary between Saxon and Briton that was much overrun at that time by Owain Glyndwr – provides background for the feeling that this 1400-version of the Gawaine poem partakes of the nature of a Border ballad. Other Gawaine romances, Celtic in character, associate themselves with this borderland between Wales and England, and some scholars have observed (although I do not know how far the observation is accepted) that in Welsh versions of Arthurian stories Gawaine is often put above his rival Launcelot or Lancelot whom English versions customarily favour. Whether or no there is tribal rivalry in the background, the significant action in the poem of *Sir Gawaine and the Green Knight* is specifically placed in the Wirral, the peninsula of land which stretches from Chester to the sea, between the two estuaries of Dee and Mersey, and consequently a tournament ground for conflicts of nations.

A prosaic view of the present-day Wirral is to regard it as 'dormitory of Liverpool', or an area to be visited for Hoylake's famous golf links. The Wirral has been captured, tamed, subordinated to modern usages. It was far otherwise when anciently Gawaine came here in his hard wintry journey to keep tryst one New Year's Day – when he had to stand passive as appointed while the Green Knight smote at him with the provenly fearsome broad-axe. I quote from Elizabeth Jenkins' book *King Arthur* a modern transcription of the hard training Gawaine went through in the Wirral:

> Half slain by the sleet he slept in his armour
> Night after night among the naked rocks,
> Where the cold streams ran clattering from the crests above
> And hung high over his head in hard icicles.

There is then the interlude at Christmas where in the bewitched castle on the route to his tryst the almost frozen Gawaine is warmed and tempted by the wife of his enemy in a way that he evades partially but not completely. New Year's Day arrives perhaps just in time for Gawaine to resume his armour and go forward through a deep and frightening deserted ravine. The listener to the poem has to brace himself, as certainly Gawaine had to brace himself, not to flinch at the terrible sound as he approaches the place where the axe is being whetted:

> What! It clattered amid the cliffs, fit to cleave them apart,
> As if a great scythe were being ground on a grindstone there.
> What! It whirred and it whetted, like water in a mill,
> What! It made a rushing, ringing din, rueful to hear.

It is no discredit to Gawaine to admit that he does flinch – the poem says he 'shunts' – at the first stroke aimed at him by the Green Knight with that awful axe. Manfully, though, he stands up to the second stroke, and receives only a flesh wound. Some blood is spilled, yet the episode ends without fatal result; and meanings and half-meanings in the symbols and magic in the poem remain to be conjectured and disputed.

Three writer-friends whom I associate with the Wirral of my own lifetime are Arthur Behrend, the late William Olaf Stapledon (who stirred us with the prophetic novel *Last and First Men*) and H. F. M. Prescott (whose mature work proved what good teaching she had received as a girl at Wallasey High School). Across the Mersey another twentieth-century novelist, Dorothy Kathleen Broster (author of *The Flight of the Heron* and *The Gleam in the North*), was born at Grassendale, but I propose here a monstrous geographical skip north over the coastline from Merseyside to Morecambe Bay, and thence into the Lake District in what is now named Cumbria. An inland course through Manchester, Lancaster, Penrith to Carlisle belongs to my next chapter, and I will not here miss much of literary history by leaping along the coast from Liverpool to the small village of Silverdale, in Morecambe Bay's north-east corner.

It is in memory of Mrs Gaskell that I particularly mention Silverdale. True, the town of Knutsford in Cheshire was where Elizabeth Gaskell (*née* Stevenson) was brought up by her aunts after her mother's death and was the scene immortalized in perhaps the most widely read of her books, *Cranford*; but I have the impression that the actual writing of *Cranford* and her other works was mostly done when she managed to withdraw from the Manchester area to Silverdale.

The view from the hill above Silverdale, where now the county line between Lancashire and Cumbria meets the coast, is famous for the spectacular sunsets which fascinated Turner and Cox, and it was a view much loved by Mrs Gaskell, whether high tide was filling the expanse of Morecambe Bay or whether the ebb was revealing to seabirds the attractions of the sands and mudflats. The 'Abermouth' of her novel *Ruth* is held to have been Silverdale, and she may have worked on that book while staying at nearby 'Wolf House', though by repute the room she was fondest of writing in was in a square building in Silverdale known as Lindeth (or Gibraltar) Tower. *Ruth* and *Cranford* were both published in the same year (1853); perhaps the previous summer at Silverdale had been especially productive. Two years before that, in 1850, Mrs Gaskell had gone on from Silverdale into the Lake District, where at the home of the Shuttleworths on the shores of Windermere she had her first meeting with Charlotte Brontë. Her subsequent visit to Charlotte Brontë at Haworth Parsonage is topographically reserved for the next chapter, but here I may note that her *Life of Charlotte Brontë*, when the two volumes of it came to be published in 1857, was of great and sympathetic influence in arousing interest in both the achievements and the tragic story of the Brontë sisters.

Before the recent alterations to England's county lines, Lancashire continued beyond Silverdale to include the whole of Morecambe Bay, and thus R. G. Collingwood, one of the most stimulating thinkers and writers of the twentieth century, could claim to be a Lancastrian, for he was born at Cartmel Fell on the eastern side of Windermere. Lancashire indeed used to take in the whole western side of Windermere, and thus included the hamlets of Far Sawrey and Near Sawrey between Windermere and Esthwaite Water which Beatrix Potter first visited in 1896. It was in 1905 that she made up her mind to purchase Hill Top Farm at Near Sawrey. She found Hill Top 'as nearly perfect a place as I ever lived in'. Beatrix Potter never wholly forgot her happiest moments in childhood when staying in the Hertfordshire home of her grandmother, and many moments revived when she was settled into Hill Top – soon the home likewise of Jeremy Fisher, Tom Kitten and Jemima Puddle-duck. When at the age of forty-seven Beatrix Potter married her neighbour William Heelis, she moved across the road to Castle Cottage, but she kept Hill Top as a private retreat, and the year before her death gave it to the National Trust. Hill Top is thus preserved for the public to visit, with many of Beatrix Potter's drawings and personal relics and the objects themselves which sometimes come into her illustrations of the stories.

Two other notable sites in this part of the Lake District which used to owe fealty to Lancashire are Hawkshead, where Wordsworth between the ages of eight and sixteen was at school, living in what became known as Wordsworth Cottage, and Coniston, where for his last thirty years John Ruskin lived, and where his grave is in the churchyard. But many of the sites which have drawn tourists to the country of 'the Lake Poets', especially after that term was used in the *Edinburgh Review* of 1817 and repeated by De Quincey, are on the eastern side of the long lake of Windermere and to the north, in the part of Cumbria which I still habitually think of as Westmorland. The John Wilson whose pen-name was 'Christopher North' lived at Elleray on the outskirts of the once small settlement of Windermere, which now links with the older Bowness as the chief town on the lake. Storrs Point, south of Bowness, was where Christopher North, after he had gone to Edinburgh and helped *Blackwood's* to its fame as a magazine, returned to organize a 'radiant procession' of 'not fewer than fifty barges' in 'one of the most splendid regattas that ever enlivened Windermere'. The date of that occasion was 15 August 1825, the fifty-fourth birthday of Sir Walter Scott, which happily brought Canning and Scott to the same house-party. 'The weather was as Elysian as the scenery', wrote Lockhart. 'The bards of the Lakes [Wordsworth and Southey] led the cheers that hailed Scott and Canning; and music and sunshine, flags, streamers, and gay dresses, the merry hum of voices, and the rapid splashing of innumerable oars, made up a dazzling mixture of sensations as the flotilla wound its way . . .' The tour from which Scott was then returning took him on to the Wordsworths at Rydal Mount, then to Southey at Keswick, and home to Abbotsford; and though of that tour he noted that it 'had been one ovation', it was, sadly, the last of such happy times.

In the twentieth century Arthur Ransome settled at Windermere in his well-earned retirement; regattas had become more crowded than in the days of Walter Scott, yet Ransome's passion for fly-fishing enabled him to find ways of escape, before his death there in 1967. Ambleside, just to the north of the lake, was where Matthew Arnold spent the last years of his life, at Fox How. Harriet Martineau had likewise, somewhat earlier (in 1845) settled in Ambleside. Wordsworth, by then at nearby

Rydal Mount, seemed to her only on occasion inspiring as a companion. 'His conversation can never be anticipated', was her record of Wordsworth. 'Sometimes he flows on in the utmost grandeur. . . . At other times we blush and are annoyed at the extremity of bad taste with which he pertinaciously dwells on the most vexatious and vulgar trifles.' It may be that Wordsworth lectured Harriet Martineau, as he had tried to lecture Felicia Hemans; but Miss Martineau, herself something of a lecturer, was not so witty as Mrs Hemans at dealing with the old man when he was tiresome. Miss Martineau was herself somewhat lacking in understanding and sympathy when she dismissed Hartley Coleridge as 'a sick child', and indeed used rougher terms than that for Hartley, who after other Coleridges had left the Lakes, stayed on as schoolmaster, on and off, at Ambleside. When Hartley was a small and physically weakly child of six, of whom 'his uncle Southey used to say he had two left hands and might have added that they were both useless', Wordsworth felt 'many fears' about him. It was one of the attractive qualities of Wordsworth that he did retain full sympathy with Hartley Coleridge. The door of Rydal Mount was ever open to Hartley, though the erratic schoolmaster's head might be prematurely grey from consciousness of having 'lost the race I never ran'.

At Ambleside I recall a paragraph once written about Hartley Coleridge:

In one thing Hartley was more fortunate than Wordsworth. He was far better loved by the country folk. They had a low opinion, in general, of Wordsworth, who seemed aloof, careless, a stranger in their midst. 'Many's the time', said an old inn-keeper whom Canon Rawnsley questioned, 'I've seed him a takin' his family out in a string, and niver geein' the deariest bit of notice to 'em; standin' by hissel' and stoppin' behind agapin', wi' his jaws workin' the whoal time; but niver no crackin' wi' 'em, nor no pleasure in 'em, – a desolate-minded man, ye kna. . . . It was potry as did it'. . . . 'As for Mister Wudsworth', said the one-time butcher's boy, 'He'd pass you, same as if ya was nobbut a stoan'. . . . And of course, as for Wordsworth's 'habits, he had noan'. He neither smoked nor drank. For 'li'le Coleridge' in and out of every cottage, in and out of every pub, ever willing to share a pipe, a discussion, an opinion, or a game, they had both reverence and love. The dalesmen enjoyed his conversation, whether they comprehended it or not. 'Aye, but Mr Coleridge talks fine', observed one. 'I would go through fire and water for Mr Coleridge', said another.

A little to the north of Ambleside is Grasmere, whose churchyard holds graves to be looked for: Dora, Wordsworth's daughter, was buried here in 1847, Hartley Coleridge in 1849, Wordsworth himself in 1850, his sister Dorothy in 1855 and his wife in 1859. It was at Dove Cottage in Grasmere that the Wordsworths lived from 1799 to 1808, a period most agreeably to be remembered, and when Wordsworth married in 1802 he brought his wife to Dove Cottage. His illegitimate daughter in France was a part of his history concealed from the neighbours; his sanctioned daughter was Dora, born in 1804. Samuel Coleridge had been tempted to settle in the Lakes by the prospect of the Wordsworths' company; in 1803 he stopped at Dove Cottage on his way from Keswick to Malta, ill in body and disturbed in mind, and there the Wordsworths nursed him for a month, Wordsworth pressing on him at parting a loan of £100, a sum considerable for both of them.

In those years Wordsworth certainly wins the affection due to a man who could yield to warm, impulsive and unselfish actions. When he and Dorothy had been on tour in Scotland they had looked up Walter Scott, who was much pleased to see them; in 1805 Scott, on a tour of the Lakes with his wife, received in return an enthusiastic welcome at Dove Cottage. In the early years at that cottage, even though Wordsworth was 'a man of fancies, ye kna' (in the words of a man who did some gardening for him) the atmosphere was one of friendliness all round. At the age of four or five Dora had, beside the other children, De Quincey – 'Kinsey' to the small folk – and Coleridge to play with. Her aunt Dorothy wrote at this time: 'D. is very pretty, very kittenish, very quick, very clever, but not given to *thought*. Coleridge often repeats to her (altering a line of William's poem of *Ruth*), "the wild cat of the wilderness was not as fair as she". To this she replies with a squall, inviting him to some fresh skirmish.'

That was when, and as if house-moving would be conducive to renewal of inspiration, Wordsworth had moved to Allan Bank at the other end of the village – Coleridge was visiting at Allan Bank; De Quincey was taking over Dove Cottage. At the earlier time of his month's illness at Dove Cottage, in the pangs of depression Coleridge drafted his ode 'Dejection', and warned Wordsworth with the prayer:

> Full seldom may my friend such vigils keep.

Wordsworth at that time had been sorry for Coleridge, confident that he himself was strong enough to hold his 'vision', but by the time of the move to Allan Bank he was himself having to face his own secret doubts and insecurities, his own

> . . . strange half-absence, as of one
> Knowing too well the importance of his theme,
> But feeling it no longer.

After 1808 it is noticeable how a seeking for his own kind of opiate grew upon Wordsworth. That there was any weakening of his own powers, or that he himself was in perplexity, he stubbornly denied;

weaknesses belonged to other people. Nevertheless, now to observe other poets' weaknesses was sometimes a threat to his own composure. Watching Coleridge, in the latter's extended stay at Allan Bank in 1808, behaving as the pale ghost of what he had been, shook Wordsworth's self-confidence; the consequent anger cooled his feelings for Coleridge. Now to assert his own superiority he began to show off weaknesses of others. When Coleridge felt that his stay at Allan Bank was becoming a strain, he proposed that he might settle with a mutual friend in London. Wordsworth took it upon himself to write to the friend to warn him of Coleridge's opium-taking and other habits – a gratuitous action which intensely hurt Coleridge. Wordsworth's own opiate of correction of others' conduct was becoming an increasing concealment from himself that his own genius was fitful. Lamb felt that after the Dove Cottage period Wordsworth had grown cold. De Quincey was angered at Wordsworth's refusal to invite him into the later homes, the reason apparently being that De Quincey and a female friend were living together without benefit of clergy. Many of Wordsworth's new characteristics which some of his old friends found unlikeable were outward manifestations of the violent inner fight to retain his 'vision'.

In Wordsworth's youth his sister Dorothy had sacrificed herself very willingly – almost too subserviently, some say – to any task that assisted in giving him 'eyes and ears', attending to the practical details on all their joint tours and goings-about. This was so also when Coleridge joined them: Dorothy was the essential partner who made the arrangements and 'did the work'. As Wordsworth aged, Dorothy's physical health, and even more her mental powers, failed prematurely. She lived on in the household in an enfeebled way – actually she was to outlive William by five years – but after her serious illness in 1828 (when she was fifty-six) she could not be the stimulant to William that she once had been.

By that time it was likely that Wordsworth's daughter Dora might become the replacement, the 'living staff' that his limping genius needed. In reading of the Wordsworths there is, on Dora's behalf, a real tremor when, about 1828, one sees her father eyeing her possessively. Is Wordsworth's 'selfishness' actually going to enslave Dora? In 1828 (Dora being then twenty-four) her hand had been spoken for by the young widower, Edward Quillinan, whom she had known since she was seventeen, and to whom she had been drawn more closely after the death, in a tragic accident, of his first wife. Dora was ready to say 'yes' to Quillinan in 1828, but Wordsworth said 'no'. He recognized that Dora and Quillinan loved each other, that if she were wishful to be a wife and mother here was her opportunity – but could he, her father, allow her not to be at his hand? He, Wordsworth, would consider it, but not yet. Before that answer Dora had been reported to be 'as happy as a lark', yet she echoed the 'not yet' to Quillinan. The faithful Quillinan accepted dismissal only temporarily; he went away, travelled abroad, returned and as years went on remained in touch and repeated his question. Wordsworth went on discovering reasons for repeating his 'not yet'.

It was not wholly accurate of De Quincey to say that Wordsworth was unable to amuse himself, that he was 'gloomily unfitted for bending to such a yoke'. By the time he was depending on his daughter Dora, he could sometimes amuse himself by actions which, if not designed to upset other people, showed little regard for others' convenience or feelings. He amused himself by barging in upon Southey at Keswick. A more notable example occurred in September 1831, when Wordsworth learned that Scott, ill, palsied, broken with the overwork with which he had attempted to pay off his debts, was under imperative orders to winter in Italy. The emergency was of national concern – a naval frigate was being prepared, at Portsmouth, to take Scott. Scott's children were rallying at Melrose to see to the many arrangements and to get the invalid off, his son, the major, having obtained leave to be in attendance for the journey.

Wordsworth had not seen Scott since the losses that had crippled him. However, at this perhaps final moment might it not cheer the invalid and those attending him if Wordsworth should arrive at Abbotsford to stay a day or two and by his presence add respect to the departure, scheduled for 23 September? Scott's son-in-law, Lockhart, is slightly cryptic in his account of the proposed visit: 'nothing could have gratified Sir Walter more, or sustained him better, if he needed any support from without.' In Wordsworth's impulse to set out for Scotland there was for him the recollection of his own visit across the Border in 1803. Coleridge had been with Wordsworth for part of that tour, and Dorothy had then been caretaker for both of them. Samuel Rogers had met them on the road, all three

in a vehicle that looked very much like a cart. Wordsworth and Coleridge were entirely occupied in talking about poetry; and the whole care of looking out for cottages where they might get refreshment and pass the night, as well as of seeing their poor horse fed and littered, devolved upon Miss Wordsworth. She was a most delightful person – so full of talent, so simple-minded, and so modest!

When Coleridge had dropped out, Wordsworth and his sister went on to call upon the Scotts at Abbotsford. It was that trip, twenty-eight years earlier, that was now to be repeated, partly for the sake, one feels, of what emotions it would recollect for Wordsworth. Sister Dorothy was replaced by daughter Dora; Dora drove the open carriage with one horse, but her orders were not to overtake or precede her father, who preferred to go on foot. Wordsworth, suffering at the time from an inflammation of his eyes, had devised for himself a dark green linen eye-shade, which he wore as he walked ahead of or beside the carriage. In a note to Scott on 16 September, giving notice of their approach, Words-worth, not without high spirits, mentions the manner of the march. ' "There's a man wi' a veil, and a lass drivin'", exclaimed a little urchin, as we entered merry Carlisle a couple of hours ago, on our way to Abbotsford.'

I can't help feeling Wordsworth's farewell visit to Scott was rather for the benefit of the visitors than for the comfort of their semi-paralysed and slightly confused host. In the last few days before Scott was to be escorted off to Italy, the family had managed, temporarily, to reopen Abbotsford. This was to support Scott's delusion that his debts were paid; to keep pretence of that, as the children gathered they tried to revive 'after a long interval, and for the last time, the old splendour of Abbotsford'. On 17 September, then, with a few of the neighbouring gentry assembled and a son there to help him, Sir Walter 'did the honours of the table' once more in his old home. On Monday the 19th the Words-worths arrived, Wordsworth, as Lockhart noted, wearing the green eyeshade indoors as well as out. An excursion for the next day was proposed, so on the next morning the carriage was ordered for a drive to Newark Castle. Wordsworth's 'Yarrow Revisited' was to be one result. Wordsworth, a year older than Scott, sixty-one to Scott's sixty, watched his host carefully. In the morning 'when we alighted from the carriage he walked pretty stoutly'. On return in the evening, as the wheels of the carriage grated on crossing Tweed's river-bed towards Abbotsford, Scott was exhausted. 'Thinking it probable that it might be the last time Sir Walter would cross the stream, I was not a little moved', said Wordsworth. That movement of Wordsworth's feelings enabled the prompt composition of the sonnet which begins:

> A trouble, not of clouds, or weeping rain,
> Nor of the setting sun's pathetic light
> Engendered, hangs o'er Eildon's triple height . . .

On the next day, Wednesday, there was a perhaps less strenuous expedition to Melrose. Scott's daughter, Mrs Lockhart, had already set out from Melrose to prepare for her father's reception in London, but Lockhart provided lunch, I think, at his house, Chiefswood. There Dora Wordsworth produced the little album she had brought with her – the album Felicia Hemans had given her – and asked Lockhart to in-scribe some impromptu verses; with that request Lockhart's pen readily complied, and all returned to Abbotsford. Both Dora and Wordsworth then pressed Scott to write, as Lockhart had done, a page of impromptu verse in Dora's book. Scott attempted to avoid the challenge, yet was pressed to take the book to his room overnight, to see what he could do. The conversation that evening in the Abbotsford library was not cheerful: 'Sir Walter said a good deal about the singularity that Fielding and Smollett had both been driven abroad by declining health, and never returned.'

Early the Thursday morning, before he came into the breakfast-room, Scott did try to write what he thought were legible stanzas on a page of Dora's album. 'While putting the book into her hand', said Wordsworth later, 'in his own study, standing by his desk, he said to her in my presence: "I should not have done anything of this kind but for your father's sake; they are probably the last verses I shall ever write".' The writing was shaky, the misconjunctions of thought and hand and eye pathetically evident, and in signing at the end Scott's pen missed any recording of the initial S in his name. The page is an exhibit, as Matthew Arnold said when he was shown it, of 'a death-stricken hand'. Yet Wordsworth wrote proudly to tell Mrs Hemans: 'We prize this memorial very much, and the more so as an affecting testimony of his regard at the time when, as the verses prove, his health of body and powers of mind were much impaired and shaken.'

Scott could not properly sign his name to the page in Dora's album, but he managed to get the date right. The effort to produce his contribution was forced from him on 22 September 1831. The Wordsworths then took themselves off. Scott was allowed to rest while the family completed the packing, and early on the morning of the 23rd, accompanied by his daughter Anne and Lockhart, he was taken from Abbotsford by carriage for the journey by easy stages to reach London on the sixth day. After a month there, with medical consultations, Scott was taken on to Portsmouth and by the frigate to the hoped-for remedial scenes of Italy. One gathers that Wordsworth walked steadily back from Abbotsford to the Lakes, with Dora driving close behind, and reached Rydal Mount (where they had been living since 1813) in excellent spirits. The result of the trip for him was a renewal of feelings which he could renew in utterances.

It had all encouraged Wordsworth to plan further trips with Dora, but Dora, it seems, after return to Rydal Mount, was less happy. Lockhart's contribution to her album had in effect asked the question: when was she going to become Mrs Quillinan? When indeed? The years passed; Quillinan was mostly abroad; he kept writing to Dora, but Dora's replies, with her father's eye on her, were restrained. Samuel Rogers, visiting Rydal in 1834, noticed something wrong: 'Their daughter Dora looks cheerful before other people, but is in a sad, melancholy way and eats nothing, says nothing, and goes nowhere.' Yet in 1836 Quillinan did return to England; he revisited the Lakes; Mrs Wordsworth burst out with the remark 'his presence was a god-send'.

A year after that, when Mrs Wordsworth and Dora were abraded by correcting proofs for the fifth edition of the collected poems, Wordsworth began to feel it might be helpful to rope in Quillinan. Thus towards the close of 1837 he formally requested of Quillinan 'that, as an act of friendship, at your convenience, you would take the trouble – a considerable one, I own – of comparing the corrections in my last edition with the text in the preceding one. You know my principles of style better, I think, than anyone else . . .'

Eighteen further months of acts of friendship emboldened Quillinan to take the newfangled 'Railroad Mail-Coach' from London. To Dora he spoke openly of the 'blest days of steam!' –

> Shy northern Maid! The laurelled copse
> Of Rydal now is no retreat;
> Up goes a silver cloud, and drops
> Your southern lover at your feet.

Openly, again, he pressed his claim to marry Dora. Wordsworth, as if to think things over, departed from Rydal Mount with Mrs Wordsworth to Bath. After what clearly was a great struggle, in the early summer of 1839 he wrote to Dora 'I must submit' – but still, throughout the remainder of 1839, throughout all of 1840, the fixing of a wedding day was postponed. Finally, almost unexpectedly, one reads a letter of Wordsworth, from Bath, dated 11 May 1841: 'This morning, my dear daughter was married in St James' in this place . . .'

When she became Mrs Quillinan, thirteen years after the asking, Dora was thirty-seven, and Quillinan fifty. They were to have only six years of married life. For the first four of those years they were mainly in the Lake District, but Dora's increasing breakdowns of health were diagnosed as 'consumption'. As soon as it was pronounced that she was in the grip of the 'Captain of the Men of Death', Quillinan took her to Portugal. Any hope of that affecting a cure was, after more than a year's trial, given up. They returned so that she might die at Rydal. After her burial at Grasmere in 1847 Wordsworth wrote: 'We see little of poor Mr Quillinan. Mrs Wordsworth seldom goes down the hill, and I have not the courage to go to his house.'

*　　*　　*

North of Windermere the next centre of importance for its literary associations is Keswick. It was here, a dozen miles from Grasmere, that Coleridge settled in Greta Hall in 1800, and it was nominally his residence until 1809, although after the completion of the second part of *Christabel* and the drafting of the 'Ode to Dejection' by 1803, he was away from Greta Hall most of the time. Charles Lamb brought his sister Mary to visit the Coleridges for three weeks in 1802. Of this highly adventurous expedition to the Lakes Lamb wrote that 'such an impression I never received from objects of sight before'. Lamb and Mary had been pushed to physical exertions by Hazlitt in Hampshire, but exertions in the Lakes transcended those: 'We have seen Keswick, Grasmere, Ambleside . . . we have clambered up to the top of Skiddaw.' The Lambs missed seeing the Wordsworths, for Wordsworth and Dorothy were at that moment on their visit to Calais, but Charles and Mary were free to inspect and approve Dove Cottage. In 1803 Hazlitt visited Coleridge in Keswick, staying long enough to paint portraits of Coleridge and Wordsworth, and just before Coleridge was to set off for Malta (pausing, as we saw, at Grasmere) his brother-in-law Southey arrived to share the residence of Greta Hall, each family to occupy its own floor. As in Coleridge's absences, in Malta and then elsewhere, remittances from him might be irregular, the reliable Southey felt responsible for looking after the Coleridge floor as well as his own. Southey worked manfully to do this. 'To think', he once expostulated, 'how many mouths I must feed out of one inkstand.' In 1809 the Coleridges moved away from the Lakes (apart from transient visits and Hartley's permanent return) and the whole of Greta Hall became Southey's possession and remained so until his death in 1843.

Southey had many visitors at Greta Hall. Shelley and his first wife Harriet stayed for some time in the winter of 1811–12, Shelley becoming increasingly scornful that Southey's once revolutionary ardours had subsided, and that he was going to be studiously attentive to the mundane routine of contributing to the *Quarterly* at £100 an article. When he accepted the appointment as Poet Laureate in 1813 (Scott had waived the honour for Southey to have it), that, for Shelley, finished Southey. But Southey by then was attracting visits from Scott, and later on from Landor, when the latter returned from Italy to revive in person the warm friendship they had always had from early days. Landor was always a steadfast admirer of Southey's merits and of his remarkably good nature. When the self-assured young Emerson toured England in 1833 'to see the faces of three or four writers' he recorded with immature scorn that Landor, when interviewed, 'pestered me with Southey; but who is Southey?' Twenty years elapsed before Landor was made aware of Emerson's question, but when aware, he then replied:

I will answer the question. Southey is the poet who has written the most imaginative poem of any in our own times, English or Continental; such is the *Curse of Kehama*. Southey is the proseman who has written the purest prose; Southey is the critic the most cordial and the least invidious. Show me another of any note, without captiousness, without arrogance, and without malignity.

Landor, whose visits to Greta Hall were perforce rare, was always warmly welcomed. Wordsworth, residing close enough to look in upon Southey more frequently, tended to consult his own convenience in making visits. Unless forewarned, Southey was apt to be immersed in work. 'Imagine me', he wrote, 'in this great study of mine from break-fast till dinner, from dinner till tea, and from tea till supper, in my old black coat, my corduroys alternately with the long worsted pantaloons and gaiters in one, and the green shade, and sitting at my desk, and you have my picture and my history.' When Southey was not writing he was apt to be occupied with his extensive collection of books, the most valued of which were put into the cloth covers specially worked by his daughters, Edith and Kate. Southey greatly cared for the condition of his books, as also for their contents; but, whatever the book, Wordsworth cared for the contents rather than the appearance. He had been known to pick up a buttery knife in order to cut the pages of a volume which, till he held it, had been in mint condition. 'To introduce Wordsworth into one's library', Southey admitted ruefully, 'is like letting a bear into a tulip garden.' And Wordsworth, when visiting, seemed to preserve what Carlyle called 'a rock-like indifference' to his host's feelings. That Wordsworth (so Landor felt) showed so little respect for Southey caused a rift between Landor and Wordsworth that never healed. (It was certainly annoying to Landor, as Southey's first and constant patron, for Wordsworth to assert to him that 'he would not give five shillings for all Southey's poetry'.) Nevertheless a verse from Southey was one of the first which Dora sought for her album, and Southey obliged by filling a page impromptu in his neat writing and signing it from 'Cat's Eden, 1 Oct. 1830'.

Cat's Eden was, I take it, Southey's study at Greta Hall. Scott was devoted to his dogs, and Southey to his cats, of whom Rumpel was a particular favourite. Rumpel died in 1834; I imagine Dora Wordsworth had been taking notice of him while Southey was writing in her little book. I don't believe there were either cats or dogs at Rydal Mount. Canon Rawnsley questioned some who knew Wordsworth about his attitude to animals. 'Wudsworth was no dog-fancier', answered one who had been a servant of the poet, 'and as for cats, he couldn't abide them; and he didn't care for sheep, or horses, a deal, but if he was fond of onything it was of *li'le ponies*.' Maria Jane Jewsbury (who wrote in Dora's book a month after Southey) thought to enliven Rydal Mount by presenting Wordsworth with some goldfish, and Dora with a pair of doves. The doves were in an osier cage; one died, but Wordsworth was pleased with the other, for, as he says in his note to 'The Poet and the Caged Turtledove', 'it was the habit of the bird to begin cooing and murmuring whenever it heard me making my verses'. Then that dove died; Wordsworth goes on to say that a neighbour's cat got in at the window and killed it. The fish were kept for some time in a bowl in the morning-room, but they did not thrive there, and were removed to 'Dora's Field'. Wordsworth's comment was: 'One of them being all but dead, they were taken to the pool under the old pollard oak. The apparently dying one lay on its side, unable to move. I used to watch it, and about the tenth day it began to right itself, and in a few days more was able to swim about with its companions.' Later, though, a sudden flood swept all the fish out of the pool in Dora's Field, and they perished. Wordsworth had bought Dora's Field, adjacent to Rydal Mount, in 1826; he gave it to Dora, and after her death the field retained her name, and still does, for ultimately the poet's grandson, Gordon Wordsworth, gave it to the National Trust. In spring the Trust reports Dora's Field to be a mass of daffodils and bluebells.

Between Rydal Mount and Keswick there are many well remembered associations. Keats, for instance, with Charles Brown, traversed this road in the summer of 1818. Windermere had surpassed Keats's expectation; they went on to Rydal Mount to call on Wordsworth, but he was out, so they left a note and went on past Grasmere to Keswick. Southey at that moment may also have been away, yet Keswick at any rate claimed Keats for I think two nights and he and Brown climbed Skiddaw before going on to Scotland. After Keats it is natural to recall Tennyson's visits to the Lake District, though he is mostly to be associated with Tent Lodge, at the head of Coniston Water. Tennyson had been in the Lake District in 1835, staying at Mirehouse with Spedding to meet Edward FitzGerald, but he came again in 1850 to Tent Lodge with his bride, for some months. While Tennyson was here the poet laureateship was offered to him and accepted, in succession to Wordsworth. Southey, at Keswick, had held that office before Wordsworth, until his health failed and he died in 1843, being buried in Crosthwaite churchyard. Carlyle, who had earlier visited Wordsworth at Rydal Mount and did not take greatly to him, was a guest of Tennyson's at Tent Lodge, and being much closer to Tennyson than to Wordsworth, thought better of the office of laureateship when his friend had it. A mile south of Tent Lodge, on the eastern side of Coniston Water, is Brantwood, where Ruskin sought retirement from 1871 until his death in 1900.

The new century was to attract more men of letters to the Lake District when Sir Hugh Walpole made Brackenburn in Borrowdale his permanent address. Walpole died there in 1941. His Lakeland saga, *The*

Herries Chronicles, is mainly set in Borrowdale, midway between
Coniston and Keswick. West of Keswick, towards the sea, is Cockermouth, where the River Cocker joins the Derwent. Here the Derwent
flows past the garden of Wordsworth House (now kept up by the
National Trust) where William, and a year later his sister Dorothy,
were born and lived in childhood. Wordsworth's 'fair seed-time' is
happily remembered at Cockermouth; in that territory of garden and
river, and 'distant Skiddaw', he recollected of Dorothy in the early
1770s that

> She gave me eyes, she gave me ears;
> And humble cares, and deliberate fears;
> A heart, the fountain of sweet tears;
> And love, and thought, and joy.

Halfway between Cockermouth and Carlisle is Wigton, and Wigton
was the birthplace of John Woodcock Graves, who is said to have produced impromptu, in 1828, the song 'D'ye ken John Peel' which has
ever since honoured his friend. The Cumberland huntsman John Peel
maintained a pack of hounds at Caldbeck at his own expense for fifty
years, until his death and burial in Caldbeck churchyard in 1854. This
northern corner of Cumbria, where it borders on the Solway Firth,
figures very materially in Scott's spirited romance, *Redgauntlet*. So
spirited indeed is the telling of that tale that it is easy to agree with
Hazlitt's special enthusiasm for *Redgauntlet*; and after seeking to identify
the location of the fray over the stake-nets for the salmon in the Solway
(where Darsie Latimer was captured) there is the further amusement of
identifying just where Scott placed the arrival, on the Cumberland
coast, of the brig *Jumping Jenny* (captained by Nanty Ewart). One of
the pleasures offered by Scott is his incidental and easy use of topographical detail, and although there may be mock-serious argument as
to the exact placing, in *Redgauntlet*, of the Place of Fairladies where the
Royal Wanderer (Charles Stuart) is (although under alias) recognized
by the reader, there can be readier agreement about the site of the inn by
the Solway where the drama came to its climax, and the last heir of the
Stuarts leant on Redgauntlet's arm as they walked towards the beach.

Stirring stuff! And was it not this identical part of the Cumberland
coast which prompted Wilkie Collins to specify it as location for the
Limmeridge House and the Limmeridge tombstone in *The Woman in
White*? Surely the precise travelling instructions given to readers of
that classic tempts some to visit Bowness-on-Solway in search for Mr
Fairlee's house, with windows which looked out upon the sea, at a site
where 'the distant coast of Scotland fringed the horizon with its lines
of melting blue'.

6. FROM CUMBRIA SOUTH THROUGH STAFFORDSHIRE

We have reached the northernmost point of this journey; the direct road from Manchester to Carlisle, and territory (including the Pennines) between that road (A6) and the Great North Road (A1) is for my next chapter; therefore on my present return to London I skip back from Cumbria to Cheshire. But first, well away west of the coast of Cumbria and rising in the Irish Sea is the Isle of Man. I have so far mentioned that the Isle of Man was haven of refuge for Charles Dickens's maternal grandfather, when that once highly respected Head of the Moneys Section of the Navy Office in Portsmouth, after discovery by auditors of his nine years of systematic embezzlement, escaped trial by fleeing beyond English legal jurisdiction. It seems clear that Dickens's mother did not lose affection for 'my father who lives abroad', for young Charles, born two years after the scandal, was named after him; but one agrees with Angus Wilson that the resulting tension hanging around his childhood home 'must have been felt by the sensitive child'. Calais, Boulogne, Cherbourg probably teemed, Wilson points out, with 'suspected felons'; it was the more ingenious of Dickens's grandfather to seek his refuge at Douglas in the Isle of Man, where he died in 1826, Dickens being then fourteen years old.

The poet Thomas Edward Brown, a native Manxman, has been mentioned earlier for the great encouragement he gave, as teacher, to W. E. Henley. Brown was born at Douglas in 1830 and brought up in the vicarage of Kirk Braddan. He earned the title of 'Manx poet' with his early *Fo'c's'le Yarns* and other narrative poems, mainly in the Manx dialect. In his twenty-eight years of schoolmastering at Clifton he returned as often as he might to the Isle of Man, and his lyrics written at Clifton refer often to feelings evoked by memories of the island – memories of the rocks and waves at Scarlett, the gorse in Glen Chase, the 'blaeberries on old Barrule' and thunder in the caves of Bradda Head. In the particular poem I am quoting, when Brown is much preferring his thoughts of his island home to the actuality of being tied to Clifton, I am puzzled by the line

But Wordsworth's castle's still at Peel – thank God!

The reference seemingly is to Wordsworth's 'Elegiac Stanzas suggested by a picture of Peele Castle, in a storm' – the stanzas containing the often-quoted line 'The light that never was, on sea or land' – but later scholars assure me that Wordsworth's Peele Castle, or more correctly Piel Castle, was not the castle at Peel on the Isle of Man, but the castle at Piel Island near Barrow-in-Furness.

The castle of 'Sodor, of Holm Peel' on St Patrick's Isle on the west coast of the Isle of Man, is thus associated with Walter Scott rather than with Wordsworth. It plays full part in Scott's *Peveril of the Peak*; it is where Julian Peveril meets with Fenella (one of the odd characters such as Scott has weakness for) and it is from this Peel Castle that Julian is conveyed to the bark which is to land him, carrying important missives, in Liverpool. Those missives were from the seventeenth-century ruler of the island, 'the princely Countess of Derby, the royal Queen in Man', and Scott makes it clear that for the purposes of his romance he has put the lady into the seventeenth-century 'Popish Plot' whereas she was in fact a French Protestant. The general picture of life in the island in that period is present in *Peveril* with Scott's usual 'big Bow-Wow strain'. Of later novelists, one who set out to study a special life and character in Manx people was Hall Caine (1853–1931) in *The Manxman*. Thomas Henry Hall Caine (in later life Sir Hall Caine) was not himself a native Manxman; he was born at Runcorn in Cheshire, but his parents came from the island, some of his childhood was spent there, and he returned to spend his last years at Greeba Castle on the slope of Greeba Mountain.

* * *

Returning to the mainland from the Isle of Man –

Mona – long hid from those who roam the main

to Liverpool, and following the same course that young Peveril pursued towards Derbyshire we pass through Runcorn, where Hall Caine started life as the son of the ship's smith, and then through Daresbury, where Charles Lutwidge Dodgson (Lewis Carroll) was born in 1832. He was brought up at the rectory, with his younger sisters and brother, until his father was transferred to Darlington. There is a memorial window to Lewis Carroll in Daresbury's church to record his childhood there, before his schoolings, first at Richmond in Yorkshire and then at Rugby; thence to Oxford to make friends with Dr Liddell and his family.

On towards Manchester, but south of the conurbation, is Knutsford, scene of the social life early in Victoria's reign as depicted in Mrs Gaskell's *Cranford*. As a motherless baby Elizabeth Stevenson was brought from Chelsea to her aunt Mrs Lumb who lived on the edge of Knutsford heath; her life until marriage was spent in Knutsford and the neighbourhood; but after marriage to the Unitarian minister

William Gaskell in 1832 her life was mostly in Manchester (with some of her writing, as has been suggested, done at Silverdale). Mrs Gaskell's publications began with *Mary Barton*, issued anonymously in 1848, and highly praised by Maria Edgeworth, Landor and Carlyle. It was after she had been a guest of Dickens, with Carlyle and Thackeray, in 1849, that she began to contribute to *Household Words* and to add the profession of authorship to her social work. *Cranford* was published in 1853; though the life described is generally taken to be pictorial of the Knutsford she had left in 1832, some touches of later date are agreeably worked in: when with dreadful unexpectedness 'Captain Brown is killed by them nasty cruel railroads' it was because he had been absorbed in the *Pickwick Papers*; and when the ladies of *Cranford* were told about Tennyson: 'This young man comes and tells me that ash buds are black; and I look and they *are* black' – no such anachronisms (if they are anachronisms) matter in the least. Each part of Mrs Gaskell's study of the human characters that attracted her deserves the epithets applied to it by Charlotte Brontë; everywhere *Cranford* is, as Miss Brontë said, 'pleasurable reading: graphic, pithy, penetrating, shrewd, yet kind and indulgent'. I should add that meticulous students of topography have placed the location of the lime-pit into which the cow fell who came out burnt and was put into a flannel waistcoat, on the Northwich road, just to the west of Knutsford. Mrs Gaskell died at Alton in Hampshire in 1865, but her body was brought for burial to the old Unitarian graveyard near the station at Knutsford.

From Knutsford I forsake the route that Julian Peveril followed on his way to Peveril Castle, as recounted in *Peveril of the Peak*. As the crow flies, Peveril Castle is only twenty-five miles due east of Knutsford, but it is on the far side of the road A6 which here links Manchester, Derby and Leicester, and so belongs to my next journey. But the Staffordshire side of A6 holds a considerable variety of associations; and indeed due south of Knutsford (but about forty miles distant in a bee-line) there is one memory, not well known, which delights me. Remember here the statue in London which I mentioned earlier, that statue in the garden of St Mary Aldermanbury in the City of London which I have always thought of as the 'publishers' shrine', set up to the two men who published the first folio of Shakespeare. The nineteenth-century gentleman who so earnestly desired a memorial to the publishers was Charles Clement Walker, and his address was Lilleshall Old Hall, Shropshire; and that's to be found forty miles due south of Knutsford, three miles from Newport, on the Salop side of the border with Staffordshire. The beautiful remains of Lilleshall Abbey in the grounds of Lilleshall Hall were presented to the nation and are open to the public, so it is no intrusion to pay a visit to Lilleshall in piety to Mr Walker.

A more direct return Londonwards from Cheshire through Stafford-shire leads quickly into the 'Five Towns' of Arnold Bennett's best-known novels. The five towns of the Potteries – it could be claimed that in actuality there were six – have since 1910 been conglomerated into the city of Stoke-on-Trent. Enoch Arnold Bennett (1867–1931) was born at Hanley, in a house in Hope Street which for a time his father had used as premises for pawnbroking. (That was a temporary expedient – Bennett's father, who it is assumed is represented by Darius Clayhanger in the novel *Clayhanger*, tried several professions before becoming a solicitor.) The family moved to Burslem when Bennett was a boy, and at Burslem, the 'Mother of the Potteries' and birthplace of Josiah Wedgwood, was the Wedgwood Institute, a school of science and art at which Sir Oliver Lodge and Arnold Bennett were both students before they went on to other schools. The house in Burslem in which the Bennetts lived from 1880, No. 205 Waterloo Road (the 'Trafalgar Road' of the novels is a not impenetrable disguise), is now the Bennett Museum. In the novels *Anna of the Five Towns*, *The Old Wives' Tale* and *Clay-hanger*, it is not difficult to identify the settings: 'Hambridge' may be interpreted as Hanley, 'Knype' as Stoke, 'Longshaw' as Longton, 'Turnhill' as Tunstall and 'Bursley' as Burslem. Growing up in the streets of the sprawling industrial towns, Bennett and his companions were not disposed to be 'soppy' about rural scenes and settings. Hence Bennett's dismissal of the Wrekin as 'a swollen bump'; yet he could perceive and express a moment of beauty in the formation of a slagheap – as in this passage from *Clayhanger*:

To the south of them, a mile and a half off, in the wreathing mist of the Cauldon Bar Ironworks, there was a yellow gleam that even the capricious sunlight could not kill, and then two rivers of fire sprang from the gleam and ran in a thousand delicate and lovely hues down the side of a mountain of refuse. They were emptying a few tons of molten slag at the Cauldon Bar Ironworks.

Arnold Bennett's paramount interest in writing led him to London, where for some years after 1889 he found office employment with a firm of solicitors. In Burslem the Bennetts had been friendly with a neigh-bouring family, the Kennerleys; Arnold married Miss Kennerley, and presently her brother, young Mitchell Kennerley, followed Arnold Bennett to chance his own arm in London. John Lane, the publisher, had at that moment just dissolved partnership with Elkin Mathews, and was publishing notable works (*The Yellow Book* and other *avant-garde* writings of the 1890s) on his own, at the sign of The Bodley Head, from an office at the Vigo Street end of Albany. It was Arnold Bennett, I believe, who steered young Mitchell Kennerley into employment with the enterprising John Lane, and Kennerley so quickly proved his aptitude that when Lane in 1896 opened an office in New York, he took Kennerley with him and left him there, aged eighteen, as New York manager. Within four years Kennerley had established himself so well in New York that he could set up his own independent publishing imprint, and for the quality of books issued under that imprint, and later for his superb management of sales at New York's famous Anderson Galleries, Mitchell Kennerley became one of the most exciting figures in New York's literary scene in the first three decades of the twentieth century. Bennett had likewise risen to have much influence in London; so that by producing Bennett and Kennerley, Burslem was proving that what was a fashion in Burslem yesterday would on the morrow be a fashion in both London and New York.

Further associations may be recalled in the neighbourhood of Stoke-on-Trent. When mentioning the novel *John Halifax, Gentleman* at Tewkesbury, I spoke of its author (Miss Mulock, later Mrs Craik) as having been born and brought up at Stoke. A few miles to the north-east on the fringe of the Peak District is Rudyard and Rudyard Lake where Kipling's parents stayed, and which they affectionately remembered when naming their son. At Newcastle-under-Lyme Vera Brittain (1896–1970) was born; her autobiographical *Testament of Youth* was so widely read in the 1930s that her also excellent novels were almost overshadowed. A dozen miles due east of Stoke and close to the Derbyshire border (the county line here follows the course of the River Dove) is Ellastone. This, it is worth remembering, is the setting for parts of George Eliot's *Adam Bede*; Ellastone is to be identified as 'Hayslope' in the novel, and from the novel there may be pictured at least the site of the Hall Farm, where Mrs Poyser had her say out to the Squire, and felt the easier for it, at least for the moment. 'There's no pleasure i'living,' said Mrs Poyser, 'if you're to be corked up for ever, and only dribble your mind out by the sly, like a leaky barrel.'

It is also to be remembered that at Wootton Hall, nearby Ellastone, overlooking the lovely valley of the Dove, none other than Jean-Jacques Rousseau often had feelings not unlike that just expressed by Mrs Poyser. It was during the years that Rousseau stayed at Wootton Hall (1766–8) that he wrote much of his *Confessions*. A comparison has sometimes been made between Rousseau and Cowper. Disregarding the many and obvious personal differences, Sainte-Beuve suggested one similarity. A chief article of Rousseau's creed was the duty of universal philanthropy, and yet Rousseau fancied himself to be the object of all men's hatred. 'Similarly, Cowper, who held that the first duty of man was the love of God, fancied that some mysterious cause had made him the object of the irrevocable hatred of his Creator.'

Ashbourne, the 'Oakbourne' of *Adam Bede*, is on the opposite side of the Dove from Ellastone. Before George Eliot's time, at Mayfield Thomas Moore had composed his 'Oriental-sentimental tales' in verse called *Lalla Rookh*, which on their appearance in 1817 had immense success. Before that, the associations of the neighbourhood of Ashbourne cluster round Samuel Johnson's friend Dr Taylor and Johnson himself. It was at the brook behind Dr Taylor's garden (the Henmore Brook?) that Boswell watched Johnson making many efforts to pole a dead cat over the dam. 'This may be laughed at', says Boswell, 'as too trifling to record.' I have mentioned before as of more importance, the Dove Dale (up river from Mayfield and Ashbourne) where Johnson found the scenery for his Happy Valley in *Rasselas*. Downstream the Dove passes beside Uttoxeter, where in rainy weather Johnson performed penance in the market-place. The story is one of those most frequently quoted from Boswell:

> Once, indeed, (said he), I was disobedient; I refused to attend my father to Uttoxeter-market. Pride was the source of that refusal, and the remembrance of it was painful. A few years ago, I desired to atone for this fault; I went to Uttoxeter in very bad weather, and stood for a considerable time bare-headed in the rain, on the spot where my father's stall used to stand. In contrition I stood, and I hope the penance was expiatory.

Hawthorne, in *Our Old Home*, paid tribute to the scene of this penance, and there is a bas-relief on the conduit in Uttoxeter market-place to commemorate it.

Stafford, where Izaak Walton was born (and nearby Shallowford, where a half-timbered cottage preserves the Walton connection), and Lichfield bring us back again towards Watling Street. Lichfield has its associations with the Johnson house, with Garrick's early home, with the house of Erasmus Darwin – and that splendid character should be appreciated not only for what he did for Richard Lovell Edgeworth and for activities with the Lunar Society but for his own poetic works, *The Loves of the Plants* and the *Economy of Vegetation* forming parts of his large *Botanic Garden*.

The birthplace of two of the Powys brothers was in Derbyshire. The youngest brother, Llewellyn Powys (1884–1939), was born in Dorchester, and all three are usually associated with the West Country and Wales. However, the older Theodore Francis Powys (1875–1953) and the oldest John Cowper Powys (1872–1963) – possibly the best-known of the three for his verse and the novels *Wolf Solent* and *A Glastonbury Romance* – were born at Shirley, just off the main road between Ashbourne and Derby.

I enter Leicestershire at Ashby-de-la-Zouch, the setting for robust episodes of the tournament in *Ivanhoe*, where Prince John had an eye for the black-eyed Rebecca, and the Disinherited Knight, entering the lists anonymously, carried off the honours. Scott may have visited the castle ruins at Ashby-de-la-Zouch if, as some say, he was one of the visitors to the nearby Coleorton Farm where Wordsworth and his wife and sister stayed in 1806–7. Nearer to Leicester, on the fringe of Charnwood Forest, is Woodhouse, where a somewhat slender connection with Robert Herrick is that his uncle and guardian, Sir William Herrick, possessed the fine estate of Beaumanor Park. Leicester itself is on the Manchester Road (the route of my next chapter) and all that I mention of Leicester here is that it was the traditional residence of King Lear and his daughters. Now my eye roves quickly from Higham-on-the-Hill, where Robert Burton (of the *Anatomy of Melancholy*) was born, to Gumley, where Evelyn Cheesman, author of *Things Worth While*, was taught by Atkins (earth-stopper to Fernie's Hunt) how to bouffle badgers. After that, by making for Northampton my course bisects the county of Northamptonshire. In a sense my journey here bisects the early associations of John Dryden, for Dryden was born in 1631 at Aldwinkle All Saints in the eastern part of the county, but after his student days at Cambridge he lived at Blakesley towards the western end of Northamptonshire (on the way to Sulgrave Manor, famous as the home of George Washington's direct ancestors and now equipped as a Washington museum), until he went off to London at the age of twenty-six, there to set up in active practice as a playwright.

There is a line of Dryden's poem 'Annus Mirabilis' which shows a thought derived from growing up in that age (often called the 'century of genius') in Northamptonshire. The time was one of much penetrative 'scientific' thinking about the nature of the cosmos, and in the general climate of thought favourable to the growth and appreciation of a Newton a particular feature, perhaps peculiar to Northamptonshire, was consideration of voyages to the moon. Dr Marjorie Nicolson in her book *Voyages to the Moon* treated with equal scholarship and charm the whole background of imaginative voyages from Lucian to science-fiction writers of today; but the noticeable stimulus towards 'aviation' in England of the seventeenth century came largely from men born or brought up in the Midlands. Dr Nicolson quoted the quatrain of Dryden's about how England, after the terrible yet wonderful period of the Great Plague and the Great Fire of London, would be leading, as no nation before, in discovering the nature of the cosmos:

> Then we upon our globe's last voyage shall go,
>   And view the ocean leaning on the sky;
> From thence our rolling neighbours we shall know,
>   And on the lunar world securely pry.

There is nothing much in the brassy John Bull sentiment of the passage to cause one's attention to linger, or to draw particular notice to the wish to pry into the moon-world – except, as Dr Nicolson pointed out, that Dryden is drawing on thoughts about the moon also expressed by Samuel Butler, deriving directly from the excitement stimulated by Francis Godwin's *Man in the Moone* and John Wilkins's *Discovery of a New World: or, a Discourse tending to prove, that it is probable there may be another Habitable World in the Moon*, two remarkable and influential books that were both published in 1638. To those who wish to follow the influence of Godwin's romance (on *Cyrano de Bergerac*, Defoe, Swift, Aphra Behn and others) and of Wilkins with his scientific approach ('Wilkins' *Discovery* established the conventions of the moon-voyage for more than a century. There is no one of the full-length English voyages that did not draw from it') I greatly commend Dr Nicolson's book – here I simply note that both of those important figures, Francis Godwin and John Wilkins, were Northamptonshire men.

Godwin (1562–1633 – his *Man in the Moone* was published post-humously) was born at Hannington, between Northampton and Kettering, and Wilkins (1614–72) was born at Fawsley, three miles south of Daventry. Wilkins was one of the many remarkable men of the Civil War period: he was vicar of Fawsley at the time of writing the *Discovery*; he married Cromwell's sister, adhered to the Parliamentary side in the warfare, was Master of Trinity College, Cambridge when Isaac Newton was expecting to matriculate, but at the Restoration of the monarchy Wilkins was expelled from his Mastership and left Cambridge before Newton's admission to Trinity. Wilkins was, however, at the centre of the group of men who formed the Royal Society; as a scientist he stood as it were halfway between Kepler and Newton, and it is sad that his too early death removed him from the Royal Society in the year that Newton became a Fellow. By curious coincidence one of Wilkins' themes (which also specially intrigued Dryden) was the discovery of strange means and routes for long-distance communication – and at Borough Hill by Daventry, within sight of Wilkins' home at Fawsley, a BBC high-power, short-wave transmitter was built in 1925 and the wireless masts there since then have multiplied.

How curious is this intensity of interest in the seventeenth century in this particular patch of the Midlands, in this pastoral inland terrain, about methods, romantic or practical, for voyaging to the moon! The world had perforce to wait a long while for practical methods, and in the middle of the eighteenth century a romantic type of science fiction was taking over, as shown by *The Life and Adventures of Peter Wilkins*. This anonymous romance was widely known and loved, said Dr Nicolson, for over a hundred years: 'Southey thought its winged men and women "the most beautiful creatures of imagination that were ever devised"; Lamb read it surreptitiously at Christ's Hospital; Leigh Hunt, Scott, Thackeray, Dickens, knew it well. Coleridge not only talked about the romance in his *Table Talk*, but both he and Shelley reflected it in their poetry.' There is no doubt that *Peter Wilkins* was in large part stimulated by *Robinson Crusoe* and *Gulliver's Travels*, but it also went back to the flying men of Godwin and John Wilkins – Dr Nicolson strongly suspected that the name Peter Wilkins was intended to remind readers of John Wilkins. The scientific heritage of the moon-world as discussed by seventeenth-century Northamptonshire worthies did not depart without other traces. Were we not watching trace-elements farther along Watling Street, in the Lunar Society of Birmingham? .

*   *   *

Northampton brings to memory Anne Bradstreet who after emigration from Boston in Lincolnshire to New England in 1630 obtained the reputation of America's (or more strictly New England's) earliest published poet. Born in Northampton, Anne married Massachusetts' Governor Simon Bradstreet. Her book of verse *The Tenth Muse Lately Sprung up in America* was printed for her in 1650 in London. She had the gift of a simple and direct rhythmic expression of true feeling. Proof of that is in the poem she wrote to her husband when she was waiting for a childbirth in which there were serious apprehensions of her dying:

> If any worth or virtue were in me,
> Let that live freshly in thy memory
> And when you feel'st no grief, as I no harms,
> Yet love thy dead, who long lay in thine arms . . .

Anne Bradstreet survived the hours and pain of that particular danger. Book publishing had already started in Boston with *Bay Psalm Book* in 1640 and the American book trade was widening sufficiently for Anne Bradstreet's second volume of *Poems* to be published in Boston in 1678.

Among Northampton's less cheerful literary connections are that when the poet John Clare had his complete mental breakdown he was an inmate of Northampton's asylum from 1837 until his death in 1864; and in the previous century one of Cowper's sombre occupations was the supplying of verses regularly for seven years to the parish clerk of All Saints Church to accompany the bills of mortality which registered local deaths. In his long period at Olney across the Buckinghamshire border Cowper could pay occasional visits to Northampton; there is a tradition that he composed his verse 'God moves in a mysterious way' after standing under 'Cowper's Oak' at Yardley Hastings, midway to Northampton, during a thunderstorm.

This present chapter has looked at Watling Street to notice what developed in the ancient borderland between Saxons and Danelaw; my next journey, along the last of my radial English routes, will carry me from St Albans into what was once upon a time the Danelaw's heartland.

A6

——

THE MANCHESTER
ROAD

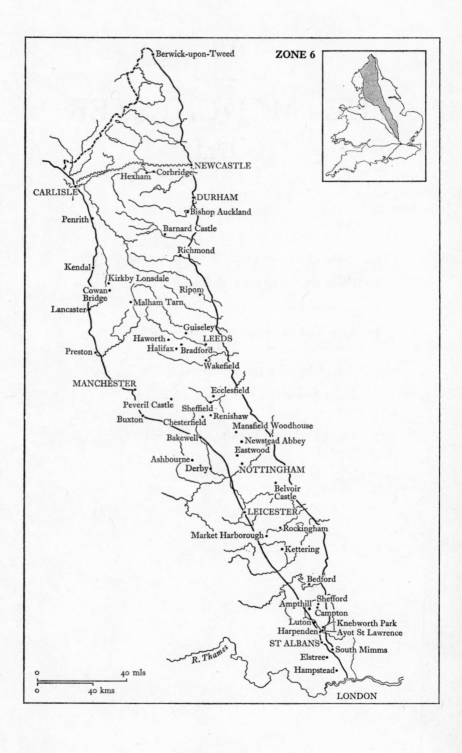

ZONE 6

Berwick-upon-Tweed

NEWCASTLE
Hexham •Corbridge
CARLISLE
DURHAM
•Bishop Auckland
Penrith
Barnard Castle
Richmond

Kendal•
•Kirkby Lonsdale
Cowan   Ripon•
Bridge
Lancaster• •Malham Tarn

Guiseley•
Haworth• •LEEDS
Halifax• •Bradford
Preston•
Wakefield•

MANCHESTER
Ecclesfield•
Peveril Castle•
Sheffield•
Buxton•   •Renishaw
Chesterfield•   Mansfield Woodhouse•
Bakewell•
•Newstead Abbey
Ashbourne•   Eastwood•
Derby•
NOTTINGHAM

Belvoir
Castle•
LEICESTER•

•Rockingham
Market Harborough•

•Kettering

•Bedford

•Shefford
Ampthill• Campton•
•Knebworth Park
Luton• •Ayot St Lawrence
Harpenden•
ST ALBANS•
•South Mimms
Elstree•
Hampstead•

R. Thames

LONDON

o
40 mls
o
40 kms

1. FROM HAMPSTEAD INTO BUNYAN'S COUNTRY

I treat now of the sixth of the most historically important arterial roads from London. Each of the other roads that I've looked at has retained an identifiable starting-place in London, and the A5, which curves into Watling Street and the Holyhead Road, is especially dignified by having a splendid ceremonial arch at either end. The distinctive and strange feature of the A6 is that this great road does not wish to have, or is not permitted to have, any identifiable starting-place at all in London. Nowhere but in the London area is the A6 shy about claiming respect. Throughout the Midlands it is the 'Manchester Road', which after Manchester goes steadily northward through Lancaster to Carlisle, romantically on to Gretna Green, importantly on to Glasgow; yet the traveller from London is not permitted to recognize the separate existence of the A6 until he reaches South Mimms.

South Mimms is topographically at the edge of the Metropolitan Police Area; it is on the perimeter of London's stockade. Is the refusal of the road A6 to reveal its identity except outside London's modern wall of officialdom deliberate? Am I to be prepared for the spirit of writers and writings emergent from the region of this road to be specifically, perhaps aggressively, 'outlaw'? Perhaps the question should be left *sub judice*, beyond preparing the mind for possible special kinds of individual eccentricity along this road, and possibly representation in literature of special kinds of Nonconformity and Dissent. There is for me another question, though, more urgent at this instant. If the road A6 has no beginning within London, where do I propose beginning? Might a reasonable starting-place be Hampstead?

Topographically Hampstead is in line for a radial route from London between A5 and A1 through St Albans, where A6 makes its avowed fresh start to Luton, Bedford and points north. Some might object that literary associations in Hampstead have become too cosmopolitan for so determinedly a British road as A6. It is true that on the way to Hampstead, between Regent's Park and Parliament Hill Fields, you will find No. 41 Maitland Park Road, where Mr and Mrs Karl Marx settled in 1875 after they left Soho, and where Marx lived for the last eight years of his life. His tomb in Highgate cemetery, topped now with its massive dark metallic bust, is much more easily to be located than when George Blake and I searched without finding it one afternoon in the 1920s. Blake, as not infrequent among Lowland Scots, had an almost morbid interest in gravestones. Later on, in the winter of 1949–50 Ivor Brown, also a Scot, reported that by perseverance he had found Marx's grave. The difficulty in those years, as Ivor Brown remarked, was that it was still, as from its beginning, 'a flat job' – meaning that there was no upright headstone. The site had been registered and used first for the body of Jenny von Westphalen, Marx's wife, who had chosen to leave her prosperous family to endure with Marx danger, exile and poverty. She was a few years older than her husband and died at Maitland Park Road, and was buried in Highgate cemetery two years before he was. The 'flat job', as it then was, was reopened to contain Marx's body also. Now the great metal bust attracts many visitors. That memory is perhaps not strictly part of Hampstead's heritage, but among other foreign visitants who came into Hampstead because it was so cosmopolitan, it is easy to recall Sigmund Freud, who came to No. 20 Maresfield Gardens, off Fitzjohn's Avenue in 1938, when the Nazi occupation of Vienna forced him to seek refuge. Earlier, what other English residence could have been more attractive to Rabindrinath Tagore than the one chosen for him at No. 3 Villas on the Heath, Vale of Health?

In the year (1915) that Tagore received his knighthood (which four years later as an ardent Indian nationalist he insisted on resigning) an English writer living in the Vale of Health (at No. 1 Byron Villas) was D. H. Lawrence. (Lawrence returned in 1923–4 to Hampstead, to No. 110 Heath Street.) The mention of Lawrence at once establishes a connection with Nottinghamshire, and hence a spiritual tendril such as I am seeking between Hampstead and the country served by the arterial road A6. It is at any rate a direct link – genius that took character from Nottingham working at least momently in Hampstead. In 1915 Lawrence's novel *The Rainbow* was being published and suppressed as obscene. The two parts of *The Rainbow*, the novel with which Lawrence's individual struggle with orthodoxy comes out strongly, take colour from the transition from Nottinghamshire to London. While *The Rainbow* was being published Lawrence was working on the sequel, *Women in Love* (not published until 1921). Here he tackled the relationship of two couples: Ursula and Birkin, and Ursula's sister Gudrun and Gerald Crich. If one agrees with the identifications suggested by Grigson's *Modern World Literature*, Ursula in *Women in Love* is more clearly Frieda Lawrence than when she appeared in the second half of *The Rainbow*, Birkin is Lawrence, and Gudrun and Gerald Crich are partly modelled on Katherine Mansfield and John Middleton Murry. Katherine Mansfield and Middleton Murry are, like Lawrence, likewise associated with Hampstead; they lived for some time in East Heath Road. It is true that Lawrence and Frieda and Murry and Katherine Mansfield flitted from place to place, so that no one locality can claim them with total possession; nevertheless one link between the country-side belonging to the road A6 and Hampstead is established. I am prompted to be sure to remember the newly restored birthplace of Lawrence at Eastwood in Nottinghamshire when this Robin Hood of a road takes me to that neighbourhood.

The cosmopolitan nature of present-day Hampstead only shows a broadening of the attraction that it has had for Britons born elsewhere. Few of even the English artists that one associates with Hampstead were actually born there. Two Hampstead painters that I happen first to think of are John Constable and Kate Greenaway: Constable a foreigner from Suffolk, Kate Greenaway a native properly of Hoxton. Of writers, to go back to the time of Leigh Hunt's 'matchless fireside companionship' at the Vale of Health, Hunt was imported from South-gate, Shelley from Sussex, Keats from Moorgate. Hampstead seems always to have welcomed strangers; probably the most prized literary memorial is Keats House. Keats's earlier lodgings in Hampstead had been in Well Walk, to which he and his two brothers moved in March 1817 partly in search of purer air for the youngest brother Tom, whose health, at the age of eighteen, was already causing worry. In the first months of the period at Well Walk Keats used to walk down the short slope of the Heath to Hunt's cottage in the Vale of Health for the chatter and 'poetic pranks' that for a time were amusing them both; but gradu-ally, and as Keats determinedly set to work on the lengthy *Endymion* (from which Hunt had tried to dissuade him), contacts with Hunt diminished. Keats was away from Hampstead for much of 1817 (at the Isle of Wight, Margate, Oxford and Burford Bridge, where *Endymion* was completed). He was at Well Walk again at Christmas and was one of the party at 'the immortal dinner' which Haydon gave in his painting room. Among those present were Wordsworth, Lamb, Monkhouse, Landseer – and 'Lamb got tipsey', and when the 'Gentleman who was Comptroller of the Stamp Office, frilled, dressed, & official' walked in after dinner, Lamb's behaviour to that dignitary, much to the 'venerable anxiety' of Wordsworth, was so frivolous that there was nothing for it but to conduct the 'tipsey' Lamb into an inner room and close the door on him. 'I felt pain', said Haydon in his journal, 'that such a poet as Wordsworth should be under the supervisorship of such a being as the Comptroller.' The laughter and sympathy of most of the party was entirely with Lamb.

Keats's brother George had taken the increasingly ill youngest brother Tom to spend that winter at Teignmouth in Devon. In March 1818 Keats changed places with George to look after Tom and bring him back to Hampstead in May. George was getting married and about to emigrate to America; Tom, when brought back by Keats to Well

L.B.—M

Walk, was so much better in health that Keats and his friend Brown set off with George and his bride to Liverpool, and having said goodbye to the emigrants, Keats began his walking tour with Brown through the Lakes and into Scotland. In Scotland, by August Keats himself was ill and forced to return to London by ship. At Well Walk Tom had suffered a bad relapse. The consumption of the lungs was now in his case, as the phrase was, 'galloping', and from the middle of August until December Keats was increasingly, and towards the end by night as well as day, Tom's nurse. Tom 'looks upon me as his only comfort', wrote Keats, and though Keats felt his own vitality ebbing away with his brother's life, none of his friends could prevent the tax that Tom's dying made on Keats's own strength. Severn, Haslam, Brown each felt (and Keats had the same premonition) that Keats was vulnerable in the same way as Tom. On the morning after Tom's death Brown took Keats away from the lodgings in Well Walk to live in Brown's own semi-detached villa in what was then Wentworth Place – the house, then surrounded by open heath, which has now turned into Keats House.

  While Brown and Keats were on their walking tour in the previous summer, Brown had let his part of the house now called after Keats to Mrs Brawne and her two daughters and son, who remained in the neighbourhood after the summer. They were sympathetic with Keats when he was wearing himself out with nursing Tom; in later life Fanny Brawne spoke of how Dryden's couplet

> The fiery soul, that working out its way,
> Fretted the pigmy body to decay

applied with sad exactitude to Keats. After Tom's death they invited Keats to spend Christmas Day with them; he broke other engagements to do so, and in the early summer of 1819 intimacies ripened when Mrs Brawne rented the other half of the semi-detached Wentworth Place. Thus by May Keats and eighteen-year-old Fanny Brawne were living in joined houses under one roof and with a garden in common. That Keats and Fanny should become engaged was almost inevitable; that his state of mind and feelings in the forthcoming months were to produce his loveliest poems was a concomitant result. The lightweight exercises indulged in with Leigh Hunt a year before were now forgotten; Keats had moved into company more suited to him – there was, one feels, immediate recognition of that in the one meeting between Coleridge and Keats early in 1819.

  There was certainly more instantaneous rapport between Keats and Coleridge than between Keats and Wordsworth. The two accounts of the meeting which Coleridge recorded years later do not precisely tally with what Keats wrote to his brother George at the time, which was that as Keats and a friend happened to meet Coleridge in Millfield Lane on the Highgate side of Hampstead Heath, they joined and strolled at an 'alderman-after-dinner pace' for nearly two miles, Coleridge's talk 'far above singing' touching on many things. Keats listed Coleridge's talk for his brother and for his own memory, and prominent in the list was the item 'Nightingales, Poetry'. Coleridge's 'conversation poem' 'The Nightingale' with its emphasis on the happiness, not the melancholy, of the bird was one with which Keats was familiar. In the spring of 1819 Hampstead's nightingales kept forcing themselves on Keats's attention. One evening when he was supposed to be with friends at the Spaniards Inn, Severn noticed that Keats had vanished, and found him outside, lying under the trees later known as 'Constable's Firs', hearkening to a nightingale. Brown reported that it was after promptings by the resident nightingale in the Wentworth Place garden that Keats on a May morning put his own 'immortal Bird' on closely written sheets of paper.

I might pause to recall the moment 'in the Spaniards Tea-gardens' when Mrs Bardell was in the chair for the celebration of the happy conclusion of the memorable affair of *Bardell* v. *Pickwick* – 'How sweet the country is, to-be-sure!' sighed one of her guests, when they had reached the Spaniards – but the surprise 'special messenger' arrested Mrs Bardell there and then, and by the sudden popping of her into the Fleet, out popped Mr Pickwick from that prison. That adventure might lead on to thinking of the Heath's other famous inn, Jack Straw's Castle, where Heath Street leads into North End Road, and there, at North End Road, I am on a reasonably direct line of departure leading onward to South Mimms to joining the as yet elusive road A6. This would be a route with a rightful feeling of independence, not beholden on the left hand or the right to A5 or A1.

So once a Londoner's attachment to A6 has been thus directly established, then is he launched on a long straight journey which will take him to the northernmost coast of Cumbria, and to that precise part of the Solway Firth to which Wilkie Collins despatched Walter Hartright, the drawing-master, at the start of *The Woman in White*. Why should Wilkie Collins, who had been at North End, Hampstead, as a baby send off the drawing-master to 'Limmeridge House, Cumberland'? Why should Collins place the departure of his story at the mother's cottage at North End (so easily identified as the scene of his own childhood) – unless he also felt, as I have now persuaded myself, that North End is an appropriate starting-place from which to approach this singular road?

*   *   *

This informal approach to St Albans, sneaking from North End past Elstree and Borehamwood, need not cause me to forget that Sir Richard Burton, impulsive nineteenth-century pilgrim to 'Al Madinah and Meccah' and famous translator of the *Arabian Nights*, was born at Barham House, Elstree. If I had veered eastward into Barnet to verify exactly where the St Albans Road forks away from the Great North Road, I should there have been close to Hadley Common, where Mrs Trollope (Anthony's mother) rented a house for the year 1836, and where Anthony, escaping now and then from the Post Office to ramble with his two companions of the 'Tramp Society', had memorable visits. A less happy recollection at Hadley Common is that Cecil Day Lewis died there in 1972, while on a visit at Lemmons – we noticed his grave in the churchyard at Stinsford in Dorset, where Thomas Hardy's heart rests also.

Coming into St Albans from South Mimms by what is now openly recognized as road A6, we have to make a sharp turn north at the town centre not to be carried off past Gorhambury (seat of none less than Sir Francis Bacon, the first Baron Verulam) and so becoming captured, almost before knowing it, by Watling Street. It is by being properly firm in St Albans and if necessary waiting for the north star to by my guide that I am now indubitably on the trail A6 towards Robin Hood.

At St Albans the A6 is locally called the Harpenden Road, for one is now launched on the direct route through Harpenden, Luton and Bedford. Harpenden made, anonymously, an earlier surreptitious entry in my narrative. When I paused at Guildford on the Portsmouth Road to talk of Ellen Terry, I mentioned the six-year period when Ellen was living with Edward Godwin in Hertfordshire. It was between Wheathampstead and Harpenden that they were living, and their son Edward Gordon Terry, later famous in the theatre world as Gordon Craig, was born at Harpenden in 1872. That period of Ellen Terry's 'resting' in the country ended when Charles Reade, on horseback in one of Hertfordshire's narrow lanes, was both startled and delighted to meet his vanished favourite Miss Terry driving her dog-cart; her return to the London stage as leading lady in Reade's play *The Wandering Heir* opened a notable new act of theatre history. Farther on, near Ampthill Park, are the ruins of Houghton House, built for the Countess of Pembroke, 'Sidney's sister, Pembroke's mother'; it may have suggested to Bunyan the 'House Beautiful' of *Pilgrim's Progress*, but a more definite link between Bunyan and Ampthill is that he was first arrested here in November 1660 for preaching at a local farmhouse. This leads me on to Elstow, famous as John Bunyan's birthplace in 1628, and to Bedford itself, where in the first part of his twelve years' imprisonment Bunyan wrote *Grace Abounding* and when re-confined, turned to composing *The Pilgrim's Progress*.

The Pilgrim's Progress is one of the great and fitting contributions to literature from Robin Hood's domain. Saintsbury dwells on the way in which for four generations after its first appearance *The Pilgrim's Progress* was sniffed at by academic critics; 'its popularity, though always great, was, so to speak, subterranean and almost contraband. . . . And so the greatest prose-book of the late seventeenth century in English had, for nearly a hundred and fifty years, the curious fate of constantly exercising influence without ever achieving praise, or even notice, from those whose business it was to give both.' The swing from such neglect was to a custom of regarding Bunyan as having been, in essentials, originator of 'the English Novel in its most characteristic form', developments brought in by Defoe, Richardson and Fielding being slighter than they look. 'Defoe may claim the parentage of a species,' said Dr Allon, 'but Bunyan is the creator of the genus.' Yet to try to pick up *The Pilgrim's Progress* with any narrow kind of forceps is surely a mistake; on a shelf with novels only it would be as much misplaced as if it were on a shelf of books for children only. Coleridge, who was one of those who in the nineteenth century drew attention to *The Pilgrim's Progress*, made a remark to be remembered: 'This wonderful work is one of the few books which may be read over repeatedly at different times, and each time with a new and a different pleasure.'

Coleridge mentions three of his separate readings of *The Pilgrim's Progress* – once as a poet, once with devotional feelings, and once as a theologian – 'and let me assure you', he said, 'that there is great theological acumen in the work. I could not have believed beforehand that Calvinism could be painted in such exquisitely delightful colours.' Coleridge's emphasis on Bunyan's 'acumen', coming from a mind as supple and subtle as his, is doubly welcome. For unless I misread comments attributed to Charles Kingsley, even when Bunyan had been drawn to the attention of university people, some of them in the nineteenth century assumed that because he was the son of a Bedford tinker he must have been a 'simple' fellow. 'Born and bred in the monotonous midland', Kingsley wrote of Bunyan, 'he has no natural images beyond the pastures and brooks, the town and country houses he saw about him.' Such a first *non sequitur* appears to have led to another, that though Bunyan had been granted singular power to rivet attention to human life and nature in an ordinary everyday guise, he was too simple to apprehend those 'complexities and contradictions of the human heart which we are now so fond of trying to unravel'. When re-reading Bunyan's works one is likely to agree more with Coleridge than with Kingsley as regards Bunyan's acumen.

Here (and partly perhaps because both men appear in this same 'monotonous midland' area) certain comparisons suggest themselves between Bunyan and Cowper. In *Grace Abounding*, Bunyan's autobiographical document recording his own 'going down into the deep', the same metaphor (that of the castaway) persists as with Cowper, and the same torment that whirled back and stuck with each of them was as told by Bunyan in the words of the Epistle to the Hebrews (xii, 17): 'For ye know, how that afterward, when he would have inherited the blessing, he was rejected; for he found no place of repentance, though he sought it carefully with tears.' This fate of Esau flew in Bunyan's face 'like to Lightning', and in the thirty pages of *Grace Abounding* allotted to those years Bunyan's spirit is portrayed as hanging 'as in a pair of Scales, sometimes up and sometimes down, now in peace and anon again in terror'. A detached and distant view shows Bunyan and Cowper close together in any wide collection of the varieties of religious experience. Bunyan's self-analysis in his own *Grace Abounding* reveals the intellect and charm of character that were not destroyed when he was re-arrested and put in gaol for a further six years.

Bedford does not now neglect to honour Bunyan. 'Bunyan's Statue stands facing where stood his jail' – the County Gaol, to which he was first committed immediately after the Restoration in 1660, used to stand at the corner of High Street and Silver Street. The initial charge under which he was indicted was that by joining and preaching in John Gifford's group of Nonconformists he had 'devilishly and perniciously abstained from coming to church to hear Divine service, and was a common upholder of unlawful meetings and conventicles'. 'O, I saw in this condition I was as a man who was pulling down his House upon the Head of his Wife and Children . . . especially my poor blind Child, who lay nearer to my heart than all I had besides . . . *yet*, thought I, *I must do it, I must do it*.' Bunyan apparently had a short period of liberty in 1666; it was in that year that *Grace Abounding* was published; if he was released for a while, he was speedily re-arrested on the old charge and returned to the same gaol. It seems that it was during a still further term of imprisonment for six months in 1675–6, this time in the Town Gaol on Bedford's Old Bridge, that he wrote the first part of *The Pilgrim's Progress*.

A more recent 'novelist of Dissent', born at Bedford in 1831, was William Hale White, who wrote under the pen-name of 'Mark Rutherford'. White was brought up in a Dissenting household and as if destined for the Congregational ministry, but when a student he was expelled from the Congregational New College because of his 'modernism'. His spiritual struggles were described in *The Autobiography of Mark Rutherford* (1881) and *Mark Rutherford's Deliverance* (1885). His novels likewise, such as *Catherine Furze*, are nowadays singled out for, as William Haley expresses it, the way they 'breathe a natural air of Dissent'. Mark Rutherford joins the company of George Eliot and Mrs Gaskell as getting 'to the heart of the Dissenting matter'.

2. FROM KETTERING THROUGH DERBYSHIRE

At Kettering the influence of Bunyan showed when William Carey, Andrew Fuller and a few others in a house now known as the 'Mission House' started, in 1792, the Baptist Missionary Society. The Society of Friends also has special allegiance to this region; George Fox, son of a Leicestershire weaver, received here his own spirit of Dissent. Religious feelings manifest in the seventeenth century were retained in the nineteenth-century Leicestershire into which the literary Thomas Babington Macaulay was born. In 1800 his father Zachary Macaulay, the West Indies merchant and philanthropist who later devoted himself to the abolition of the slave trade, had brought his wife to stay for her confinement with his sister, who had married into the ancient family of the Babingtons, and whose house was the Elizabethan mansion of Rothley Temple, five miles north of Leicester. At Rothley Temple, then, Macaulay was born, and he maintained that the two seventeenth-century minds of the greatest influence in his upbringing were Milton and Bunyan, because 'one of those minds produced the *Paradise Lost*, the other *Pilgrim's Progress*'. Macaulay's own literary career began with his essay on Milton in the *Edinburgh Review* in 1825, but he felt his own vivid style of writing (so much praised when his *History of England* began to appear) owed most to his memory from boyhood of *The Pilgrim's Progress*. 'There is no book in our literature', said Macaulay, 'on which we would so readily stake the fame of the old unpolluted English language, no book which shows so well how rich that language is in its own proper wealth, and how little it has been improved by all that it has borrowed.'

My personal affection towards Macaulay derives not so much from his prose writings as from one of his ballads in the *Lays of Ancient Rome*, namely 'Horatius'. *The Lays of Ancient Rome* appeared in 1842.

At first, and for years afterwards [those verses] were favourably received both by critics and others. But it pleased Mr Matthew Arnold, to whom Macaulay was the embodiment of his enemy the Philistine, and who did not like the ballad metre for ancient themes, to speak with the utmost contempt of them, and generation after generation of critics has echoed this contempt.

The critic who wrote that was Saintsbury, who added that it was simply silly of Arnold to deny the thrill of verses beginning:

> Lars Porsena of Clusium
>   By the Nine Gods he swore
> That the great house of Tarquin
>   Should suffer wrong no more.
> By the Nine Gods he swore it,
>   And named a trysting day,
> And bade his messengers ride forth,
> East and west and south and north,
>   To summon his array.

The gathering of that array

> From many a lonely hamlet,
>   Which, hid by beech and pine,
> Like an eagle's nest, hangs on the crest
>   Of purple Apennine

with its visual details –

> And in the vats of Luna,
>   This year, the must shall foam
> Round the white feet of laughing girls,
>   Whose sires have marched to Rome

– is superb invitation to an interesting story, put into such catchy rhythm as to be permanently memorable. 'How well Horatius kept the bridge/In the brave days of old' may be 'poetry for the million', said Saintsbury, 'but not the less poetry'.

Elizabeth Barrett, two years before she met Robert Browning, wrote in a letter to a friend: 'You are very right in admiring Macaulay; he has a noble clear, metallic note in his soul, and makes us ready by it for battle. I very much admire Mr Macaulay, and could scarcely read his ballads and keep lying down. They seemed to draw me up to my feet as the mesmeric powers are said to do.' Presently Elizabeth Barrett was susceptible of being drawn to her feet by Browning with his 'The Pied Piper of Hamelin'; and soon in many a Victorian nursery there was athletic pleasure in the chanting of the contemporary ballads, all readily designed to be 'learned by heart' – 'Horatius', and 'The Pied Piper', and Tennyson's 'The Charge of the Light Brigade' and his naval ballad beginning 'At Flores in the Azores Sir Richard Grenville lay'.

It is intriguing to speculate what instigated Macaulay, regarding himself as certainly a man of letters yet not necessarily a poet, to turn into ballads the Roman stories that appealed to him. Macaulay dated his conscious impulse as rising largely from Sir Walter Scott, of whom he spoke as 'the great restorer of our ballad-poetry'. There is no reason to doubt that Scott was an effective trigger to Macaulay; but common to both and perhaps working in an underground way was childhood in surroundings where there was companionship with ballads and where ballad-poetry was native to the environment. The way balladry sprang up spontaneously on the Scottish Border needs no emphasis; to answer the question 'What is a ballad?' Professor Ker was wont to point to 'Sir Patrick Spens' and 'Lord Randal' and other 'things of that sort' – his interest at that moment being primarily in the Border ballads. Yet also into an early period there came the Robin Hood ballads. These were distinctively native to the heartland of what had been the Danelaw, and of those ballads there is a selection in *The Oxford Book of Ballads* and in other popular anthologies. It is, however, strange that the *Oxford Book* and other collections limit themselves to ballads of the early period, as if there were no worthy and remembrable 'things of that sort' composed in England after Tudor times.

A fact that needs emphasis is that Marvell in the seventeenth century and Gay, Swift, Pope, Cowper in the eighteenth regarded ballads as a living form of versification whether for lively recitation of some story or episode, or for propaganda. Two of those men inherited a taste for ballads from parents in this part of the Danelaw area. Swift's mother was a native of Leicester, and he was cousin to Dryden of Northamptonshire. After leaving Trinity College, Dublin, he joined his mother at Leicester and for more than twenty years continued to visit her there, until her death in 1710. His mother (Abigail Erick) is thought to have encouraged Swift's versifying, more than did Dryden, who is supposed to have remarked: 'Cousin Swift, you will never be a poet.' Swift's own ballads were mostly prompted by instances of oppression. This accorded with Danelaw tradition, which Byron followed a century later when Nottinghamshire weavers were thrown out of work and he used the street-ballad form to defend them 'with an irony and gusto worthy of Marvell and Swift' (*The Common Muse*, edited by V. de Sola Pinto and A. E. Rodway). The other tradition of using the ballad form for graphic recital of a good story was one which Cowper said he learned from his father. Perhaps growing up in a household familiar not only with Cowper's serious poems but with *John Gilpin*, made it natural for Macaulay to try his hand, for the fun of it, with the *Lays of Ancient Rome*. 'Horatius' is too closely allied to schoolroom lessons to count as 'genuine popular poetry', yet the straightforward praise for the supposedly simple moral code 'in the brave days of old' accords well with the spirit of the local traditional ballads.

I have harped a great deal on the conscious opposition of the Robin Hood legend to the legends of Arthurian heroes. Territory in which loyalty to Robin Hood is native and dominant extends along my present road A6 as far as the forest of Englyshe-wood or Inglewood surrounding Penrith and 'merry Carlisle', but the heart of it was the Sherwood Forest surrounding Nottingham, and his demesne stretched north-eastward through the forest of Barnsdale and on through Yorkshire to the east coast beside Whitby. (I am reminded how intuitive it was of Wilkie Collins to seize upon 'merry Carlisle' and the Robin Hood part of the Yorkshire coast for the starting-points of his two classics of mystery and crime.) The large number of Robin Hood ballads share the perennial appeal of a 'Wild West' with satisfaction of frontier virtues and a general intention of getting the better of authority. There is the joy of the green-wood background in the early ballads:

> In somer, when the shawes be sheyne,
>   And leves be large and long,
> Hit is full mery in feyre foreste
>   To here the foulys song:
>
> To se the dere draw to the dale,
>   And leve the hilles hee,
> And shadow hem in the levës grene,
>   Under the grene-wode tre.

Those deer belonging to the king belong equally to Robin Hood and Little John and to any, such as the financially embarrassed knight, Sir Richard at the Lee, who are in need of help from the outlaws. The particular meeting whereby that knight was saved from the legal clutches of the avaricious Abbot of York occurred in the Barnsdale region between Pontefract and Doncaster. The more than 450 verses collected under the title of the *Little Geste of Robin Hood* tell of various instances of Robin Hood's sympathies with the underdog and his perpetual hostilities with the sheriff of Nottingham – local authority is outwitted on occasion by Robin's direct appeal to the king, and whenever the king is irritated by Robin, the queen intercedes for him. The final verses of that long ballad briefly record Robin Hood's death at the Cistercian nunnery of Kirksley (Kirklees) near Wakefield, where the wicked prioress, although of his own kin, contrives that he should die by being over-bled.

Many other of the medieval ballads express the grief for the death of Robin Hood,

> For he was a good outlaw,
>   And did poor men much good.

In general the stories recited fit in with the spirit which broke out in the

Peasants' Revolt of 1381, and also perpetuate the wish for 'permissive' society. Robin Hood's birth is placed as specifically as his death: he was born 'in merry sweet Locksly town, in merry Nottinghamshire'. His father is usually reported to have been the forester who with his lusty strong bow outshot in competition even Adam Bell, Clym of the Clough, and William of Cloudesley – though the last-named, before William Tell copied the feat, had sent an arrow, from a distance of six score paces, through an apple placed on the head of his seven-year-old son. Either from necessity or choice Robin himself (whose skill with the bow was to exceed that of his father) created his own free life in the greenwood. He lived by hunting, and when spoken of as 'Earl of Huntingdon', 'knowing' hearers might approve the pun. The adventures of Robin Hood which ballad-makers seemed most to enjoy were those in which the proud were humbled and the rich were fleeced to benefit the poor. The attitude to the Church throughout all the Robin Hood ballads indicates that 'a natural air of Dissent' was being breathed throughout his territory; just as we have several times noticed that same air inspiring people of other subsequent generations in this same area.

* * *

In 1913 a writer then not yet widely known, named D. H. Lawrence, published an autobiographical novel, *Sons and Lovers*. In Lawrence's opening paragraphs indicating that the novel will deal with life in a Nottinghamshire mining village (the name 'Bestwood' in the novel signified Lawrence's birthplace, Eastwood) the noticing reader picks up two clues: the company's mines are 'on the edge of Sherwood Forest' and the railway that serves them passes 'Robin Hood's Well'. These clues link Lawrence's individual exploration of Dissent with the temper indigenous since Robin Hood to this territory – the territory to which Lawrence often referred as 'the country of my heart'. George Eliot had written of middle-class Midlanders, so Lawrence was to write of the working-class Midland miners, 'but with more poetry'. In *Sons and Lovers* vivid awareness of the beauty of the countryside is background to the terrible human fights between Paul's parents:

The sun was going down. Every open evening, the hills of Derbyshire were blazed over with red sunset. Mrs Morel watched the sun sink from the glistening sky, leaving a soft flower-blue overhead, while the western space went red, as if all the fire had swum down there, leaving the bell cast flawless blue. The mountain-ash berries across the field stood fierily out from the dark leaves, for a moment. A few shocks of corn in a corner of the fallow stood up as if alive; she imagined them bowing; perhaps her son would be a Joseph. In the east, a mirrored sunset floated pink opposite the west's scarlet. The big haystacks on the hillside, that butted into the glare, went cold.

With Mrs Morel it was one of those still moments when the small frets vanish, and the beauty of seeing things stands out, and she had the peace and the strength to see herself. Now and again, a swallow cut close to her. Now and again, Annie came up with a handful of alder-currants. The baby was restless on his mother's knee, clambering with his hands at the light. . . .

Her heart was anxious.

'I will call him "Paul"', she said suddenly; she knew not why.

. . . that day, at least, ended peacefully.

The 'Lawrence House' in Victoria Street, Eastwood, where David Herbert Lawrence (self-portrayed in *Sons and Lovers* as 'Paul') was born in 1885, has been restored as a memorial. It is fitting to be reminded of Lawrence's birthplace, for despite outward changes, there is in much of his work a deep reflection of ancient Nottinghamshire feelings. The gamekeeper in *Lady Chatterley's Lover* is a modern representative of the forester who in the medieval ballad made love to 'Earl Richard's daughter' so that they were in woodland-contract 'like proper paramour': the feeling in the novel is close to the ballad of the birth of Robin Hood 'in gude green-wood'. His Nottinghamshire heritage impelled Lawrence to repeat that 'life itself' came from 'the working class' which on occasion, as in the ballad, might combine well with family 'of high degree'.

During the years that Lawrence was growing up at Eastwood, twenty miles due north, at Renishaw Hall, Edith Sitwell and her two brothers were reared in a family representative of an opposite side of the industrial picture: the inheritance of land in the coal-mining district of Derbyshire had brought wealth to the Sitwells. They were owners, where Lawrences were 'workers'. On my return journey I must come back to the contrast of Lawrence and the Sitwells, who when young were geographically close together, and yet in circumstance were greatly different. Common, however, to the fourth child of the Lawrences and the two years younger Edith Sitwell was their inventive and insistent urge to write. As time went on each of these eccentric individuals sought actively to taunt and to express defiance of the dullness of the all-too-ordinary dead-weight of the powerful, complacent mass of people in between their own respective social settings. The dominant Edith Sitwell enlisted her brothers into the activity, to which Lawrence from his opposite covert was equally inclined, of shooting off arrows at middle-class targets.

Most of Nottinghamshire lies in between the roads A6 and A1, and awaits my return from the outward journey, which at this point is carrying me west of Nottingham, through Derby and thence across the Peak District to Manchester. The literary history of Derby itself indicates that middle-class representatives, when gifted with 'liveliness of mind' (Jane Austen's expression) can manage not too badly in competition with such archers as just mentioned. George Eliot is spoken of as standing up for some of the ideas provided by middle-class Midlanders: Derby appears as 'Stoniton' in *Adam Bede*, and Herbert Spencer, the friend who provided many ideas that influenced her, was born at Derby. In the previous century Samuel Johnson and Mrs Elizabeth Porter selected St Werburgh's Church, Derby, as the place for what I suppose might be called their lower-middle-class wedding. It is interesting that both Walter Scott and Jane Austen selected Derbyshire as a county in which marriages of people of different heritage might be brought about. (The thought occurs that both of them had sympathy with Richardson.) Surely the greatest challenge to Jane Austen's skill as novelist was to arrange with credibility, and in spite of all the obstacles so expertly detailed, the union of Elizabeth Bennet and Fitzwilliam Darcy. In the final sentence of *Pride and Prejudice* Jane Austen alludes with pleasure to the scheme of Elizabeth's visit to Derbyshire as the means for achieving the marriage, and, as one re-reads that novel, one may pause to admire the neatness with which Derbyshire serves the novelist's purpose.

As regards *Pride and Prejudice*, I would hesitate to try to locate Pemberley, the country estate of Mr Darcy, on the map of Derbyshire with any exact precision. It is true that the general great change of atmosphere from Elizabeth's home and surroundings in Hertfordshire to Darcy's country home is to be much in mind. Though Jane Austen attends more closely to people's behaviour than to topography, her general feelings for 'place' are acute. Elizabeth's uncle and aunt had at first designed to take her for a tour of the Lakes, but the curtailment of that scheme and the substitution of Derbyshire, though disappointing to Elizabeth, is the making of the story. Since the aunt had less interest in 'all the celebrated beauties of Matlock, Chatsworth, Dovedale, or the Peak' than in the little town of Lambton where some of her friends still remained, the visit to Pemberley, because that estate is within five miles of Lambton and connected with many of their acquaintance, is perfectly plausible; so is the testimony of the housekeeper at Pemberley, so necessary to the improvement of feelings towards Darcy; and natural also is Darcy's appearance in the flesh, and friendliness to the uncle and aunt (very necessary to the plot). One of the pleasures of journeying through Derbyshire is thus the general memory of how smoothly and successfully the machinery of *Pride and Prejudice* is worked. In the end Elizabeth is able to say in playfulness to her sister Jane that her happiness 'must date from my first seeing Pemberley'. 'It is not the object of this work to give a description of Derbyshire', said Jane Austen, but nevertheless it is the tour in Derbyshire which remains the novel's turning-point. The reader shares with Elizabeth Bennet her 'thanks for not going to the Lakes'.

The arterial road A6 for Manchester proceeds through Matlock, Bakewell and Buxton to where it is joined, near Whaley Bridge, by the road coming in from Sheffield through Castleton, and there, perched on its limestone crag, is what remains of the Norman keep of Peveril Castle. Those ruins are a visible reminder of *Peveril of the Peak*, in which romance Scott makes a spirited effort to render plausible, after the Restoration, the marriage of Julian Peveril and Alice Bridgenorth, representatives of Cavalier and Puritan families. If Scott had been really interested in Julian and Alice as people, *Peveril* would have had elements of comparison with *Pride and Prejudice* (which Scott had read ten years before he wrote *Peveril*), but his famous and frank admission that Jane Austen's 'talent for describing the involvements and feelings and characters of ordinary life' was something beyond his own powers, made him dodge persenting Julian and Alice as anything other than puppets.

What remains superb in *Peveril* is the general zest and sweep with which, for instance, the opening episode is described – the feast at Martindale Castle to celebrate the king's Restoration. Here Scott's own talent is inimitable: Peveril prescribes the celebration but hares off to Whitehall on his own ploy, leaving it to his lady not only to obtain provisions but to keep the peace between the hostile factions of Royalist and Roundhead guests. A comedy concealed from some of Scott's readers at the time was that while embarking on *Peveril* he was also immersed in the hurried arrangements for the reception in Edinburgh of King George IV; the two weeks' visit of that monarch in August 1822 was the first time, since Charles II, that a sovereign had appeared in the northern capital; the flurry of excitement in Edinburgh was prodigious and (as in the lesser goings-on at the entertainment at Peveril's castle in the novel) there were some violent mixed feelings of which Scott, in the Edinburgh of 1822, was aware. (Thomas Carlyle, for one, rather than to have to hold his tongue at 'such efflorescence of the flunkeyisms' took himself off in dudgeon for the duration of the royal visit.) In *Peveril* the comedies of dealing with frictions at a feast supposedly of reconciliation are treated with accents of experience.

3. MANCHESTER AND TO THE NORTH

Manchester's literary associations might be expected mainly to tie in with the social tempers that arose with the rapid increase of factory work in the Lancashire cotton industry. From the end of the eighteenth century the speed with which mills and machinery were turning 'the largest village in the country' into 'Cottonopolis' added unforeseen and intolerable tensions to many lives in Manchester. After the 'massacre of Peterloo' in 1819, when a mass meeting of protest against workers' distress caused a mayor of Manchester to cite the Riot Act and call upon armed yeomanry to disperse the mob – apart from those injured, eleven people were killed in that street-fighting – it was natural for most people to have considerable concern with social reforms. A newspaper, the *Manchester Guardian*, was founded in 1821 to carry on traditions of liberalism. Engels came from Germany to settle in Manchester; Marx came to visit. Meanwhile English novelists, whom Charlotte Brontë and Mrs Gaskell represent in this part of England, were supporting liberal feelings. However, it was not until the middle of the nineteenth century that Mrs Gaskell was vividly picturing painful features of Manchester life; before her time Harrison Ainsworth, born in Manchester in 1805 and educated at Manchester Grammar School, had been content to imitate Scott with historical romances imbued with schoolboyish melodrama: his first novel, *Rookwood* (1834), had Dick Turpin as its hero and was immensely popular in its time, although by now it may be for the cloak and dagger romance of *The Tower of London* (1840) that Ainsworth is chiefly remembered.

Before Ainsworth another notable native of Manchester was Thomas De Quincey (1785–1859), author of the *Confessions of an English Opium-Eater*. In early boyhood De Quincey, son of a Manchester merchant, was protected, like Ainsworth, from the rougher side of life; except that after the father's death when the boy was seven the eldest of what De Quincey later called his 'horrid pugilistic brothers' tried to make him fight with factory children in the streets of Salford. The cleverest but least robust of the six children who were left in charge of their mother and four other legally appointed guardians, De Quincey was soon taken away from Manchester to preparatory schools in Bath and Wiltshire, but the dominant guardian saw to it that the boy of such scholarly aptitudes should be entered as a boarder at Manchester Grammar School at the age of fifteen. It was expected that he would proceed to Oxford three years later with an easily earned scholarship. The boy found the prescribed schoolwork too easy; he spent some spare time reading Hebrew with a Lady Carbery, who had taken notice of the boy and his mother at Bath; but with half of his prescribed term at Manchester Grammar School completed (nineteen months of the thirty-six required) De Quincey, not yet seventeen years old, made up his mind, as he phrased it, to 'elope'. It was not that he had designs of escaping from Manchester with Lady Carbery; she helped, though, by giving him £10 with which to get away from school and see the world. The year was 1802; De Quincey had already been excited by the Lake poets and had an adolescent idea of joining them; but an accident directed his footsteps first to Chester, where his mother was staying, and thence he simply wandered off footloose for a period in North Wales. Living rough in Wales ended when he climbed on the Holyhead coach for London, there to seek help to claim some patrimony independent of his guardians, and so perhaps to go to Oxford on his own.

It was when De Quincey, still a boy, reached London as a drop-out, that his periods of living really rough began. It must be remembered that the *Confessions of an English Opium-Eater* that appeared in the *London Magazine* in 1821 were written nearly twenty years later than De Quincey's first London experiences. Even Lamb's *Essays of Elia*, then also being written for the same periodical, contain a certain amount of embroidery in autobiographical reminiscence: embroidery, in the personal essay, was in the fashion. It was on the 1821 visits to London that De Quincey used to be sought for and captured by Tom Hood (assistant editor of the magazine), conveyed to and imprisoned in the back room of Bohn the publisher's premises at No. 4 York Street, Covent Garden, until his forthcoming portion of *Confessions* was completed. In that back room Hood provided pen, paper and *quant. suff.* of the proper stimulant to encourage the narrative; as a reminder of that intercourse with De Quincey Hood kept some of the manuscript of the opium-eater's papers 'showing the stain of a "purplish ring" where his tumbler of laudanum had stood'.

De Quincey's experiences of squalor and starvation in Soho, his companionship with the young streetwalker Ann, and his repetitions of such experiences and ineffectual searchings for Ann as he remembered her, all going on both before and during the long period of his supposed continuous residence at Worcester College, Oxford, to which he did, at the age of eighteen or so, obtain admission – all of this, reformed and retouched, redreamed perhaps for publication as an anonymous casebook (the anonymity of the Opium-Eater was at first carefully preserved), was set down in the purplish-stained manuscript with an individual humour which makes one envious of those who have the joy of meeting it for the first time. What quotation would illustrate De Quincey's humour? I select the passage where, not without alarm for himself, the Opium-Eater discusses whether an overdose might produce spontaneous combustion, adducing as one example that of the man who 'blew up in the dark, without match or candle near him, leaving nothing behind him but some bones, of no use to anybody, and which were supposed to be *his* only because nobody else ever applied for them'.

No more than with Charles Lamb can De Quincey's individual humour be conveyed by quoting a single brief sentence; yet it is a reminder to refresh acquaintance with one of Manchester's remarkable natives. It must, though, be admitted that De Quincey was not overfond of his native city. It occurred to him to write 'Vision of Sudden Death' in a Manchester tavern, but he lives on more for what he wrote else-where. After his first London experiences, continued during the lengthy but intermittent tenure of the college rooms in the Oxford which he eventually left without taking a degree, he managed in 1809 to put into effect his early notion of settling at Grasmere, in the Lake District, and his headquarters were to be there or thereabouts until in 1830 he made a final move to Edinburgh.

Among other remarkable writers who were born and brought up in Manchester but whose best-known writings were produced elsewhere was Frances Hodgson Burnett. She was born in 1849 and lived as a child in the same district, Salford, as De Quincey, but hers was an era in which her widowed mother lived in shabby gentility, and the family's reduced circumstances produced dreams of sudden transformations from poverty to grandeur. When Frances was sixteen the family emigrated to the United States, where not altogether good fortune presently settled them into a log cabin in Tennessee. In pressing need for money, Frances turned to writing for fiction magazines; from the age of nineteen her stories found publication. In 1886, after she had married, raised children and divorced her husband, she dressed her younger son Vivian in the velvet suit and lace collar that set off his golden curls and (much to his own later chagrin) used him as model for *Little Lord Fauntleroy*. That novel was an instantaneous and in its time a pheno-menal bestseller. A second marriage when she was fifty proved disas-trous, but with her ability to earn a handsome income she returned to England in 1898 to make her home at Maytham Hall in Kent. After nine years there she found that after all she preferred to be near New York and moved to a new italianate villa built to her wishes at Plandome, Long Island. There, out of what her son called her 'regretful feeling' on hearing that new owners of Maytham Hall in Kent were altering the walled rose garden that had been her special favourite, she started on what remains now her finest book, *The Secret Garden*. That novel was not wildly admired when published in the period before the First World War, but it has established itself above all her other works as a lastingly pleasure-giving story.

Two young men, approximately ten years younger than Mrs Burnett, arrived in Manchester to become students at Owens College (the nucleus later of the Victoria University of Manchester) a few years after the hard times had forced her emigration. One was George Gissing (1857–1903) who came from Yorkshire and seemed on the way to a brilliant academic career when amorous troubles brought him into collision with authority; seemingly forever disgraced in Manchester he too lit out for the New World. Still in his teens he lived a wandering and frequently penniless life in the United States, but at twenty returned to the Old World to study awhile at Jena and thence presently to London. He drew on his own experiences in writing his first novel, *Workers in the Dawn*, which was published when he was twenty-three. It drew attention, as did his later novels (the best-known perhaps was *Demos*), to degradations and disintegrations forced on men and women by the struggle against extreme poverty. Among the friendships which Gissing's writings created was a warm and lasting one with H. G. Wells, but pneumonia caused Gissing's death at the age of forty-six – his autobiographical work, the *Private Papers of Henry Ryecroft*, was published in the year of his death.

It was for medical training that Gissing's contemporary Francis Thompson came to Manchester from Preston, but his gifts were not adapted to practical doctoring. After six years of attendance at college and a third failure to pass examinations he broke away from any further endeavour to earn a living from medicine or any other profession. It is said that among books given to Thompson by his mother was De Quincey's *Confessions*. At any rate, like De Quincey, Thompson drifted to London; like De Quincey, became a habitual opium-eater; like De Quincey, but in perhaps deeper despondency, was a street waif. After a period of seemingly complete waste a small turn of fortune happened in 1888, introduced by the compilation *Merry England* which printed contributions from him in both prose and verse. Thompson came then to the attention of Wilfred and Alice Meynell who, by 1893, helped in the publication of his *Poems*, including *The Hound of Heaven*. With the help of the Meynells he partly broke the opium habit, but he was already doomed to die of consumption. One Roman Catholic sanctuary after another did its best to care for Thompson in his long illness, but his death occurred in 1907.

The singular part that Manchester played in the life of the Brontë family is now worthy of special attention. The fortune of the Brontës turned upon the writing of *Jane Eyre*; that novel began to be written in Manchester in the year 1846. At Haworth parsonage in West Yorkshire the year 1845 had brought acute worries, soon to grow much worse, to the three Brontë sisters, Charlotte, then aged twenty-nine, Emily (twenty-six) and Anne (twenty-three). At the start of that year, Charlotte and Emily had been hoping to set up a school as the only way of obtaining some small income. Before they could attempt any alterations to the parsonage so as to take in pupils (possibly foreign girls) with 'the board and English education at £25 per annum', the plan had to be discarded. Mr Brontë, the hard-bitten indestructible widowed father (destined to outlive all of his children), was sixty-eight, and with rapidly increasing blindness required increased care; but another interruptive emergency was that the twenty-seven-year-old Branwell Brontë, the erratic only son, was dismissed in disgrace from his employment as tutor and returned home needing solace for his sense of total failure. Branwell's method of escape was opium, though he drank spirits as well whenever he had opportunity. Over the next three years, until his final collapse and death, he managed to obtain supplies sufficient to produce, towards the end, very frightening attacks of delirium tremens. The year 1845 ended at Haworth parsonage with the dominating but half-blind father instituting that the feckless Branwell should sleep of nights in the same room with him, and it grew to be a habit with the three daughters, when the men were thus locked away, to walk one after the other round the table in the parlour, night after night. It was the daughters' restless way of discussing between themselves all possible projects for coping.

One project that Charlotte, Emily and Anne discussed was that they might become authors. Each had written poems and a selection was put together, their own names veiled under the pseudonyms of 'Currer', 'Ellis', and 'Acton Bell'. Charlotte took charge of writing to publishers; with less delay than might nowadays be expected, a publisher was found, and about the end of May 1846 the slender cloth-bound *Poems* was offered to the reading public. The writers hoped that the *Poems* would open the way for publication of three prose works. Charlotte had already completed a novel, *The Professor*; Emily had *Wuthering Heights* ready for publication; Anne's contribution was *Agnes Grey*. Round and round the parlour table on those summer nights, after Branwell and their father had been put to bed, the sisters performed their walking routine – but soon any hopes of achieving reward from their writings were diminishing. True, the poems had been printed, but they had found no buyers, and Charlotte's *The Professor*, when sent to the publisher, was promptly declined. As that manuscript, successively sent on to other publishers, was successively rejected, the sisters finally lost all the hopes that Charlotte had raised.

In that summer other trials continued to haunt the nightly walks around the parlour table. On 17 June Charlotte recorded: 'Branwell declares that he neither can nor will do anything for himself; good situations have been offered him, for which, by a fortnight's work, he might have qualified himself, but he will do nothing except drink and make us all wretched.' By July 1846 the cataract in the elderly father's eyes had resulted in such increased blindness that an operation seemed imperative. Thus Manchester entered the story. Charlotte and Emily set off there to find the right surgeon. They made arrangements with a certain Mr Wilson, and having returned to Haworth, towards the end of August Charlotte conducted her father to Manchester for the operation. She arranged for the subsequent stay in lodgings, where the patient would be at first confined to bed in a dark room, for convalescence of a month or six weeks. 'I wonder', Charlotte wrote from those lodgings on arrival on 21 August, 'how Emily and Anne will get on at home with Branwell. They, too, will have their troubles.' On 26 August she wrote:

The operation is over; it took place yesterday. Mr Wilson performed it; two other surgeons assisted. . . . Papa displayed extraordinary patience and firmness; the surgeons seemed surprised. I was in the room all the time, as it was his wish that I should be there; of course, I neither spoke nor moved till the thing was done, and then I felt that the less I said, either to papa or the surgeons, the better.

Gradually, when thinking about this surgical operation, one begins to appreciate the ordeal for all who were in the operating room on that day in August 1846. The date is important. I am told that nowadays surgeons often prefer not to operate on both eyes at once, but apparently Mr Wilson, in 1846, thought that could be done, and did so. Anaesthetic? Here I am subject to correction from historians of medicine, but I am not told of Mr Wilson having the aid of a general anaesthetic – chloroform, for instance, was not in use in England until 1847. Such local anaesthesiant as cocaine? Cocaine did apparently create almost a revolution in ophthalmic surgery – but not until the 1880s. So I speak in ignorance of what aid there may have been for Patrick Brontë's firmness beyond the comfort, for him, of having his daughter present. As for Charlotte, I think one agrees with her that it was an ordeal about which the less said the better.

Mrs Gaskell records, in her *Life of Charlotte Brontë*, that on the same morning on which Charlotte was to sit quiet and motionless in attendance at the operation the manuscript of her first novel (*The Professor*, by 'Currer Bell') was again returned to her with another curt note of rejection; Mrs Gaskell quotes Charlotte's own words that on that score 'something like the chill of despair' was invading her heart. Rightly, then, Mrs Gaskell praises the courage and spirit with which Charlotte in that enforced stay for her father's slow recuperation in one of those 'streets of small monotonous-looking houses in a suburb' of Manchester, plucked herself up to repel the chill of despair and start to write a second novel despite the failure with the first. Mrs Gaskell expresses the depression of the setting: 'in those grey, weary, uniform streets where all faces, save that of her kind doctor, were strange and untouched with sunlight to her, – there and then did the brave genius begin *Jane Eyre*'. Somehow in Charlotte Brontë's small physique – 'stunted' was the word she applied to herself – adrenalin began to flow. Perhaps successfully standing up to the ordeal of her father's eye operation was in some way a stimulant; at any rate, acutely aware that repair of the family fortunes depended on what she could do, away she started on the tale of little Jane Eyre, equally conscious of 'physical inferiority' and equally determined not to give in. The completion, publication and instant success of *Jane Eyre* then opened the way for the publications of Emily (*Wuthering Heights*) and Anne and started the fame of the Brontë family – fame that for most of them was posthumous, for after 1849 the only ones left alive were Charlotte and her father (his sight for a while materially restored). I confess that thoughts about the circumstances in the Manchester boarding-house in which *Jane Eyre* was written, made me pick up the novel for re-reading with more interest than hitherto.

*   *   *

If there is pleasure in re-reading *Jane Eyre* (and likewise in Charlotte Brontë's *Shirley* and *Villette*) there is also much pleasure in reviving acquaintance with the contrasting personality of Mrs Gaskell, of whom we had a glimpse at Knutsford. The motherless girl Elizabeth Stevenson who grew up there in charge of her aunt, married at the age of twenty-two the Scottish Unitarian minister from Manchester, William Gaskell. Both Elizabeth and Charlotte give touches of self-portraiture in their novels, and there is physical contrast between the short, dumpy figure of Miss Brontë with her plain face, 'sensible, not handsome' – a face most notable for its 'lines of force' – and the tall and more commanding presence of the handsome Mrs Elizabeth Gaskell, who if her feelings were outraged swept out of the room 'with the noiseless grace of an offended princess', 'throwing her head back with proud disdain, till her throat curved outward like a swan's'. Yet of the two it was the handsome Elizabeth who was much the milder, gentler person. Had Elizabeth died first, I doubt if it would have occurred to Charlotte to write a Life of her; but the warmth of affectionate admiration which made Elizabeth write her *Life of Charlotte Brontë* is like that of a devoted younger sister. Elizabeth Gaskell was in fact the elder by six years.

Charlotte Brontë became a professional author by persistent determination and as the only way of keeping things going at Haworth parsonage. Mrs Gaskell's first novel *Mary Barton* (published shortly after *Jane Eyre*) had been written more or less by accident. When she had left Knutsford to become a minister's wife in Manchester in 1832, in addition to sharing the incessant social and welfare work for which there was more than abundant need, she took on the full-time duty of childbearing. The first birth was of a stillborn girl; three healthy girls followed, and then the parents had the joy of a son. It was when this only son caught scarlet fever at ten months and died that Elizabeth seemed heartbroken. Childbearing was tried once more, but the sixth child was another daughter. Then, apparently at Mr Gaskell's suggestion as a way of dealing with her recurrent grief over the death of the boy, *Mary Barton* was written. The novel's success on publication was, to the Gaskells, a matter of surprise. It was flattering to have Dickens at once asking her for further writings. Without previous expectation, Mrs Gaskell was swiftly pushed into a literary career. Her earnings were useful to the family; from cramped quarters in Upper Rumford Street, Manchester, they moved to No. 84 Plymouth Grove. Living and working in Manchester continued to fascinate and repel Mrs Gaskell, and that love-hate relationship is pictured in the character of Margaret Hale in *North and South*. The problem of being both woman and professional writer, for one who wished likewise to be a thoroughly dutiful wife and mother, was far from easy. In addition to his ministry William Gaskell was professor of English history and literature at Manchester New College; he was in demand for lecturing at Owens College and for lecturing to factory workers; as a matter of course he had a room of his own wherein to be undisturbed while composing lectures, sermons, and the hymns which were later included in Martineau's collection. A touch of envy enters one of Mrs Gaskell's letters: 'One thing is pretty clear, *Woman* must give up living an artist's life, if home duties are to be paramount. It is different with men. . . .'

Mrs Gaskell used to be portrayed as having the gift of combining with perfect ease the life of a literary personality (she enjoyed being lionized) and simultaneously the domestic life in which she was the central figure around whom husband and daughters revolved. After the publication of *Mary Barton* there were, however, increasingly, periods of escape from Manchester. We saw her search for a room of her own at Silverdale, on Morecambe Bay. Nothing indicates that William Gaskell felt at all neglected during his wife's long and frequent absences, or by the way her thoughts seemed to be totally wrapped up with the Brontës after she had met Charlotte at the house-party beside Windermere in 1850. Yet some drifting apart can now be detected. In her writings Mrs Gaskell touches very often on temperamental and scenic differences between 'North' and 'South' in Britain. Sometimes 'North' is for her identified entirely with industrial Lancashire and northern people as those descended from stock of the ancient Danelaw. Mr Gaskell appears as almost wholly immersed in daily life of the 'North' and with no wish to get away, yet Mrs Gaskell's own identifications with 'North' do not stifle her longings for what she felt to be a more idyllic country, the 'South'. South to her was southern England, south of the old rampart of Watling Street.

Mrs Gaskell's *North and South* was commissioned by Dickens for his periodical *Household Words*, where in 1854 it followed immediately on Dickens's own serial, *Hard Times*. In her novel there are a number of touches on the beauty of countryside in the southland that had been King Alfred's country. Her heroine is imagined as coming to the 'North' from Hampshire:

'Do you remember the matted-up currant-bushes, Margaret, at the corner of the west-wall at the garden at home?'
Did she not? Did she not remember every weather-stain on the old stone wall; the grey and yellow lichens that marked it like a map; the little crane's-bill that grew in the crevices!

Ten years after the book publication of *North and South*, Mrs Gaskell used the money advanced for her subsequent and final novel, *Wives and Daughters*, for the purchase of a house of her own in Hampshire. That novel, containing the very best of her character-drawing (e.g. the superbly drawn Mrs Kirkpatrick), was not destined to be proof-read by her. The house, called The Lawn, was (and is) in the village of Holybourne, between Alton and Farnham. Oddly, Mrs Gaskell seems not to have mentioned the purchase to her husband. In the autumn of 1865 Mr Gaskell was sixty; he was much wrapped up in his activities in Manchester and there is no hint that he was likely to contemplate a move south, then or later. Nevertheless in that autumn Mrs Gaskell, five years younger than her husband, quietly moved into the Hampshire house to get it to her liking. The impression created at Holybourne was that she was there to stay. On the morning of the second Sunday in November she went as usual to the parish church, but on return to her house suffered a sudden heart attack and died.

There is no reason whatever to cast doubts on the happy and united homelife of the Gaskell family in Manchester. Mrs Gaskell could afford two houses, and if she wished one with a secret garden in the south, why not? The proposed surprise of the Holybourne house as a Christmas present to husband and family might well have been just that, had the heart attack not intervened.

* * *

The bitter conflicts between 'masters' and 'hands' in Lancashire's factories in the winter of 1853–4 made a theme which Dickens felt to be appropriate for the weekly journal *Household Words* of which he had been editor and part owner since 1850. The particularly long-drawn-out battle of strike and lockout fought at Preston between hands and owners of the cotton mills caused Dickens to pay a visit to form his own opinion of the contest. He arrived at Preston in January 1854, and though many of the unemployed could only 'sit at home and mope' – the duration at Preston was to last for twenty-three weeks – Dickens found, and was able to attend, a meeting of the strike committee. On his return to London he at once contributed an article to *Household Words* in which he praised the efficiency, orderliness and moderation of the strike committee, and then recounted how he himself had defended the strikers on his railway journey from a fierce old gentleman who fumed, 'They wanted to be ground . . . to bring 'em to their senses.' Two months later the opening chapter of his novel *Hard Times* was to state the main thesis, that 'masters' (of any kind) ought to be better educated than merely 'according to Cocker': the novel was to show that a completely materialistic mastery of anybody by 'arithmetic' is death-dealing to each character who subscribed wholly to that system. ('According to Cocker' was a title Dickens had first thought of for his story; the phrase, derived from Edward Cocker's schoolbook of arithmetic, had been popularized in the theatre.)

Preston, halfway between Manchester and Lancaster, appears in *Hard Times* as 'Coketown', yet Dickens in this novel takes no trouble at all to picture Coketown as a real place; the factory town is nothing but a shadowy backdrop, in front of which he seems to wish his characters each to overact the parts that he has assigned in the melodrama. *Hard Times* has been admired by some, including Bernard Shaw and F. R. Leavis, but I feel with Angus Wilson that its claim to be considered among Dickens's masterpieces 'can hardly be sustained'. Dickens suggests potentials in the labour-relations theme and in some of the characters which he vexatiously neglects in favour of a quick-moving serial ruthlessly cheapened for the weekly magazine. I very much agree with Angus Wilson that the heroine, Louisa Bounderby, is 'potentially one of Dickens's most successful women', but in *Hard Times* the imposed overacting hides the real person. At the time of publication Ruskin expressed his vexation with Dickens: 'I wish that he could think it right to limit his brilliant exaggeration to works written only for public amusement; and when he takes up a subject of high national importance, such as that which he handled in *Hard Times*, that he would use severer and more accurate analysis.' It was to Mrs Gaskell's immense advantage that her *North and South* followed immediately on *Hard Times* in *Household Words*, for comparison of the two novels favoured hers.

4. THE WALL AND SOUTHWARD ACROSS THE HIGH MOORS

Except for the distant respect due to 'Old John of Gaunt, time-honoured Lancaster' and because more recently Laurence Binyon was born here, Lancaster recalls to me no very special literary associations; but a detour to the east before Kendal introduces Kirkby Lonsdale, the 'Lowton' of *Jane Eyre*. The road across country from Leeds to Kendal crosses Cowan Bridge where parts of the old Clergy Daughters' School remain – the school at which Charlotte Brontë was a pupil, and of which in *Jane Eyre* she gave an account under the name 'Lowood'. Thirty years later, when writing her *Life of Charlotte Brontë*, Mrs Gaskell was pleased with the sight of Cowan Bridge when she made a summer visit:

It is prettily situated; just where the Leck-fells swoop into plain; and by the course of the beck alder-trees and willows and hazel bushes grow. The current of the stream is interrupted by broken pieces of grey rock; and the waters flow over a bed of large round white pebbles, which a flood heaves up and moves on either side out of its impetuous way till in some parts they almost form a wall. By the side of the little, shallow, sparkling, vigorous Leck, run long pasture fields, of the fine short grass common in high land; for though Cowan Bridge is situated on a plain, it is a plain from which there is many a fall and long descent before you and the Leck reach the valley of the Lune. I can hardly understand how the school there came to be so unhealthy, the air all round about was so sweet and thyme-scented, when I visited it last summer. . . .

The account of 'Lowood' school, at which Jane Eyre at the age of ten was assigned to stay throughout vacations as well as during school terms, tells how it was so severely afflicted with 'the typhus fever' that inquiry was made which revealed many and various examples of bad management. Four of the Brontë daughters were sent to that Clergy Daughters' School at Cowan Bridge, pictured as 'Lowood'. Mrs Gaskell supposes it provided the best education that Patrick Brontë could afford. Maria and Elizabeth Brontë both died, in their twelfth and eleventh years of age respectively, and though neither death was directly attributed to school conditions Mrs Gaskell does wonder that Charlotte did not remonstrate against her father's decision to send her and Emily back to Cowan Bridge after the two other sisters had failed to survive.

At Kirkby Lonsdale one used to enter Westmorland, but that county, and Cumberland, and what used to be an important portion of Lancashire, are now lumped into the large administrative bloc called Cumbria. In 1844 the project of building from Kendal, largest of the Westmorland towns, a spur of railway to Windermere caused Wordsworth to utter two sonnets of disdainful protest. 'Mountains, and Vales, and Floods, I call on you', cried Daddy Wordsworth, to repulse the 'triumphal car', 'Hear YE that Whistle?' One cannot help but feel that part of the anguish of the sonnets was Wordsworth's awareness that his daughter Dora's 'southern lover', Edward Quillinan, was brought to Rydal Mount more quickly by the railway. The main line of the railway northward from Kendal parallels the road A6 in making the long climb up Shap Fells to the quarrying village of Shap, with the corresponding descent to Penrith (where Wordsworth and his sister Dorothy at one time attended school, and where their mother was buried). From Penrith A6 and the recent motorway M6 and railway all travel side by side through the ancient Inglewood Forest, the Englyshe-wood wherein Adam Bell, Clym of the Clough and William of Cloudesley in the old ballad,

> They were outlaw'd for venyson,
> These yemen everych-one.

All those routes lead in the same direction that those three yeomen of the north country took, straightway into 'merrie Carlisle'. In the letter to Scott quoted in my previous chapter Wordsworth referred to himself and his daughter Dora as passing through 'merry' Carlisle, for so the county town of Cumberland was celebrated in the ballads with which both men were familiar, and so the epithet was used for Carlisle in Scott's *Lay of the Last Minstrel*.

Carlisle had a special claim to be 'merry' for Walter Scott, for he was married there, on Christmas Eve 1797, to the sprightly French lady, Charlotte Charpentier, who with her brother had been settled in England as wards of Lord Downshire, to escape from the French Revolution. Scott, twenty-six years old, had completed his fifth year of practice at the Bar that summer and he and his friend Fergusson set out on a tour to the English Lakes. On their way back, the route of Hadrian's Wall from Carlisle brought them to 'the then peaceful and sequestered little watering place of Gilsland' – the little spa is at the edge of Walk Forest, in the Irthing valley, and the 'waters' still derive from sulphur and chalybeate springs. As Lockhart tells the story, Scott's law practice and dependence on his father, that elderly Writer to the Signet, was as drawn in the portraits of the elder and younger Fairford in *Redgauntlet*; and the romantic attraction of 'the lady of the green mantle' in that tale arose from Scott's own infatuation with the young lady in Edinburgh who wore that mantle with bewitching grace in church. However, by 1797 she of the green mantle had given her hand to a baronet of higher station and greater wealth than Walter; in part the summer tour was to recover from that disappointment; and suddenly, at Gilsland, the cure was instantaneous. 'Riding one day with Fergusson, they met, some miles from their quarters, a young lady taking the air on horseback. . . .' There was to be a ball at Gilsland that evening. Both Scott and Fergusson had been smitten by sight of the lady, and with 'no little rivalry' put on their dress uniform of the Edinburgh Volunteers – but this time Captain Scott was not to be outgunned by his rival, and what began as a contest in flirtation was very soon for Scott and for Miss Charpentier the real thing.

Thirty years later (and five years before the final visit of Wordsworth and Dora to Abbotsford) the widowed Sir Walter Scott mourned in genuine and lasting grief for the wife whom he had met so accidentally at Gilsland, and with whom initial flippancy turned so quickly into serious passion. They had been quickly married – the ceremony was performed by the Bishop of Carlisle in Carlisle's cathedral within four months of their first seeing each other. Since I gave a sketch of the widowed Scott at the time of enfeeblement it is but fair to quote Lockhart's description of Miss Charpentier (or Miss Carpenter, as Lockhart calls her) at the time of the wedding:

Without the features of a regular beauty, she was rich in personal attractions; 'a form that was fashioned as light as a fay's'; a complexion of the clearest and lightest olive; eyes large, deep-set and dazzling, of the finest Italian brown; and a profusion of silken tresses, black as a raven's wing; her address hovering between the reserve of a pretty young Englishwoman who has not mingled largely in general society, and a certain natural archness and gaiety that suited well with the accompaniment of a French accent. A lovelier vision, as all who remember her in the bloom of her days have assured me, could hardly have been imagined; and from that hour the fate of the young poet was fixed.

Now, as I turn eastward from Carlisle to spy out the land between A6 and the famous Great North Road, it is Hadrian's Wall that demands attention, that Wall which in Roman times stretched from what is now Bowness-on-Solway through the outskirts of present-day Carlisle almost due east across the island to Newcastle-upon-Tyne and Wallsend. Not just *a* Wall – it is *the* Wall: that was how Kipling expressed its dynamic effect on his imagination; and I for one have never ceased to be grateful to Kipling for transmitting his vision in the three chapters that he devoted to the Roman centurion in *Puck of Pook's Hill*. As a boy one read those three chapters with boyish excitement and took them for granted. Returning in maturity to Kipling's insight into the ancient life along that Roman Wall one realizes with T. S. Eliot that 'at times Kipling is not merely possessed of penetration, but almost "possessed" of a kind of second sight'. A story that Eliot calls 'a trifling curiosity in itself' caused him, as I well remember, hearty laughter: it was that at the time of publication of *Puck of Pook's Hill* Kipling was reproved for having placed in defence of the Wall a Roman legion which historians declared had never been near it – but that later discoveries proved to have indeed been stationed there. 'That is the sort of thing one comes to expect of Kipling', said Eliot.

Turning eastward from Carlisle to have a glimpse of what remains of Hadrian's Wall, I am proud to re-inspect how Kipling brings it alive with his powerful double action of prose and verse. Kipling's 'Centurion of the Thirtieth' told his story of the Long March from the south of Britain, advancing up the Great North Road at Rome's pace, twenty-four miles in eight hours, neither more nor less:

.. The hard road goes on and on – and the wind sings through your helmet-plume – past altars to Legions and Generals forgotten, and broken statues of Gods and Heroes, and thousands of graves where the mountain foxes and hares peep at you. Red-hot in summer, freezing in winter, is that big, purple heather country of broken stone.

Just when you think you are at the world's end, you see a smoke from East to West as far as the eye can turn, and then, under it, also as far as the eye can stretch, houses and temples, shops and theatres, barracks and granaries, trickling along like dice behind – always behind – one long, low, rising and falling, and hiding and showing, line of towers. And that is the Wall!

... But the Wall itself is not more wonderful than the town behind it. Long ago there were great ramparts and ditches on the South side, and no one was allowed to build there. Now the ramparts are partly pulled down and built over, from end to end of the Wall; making a thin town eighty miles long. Think of it! One roaring, rioting, cock-fighting, wolf-baiting, horse-racing town, from Ituna on the West to Segedunum on the cold eastern beach! On one side heather, woods and ruins where Picts hide, and on the other, a vast town – long like a snake, and wicked like a snake. Yes, a snake basking beside a warm wall!

Corbridge, closer to Newcastle than to Carlisle, is perhaps where Kipling's centurion reined up his horse, and his men grounded their spears, at the station where at one time one lane of the Great North Road had run under an archway into what some governor might have thought to be a new province of Valentia; but that arch had been bricked-up because of the Picts, and on the plaster some hand had scratched '*Finis!*' Corbridge, or even better the nearby Hexham, is a centre from

which to explore the best-known and well-exhibited remnants of Roman
life along the Wall. In Hexham's famous Priory Church, or Abbey, is
the monument of the Roman standard-bearer whose horse tramples a
prostrate Pict; that statue has often been commented on in connection
with 'A Pict Song':

> Rome never looks where she treads,
> Always her heavy hooves fall . . .

which Kipling placed at the end of his three chapters in *Puck of Pook's
Hill*. The stonework of the Wall itself, diminished by eighteen or so
centuries of weathering, and all the relics retrieved from the many
excavations, bring much to mind the hard, tough, enslaved, but in the
end unbeatable Little Folk (those often unseen Hooded Ones, the
cucullati) whose curse is summarized in the last two lines of Kipling's
song:

> But you – you will die of the shame,
> And then we shall dance on your graves!

*   *   *

The Inglewood Forest (Englyshe-wood) at the western end of Hadrian's
Wall was so thickly wooded in the time of Adam Bell, Clym of the
Clough and William of Cloudesley that red squirrels (or in Roman times
such edible dormice as escaped the pot) might travel on interlacing tree-
branches from Carlisle to Penrith without ever touching the ground.
Towards the east and north of the Wall the wide area towards the present
Border Region of Scotland – the area that Kipling spoke of as the un-
conquered province of Valentia and which is now Northumberland –
was ever perhaps a somewhat more open land of moors and fells. If the
slacks, haggs, gills and especially each howe (a 'howe' is the site of a
tumulus, of which there are hundreds on the northern moorlands) are
likely to be haunted by the Hooded Ones, where there once was Inglewood Forest the stranger is fully as likely to encounter the 'Wild
Huntsman' with his phantom followers and hounds.

> Though Inglewood vanish mid chimneys and smoke,
> Her thickets uprooted, and felled her last oak,
> Our spirits shall haunt her, and men yet unborn
> Shall quake at the blast of the Wild Huntsman's horn.

The *Northumbrian Decameron* by Howard Pease shows that terror of
nightly attack from real marauders was for centuries fully as common
in these parts as supernatural fears:

The first thing a Northumbrian did when he woke in the morning, it has been said, was to put his hand to his throat to see if it had been cut in the night. On either side of the March line the conditions were alike – either nation lived by taking in each other's cattle – and the 'Fire the Fells' and 'Hard-riding Dicks' loved the life. The Robsons might run a raid into Liddesdale in order to 'larn' the Armstrongs and Elliotts that 'the next time gentlemen came to take their sheep they were no to be scabbit'. . . .

It is supposed that after 1603, when James VI of Scotland became James I of Great Britain, the Border battles and raids and counter-raids, so frequently celebrated in ballads, began to die away; in course of time the hunting that pleased hard-riding gentry was foxhunting, and the literature that grew out of that in this north country is indicated by 'D'ye ken John Peel', composed in 1828 in honour of the Cumberland hunts-man, and, on the eastern side of Northumberland, by the hunting characters of Belford immortalized by the younger Surtees in 1838 in *Jorrocks's Jaunts and Jollities*.

The literary associations of the Borders Region are more plentiful on the Scottish side of the Cheviot Hills, but that is country that belongs in my next chapter. Here I return southward from Hadrian's Wall over the high fells of County Durham into the part of North Yorkshire which lies between the Pennines and the Great North Road. One delightful exploration is from Hexham (did I mention that Rupert Brooke's poet-friend Wilfred Gibson was born at Hexham?) southward through sur-prising Blanchland and presently over the ups and downs and lights and shades of the moors to the wide and pleasing streets of Barnard Castle

When Dickens, still in his twenties, was on a flying trip with 'Phiz' in 1838 to look into such Yorkshire schools as the 'Dotheboys Hall' of *Nicholas Nickleby*, that high-spirited pair stayed at the King's Head at Barnard Castle; and some years earlier Walter Scott is mentioned as using a stable-loft in the yard of the King's Head as a temporarily undisturbed writing-room. I cannot now verify the anecdote that it was Scott's practice to have the ladder to that stable-loft removed until he had done his stint of writing, and then to shout for release. More easily verified is that the scene of Scott's long poem *Rokeby*, after opening near Greta Bridge, then shifts to Barnard Castle and its vicinity. Scott's son-in-law, Lockhart, admitted: 'I never understood or appreciated half the charm of this poem until I had become familiar with its scenery.' Maria Edgeworth, though, was mostly captivated by the heroine Matilda, and when Scott's reply indicated that Matilda had been drawn from 'his own unfortunate first love' and that he had felt himself to be the youth who lost her to his competitor, Lockhart agreed the narrative-poem contained 'something more than a mere shadow'.

Ten miles due south of Barnard Castle (though slightly more by the road over Scargill High Moor) is Marrick Priory, the scene of much of the action in the great historical novel *The Man on a Donkey* by Hilda Prescott – I repeat here my admiration for that magnificently reconstructed story of the Pilgrimage of Grace. If I go on southwards towards Harrogate, anecdotes in this western part of what is now designated 'North Yorkshire' might lead me across Wensleydale, past Coverham (birthplace of Miles Coverdale, translator of the Coverdale Bible) to Dacre, where Alfred Richard Orage was born. Orage's name deserves the particular attention of anyone specially interested in writings produced during the 1914–18 war and in the 1920s; as editor of the *New Age* and also after that, his importance as an effective catalyst is known to those who see behind the surface of the literary scene. Yet what also suddenly suggests itself is an adventurous expedition into the Pennine wilds west of Harrogate (and north of the cross-country road from Leeds to Kendal) to search for Malham Tarn. Six miles north-east of Settle and now a National Trust property, this lonely tarn is within the wide region which once belonged to the monks of Fountains Abbey. In the mid-nineteenth century it was owned by a wealthy Yorkshireman, Walter Morrison, who built a house among the oak woods on the north side of the small natural lake – that house is now let to the Field Studies Council. My expedition is because among Morrison's Victorian house-guests at Malham Tarn were Ruskin, Charles Darwin and Charles Kingsley. Between the little village of Malham and the Tarn is Malham Cove, a spectacular sheer white limestone cliff, curving in almost a semicircle; from the base of the cliff there trickles out a streamlet, the beginning of the River Aire. When Kingsley observed that there were black streaks down the white cliff of Malham Cove, he remarked it was as if a chimney-sweep habitually fell over the edge. That fancy is held to have prompted him to start the writing, at Tarn House, of *The Water Babies*.

I don't know how many readers there are nowadays for Kingsley's novels. Snatches from his songs remain, sometimes perhaps for mockery, in common memory:

> O Mary, go and call the cattle home,
>   And call the cattle home,
>   And call the cattle home,
> Across the sands o' Dee . . .

or

> Be good, sweet maid, and let who will be clever;
>   Do noble things, not dream them, all day long . . .

or

> I once had a sweet little doll, dears,
>   The prettiest doll in the world . . .

or

> When all the world is young, lad,
> And all the trees are green . . .

The best of Kingsley's songs, said W. E. Henley, 'will take rank with
the second best in the language', and such a silver medal meant in his
time no dispraise. Henley and R. L. Stevenson read all of Kingsley's
works, not only the *Westward Ho!*, *Hypatia* and *Hereward the Wake* that
were familiar to boys of a later generation but also his thirty-five other
publications. He was, said Henley, 'one of the good influences'. Stevenson's tribute was expressed in a letter to Sidney Colvin: '*Treasure Island*
came out of Kingsley's *At Last*, where I got the Dead Man's Chest –
and that was the seed.'

I was recently reminded by Gillian Beer's BBC talk (Radio 3, printed
in *The Listener*, 17 April 1975) that of Kingsley's prose works the most
interesting to us now might be *The Water Babies*. What Miss Beer calls
'the primary fairy tale' of *The Water Babies*, 'told with marvellous
spontaneity', is readily to be associated with the surroundings of Malham
Tarn, and probably with Kingsley's stay at Tarn House in 1858. Little
Black Tom, the chimney-sweep's climbing boy, made to climb through
the chimney-flues in the great house by the wicked Mr Grimes, comes
down the wrong chimney 'into a little girl's bedroom, is hunted off the
estate like an animal, slides down a great cliff and comes to an old dame's
schoolroom. Feverish and hallucinated, he wanders from the outhouse
where he is laid to sleep; and, driven by the obsession that he must be
clean, he steps down into the river.' So Miss Beer relates; Kingsley
continues:

He went on to the bank of the brook, and lay down on the grass, and looked
into the clear, clear limestone water, with every pebble at the bottom bright
and clean, while the little silver trout dashed about in fright at the sight of his
black face; and he dipped his hand in and found it so cool, cool, cool; and he
said: 'I will be a fish; I will swim in the water; I must be clean, I must be
clean . . .' And he put his poor hot sore feet into the water; and then his legs;
and the further he went in, the more the church bells rang in his head.

Now the primary fairy tale expands. Kingsley, in Miss Beer's analysis,
'seeking for a way of preserving religious meaning in a world he felt to be
saturated with cruelty and beauty, found it through the idea of transformation'. The poverty-stricken working-class child Tom slips into
the river, wakes to find himself with gills, a water baby, 'swimming in an
all-encompassing element . . . back at the beginning of the evolutionary
cycle, living as all primitive life first lived, in the sea, with time to grow
afresh'. The tale, if Kingsley had started it in 1858, was greatly deepened

by his study of *The Origin of Species* on its publication in 1859. To quote Miss Beer again: 'It is hard, I think, to over-emphasize the richness of Kingsley's recognition of mythic elements in the ideas of development and mutation, of "metamorphosis" as Darwin sometimes calls it in *The Origin of Species*.' If scientists, in Kingsley's own words, 'have got rid of an interfering God', evolutionary theory as he understands it requires what Miss Beer calls 'a sustaining and inactive presence which expresses godhead through fecundity' – in Kingsley's book such a female presence increasingly haunts Tom's adventures. In *The Origin of Species* Darwin personifies Nature as 'She', and in *The Water Babies* 'the Irishwoman' who watches over Tom at the beginning transforms into Mrs Doasyou-wouldbedoneby and Mrs Bedonebyasyoudid and towards the end, in the thronging world of the deep sea, Tom finds her enlarged into Mother Carey:

From the foot of the throne there swam away, out and out into the sea, millions of new-born creatures, of more shapes and colours than man ever dreamed. And they were Mother Carey's children, whom she makes out of the sea water all day long. . . . She sat quite still with her chin upon her hand, looking down into the sea with two great grand blue eyes, as blue as the sea itself.
'I heard, ma'am, that you were always making new beasts out of old.'
'So people fancy. But I am not going to trouble myself to make things, my little dear. I sit here and make them make themselves.'

After the first promptings of the story of the chimney-sweep and his boy Tom, a great deal of heft was added before Kingsley released for publication, in 1863, the many things that Tom had learnt 'when he was a water baby, under the sea'. He may initially have been prompted by his 1858 visit to Malham, but as the book developed during the five years of composition many fables, mostly relating to the 'evolutionary debate', came crowding in. An interest in looking again at *The Water Babies* (apart from noticing much that one had naturally missed in childish readings) is that whereas the fables are presented in Victorian costume, there is a background feeling which is often expressed, in other language, at the present day. More than a century after *The Water Babies* Arthur Koestler writes of those, creative artists and creative scientists alike, whose 'exploratory drive' brings to them experience in which curiosity and wonder combine in satisfying partnership. 'Experiences of this kind', writes Koestler, 'always combine intellectual satisfaction with emotional release – that quasi-mystical "oceanic feeling" in which for a brief moment the mortal self seems to dissolve like a grain of salt in the ocean.' More than word-play links Kingsley's *The Water Babies* with other mystiques of 'oceanic feeling'.

When I recently re-read *The Water Babies* I paused at Kingsley's description of the proud otter who 'stood upright half out of the water, grinning like a Cheshire cat'. I was puzzled rather than satisfied by the explanation of the phrase by the Rev. Dr Brewer in his *Dictionary of Phrase and Fable* – that in former generations in Cheshire, cheeses were customarily 'moulded like a cat', and such cheese-cats had sculptured grins; hence 'grinning like a Cheshire cat' was a description applicable to anyone who noticeably displayed teeth and gums when smiling. There would seem to be some other possible allusions behind the phrase. Perhaps in Cheshire, as sometimes on England's east coast, a stuffed white cat in a window was a signal to smugglers that the coast was clear ? Or what other, perhaps simpler, meanings lie behind the grin of the Cheshire cat ? The Cheshire cat's grin is referred to by 'Peter Pindar', the pseudonym of John Wolcott, who in the last twenty years of the eighteenth century was lampooning George III, Tory ministers 'and things and persons generally'. The phrase was commonly used in the 1850s, for instance by Thackeray in *The Newcomes* (1855). There is thus no special novelty in Kingsley's mention of the Cheshire cat in *The Water Babies* in 1863. Yet the phrase in that place caught my attention, making me fancy that it was from *The Water Babies* that Lewis Carroll's young companions, the daughters of Dean Liddell, had made acquaintance with the Cheshire cat. It was, I felt, characteristic of Lewis Carroll (and Tenniel) to build on and add to, in the story of *Alice* (published in 1865), things to which the children had already and in other connections been introduced.

5.   BRONTË COUNTRY AND SHERWOOD FOREST

The headwaters of the River Aire, after emerging from Malham Cove and serving Kingsley as the setting for Tom's metamorphosis into a water baby, flow south and east past Skipton, through Airedale. When, in company with a canal, the Aire has passed Keighley, it bends a little to the north of Bradford before becoming captured and forced to pass through Leeds on its course to Humberside. Just above that northern bend of Airedale, between Shipley and Otley and to the east of far-famed Ilkley Moor, is Guiseley. One reason for locating Guiseley with such precision is that in the churchyard of the old church several generations of Longfellow's ancestors are buried. Longfellow is one of the New England poets to whom there is a memorial in Westminster Abbey, where the sculptured bust does its best to record Kingsley's opinion – Kingsley said that Longfellow's was the most beautiful human face he had ever seen. But another reason for mentioning Guiseley's church is that this part of Yorkshire is 'Brontë country' and it was in this church that Patrick Brontë and Maria Branwell were married on 29 December 1812.

Patrick Brontë was then thirty-five. The first two daughters, Maria and Elizabeth (destined to die during their school years), were born while his parish was at Hartshead, south of Bradford and near Kirklees, site of the Cistercian nunnery with the legendary grave of Robin Hood. Brontë then moved the few miles west to Thornton, south of Keighley, where in quick succession Charlotte, Branwell (the only son), Emily and Anne were all born. When the oldest of the six children was scarcely more than six years old the family moved into Haworth parsonage, another five miles westward and higher in the moors. This parsonage is now the Brontë Museum, containing many relics and manuscripts. I prefer to attend to memories of the parsonage when it, and the flat gravestones not screened from its front windows, symbolized much loneliness. Eighteen months after the move to Haworth, Mrs Brontë died. Patrick Brontë, according to Mrs Gaskell, was not naturally fond of his children; he had 'felt their frequent appearance on the scene as a drag both on his wife's strength, and as an interruption to the comfort of the household'. Patrick 'did not require companionship'; even before his wife's death he had begun to take his dinner alone – 'a habit which he always retained'. He retained other habits: at all times of day, even when preaching in church, he carried a loaded pistol in his pocket 'just as regularly as he puts on his watch'. When Mrs Gaskell visited Haworth to see Charlotte and her father in 1853 she was startled to observe the then elderly parson's pistol accompanying him at family prayers at night and at breakfast in the morning.

Mrs Gaskell's visit to Haworth parsonage was described by her in a letter which Clement Shorter added to the World's Classics edition of her *Life of Charlotte Brontë*. The month was September; after 'skirting the pestiferous churchyard' and 'half blown back by the wild vehemence of the wind' the visitor was warmly welcomed by Charlotte. 'We dined – she and I together – Mr Brontë having his dinner sent to him in his sitting room according to his invariable custom, (fancy it! only they two left).' On the four days Elizabeth Gaskell was at the parsonage the routine was unvaried: 'breakfast at 9, in Mr Brontë's room, which we left immediately after.' At twelve o'clock Charlotte and Elizabeth went out to walk. At two they dined; at four went out again; at six they had tea. At half past eight they went into Mr Brontë's room to prayers – 'soon after 9 every one was in bed but we two' and 'we sat over the fire and talked – talked of long ago when that very same room was full of children: & how one by one they had dropped off into the churchyard close to the windows'.

After the two eldest Brontë girls had died at the ages of twelve and eleven (they died 'of the fever at the Clergy School' was Elizabeth's then impression) the others grew up, Charlotte feeling a main responsibility, until the shocking year towards the end of the 1840s when Branwell, aged thirty, Emily, aged twenty-nine, and Anne, aged twenty-seven, all died within eight months. Then Mr Brontë in his own room (with his pistol as companion) and Charlotte in the dining-parlour were alone in the parsonage; alone when, after prayers, the two servants Tabby and Martha had retired. Tabby was nearing ninety at the time of Elizabeth Gaskell's visit, but Martha revealed how at night Charlotte continued to the end the dining-parlour routine of 'walking'.

For as long as I can remember [said Martha] – Tabby says since they were little bairns – Miss Brontë & Miss Emily & Miss Anne used to put away their sewing after prayers & walk all three one after the other round the table in the parlour till near eleven o'clock. Miss Emily walked as long as she could, & when she died Miss Anne and Miss Brontë took it up – and now my heart aches to hear Miss Brontë walking, walking, on alone.

After Martha had told her about the walking, Elizabeth Gaskell listened each night. She could not avoid detecting that Charlotte, after seeing her to the upstairs bedroom and bidding goodnight, did return downstairs again to begin 'that slow monotonous incessant walk'. In the bedroom over the parlour, Elizabeth, as she lay in darkness, with the wind 'piping & wailing and sobbing round the square unsheltered house in a very strange unearthly way', felt compelled to go on listening for the footsteps beneath. Was there the feeling – or only the wind? – of footsteps other than Charlotte's? 'I am sure', Elizabeth wrote afterwards, that in such walking 'I should fancy I heard the steps of the dead following me'. Was there indeed any doubt about the walking of the dead at the end of *Wuthering Heights*, the most powerful of the Brontë novels? Did not the hauntings of 'unquiet slumbers' bring back the walkings of the lone Emily – the 'wholly lone' Emily night-walking on the moor with 'that other ghost'? Whatever the dark wind that stormed around the parsonage, walkings went on, walkings of Heathcliff or others, and they were such as the innocent shepherd boy with his innocent lambs continued to 'darnut pass 'em'. Around Elizabeth's bedroom there was the piping, wailing, sobbing of the night wind as she hearkened to Charlotte's steps round and round for the hour or so. One morning Elizabeth ventured to question Charlotte about the 'walking', and apparently Charlotte merely said she could not sleep without it. The context of that conversation indicates that the companion most real to Charlotte was, to the end, Emily.

After that last glimpse of Charlotte Brontë as recorded by Elizabeth Gaskell, Charlotte herself had only another eighteen months to live. In those last months she married the curate at Haworth, Mr Nicholls, but they had scarcely settled into keeping house at the parsonage for her father when Charlotte died. Her life-span had been the same as that of her mother, each dying in her thirty-ninth year. Old Patrick Brontë went on living at Haworth parsonage for six years after Charlotte's death; he was eighty-four when he died in 1861.

* * *

If this part of Yorkshire is 'Brontë country', other associations are also thick on the ground. Novelists Oliver Onions and J. B. Priestley were both born in Bradford; at the start of *The Good Companions* it was from Bradford ('Bruddersford') that Jesiah Oakroyd, joiner and carpenter by trade, set forth eastward to journey on the Great North Road. The journalist and author Arthur Ransome was a citizen of Leeds by birth, though by degrees he gravitated to the Lake District. But it is not the large conurbations such as Bradford and Leeds that appeal to me so much as – and for a curious crescendo of reasons – the town named Wakefield. A first small reason is that a certain man whom Sterne caricatured as Dr Slop in *Tristram Shandy* is supposed, by one school of scholars, to have been John Burton from Wakefield. Thus there is the whisper of a link between Wakefield and the part of Yorkshire wherein Sterne's pen placed *Tristram Shandy*. Hearkening to that whisper, I find another link between Wakefield and Yorkshire's Vale of Pickering in Goldsmith's *The Vicar of Wakefield*. Before discussing *The Vicar of Wakefield* I have to dismiss two other items about Wakefield, one that George Gissing was born here, and the other that Charles Waterton, one of the most engaging of genuine English eccentrics, inherited and lived at Walton Hall nearby. To enlarge on Waterton, whose *Wanderings in South America* remains a nineteenth-century classic (and not merely for the narrations of his riding on a cayman and of the offering of his toes to vampire bats), would be altogether interruptive, though to dismiss him causes pangs. I do so for the reason that at Wakefield (and Goldsmith's Vicar will assist me to recognize it) I feel the continuing presence in this part of England of the spirit of Robin Hood.

In this part of Yorkshire which Gordon Bottomley spoke of as belonging to 'Iron-Founders and Others' how do I propose to exhibit that the spirit of forgotten Robin Hood has from time to time continued to show up? I counter that question with another: why did Goldsmith call his masterpiece *The Vicar of Wakefield*? Why Wakefield? I notice that Mr Doble, when editing an Oxford edition of *The Vicar of Wakefield* a couple of generations ago, commented that an answer to that query was far from obvious. It was easy enough to assume that in 1762, when Goldsmith was writing the tale, Wakefield was known to him from his travels in Yorkshire as a pleasing town with an impressive bridge over the River Calder – the bridge, as is now seen on old prints, carried on it an imposing stone chantry, very noticeable in Goldsmith's day. However, none of the features of Wakefield are put forward by Goldsmith and the place itself plays little apparent part in his story. Mr Doble stressed the point:

In the first chapter its name is merely mentioned; in chapter ii we are told that there were three strange wants there: 'a parson wanting pride, young men wanting wives, and ale-houses wanting customers'; in the third chapter the Vicar and his family migrate to a distant neighbourhood. There is probably no trace of any direct connexion between Goldsmith and Wakefield now discoverable. . . .

Again, why Wakefield?

I do not know if Samuel Johnson, or other readers in the eighteenth century, needed to have overt instruction that Robin Hood's grave at Kirklees was close to Wakefield. Possibly, in that enlightened period, any reader would recognize that the name Wakefield 'placed' the tale in Robin Hood's country, that it would be a greenwood story, one that belonged to the region of legend. Let me repeat that the spirit of Robin Hood was then (and is now) everywhere to be remembered in the great geographic shoulder of Yorkshire that stretches from the grave near Wakefield across the Vale of Pickering and the North York Moors to Robin Hood's Bay. Now although Mr Doble when editing *The Vicar of Wakefield*, momently forgot to mention Robin Hood, he did draw attention to the work of an ingenious topographer (Edward Ford) who pointed out the other clues that Goldsmith used in shaping the tale as a conscious duplication of a Robin-Hood-type scenario. For when the Vicar and his family move from the initial position near Robin Hood's shrine, their course is by no means haphazard 'in any old direction'. Goldsmith put into the text travel information and distances, clues whereby the reader may trace the actual journeying. What then is the course of the Primrose family in *The Vicar of Wakefield*? Briefly, it is north from Wakefield to Boroughbridge – Edward Ford made it clear that the 'rapid stream' where Sophia Primrose was rescued from drowning by Mr Burchell was the confluence of the Rivers Swale and Ouse beside Boroughbridge. And Mr Burchell? Of whom is that character, rescuer of Sophia, rescuer presently of the Vicar and others, to seem reminiscent? The movement of the tale goes on into Yorkshire's Vale of Pickering, past Sterne's Coxwold and through the precise locality described in Herbert Read's *The Innocent Eye* – Read in our time was thoroughly aware that this area was the heart of Robin Hood's domain. The climactic scene at the end of *The Vicar of Wakefield* is Dr Primrose's imprisonment at Pickering; and the rescue from that and the relief of every other worry reveals the true character of Mr Burchell, who is surely not merely an eighteenth-century aristocrat and anarchist but an actual double, or stand-in, for Robin Hood himself.

What I am suggesting is that Goldsmith's 'novel' of *The Vicar of Wakefield*, every scene of which is pictured in country identified with Robin Hood, is in effect the retelling of a Robin Hood ballad in eighteenth-century dress. On a re-reading, many touches in the charming ripple of Goldsmith's prose support this feeling, not least the several mentions of balladry, and the pervasive 'greenwood' atmosphere: 'Our little habitation was situated at the foot of a sloping hill, sheltered with a beautiful underwood behind, and a prattling river before: on one side a meadow, on the other a green. . . .' The 'little republic' to which Dr Primrose gave his rules, and the various adventures, are all so much in alliance with ancient legends about Robin Hood that I might even think that the comedy of the purchase of the 'groce of green spectacles' is a laughing hint of Goldsmith's for the reader to look through them – and, by looking through them, to become more aware of beauty in

> the levës grene
> Under the grene-wode tree.

* * *

South of Wakefield I travel through Barnsley – 'bleak and black' was the phrase outsiders sometimes applied to Barnsley – to Sheffield. Before reaching Sheffield, though, a literary pilgrim ought to pause at Ecclesfield to recall the clergyman Alfred Gatty, his wife Margaret Gatty, and their daughter, who was born at the vicarage at Ecclesfield, and who became Mrs Juliana Horatia Ewing. These names became happily well known before the end of the nineteenth century. When Mrs Gatty and Juliana Horatia started *Aunt Judy's Magazine* in May 1865 they started one of the best-ever periodicals for childhood reading and prototype for others.

Margaret Gatty was the daughter of Alexander John Scott, who in Nelson's time had been the naval chaplain to the *Victory*; he had served at Trafalgar and attended Nelson at his death, which explains the choice of Horatia as the middle name for her daughter. After Ecclesfield had become Alfred Gatty's parish, Mrs Gatty's contribution to social work by writing *Parables from Nature* was enlarged when her publishers agreed to her editing a periodical for Victorian nurseries. Mother and daughter joined in providing material and in dragooning contributors. A contribution to be noted in the first volume is the spirited poem 'The Wives of Brixham' by M. B. Smedley, a piece very often since selected for dramatic declamation.

The Rev. Alfred Gatty was well known for his hymn-writing, and when Major Alexander Ewing was stationed nearby, hymn-writing was the common interest which brought together the soldier and the vicar. The younger man had already been known as the composer of 'Jerusalem the Golden'. Ewing was thus made welcome to the vicarage, and soon in *Aunt Judy's Magazine* a song by 'J.H.G.', such as Juliana Horatia had formerly had set to music by her father, is now provided with 'Music by Alexander Ewing'. In 1867 J.H.G. became Mrs Ewing, and when the Major's regiment moved the young married couple also moved from Ecclesfield. Mrs Gatty laboured on with the magazine until she died in 1873. One of the splendid serials that ran throughout 1868 was *Scaramouches* by Miss Rodd – the adventures of the four naughtiest children that ever were sent from Dublin to schools in England. (Those who in childhood read of Joanna, Edward, Clorinda and Patrick do not forget them.) Mrs Ewing's own works included many soldier-stories and *A Flat Iron for a Farthing*, *Jan of the Windmill* and *Jackanapes*.

Sheffield, still one of the largest of Yorkshire's large cities, is more notable for its art collections (the picture gallery was due largely to the endowment of J. G. Graves, and the Ruskin Museum was founded here by John Ruskin in 1875) than for literary associations. Ever since the time when the miller in Chaucer's tale bore 'a Sheffield thwitel in his hose' the production of steel has remained Sheffield's greatest occupation. Ebenezer Elliott (1781–1849), the 'Corn-Law Rhymer' (of whom there is a statue in Sheffield's Weston Park) may be respectfully remembered. Elliott was himself put early to work in an iron foundry and later became a master-founder. His feeling for natural beauty stirred him in his teens to writing poems (much influenced by Crabbe) and he was one of the many young poets with whom Southey corresponded. Years later, when Southey's politics had changed colour, he wrote of Elliott: 'I mean to read the Corn-Law Rhymer a lecture, not without some hope that as I taught him the art of poetry I may teach him something better.' What came to stick in the craw of Southey, Wordsworth and indeed, later on, of Professor Saintsbury, was that when Elliott had become a not un-prosperous ironmaster, he continued to share and to stand up for the angry feelings of the 'hands'. The fact that Elliott 'espoused the extreme views of social, economical, and political matters which infected the working classes between Waterloo and the middle of the century' was to Saintsbury hard to understand 'especially as he had no excuse of personal suffering'. Elliott's virulence against the Corn Laws and his taking the side of 'workmen against landowners and men of property' made him, as an employer, 'a traitor to his class'.

Elliott of Sheffield was a forerunner of what many people came later to identify as a Manchester spirit – Engels, De Tocqueville, Carlyle were drawn to study Manchester, and Mrs Gaskell and Dickens, after the Corn Laws had been repealed in 1847, were moved to write of the continuing hard times for workers in Manchester. The Corn Laws were seen as a move to keep up the price of bread for the benefit of landowners regardless of famine for out-of-work foundry workers; the battle against them was fought as strongly by Elliott in Sheffield as by anyone in Manchester. Saintsbury allows that Elliott's anti-Corn-Law 'Battle Song' 'is as right-noted as it is wrong-headed', yet it is possible that some of his simple songs did more to arouse sentiment for the un-employed:

> Child, is thy father dead?
>   Father is gone!
> Why did they tax his bread?
>   God's will be done!
> Mother has sold her bed:
> Better to die than wed!
> Where shall she lay her head?
>   Home we have none!

The switch from writing of feelings that he received from country lanes, streamsides and Yorkshire's moors to feelings roused by the bread-tax may not have improved Elliott's poetry. After becoming involved in social welfare and politics 'My feelings', he said, 'have been hammered until they have become *cold-short*, and are apt to snap and fly off in sarcasms.' Yet if for many industrial workers the hard times were to continue, Elliott could at least rejoice before his death at the repeal of the Corn Laws.

Ten miles south-east of Sheffield is Renishaw, and I promised to return to Renishaw Hall for further mention of the three literary Sitwells of recent time. The Corn-Law Rhymer of Sheffield had been '*cold-short*' with aristocratic landowners if they had no feelings for the lives of industrial workers; the name of the town of Chesterfield south of Sheffield is a reminder of the Lord Chesterfield whom Dr Johnson pilloried, and whom one feels that Dickens seized upon for caricature as Mr Chester in *Barnaby Rudge*, and whom Wilkie Collins, though he thought *Barnaby* 'the weakest book that Dickens ever wrote', seems likewise to be caricaturing in the selfish affection of Mr Fairlie in *The*

Woman in White. All those remindings indicate that hostilities against well-to-do property-owners who are thought to be dilettante are easy to invent. Thus it was an interesting task for John Lehmann, when writing his book about 'The Sitwells in their Times' titled *A Nest of Tigers*, to convey to the unconverted that Dame Edith Sitwell and her brothers Sir Osbert and Sacheverell ('all three suddenly emerging from an aristocratic background to be in the front of an avant-garde revolution') could be engaging and sympathetic characters.

The scene from which emerged the 'delightful, but deleterious trio' (as Sir Edmund Gosse called the Sitwells in the early 1920s) was the 'large ancestral home set in the coal-mining district of Derbyshire, not far from the town of Chesterfield'; the name of the home, Renishaw Hall; and in John Lehmann's description:

The house itself is, in the main, Jacobean with Regency modifications and additions. A long line of battlements and pinnacles crowning its many-windowed grey-stone mass, it stands on a plateau dominating the surrounding country-side, with chimneys far away that indicate the industrial riches on which the Sitwell fortunes were founded. Elaborately designed formal lawns stretch down, terrace by terrace, in front of the house to the lake at the furthest descent, and the valley of the Rother in the distance. . . .

Edith Sitwell remembered every detail of childhood at Renishaw Hall, where her special first love was her peacock; they were of the same height, and with him she walked round the large gardens, her arm 'round his lovely neck, that shone like tears in a dark forest', until he jilted her in favour of a newly bought peacock-bride, and that, she said, remained an indelible impression of faithlessness. The not completely successful consolation was a baby owl that had fallen out of its nest, 'which used to sleep with its head on my shoulder, pretending to snore in order to attract mice'. To Sir Osbert Sitwell also 'my home always meant Renishaw'. Renishaw 'inspired idyllic prose descriptions from all three', and one of the most stirring of John Lehmann's quotations is the recollection of an early September morning at Renishaw, taken from Sacheverell Sitwell's *All Summer in a Day*. The passage begins: 'It seems misty and cloud-bound all the year among the Derbyshire hills, and this actual month is the dimmest and most distance-hiding of the seasons. . . .' No statue or human figure – gardener or woodsman – could be seen at a further distance than ten yards as the youngest of the Sitwell trio passed through the gardens and terraces in the mist that morning, making for the last of the gates to be passed through before the driveway from the house joined the highroad:

As one opened this last gate, and then turned round to shut it so that none of the sheep wandering in the field could escape on to the public road, one looked invariably a little to the right down the slope, where the lake should have showed blue and shimmering beyond the fields. But it was not there to-day: or, at any rate, not yet. Instead, the hollow that those sparkling waters should have filled lay absolutely hidden under the fleeces of mist. It looked stark and despairing down the meadows, sopping wet to the feet, and cold as ice when one's hand touched the iron of a gate. And indeed the clanging and cold of the metal brought one quickly out of these reveries across the public road to another gate on the far side. Coming down the road there were a whole straggling convoy of miners, carrying their bundles, and showing faces of an intensified blackness against the hedges.

The contrast between those brought up in the grey-stone house with battlements and pinnacles and the miners with faces of 'intensified blackness' walking the public road could hardly be more vivid; yet it is possible to feel a recognition of each other in the writings of the Sitwells and of D. H. Lawrence, son of one of the miners to be seen in a similar straggling convoy in the Nottingham part of the same coalfield. Is one to fancy common elements of heritage between these who belong to the country which once was Sherwood Forest?

Sherwood Forest does provide some curious conjunctions. Earlier I was recalling Jane Austen's *Pride and Prejudice*, though avoiding any attempt precisely to locate Mr Darcy's country estate of Pemberley in Derbyshire. At the very end of that novel is the statement that Darcy's friend Bingley 'bought an estate in a neighbouring county to Derbyshire' within thirty miles of Pemberley. I wonder if, at the time of winding up the various matters of *Pride and Prejudice*, Miss Austen happened to look at a map? Supposing the question idly arose of where was that estate of Bingley's, what else on the map would sharp eyes see and finger point to, thirty miles from Darcy's part of Derbyshire and in the neighbouring county of Nottingham, but the place-name of Mansfield Woodhouse – as noticeable in Miss Austen's time as now? May I here recall that when Miss Austen was getting *Pride and Prejudice* off her hands in 1813 she had already begun to plan *Mansfield Park*? And *Emma*, the story of Emma Woodhouse, belongs to the same period. Names that an author is going to turn to his, or her, own use come to that author's attention and are somehow kept at the back of the mind. Where else except at Mansfield Woodhouse are *Mansfield* Park and Emma *Woodhouse* seen to be arriving as a pair of name-tapes, both in one small packet to be put into the reticule and later brought out and stitched to service where appropriate? The 'Mansfield Park' of Jane Austen's novel is seen, from the first sentence of Chapter 1, to have been translated to 'the county of Northampton', and the adventures of 'Emma Woodhouse' take place largely in Surrey; yet those could be conscious transferences. It is the odd coincidence of the names occurring together just where and when Jane Austen was putting final touches to *Pride and Prejudice*, that gives the feeling that the Nottingham place-name might have got into her work-bag.

Such gossamer speculation can be quickly dismissed by passing on from Mansfield to Nottingham; midway is Newstead Abbey, and there is no doubt about that having been the ancestral home of Lord Byron. By such pressing ahead towards Nottingham I have said farewell to Derbyshire, conscious of several regretted omissions – Hathersage, south-west of Sheffield, retains in its churchyard the grave of Robin Hood's 'Little John'; in the church are the brasses of the Eyre family from which Charlotte Brontë is supposed to have taken her heroine's name; North Lees Hall, close by, is the chief claimant to have been the 'Manor House' of *Jane Eyre*, and the 'Whitecross' of the novel has been taken to be Grindleford, on the road south from Hathersage toward Bakewell. Then in my haste to connect Mansfield Woodhouse with Jane Austen I bypassed such notable sites, on the Derbyshire side of the county line, as Bolsover Castle, where in 1634 the performance of a second version of Ben Jonson's *Love's Welcome* greeted Charles I and his queen. Also, south of Bolsover, I bypassed the noble Elizabethan mansion of Hardwick Hall. 'Hardwick Hall, more glass than wall' was a familiar saying, from the fame of its vast display of windows; the portraits in the picture gallery are likewise famous, and a chief literary association is that Thomas Hobbes, author of *Leviathan*, was provided with a home at Hardwick Hall for the last years of his long life. He died at the age of ninety-one and was buried in the little church of Ault Hucknall on the north verge of Hardwick Park. The pulse of traffic on the motorway M1 throbs a mile to the west of Hardwick, not disturbing the serenity of Auld Hucknall.

6. FROM NEWSTEAD ABBEY TO THE VALE OF BELVOIR

Midway between Mansfield and Nottingham is Newstead Abbey in the heart of Sherwood Forest, ancestral home of George Gordon, sixth Lord Byron. The poet was not born here. His father, Johnny Byron or 'Mad Jack', disported himself in the 1780s mainly in France; he had thither eloped with the wife of Lord Carmarthen, and their daughter Augusta, Byron's half-sister, was born in 1783. Five years later Mad Jack's first wife had died and her fortune had been exhausted; Catherine Gordon, aged twenty and with a moderate fortune of £23 000, had been persuaded to become his second wife; and her child who was to become the poet was born in lodgings in London in 1788 with a lame foot.

It is debatable [says Lady Longford, Byron's most recent and perhaps most understanding biographer] whether Byron was more affected by his ancestry or his deformity. . . . Certainly the lame right foot, today thought to be dysplasic or clubbed, distorted Byron's life. From earliest childhood he learned to bear pain. In proud youth his deformity taught him shame and concealment. When he grew to manhood it introduced him to the problem of evil; who or what caused such unmerited suffering? Without deformity he might never have developed his compensatory talents for boxing, swimming, riding, target-shooting and love-making. Would there have been any need to rival Leander at the Hellespont?

As for Byron's heredity, Lady Longford does not neglect his mother,

A Celt, it seemed, if ever there was one. She once bit a piece out of a saucer and her temperament would produce hysterics at the theatre, an excitability which her little boy probably inherited.

Mad Jack, Byron's father, died when the boy was three years old; he had spent Catherine's dowry before deserting her, and her lawyers were able to retrieve for her less than £150 a year out of her fortune. The poet's great-uncle, known as the 'Wicked Lord Byron', occupied the family home of Newstead Abbey, living there 'as a scandalous recluse' in the only quarters he found habitable – the scullery – 'with "Lady Betty", a servant girl'. That fifth Lord Byron cared little for the 'Geordie Gordon' who was now heir to the barony, and until Geordie was ten years old he and his mother lived as best they could on her slender means in Aberdeen. Then the 'Wicked Lord' died, and Byron came in for his English inheritance, as Lady Longford describes:

Newstead Abbey might have been created for Byron and his mother. Stuffed as they both were with Gothic tales like Mrs Radcliffe's *Mysteries of Udolfo*, it was their dream of a perfect ruin. They arrived at the end of August 1798, thus exploring it in the autumn, most Gothic of seasons. They were entranced by the lofty stone façade of the ancient priory (never in fact an abbey). Behind the 'yawning arch', traceried windows, high gables and carved finials was – nothing. All hollow. What else should a Gothic ruin be? . . .
Before the dilapidated mansion stood a fountain, and beyond that a long sheet of water complete with waterfall and the required eighteenth-century forts and follies. The remains of Sherwood Forest surrounded the denuded 3000 acres of the estate. The young lord fell headlong in love with Newstead's haunting beauty and was to fight a losing battle for many years to avoid selling. His mother's income had fallen to £135, and though Byron's elevation to the peerage produced a state pension, it was only £300.
Since his lameness had not improved, he was sent early in 1799 to Notting-

ham where he attended a quack named Lavender, trussmaker to the Infirmary, who screwed his leg into a painful wooden frame. His nurse [who had come with them from Aberdeen] varied her affairs with chaise-boys by hopping into bed with Byron. 'My passions were developed very early', he recalled. . . .

Byron's mother recognized that if Newstead was to be restored by Byron's twenty-first birthday, it had to be let in the meantime; so for ten intervening years Newstead was let to Lord Grey and the Byrons had various lodgings elsewhere. In the autumn of 1808 the tenancy expired and Byron and the tame bear which he had acquired at Cambridge installed themselves at the so-called Abbey. The bear and other of Byron's whims and indulgencies were part of the youthful high spirits of what in *Childe Harold* Byron called his 'repugnant youth' and in *Don Juan* his 'hot youth'. Though intending to exercise every right of a seigneur he had no wish at that moment to stay long at Newstead; some hidden reason, real or fancied, made him try to get out of England; and though the regular European 'Grand Tour' was ruled out by the Napoleonic wars, he set his mind on Greece. So though in January 1809 Byron shunned the traditional junketings of the coming-of-age of a new lord at Newstead (shy at that stage of sharing ale and punch with tenants of the estate or of making, as he said, '*Uproar*' with the 'rabble') he is seen in April giving a riotous farewell party at Newstead for his particular friends of Cambridge days. This was a party, Lady Longford's biography suggests, that set off legends about Byron's orgies at Newstead – the participants 'masquerading as monks' and 'entertaining his "Paphian girls" whom Thomas Moore astutely guessed were in reality the Newstead housemaids. (Byron had already got a son by 'Lucinda', and provided her with £100 a year.)' Then, having managed to raise a loan, Byron set forth, with his friend Hobhouse and three servants, for his first expedition to Greece.

It was a twenty-three-year-old Byron who returned to Newstead in August 1811. He had sailed back from Greece with what Lady Longford neatly calls 'a distinctly Gothic collection of diseases and trophies: "an *Ague* & a *Clap*, and the *Piles*, all at once", four Athenian skulls, four live tortoises, a serpent-ring carrying a drop of poison in the golden jaws and a draught of the Attic-type hemlock which had killed Socrates'. His mother had died a week before his arrival home. That, and other deaths, made Byron feel, at Newstead, that 'Some curse hangs over me and mine'. These were months when he was out of sorts; he felt 'as old at twenty-three as many men at seventy'; a Newstead servant girl whom he particularly favoured left his bed for that of a rival; Byron's life was not worth living. Nevertheless in the same period sympathetic friendship with his half-sister Augusta was restored; Byron invited her to stay with him at Newstead; and, however much he pretended to be doing nothing but 'yawning', he indisputably was managing to put the first two cantos of *Childe Harold's Pilgrimage* in shape for publication. In November, though still in deep mourning for his mother, he was having a 'literary dinner', with Thomas Moore and Thomas Campbell, at the London home of Samuel Rogers, the banker-poet. Byron was likewise learning about politics at the Whig headquarters, Holland House in Kensington, and at the end of February 1812 made his maiden speech in the House of Lords, denouncing a government bill extending the death penalty to 'Luddite' machine-breakers when such of the unemployed had been, in Byron's phrase, 'famished into guilt'. It was less than a fortnight after that political début that for his other capability, as poet, he was enabled to make his remembered remark: 'I awoke one morning and found myself famous.' The beginning of 'Byron's *reign* in the spring of 1812' was the instant after the publication by John Murray of the first two cantos of *Childe Harold's Pilgrimage* on 10 March.

The adulation and hysteria about Byron, or for what seemed imaged of him in the portraiture of Childe Harold, affected three young women in particular: Caroline Lamb, Annabella Milbanke, and his own half-sister, Augusta Leigh. Byron's tanglings with Caroline, incompatible marriage to Annabella and affinity with Augusta have been matters both for light gossip and careful academic study ever since. At Newstead, it is of Byron's relations with Augusta that one thinks especially. Childe Harold was portrayed, as Lady Longford points out, as a self-outcast from society, 'having drugged himself into world-weariness through the "concubines and carnal company" kept at his ancestral abbey'. I pick up also what Lady Longford has to say about Augusta: how when Byron had returned to Newstead his feelings of sorrow – and guilt – at his mother's death before he could get to her had brought renewal of affection from the half-sister (five years his elder) for the formerly baby brother, the 'baby Byron' who needed comforting. In Byron's unhappy autumn of 1811 the 'loving and lively correspondence' that developed with Augusta brought unfeigned release. She was married, though none too happily; the invitation of 1811 for her to come to stay with him at Newstead so as to cheer each other up was one that could be repeated. In the prodigious frenzy about Byron in the London season of 1812 he could often talk things over with Augusta; who, for talking about love-affairs, was more appropriate than a fond half-sister? Consultations developed, almost certainly beyond the initial intentions of either, into 'an entirely new scrape', sexual intimacy despite their relationship. Lady Longford's account is unequivocal:

Ill-treated by her husband, Augusta would do anything her 'baby Byron' wanted. It is as certain as these things can be that she was his lover. Her unthinking acquiescence in his crime must have increased his guilty torment.

Whither was he leading his 'Guss', his 'Goose'? The very innocence of her pet names was a reproach.

A visit of Augusta's to Newstead Abbey at the beginning of 1814, for the cold three weeks from 17 January to 6 February, was spent by her mainly within doors, partly because Newstead was 'snowbound and thaw-swamped', partly because of her condition.

Augusta was heavily pregnant, having conceived at the height of that first season with Byron. Before taking her to Newstead he had confessed to Lady Melbourne that this love of theirs, because forbidden, made other loves seem 'insipid', but 'it had a mixture of the terrible'. Their intentions, however, had been 'very different'; and when they failed to adhere to them it had been her 'weakness' but his 'folly' – or worse. 'Pray do not speak so harshly of her to me – the cause of all.'

On 14 April 1814 Augusta Leigh, at her husband's home at Six Mile Bottom, gave birth to a daughter, Elizabeth Medora Leigh. Lady Longford discusses the often-asked question, 'Was Byron the father?' There are, she concludes, arguments for and against his paternity. It is possible that Byron and Augusta remained doubtful. I am more inclined to pass on to notice the abiding affection that continued between the half-brother and half-sister. Their mutual dependence on each other was commented on by many. In the April of 1816, just before Byron was to shake the dust of England from his feet, he and Augusta both wept copiously at their parting. There is perhaps nothing of much significance at Byron's being over-emotional and generally overacting in those last few days before he was to climb into his dark green Napoleonic travelling-coach for the drive to Dover. One action, for instance, in the week before Byron's leaving was his satisfying the desire of the seventeen-year-old Claire Clairmont, stepsister of the Mary Godwin who was living with Shelley. Apparently Claire did the arranging for the assignation some-where outside London, and Byron's complaisance was to result in due course in the birth, to Claire, of his illegitimate daughter Allegra. Yet the continuing lifelong mutual affection between Byron and Augusta contrasts completely with the efforts he was soon making to avoid Claire – Allegra he tried to care for, but not her mother. The attachment to Augusta was something deep and different. However the tie between Byron and Augusta is to be described, it was not a slip knot.

Mutual and abiding memories of Newstead Abbey played a part, I feel, in keeping up the correspondence between Byron and Augusta. The weeks of being housebound together, snowbound and thaw-swamped at Newstead, she heavily pregnant and he nervous with guilt and worry, had not made them hate each other, nor hate the house. They never saw each other after 1816, but separation did not separate them. One feels the rightness of Lady Longford's remark: 'it was her being a Byron which drew him closest: her having his shyness, his laughter.' A shared feeling for the ancestral home was an integral part of 'being a Byron'. When Byron was in Venice, indulging like Don Juan in distractions and dissipations, news that Newstead had at length been sold was cheerfully received in so far as the price received of £94 500 appeared to relieve him of financial anxiety – Byron accordingly stepped up self-indulgence of all kinds – and yet as hectic seasons passed and he moved from place to place, memories of Augusta and repeated thoughts of Newstead continue to reappear. After Shelley's death, the cantos of *Don Juan* to which Byron was returning were the 'English cantos', in which, from Canto XIII on, Newstead is much the centre of the scene. Then in April 1823, when Byron's attention draws away from *Don Juan* to focus on forming the 'Byron Brigade' to fight in Greece, another touch recalls both Newstead Abbey and Augusta: in packing up to lead the expedition to Missolonghi, Byron took with him the bedside Bible that Augusta had given him. Byron's study of the Bible at the time of packing for Greece may have been only to take on in argument the earnest Calvinist doctor of the garrison and, by the time they reached Missolonghi, to beat him. There was much disputatious byplay among the officers of the brigade, and some suggested that Don Juan might become a Methodist in a succeeding canto. At Missolonghi an attack of fatal fever meant that Byron was not to die in battle but, like Robin Hood, from being over-bled. 'Bleeding' was the cure-all used by what Byron called the 'Damned Doctors'; at the end he was unable to resist the treatment. On his deathbed his final mutterings were too confused to be fully understood; his valet averred that among the few names that Byron mentioned were 'Augusta and her children'.

It was the sudden recognition of the accidental similarity of Byron's death to Robin Hood's that made me rehearse some of the links that connect the memory of Byron with Sherwood Forest. One of Max Beerbohm's most delightful cartoons was of the young Byron on the cliffs of Dover, the disdainful insouciant shaking the dust of England from his feet. In the last year of his life, though, Byron sometimes thought of his own dust returning. To Lady Blessington he confessed one possible expectation: 'a marble tomb in Westminster Abbey – an honour which . . . I suppose could not be refused me.' In fact Byron's remains came back to the Byron family vault at the church of Hucknall Torkard, nearby Newstead Abbey. One of the few distant tributes was a slab of *rosso antico*, sent by the King of Greece to Sherwood Forest to be placed in the church floor above the Byron vault. The memorial on the church wall at Hucknall Torkard, and the inclusion of Byron's head in one of the stained glass windows, indicate Sherwood Forest's acceptance of the prodigal son. A personal tribute to be respected was paid in 1866 by the then eighty-three-year-old Miss Elizabeth Pigot; she arrived at Newstead Abbey with some of the curls from Byron's head, locks that had been exchanged for an equal number of hers, sixty and more years before. Her feeling was that Byron memorials rightly belong at Newstead.

*　　　*　　　*

Have I been enlarging too much the image of the legendary Robin Hood, by noticing in this part of England the emergence at different times of various characters each in one way or another showing moments of affinity with the original prototype outlaw? Yet what other tutelary spirit of the Danelaw is so representative of Danelaw dissenters in their wide variety?

At this point – as I move geographically the short distance south from Nottingham to Leicester – a shout from faraway Scotland, from no less a voice than Thomas Carlyle's, announces emphatic disagreement that so eminent a Dissenter as, for example, George Fox, who though just as truly born and bred in the Danelaw as ever was Robin Hood, could be regarded as having any unity with lighthearted outlaws of Sherwood Forest. Their very clothings kept them apart: George Fox the Quaker, with what Carlyle much emphasizes as 'his perennial suit of Leather', seems not to fit with the forestry garb of Lincoln 'grain' – whether the colour of that 'grain' were green or scarlet. Let us hearken a moment to that wonderful interruptive shout of Carlyle's, at the opening of Book III of *Sartor Resartus*, calling on everyone to halt at Leicester and think there about George Fox.

'Perhaps the most remarkable incident in Modern History', says Teufelsdröckh, 'is not the Diet of Worms, still less the Battle of Austerlitz, Waterloo, Peterloo, or any other Battle; but an incident passed carelessly over by most Historians, and treated with some degree of ridicule by others: namely, George Fox's making to himself a suit of Leather. This man, the first of the Quakers, and by trade a shoemaker . . . sitting in his stall; working on tanned hides, amid pincers, paste-horns, rosin, swine-bristles, and a nameless flood of rubbish, this youth had, nevertheless, a Living Spirit belonging to him; also an antique Inspired Volume, through which, as through a window, it could look upwards, and discern its celestial Home. . . .

'That Leicester shoe-shop, had men known it, was a holier place than any Vatican or Loretto-shrine. . . . Let some living Angelo or Rosa, with seeing eye and understanding heart, picture George Fox on that morning, when he spreads-out his cutting-board for the last time, and cuts cowhides by unwonted patterns, and stitches them together into one continuous all-including

Case, the farewell service of his awl! Stitch away, thou noble Fox . . . greater than Diogenes himself . . . greater is the Leather Hull, for the same sermon was preached there, and not in Scorn but in Love.'

Even with such cutting the vibrance of Carlyle's outburst over George Fox at Leicester comes through; the condensed quotation is a reminder to look again at *Sartor Resartus* and notice the use that Carlyle (with his green spectacles) makes of Fox's own plain-spoken *Journal*. In his own words Fox does tell of being as a young man indentured at Leicester, 'a shoemaker by trade', but the portrait Carlyle suggests of Fox's 'perennial suit of Leather', the cowhide stiff enough to form a Case or 'Leather Hull', may seem exaggerated to other readers of the Quaker's *Journal*. True, Carlyle is suggesting metaphorically that Fox's spirit had encased itself in a whole armour of such texture that when the serving-man came at him with a naked rapier Fox could tell him to put the sword aside – it was 'no more to me than a straw'. Yet, metaphor aside, the literal account that Fox gives of his clothing restricts the mention of leather, I think, to his 'leather breeches'. Near Whitby in Yorkshire, priests and professors trembled, when they were told 'the man in leathern breeches is come'. It is true that in Fox's late twenties he appears to have had pride in showing off those leather nether garments – was it in Yorkshire or at Swarthmoor that he recounts, 'I held up my coat and said "Here are my leather breeches which frighten all the priests and professors"'? Carlyle's elaboration of Fox's 'one perennial suit of Leather' is reduced by Fox himself to breeches only.

Perhaps, though, Fox's breeches are as appropriate to Sherwood Forest as, to other forests, were the Bavarian lederhosen or Fenimore Cooper's 'Leatherstocking'. Not that Fox ascribed undue importance to costume – 'our religion lay not in meats, nor drinks, nor clothes, nor Thee nor Thou' – or that he could not make allowance for others' conduct. Fox's friendly action with John Story, 'lest he should say "I had not unity with the creation"', was one which I imagine many of Robin Hood's chosen companions would have appreciated and applauded.

* * *

I must not forget that at the north-east corner of Leicestershire the county line dividing it from Nottinghamshire follows the Vale of Belvoir, and Belvoir Castle, imposing seat of the Duke of Rutland, in addition to its famous collection of paintings comes into literary history for the part it played in the career of George Crabbe. Different phases of Crabbe's long life (from birth on Christmas Eve 1754 at Aldeburgh in Suffolk to death in 1832 at Trowbridge in Wiltshire) have been touched on earlier – the struggles of his upbringing in Suffolk (and near-drowning in the Waveney); the near-death a second time in London (rescued by Edmund Burke's quick-sighted and generous patronage); and then, twenty-two years after his first poetic output seemed to have ended, the surprise of his successful resumption of verse-narratives in his autumnal last decades in the West Country. I welcome Crabbe's numerous appearances in my narrative for, as Edward Arlington Robinson said in his sonnet on Crabbe, 'his hard human pulse is throbbing still'. It is the middle period in Crabbe's life, and what has been called 'the strange gap in his publication', which is brought to mind at Belvoir Castle.

Byron's old friend John Galt greeted *Don Juan*, when the first two cantos were published, as 'a poetical novel'; that is to say, though the story might be told with wit and hilarity, it was closer to real life than a 'romance'. Though, in Byron's words, an intent was to be 'a little quietly facetious upon everything', it was also distinguished for – to those who enjoyed *Don Juan* – its absence of 'cant'. Byron's detestation of 'cant' was similar to Samuel Johnson's ('My dear friend, clear your mind of cant'), and for this reason Byron and Johnson, differing in many other respects, both respected George Crabbe's narratives in verse. Stories, if observed directly from real life and not romanticized, were what discerning readers (Burke, Johnson, Jane Austen, Macaulay and others in each generation since) felt to have all the more effect when presented in Crabbe's relatively plain manner. Crabbe's own 'poetical novel' *The Borough* may be both compared and contrasted with *Don Juan*: there is the same shared avoidance of humbug in the telling, but the avoidance is achieved by totally opposite means.

As a contemporary of Byron's noted, *Don Juan* captivated instantly with its 'sweet, fiery, rapid, easy – beautifully easy – anti-humbug style'. Crabbe, by contrast, is dealing with topics unfamiliar to 'persons of quality', and to set the tone for the dreary pathos of his tragedies he chooses a tuning fork that gives fair warning. When the poor of the borough are to be described, the documentary is to be honest: the life of the poor at best is dull as is the food, when there is food,

> Homely, not wholesome, plain, not plenteous, such
> As you who praise would never deign to touch.

The end of the road for worn-out common labourers is the poorhouse; efforts by thievery to put off such an end lead in the end to ruin from which the 'no escape' is emphasized by the scenery of eighteenth-century Aldeburgh, the restless cold sea in front, mudbanks and marsh-dykes hemming in that borough from behind. In the forefront of that dreary background Crabbe's pictures, said Leslie Stephen, 'stamp

themselves on our minds indelibly and instantaneously'. When it comes
to 'tragedy of a deeper dye', of all haunted murderers in fiction 'it is not
easy to think of a case where the horror is more terribly realized' than in
Crabbe's portrait of Peter Grimes. Peter Grimes was doubtless a close
relation of Wordsworth's Peter Bell, said Stephen; adding that 'looking
simply at the sheer tragic force of the two characters, Grimes is to Bell
what brandy is to small beer'.

When Byron called Crabbe 'nature's sternest painter, yet her best'
the remark applied more widely than to Crabbe's descriptions of
Suffolk's sea-coast landscape; it was tribute also to Crabbe's paintings
of human nature, and not only in Suffolk. It was after Crabbe had been
taken up by Edmund Burke that for the years 1782–5 he became
domestic chaplain at Belvoir to the Duke of Rutland. Crabbe was entering his thirties when he was thus translated from Aldeburgh to the
highly mannered and complexly structured life at the Duke's castle.
During the first months of residence at Belvoir Crabbe had nearly
completed for the press his poem *The Village*, which, greatly liked by
Burke, Reynolds and Johnson, caused much sensation after its publication in May 1783. Part of Johnson's satisfaction with *The Village* was
that it was a corrective to Goldsmith's *Deserted Village*, in that it depicted rural life in England of the eighteenth century stripped of any rose-
colour. It is to the credit of the Duke of Rutland that he continued to
lend his friendly hospitality to the household chaplain who, outspoken
to guests and servants alike, seemed often hostile to the whole social
system that was now feeding him.

> Why make the Poor as guilty as the Great?
> To show the great, those mightier sons of pride,
> How near in vice the lowest are allied . . .
> So shall the man of power and pleasure see
> In his own slave as vile a wretch as he;
> In his luxurious lord the servant find
> His own low pleasures and degenerate mind. . . .

'Superiority of talent is apt, without intention, to betray occasional
presumption' is the gloss which, much later, Crabbe's son was to apply
to his father's conduct in the years when he was suddenly translated
from Aldeburgh to Belvoir Castle.

Mr Crabbe could never conceal his feelings, and he felt strongly, nor, perhaps,
did he at all times put a bridle to his tongue, for he might feel the riches of his
intellect more than the poverty of his station.

. . . It is also probable that, brought up in the warehouse of Slaughden, and
among the uneducated, though nature had given him the disposition of a
gentleman – the politeness of a mild and Christian spirit – he may at that

early period have retained some repulsive marks of the degree from whence he had so lately risen; he could hardly have acquired all at once the ease and self-possession for which he was afterwards distinguished. I must also add, that although he owed his introduction to Burke, his adherence, however mild, to the Whig tenets of Burke's party may not have much gratified the circles of Belvoir.

The Duke, it seems, stood up for Crabbe against the scarcely concealed hostility of the servants and fellow-retainers at Belvoir, and at the end of 1783, when the Duke was appointed Lord Lieutenant of Ireland and he and his immediate family moved to Dublin, provision was made for Crabbe 'to claim the long-pledged hand of Miss Elmy' – of whom we had a previous glimpse at Beccles – and for the couple to go on living in apartments of their own at Belvoir Castle. Yet with the Duke removed from the scene, the Castle, as Crabbe's son points out, was less hospitable:

although the noble owner of the seat had given the most strict orders that their convenience should be consulted in every possible manner by his servants, it was soon found to be a disagreeable thing to inhabit the house, and be attended by the domestics, of an absent family. . . .

The Crabbes presently moved into the nearby parsonage of Stathern, and from that country retreat Crabbe sent to press his satirical poem, *The Newspaper*. By 1785, when the poem was published, there were no less than seventy-nine examples of such newfangled productions being issued in Great Britain and Ireland. 'It must be confessed', Crabbe wrote in his Preface, 'that these things have their use . . . but this does not outweigh the evil they do to society, and the irreparable injury they bring upon the characters of individuals.' Then, after the appearance of *The Newspaper*, Crabbe refrained from publishing any further poetry for twenty-two years; from his thirty-first year to his fifty-second he appeared to be largely preoccupied with domestic and parochial duties, which he interpreted to include medical attention to parishioners. During Crabbe's long abstention from publishing there were signs, however, of concealed literary activity. One dramatic outdoor bonfire is recorded at which the sons assisted Crabbe to burn quantities of manuscript notebooks and writings with which he had become dissatisfied. Another sudden impulse caused Crabbe to ride sixty miles away from some other duty in order to walk upon the shingle beach at Aldeburgh. Crabbe's sister had remained at Aldeburgh, yet that impulsive visit seems to have resulted from a renewed wish to produce poems. After another and lengthier sojourn in Suffolk Crabbe resumed his public career with publication of *The Parish Register* in 1807 and, soon after, the most durable of all his works, *The Borough*.

It was in 1814 that Crabbe at the age of sixty was suddenly presented with the comfortably supported living at Trowbridge in Wiltshire. Rather unkindly, Crabbe's vestry in the Vale of Belvoir rang the church bells to welcome his successor before Crabbe had departed.

7. FROM DICKENS'S ROCKINGHAM TO SHAW'S CORNER

The territory between the roads A6 and A1 narrows as one's eye traces it southward. Between Market Harborough and Stamford is Rockingham. Here Dickens was prompted to make use of the stone-built village and the once royal property of Rockingham Castle when he came to write *Bleak House*. It was Dickens's visit to Switzerland with his wife Catherine and sister-in-law Georgina in the summer of 1846 that in a roundabout way led to his association with Rockingham. At Lausanne he had much pleasure and success from reading *Dombey* episodes aloud in a salon, and a friendly and wealthy young couple, the Honourable Richard Watson and his wife, promptly attached themselves to Dickens, Catherine and Georgy in what proved to be for all an enjoyable companionship. Together they all climbed to the Great Saint Bernard, and soon after the travellers had returned to England the Dickenses were persuaded to stay at the Watsons' Northamptonshire house of Rockingham Castle.

Dickens was instantly fascinated, not only by the house at Rockingham and the history of the ancient demesne – it had been royal property continuously from the time of William the Conqueror to that of Elizabeth – but also because the Watsons gladly supported his increasing passion for organizing amateur theatricals. This passion we shall soon see to be abetted by Bulwer Lytton in the 1850s; in the 1840s the mainspring of the theatricals was the sheer pleasure and conviviality which they gave to Dickens and which he stimulated in all concerned. The Watsons were in every way convivial and Rockingham Castle became the scene of Dickens's happiest amateur theatrical ventures. Later, for the public tours of the Dickens Dramatic Company, professional actresses were engaged to play in the melodramas written by Wilkie Collins (an early member of the company), while Dickens assumed, with great effect, the 'heavy' roles; but in the private performances at Rockingham of old plays and the farces which Dickens delighted in composing, the ladies of the neighbourhood, and Catherine and Georgina as visitors, all joined in the acting under Dickens's management.

Rockingham Castle played a part in suggesting to Dickens the 'Chesney Wold' in *Bleak House*, and the Sondes Arms Inn in the village street of Rockingham is also in the novel as the 'Dedlock Arms', yet for the purpose of the story of *Bleak House*, 'Chesney Wold' –

with so much of itself abandoned to darkness and vacancy; with so little change under the summer shining or the wintry lowering; so sombre and motionless always – no flag flying now by day, no rows of lights sparkling by night; with no family to come and go, no visitors to be the souls of pale cold shapes of rooms, no stir of life about it

– the great house of 'Chesney Wold' where passion and pride, even to the stranger's eye, had to be presented as having died away, had to be transported far away from Rockingham and placed in a relatively foreign county with which Dickens had less connection, Lincolnshire.

The space between A6 and A1 now narrows again as the eye follows those roads southward across Bedfordshire. South of Bedford, between Clophill and Biggleswade, are Campton and Shefford. I have mentioned Campton before as the village where Robert Bloomfield (author of *The Farmer's Boy*) was buried. In Shefford a building known as Le Cokke is supposed to be a relic of the guesthouse of the ancient Chicksands Priory. At Chicksands House the seventeenth-century Dorothy Osborne was born and lived until the time came when she, daughter of a high-placed and ardent Royalist, was able to marry the William Temple whose father, when the courtship commenced, was of the Parliamentary party and was sitting in the Long Parliament. It was about seven years before the obstacles put in the way of the marriage could be overcome; for that period the lovers were mostly separated, yet the correspondence which kept their hearts together has charmed perceptive readers ever since.

Not many of the letters from each to each have survived – the letters of young William, later the great Sir William Temple, famous statesman and author, to whom Jonathan Swift became secretary at Moor Park, are scarcely represented – but such as there are of Dorothy Osborne's letters convey the characters to later generations. She was the older of the two, and though the disparity was no more than a year, she felt sensitive about the way she was ageing (into her late twenties) before the marriage could take place. When William, from Ireland, repeated his wish to have her portrait, it caused her to reflect: 'There is a beauty in youth that every one has once in their lives; and I remember my mother used to say there was never anybody (that was not deformed) but were handsome, to some reasonable degree, once between fourteen and twenty.' Alas, by the time of her letter to William, she was past that prime – 'as my Lady says, my time for pictures is past' – yet she does relent and sends him the best portrait she had, 'because you wished for it. . . . Put it in some corner where no eyes may find it out but yours, to whom it is only intended. 'Tis not a very good one, but the best I shall ever have drawn of me. . . . It must hang with the light on the left hand of it; and you may keep it if you please till I bring you the original.'

In one of Dorothy's letters is a famous passage about daily life at Chicksands in Bedfordshire in 1653, a pastoral picture which has reminded many of passages written independently, of the same summer and about the neighbouring county of Hertfordshire, by Izaak Walton. 'You ask me how I pass my time here', Dorothy writes to William from Chicksands; here is part of her answer:

The heat of the day is spent in reading or working, and about six or seven o'clock I walk out into a common that lies hard by the house, where a great many young wenches keep sheep and cows, and sit in the shade singing of ballads. I go to them and compare their voices and beauties to some ancient shepherdesses that I have read of, and find a vast difference there; but, trust me, I think these are as innocent as those could be. I talk to them, and find they want nothing to make them the happiest people in the world but the knowledge that they are so. Most commonly, when we are in the midst of our discourse, one looks about her, and spies her cows going into the corn, and then away they all run as if they had wings at their heels. I, that am not so nimble, stay behind; and when I see them driving home their cattle, I think 'tis time for me to return too. When I have supped, I go into the garden, and so to the side of a small river that runs by it, when I sit down and wish you were with me (you had best say this is not kind neither). In earnest, 'tis a pleasant place, and would be much more so to me if I had your company. I sit there sometimes till I am lost with thinking; and were it not for some cruel thoughts of the crossness of our fortunes that will not let me sleep there, I should forget that there were such a thing to be done as going to bed.

Macaulay, writing in the *Edinburgh Review* about the early history of Sir William Temple and Dorothy Osborne, mentioned that it was only about a year or so after Dorothy was writing the above letters, and sending William the portrait, and musing on the beauty 'that every one has once in their lives', that there came to her almost the worst of calamities – smallpox. 'Though she escaped with life', said Macaulay, 'she lost all her beauty.' The calamity did not put off the marriage. That took place early in 1655; and Jonathan Swift, who joined the Temple household nearly forty years later and remained after Lady Temple's death, never indicates that the Temple marriage was other than a most happy one.

* * *

Towards the southern tip of the angle where the roads A6 and A1 join at St Albans, many associations, ancient and modern, screen themselves conformably between Hertfordshire's winding lanes. The sixteenth-century mansion of Knebworth Park, ancestral home of the Lyttons, came into literary history mainly for the remarkable Bulwer Lytton (1803–73); although the most famous of his novels, *The Last Days of Pompeii*, was written largely while he was in Italy, much of the writing which he managed to combine with his political life was done at Knebworth House.

At the age of twenty-four Edward Bulwer Lytton, against his mother's wishes, married Rosina Wheeler; the mother's objection was not so much that Rosina was slightly older than Edward but that she showed signs of an excitable temperament. Yet the marriage took place, and for some years Bulwer Lytton earned necessary income by energetic writings in periodicals of all kinds, from quarterly reviews to 'Keepsakes'; as well as incessant journalism he produced novels and became a Member of Parliament. In politics he began as a reformer and a strong supporter of authors' copyrights and removal of taxes on literature, and it was natural that his speeches in the Commons were attractive to the young shorthand reporter of debates named Charles Dickens even before the latter had personal interest in copyright protection.

Bulwer Lytton's marriage, however, worked out as the mother predicted; the separation was made legal in 1836, after which the discarded Lady Lytton spent many of her remaining years (she lived to be eighty, outliving her husband by a decade) in lawsuits against her husband and in publishing a long series of attacks upon him – *Cheveley, or the Man of Honour*, a novel in which she made her husband the villain, created attention when published in 1839. Sir Edward Bulwer-Lytton, a baronet (hyphenating his name) since 1835, came into full possession of the family estate in 1844; he quickly had most of the exterior of Knebworth House remodelled on Victorian Gothic lines. Presently Dickens, Disraeli and other literary figures were frequent visitors. Bulwer-Lytton and Dickens were soon in cahoots devising the once greatly heralded Guild of Literature and Art. This scheme, on which Bulwer-Lytton and Dickens both expended much energy, was to establish on the grounds of the estate at Knebworth a colony wherein writers and others might be helped to spend their closing years in companionable decency. Money was to be raised for the Guild by theatrical performances produced by Dickens, the performances in the first instance to be given in the fine Tudor hall of Knebworth House. With even more energy than he had shown at Rockingham Castle Dickens threw himself into the productions in 1850, and by them and subsequent performances on tour, a respectable sum of money was raised. Bulwer-Lytton forced a charter of incorporation through the Commons, but that was not granted till 1854 and then a period of seven years, by law, had to pass before pensions could be granted. Angus Wilson sadly comments that when the time eventually arrived for the colony to get started, 'as so often happens where the organizing of the lives of artists is concerned, few writers of the desired kind were willing to take up the offer, and what could have been a remarkable scheme of welfare necessarily petered out'.

Two years before his death, Bulwer-Lytton, having by then been elevated as Baron Lytton of Knebworth, published anonymously a prophecy of future society called *The Coming Race*. It is a book oddly but often remembered at second hand. In *The Coming Race* Lytton claims, 'These people consider that in vril they have arrived at the unity in natural energic energies' – and his word *vril* for this creative force was taken up in the naming of the much-to-be-advertised meat essence Bovril. It is probable, said Saintsbury, that if Bulwer-Lytton's entire works were ever collected few, if any, authors of the nineteenth century would equal him in volume; 'while it is certain that very few indeed could produce more numerous testimonials of the kind given by the immediate, and not merely immediate, success of separate works'. Yet Saintsbury proceeded to argue that 'the very keenness, the very delicacy of his appreciation of the shiftings of popular taste' characterized his possession of 'a certain shallowness of individual soil, a literary compost wherein things spring up rapidly because they have no depth of earth, but, also because they have no depth of earth, rapidly vanish and wither away'. A solemn thought which this part of Hertfordshire insists upon bringing to mind is that a century after the death of Lord Lytton the prodigious applause which greeted his writings and plays in his lifetime is nowadays – except for here and there an individual enthusiast – unheard.

Bulwer-Lytton was automatically a resident of the part of Hertfordshire that I have reached, but George Bernard Shaw came to live here almost by accident. The two men were of different generations but Knebworth House and Shaw's Corner at Ayot St Lawrence are within a few miles of each other. By the fact of neighbourhood and by their incessant energy as writers, comparison is invited. Bulwer-Lytton, perhaps because he had been relatively born to the purple, seems not to have worried unduly about posterity's opinion; but G.B.S. (as Shaw's contemporaries often referred to him) showed some concern. As a dramatist, said G.B.S., he would either be remembered 'as long as Aristophanes and rank with Shakespeare and Molière, or I shall be a forgotten clown before the end of the century'. He made it clear that he would prefer the first fate.

An interesting contemporary impression of Shaw was that of Yeats, to whom in a dream Shaw appeared in the form of a sewing-machine, and in the dream 'the machine smiled, smiled perpetually'. Yeats received that impression in 1894 when G.B.S. was a bachelor of thirty-eight, still boarding with his mother and sister, as he had been doing ever since coming to London from Dublin at the age of twenty. His mother's success in teaching music had enabled her to live by then at No. 29 Fitzroy Square. That address has several associations: in his later prosperity Shaw bought the remaining lease of that house for his mother; later still Virginia Stephen and her brother Adrian lived there. It was at No. 29 Fitzroy Square that Lytton Strachey in 1909 proposed marriage to Virginia Stephen (though she presently preferred to become Virginia Woolf).

It was G.B.S.'s own marriage to Charlotte Payne-Townshend which removed him from Fitzroy Square. Daughter of an Irish barrister, Charlotte was 'a woman of wealth' who through the Webbs had become interested in the Fabian Society and the London School of Economics; that latter-named new-formed school was then located at No. 10 Adelphi Terrace. Charlotte contributed handsomely to the School and rented the two top floors of the Adelphi Terrace house for herself. The Webbs had introduced G.B.S. to Charlotte in 1896; in a few days they became and remained constant companions. He was forty-two and she forty-one when they were married in the Strand Register Office in 1898 and afterwards walked round the corner for him to exchange boarding with his mother for boarding with his wife. In her Adelphi Terrace flat the plan seemed to be for the 'sewing-machine' to hum and smile with even greater regularity, with improved office-space and efficient secretaries.

One gathers that Charlotte was secretary for a brief while only. She had thoughts of travel, and they increased as she grew older. She, more than he, liked moving about. She had never been hampered for money; at the time of their marriage her income was much larger than his earnings, but his earnings were rapidly increasing. There was no reason why they should not have a house in the country as well as the Adelphi office-flat. Shortly after the marriage Charlotte, I imagine, instigated the country-home search. They rented a house first in Haslemere; moved then to Hindhead; even more adventurously, lived for a while as far away as Ruan Minor in Cornwall. Returning after that to Haslemere, their next rented house was near Guildford; then they experimented near Woking; then, north of London, near Welwyn; and, in 1906, moved into the New Rectory at Ayot St Lawrence. They had not committed themselves to any more than temporary tenancy by rental, and neither of them admitted to having pleasure in the villa, or the village of Ayot St Lawrence, or in their neighbours, or in the Hertfordshire countryside. Yet after the many movings, G.B.S. at least was prepared to alter the name of the New Rectory to Shaw's Corner, and to dig in. Charlotte therefore bought furnishings, engaged a housekeeper so that she herself need not be tied all the time to Shaw's Corner, and the place, rather from inertia on their part than from positive love for it, became a permanency. By the time of the 1914–18 war the landlord wished to sell, and the Shaws then bought it.

My impression is that by the 1920s Charlotte had given up any hope of moving the 'sewing-machine' from Shaw's Corner. There was a move of their town quarters. As a result of a deplorable property deal Adelphi Terrace was torn down, but the London move forced on the Shaws pleased Charlotte: it shifted them to Whitehall Court, somewhat like a hotel, with no more bother of housekeeping than inspection every morning of the restaurant menu. In 1943 and at the age of eighty-six, Charlotte died at Whitehall Court. In her will she had specified that her ashes should be taken to Ireland and scattered on the Three Rock Mountain outside Dublin. This was a problem in wartime; G.B.S., though, kept her ashes. He had never apparently cared much about his physical surroundings, but in age he showed more pleasure in the house and garden at Shaw's Corner than heretofore; especially, after Charlotte's death, the garden. He proposed that when the time came for his cremation, Charlotte's ashes should be mingled with his and the mixture scattered in that garden. This was done in 1950, after Shaw, at ninety-four, had died at Shaw's Corner.

It was found in Shaw's will that Shaw's Corner, just as it was, had been left to the National Trust, although apparently there was no specific provision from his own moneys for maintenance of villa and garden in the order in which he left them. His whims as to how the place should be kept up were, though, thought to be well known. It suited his wishes for Shaw's Corner to become a showplace. Charlotte had always avoided publicity; G.B.S. admitted that he courted it. He would quote that Charlotte told him, 'You are always acting' – it was an observation that he accepted smilingly. I am not sure that Charlotte's ghost enjoys comment on her furnishings but there is nothing alien to G.B.S.'s vanity in having many of his hats on show in the entrance hall, or the basket chair he sat in for the putting on of outdoor shoes, or the bicycling machine he used for indoor exercise, or his Bechstein piano. The careful and scrupulous stage-setting of his plays is echoed by the desk and filing cabinets in the study, the miscellaneous awards and busts and the replica of Shaw's hand in marble in the drawing-room, and by the pen, pencil and steel-rimmed spectacles (reminder of his reading and making notes at meals) in the dining-room at Shaw's Corner.

At the bottom of the garden there is a summer-house, one of those small revolving huts into which a man might go by himself and without viewers or audience or any triggers that release some or other kind of showing-off, might for the moment meditate (should he so wish) on the mutability of writers' reputations. A mistake has been made, I feel, to force that little revolving summer-house at Shaw's Corner into being part of the stage-set. It is arranged for the ghost to be seen in – the wicker chair in place at the flap table, even another of G.B.S.'s hats in place beside the pencils, erasers, and other writing tools. Yet might it not have been better to have allowed Shaw's Corner to have some bit of a corner, that summer-house perhaps, where Shaw could be thought of alone, unwatched? Shaw asked himself, and us, an awkward question. Is he as dramatist to be ranked with Shakespeare and Molière, or else? Surely we need not be bullied, nor need Shaw be bullied either, into accepting the terms of the antithesis that he flung out.

Such circumstantial evidence as hats and writing tools have little bearing on the questions Shaw might have asked when alone in the summer-house hideaway. The external accessories are irrelevant; one might even disparage them or dislike them and yet admire Shaw and his work all the more. His contemporary Chesterton said that about his own feeling for Shaw: 'Everything is wrong about him except himself.'

SCOTLAND

Western Isles and Outer Hebrides

Isle of
Skye   Raasay

Glenelg

INVERNESS

Cairngorm
Mountains   Braemar   Stonehaven

ABERDEEN

Fort William   Kirriemuir

Glencoe   Rannoch
Moor   Perth   Dundee

Isle of
Mull   Oban   St Andrews

Iona   Inveraray   Stirling

Drymen   Kirkcaldy

Dunfermline

Greenock   GLASGOW   EDINBURGH

Irvine   Kilmarnock   Melrose   Kelso   Berwick-
upon-Tweed

Tweedsmuir

Tarbolton   Mauchline   Selkirk   Abbotsford

Ayr   Auchinleck   Jedburgh

Alloway   Ochiltree   Ettrick

Ailsa Craig   Moffat

Craigenputtock   Ecclefechan

Dumfries   Gretna Green

Stranraer

Wigtown

0   40 mls
0   40 kms

1. THE BORDERS REGION

It was my friend George Blake who (with a Scotsman's right) simplified for me the map of Scotland. Upon the map he placed a transparent rectangle of celluloid with its lower edge on the line of the Border with England (the line from Gretna to the North Sea coast near Tweedmouth) and its upper length on the almost straight line from Dumbarton through Stirling and Perth to the east coast at Stonehaven. That rectangle, said Blake, contained (roughly speaking) Scotland's Lowlands; all else to the north was the Highlands and Islands.

Within the eastern half of that rectangle and south of the Firth of Forth the area now for administrative purposes called the Borders Region merges with the Lothian Region surrounding Edinburgh. Within this area are relics of early poets such as the thirteenth-century

Thomas of Erceldoune (now Earlston), also called Thomas the Rhymer, as well as of other minstrels whose works were diligently collected by young Walter Scott. Also within this area, in the early seventeenth century, lived Drummond of Hawthornden, who was certainly visited there in 1618 by Ben Jonson (though I cannot vouch for the truth of the rumour that Jonson himself was born in Border country). Later, and with the help of the Great North Road, Edinburgh achieved pre-eminence in Scotland for the printing and distribution of books, and so drew Robert Burns from Ayrshire in 1786 to arrange for a second edition of his poems. Shortly after, intimate involvement with the fortunes of the Edinburgh publishing house of Constable and Ballantyne, in triumph and disaster, was to tie Scott to that neighbourhood. The Great North Road, 'dull, but useful' as Scott called it, aided the development of Scottish letters when the *Edinburgh Review* began its long career in 1802 and *Blackwood's Edinburgh Magazine* the even longer career which started in 1817. Thus it is fitting for me to enter the Borders Region at the point where the Great North Road passes through Berwick-upon-Tweed.

*   *   *

George Borrow, Englishman of Cornish heritage, was introduced to Scotland at Berwick-upon-Tweed at the age of ten in 1813; and a memorable introduction it was. His father, a soldier, was being moved northward from one station to another on the Great North Road; wife and son went along. On one beautiful morning of early spring the boy found himself on the bank of a river that was new to him, 'and', he wrote of it thirty years afterward in *Lavengro*, 'a goodly scene it was!'

Before me, across the water, on an eminence, stood a white old city, surrounded with lofty walls, above which rose the tops of tall houses, with here and there a church or steeple. To my right hand was a long and massive bridge, with many arches and of antique architecture, which traversed the river. The river was a noble one, the broadest that I had hitherto seen. Its waters, of a greenish tinge, poured with impetuosity beneath the narrow arches to meet the sea, close at hand, as the boom of the billows breaking distinctly upon a beach declared. There were songs upon the river from the fisher-barks; and occasionally a chorus, plaintive and wild, such as I had never heard before . . .

The intervention of thirty years tempted Borrow to make additions to what he first saw as a boy. For romantic readers of *Lavengro*, he makes the viewer think 'of how many feats of chivalry had those old walls been witness, when hostile kings contended for their possession? – how many an army from the south and from the north had trod that old bridge? –

what red and noble blood had crimsoned those rushing waters?' He compares the Tweed with the 'stately Danube' and the 'beauteous Rhine', and points out the Tweed has no need to envy them, and far less need to envy 'the turbid Tibur'. Then, happily, Borrow's narrative returns to what the ten-year-old boy actually saw and did. From the river-bank he watched several fishermen knee-deep in the water as they hauled in a salmon seine. 'So goodly and gay a scene' as was altogether provided 'had never', said Borrow, 'greeted my boyish eye'. In response that boyish eye suddenly filled with tears, and they began to trickle, and presently he lay there on the bank weeping outright. 'I was crying because I could not help it.' When one of the fishermen noticed the boy in tears, there was no explanation except it was tribute to the beauty of the Tweed.

North of Berwick-upon-Tweed, the Great North Road follows the coastline and crosses the Border three miles north of the river, at Lamberton Bar, where in old days Scottish marriages were performed for runaway couples from England, with readiness equal to that at the western end of the border at Gretna Green. The coast road would take one on to Dunbar, with recollections there of Mary, Queen of Scots, and also of Cromwell a century later; and for literary association the coast road would lead onward to Tantallon Castle, where the curving coast of Lothian faces outward to the Bass Rock – Tantallon Castle is the scene of much of Scott's *Marmion*. But I choose instead to follow the Border itself along the valley of the Tweed away from the coast to Coldstream. Norham Castle on that stretch of the river also appears in *Marmion*, while the climax of that poem is at the famous site of Flodden, just to the south of Coldstream. North of the Tweed the town of Duns is traditionally associated with Joannes Duns Scotus, the thirteenth-century *Doctor subtilis*, whose followers were so obstinate that for them the word 'dunce' was invented. Tradition goes on to say that Duns was Professor of Divinity at Oxford in 1301, that he was also regent of Paris University, and possibly died at Cologne, with the sensational addition of the story that there he might have been sealed into his tomb while yet alive. For all that I confess I have never found anything much connecting Duns Scotus with Duns, except the name.

Curiously, the macabre theme of 'burial alive' is one that is repeated in this Border country. At the beginning of the nineteenth century, at Coldingham on the coast north of Berwick-upon-Tweed, a woman's skeleton was discovered bricked in, upright, in the walls of the Benedictine priory. It is supposed that talk about that stimulated Scott to use the 'burial alive' theme in *Marmion*. Other tales of the practice may well have been told in Scott's hearing in his childhood in the Tweed valley above Coldstream.

As a boy Walter Scott attended the grammar school at Kelso, a few miles farther up the Tweed valley. As with Byron, an important question is: what was the effect on Scott of his deformity? The half-Scottish boy who became Lord Byron was born with a clubbed foot; Walter Scott's handicap was less extreme. From his own account of his trouble, it sounds to a layman as if the disease that struck him as a baby of eighteen months was poliomyelitis. At any rate, after a fever the child, before he was old enough to remember otherwise, was unable to use his paralysed right leg. Scott tells us that his first self-consciousness began when, two or three years after his birth in Edinburgh in 1771, he was taken to his grandfather's farmhouse of Sandy-Knowe, near the Tweed below Kelso. There – in successful maturity he is able to write lightly –

I recollect distinctly that my situation and appearance were a little whimsical. Among the odd remedies recurred to to aid my lameness, some one had recommended, that so often as a sheep was killed for the use of the family, I should be stripped, and swathed up in the skin, warm as it was flayed from the carcase of the animal. In this Tartar-like habiliment I well remember lying upon the floor of the little parlour in the farmhouse, while my grandfather, a venerable old man with white hair, used every excitement to make me try to crawl.

There was also a benevolent old soldier, ex-colonel of the Greys, who in full military uniform would kneel on the ground before the three-year-old, dragging his watch along the carpet to make the sheepskin-wrapped child try to follow it.

Largely through his own continuing determination not to be handicapped, Scott's lameness was in maturity to a great extent overcome. Nevertheless in his development it is a factor to be thought of. Visits to Bath as a child for treatments available there had no rapid effect. He had to learn to cure himself. The lameness may to some extent have pushed him to outdo, in whatever ways he could, his grammar-school companions at Kelso. Older friends, and those who taught him to chant ballads and told of exciting traditions, appear more in his account of his youth than do school companions of his own age. The relations with his older brother are interesting. Scott's parents had twelve children, though only five survived very early youth. The oldest brother, Robert, bred to serve the king in the Navy, was much admired by Walter. Robert 'had a strong turn for literature, read poetry with taste and judgment, and composed verses himself, which had gained him great applause'; when in bad humour, however, Robert kicked and cuffed Walter and others without mercy. If Walter could not rival Robert physically, he might yet outdo him in minstrelsy. Yet physical rivalry was also of extra importance to Walter Scott, as likewise it was to Byron.

As Scott came to manhood he vied strenuously in outdoor sport; he strove for noted feats of endurance, working up to riding as much, he boasts, as a hundred miles in a day and, lame or not, walking for as much as thirty miles.

Scott was forty-four when he met the twenty-seven-year-old Byron at John Murray's house in London. Byron's juvenile remarks about Scott in *English Bards and Scotch Reviewers* had been by both men forgotten; they met, and met again, at morning sessions with John Murray, and then together the two lame poets would go 'thumping downstairs side by side'. Their quick intimacy, as Lady Longford noted, was 'unaffected by Byron's trick of "mischief-making" and "mystifying" or by differences over religion and politics'. They exchanged gifts, but deeper than outward exchanges between Scott and Byron was the lasting impact the younger poet made upon the older. There was often straightforward fun in the companionship with Byron, and that was far from transitory – many years later Scott recalled in his journal an early dinner at Long's in 1815 with Byron present, and 'a most brilliant day we had of it. I never saw Byron so full of fun, frolic, wit, and whim; he was as playful as a kitten.' There were also periods when Byron seemed lost in gloom, in which case the older man would wait, unhurrying, for a right moment to reopen conversation, 'when the shadows almost always left his countenance like the mist rising from a landscape'. Lady Longford comments on the 'knack' with which Scott 'managed' Byron. 'If only young Lady Byron could have had the same knack', says Lady Longford. 'But as the valet Fletcher was to say: "I never yet knew a lady that could not manage my Lord, *except* my lady."'

In the pleasure of looking at the two lame poets side by side, I don't wish to overlook what I called Byron's lasting impact on Scott. I am not referring to any direct correspondence between the men during Byron's years of exile, though neither forgot the other. Byron's drama *Cain*, completed the month after Shelley's visit to him at Ravenna, was dedicated in 1821 to Scott; Scott in Scotland happily accepted that friendly and 'flattering proposal'. The impact I speak of was in fact made before the two men met in person, though it increased after their meeting, and was spoken of by Scott in the last year of his life, long after Byron's death, when in 1831, with the help of many well-wishers, he was making valiant efforts to recuperate after his first series of strokes. The travel to Italy had been arranged, and on arrival at Naples Scott was to see much of Sir William Gell, a contemporary 'who had long been condemned to live in Italy by ailments and infirmities not dissimilar to his own'. The two invalids readily compared notes and exchanged confidences such as possibly might not have been confessed to others. By 1831 Scott was under the impression that his liability for debt of £130000, as shockingly revealed five years before, had been at last paid off. (Nearly two-thirds of the debt had indeed been cleared by his own and unremitting efforts, and the gap of £50000 or so no one wished to reveal to the sick man.) There was a moment when Scott remarked to Sir William Gell (as Gell later repeated to Lockhart) how he wished to use his emancipation:

He told me, that, being relieved from debt, and no longer forced to write for money, he longed to turn to poetry again. I encouraged him, and asked him why he had ever relinquished poetry? – 'Because Byron *bet* me', said he, pronouncing the word, *beat*, short. I rejoined, that I thought I could remember by heart as many passages of his poetry as of Byron's. He replied – 'That may be, but he *bet* me out of the field in the description of the strong passions, and in deep-seated knowledge of the human heart; so I gave up poetry for the time.'

It was more than a year after Scott took up residence at Abbotsford that one sees him feeling that if Byron had '*bet*' him out of the field of poetry, Maria Edgeworth had opened the gate into another field of writing. In 1813, in direct emulation of (in his words) 'the admirable Irish portraits drawn by Miss Edgeworth', he searched for and found the beginning of a prose manuscript which he had laid aside, and to the opening scenes in England he added the Scottish scenes 'which are what really matter' – that was the tremendous fresh start of *Waverley*, and of all the Waverley novels. Yet before glancing at Scott as a kind of all-round athlete who if beaten at poetry could turn to novels, I ought to remark how all of this Border country, from Kelso up the Tweed into Tweeddale, and from Carter Bar in the Cheviot Hills west into Ettrick Forest, has through the centuries,

Betide, betide, whate'er betide,

been a notable producer of poets, among them Thomas the Rhymer, from whom that line comes. The poet James Thomson was born in 1700 at Ednam, a village two miles north of Kelso; an obelisk was set up on Ferney Hill, nearby Ednam, to record his birthplace. Another of the Border poets – James Hogg, 'the Ettrick Shepherd' – was born in Ettrick village (a monument shows where) and the churchyard there is where Hogg was buried.

It was in 1802 that Scott, already 'shirra' (i.e. sheriff) of Selkirk, still 'a lively partaker in the business of the yeomanry cavalry' and most of all an ardent ballad-hunter in the field, bent on adding to the store of his volumes of Border *Minstrelsy*, met Hogg and gave him a warm invitation to visit the Scotts at their then home at Lasswade, near Edinburgh. Lockhart tells how Hogg took up the invitation:

When Hogg entered the drawing-room, Mrs Scott, being at the time in a delicate state of health, was reclining on a sofa. The Shepherd, after being presented, and making his best bow, took possession of another sofa placed opposite to hers, and stretched himself thereupon at all his length; for, as he said afterwards, 'I thought I could never do wrong to copy the lady of the house'. As his dress at this period was precisely that in which any ordinary herdsman attends cattle to the market, and his hands, moreover, bore most legible marks of a recent sheep-smearing, the lady of the house did not observe with perfect equanimity the novel usage to which her chintz was exposed. The Shepherd, however, remarked nothing of all this – dined heartily and drank freely, and, by jest, anecdote, and song, afforded plentiful merriment. As the liquor operated, his familiarity increased; from Mr Scott, he advanced to 'Sherra', and thence to 'Scott', 'Walter', and 'Wattie' – until, at supper, he fairly convulsed the whole party by addressing Mrs Scott, as 'Charlotte'.

The readiness of 'the Ettrick Shepherd' to drop his crook and take up the pen led him into a life of ups and downs, not all literary folk being as tolerant of his behaviour as Scott. Hogg's songs are not now much remembered; what is recalled is that he was one of the group which started *Blackwood's Magazine* in 1817 and 'the Ettrick Shepherd' became one of the characters in *Noctes Ambrosianae*; further to that, *The Confessions of a Justified Sinner*, which, whether or no he wrote it unaided, remains one of the most remarkable prose fictions of the nineteenth century, suggesting close analogy with *Wuthering Heights*.

Scott's country home in the first years of his married life had been at Lasswade, close to Edinburgh, but for the period 1804 to 1812 in which *The Lay of the Last Minstrel*, *Marmion* and *The Lady of the Lake* established his fame as a poet, the couple moved to Ashiestiel on the Tweed, convenient for Scott's duties as sheriff in Selkirk. His sheriff's clerk was the earlier Andrew Lang, grandfather of the man of letters who proudly claimed Selkirk as his birthplace. Selkirk has other literary associations, not least that Oakwood Tower, above the road between Selkirk and Ettrick, is on the site of the home of Michael Scot the Wizard – it may be noted that the Wizard, and Thomas the Rhymer, and Merlin's grave and Arthur and his knights in their enchanted sleep beneath the Eildon Hills (and indeed Arthur's Seat in Edinburgh) are all indicative of the romance indigenous to this particular part of Scotland.

The visits of Robert Burns in this region in the summer of 1787 are often recorded, as at Coldstream and Selkirk, by tablets, though the house that he stayed in at Jedburgh has been demolished. The Words-worths, William and Dorothy, made their leisurely tour in 1803; Peebles, 'an old town built of grey stone', pleased Dorothy particularly as 'very pretty' On that first trip to Scotland, after they had met Scott and had been advised by him where to go, Wordsworth commented that wherever they appeared 'in the character of the *Sheriff's* friends' they received a hearty welcome.

In 1803 the young sheriff was popular not only with farmers and country folk but with the 'souters' (shoemakers) of Selkirk, the weavers of Hawick and townsfolk generally; but in the years after the Napoleonic wars, when Scott had moved into Abbotsford and rebuilt the house with many turrets and gables and parts copied from elsewhere, and was at first preoccupied with the Waverley novels and the fortune they achieved and later with the catastrophic debts resulting from the publishers' failure, the industrial workers in particular felt that Scott's Tory loyalties had made him cold and alien to their own bitter distresses. In 1831 reform was in the air in the Scottish Lowlands with as much strong feelings as in England, and by then there was less of a hearty welcome for the sheriff in Jedburgh, where he went to support the Tory candidate in the election, than when he had conducted Dorothy and William Wordsworth there in 1803. In the summer of 1831 Scott was indeed in no physical condition to attend a rowdy election, yet on this occasion clearly he was 'highly imperative', hung down his eyebrows, and no one durst disobey his intention. At seven in the morning on 18 May Scott's open carriage was at his door and he was impatiently ordering Lockhart to go with him to the scene of action. At Jedburgh:

We found the town [wrote Lockhart] in a most tempestuous state; in fact, it was almost wholly in the hands of a disciplined rabble, chiefly weavers from Hawick, who marched up and down with drums and banners, and then, after filling the Court-hall, lined the streets, grossly insulting every one who did not wear the reforming colours. Sir Walter's carriage . . . was pelted with stones; one or two fell into it, but none touched him. . . .

As Scott then walked to the hall with his 'uneven step', a companion supporting him on either side, 'he was saluted with groans and blasphemies all the way', said Lockhart, ' – and I blush to add that a woman spat upon him from a window; but this last contumely I think he did not observe.'

There was a prettier scene in the July of that year, on the last occasion on which Scott, with Lockhart's assistance, could make a fairly extensive tour in his open carriage up the Tweed and into Lanarkshire, so that he might refresh his memory of Douglasdale. Alongside the Tweed then went the carriage, 'passing in succession Yair, Ashiestiel, Innerleithen, Traquair, and many more scenes dear to his early life, and celebrated in his writings'. It was on that expedition, which was to take Scott and Lockhart across the moorland ridge between Tweed and Clyde, that Lockhart saw Scott's bodily weakness releasing control over 'the softer

and gentler emotions which now trembled to the surface'. Scott on
that expedition wept at emotions evoked just by the scenery itself, 'the
rushing of a brook, or the sighing of the summer breeze, bringing the
tears into his eyes not unpleasantly'.

It was a nice touch for Lockhart to record the Tweed responding, as
it were, when Scott had been brought back from Italy and in September
1832 was on his deathbed at Abbotsford. All his children were present,
said Lockhart, as Scott breathed his last. 'It was a beautiful day – so
warm, that every window was wide open – and so perfectly still, that
the sound of all others most delicious to his ear, the gentle ripple of the
Tweed over its pebbles, was distinctly audible as we knelt around the
bed.' Scott's great-grandfather had seen to it that the family retained
the right to 'stretch their bones' beside Dryburgh Abbey, and there
'within a lovely loop of the Tweed amid handsome trees' Sir Walter
Scott was buried.

2.   EDINBURGH

In this Abbotsford neighbourhood are the Eildon Hills, after the Tweed
Scott's favourite sight. The hills are three conspicuous volcanic summits
– conspicuous in that their beauty draws the eye, and has done so since
prehistory. Consequently they have become famous in legend, and in
legend the Eildon Hills were divided into three by fairly recent necro-
mancy, by command of that same magician Michael Scot who resided
at the Tower of Oakwood, on the Ettrick above Selkirk. Walter Scott
refers to the magical charm that did this, in the *Lay of the Last Minstrel*:

> The words that cleft Eildon hills in three,
> And bridled the Tweed with a curb of stone.

Scott and other poets also fostered the legend that Arthur and his
knights lie all in armour in caverns beneath the Eildon Hills, in enchanted sleep.

One of the main observations to be made about this Lowland country
south of Edinburgh, hill-land of streams and moors and heather,
country of soft yet strong contours, is that a gift for singing spread here
like seeds on the wind and presently became indigenous. In early days
it might be ballads that cropped up hereabouts like wild flowers:

> O waly, waly, up the bank,
> O waly, waly, doun the brae . . .

Later, and most especially in the eighteenth century, lyric-singing came
into being hereabouts, as spontaneous and natural as birdsong.

Professor Minto said long ago what should be repeated here:

The passion for song-writing which seized upon Scotland in the eighteenth
century may be compared – if small things may be compared with great – with
the passion for play-writing which seized upon England in the latter days of
Queen Elizabeth and throughout the reign of her successor. In both periods
we have a supreme outcome, the plays of Shakespeare in the one case and the
poetry of Burns in the other; but the excitement by which the powers of these
central figures were stimulated was general.

The point is well made that Burns was born in a part of the world and
at a time propitious for the kind of song-writing at which Scots aristocracy and peasantry competed, and at which Burns, when he came
along, proved supreme. Professor Minto (who was himself attached to
Aberdeen) maintained that the eighteenth-century passion for song-
writing was active in the north of Scotland also, and of that there are
excellent examples; but it was in the Lowlands that competition was
most extraordinary. 'Peers, members of the Supreme Court of Law,
diplomatists, lairds, clergymen, schoolmasters, men of science, farmers,
gardeners, compositors, pedlars – all were trying their hands at patching
old songs and making new songs', as Minto proved. Women and men
were involved equally – the writer of 'Auld Robin Gray' was a daughter
of the Earl of Balcarres, and the writer of one of the choicest lyrics of all,
'Ca' the Yowes to the Knowes', was an Ayrshire 'lucky' by name Tibbie
Pagan, who kept an alehouse and sold whisky without a licence, and
was regarded as formidable from her 'saturnine temper and dissolute
habits'. It is often the Scottish women whose appeal to the melancholy
romantic side of Scotch character has lasting success: two plaintive
songs both named 'The Flowers of the Forest' were eighteenth-century
compositions, one by Miss Jane Elliot of Teviotdale and the other by
Mrs Alison Cockburn, born at Fairnilee on the Tweed but later to move
to Edinburgh.

Allan Ramsay, migrating to Edinburgh from Lanarkshire in the first
year of the eighteenth century to start the first circulating library in
Scotland from his bookshop in the High Street, encouraged one of the
earliest groups of song-writers; yet contributions to his *Tea-Table
Miscellany* were less active stimulants than a song that came from John
Skinner, 'a persecuted Episcopalian clergyman in Aberdeenshire' and
author, to quote Burns, 'of the best Scotch song Scotland ever saw –
Tullochgorum's my delight!' Another writer of a generation later than
Ramsay and Skinner was Robert Fergusson, whose short life began in
Edinburgh in 1750 and ended in madness twenty-four years later;
there is no doubt of the impetus that Burns found in Fergusson's poems.
The stone which Burns commissioned to be placed over his grave in

Edinburgh is still there, on the west side of Canongate Kirkyard, with the date of Fergusson's birth given wrongly as 1751 instead of 1750, but with Burns's tribute on it.

The transit from Arthur's resting-place under the Eildon Hills to Arthur's Seat in Edinburgh has brought me into the capital past Lasswade, where Scott and his wife had their first country residence. A hundred and fifty years before that, William Drummond of Hawthornden was buried in the churchyard at Lasswade – the mansion of Hawthornden, where Ben Jonson stayed with Drummond, was about two miles farther up the valley of the Esk. A little farther to the west, a few miles out of the old city and on the northern edge of the Pentland Hills, was the manse where Robert Louis Stevenson spent boyhood holidays with his grandfather, the period which R.L.S. later referred to as his 'golden age'. Swanston, Colinton (off the A70 and beside the Water of Leith) and Glencorne are villages which Stevensonians locate – Swanston plays a part in *St Ives*. Yet Edinburgh has so much enlarged itself since Stevenson's time that Colinton and Swanston are now within the city. In the eighteenth century the city of Edinburgh covered no more than the square mile inclusive of the 'Ancient Royalty'; within that confine I may select a few of the memories that jostle.

Edinburgh's 'Royal Mile', stretching down the ridge from castle to palace, was mentioned by Defoe in 1724 as 'perhaps the largest, longest and finest street for buildings and number of inhabitants, not in Britain only, but in the world'. Others did not hesitate to say that to walk in that street enforced holding the nose and treading with extreme care. The walking remained 'pretty perilous' by night throughout the eighteenth century: when late on an August evening of 1773 Boswell exulted at the message that Dr Johnson had arrived at Boyd's Inn off the Canongate ('I now had him actually in Caledonia'), escorting him to the house in James Court, Lawnmarket, where Boswell was a tenant of David Hume's, made him wish Johnson had no sense of smell. The 'evening effluvia' (Boswell's phrase) 'could not be masked: As we marched slowly along, he grumbled in my ear, "I smell you in the dark!"'

Thirteen years later, Robert Burns, at the end of his two-day journey from Mauchline in Ayrshire, riding on the pony which he had borrowed from a farmer friend, arrived at the north side of the Lawnmarket a little below James Court. Burns paid less attention to the smells of Edinburgh's Lawnmarket than Johnson, partly because they were less active at the end of November than in August, and partly because Burns at that moment of his twenty-seventh year was very tired. Presently, when my journey reaches Ayrshire, I can catch up with some of the troubles, angers and griefs which had haunted Burns throughout the year 1786. There had been in that year times of panic at 'the consequences of his follies'; yet despite the shames and sorrow he had had better fortune too, and a chance, it might be, of escape from what he had left behind him. The young farmer – whose consolation was that a first printing of a selection of his poems at Kilmarnock had sold out – began to think of Edinburgh. Wilson, the Kilmarnock printer, refused to venture on a further printing; but in Edinburgh there were professionals. Thus Burns had set about making himself presentable in new buckskins, a coat of good blue cloth, a waistcoat of blue and canary stripes and a pair of proper top-boots, and, on the borrowed pony, had set off from his farm. He was to share lodgings with his friend Richmond, a lawyer's clerk, but for how long depended on what reception Edinburgh gave him. Earlier in the year the only way out of his troubles at home had seemed to be emigration to Jamaica. Now, and before setting off for Edinburgh, he had made sure there was a ship (the *Roselle*) sailing from Leith for Jamaica in December. With that conceivable escape, he started his journey but stopped at one Lanark farmhouse for supper and at another where he was to spend the night and so, one gathers, made quite a night of it. When by the following evening Burns was greeted by John Richmond in Baxter's Close, Lawnmarket, he was so tired that the whole of his first day in Edinburgh was spent by him in bed.

The lodgings at which Burns had arrived were kept by Mrs Carfrae, 'a staid sober, piously disposed, skuldudery-abhorring widow'. Mr E. F. Catford, in his *Edinburgh: The Story of a City*, remarks that Mrs Carfrae's house 'has long ago disappeared, but its approximate position is marked by an inscription on the wall of No. 479 Lawnmarket'. It is right that the site should be marked, for what happened there to Burns was as dramatic as Byron's waking to find himself famous. While Burns himself felt insecure about getting out of bed, putting on his finery and showing himself upon the Royal Mile, the literary loungers of the Royal Mile were becoming eager to have sight of the Ayrshire ploughman-poet. On 3 November there had been a first long, laudatory article about him by James Sibbald in the *Edinburgh Magazine*, with extracts from the poems; in the last week of November the well-informed knew that Sibbald's second important article with a second instalment of Burns's poems was to be the feature of the magazine's December issue. More than that, there was information that Henry Mackenzie (the critic 'whose pronouncements on matters of literary taste were final for Edinburgh') was devoting an issue of *The Lounger*, early in December, to a most cordial appreciation of the new poet. Burns might be hesitant to meet Edinburgh, but Edinburgh was eager to meet him.

On his second day in the city Burns rose to the challenge. Possibly fortified by an early short visit with Richmond to Johnnie Dowie's tavern, he set out to present the introductions he had brought from

Ayrshire. With astonishing speed one thing led to another: before he knew it Burns was snatched up by top people and exposed to every danger of the latest society toy. The women of Edinburgh were fully as quick as the men – the Duchess of Gordon was in the lead to whisk him off 'to dancing assemblies, entertainments and social gatherings of all kinds'. The greatest of surprises was the way Burns kept his head; for that Carlyle later praised him in his *Lectures on Heroes*:

If we think of it, few heavier burdens could be laid on the strength of a man. So sudden; all common *Lionism*, which ruins innumerable men, was as nothing to this. . . . Burns, still only in his twenty-seventh year, is no longer even a ploughman; he is flying to the West Indies to escape disgrace and a jail. This month he is a ruined peasant, his wages seven pounds a year, and these gone from him: next month he is in the blaze of rank and beauty, handing down jewelled Duchesses to dinner; the cynosure of all eyes! Adversity is sometimes hard upon a man; but for one man who can stand prosperity, there are a hundred that will stand adversity. I admire much the way in which Burns met all this. Perhaps no man one could point out, was ever so sorely tried, and so little forgot himself. . . .

Mrs Alison Cockburn, a contemporary who kept a shrewd eye on the behaviour of fellow-poets, likewise applauded Burns:

The town is at present agog with the ploughman poet who receives adulation with native dignity and is the very figure of his profession, strong and coarse, but has a most enthusiastic heart of love. He has seen Duchess Gordon and all the gay world. . . . The man will be spoiled, if he can spoil; but he keeps his simple manners and is quite sober.

The Lord Glencairn who had introduced Burns to the Duke and Duchess of Gordon also introduced him to the Faculty of Advocates; ten days after Burns's arrival he wrote back to Ayrshire that Lord Glencairn and the Dean of the Faculty 'have taken me under their wing; and by all probability I shall soon be the tenth Worthy, and the eighth Wise Man, of the world'. It is remarkable that despite all the social engagements arranged for Burns, he was able to attend to his personal business composedly and to good effect. As 'eighth Wise Man' he struck while the iron was hot. It was on 9 December that Henry Mackenzie pronounced him in *The Lounger* 'a genius of no ordinary rank'. By the middle of December Burns, with Lord Glencairn behind him, cornered William Creech, then Edinburgh's foremost publisher, and made him promise £500 for the copyright of a new edition of poems. Through the further good nature of Lord Glencairn it was arranged that if Burns dedicated the volume to 'The Noblemen and Gentlemen of the Caledonian Hunt', the Caledonian Hunt would engage to subscribe for a hundred copies – it seems Burns understood that proposal to mean an additional fee to him of a hundred guineas, and he hastened to agree. This was prosperity indeed, for the man who earlier in the year had been unable even to count on wages of £7 a year, and had been planning to go off to the West Indies 'to escape disgrace and a jail'. No wonder Burns commissioned a memorial stone for Fergusson, whose example had encouraged his poems. The ship *Roselle* sailed from Leith for Jamaica, and at that moment it seemed as if the former part of Burns's life was departing with her while the famous and successful Burns accepted plaudits up and down the Royal Mile.

It seems fitting that at Edinburgh the most prominent feature of the East Gardens beside Princes Street should be the Scott Monument; the Burns Monument, as may befit a country cousin, is less conspicuously farther to the eastward, below Calton Hill. In life, Scott as a boy of fifteen did once meet Burns, during the winter of Burns's first visit. Scott's letter to Lockhart recalling the episode was written forty years later and confirms the very favourable impression Burns made in general conversation. His 'perfect self-confidence, without the slightest presumption' made memorable impact on the young Walter Scott. Elsewhere Scott makes a mention of the way Burns's eyes seemed to light up (his eyes, Scott said, could 'blaze') and he records the effect of the sight of a print depicting a dead soldier and widow and child, apparently in Canada. 'Burns seemed much affected by the print, or rather the ideas which it suggested to his mind. He actually shed tears' – the tears made Scott perceive the intensity of whatever it was of which Burns had been reminded. (Is it conceivable that 'the ideas which it suggested' were connected with the exile overseas with Mary Campbell that had so nearly happened?)

Thirty-five or so years after Scott's meeting with Burns, and when Scott himself was at the zenith of his career, he was one of those who organized the welcome for the reigning monarch, George IV, on his visit to Edinburgh. To add a comic touch to Scott's distractions at the time, on the very day of the king's arrival, who should turn up from the south of England, oblivious of what else was going on, but the now elderly and widowed poet George Crabbe.

'Perhaps no Englishman of these recent days', wrote Lockhart, 'ever arrived in Scotland with a scantier stock of information about the country and the people than (judging from all that he said, and more expressively looked) this illustrious poet had brought with him in August 1822.' Crabbe's garb as an English clergyman singled him out when he was thrust into a sumptuous dinner at Lord Glengarry's, the great chief and officers of his company all in the Highland costume, and all joining in the singing of Scots songs and ballads. Scott at that dinner, as recorded in Crabbe's journal, 'was the life and soul of the whole'. Early next morning Scott, fully arrayed 'in the garb of old Gaul', returned from fulfilling an outside engagement to greet guests whom he had invited to six o'clock breakfast. On entering his parlour he found those guests, all in their full costume, being entertained by Crabbe speaking with them 'in what was at least meant to be French'. The polite old man, not having been warned about such company and hearing them speak to each other in an unknown tongue, had adopted what he considered as the universal language. The 'gallant Celts' for their part, eyeing Crabbe's costume, considered him some foreign *abbé*, until Scott straightened it all out.

The royal visit involved Scott in so many entertainments that it fell largely to his son-in-law Lockhart to look after Crabbe. On one occasion Lockhart took him to a dinner of the group which produced *Blackwood's Magazine*, and Crabbe was impressed by the behaviour of 'the Ettrick Shepherd', who called out loudly for his can of ale, scorning the 'champagne, claret and other choice wines' that were in circulation. The 'Shepherd' was one who had paid no attention to the edict of the Town Council, that for the king's entry into Edinburgh all those not entitled to the wearing of a kilt should be 'carefully well-dressed, black coat and white trousers if at all convenient'. Lockhart criticized the sudden and wholly disproportionate preponderance of kilts. Another individual (not of the *Blackwood's* group) who scorned the Town Council's edict on costume was Thomas Carlyle. He 'resolved rather to quit the City altogether and be absent and silent in such efflorescence of the flunkeyisms'. Perhaps this relates to the conception, in Carlyle's mind, of *Sartor Resartus*. Certainly for the duration of the king's stay in 1822 Carlyle took himself off in a huff to Dumfriesshire, and, at Ecclefechan, explained that his presence there was a result of Edinburgh's edict on clothes.

Saintsbury remarks that Carlyle, in the guise of his account in *Sartor Resartus* of the German philosopher Diogenes Teufelsdröckh and his 'philosophy of clothes', had borrowed that philosophy from Swift. It may, though, seem that Carlyle had no need to borrow. Saintsbury points to a good deal of autobiography in *Sartor Resartus*. 'Entepfuhl is Ecclefechan': at Ecclefechan Carlyle, on his own, had a spell of brooding on Edinburgh's sartorial behaviour. Saintsbury mentions another autobiographical hint in *Sartor Resartus*: 'The spot of the revelation of the "Everlasting No", nominally the Rue St Thomas de l'Enfer in Paris, has been authoritatively identified with the junction of Leith Walk and Pilrig Street, on the outskirts of Edinburgh.' Saintsbury was in a position to verify that identification, for though he was born in Southampton, he was Professor of Rhetoric and English Literature at Edinburgh University from 1895 until 1915.

Other individuals begin now to spring to mind through a casual connection of dates. Before Scott died, De Quincey came to settle in Edinburgh; there he continued writing for periodicals, yet as old friends fell away, spent his latter years at No. 42 Lothian Street more and more as a recluse. De Quincey died in 1859; in that year there were born in Edinburgh two writers representative of an altogether different period – Kenneth Grahame and Arthur Conan Doyle.

Kenneth Grahame was born at No. 30 Castle Street, opposite the town house which Scott had occupied for many years (and where George Crabbe was entertained). There was a tradition in Edinburgh for writing books for young readers: I need only mention R. M. Ballantyne's *The Coral Island* and Helen Bannerman's *Little Black Sambo*. Grahame left Edinburgh, though, before practising as a writer; at the age of nineteen he was in employment at the Bank of England, and it was not until 1908 that at Sonning on the Thames he wrote the book for which he is mostly remembered, *The Wind in the Willows*. Arthur Conan Doyle's home was in Edinburgh until he had obtained his medical degree. He had many boyhood memories of his birthplace at No. 11 Picardy Place, between York Place and Leith Walk, including one of a visit of Thackeray to Picardy Place. Thackeray knew the Doyles through 'Dicky' Doyle, the *Punch* artist who had done much illustrating for him, for *The Newcomes*, for example. 'Dicky' Doyle was Arthur's uncle; the child remembered that when Thackeray was brought to visit he sat on the visitor's knee while the novelist made his gold repeater watch strike one hundred o'clock for their mutual enjoyment. Thackeray died in 1863, so Doyle himself could not have been more than four years old. Doyle remained proud of the memory, and felt immensely flattered when an early piece of his own was accepted for the *Cornhill Magazine* which Thackeray had founded. Doyle's mother kept him in fairly strict discipline in Edinburgh; when he entered the university for medical training, she saw to it that he worked more steadily than another Irish medical student, Oliver Goldsmith, had worked at Edinburgh in the century before. Two lasting results of Doyle's academic training were that he turned one of his teachers (Dr Joseph Bell) into Sherlock Holmes and that he appeased his own poor record in mathematics by turning Sherlock Holmes's arch-enemy, the wicked Moriarty, into a professional mathematician.

Nine years older than Grahame and Doyle, Robert Louis Stevenson (1850–94) was born at No. 8 Howard Place (now the Stevenson Memorial House). The family moved later to No. 17 Heriot Row, where Stevenson lived from the age of seven until his twenties when he started on the career of a writer. When Stevenson came to be writing *A Child's Garden of Verses* he recalled the childhood at No. 17 Heriot Row, as for instance in 'The Lamplighter':

For we are very lucky, with a lamp before the door,
And Leerie stops to light it as he lights so many more;
And O! before you hurry by with ladder and with light,
O Leerie, see a little child and nod to him tonight!

When Stevenson was twenty-two an essay of his was accepted by Leslie Stephen for the *Cornhill*, and the acquaintance so made led Stephen to collect the young Stevenson for a visit to W. E. Henley, who had been taken to the Old Infirmary of Edinburgh for treatment there by the great Sir Joseph Lister. Henley was a year older than Stevenson; we have seen in Gloucester how tubercular bone-disease had caused the amputation of one foot in his youth: it was in the hope that Lister could save the other leg that Henley was willing to lie for two years in 'the cold, naked, clean, half-workhouse and half-jail' in Edinburgh. From the Old Infirmary Henley had likewise submitted contributions to the *Cornhill*. The long stay in hospital did in fact check the disease: Henley's other leg was saved and the lifelong friendship with Stevenson, of great benefit to both of them, began. Ten years later, when Stevenson was writing *Treasure Island* – it was after his marriage, when staying at Invercauld, between Balmoral and Braemar, that he put that tale on paper and so first won fame – he deliberately gave Long John Silver many of Henley's characteristics, though leaving out, he explained, Henley's redeeming features. Henley and Stevenson proceeded to collaborate in play-writing; they were both much intrigued by the eighteenth-century criminal trial in Edinburgh of Deacon Brodie. The case of the notorious Deacon Brodie certainly played a part in prompting Stevenson's *Strange Case of Dr Jekyll and Mr Hyde*.

3. AYRSHIRE

It is to pay attention to Burns's early life that I now head from Edinburgh west to Kilmarnock and Ayr. The father pronounced his name 'Burness' and spelled it Burnes. The mother, 'fiery' Agnes, pronounced the name 'Burrens' and she wrote it – almost all she could write – as Burns. The son Robert was born on 25 January 1759, in the cottage built of clay which, by getting into small debt to his employer, William Burnes had been enabled to buy. Six years later, after the birth of another boy Gilbert, and then of two girls, William got into larger debt by leasing a seventy-acre farm, Mount Oliphant, two miles above Alloway. It was a poor farm; the twelve years on the bleak upland acres of Mount Oliphant were summed up by Burns in four words: 'We lived very poorly.' Robert had some troubles, nervous and rheumatic, which recurred, but provided the boys kept up with all farm chores, the increasingly worried father did not reproach them at meals – meals seemingly always of skim milk and porridge of oats or barley – if they sat 'with a book in one hand and a spoon in the other'. The book was whatever might be left by the itinerant but talented young dominie who served a circuit of farmsteads; and Robert was the dominie's special favourite. He inspired Robert to memorize poems, just as his mother awakened him to the memorizing of songs; then, at the age of fourteen, the boy wrote his own first love-song, composed 'in a wild enthusiasm of passion' for a fair-haired country girl who came at harvest-time to help with the gleaning (she got a thorn in her hand which he had to take out). So his career as a poet started.

After the twelve years at Mount Oliphant and when Robert was eighteen, William Burnes achieved one further and disastrous move. The plunge was into leasing a larger farm, Lochlie, near the weaving village of Tarbolton. A scheme, of which there were great expectations, was to grow flax; presently, when their crops were plentiful, Robert would visit the seaport of Irvine, centre of the flax trade, to become a skilled flax-heckler; then the farm produce could be sold direct to local weavers. The move was exciting for the whole family; Robert, now a personable young man, though at times moody and at times ebullient, joined other young farmers in forming a 'Bachelors' Club' at Tarbolton. In part, the Bachelors' was a debating society (Burns proved himself an easy and applauded speaker); in part it was a club that promoted dancing (of which Burns, in open disobedience to his father, had become 'distractedly fond'); and in part each member was to qualify as 'a professed lover of one or more of the female sex'. As an esteemed leader of the Bachelors', Burns was also inducted into the Tarbolton Lodge of the Freemasons, and his presence there was noted with approval by Gavin Hamilton of Mauchline, a well-connected and prosperous country lawyer and a Freemason of importance.

The social results of the move to Lochlie were better than the farm results. The flax was harder to grow than expected. Burns was twenty-two before Lochlie had enough flax under cultivation for him to take time away at Irvine to learn about heckling. By then his social prowess had received a bump: the love that as a leading Bachelor he had professed to 'Mary Morison' (probably Alison Begbie) was spurned by her. That stung his pride. He could and did assuage himself in poems, and the resonance of the 'Mary Morison' poems first shows his true gift. Nevertheless, his pride as a bold lover needed restoration, and as soon as he was on his own at Irvine (lodging in a flax-dresser's house in Glasgow Vennel right above the heckling room) he was glad to regain confidence by going around with a newly met companion, Richard Brown, six years older, well educated and an experienced seaman, as well as 'a wild, bold, generous fellow' with women.

Burns himself later implied that it was Brown who taught him to treat sex affairs 'with levity' – an imputation which Brown, when he had become a captain of West Indiamen and was respectably married, denied with vehemence. Be that as it may, Brown's contribution to literature was his praise of Burns's verses. The better-educated companion whom Burns admired 'to a degree of enthusiasm' was emphatic that verses of such merit ought to be sent to a magazine, and ''twas actually this' that was a trigger for Burns to strive to become 'a Poet'. The intoxication of thinking himself 'a Poet' was promptly stimulated by studying the works of Ramsay and Fergusson:

> Ramsay an' famous Fergusson
> Gied Forth an' Tay a lift aboon,
> Yarrow an' Tweed, to monie a tune,
>   Owre Scotland rings,
> While Irwin, Lugar, Ayr an' Doon
>   Naebody sings.

This was a field, other than farming, which Burns could feel to be open when he recovered from the attack of serious illness (possibly endocarditis) that he had at Irvine. Yet at the instant he had to gird himself to cope with the sorry state of things at Lochlie.

This sorry state included the likelihood of William Burnes's arrest and probable imprisonment for debt as a result of his counter-actions against the landlord of Lochlie. Robert apparently turned for advice to his friend and fellow-Mason, Gavin Hamilton, whose probable estimate was that the father, though only as yet in his sixties, was in too bad shape to live much longer. He therefore advised and made it possible for the sons to have as many of the family assets as possible in their own names and diverted into investment that the father's creditors could not touch – namely, investment in one of Hamilton's properties, a farm called Mossgiel. William died in February 1784, and after the burial in accordance to his wish in Alloway churchyard, the family found sanctuary at Mossgiel, two miles away from Lochlie and nearer to Mauchline village. The house, facing south-west to look over the wooded valley of the Ayr, was a great improvement on any previous home. As master of Mossgiel Robert chose for himself an attic room and placed a writing table beneath the sloping skylight. A reliable hero-worshipper, his brother Gilbert was delighted that Robert's first entry in the new book for the Mossgiel farm accounts was – a poem.

It was a prophetic action, for Robert's verses were the family's chief asset. The first harvest at Mossgiel was a failure: in 1784 Robert had a return of the nervous depression that had afflicted him at Irvine. Ease to worry was that Hamilton was landlord, and Hamilton, 'jovial, free-living young married man', took delight in Robert's company and especially in the assistance of Robert's pungent and rollicking satires against Hamilton's opponents in the Kirk. Robert heartily sided with exponents of the New Licht, they being more 'permissive' than the elders of the Auld Licht, the 'Unco Guid'. The young master of Mossgiel, tying his hair in a queue with a ribbon to cut a dash at Mauchline either with the Hamiltons and their friends or with a crew of his own admirers at the favoured Mauchline alehouse, found it not hard to shrug off that first bad harvest. Some elders, however, who had gossiped about the way the transfer to Mossgiel had evaded Lochlie debts, found a further target when in the spring of 1785 Lizzie Paton of Largieside was reported to be with child, and Robert Burns of Mossgiel admitted fatherhood. Mrs Carswell has described the penance in her biography:

In due course he and Lizzie had to submit to the discipline ordained by the Kirk for the punishment of unchastity – that is, they had to sit upon the sinners' seat, or 'cutty stool', before the assembled congregation throughout the service on three successive Sabbaths and at one point to rise and face the minister as penitents under a reprimand which might be as lengthy as was thought fit.

Robert (and indeed Lizzie) went through this public exhibition of the 'fault' with less penitence than bravado. Lizzie had lived with the Burns family as a servant during the last winter at Lochlie; Burns's mother liked Lizzie, had kept in touch, and would have been glad for Robert to marry her; there was no general astonishment at her becoming pregnant by him. The performance at the 'cutty stool' had the merit for Burns of putting him level with two admired Mauchline cronies who had each been treated to that Kirk penance – one of those cronies was the John Richmond, law-clerk in Gavin Hamilton's office, with whom Burns would later share lodgings in Edinburgh. The birth in May of black-eyed 'dear-bought Bess' (named after Lizzie) gave Burns enormous paternal pleasure; he proudly wrote out several versions of 'A Poet's Welcome to his Bastart Wean' and one copy was sent off boastfully to Richard Brown of Irvine. Yet the harvest at Mossgiel in that year was worse than in the previous year, and the ploughman, having again for his comfort turned to an 'Almighty Love', was now frightened. Why, in the writing in November 1785 of 'To A Mouse', should the poem end with the quatrain:

But, och! I backward cast my e'e
On prospects drear!
An' forward, tho' I canna see,
I guess an' fear!

It is fairly clear that Burns foresaw standing up again in Mauchline Kirk to be cited – this time with Jean Armour – and now found nothing to laugh at.

A quick summary of Burns's often panicky activities in the short twelvemonth between writing the above four lines and his entry into Edinburgh almost inevitably renders a comic strip of a story into which, through recklessness, there certainly enters, for some of those involved, real human grief. When Burns and Jean Armour began having intercourse, she still under age and in parental custody, it was obvious to both that her father James Armour, dour purse-proud master mason and contractor of Mauchline, pillar of the Auld Licht in the Kirk, would if he knew be outraged; perhaps that added spice. The first hint of her pregnancy caused Burns a little more thought: he drew up a paper, purporting to be a declaration of intent of marriage, which he and Jean both signed, and which, when shown to her father, would supposedly make everything all right. In March 1786 Jean confessed that she was pregnant to her mother, who told Mr Armour. He fainted, and Mrs Armour had to 'run for a cordial'. Jean then produced the 'marriage paper'. Armour, instead of being placated, was all the more incensed – the 'contract' was repudiated with scorn and anger as a blatant attempt by Burns to save affairs at disgraced, debt-ridden Mossgiel by a forced alliance with the Armours. The Armours packed Jean off for a time to 'friends at Paisley', but the 'holy beagles' (as Burns called them) of the Kirk Session at Mauchline were bound to sniff out the reason. No more than a year after the Lizzie Paton scandal Robert and Jean would face three public rebukes in the kirk: the Armours would see that they did, though even after that the match would be repudiated.

When Burns, in April, learned from Jean the extent of the Armours' scorn for him, he assuaged his injured feelings in the way that Mrs Carswell interpreted, I think, correctly: 'In a strange letter written that month, he describes himself as lunatic with rage. He has "lost a wife". Well, he will revenge himself upon her and the world in general by getting forthwith "another wife".' Mary Campbell, then in service at Montgomerie Castle near Tarbolton, was the girl promptly and not unwillingly promoted into becoming the other wife. The trysting day with Mary was by appointment 'the second Sunday of May, in a sequestered spot by the banks of the Ayr'; and on that day the future was totally agreed: Robert and Mary, as husband and wife, would escape for ever from Ayrshire by sailing off that autumn from Greenock for Jamaica.

Burns had already obtained the offer of a post as overseer on a Jamaican plantation; he had already arranged with the printer in Kilmarnock for the printing of his book of poems – subscription blanks had been ready since mid-April – and as soon as the book was ready and the moneys paid in (six hundred copies at three shillings apiece) there would be funds in hand for their honeymoon voyage to the Indies to be made in style. There is little doubt that Robert pictured all this so vividly that he believed it. Mary's parents lived in Greenock; her part in the compact was to give notice to her Ayrshire employers, take what wages were due, and return home to wait for Robert to arrive at Greenock in honour of his vows.

Without disclosing Mary's part in the plan, Robert told his family and friends, all busily collecting subscriptions for the book of poems, about his thoughts of Jamaica. Gavin Hamilton, to whom the book was dedicated and who was busily obtaining subscriptions for it from Ayrshire's nobility and gentry, utterly refused to comprehend why Burns, on the eve of a literary success which would lead him straight to Edinburgh, should prate about the West Indies. Not only Hamilton but every other companion reasoned with Burns that Jamaica was a daft idea. By 31 July, date of publication for the book at Kilmarnock, it was indeed hard to deny the daftness of wrecking his career as poet by self-banishment: of the Kilmarnock edition 612 copies had been printed, all but thirteen had been sold before publication, and those thirteen and any 'returns' would clearly be snapped up. Coincidental with this success Jean Armour, who was now near her time, had returned to Mauchline, to stand up publicly in the kirk with Burns for the compulsory rebuke – and the betting was that she looked forward to it. The dates for those performances in the kirk were 23 and 30 July and 6 August. Since the disclosure of pregnancy to her father, Jean had become eighteen; she was now of age, out of her father's custody; if the Kirk permitted, she could do as she wanted. True, that during her father's first tempest of anger she had been forced, at that moment, to renounce Robert's proposal; but now as adult she could renounce that renouncement – and why not? What earthly reason was there for Burns not to give up his wild talk of the Indies and stay and marry her?

But Burns had packed his trunk and it was corded and on its way to Greenock even before the appearance in Mauchline Kirk, and the situation was wholly reversed from what Jean imagined or from what he could confess. The tryst that he had made – to the Indies with Mary – might seem now, even to himself, a suicide pact. It held perhaps precisely that validity. The imperative for Burns to obtain from the Mauchline performances was the certificate that he was a single man. With that, he could follow his trunk to Greenock. I am not prepared to debate whether

Burns as yet knew that Mary, in Greenock, was likewise pregnant.

The tragic story grew more complex by a new round in the fight between Burns and Jean's father. Success of the Kilmarnock publication had caused Burns to make a will by which provision was made, through Gilbert as trustee, for the little 'bastart' Bess, the child of Lizzie Paton. Jean's father, getting wind of this and alarmed at mentions of Burns's proposed journey, applied for a writ to slap Burns in gaol until he had provided for maintenance of Jean's expected baby. Mr Armour used his pencil; he figured Burns's book must be bringing him in as much as £50; he was as set as ever against the marriage, but maintenance for the infant he would have.

The three Sabbath penances were over. Burns was a single man. Armour's writ was not served, but that was not what stopped Burns from hastening to Greenock. Throughout August, though continuing to talk about sailing dates for Jamaica, he remained close to Mossgiel. The assumption is that as Jean's time for childbirth was close, Burns was waiting in genuine anxious concern for word that all was well. That word came on 3 September: Jean safely delivered of twins. With unbounded elation Burns wrote to Richmond in Edinburgh that same night: 'Armour has just brought me a fine boy and girl at one throw. God bless the little dears!' This part of the story can be wound up by saying it was presently arranged that the boy-twin, Robert, was to be brought up by the patient brother Gilbert at Mossgiel, and the girl-twin, Jean, by the Armours.

The story of Mary Campbell, waiting at Greenock for the Burns she never saw again, is less easy to tell. Her pregnancy was probable, and probably Burns knew of it, or suspected. Jean was due first, yet after 3 September and into October there is just no evidence bearing on contacts with, or any motions towards, Greenock. Had Burns's trunk actually gone to Greenock? Nobody knows. A noticeable gap in Burns's correspondence has been pointed out between 8 October and 13 November 1786, and there are perhaps some other indications that it was at that time that Burns had word of Mary's death. It does not seem that he had any word beforehand about the sudden fatal illness. From later information it is learned that Mary died of a 'malignant fever', perhaps typhus, contracted at Greenock. Mrs Carswell commented: 'if the girl was some months gone with child, she would be practically certain', according to medical opinion regarding any case of high fever, 'to give birth to a premature infant'. Mrs Carswell felt that in the contents of the letter from Greenock about Mary Campbell, when Burns did receive it, 'there was that in her death which made her parents blame him and he yet more himself'.

After this noticeable gap in Burns's correspondence there is in mid-

November a letter mentioning that he is off to Edinburgh in a week or two 'to throw off a second impression of my book' – which returns me to the moment in Edinburgh at which I brought Burns in.

4. DUMFRIES AND THE GALLOWAY REGION

When the ploughman-poet had ceased to be a new toy, Edinburgh society dropped its exaggerated fervour about him. Among his continuing friends were Lord Glencairn and the eccentric banker, Patrick Miller; among women, one was Margaret Chalmers.

Patrick Miller made his presence known within two weeks of Burns's arrival in Edinburgh. Surmising that the ploughman-poet might need some actual cash, Miller, anonymously and through the hand of the editor of the *Edinburgh Magazine*, made him a gift of ten guineas. When Burns discovered the identity of his unknown friend and was invited to Miller's house for a glass of claret, the banker told him of his estate in the valley of the Nith near Dumfries, and remarked that if Burns should ever think of farming in that neighbourhood, he should let him know. Burns filed that thought; at the moment he was probably over-estimating the earnings of his pen. He was certainly anticipating that payments for the *Poems* would come more quickly than they did. Glencairn saw to it that the florid dedication of the first Edinburgh edition to the Caledonian Hunt was accepted by the Hunt, and the Hunt minuted that £25 should be paid to the author on publication. Burns had misinterpreted: the payment was not quite the hundred guineas, nor coming quite so quickly, as first hoped. Payments on publication were the harder to wait for because Creech kept on delaying the publication date.

Burns was learning that William Creech, that 'upright, pert, tart, tripping wight', was a man of two characters, one sociable and rushing him 'into all public matters', the other uncommonly unable to pay out any money. Before Burns had payment Creech went off to London for a spell of business. The poem 'To William Creech' which Burns sent after him to London, supposedly recording 'Edinburgh's distress' at the temporary loss 'of her darling bird that she lo'es best – Willie's awa'!', was not exactly the graceful compliment that, on the face of it, it looks. However, the book at last was out, the Caledonian Hunt made their payment, and Burns and Bob Ainslie could for the moment laugh at Creech and set off themselves, in May, for a tour of the Borders.

When Ainslie had returned to Edinburgh Burns continued his

travels, in the summer of 1787, the fame of his book preceding him. He was highly pleased that at Dumfries, on his arrival on 4 June, he was received as an honorary burgess. That created in Burns a special feeling for Dumfries. It was probably there that a less pleasing letter caught up with him from May Cameron, a servant girl from Edinburgh, protesting that he had left her in trouble. Burns wrote instantly to Ainslie (who was in fact in similar 'paternal predicament'). Burns made no denial; he asked Ainslie to see her: 'Call immediately, or at least as soon as it is dark, for God's sake, lest the poor soul be starving. Ask her for a letter I wrote her just now, by way of token – it is unsigned.' I have no intention of pursuing many of Burns's 'mischiefs' – the curious will find pointers in *The Burns Encyclopedia* by Maurice Lindsay. One episode which does claim mention here was his return in that summer to Mauchline. There Burns felt that because of his new prosperity his former enemy, James Armour, was changing his tune. Burns was disgusted at such 'new servility' and, as if to teach the Armour family a further lesson, he invited Jean to walk with him and renewed lovmaking with no profession whatever that it would lead to marriage. Jean herself could never succeed in putting conditions on his wooing.

Back in Edinburgh, Burns drew money from some source, for with a schoolmaster friend, Will Nicol, he rolled out of Edinburgh in high style, in a hired chaise, to visit the northern Highlands. On his return he renewed his siege of Creech. He also pursued the application, which had been in his mind for some time, for a position in the Excise and was actively assisted in this by Lord Glencairn.

A further thought, much in Burns's mind towards the end of 1787, was of making a good marriage. 'Of all the young women he had met in Edinburgh's drawing-rooms', says Mrs Carswell, the one 'best calculated to fill the part of Mrs Robert Burns' would have been Margaret Chalmers. Peggy Chalmers was 'a farmer's daughter of the higher sort, cousin to Gavin Hamilton, attractive, sympathetic, and well-educated'. Burns had possibly met Peggy through the Hamiltons at Mauchline – her father had a nearby farm – and it seems to be agreed that she was the 'dear Countrywoman' whom he had met again in Edinburgh, and who knew about his 'black story at home'. On Burns's Highland tour he spent eight happy days at Harvieston, Peggy Chalmers being there. He proposed marriage. She was sensible and refused him, yet not so unkindly as to destroy his admiration: she remained his trusted confidante. When both were back in Edinburgh in November, Burns confessed to her the new mess he had made of things at Mauchline. He had received news that not only was Jean Armour in five months going to make him yet again a father, but that this time Jean's parents in their anger had expelled her from home. Burns was arranging temporary refuge for Jean with friends of his near Tarbolton. Peggy reiterated previous advice of hers, that Burns ought to marry Jean and take up Mr Miller's offer of a farm at Ellisland near Dumfries.

Burns appeared to accept Peggy's advice. Then, at a tea-party on 4 December, he met Mrs M'Lehose. Agnes M'Lehose, Nancy to her friends, was a plump grass-widow. She had a husband in Jamaica, but herself lived with three small children in a southern suburb of Edinburgh. Very soon after the first meeting Burns wrote to his old friend Richard Brown of Irvine that 'Almighty Love still "reigns and revels" in my bosom'. He wished Brown to know he was 'ready to hang' himself for Nancy, who in the flirtation archly named herself Burns's 'Clarinda'. Until the middle of February both had fun with 'Almighty Love', but then the behaviour attracted attention. Clarinda was terrified by a 'haughty dictatorial letter' from the guardian of her income. Burns was likewise given danger signals. He now had in his pocket the long-awaited nomination to the Excise service, for which he could thank Glencairn. Glencairn seems to have made it clear that any serious scandal would upset the hoped-for appointment. It finally came over Burns that attention to his responsibilities at Mauchline was overdue. Off he then went from Edinburgh to visit the now very pregnant Jean.

On this trip home Burns's behaviour was like that of a spoiled boy whose fun was being interrupted. To Jean and the Armours he was businesslike and curt. Jean had been unhappy in the refuge at Tarbolton; Burns arranged for her to have bed and board in a room of her own in the Backcauseway. He then managed to have a commonsense interview with the Armour parents and persuaded Mrs Armour to play a mother's part. That being that, with a perfunctory parting embrace for Jean, he was away to his own house at Mossgiel, and thence to Edinburgh to be on hand there for his interview with the Excise authorities. His mood at the moment was that he had done enough for Jean: 'I have done with her, and she with me.'

Within six weeks, events changed Burns's actions. First, he heard that Jean at Mauchline had again presented him with twins, and twins, to Burns, were a special gesture. Then at his interview the authorities suggested that work as an Excise officer at Dumfries would readily combine with farming at Ellisland. Further, the adviser he had sent to inspect the farmland at Ellisland reported favourably. On top of this, with Glencairn and Peggy both pressing that he should regularize matters with Jean, the news from Mauchline came that Jean's twins had died, one after the other, within weeks of birth. It is conceivable that to Burns's emotional nature this loss called on him to make amends. At any rate, after working himself into a pother of being 'positively crazed' and 'fevered' and 'under a load of Care almost too heavy for his shoulders', Burns's mood was now, with heroic self-sacrifice, to accept the post of Exciseman and the tenancy of the farm at Ellisland, and to make the amendment of marriage with Jean. In April, at Gavin Hamilton's house, Burns and Jean signed the legal document that they were married; their joint appearance at the kirk the following Sunday completed the ceremony; then Burns went off promptly to Ellisland to see to the building of the house to be lived in there.

All this detail has been leading up to the period, at Ellisland, of some of Burns's very best writing. It was to be more than a year before the house at Ellisland was habitable. For that time Jean was to remain at Mossgiel, learning about dairy-work. Burns, while being taught his work for the Dumfries Port Division of the Excise and studying how to combine that work with farming, lived alone, or 'dossed', in a damp 'rickety hovel' half a mile above Ellisland on the River Nith. He had at least one bad attack of influenza in the first autumn, and that and the continuing poor living conditions were bad for his now chronic endo-carditis. Nevertheless, away from the 'Dissipation and business' of Edinburgh his spirit turned a new leaf. Clarinda, out of sight, seemed almost out of mind. He had never faced up to telling Clarinda about his departure and marriage; he had asked Bob Ainslie to call upon her and put things right. That made Clarinda 'very angry' and so – for some years – correspondence with her ceased. Contrariwise, Burns's letters to Jean, light-hearted, practical and affectionate, show him in this period at his very best, and the special songs that he spontaneously wrote for her ('Of a' the airts the wind can blaw' and 'I hae a wife o' my ain') must have given her special pleasure.

The double strain of attempting to farm Ellisland by himself and covering for the Excise his round of two hundred miles each week on horseback, with exact accountings, had a worse effect on Burns's physique, at the age of thirty, than he or others recognized. Yet while dossing in his rickety hovel Burns managed to send 'song cargoes' to his Edinburgh friend and partner, James Johnson, for the *Scots Musical Museum*. From this time on Burns became, as Maurice Lindsay emphas-izes, 'virtually the real editor of the *Museum*, contributing about 160 songs of his own, and mending and patching many others'. Burns's wonderful lyric gift, spontaneous but also most industriously cultivated, was actually now to burgeon in the few remaining years of his life. The period at Ellisland, ruinous for Burns's health, produced his 'Tam o' Shanter' and 'Willie brewed a peck o' maut'.

Having followed Burns to the time of his fullest poetical writings, I shall consider the routes through the Lowland country which produced not only Burns but other writers also.

*   *   *

Tibbie Shiel's Inn at an end of St Mary's Loch has often been a place to halt between the eastern Borders and the south-west. There I think of Carlyle, trudging on foot over the high moors, to and fro between Ecclefechan and Edinburgh. I might also have been thinking (to skip a century) of John Buchan and *The Thirty-nine Steps*. Over the moors to the west of St Mary's Loch is Talla Reservoir – the road between is spoken of as about the wildest and loneliest in southern Scotland – and thereby is the hamlet of Tweedsmuir. When John Buchan was raised to the peerage the title he chose was Baron Tweedsmuir. Although in *The Thirty-nine Steps* the moorland adventures of Richard Hannay began far west in Galloway, they led him eastward across country to Buchan's favourite 'upper waters of the River Tweed', and after Richard's first escape from the ferociously sinister enemy who 'could hood his eyes like a hawk', it was from near Tweedsmuir and Tweedshaws that in shining blue June weather the hero's return journey began. It is exciting indeed to follow Buchan's hero as he goes with the cattle drover over the pass and down the sunny vale of Annan, through 'a constantly changing prospect of brown hills and far green meadows, and a continual sound of larks and curlews and falling streams', to take the night express train to the south from its halting-place near Moffat, and so to complete that volunteer's best service to his country before he 'put on khaki'.

But it is for Burns again that I now go directly from Edinburgh to Kilmarnock, just south of Glasgow. The red sandstone Kay Park Monument at Kilmarnock houses a Burns museum and one of its chief items is a copy of the first (Kilmarnock) edition of the poems. I am now in the region where, in all directions, are Burns reminders. At Irvine on the coast there is a tablet at the site in Glasgow Vennel where the flax-heckling workshop went up in flames at Hogmanay; at Mauchline (on the road south from Kilmarnock) the present church is on the site of the older kirk which played so much part in Burns's story. Four of Robert and Jean's children are buried in this Mauchline churchyard – Burns and Jean and later children were buried at Dumfries. Between Mauchline and Ayr, on the northern side of the valley of the River Ayr, are Mossgiel and Tarbolton where the meeting-place of the Bachelors' Club, which remained active for some years after Burns had left the district, is now kept as a museum.

A different set of literary associations, however, are found by pursuing the main road from Kilmarnock past Mauchline to the south side of the Ayr valley where one comes soon to Auchinleck. Here was the country seat of James Boswell's father, and it was early in November 1773 that Boswell and Dr Johnson came in a post-chaise from Kilmarnock to Auchinleck to fulfil Boswell's wish that Johnson and his father should meet. The visit was to last a week, and for the first four days all was harmonious; but on the fifth day Boswell, unable to keep his elders any longer off the danger subjects of Whiggism and Presbyterianism, had a collision to report which gave him good material for the last pages of his *Tour to the Hebrides*. Nineteen years younger than Boswell, Burns never met his fellow-countryman. He hoped for a meeting in 1788, and copied a ballad and one or two 'fugitive Pieces' for an intermediary to pass on to the Laird of Auchinleck, as Boswell was by that time, but there is no record of Boswell receiving Burns's missive. Boswell was then forsaking Ayrshire permanently for London, to get on with completing his *Life of Samuel Johnson*.

Between Auchinleck and Ayr is Ochiltree. Here there is recollection of a powerful novel of the beginning of the twentieth century, *The House with the Green Shutters*. The author, George Douglas Brown, was born on his father's farm at Ochiltree in 1869. By the time he grew up he was disgusted with Scottish novelists of the 'Kailyard School' who prettified rural life, so under the pen-name of 'George Douglas' he provided in 1901 the still memorable novel based on life that he had seen. His promise as a novelist was cut short by his death, soon after his first book, at the age of thirty-three.

Moving now to Ayr, and two miles south of Ayr to Alloway, one is at the heart of the area where mementos of Burns are once again transcendent. Burns's birthplace, the now well-kept cottage at Alloway, has been much rebuilt since the night ten days after his birth when a gale from the Atlantic blew in the bedroom end, and Agnes Burns and her baby Robert had to find refuge with neighbours. Alloway's Auld Kirk was a ruin even before Burns's time. In Burns's years at Ellisland and Dumfries he often thought back to earlier memories and of those with whom he had 'paidl'd i' the burn' in auld lang syne, and perhaps memory of Alloway's ruined kirk produced, at Ellisland, the tale of 'Tam o' Shanter'. The starting-point of Tam's ride was, of course, in Ayr, a town ever unsurpassed 'for honest men and bonnie lasses': Ayr's High Street has the Tam o' Shanter Inn, another of the many Burns museums. From Ayr it was through Alloway that Tam was riding when through the window of the ruined kirk he witnessed the dance of the warlocks and witches with such excitement as to roar out 'Weel done, Cutty-sark!' Tam's instant flight then over the Brig o' Doon (the single arch below the Grecian-style Burns Monument) just barely saved him by the good fortune that witches cannot follow beyond the middle of the next running stream.

In the Burns Monument at Alloway is the little two-volume Bible that Burns gave Mary Campbell. On the flyleaf of each volume Burns wrote a quotation – in the Old Testament volume, Leviticus xix, 12, and in the volume with the New Testament, Matthew v, 33 – about not swearing falsely and true performance of oaths. The Bible that Mary gave to Burns at their appointed secret troth on the second Sunday in May 1786 is not known now to exist; this Bible that Burns gave to Mary was preserved by her mother. When Burns at Ellisland was reviewing memories he expressed his lasting remorse for Mary in the poem he wrote in 1789, called by later editors 'To Mary in Heaven', though Burns left it untitled. Later Burns's memory was again with Mary when in 1792, given an older tune to which to set words, he wrote 'Highland Mary'. That Bible deserves its place within the Burns Monument.

*   *   *

Tam o' Shanter and his mare in their escape from Alloway had been scared enough, after getting across the Brig o' Doon, not to pull up till they had gone on the ten miles or so southward to Kirkoswald. My purpose is now to go farther and follow the coastal road on past Kirkoswald and circle the south-western corner of Scotland to Dumfries. In the opposite direction Keats and his friend Charles Brown traversed the coast on foot, in the summer of 1818, from Dumfries to Alloway. Keats was intensely interested in Burns's lyric gift, and perhaps it was unfortunate that his walking tour was directed from Burns's deathplace to his birthplace: in 1818 it had been bruited about that Burns's life had been ended at Dumfries by drink and debauchery, and if that was Keats's belief it was easy for his impressions of Burns at Dumfries as 'poor unfortunate fellow' to colour Burns's life throughout.

The sight of Ailsa Craig, 'craggy ocean pyramid' as Keats called it, out at sea from Girvan, reminded me of the walking tour of Keats and Brown in these parts. In 1818 they were being almost unduly circuitous, after leaving Dumfries, for having gone west to Portpatrick they took ship there for Ireland. A single night in Ireland was enough for them; it was after returning to Portpatrick the next day that they walked north beside the Ayrshire coast. They did not always stick to the road; the entrance to Glen App was 'like an enchanted region', and from the hills at the head of that glen Keats had his first sight of Ailsa Craig:

. . . we had a gradual ascent and got among the tops of the Mountains whence in a little time I descried in the Sea Ailsa Rock 940 feet hight – it was 15 Miles distant and seemed close upon us – the effect of ailsa with the peculiar perspective of the Sea in connection with the ground we stood on, and the misty rain then falling gave me a complete Idea of a deluge. Ailsa struck me very suddenly – really I was a little alarmed.

Keats wrote his sonnet 'To Ailsa Rock' at Girvan and thence he and

Brown went on to Alloway, but I am moving the opposite way, through Wigtown and Kirkcudbright to Dumfries.

On the south coast of Wigtown there is association with the naturalist, artist and writer Gavin Maxwell (1914–70). Maxwell was born at the hamlet of Elrig, and his books *Ring of Bright Water* (1960) and *The House of Elrig* (1965) will long continue to make friends for this part of Luce Bay. Then eastward past Newton Stewart I can again pick up and follow the moorland adventures of Richard Hannay in *The Thirty-nine Steps*. In the moors of Kirkcudbright that Hannay crossed, between the Big Water of Fleet and the bigger waters of Dee, is Laurieston Forest – this is the country of which S. R. Crockett wrote, notably in *The Stickit Minister* (1893). Crockett was a native of Laurieston. Farther eastward, lower Nithsdale and Dumfries itself return me to the story of Burns in the last eight years of his life.

I mentioned that Keats appeared to accept a view of Burns's life at Dumfries that to scholars nowadays seems much too sombre. Keats and Brown were not in the best of moods when in their walking tour of 1818 they crossed the border from Carlisle to Dumfries. They were footsore when they reached Carlisle, and Carlisle was not merry 'to our thinking'. They agreed the country between Carlisle and Dumfries would be dull, and having decided to cover it by coach, were inclined to believe the dullness. Gretna Green was 'a sad ominous place for a young couple, poverty-struck and barren'; Dumfries 'did not wear the air of comfort', and all that Keats got out from the sight of the Burns Mausoleum was 'the feel of not to feel it'. A cloud of numbness settled on Keats in Dumfries, and that may have induced an assumption that the town had a likewise deadening effect on Burns. 'Poor unfortunate fellow', Keats reflected. 'How sad it is when a luxurious imagination is obliged in self defence to deaden its delicacy in vulgarity. . . .' Keats (to Reynolds) soon enlarged on Burns's 'Misery' – 'he talked with Bitches – he drank with blackguards, he was miserable – We can see horribly clear in the works of such a Man his whole Life, as if we were God's spies'. Keats felt it all so vividly that it was 'a dead weight upon the nimbleness' of his own quill.

By the beginning of the twentieth century, George Saintsbury, among other historians, was pointing out that too much 'Misery' had been imputed to Burns's last years in Dumfries, for though he died at the unduly early age of thirty-seven, his poetical powers were 'to the very last' in fullest perfection. Then in the 1930s the brilliant portraiture of Catherine Carswell and the meticulous scholarship of Franklin Bliss Snyder gave to the general reader a fairer picture of Burns than had been available before. Certainly in the first bad winter of 1788–9 at Ellisland before the house was built and Jean had come to look after

him, it is possible to suspect recurrences of 'rheumatic fever', the
reputed cause of Burns's death in 1796. Yet at Ellisland, both before
and after Jean joined Burns there and they tried to make a go of dairy
farming, life was not all hardship. Burns himself was circulating in a
wide range of local society. He was still on good terms with his banker-
friend and landlord, Patrick Miller of Dalswinton – Burns was almost
certainly one of the distinguished people invited to be passengers in
William Symington's pioneer steamboat, financed by Miller and tried
out on Dalswinton Loch in 1788. In 1788 Burns was entering into warm
friendship with Captain Robert Riddell of Friars' Carse; Riddell and
Burns combined in forming the communal library scheme called the
Monkland Friendly Society, whose main purpose was 'to store the minds
of the lower classes with useful knowledge'.

The landed gentry with whom Burns went to dinner were accustomed
to hard drinking, and as Burns got drunk easily and was then all the
more amusing, he had numerous times of excess. Nevertheless any
notion of perpetual excess is countered not only by the quantity and
quality of his song-writing but by the regularity of his work for the
Excise and his promotion in that service. When towards the end of 1791
he gave up the losing battle of farming at Ellisland and moved into
Dumfries, the promotion increased his responsibilities and doubled his
Excise earnings. Once later, Burns's position in the Excise was seriously
threatened, but that was for his political expressions: in 1792 he was
among those most enthusiastic for the French Revolution and vaguely
for the 'rights' of Common Man in general; in arguments he would
quote that other renegade Exciseman, Tom Paine, and, at war with
France, was not above proposing disloyal toasts. Such romantic 'radical'
behaviour lost Burns a number of his old friends, and brought on him,
at the end of 1792, an official inquiry into his conduct.

This official inquiry came upon Burns 'like a thunderclap', said Mrs
Carswell. He got 'into panic' and felt himself forced to make 'grovelling
apologies'. These were in fact accepted; Burns 'was let off with a severe
reprimand'; yet it was an episode very unnerving to the normal routine
of his life. The Burns family were at that time still quartered in their
first home in Dumfries, a second-floor flat in Wee Vennel, now Bank
Street, and Burns described his routine as 'Hurry of business, grinding
the faces of the publican and sinner on the merciless wheels of the
Excise, making ballads, and then drinking and singing them; and,
above all, correcting the press of two different publications'. The two
publications were Johnson's *Scots Musical Museum* and Thomson's
Select Scottish Airs. The regularity of Burns's 'making ballads' is
proved by the number he produced, 160 songs for Johnson and
about 114 for Thomson, after the Thomson connection began in 1792.

Still other songs Burns touched up, polished or rewrote under other titles for both collections.

Before Burns's Dumfries routine had started, he had been to Edinburgh to see and to say farewell to Mrs M'Lehose. In November 1791 he heard from Ainslie that she was soon to sail for Jamaica, possibly there to be reconciled to her husband. Since Burns's 'perfidious treachery' three years earlier, he and Clarinda had only exchanged icy letters at long intervals; there had been no meeting. Both felt, though, this final parting called for a last farewell. In Edinburgh on 6 December the lovers met, not now 'Sylvander' and 'Clarinda' but Robert and Nancy. 'Ae Fond Kiss', which Burns sent from Dumfries to 'my Nancy' on 27 December is a poem as genuine as the nine songs which Sylvander wrote to Clarinda are artificial, and neither of them forgot the other. Exactly forty years later, when Nancy was seventy-two, she wrote in her journal under the date 6 December 1831: 'This day I can never forget. Parted with Burns, in the year 1791, never more to meet in this world. Oh, may we meet in Heaven!' Burns had less than five years to live after the parting, but his continuing thought of Nancy is recorded by the story which Mrs Carswell found to be 'credibly handed down in Dumfries':

When Burns lay dead, the tale goes, Jean was distressed to find him wearing under his shirt a wax profile of Mrs M'Lehose which he had long since discarded. In her vexation she first snapped the wax across, then, regretting her action, put the pieces away in a little box. Certainly the wax profile which Mrs M'Lehose gave Burns, and which is now in the Cottage Museum, has at one time been snapped across.

The year 1793 'began, continued, and ended in misfortune' for Burns.

Its early days [wrote Mrs Carswell] saw his humiliation before the Excise Board, and in April he had an attack of rheumatic fever that sensibly aged him. This illness, combined with the necessity he was now under of keeping a strict guard upon his Jacobin tongue in public, frayed his nerves and made him increasingly miserable.

There were good moments: in September he adds 'one song more' to a letter to Thomson, a third revised version of 'Auld Lang Syne'. Earlier in that year he had told Thomson how essential song-writing was to him – 'You cannot imagine how much this business of composing for your publication has added to my enjoyments.' Incidentally, never since his early dealings with Creech had Burns accepted money for his poems; a pathetic financial panic at the very end of his life forced him to ask for small loans from his publishers, but until then his songs were all for love. After his illness in the spring of 1793 the Burns family had moved

L.B.—P

into the self-contained house in Mill Street, now Burns Street. This
house (now preserved as a Burns museum) 'was of a good order, such
as were occupied at that time by the better class of burgesses'. But at
the very end of 1793, or at the start of 1794, at the Hogmanay party
staged by Captain Riddell of Friars' Carse, Burns behaved when drunk
in a way (not precisely recorded) which caused him much subsequent
shame and remorseful apologies. Estrangement with the one member
of the Riddell family that Burns most cared for (Maria Riddell) was in
time overcome; yet he consoled his anger over the Hogmanay mis-
behaviour in ways not happy either for his homelife or his health.

Nevertheless, song-writing went on. 'Scots Wha Hae', the 'kind of
Scots Ode' which he had composed in 1793, was one of the ballads he
sang with even more enthusiasm when a French invasion of Britain was
heralded in 1794. Burns was one of the first then to enrol in the Dumfries Volunteer Corps. Before that year's end he was also temporarily
made acting supervisor in the Excise. Yet the rheumatic fevers and
endocarditis were by now acute. During 1795 his health went from bad
to worse: by the spring of 1796 Burns looked 'gaunt, of sickly aspect'.
As late as February 1796 he was promising Thomson verses 'for twenty-
five Irish airs', but from then on the story is mostly of 'the reper-
cussions of PAIN! Rheumatism, Cold, and Fever . . .' He was placed on
sick-leave, and was sent off in June for 'cure' at the nearby little spa of
Brow Well. There, in loneliness and worry, he tormented himself with
unnecessary financial panic. He was lonely at Brow Well, Jean being
then, as so often, in an advanced state of pregnancy. Towards the end
of July he managed to get himself driven from Brow Well home to
Dumfries, where three days later he died.

Burns was given a military funeral at Dumfries: his body was carried
to St Michael's churchyard to Handel's 'Dead March', and the Volunteers fired a volley in salute at the grave. 'At the same time as his body
was lowered into the grave', Mrs Carswell adds, 'Jean gave birth to yet
another boy.'

Two favourite taverns of Burns in Dumfries were the Globe Inn in
High Street and the Hole in the Wa' in Queensferry Square. 'Anna of
the gowden locks' (Anna Park) was barmaid at the Globe, though after
having a daughter by Burns she disappears from history. It seems to
have been naturally accepted by Jean that Anna's baby (born in 1791)
should be brought up in the Burns household along with her own
children. A boy of Jean's own was born only a few days later and, Mrs
Carswell remarks, Jean was used to nursing twins. But I linger no more
over Burns associations with Dumfries than to add that in 1803, when
Wordsworth and Dorothy visited the corner of the churchyard in which
Burns's grave was grass-grown (and so recorded in the first of three

poems that were suggested to Wordsworth), the Mausoleum (so little to Keats's taste) had not yet been erected. The classic structure was put up in 1815 to house the remains of Burns and Jean and five of their children.

Ecclefechan is, as the crow flies, a dozen miles east of Dumfries, and there the long life of Thomas Carlyle, which did not end until 1881, began in the year before Burns's death. In *Sartor Resartus* Ecclefechan appears as 'Entephfuhl' and the Arched House there is now a Carlyle museum, but *Sartor Resartus* was actually written at the moorland farm at Craigenputtock, also a dozen miles from Dumfries but northwest. The farm at Craigenputtock had been inherited by the brainy and self-willed Jane Welsh who, when she married the penniless dyspeptic Carlyle in Edinburgh, was gossiped about for throwing herself away on a husband whom only she fancied to be a genius. The two lived at the farm from 1828 till 1834, with just sufficient support from her income for Carlyle to spend his time reading German and with Jane reading Tasso and Cervantes. The work of the farm was done by others, though on occasion Jane would milk the cows and bake loaves of bread – sometimes a point was made of her doing so, to impress such a visitor as Ralph Waldo Emerson. In the six years at Craigenputtock both Carlyles read, and wrote, and consulted – it is a moment happy to remember when Jane, finishing the last page of the manuscript of *Sartor*, exclaimed, chary of praise though she always was, 'It is a work of genius, dear.' London had yet to be convinced; London as yet showed not much sign of obeisance; London then should be assaulted, invaded, conquered from within. Froude gave a biased view of the Carlyles, intimating that Carlyle 'dragged' Jane Welsh to an unhappy life in London, but her letters show her own moving spirit for the shift from Craigenputtock to Chelsea. 'Burn our ships' was her gay remark signalling the departure; '*i.e.* dismantle our house; carry all our furniture with us.'

5. GLASGOW

The road north from Dumfries up Nithsdale would take me not only past the Burns farm at Ellisland but also, farther on, past Maxwelton House, near Thornhill, which was the birthplace and home of Annie Laurie. Annie Laurie's boudoir and a Folk Museum are there to be seen. To the west of the Nith valley are two reminders of Scott's novels: in the churchyard at Irongray Scott caused a stone to be erected in honour of Helen Walker, the woman from whom he drew the character of Jeanie Deans in *The Heart of Midlothian*, and north of Irongray is the ruin of the tower of Lag, all that remains of the mansion of the man whom Scott made into the fictional Sir Robert Redgauntlet. But the whole of this countryside north of the Solway Firth is happy hunting ground for features used by Scott – south of Dumfries on the coast of the firth is the ruin of the red sandstone Caerlaverock Castle, the 'Ellangowan' of *Guy Mannering*; and in the churchyard of Caerlaverock is the grave of Robert Paterson, the stonecutter widely known as 'Old Mortality' who travelled hither and yon to repair the graves of Covenanters, and whose nickname Scott used as title. But a thorough study of Scott's topography has pleasurably occupied whole lifetimes. I escape from that, and from Dumfries, not by the road up Nithsdale towards Kilmarnock but by the road past Moffat and Uddington, because that is the road whereon the place-name Lesmahagow is a sudden reminder that Tobias Smollett passed here on this most direct route between Glasgow and London.

How adequately to record the literary associations of Glasgow, Scotland's largest city? It is easy to observe the literary memories that Glasgow, of its own choice, offers. George Square, designed in 1781 to become the heart of future Glasgow, was named for George III, and a column eighty feet high was put up in the centre, intended, so the story goes, to bear a statue of that monarch. One of Glasgow's secrets is how that plan was thwarted, and a Scottish hero chosen instead to stand on high in the place of honour in George Square. Who, then, was Glasgow's choice for the effigy to top the column? Who but Walter Scott, wearing the plaid (and wearing it, as his custom was, on the wrong shoulder)? Part of the scene of Scott's *Rob Roy* was in Glasgow, and perhaps it was pawky wit that contrived that Scott's statue should enact, in charade, the title of his novel. The other literary figure to whom Glasgow gave a statue in George Square is, also predictably, Burns. In a sense Glasgow is more closely a spiritual home for Burns than Edinburgh; two of his best biographers – Catherine Carswell and Maurice Lindsay – were Glasgow-born. The monuments in both Edinburgh and Glasgow demonstrate that Burns and Scott exert a supremacy as national figures which no other Scottish writers have yet approached.

*   *   *

One writer whose upbringing was closely associated with Glasgow was Tobias Smollett (1721–71). Smollett was born at the grange of Dalquharn, near Renton, between Dumbarton Rock and Loch Lomond. The Smollett family was well established in that part of the Vale of Leven, yet as a younger son of a younger son, Tobias, after early schooling at Dumbarton, was pushed out to make his own way in the world. In his first novel, *Roderick Random*, he may be drawing on childhood memories of a domineering grandfather's harshness to younger grandchildren; certainly the character of the young Scotsman in that novel, 'arrogant, unscrupulous, and not too amiable, but bold and ready enough', seems a sharply observed self portrait. Smollett's own adventures began when he was apprenticed at the age of fifteen to a Glasgow surgeon; the apprenticeship and study at the university were intended to fit him for a medical career; yet by the age of eighteen he preferred to become a dramatist, and with the draft of a dramatic tragedy in his pouch, broke his indentures and set off on foot from Glasgow to London to make his fortune. After a year of living rough his smattering of medical training obtained him a hammock as surgeon's mate aboard a man-of-war. That took Smollett to the West Indies, where after leaving the service he remained for some years, married, and then returned to his original ambition and to London, to seek fame by writing. Dr Smollett's surgery in Downing Street succeeded in enabling him, at the age of twenty-seven, to write his zestful and immediately popular *Roderick Random*. The most memorable of his subsequent novels, *Humphry Clinker*, came nearly a quarter of a century later. Having achieved literary fame, he revisited scenes of his childhood in Scotland; he had not forgotten in his wanderings the places and names of his youth. Lesmahagow on the road into Glasgow reminded me of Smollett: when at eighteen he was escaping from Glasgow his first day's march took him to Lesmahagow. At fifty his mind suggested the name – the Scots soldier of fortune in *Humphry Clinker* is, in the eighteenth-century spelling, Captain Lismahagow.

Boswell, of the generation after Smollett's, was first a student at Edinburgh University and then attended Adam Smith's lectures at Glasgow. Thomas Campbell, of the generation subsequent to Boswell's, switched the other way: born in Glasgow in 1777, after school and university there he went to study law at Edinburgh – though his real intention was poetry. Success came to him too easily with a long poem, *The Pleasures of Hope*, published when he was twenty-one. What was new in that year was the *Lyrical Ballads*, and being strangely new their sale was slow, while Campbell's *The Pleasures of Hope*, safely within the old fashion, passed through four editions within the year of its publication. Discussing Campbell with Washington Irving later, Scott pointed out that the brightness of Campbell's early success had been a detriment to his further efforts: 'He is afraid of the shadow that his own fame casts before him.' The songs for which Campbell is mostly remembered ('Ye Mariners of England' and 'Hohenlinden' among them) date from the period of the Napoleonic wars.

Scott was more respectful to Joanna Baillie (1762–1851). She was born at Bothwell Manse, south-east of Glasgow, on the road to London; at the age of twenty-two it was to London that she migrated, where as a dramatist she had much more success than Smollett. In 1810, her reputation having been established in London, the Edinburgh Theatre gave her a first production 'in her native kingdom', and Scott took special delight in attending to all details of costume, in being present at all rehearsals, and in supplying the prologue. Joanna Baillie revisited Scotland from time to time, but made her permanent home in London, where she lived till her ninetieth year in Hampstead.

Three nineteenth-century writers to be recalled in Glasgow are Michael Scott, James Thomson and Francis Bret Harte. Michael Scott (1789–1835) was born at Cowlairs, went roving to the West Indies (memorials of him are to be seen now in Jamaica), and when he had returned to Glasgow in 1822, presently began to compose two highly individual travel narratives, *Tom Cringle's Log* and *The Cruise of the Midge*. Not long before his death in middle age these were published in *Blackwood's Magazine*, but he did not live to see them in book form. *Tom Cringle's Log*, in itself a considerable curiosity, rather curiously made its first appearance in book form in an anonymous printing in Paris, a year after Michael Scott's death. A year before Michael Scott died, James Thomson was born at Port Glasgow to a life destined to be just about as short as Michael Scott's but much less cheerful. Thomson's early verses were printed over the initials 'B.V.', standing for 'Bysshe Vanolis', the first name expressing his admiration for Shelley, and the second, cryptically, for the German poet Novalis. Thomson's long poem *The City of Dreadful Night*, printed in 1874, was perhaps his chief consolation and stay against an extremity of self-disgust; the sermon he communicated was

> O Brothers of sad lives! they are so brief;
> A few short years must bring us all relief:
>   Can we not bear these years of labouring breath?
> But if you would not this poor life fulfil,
> Lo, you are free to end it when you will,
>   Without the fear of waking after death.

In fairness to Glasgow it must be said that most of Thomson's melancholic maturity was lived in Victorian London. *The City of Dreadful Night* was contributed to the periodical promoted by the freethinker Charles Bradlaugh; the poem was published separately in 1880. By that time Francis Bret Harte (whose reputation had preceded him for such stories of Californian gold-rush days as *The Luck of Roaring Camp* and such poems as 'The Heathen Chinee') was American consul in Glasgow, which led, when he left the service, to his living in London. Bret Harte was thus following Thomson's footsteps, but to him both Glasgow and London were so far from dreadful that he remained in Britain for the rest of his life.

In the twentieth century there was an interesting period of affectionate intimacy between writers in Glasgow and counterparts in New York, to a large extent initiated by the friendship of the Glasgow shipmaster Captain David Bone (who in due course became Commodore of the Anchor Line) and Christopher Morley, who was at the beginning of that friendship one of New York's lively newspaper columnists. (Readers of my brother Christopher's novel *Where the Blue Begins*, published in 1922, recall that one of its characters was drawn from David Bone.) In the 1920s various writing-friends of my brother's, Vachel Lindsay, Hulbert Footner, Don Marquis, William McFee – the list of names could be expanded – established a habit, followed by others, of making Glasgow their port of arrival in Britain. Among British writers who in the 1920s made westbound sea-crossings from Glasgow to New York with David Bone were Joseph Conrad and Walter de la Mare.

Glasgow naturally drew writers from the nearby countryside, whether Lowland or Highland. Neil Munro, author of *John Splendid* and *The New Road*, was born in 1864 at Inverary in Argyll. (Hugh Hector Munro, who wrote under the pseudonym of 'Saki', is not to be confused with Neil. 'Saki', six years the younger, was born in Burma, but brought up in, and identified with, Devon.) Neil Munro wrote of the Highlands, yet from 1918 to 1927 was in Glasgow as editor of the *Glasgow Evening News*. Edwin Muir (1887–1959), poet and novelist, came from farther afield; he was born in Orkney but worked from 1901 to 1919 in Glasgow before marrying Willa Anderson and going to live in Prague for ten years, which led to the introducing and translating of the novels of Kafka. John Davidson (1857–1909) of Barrhead south of Glasgow, preferred, as poet, to try his luck in London, where he partnered Yeats in starting the Fleet Street Rhymers' Club. The contemporary poet, William Sharp of Paisley, remained in Glasgow and wrote in both his own name and as 'Fiona MacLeod'. George Blake, novelist of a later generation, was born in Greenock but lived mostly in Glasgow. The actual home-born and home-grown talents of Glasgow have been well represented in our time by Catherine Carswell and 'James Bridie' the playwright (who retained his professional medical practice under his own name, Dr Osborne Henry Mavor). Nor do I forget that the slightly earlier and massive literary work *The Golden Bough* owed its origin – at least its author did – to Glasgow. The twelve volumes of *The Golden Bough* appeared between 1890 and 1915, when the author, Sir James Frazer, was at Cambridge; but he had been born

and brought up in Glasgow, and was at Glasgow University before
Cambridge tempted him.

I now intend to leave the rectangle of Lowlands, and head from
Dumbarton Rock through Stirling and Perth to the east coast at Stonehaven and Aberdeen. Yet I am not to leave the Firth of Clyde without
a reminder that at Greenock the grave of Mary Campbell – Burns's
'Highland Mary' – is in the cemetery at the top of Nicolson Street, and
that a statue to her is at Dunoon, across the Clyde in Argyll, recording
her birthplace.

6. THE EASTERN HIGHLANDS

It is traditional for a 'literary' inspection of the Highlands to move into
the Eastern Highlands before assaying the west coast. By that circuit
Boswell conducted Johnson, and after leaving the Clyde at Dumbarton
I propose partly to follow their route. I have already mentioned Smollett
at Dumbarton; a far earlier association is that St Patrick is said to have
been born there before being captured and taken to Ireland by maraud-
ing raiders. Loch Lomond lies north of Dumbarton, and Smollett (in
Humphry Clinker), Scott (in *Rob Roy*) and Keats on his walking tour
may all be looked to for its praises. Yet I choose the road which bends
away from the loch – partly because this takes me through Drymen,
where Walter Scott lived at Ross Priory while writing *Rob Roy* and
where in this century 'James Bridie' lived at nearby Finnich Malise –
and partly because the Royal Burgh of Stirling, dominated by the castle
on its imposing rock, commanded for many centuries the central
gateway to the Highlands.

If now from Stirling I keep to the north of the Ochil Hills I come
directly to Perth, where apart from scenes from *The Fair Maid of Perth*
there are other memories of literary interest; one notable event was
John Ruskin's marriage to Effie Gray in 1848 at the house of Bowerswell,
across Perth Bridge on the Bowerswell Road. Ruskin had visited Perth
in boyhood, with his parents, and 'Effie' (Euphemia Chalmers Gray)
was the daughter of a lawyer of Perth, an old friend of the Ruskin
family. In 1875 John Buchan was born at Perth, the son of a minister of
the Free Church of Scotland. The mention of the Free Church may be
a reminder that the Reformation was effectively launched (many say) by
the famous sermon preached in Perth by John Knox in 1559. Perth is
also the birthplace of William Soutar, a poet of our time, who died in a
house in Wilson Street (marked by a tablet) in 1943. Perth's literary
memorials are, however, dominated by Scott, of whom there is a statue

beside Kings Place, and the house where the 'fair maid' (Catherine Glover) of Scott's novel lived in 1396 – or at least a house restored upon the same site – is open for inspection.

But if from Stirling I travel due eastward following the coastline of the Firth of Forth, on the way to St Andrews I would see the 'Dunfermline toun' of balladry:

> The king sits in Dunfermline toun,
>   Drinking the blude-red wine;
> 'O whare will I get a skeely skipper
>   To sail this ship o' mine?'

Sir Patrick Spens was the 'skeely skipper' of that ballad but there are other names to be recalled here: the fifteenth-century lyric poet Robert Henryson (or Henderson) is believed to have been a native of Dunfermline, and Andrew Carnegie (if not himself a 'man of letters', one who did much to help others to become so) was certainly born at Dunfermline in 1835, in a small cottage which is now a museum. Most fittingly, the first of nearly three thousand Carnegie libraries was started here in 1881. Kirkcaldy, east of Dunfermline on the Firth of Forth, is where Adam Smith, author of *The Wealth of Nations*, was born in 1723, and five years later Robert Adam, the architect who with his brothers built (among their other memorable achievements) the Adelphi in London, was likewise a native of Kirkcaldy. Both Adam Smith and Robert Adam went to the now-demolished Burgh School, where later (during 1816–19) Carlyle had an unhappy period of schoolmastering – 'it were better to perish than to continue' was Carlyle's parting remark. Farther up the coast of Fife is Largo, where the statue of Alexander Selkirk near the harbour of Lower Largo is a reminder of the shoemaker's son who went to sea, was marooned on the Pacific island, and after five years of solitude was rescued by Woodes Rogers, for his experience to be transformed by Defoe into *Robinson Crusoe*.

We are then on the road by which Boswell and Johnson reached St Andrews in the summer of 1773, and I pause to recall that Andrew Lang (1844–1912), born at Selkirk and living for his middle life in London, chose for his later years to live at St Andrews. In early life, in farewell to student days he had written:

> St Andrews by the northern sea,
> A haunted town it is to me!
> A little city, worn and grey,
> The grey North Ocean girds it round . . .

There he returned, and though he died at Banchory on Deeside west of Aberdeen, his body was brought back to St Andrews for burial.

By Lang's time, and by ours, the grey city, enlivened by the red gowns of the university students, had made much recovery from the subdued atmosphere felt by Johnson and Boswell as they passed through St Andrews on their journey from Edinburgh north to Aberdeen, thence westward to Inverness and the Hebrides. It is good to have a picture in mind of the travellers as they set forth from Edinburgh, the dapper Boswell at the age of thirty-three and the large heavy-built Dr Johnson in his sixties clad in plain brown clothes, with twisted hair-buttons of the same colour, a large bushy greyish wig, a plain shirt without frill, black worsted stockings and shoes with silver buckles. So long as the pair journeyed by chaise through the East Lowlands to Aberdeen there was no great need for the boots, the very wide brown greatcoat with enormous pockets, and the large English oak stick, with which Johnson had equipped himself for the real wilderness; but all his travel gear was fully needed after the venturers had swung away from the east coast through 'Bamff' (as Johnson spelled it) and Elgin, Nairn and Fort George to Inverness – and after they had departed from Inverness by horseback along the roughly traced Wade's Road through the Gaelic part of Scotland towards the Western Highlands and Islands.

On the early stages of their journey there were some good moments; of the ruined monastery at Aberbrothick (as Arbroath on the coast of Angus was then called) Johnson wrote, 'I should scarcely have regretted my journey, had it afforded nothing more than the sight of Aberbrothick.' There were plenty of occasions when Boswell's 'facility of manners' (the phrase Adam Smith so well applied to Boswell) had fine play, and at Aberdeen in particular Johnson was well received by the professors, and by the burghers who made him a freeman of that city; it was also at Aberdeen that Johnson discovered an affinity with Scotch broth. Yet Moray McLaren in his book about the 'immortal journey' (*The Highland Jaunt*, 1954) was surely right: the most important part of Johnson's *A Journey to the Hebrides*, and of Boswell's *Journal* of the same tour, begins after their departure from Inverness.

Before leaving the north-eastern corner of the Lowlands I should look at the inland road from Perth to Stonehaven and Aberdeen, as well as at the coastal route. It is possible that Boswell wished Johnson to avoid Perth, for not far to the west of Perth is the Sma' Glen, between Crieff and Amulree, where a large flat stone shows the resting-place of the remains of Ossian. It was all very well for Wordsworth in 1803 to reflect on the grave of the legendary bard, claimed by both Scotland and Ireland, and to remark that

> In this still place, remote from men
> Sleeps Ossian, in the Narrow Glen.

The 'Ossianic controversy' of the eighteenth century, on the authenticity of James Macpherson's translations, had been settled by Wordsworth's time; but it was Johnson who had played a large part in the exposure of Macpherson as an impostor, and if Boswell wished to steer Johnson away from Ossian he may have been wise. Yet shortly after leaving Perth by the inland road to Stonehaven there is Dunsinane Hill, crowned with the remains of an ancient fort, which would have interested Johnson as a possible relic of Macbeth's castle. The nearby Pass of Birnam, 'mouth of the Highlands', whence Malcolm's force emerged for final battle with Macbeth, boasts some fine old trees beside the River Tay, said to be survivors of the Birnam Forest from which Malcolm's troop hewed down their branches and thus brought Birnam Wood to Dunsinane. Glamis is also along the route between Perth and Forfar, and it is only a short sidestep from Glamis to Kirriemuir, the 'Thrums' of J. M. Barrie. Here Barrie was born in 1860, and the National Trust maintains the house as a Barrie museum. After Barrie's death in 1937 his body was brought here for burial in the cemetery at the top of the town.

Beyond Forfar the road to Aberdeen passes Fettercairn where, in the home of Boswell's executor, a cache of Boswell's *Journals* and letters of Johnson was a sensational discovery in 1930. Towards the coast is Arbuthnott, in the district where James Leslie Mitchell (1901–35), writing under the pseudonym 'Lewis Grassic Gibbon', was in the 1930s pouring out the trilogy of rhapsodic novels which were later, posthumously, published collectively as *A Scots Quair*. A Gaelic heritage lays rightful claim to all that is on the inland side of the road I have been traversing. Indeed, it was at Aberdeen that Byron felt to the full the Highland spirit to which, from his mother's side, he was entitled; and he dated his love of mountainous countries from the period when he spent school holidays at farms in Aberdeenshire's Dee valley near Ballater. There Byron learned to swim in 'the billows of Dee's rushing tide', and in 'The Island' he claimed never to have forgotten how 'the Highland's swelling blue' first taught his eye:

> Long have I roamed through lands which are not mine,
> Adored the Alp, and loved the Apennine,
> Revered Parnassus, and beheld the steep
> Jove's Ida and Olympus crown the deep:
> But 'twas not all long ages' lore, nor all
> *Their* nature held me in their thrilling thrall;
> The infant rapture still survived the boy,
> And Loch-na-gar with Ida look'd o'er Troy,
> Mix'd Celtic memories with the Phrygian mount,
> And Highland linns with Castalie's clear fount.

Byron apologized to Homer and to Phoebus for the digression to explain how 'the north and nature' had taught him to adore 'their' scenes. He had reason to remember one Highland linn in particular, the Linn of Dee above Braemar, for there as a boy his lame foot tripped him in the heather and he was barely saved by a companion from a bad fall into the rocky cleft. The unforgotten Lochnagar of Byron's verse dominates the mountain range behind Balmoral Forest.

At Braemar, which is reached by road either due north through the mountains from Perth or due west through Deeside from Aberdeen, Robert Louis Stevenson stayed for some months in 1881, and the cottage in Castleton Terrace is rightly marked with a tablet, for it was there that *Treasure Island* was born. What happened was that on (I believe) a rainy day at Braemar Stevenson's stepson, Lloyd Osbourne, then a boy of thirteen, had been drawing a map of an imaginary island, the which, when Stevenson noticed it in outline, caused him to fill in some names with his own pencil and to write the caption 'Treasure Island' across the top. A letter to his friend Colvin in 1884 (by which time the published book was famous) told the origin of some of the names in *Treasure Island*: 'T.I. came out of Kingsley's *At Last* where I got the Dead Man's Chest – and that was the seed – and out of the great Captain Johnson's *History of Notorious Pirates*. The scenery is Californian in part, and in part *chic*.' His lion-hearted friend Henley, as I have likewise mentioned before, came promptly to Stevenson's mind, suggestive for John Silver; and so, and with gusto, the story began to be written at Braemar and was completed after the Stevensons had moved on to Davos in Switzerland.

I should not leave Deeside without remembering that Norman Douglas, author of *Old Calabria* and the famous novel *South Wind*, was born at Tilquhillie; but another wind altogether has given me a special wish to travel north to Huntly. Two books that I recall from nursery days are *At the Back of the North Wind* and *The Princess and the Goblin*, both written by George Macdonald (1824–1905). Although professional historians of literature tend to neglect Macdonald – even the generous Saintsbury credits him with only 'very great but somewhat unconcentrated gifts' – I find a pleasure in paying respect to Huntly as his birthplace. Macdonald lived for a time at Cullen on the north coast of Banffshire, and it was at Cullen that when Johnson and Boswell were served with dried haddocks broiled for breakfast, Johnson 'was disgusted by the sight of them, so they were removed'. But with all customs native to the fisherfolk of Cullen Bay and nearby Lossiemouth, Macdonald, when he came to write novels, was more sympathetic. After taking his degree at Aberdeen, he moved to Manchester, where he was much admired as a lay preacher and where his first published narrative poem won praise from both Lady Byron and Tennyson. His writing soon turned to prose fiction; in 1860 he moved to London, where among his personal friends were F. D. Maurice, Ruskin, Carlyle, William Morris, Tennyson and Browning, when the widowed Browning returned from Italy to London. Macdonald's own literary output continued to be voluminous, varied by lecture tours in America; but I now confess that having searched for and re-read the works which gave great childhood pleasure, I accept the justice of Saintsbury's remark, that Macdonald's gifts were unconcentrated: the stories, of which the beginnings remain forever memorable, do wander and fade before the end.

The road inland from Fort George is the route of entry into Inverness used by Boswell and Johnson; yet no entry by road exerts to my memory the thrill ofentering Inverness after an all-night ride from London in one of the old -fashioned trains – old-fashioned because drawn by one of those nobly snorting steam engines which gave to the whole journey such an animated character. Nobody provides a better reminder of the feel of reaching Inverness by steam-train than Elizabeth Mackintosh (1897–1952) who was born here, and who wrote her plays (including *Richard of Bordeaux*) in the name of 'Gordon Daviot' and her novels under the pseudonym 'Josephine Tey'. After the night-train had steamed out of King's Cross, Josephine Tey describes, in her novel *The Man in the Queue*, how Inspector Alan Grant's arrival at Inverness, 'as the train rattled and swerved and swung in its last triumphant down-rush to Inverness', brought him nothing but exhilaration.

The characters in *The Man in the Queue* with whom Josephine Tey was concerned left the comfort of the 'through' train from London and crossed the platform at Inverness to get into 'a little local affair that for the rest of the morning trundled from the green countryside back into a brown desolation . . . West and still farther west they trailed, stopping inexplicably at stations set down equally inexplicably in the middle of vast moors devoid of human habitation', until by afternoon each of those characters had been bundled out on to a sandy platform, the train then wandering off by itself into some desolation even more remote. Yet by the twentieth century a single day sufficed for the traveller by train and mail-car to cross the north-west Highlands from Inverness to almost any point upon the west coast. For Samuel Johnson, whose stout form in its enormously wide greatcoat with outsize pockets seemed completely to dwarf the small Highland pony provided for him to ride on, a first day brought him from Inverness along the length of Loch Ness to Fort Augustus, but it was then a matter of two more days, having as Johnson said bidden 'farewell to the luxury of travelling' and entered 'a country upon which perhaps no wheel has ever rolled', before he and Boswell could get as far as the coast at Glenelg, thence to be ferried to Skye to begin their tour of the Hebrides.

7. THE WESTERN HIGHLANDS AND ISLANDS

Josephine Tey loved the Badenoch region and the Cairngorms south of her native Inverness. Especially in *The Singing Sands*, the last of her books (the manuscript was found among her papers after death), she keeps returning to well-remembered places in the Highlands which are at once particularized and concealed in the writing. The lyrical gift of conveying with simple directness a true burst of feeling at seeing again a much-loved scene is often possessed by the Celtic Highlander – was it not a Welsh Highlander (Eifion Wyn) who said: 'Oh God, why hast thou made Cwm Pennant so beautiful and the life of an old shepherd so short?' Again and again in the first part of *The Singing Sands* Josephine Tey conveys such Celtic feeling for parts of 'the long rampart of the Highland line, white and remote against the calm sky'; sometimes it is Strath Tay of which she speaks, sometimes her 'great clean Highland country' is Badenoch and the Cairngorms, and sometimes Strathspey. Particularly in that story she brings together many poignantly remembered Highland scenes.

Josephine Tey also has a special feeling for the Western Isles, the Outer Hebrides. Below the surface Highlanders know a heritage of ancient feeling that islets far out into the Western Ocean are on the way to Tir nan Og, the Gaelic version of the Hesperides, the fabled Happy Islands of the Blest. To that deep undertow of 'oceanic' feeling, shared by the Welsh who remember Madoc and the Irish who remember St Brandon – and shared perhaps by all peoples who have lived on Europe's western seaboard – there is the added symbolism of the Hebrides as the homeland from which the Scottish Highlander may have been forced to emigrate. The 'Canadian Boat Song' expresses this:

> From the lone sheiling of the misty island
>   Mountains divide us, and the waste of seas –
> Yet still the blood is strong, the heart is Highland,
>   And we in dreams behold the Hebrides.

This version of the song in English may have been based on a Gaelic original; the English version is generally credited to John Galt, who was born at Irvine in Ayrshire, and who after visits to Canada settled at Greenock. It was printed in *Blackwood's Magazine* in 1829; a good many years later Andrew Lang, in an irreverent moment, parodied the sentiment in a verse 'To Fiona':

From the damp sheiling on the draggled island
Mountains divide you, and no end of seas.
But, though your heart is genuinely Highland,
Still, you're in luck to be away from these!

Highlanders, among them Josephine Tey, see both sides of the picture. In *The Singing Sands* the herring fleets of Lewis, the cliffs of Mingulay, the songs of Barra, the hills of Harris, the wild flowers of Benbecula, and 'the sands, the endless wonderful white sand, of Berneray' are all, I think, readily identified; but of the particular island of 'Cladda', since it is not identifiable, Josephine Tey can offer the bad in equal measure with the good. At the Cladda Hotel, for a first meal, her hero hoped for the lobster for which the isle was famous; or failing that, some herring fresh from the sea, split and fried after being dipped in oatmeal. The meal in actuality

consisted of a couple of bright orange kippers inadequately cured and liberally dyed in Aberdeen, bread made in Glasgow, oatcakes baked by a factory in Edinburgh and never toasted since, jam manufactured in Dundee, and butter made in Canada. The only local produce was a pallid, haggis-shaped mound of crowdie; a white crumbly by-product without smell or taste.

So, to set out for the threshold of Tir nan Og, the Gaelic Paradise, and fetch up at the Cladda Hotel has for Josephine Tey 'an exquisite ridiculousness' – exquisite, because she makes the sentiment of 'we in dreams behold the Hebrides' survive despite ridicule.

Neil Gunn, author of *Morning Tide* and other writings, was a Highlander who knew the Islands. He was living at Inverness in the years between the two world wars when George Blake and I, and on one occasion T. S. Eliot also, were privileged to stay overnight with the Gunns in their pink house. Now I should have liked to discuss Compton Mackenzie's island of 'Todday' in *Whisky Galore* with Gunn, for Gunn by profession, like Robert Burns before him, was an officer in the Excise service. Yet at that time *Whisky Galore* had not been written. One item I remember from that between-wars drive from Glasgow to Inverness with Eliot was the pause we made on Rannoch Moor. It was some weeks later that Eliot handed me his short poem, one of the few 'Landscapes' that he cared to preserve, called 'Rannoch, by Glencoe'. On that same trip, after Glencoe, Blake took us on the route to Inverness that Brown and Keats had followed in the summer of 1818, but Blake did not make us climb Ben Nevis, the task to which Brown and Keats had been persuaded. 'Never again', was Keats's verdict; he wrote to his brother: 'I am heartily glad it is done – it is almost like a fly crawling up a wainscoat – Imagine the task of mounting 10 Saint Pauls without the convenience of Stair cases.'

Keats had at the time a bad sore throat; he was 'thin and fevered' after the considerable exertions on the walking tour; at Inverness his throat forced him to consult a doctor, and the doctor promptly forbade him to continue journeying into increasingly difficult country. So, for Keats, passage home by sea from Cromarty was arranged and though beyond 'a little Qualm now and then' he was not seasick, the nine days' sail to London Bridge was not made more pleasant by a spell of tooth-ache. On arrival at Hampstead on 18 August Keats himself was not in the best of shape to receive the shock of his younger brother Tom's most serious relapse. From then till December Keats was nurse, without let-up, to the restless boy, who was not dying easily but dying 'with an exquisite love of life', and his brother his 'only comfort'.

*   *   *

From Inverness we may nowadays cross to the western coast of Scotland with less effort, as I have noted, than had to be made by Samuel Johnson; but in a search for spontaneous local contributions to literature in English, the north-western Highlands seem to continue to offer, as for Johnson, a proud indifference. North-eastern Caithness and the Orkney and Shetland Islands are as if an area apart. Scott plays on the Scandinavian heritage in 'Zetland' in his novel *The Pirate*, which few would claim to be one of his best (yet the shipwreck at the cape of Sumburgh and the adventure at Fitful Head and the final scenes in Orkney have good moments). I don't forget that in our time Orkney has produced both Edwin Muir, who was born at Deerness, and Eric Linklater; but on the north-western mainland, areas of Sutherland and Ross and Cromarty, though large, are sparsely populated and native writers using English are also sparse. (Of writings and oral tradition in the Gaelic I am wholly unable to speak; in the Scottish Highlands I am aware of my ignorance of Gaelic as, in North Wales, I was aware of my ignorance of Welsh.) There is an immense number of books about Highlanders and the Highlands which, if looked into, you find to be written by visitors rather than natives. About the Hebrides, for instance, as Josephine Tey pointed out, there is 'a whole literature'. She made one of her characters remark: 'It's a distinction in Scotland not have written a book about the Islands.' The edge in the remark is that the Highlander is 'above' such writing; if a Scotsman is a writer of such books in English, it is probably a mark that he is a Lowland Scot. One may still feel the Highlander's pride that preserves his separateness, now as in Johnson's day. 'I asked a very learned minister in the islands', wrote Johnson, 'which they considered as their most savage clans; "Those", said he, "that live next the Lowlands".'

The poetry and song of Scotsmen who chose to write in English flowered superbly with Burns and Scott – and Byron. If Lowlanders, or those living 'next the Lowlands', could so well express themselves, should one not surmise at least equal talents for expressing gaiety and sorrow among Highlanders who preferred their own language, the Gaelic? Here I quote Moray McLaren:

Wherever Gaelic is the predominant language in the islands or on the main-land there exists a deep but inextinguishable underground movement of poetry, romance and hidden gaiety. It is like a thread of gold ore running through the heart of a rock which flashes to the surface only when that rock is struck, or which gleams at some unexpected corner or side of it where the ceaseless flow of water has worn the rock thin. This underground movement, this thread of hidden gold in the character, even in the demeanour, of the most indrawn, withdrawn Highland Gael, is indestructible. As the mountain peaks of Skye, hidden for so much of the year in the mist and clouds, are themselves indestructible and are always there far above us when we cannot see them, so, deep below, there lies in any company of Gaelic-speaking Celts from the West and the Western Isles this underground movement of poetry and song and gaiety. And in the temperament of each of them there runs this thread of gold.

Other possessors of the Gaelic assure me, with the same or similar metaphors, of the preservation, especially in the Western Isles, of poetry of Gaelic oral tradition. Moray McLaren speaks of the island of Raasay in particular for tales and songs 'full of the pride and poetry of the remote Celtic past', but he points out the secrecy with which the gold is hidden. 'Some of the oldest and best of the poetry of Gaelic oral tradi-tion is still preserved on Raasay only to be spoken and passed on when no stranger is there and when no ministerial frown is to be seen, or no tight-lipped disapproval to be felt to check its flow.'

The contrast between the pessimism on Raasay nowadays and the spirit of the Raasay that greeted Johnson in the eighteenth century makes one re-read Johnson's *Journey* and Boswell's *Journal* with renewed attention. It will be remembered that on the steep rough road leading down from Mam Rattachan to Glenelg, in the increasingly dark evening of 1 September 1773, both Dr Johnson and the horses became thoroughly fatigued. Johnson's weight was such that his guides, who led the ponies' heads, forced him to keep getting on and off that he might be carried alternately, and one pony in particular in going downhill did not go well. Johnson was scared of falling and grumbled. Boswell, too, was out of temper, and they had their first and only serious quarrel of their tour. Matters were not mended by finding the inn at Glenelg miserably unprepared for visitors. There was (says Boswell) 'not a single article that we could either eat or drink', and in a damp and dirty

room into which they were shown 'out of a wretched bed started a
fellow from his sleep'. Johnson's phrase for the poor tinker ejected from
the bed is more graphic; the man evicted was 'black as a Cyclops from
the forge'. Johnson's account continues, 'Other circumstances of no
elegant recital, concurred to disgust us.' The tired and disgruntled
travellers spent that night in separate rooms, their Highlanders having
managed to scrounge for each of them a bundle of hay. Johnson records
that he slept on the hay in his wide riding coat but 'Mr Boswell, being
more delicate, laid himself sheets with hay over and under him, and
lay in linen like a gentleman'.

The sudden violent hostility between Johnson and Boswell on that
unhappy evening and night was outwardly smoothed over, with mutual
apologies between the friends in the morning; yet it is a full week before
one feels that complete and easy amity was wholly resumed. The behaviour of both Boswell and Johnson as well as that of their Macdonald
hosts at Armadale in the introductory days on Skye gives an impression
that everybody, guests as well as hosts, was out of sorts. It is not until 8
September, when setting forth in 'Raasay's Carriage', the Norwegian-
built boat belonging to the Macleods of the House of Raasay, for the
stay in that faithfully Jacobite household on the island of Raasay, that
both Johnson's *Journey* and Boswell's *Journal* begin again to communicate the happiness that after two centuries is fresh as a daisy. From the
moment of embarking in the open boat for the pull against the high wind
across the sound to Raasay gaiety returned: 'Dr Johnson sat high on the
stern like a magnificent Triton.' There was, as he said, 'something wild'
in the misadventure that his spurs, being removed from the magnificent
Triton's boots, fell overboard and were lost, but he quickly regarded
that as fulfilment of a dream he'd had and that led to talk of the 'second
sight'. To encourage the four stout rowers as they pulled into the rough
head-sea, their pilot and host, Malcolm Macleod, burst into a Gaelic
song, to which the boatmen chorused, and all went well. 'I should tell a
tea-table in London', he merrily went on shouting, 'that I have crossed
the Atlantic in an open boat!' and to the wind that 'blew enough to give
the boat a kind of dancing agitation' he shouted the whole of Horace's
Ode 'Otium divos'.

The song into which Malcolm Macleod had burst was the famous
Jacobite war-song called (in translation) 'Sound the Pibroch'. It is worth
recalling Boswell's portrait of that singer, who had been guide, friend
and guardian of Prince Charlie in 'the forty-five'. Here, then, is that
Macleod of the Raasay family:

He was now sixty-two years of age, hale, and well-proportioned, – with a
manly countenance, tanned by the weather, yet having a ruddiness in his
cheeks, over a great part of which his rough beard extended. His eye was

quick and lively, yet his look was not fierce, but he appeared at once firm and good humoured. He wore a pair of brogues; tartan hose which came up only near to his knees, and left them bare; a purple camblet kilt; a black waistcoat; a short green cloth coat bound with gold cord; a yellowish bushy wig; a large blue bonnet with a gold thread button. I never saw a figure that gave a more perfect representation of a Highland gentleman.

It was past six o'clock when the boat arrived at the little bay and harbour before Raasay House. There the guests were welcomed by the Laird of Raasay and introduced into the house 'with politeness' (Johnson reported in a letter to Mrs Thrale) 'which not the Court of Versailles could have thought defective'. There was a large company, and within the house the Doctor and Boswell were made welcome by Lady Raasay and her three sons and ten daughters. Boswell noted that not only was a dram of excellent brandy served round immediately, but that also 'on a sideboard was placed for us, who had come off the sea, a substantial dinner, and a variety of wines'. He was delighted to observe in the room 'several elegantly bound books and other marks of improved life'.

Johnson vied with Boswell to express the pleasure of the reception at Raasay. Says Johnson's *Journey*: 'We found nothing but civility, elegance, and plenty. After the usual refreshments, and the usual conversation, the evening came upon us. The carpet was then rolled off the floor; the musician was called, and the whole company was invited to dance, nor did ever fairies trip with greater alacrity.' Says Boswell: 'Raasay himself danced with as much spirit as any man, and Malcolm bounded like a roe.' Boswell watched to see what effect the 'little ball' was having on the Doctor who was 'sitting by, while we danced', Johnson had likewise observed the books, and had clutched hold of Hooke's *Roman History*; in the general jovial noise he was seen to be sometimes meditative, sometimes smiling complacently, sometimes looking upon Hooke's *Roman History*, and sometimes talking with Mr Donald M'Queen. Then, says Johnson: 'When it was time to sup, the dance ceased, and six and thirty persons sat down to two tables in the same room. After supper the ladies sung Erse songs, to which I listened, as an English audience to an Italian opera, delighted with the sound of words which I did not understand.' In his letter to Mrs Thrale Johnson adds a final thoughtful comment on the happy evening:

At twelve it was bed time. I had a chamber to myself, which, in eleven rooms to forty people, was more than my share. How the company and the family were distributed is not easy to tell. Macleod the chieftain, and Boswell, and I, had all single chambers on the first floor. There remained eight rooms only for at least seven-and-thirty lodgers. I suppose they put up temporary beds in the dining room, where they stowed all the young ladies. There was a room above stairs with six beds, in which they put ten men.

No longer, mourns Moray McLaren, is there a laird's house on Raasay where they dance like that every night all the year round and offer the gay hospitality of song and wit and flowing conversation.

Before the disasters which began two hundred years ago Raasay had a name for gaiety, contentment, gallantry and romance which was known afar in the other islands and on the Gaelic-speaking mainland. From Raasay there came poetry and song and deeds of valour the origins of which lie far back in the mysterious depths of Gaelic oral tradition. Raasay long before 1773 long, before the great days of 1745, had been a pearl amongst the Western leiss; and the two travellers were fortunate enough to catch the gleams from it just before its lustre faded.

McLaren then quotes Neil Munro's 'Lament for Macleod of Raasay'.

> Gone in the mist the brave Macleods of Raasay,
>   Far furth from fortune, sundered from their lands,
> And now the last grey stone of Castle Raasay
>   Lies desolate and levelled with the sands.
> But pluck the old isle from its roots deep-planted
>   Where tides cry coronach round the Hebrides,
> And it will bleed of the Macleods lamented
>   Their loves and memories!

Johnson and Boswell returned to Skye, and Johnson slept 'in Prince Charles's bed in the house of Miss Flora Macdonald' and proceeded to nine happy days at Dunvegan Castle, where the power of Johnson's talk 'luxuriated in a sense of civilized enjoyment'. Johnson at length left Skye – leaving 'with some heaviness of heart an Island which I am not likely to see again' – for further adventures. On the way to Mull a sudden and dangerous 'tempest' forced the boatload to find shelter in Coll. There, for exploration of the island, Johnson was supplied with what nowadays might be called a 'Shetland pony'.

If there had been many spectators [Johnson wrote] I should have been somewhat ashamed of my figure in the march. The horses of the islands, as of other barren countries, are very low: they are, indeed, musculous and strong, beyond what their size gives reason for expecting; but a bulky man upon one of their backs makes a very disproportionate appearance.

A final proper act of piety was the visit to Iona, on the islet off the coast of Mull. There, since there was no other means of landing, 'our Highlanders carried us' through the water to dry land. For Johnson the inspection of Iona was the climax of the journey to the Hebrides. 'That man is little to be envied, whose patriotism would not gain force upon the plain of Marathon, or whose piety would not grow warmer among the ruins of Iona.' That famous sentence of Johnson's is evidence that his piety was rewarded, but his search for evidences of Gaelic literature, though he questioned eagerly wherever he went, were unsuccessful. His considered conclusion about the Highlanders was that 'the antipathy between their language and literature' was one that would continue until their Gaelic language 'begins to teem with books'.

If that be so, the literary associations to be looked for in the Highlands and Islands are associations with outsiders, or with what writings the lovely terrain and its Gaelic peoples have suggested to visitors. Certainly there has never been a more interesting pair of visitors than the Staffordshire man Johnson and the Lowland Scotsman Boswell. After fitting respect had been paid to Iona, they returned to the mainland at Oban, 'this small village' as it was to them: and then, still having to rely on small 'musculous' Highland ponies to carry them across country, they made their way, after being ferried across Loch Awe, to Inveraray. More recently as I have mentioned, Inveraray was the birthplace of Neil Munro, and not only are scenes in his novels laid here, but also scenes in Stevenson's *Catriona*, the sequel to *Kidnapped*. Boswell's wish was that if Dr Johnson's presence at the inn of Inveraray were made known to the Duke of Argyll, that fifth duke (even though his wife despised Boswell) might invite them to dine at Inveraray Castle. Boswell chose a right moment for presenting himself at the castle, and obtained the desired invitation; though the Duchess remained at daggers drawn with Boswell, the Duke was notably amiable to Johnson. When Johnson mentioned the troubles he had with the smallness of Highland ponies, the Duke insisted on supplying a proper steed from his own stables, which presently carried Johnson with fitting dignity past the seat called Rest-and-be-thankful in Glen Croe and on by the west side of Loch Lomond to Dumbarton. The 'difficulties of peregrination' had ended, Johnson said, at Inveraray; and from Dumbarton a post-chaise conveyed the travellers luxuriously to Glasgow.

In the annals of Johnson and Boswell I find no mention of how the steed, so generously lent to the Doctor by the Duke of Argyll, was returned. It is possible that an attendant groom returned the horse not to the stables at Inveraray, but to that other property which, in *The Heart of Midlothian*, Scott designates as 'Roseneath'. At Roseneath were set the closing scenes of that novel, and Scott takes pains to describe the picturesque beauty of that 'island': 'the Earls and Dukes of Argyle, from an early period, made it their occasional residence, and had their temporary accommodation in a fishing or hunting-lodge which succeeding improvements have since transformed into a palace'. Later, the hunting-lodge of the Dukes of Argyll which made for a happy ending to Scott's novel became the Rosneath Castle on Gare Loch where Churchill, Eisenhower and Montgomery met in 1944 to concert

plans for the invasion of France. (Information reaches me, though, that
the Rosneath Castle of the Second World War has since been demolished.)

The large-scale map of Scotland on which I have been tracing the
whole Scottish journey of Johnson and Boswell serves also for tracing,
in accordance with the data carefully supplied, the even more hazardous
journey, twenty-two years before theirs, of Stevenson's well-remembered
characters David Balfour and Alan Breck in *Kidnapped*. Johnson and
Boswell, after the visit to Iona, found it safe enough to return to the
mainland at Oban and to travel directly through the heart of Campbell
country to Glasgow and 'home'. Yet twenty-two years earlier when the
brig *Covenant* bearing Alan Breck and David Balfour had cleared Iona
but had struck and been lost on the Torran rocks (which for Stevenson's
convenience crept closer to Mull than the map may show), for them to
be castaway in a land of the Campbells kept up the tension. 'Set me on
dry ground in Appin, or Ardgour, or in Morven, or Arisaig, or Morar;
or, in brief, where ye please, within thirty miles of my own country',
said Alan, 'except in a country of the Campbells.' Thereafter the route
of the travellers in *Kidnapped* may be traced from Glen Coe eastward
across the Rannoch Moor and south from Ben Alder to the Braes of
Balquhidder, all of which brings a reader into territory made familiar
by Walter Scott.

The setting of Scott's *The Lady of the Lake*, and some of the scenes of
Rob Roy, in the beautiful country of the Trossachs and Loch Katrine,
holds me hereabouts. John Freeman, in his *Literature and Locality*,
reminds me that the marvellous scene beside the waterfall in *Waverley*,
where Flora MacIvor, accompanying herself on the harp, sings lofty
Highland battle-songs to the susceptible Englishman, is placed on the
north side of Loch Ard, a few miles west of Aberfoyle. (Scott refers to
the placing of the waterfall in a note to *Waverley*, and adds: 'The
appearance of Flora with the harp, as described, has been justly censured
as too theatrical and affected for the ladylike simplicity of her character.
But something may be allowed to her French education . . .') Yet not
even recollections of *Waverley* should at this point deter me from pursuing the final happy stages of the fugitives' route in *Kidnapped*. Alan
Breck and David bypassed Stirling, made their way along the north
shore of the Firth of Forth and were enabled to cross the Firth by the
very fine lass from whom they bought some bread and cheese. When
they had been landed near Carriden, they were close-handy for the
final episode at the House of Shaws, which Stevenson had placed in the
countryside familiar to him from his boyhood holidays. For the parting
with Alan, David walked with him towards Edinburgh as far as the hill
of Corstorphine, and there was the halting-place bearing the same name

as the halting-place Dr Johnson had noticed at Glen Croe – Rest-and-be-Thankful.

'Rest-and-be-Thankful' – the worthy phrase marked Johnson's farewell to his Scottish peregrination. It was also chosen by Stevenson to salute the end of *Kidnapped*. I feel it may fairly mark the completion of my survey of some of the literary associations of Britain's mainland.

IRELAND

From James Joyce I learned the inadvisability of any outsider presuming to offer guidance to literary sites in Eire. This I might have learned from the writings of plenty of Irishmen, ancient or modern; yet the personal instruction came to me first-hand from Joyce, and to explain that brings in some by now fairly distant memories.

Two powerful explosions which rocked some of us in the early 1920s were *Ulysses* and *The Waste Land*. Reading and re-reading *The Waste Land* in a quarterly periodical called *The Criterion* after a while brought me into a sort of younger-brother companionship with T. S. Eliot; several years later that led to personal contacts with Joyce. Eliot first met Joyce when Wyndham Lewis and Eliot visited Paris in August 1920. (Ezra Pound had commissioned Eliot to convey to Joyce from London a nondescript brown-paper parcel which, when Joyce arrived at the meeting-place to open it, proved to contain, wrapped within trousers, a pair of old brown shoes.) Later, Eliot sometimes mentioned various other adventures on that visit to France with Lewis, but Lewis (in *Blasting and Bombardiering*) wrote mainly of the first evening with Joyce. Lewis thought that Joyce was 'playing the Irishman a little overmuch perhaps, but in amusingly mannered technique'. Eliot's opinion, recorded by Lewis, was that Joyce on the surface was highly polite yet underneath was exceedingly arrogant. In later expressions Eliot described Joyce as a kind of polar opposite of Ezra Pound – Joyce, 'concerned with nothing except his own writings', was the most egocentric of all men that Eliot had known. As for Joyce's writings, however, Eliot perceived as instantly as Pound how worthy of concern they were. There is an account by Virginia Woolf of Eliot coming to tea at the Hogarth Press after *Ulysses* had been published in Paris, and in discussing *Ulysses* she found him, for the first time in her experience, 'rapt, enthusiastic'. 'How could anyone write again after achieving the immense prodigy of the last chapter?' was an opinion of Eliot's that Virginia Woolf recorded.

As a periodical edited by Eliot, *The Criterion* had been started with the financial backing of Lady Rothermere; when after the first three years that backing was withdrawn, it was my good fortune to be in a position to organize the quarterly's continuance. (No trumpet need be blown for that – it was merely a matter of getting together some of *The Criterion*'s well-wishers.) It so happened that at that time Eliot and Joyce were corresponding over printing some sections of Joyce's 'Work in Progress' in *The Criterion*, and the saving of *The Criterion* meant continuance of that correspondence. Involved in the formation of the publishing firm of Faber & Faber, I was brought into sharing an office-room (and for a period of confusions, sharing a single telephone) with Eliot.

I was then beginning to arrange for publication of some shilling pamphlets, and it was easy to think that portions of 'Work in Progress' might appear in London in pamphlet form. In the summer of 1929 James and Nora Joyce were in England; Stuart and Moune Gilbert had travelled with them from Paris and all four were at Torquay for the two months that Gilbert and Joyce were working over and completing the text of Gilbert's book, *James Joyce's Ulysses*. Eliot was in touch with the Joyces and Gilberts that summer, and to a lesser extent I was involved: Faber & Faber were to publish Gilbert's book in 1930. It is perhaps right to record that Joyce expressed high pleasure at my suggestion of the shilling pamphlets; his *Anna Livia Plurabelle* was prepared for separate publication in 1930 and *Haveth Childers Everywhere* for 1931, two of the parts to be later incorporated in *Finnegans Wake*. Joyce was indeed elated to the point of composing and sending us verses with which to advertise the publication of each pamphlet – the advertisement that he sent for *Anna Livia* was as follows:

> Buy a book in brown paper
> From Faber & Faber
> To see Annie Liffy trip, tumble and caper.
> Sevensinns in her singthings,
> Plurabelle on her prose,
> Seashell ebb music wayriver she flows.

Joyce, I think, hoped to see his advertising-copy well displayed in all national newspapers: he did complain a bit (some authors do) that there wasn't enough advertising. Throughout the 1930s there were sometimes occasions for Eliot to visit Paris – meaning sequences of lunches, dinners and late sessions with Joyce and companions – and the custom was for me to go along to share the fray. So much for the explanation of palaverings with Joyce.

On occasion in Paris Joyce did not hesitate to comment on other Irish writers. By Irish writers I don't mean only those who in fealty to the Gaelic League were communicating in an indigenous Irish language; as I have confessed before, in Wales and Scotland, writings in the various forms of the Gaelic are to me a sealed book. What Joyce (and indeed Yeats) regarded as Irish writers were Irish-born writers writing in English yet deriving what they wrote about from native sources. On such Irish writers in the eighteenth century Samuel Johnson had commented that they were not in a conspiracy to puff up their countrymen. 'No, Sir,' was Johnson's remark, 'the Irish are a *fair people*; – they never speak well of one another.' In the twentieth century many Irish writers – George Moore, Yeats, George Bernard Shaw, Joyce – have often proved themselves 'fair people' in Johnson's sense. Yet apart from the Irishman's right to speak, if he so wished, 'not well' about his compatriots, I recall Joyce commenting on how few Irish writers had managed, or even cared, to remain in Ireland. As Joyce himself had since the age of thirty pronounced himself to be a confirmed exile from Ireland, one tended to take that opinion with a pinch of salt. Nevertheless, at this point it is a comment worth pondering. So far in this book I have mentioned Irish writers only as they have put in appearances on the main island of Britain – but hasn't that already encompassed many Irish names? How does one test Joyce's hint, that fertile as Ireland has been at giving birth to literary talent, the careers of Irish writers led many of them abroad?

Of the eighteenth-century names that may come most quickly to mind – Steele, Swift, Goldsmith, Sheridan, Burke, Sterne – Swift is an exception to Joyce's argument, in so far as he did return to Dublin as Dean of St Patrick's Cathedral, and both he and Stella were buried there. Associations with the other names are mostly within England. The agrarian, commercial and political grievances of Ireland caused the flight of soldiers of fortune, 'the wild geese', into every foreign army; the tradition for the literary wild geese was to be 'passengers to London'. Diminutive Maria Edgeworth – on all social occasions she managed valiantly to improve her height of four feet seven inches by wearing enormous hats – continued into the nineteenth century the fight to increase the awareness of Irish landlords' responsibilities for staying at home. The publication of her novel *Castle Rackrent* in 1800 was a matter of importance. Nevertheless the poet and singer Thomas Moore drifted naturally to London and to English companionships, notably with Byron. Maria Edgeworth's prompting of Scott to begin his

Waverley novels was paralleled by a less happy influence that she had
on later Irish storytellers. The subtitle of *Castle Rackrent* when first
published was 'An Hibernian Tale', and it and some of her further
novels made use of episodes of family history around Edgeworthstown
and stories which her father's great talent for mimicry had made highly
amusing.

However, a later tradition of 'Hibernian tales', as it developed and
coarsened, degenerated into the 'stage Irishry' which towards the end
of the century came to be thoroughly offensive to those who (like Yeats
and Padraic Colum) believed in Ireland as a mystical entity. After a
great surge of nationalism and the setting-up of the Irish Free State,
such nineteenth-century 'Hibernian tales' as those of Samuel Lover,
whose *Handy Andy* was published in 1842, were touchily regarded as
having made out that Ireland was 'the Empire's favourite buffoon'.
Maria Edgeworth can be cleared of that charge, and interest in her
as a serious novelist is now reviving, despite disfavour to some of the
Irish novelists who followed her.

Joyce pointed out that his first flamboyant thought of emigrating to
Paris was because so many of his immediate predecessors (Wilde, Shaw,
Yeats) had gone to London. Yeats alternated between England and
Ireland, yet such a Dublin companion of his as George Moore proceeded
to settle in London. J. M. Synge's unpopularity in Dublin was such that
he might have been exiled, but ill-health waived that issue: Synge died
in middle life, at thirty-eight, and is buried in Dublin. More than a
decade after that, the production of Sean O'Casey's plays at the Abbey
Theatre caused riotings in the 1920s; O'Casey presently settled for the
rest of his life in England. Former centres of literary life in Dublin
lost a good deal of sparkle when Oliver St John Gogarty, after his period
as senator, spent much of the latter part of his life in the United States,
and when George William Russell (widely known as 'AE') left Dublin
in 1932 to spend his last years in Bournemouth. Among other more
recent Irish writers, pre-eminent to the outside world has been Samuel
Beckett, born in 1906, who won his Nobel Prize for Literature in 1969;
he is one of the Dublin-born writers who found his cultural centre in
Paris. The slightly younger Brian O'Nolan (1911–66), who was born
in Ulster but moved to Dublin, used the pseudonym 'Flann O'Brien' for
his novel *At Swim-Two-Birds*, which made its original impact in 1939.
'Flann O'Brien' has gained widening recognition ever since. Still other
present-day writers that I might mention (except that living writers are
not within my terms of reference), are Sean O'Faolain, Liam O'Flaherty,
John McGahern, William Trevor, and, not least among contemporary
poets of Northern Ireland, Seamus Heaney. Yet my particular purpose
is to notice what Irishmen say about 'sense of place' and topographical

associations. Therefore I go to Brendan Behan (1923–64), who was born in the same area of Dublin as Sean O'Casey, with whose talents Behan's were in some ways comparable. *Brendan Behan's Island* (1962) is a work I would specially mention; that, and James Plunkett's book *The Gems She Wore* ('A Book of Irish Places', 1972), prove the contention that writings about Ireland to be recommended are books written by Irishmen, not by outsiders.

By the age of thirty Joyce pronounced his exile from Ireland. Ten years before that he had made his first experiment of living in Paris, in the mood recalled in *Finnegans Wake* : 'He even ran away with hunself and became a farsoonerite, saying he would far sooner muddle through the hash of lentils in Europe than meddle with Irrland's split little pea.' When his mother was dying he was called home to Dublin. After that he lodged for a time in the Martello tower at Sandycove with Gogarty and Trench, but this was cut short when one of Trench's nightmares waked Gogarty, whose remedial action was to fire a fusillade of revolver shots; the bullets knocked down pots and pans over Joyce's bed. That tower at Sandycove provided the opening scene of *Ulysses*, and now houses a small museum; it is spoken of as 'James Joyce's Tower', though in fact the night-time gunfire had shot him out of it at speed (Joyce was often terrified of ordinary thunderstorms). Soon after, Nora Barnacle sauntered into Joyce's life. Then Joyce, having composed a broadside (*The Holy Office*) excoriating each of his literary compatriots – Yeats, Synge, Gogarty, Colum, Roberts, Starkie, Russell, the lot – borrowed whatever he could from those he lampooned and induced the much-enduring Nora to elope with him to Paris, Zürich and Trieste.

In the 1930s, the period of my brief reminiscence, Joyce was living in Paris. He and Nora spent six months of 1931 in England to establish domicile, and a register office marriage took place in Kensington, both of these formalities having been suggested by Joyce's lawyers. I recall, though, no talk of any wish of Joyce's to return to Dublin. The character of the Dublin that Joyce dwelt upon in memory was, to the minutest detail, permanently fixed; it had become a Dublin transfigured into myth, even as the River Liffey was transfigured into Anna Livia Plurabelle. It became clear that to visualize Joyce's Dublin you had to be, as he was, unconfused by any changes which might take place to subtract from his 'out-of-date' fixed picture. *Ergo*, Joyce's advice was that if you wished to enjoy *Ulysses*, you should not make the enjoyment more difficult by going to look at a changed Dublin. By the same token, to look at the actual present-day River Liffey may not so much assist as confuse your reception of the Anna Livia dreamed in *Finnegans Wake*. A further point of Joyce's was that myth is so all-important in Ireland

and the where and when and how myth and actions and words cor-
respond within Ireland are matters so much better comprehended by
the Irish-born than by those not born-to-it that the wise outsider knows
better than to comment. I have suggested a couple of books about
Ireland by Irishmen, and very good they are for the literary associations.
Read them, and the likes of them, as readers' guides to Ireland. Such is
my interpretation of Joyce's advice. Casting my mind back to the first
meeting of Lewis and Eliot with Joyce, it may have been such advice
that caused Eliot to call Joyce arrogant, yet we came to respect Joyce as
a teacher.

'Yeats, funny fellow,' I remember Joyce saying, 'calls himself Yates, it's
really Yeets.' I am not at all sure what the cryptic remark implied. It is
possible there was some reference to Ireland's landed gentry, some
query being suggested by Joyce as to whether Yeats was or was not
securely of that social class. Yeats was sometimes recorded (for instance
by George Moore) as thundering against the 'middle classes' as if from
the standpoint of an aristocrat by birth. 'We asked ourselves', wrote
Moore in *Hail and Farewell*, 'why Willie Yeats should feel himself
called upon to denounce the class to which he himself belonged essentially . . . we had laughed at the story . . . that on one occasion when
Yeats was crooning over AE's fire he had said that if he had his rights
he would be Duke of Ormonde . . .' An avowed ambition of Yeats was
so to conduct the Abbey Theatre in Dublin that there would arise a
burst of positive national expression, and this burst of 'indomitable
Irishry' would not come from Irish urban *bourgeoisie* and middle class
but from a renewal of the fusion of aristocrats and peasantry. Reviewing
his effort later, Yeats wrote:

> John Synge, I and Augusta Gregory, thought
> All that we did, all that we said or sang
> Must come from contact with the soil, from that
> Contact everything Antaeus-like grew strong.
> We three alone in the modern times had brought
> Everything down to that sole test again,
> Dream of the noble and the beggar man.

Yeats directed Synge to the west of Ireland and the Aran Islands, which
became the source of Synge's most famous plays. Yeats's own plays
were not so deeply taken to heart by Dublin's audiences; when later,
in the 1920s, Sean O'Casey brought Dublin's tenements and 'themes
white-hot from Ireland's immediate past' to the Abbey, the passions
aroused were so violent that they led to the quarrel which caused

O'Casey's exile – like Shaw, Joyce and subsequently Samuel Beckett, he moved away from Ireland for ever.

It does not seem unnatural that when Yeats's painter-father had brought the family to London and a not very inspiring life in alien side-streets of Hammersmith and Bedford Park, Willie Yeats and his sister Lily, who had been born in Sligo, should have had fantasies, when life seemed grey and dull, of an Irish ancestry which should have provided a proud right to better things. The father had talked and acted as if entitled to inheritances, and Yeats later spoke of his sister sharing and feeding his boyish feelings until he longed 'for a sod of earth from some field I knew, something of Sligo to hold in my hand'. It was when Yeats was in London in his twenties, according to an autobiographical passage written at the time, and caught in a crush in the Strand, that the sound of a little water-jet balancing a wooden ball in a shop window brought the swift vision of a cataract in Galway 'with a long Gaelic name'; soon after, gazing at the osier-fringed Chiswick eyot in the Thames on a Sunday morning stroll caused his best-known poem of that period, 'The Lake Isle of Innisfree'. A self-induced conviction of being by right one of Ireland's top landed gentry need not depend on having land, though to do without horsemanship or hunting might be more difficult. George Moore (if his story is believed) thought that Yeats as incarnation of a Duke of Ormonde was going a bit too far. Yet in 1917, when Yeats at the age of fifty-two married Dorothy Pound's cousin, nicknamed 'George', his boyhood wish to hold 'something of Sligo' strongly returned, and the desire for contact with the soil so integral to his 'Irishry' came out in his purchase of the Thoor Ballylee, a sixteenth-century stone tower beside a river bridge near Gort in Galway. The tower had fallen into such dilapidation that Yeats was able to buy it for £35, and it could only be fixed up 'With old mill-boards and sea-green slates' for use as a summer home for his wife and presently the children. To Yeats the tower in the west continued to satisfy a deep need for many years. Even though the Thoor Ballylee eventually ceased to be even a possible vacation-home, it had restored Sligo to Yeats, and when at the end of his life he was dying in the south of France he made plans to be buried in the neighbourhood of Sligo.

Myth, I have said, is all-important in Ireland, and Irish myth is to be spoken of by Irishmen. I was advising the reading of James Plunkett's *The Gems She Wore* for impressions that he had a right to give, felt beside the gravestone of Yeats in the churchyard of Drumcliffe. Ben Bulben, legendary mountain, rises high above Drumcliffe Bay and above Yeats's resting-place. Ben Bulben was the hunting ground of the great heroes of myth, and the scene of the death of Diarmuid; quietly James

Plunkett rehearses for you the myth of the immortal huntsman, and quietly as he comes to the gravestone he reminds you also of Yeats's Three Songs to the One Burden, 'From mountain to mountain ride the fierce horsemen'. 'Huntsman', 'horseman', the symbols twine together, as they were twining for Yeats in the last weeks of January 1939 when he was dying in the south of France. Without overtly saying so, Plunkett has thus prepared you for that memorable letter of Yeats to Ethel Mannin saying that he had arranged about his burial:

> Cast a cold eye
> On life, on death
> Huntsman, pass by.

In that letter, Plunkett reminds you, the word 'Huntsman' was struck out and the word 'Horseman' which is carved on the plain gravestone was substituted. Irish myths, ancient and recent, huntsman and horse-man, coalesce as you turn from the remote churchyard to the sight of Ben Bulben.

Both James Plunkett and Brendan Behan lead a visitor on from Sligo to the Aran Islands off the coast of Donegal. Behan discovered that the islanders felt that Synge had been 'patronizing', 'but', Behan continues, 'but they are very touchy and no matter what is said about them in any part of the world, they find out about it. For instance, they will certainly know everything I've said about them here, but it's said with love and respect and I hope it won't come between us.' I take to heart that gentle warning. I have said that Irish men of letters have also been, as Behan phrased it, 'touchy'. The late St John Ervine, writing of George Bernard Shaw, expressed that vividly. 'Wilde, Shaw, Yeats, George Moore were incompatible. They seldom met, and disliked each other's work. None of them lived in Ireland any longer than he could help. The single Irishman of any quality in letters who lived in Dublin was the Ulster poet, George Russell (AE) and even he, shortly before he died, could endure it no longer' – St John Ervine must have been an Irishman, perhaps an Ulsterman, to speak so strongly.

The Aran Islands of Donegal remind me that the Province of Ulster is next door. Again, one met the writers from Northern Ireland mostly abroad – the scholar Helen Waddell at Oxford, the novelist Forrest Reid and essayist Robert Lynd in London, the poet Louis MacNeice at Birmingham, and the writer of my almost-favourite detective stories, Freeman Wills Crofts in Surrey. For guidance to the associations and the sense of place in the north of Ireland the same maxim holds as for the south: the wise outsider leaves comment, with love and respect, to the native-born.

INDEX OF PERSONAL
NAMES

INDEX OF PLACES

Note : Figures in **bold** type indicate the page numbers of maps showing the places noted. Places which do not appear on the maps are approximately located in parentheses with regard to those places which do, and with the page numbers of the appropriate map indicated similarly in **bold** type.